MW00780129

S SHOOTING TO
URVIVE

How to Fight with a Pistol

SHOOTING TO
SURVIVE

How to Fight with a Pistol

Timothy D. Blakeley

POLICE TECH
PUBLICATIONS

Copyright ©2013 by PoliceTech Publications

All rights reserved. No part of this book may be reproduced in any form or by any electronic or mechanical means including information storage and retrieval systems, without permission in writing from the author. The only exceptions are a reviewer, who may quote short excerpts in a review, and under the fair use law.

PoliceTech Publications
PO Box 1449
Carthage, North Carolina 28327
A division of PoliceTech LLC
E-mail: info@policetech.com
www.PoliceTech.com

PoliceTech is a registered trademark.

Printed in the United States of America

Edited by Jeanette J. Blakeley

Library of Congress Cataloging-in-Publication Data
Blakeley, Timothy D.,
Includes endnote references and index.
1. Sporting, 2. Firearms, 3. Self-defense

2010943359

ISBN 978-0-9827748-9-2

First Edition

To operators that willingly go into harm's way.

ACKNOWLEDGMENTS

I have been supported during my career by my wife, sons, family members, best friend, friends, trainers, and colleagues. My father, Elworth Blakeley will always be my hero, and I miss him every day of my life. My wife, Jeanette Blakeley who tirelessly supports me is my heroine, and without her this book would not exist.

I have enjoyed unique opportunities to learn, practice, and teach firearms self-protection techniques in the United States and foreign countries. I am indebted to those trainers and students in my life whose influences are also found throughout this book.

Thank you to those individuals whose guidance helped shape my understanding of organizational and operational survival: Field Training Officer Don Robb (Dallas Police Department); Police Instructor Richard Perez (Dallas Police Department); Tactical Officer Steve Claggett (Dallas Police Department); Special Agent Charles Massey (North Carolina State Bureau of Investigation); and Team Lead Jason Collins, (Civilian Police Program, Afghanistan).

Deserving of recognition and compliment is Gaston Glock, founder of Glock Inc., for having the imagination, determination, and perseverance for designing, building, and marketing pistols that perform to the moniker of "Glock Perfection."

A special thank you is in order to Alan Ramsey, Director of Training at Glock Inc., who is certainly one of the reasons for the company's reputation of exceptional customer service and training. Alan as a matter of practice provides selfless assistance to operators who knowingly go into harm's way.

There would not be training without those companies that make quality products or provide services that promote the survivability of armed civilians, police officers, and military operators. Those companies have my appreciation, and some of their products and services are referenced throughout the endnotes in this book.

I also wish to acknowledge with gratitude the following organizations whose influence, training, or materials contributed to the breadth and scope of this book:

- American College of Emergency Physicians
- Bureau of Alcohol, Tobacco, Firearms and Explosives
- Calibre Press

- Dallas Police Department, Texas
- Department of Health and Human Services
- Department of Justice
- Department of State
- Drug Enforcement Administration
- Federal Bureau of Investigation
- Federal Law Enforcement Training Center
- Force Science Institute
- Glock Inc.
- Glock Sport Shooting Foundation
- Immigration and Customs Enforcement
- International Association of Chiefs of Police
- International Association of Law Enforcement Firearms Instructors
- International Defensive Pistol Association
- International Practical Shooting Confederation
- Israel Defense Forces
- Israel Police
- Line of Duty, Inc.
- Marshals Service
- National Rifle Association
- National Rifle Association Action Pistol: Competitive Shooting Division
- National Rifle Association Law Enforcement Division
- New York City Police Department, New York
- North Carolina Justice Academy
- North Carolina Private Protective Services Board
- North Carolina State Bureau of Investigation
- Secret Service
- United Kingdom British Army
- United Kingdom Police Force
- United States Air Force
- United States Army
- United States Marine Corps
- United States Navy
- United States Practical Shooting Association

Timothy D. Blakeley

TABLE OF CONTENTS

A CAUTION TO THE READER

Follow the Four Rules for Firearms Handling to help prevent *mistaken* property damage, personal injury, or death.

1. **Firearms are considered loaded until proven empty.**

2. **Keep the muzzle pointed in the appropriate direction.**

3. **Keep the trigger finger on the receiver unless firing.**

4. **Fire when reasonable in view of the circumstances.**

Fighting with a pistol is *not* an easy endeavor. Anyone who decides to acquire skills necessary to fight with a pistol should be willing to expend the necessary time and effort to obtain competency. Fighting with a pistol is a matter of life-and-death that has resulted in some operators successfully defeating their adversaries while other operators have died.

This book is for providing information to armed civilians, police officers, and military operators on fighting with a pistol and operational survival. The sale of the book is with the understanding that the publisher and author are *not* engaged in rendering legal or other professional services by way of this book. If legal or other expert assistance is required, seek the services of a competent professional.

Sources of information used in this book unless otherwise noted are under the *fair use law* in sections 107 through 118 of the copyright law (title 17, U. S. Code) for purposes of illustration or comment. Works are documented for research and comment with accompanying endnotes giving authors credit due. The reader should consider for further study acquiring the material by those authors listed in the endnotes and tailor that information to individual needs. This book also includes quotation of short passages in scholarly or technical work for illustration or clarification of the author's observations.

Efforts were made to make this book as complete and as accurate as possible. However, there may be mistakes, both typographic and in content. Please report typographical or content errors to info@policetech.com. Glock pistols were used to test the techniques in this book and some of the techniques may *not* be applicable to other brands of pistols. Therefore, this book is a general guide for fighting with a pistol and operational survival information. This book also contains information on fighting with a pistol and operational survival current only up to the printing date.

The author and PoliceTech Publications expressly disclaims any warranties, liabilities, losses, cost, claims, demands, suits, or actions of any type or nature whatsoever, arising from this book or any claim that a particular technique or device described in this book is legal or reasonable in any jurisdiction. The reader assumes sole responsibility for his or her actions. The information contained herein is subject to change without notice.

Information and Precautions

NOTE: Important information related to the equipment, materials, operators, or bystanders.

CAUTION: Potential damage to equipment and materials.

WARNING: Potential injury to operators involved or bystanders.

DANGER: Life-threatening situation to operators involved or bystanders.

The term *operator* represents an *armed civilian, police officer,* or *military operator*.

The term *police officer or officer* represents any *law enforcement officer* (municipal, county, state, federal, or national).

The term *deputy* represents a specific *law enforcement officer* (county or parish).

Trademarks

GLOCK® and Safe Action® are registered trademarks of Glock Inc., 6000 Highlands Parkway, Smyrna Georgia 30082 USA.

PoliceTech® is a registered trademark of PoliceTech LLC, P.O. Box 1449 Carthage, NC 28327 USA.

PREFACE

Combat shooting utilizes firearms for the protection of human life or preventing serious bodily injury especially from an adversary. One firearms manufacturer recommends *combat* oriented training for police officers and military operators.[1] There may be concern about using the term "combat shooting." Some may believe the term "combat" has a connotation of destroying property and killing people. However, in our context the word *combat* is a fight between two or more people. In combat situations (commonly called *deadly force encounters*) police officers try to minimize property damage and use reasonable force to stop criminals. Officers must keep clearly in their mind they are not at war with the citizenry.[2]

Although police officers and military operators are not at war with a country's general population, any deadly force encounter is most definitely a war of a personal nature. Moreover, those waging war against the police see them as the enemy.[3] In that war just like any other—a winning attitude is required. The armed civilian, police officer, or military operator cannot afford to lose. Losing will likely mean dying.[4] Even when injured the *will* to fight must demand the *body* continue to fight. Those who protect the innocent must accept that cuts can be stitched, and broken bones set. The body can take a great deal of damage and continue to function. Many times even a severely damaged body can be put back together. A life lost is gone forever.

The combat shooting techniques contained herein are from research of shootings and the experiences of armed civilians, police officers, and military operators. Tragically, some of the officers' experiences are a part of the Federal Bureau of Investigation's publication Law Enforcement Officers Killed and Assaulted. In addition are the author's experiences while working as a patrol officer in the crime laden

---

[1] Glock Inc., Instructions for Use Glock Safe Action Pistols All Models, (Smyrna, GA: March 2011), 1.

[2] *Holland v. Harrington*, 268 F.3d 1179 (10th Cir. 2001).

[3] U.S. Department of Justice, *Violent Encounters*, 2006, (Washington, DC: FBI, 2006), 131.

[4] George T. Williams, "Reluctance to Use Deadly Force," *FBI Law Enforcement Bulletin*, (October 1999): 3-4.

Southwest and Southeast Divisions of the Dallas Police Department in Texas, as a chief of police in a gang and drug ridden community in North Carolina, and as a police adviser and trainer in southern Afghanistan during Operation Enduring Freedom.

There may be those who have differing opinions about the practices outlined in this book. Nevertheless, each person should be able to learn *something* usable for defeating a violent adversary. For those of us who had that experience—some of the information may be heartfelt. The point of view is equally applicable to an armed civilian, police officer, and military operator. Given the choice, it is preferred to use a long gun (carbine, shotgun, or submachine gun) to engage an adversary.[5] However, because of convenience or circumstances of the situation the pistol may be the weapon deployed.[6]

Combat shooting techniques must emphasis accuracy of shots fired with extreme speed. The ultimate evaluation of a training program is the number of adversaries that are stopped by being wounded or killed versus the actual number of deadly force encounters. The desired statistic for a deadly force encounter is a minimum ratio of 1-to-1. A deadly force encounter should result in at least one adversary being struck by gunfire.[7] An organization not achieving this goal may want to reevaluate its firearms training program. The goal of combat shooting is the incapacitation of an adversary thus preventing injury or death to the armed civilian, police officer, or military operator.

[5] U.S. Department of Justice, Federal Bureau of Investigation, Firearms Training Unit, *Wound Ballistic Workshop "9mm vs. .45 auto"* (Quantico, VA, September 15-17, 1987), 19.

[6] U.S. Department of Justice, Federal Bureau of Investigation, Firearms Training Unit, FBI Academy, *Handgun Wounding Factors and Effectiveness* (Quantico, VA, July 14, 1989), 2.

[7] Department of Justice, *Violent Encounters*, 2006, (Washington, DC: FBI, 2006), 48.

SHOOTING TO SURVIVE

How to Fight with a Pistol

OPERATIONAL SURVIVAL

1

Operational survival is the ability to do what is right in combat while avoiding mental trauma, physical injury, and death. Operational survival not only promotes preservation of self, but also the team and the mission. Operational survival is applicable to armed civilians, police officers, and military operators. In this book, operational survival for the armed civilian is lawful self-protection. Operational survival for the police officer is performing law enforcement duties. Operational survival for the military operator is performing combat missions. Although the three groups vary in operational duties and requirements—operational survival is of equal importance.

The development of operational survival consists of a triad with each of the three sections consisting of two parts. The two parts work in unison with each other: mind-set and fitness, training and tactics, and equipment and weapons. First, the foundation begins with the proper *mind-set* to accept the dangers of the operation combined with a *fitness* level to overcome environmental obstacles. Second, *training* for specific operational requirements combined with *tactics* that are effective against an adversary to ensure success. Third, *equipment* necessary to complete the operation combined with *weapons* that provide superior firepower to protect personnel executing the operation. Maintaining the operational survival triad cannot guarantee a successful operation, but not maintaining it will guarantee a higher probability of failure. (Figure 1-1)

In the scope of operational survival, failure means a great deal more than something not accomplished does. Failure by an operator or team will likely mean the *unintentional* loss of life. That life lost may be an operator, family member, team member, or a hostage. To prevent failure each operator must be prepared for the requirements of the operation.

Figure 1-1 *Operational Survival Triad*

Operational requirements vary by an operator's role and the organization tasked for the mission. A private citizen with a concealed carry permit will have different operational requirements than a police adviser in a foreign combat zone. Each operator in both cases must commit to setting time aside to practice in order to meet the requirements of their particular mission.

Some of the requirements for an armed civilian with a concealed carry permit are as follows: (1) have the mind-set to take a human life, (2) accept the dangers of being shot, (3) safely handle a pistol in locations frequented (residence, place of business, etc.), (4) carry out necessary tactical skills (cover, concealment, etc.), and (5) accurately fire a pistol. These things are usually done while wearing civilian clothing, magazine pouch, holster, and pistol.

Some of the requirements for a police adviser in a foreign desert combat environment are as follows: (1) have the mind-set to take a human life, (2) accept the dangers of being shot, (3) accept the dangers of being blown up, (4) safely handle a pistol and carbine in and around unfamiliar surroundings and armored vehicles, (5) complete rigorous vehicle evacuation training, (6) perform bounding drills to break contact with heavily armed and committed terrorists, and (7) accurately fire an automatic carbine and semiautomatic pistol. These things may have to be done in 120-degree Fahrenheit (48.8-degree Celsius) heat and while wearing 50 pounds (22.6 kilograms) of equipment.

Mission requirements dictate acceptable thresholds for each of the six areas of operational survival. As the two previous examples show, thresholds can vary greatly. After meeting the initial thresholds, individual competence will likely be the determining factor for a successful operation. This is especially true of an operation that has gone wrong. Individual competence from the men and women on the ground is what will turn the tide of a seemingly failed operation. This lesson has been learned repeatedly throughout history.

MIND-SET AND FITNESS

Mind-set for the Fight: Mind-set consists of a "…fixed mental attitude or disposition that predetermines a person's responses to and interpretations of situations."[1] A person's attitude about a situation directly affects how he or she responds to the situation. Training and experience is worthless if the mind is not in the game. Operators need to be mentally and physically capable of saving their own lives in a violent encounter.[2] The only certainty is the operator's ability to defend him or herself and others. To think that a partner or others will always be there to help is being naive.[3] Safety and survival is directly dependent on individual *competence,* and not just *confidence.*[4] "It's not the will to win that matters—everyone has that. It's the will to prepare to win that matters."[5]

Attacks occur many times when conditions are most advantageous to the attacker and least advantageous to the person being attacked. The victim denying that an attack is even occurring perpetuates an already grave situation. The final confirmation of the attack for the victim usually comes in the form of getting hurt. In a 10-year period about half the law enforcement officers feloniously killed did *not* use or attempt to use their own gun.[6] The threat of an attack must be reacted to and not just the actual attack.[7] Instant feedback usually occurs from bad tactics in some form of a physical injury. The effectiveness of good tactics usually comes in the form of defeating the adversary. Most of the time making some kind of a decision improves the situation.

Any person that has an aversion to violence should *not* be placed in situations in which violence is the likely outcome. There is a saying in law enforcement, "Not everybody is meant to drive a police car." The author explained it to his sons in this manner, "Sometimes your best is not good enough—you have to do what is required. If you cannot do what is required—step aside and let someone who can."

The fact is not everybody has the mind-set to run toward a volatile and violent situation. Those who do have the mind-set know the more their fear is confronted the easier it is to face. Police officers and military operators by the thousands face fear every day. Such men and women do possess the proper mind-set to fulfill their sworn duty. It is not a lack of fear, but a commitment to do the right thing that keeps them running toward certain danger. There are times an operator without hesitation must inflict violence.[8]

An operator can be a highly trained person, but without the mind-set to take a human life that training is of little use. Legally the armed civilian and police officer are *not* trying to kill the attacker, but to stop any act of aggression likely to cause serious bodily injury or death.[9] However, it "...is often very difficult to successfully produce incapacitation without producing death."[10] Any person who knows deep inside they cannot take a human life should not carry a firearm personally or professionally.[11] The adversary if at arm's reach would likely take the firearm and have the resolve to kill the victim and do just that. It is not a chance worth taking.

An adversary's personal weapons, edged weapons, or firearms are not the only things that can kill. Death can come as quick from panic, indecision, and carelessness. Questioning the reality of an attack dramatically affects reaction time. When recognizing that something is wrong—without hesitating make the necessary adjustments. Likewise, keep emotions in check while making the adjustments. When emotion goes up—judgment has a tendency to go down. The mind and body must seamlessly work together ensuring the greatest probability of survival.

The mind will only give the body commands calculated to be achievable. The body's previous successes and failures provide the threshold for the mind. The mind learns the physical limits of the body during training and past operational experiences. The key is to provide the mind with a fit body that can perform at peak efficiency. As one antirape instructor pointed out, a person's body should be an ally and not a self-imposed enemy.[12]

Fight-or-flight

Fight-or-flight is "...the response of the sympathetic nervous system to a stressful event, preparing the body to fight or flee, associated with the adrenal secretion of epinephrine."[13] The body's physiological changes are "…characterized by increased heart rate, increased blood flow to the brain and muscles, raised sugar levels, sweaty palms and soles, dilated pupils, and erect hairs."[14] A University of Oxford professor, William McDougall in his book, "An Introduction to Social Psychology," published in 1908, developed the idea for the fight-or-flight reaction theory popularized by a Harvard University professor, Walter B. Cannon.[15] Professor Cannon in his book "Bodily Changes in Pain, Hunger, Fear and Rage" published in 1915, wrote:

> "McDougall has developed this idea systematically and has suggested that an association has become established between peculiar emotions and peculiar instinctive reactions; thus the emotion of fear is associated with the instinct for flight, and the emotion of anger or rage with the instinct for fighting or attack."[16]

No matter the level of an operator's training or capabilities to handle stressful situations, he or she will experience to some varying degree involuntary physiological changes associated with the fight-or-flight reaction. Professor Cannon wrote that physiological changes associated with the fight-or-flight reaction are actually favorable for self-preservation:

> "The increase of blood sugar, the secretion of adrenin, and the altered circulation in pain and emotional excitement have been interpreted in the foregoing discussion as biological adaptations to conditions in wild life which are likely to involve pain and emotional excitement, i.e., the necessities of fighting or flight. The more rapid clotting of the blood under these same circumstances may also be regarded as an adaptive process, useful to the organism. The importance of conserving the blood, especially in the struggles of mortal combat, needs no argument.[17]…And increased blood sugar, increased adrenin, an adapted circulation and rapid clotting would all be favorable to the preservation of the organism that could best produce them."[18]

An operator that is maintaining his or her situational awareness will usually perceive a threat before the attack actually occurs. An operator's body will still instinctively go into a fight-or-flight reaction preparing for self-preservation even with the advance knowledge of a possible attack. The fight-or-flight reaction can also be experienced even in training as documented by a police trainer using a heart rate monitor on a police cadet. The police cadet's heart rate reached an astounding 239 beats per minute during marking cartridge scenario training.[19]

Excellent physical conditioning is paramount to deal with the physiological changes on the body. Operational experience can also influence physiological changes. Police officers with more experience working the streets were consistently found to have a heart rate of 40 to 50 beats per minute lower.[20] This is similar to the U.S. Army's acknowledgement that "…combat skills and high stress tolerance are maintained when frequent successful combat actions occur."[21]

When an operator is in poor physical condition and placed in a physically demanding situation the mind is preoccupied with the body's distress. Some of the thoughts could be shortness of breath, weight of the equipment, and distance to travel. Allowing the mind to be preoccupied with such thoughts in an operational environment is dangerous. The mind needs to be free of preoccupation. Excellent physical conditioning frees the mind to concentrate on tactical issues: Where is the adversary located? Where are positions of cover to fight effectively? Are members on the team accounted for and present? In general, what can hurt or kill me? These things require the mind's full attention so an operator can survive in a combat environment.

An operator's physical conditioning and combat capability will influence the mind's decision to fight or flee. There are other decisions that could be made: *freeze, submit,* or *posture.*[22] In combat, it will likely come down to either stand and fight or break contact by systematically fleeing away from the perceived danger (flight). Systematically breaking contact consists of a bounding maneuver in accordance with an organization's standard operating procedures (SOPs).[23] The bounding maneuver is repeated until all operators are out of the danger area. The operators although fleeing the area would immediately and with outright aggression, stand and fight again *if* cornered by their adversaries.[24]

Levels of Situational Awareness

Situational awareness *is* an operator's first line of defense. Levels of situational awareness are the degrees in which an operator observes what is going on around him or her.[25] The operator in other words knows his or her circumstances. The operator can make reasonable decisions to produce positive outcomes by perceiving and understanding the operational environment. Specifically, what activities are people involving themselves? What is the climate of the operational environment? What sights, sounds, and smells are identified? Is the operator's intuition subconsciously warning of potential danger? The operator cannot act reasonably without first assessing the circumstances.

NOTE: Situational awareness results in two states of the human body: *relaxed state* (parasympathetic nervous system) or *heightened state* (sympathetic nervous system).[26]

An operator's daily routine may place him or her in a variety of operational environments and in contact with innocent civilians, other operators, and adversaries. People well known by an operator and secure areas are considered reasonably safe. Other people *not* known and unsecured areas are considered unsafe or hostile. Therefore, the operator's level of situational awareness will vary and rightfully so. The three levels of situational awareness are *low, moderate,* and *high.*[27] The author as an example used three levels of situational awareness while working in Afghanistan.

The author spent time in a single person room at a Regional Training Center (RTC) that was a secured facility. In the room behind a locked door he relaxed and recharged, but maintained a low level of situational awareness. He also kept a pistol and carbine within reach. Anytime he left the room and entered the compound his level of situational awareness went to moderate. He was familiar with the compound and security personnel. However, he consciously evaluated the local police recruits, as they were unknown to him. Anytime he left the compound in a vehicle, his level of situational awareness went to high and remained there. He would consciously evaluate the area, vehicles, and people by listening for sounds and watching for anything that might pose a threat. Maintaining a high level of situational awareness is mentally and physically exhausting, but becomes less so when practiced daily. The mind and body adapts to the intensity and the fatigue threshold increases.

An operator when in familiar surroundings has the ability to subconsciously accept what is normal, but consciously respond to what is abnormal. An operator in unfamiliar surroundings or in contact with unknown people must consciously evaluate both and be prepared to respond to danger. There are certain things that are obviously dangerous, but there are also dangerous things that are not so obvious. In police work it is not necessarily what is wrong, but something is not quite right. An Israeli antiterrorism instructor explained it as being able to identify the *irregular* within the *regular*.[28]

As an example, while working a violent crime task force the author had noticed a car with an equipment violation (no front license plate). He and his partner performed a traffic stop. The author ran the violator's license by name and date of birth, but did not get a return from National Crime Information Center (NCIC). He ran the driver's license by number and it came back to a different person. He knew from his training and experience the violator was likely a *professional* criminal. It would be unlikely that an amateur criminal would have a forged driver's license that appeared authentic.

The author with his pistol in hand walked back to the driver's door. He ordered the violator to get his hands up. He told the violator to do exactly as instructed and doing anything different would get him shot. Keeping the pistol in a retention position, he opened the car door and ordered the violator to step out, look straight ahead, and not to turn around. The author holstered his pistol, jammed the violator in between the open door and windshield post, and handcuffed him. Fingerprinting and interviewing the violator confirmed his identity and exploits of committing bank robberies in the Dallas (Texas) area.

What began as a traffic violation ended with the solving of 18 bank robberies. The mismatched driver's license number within the other information is an example of something irregular (incorrect number) within the regular (authentic appearing license). The author was at a high level of situational awareness, trusted his police instincts, and acted accordingly. The author's preparation and actions reflected his assessment of the circumstances at that time and proved to be correct—a professional criminal.

Actions taken by an operator are evaluated from three viewpoints: (1) *operator*, (2) *adversary*, and (3) *third party*. Consider the three viewpoints as *your* side, *their* side, and for practical purposes the *right* side. The third party or right side may consist of family members, peers, supervisors, agency head, judge, jurors, public, and the media. Acceptance by the right side requires the operator to have *assessed* the circumstances correctly, *prepared* accordingly, and *acted* in a reasonable manner. An operator *not* assessing the circumstances correctly is basing his or her preparation and actions on inaccurate information.

To collect and process accurate information the operator must utilize his or her senses and intuition: sight, smell, touch, and hearing combined with training and life experiences. Training may provide a positive or negative effect on the situation. Life experiences may be the operator having been in a prior crisis that resulted in a favorable or unfavorable outcome. An operator in a life-threatening situation and second-guessing his or her actions may become another statistic caused by hesitation. The operator's past accomplishments or future endeavors in combat do not matter. The operator's actions at that moment in combat are what matters. Those operators that wish to survive will commit to maintaining the appropriate level of situational awareness and act accordingly.

The ability to maintain awareness is a choice resulting in learned behavior. An operator that chooses to be aware half the time has a 50 percent chance of survival. Many times police officers recount as being surprised when attacked.[29] A surprise attack is successful sometimes because of undetected movement. The police officer may not have been aware and failed to detect an adversary's subtle or abrupt body movement. [30] This can include the eyes (target glancing), facial expressions, shoulder drop, or the blatant act of stepping back with a foot. Such movements are many times precursors to an attack, especially the act of stepping back with one foot (fighting stance). Maintaining situational awareness allows the operator to detect such movements providing an opportunity to intervene and defeat the attack before the act stage is initiated by the attacker.

NOTE: About 65 percent of communication is nonverbal behaviors.[31] An adversary using compliant language may attempt to disguise a hostile intent, but closely examining body language will likely reveal the truth.

There are techniques to use while in a high level of awareness to deter a violent attack. Instincts must be trusted and the inner voice followed. Recognize the signs of danger and be suspicious of everything. Scan a person's *face*, *hands*, and *waist* to determine whether a potentially dangerous threat is approaching. This method of scanning is necessary because people starring have a tendency to see what they expect.[32] Make a determination, take decisive action *if* necessary, and move on to the next potential threat. The operator must be willing and capable of using deadly force when it is reasonable to do so.

In the law enforcement profession a uniformed officer is at the greatest risk.[33] The patrol officer is usually the first to respond with only limited information to a situation where many times emotions run high. Frequently the patrol officer is alone. Patrol officers on duty must remain in a moderate to high level of situational awareness to maximize their survivability. A moderate to high level of awareness begins the moment the police officer puts on a badge and gun and walks out the door. The fact is danger exists everywhere.

NOTE: The way to win a violent encounter is to produce more violence than the adversary does.[34]

Stress the Silent Killer

What is stress? Stress is *mental* or *emotional* strain that can result in *physical* symptoms of raised blood pressure or depression.[35] Stress can cause the brain to undergo "...structural remodeling, thereby impairing memory and increasing anxiety and aggression. This can lead to operators becoming distant from spouses, children, other family members, and friends because they are too drained to give to anyone else."[36] What causes stress? Anxiety associated with life's changes, traumatic events, or being overworked causes stress. Stress can also result from a person not being ethical in his or her personal and professional life.

Ethics is more than doing what is legally required. Ethics is doing the right thing at the right time. There is a difference between what a person has a right to do, and what is the right thing to do. The circumstances of a decision published on the front page of a newspaper will reveal the ethicality. Likewise, family members and friends' reactions to a decision can be telling. Not doing what is right will cause stress[37] and sometimes doing the right thing can cause stress.

Personnel in a combat zone may experience a *combat stress reaction*:

"Combat [stress] reaction consists of behavior by a military operator under conditions of combat, invariably interpreted by those around him [or her] as signaling that the military operator, although expected to be a combatant, has ceased to function as such."[38] This reaction is because of the massive stress levels that operators are exposed. "The imminent threat of death and injury, first and foremost, but also the sight of death and injury in others; the loss of commanders and buddies; the physical deprivations of food, water, and sleep; the discomfort of the burning sun and cold nights without adequate shelter; and the lack of privacy, on the one hand, and of the support of family and friends, on the other."[39]

Some people deal with stress by overeating, starvation dieting, smoking, chewing tobacco, drinking alcohol, gambling, taking drugs, and pornography. Each can be a destructive behavior making the current situation even worse. According to the American Heart Association, stress may be linked to heart disease risk.[40] Among law enforcement officers, job related illness is the third largest killer only behind vehicle crashes, and murder.[41]

The healthy way to handle stress is to get adequate sleep, eat a balanced diet, abstain from tobacco products, abstain or drink alcohol in moderation, abstain or gamble in moderation, use medication as prescribed, and maintain a healthy personal and intimate relationship with your husband or wife. Take one problem at a time. Be flexible and have a hobby. Do not invest time and energy in a relationship that is physically abusive or emotionally strangling.

NOTE: Without *effective* communication, relationships are susceptible to falling apart.

Arguably, the best stress reliever is to have a person to talk with while not having to worry about maintaining an appearance. Normally that person will be a spouse. Talking with other like-minded operators can also be helpful. Emotionally confiding in a person of the opposite sex other than a spouse is a recipe for an extramarital affair. Such confiding will only add to the stress already felt. The continued buildup of stress gone unresolved will likely result in a blow up.[42]

A severe blow up can destroy a relationship and breakup a family. What does it profit a person to achieve professional success, but at the cost of his or her family? When retirement comes knocking few people will care. There will be peers standing in line to get the retiree's previous position, equipment, weapons, vehicle, etc. Family members will be there for the retiree long after the retirement party that included slaps on the back and handshakes. Make sure the job is what you do and *not* who you are.

Fit for the Fight

In America, nearly 35 percent of the general population is obese.[43] This problem is also an issue in the law enforcement community. Surprisingly, even one of the best fighting units in the world is feeling the effects of overeating. A U.S. Marine Corps Master Sergeant in Afghanistan noted to the author that even Marines on average are carrying more body fat than in previous years. The discussion of a proper diet and workout program is included because obesity is a *prevalent* problem and fitness is a *critical* component of operational survival.

Functional conditioning is a fitness lifestyle that operators need to embrace. It is not necessary to spend hours in a gym to obtain functional conditioning. *Functional conditioning* is a fitness program developed around the physical requirements of the operational environment.[44] It is a matter of form follows function. In law enforcement, foot pursuits are a good example for functional conditioning. How many police academies require recruits to run 2 to 5 miles (3 to 8 kilometers) at a slow to moderate pace? How many police foot pursuits are ran at a slow pace? Foot pursuits are an all-out race—win or lose.

One of the author's police foot pursuits began with him jumping out of his vehicle, running flat-out for 250 yards (228.6 meters). He ran over a washed out graveled road, jumped two ditches, crossed a yard, and finished the pursuit in the woods. The outside temperature was about 35 degrees Fahrenheit (1.6 degrees Celsius) on that day. His lungs felt like they were going to explode. He had to drink hot water to warm his core. No doubt if his heart had a weak valve, it would have blown out. There were a couple of problems for the author: being overweight, and not sprinting in adverse weather.

Academies would be better suited to have recruits chase one another over obstacles. A streaming flag could be attached using a hook-and-loop fastener[45] to the waist of the role-playing suspect. Similar to flag football the pursuing officer would grab the flag signifying contact.

Another variation would be to chase a fleeing suspect using two, three, or four role-playing officers. Police officers at the agency and academy staff members will have plenty of variations of real-life incidents. This training is a good example of functional conditioning. In addition, the training allows the recruits to learn their physical limits while wearing equipment. To break the daily routine of the academy, hold the training off-site (city park, commercial complex, etc.).

WARNING: Instructors will need to inspect the training area for hazardous debris to ensure the safety of participating recruits.

Examining the physical requirements of police officers in the law enforcement profession provides the necessary information to establish a fitness program.[46] Some of those requirements are as follows: (1) life-and-death fighting with personal weapons (hands, feet, etc.), (2) step from a vehicle using one leg, (3) run full speed, (4) squat behind cover, (5) lay behind cover and quickly get up, (6) climb over a 4-foot (1.21-meter) obstacle (fence, wall, etc.), (7) climb over an obstacle taller than 4 feet (1.21 meters), (8) climb through a window, (9) step or jump from or to an elevated surface, and (10) drag an unconscious person. With some of the physical demands of a police officer established, a suitable training program can be recommended. That program consists of functional conditioning that is *anaerobic*, not aerobic. However, a demanding anaerobic program does have aerobic benefits.

Anaerobic exercise calls for the body to work until it is lacking oxygen (out of breath). Anaerobic training is performed in short all-out efforts. Is this starting to sound familiar in relation to what a police officer does? Anaerobic is the physiological effect endured during a foot pursuit or physical fight.[47] Accepting the need for anaerobic training allows the making of general recommendations that are suited for law enforcement operations. The example is for a police officer, but the program is equally suited for others wanting to achieve a high-level of fitness.

WARNING: Check with a health care provider before beginning any physical activity or workout program.

A balanced fitness program includes stretching for flexibility, striking and kicking for power, weight training for strength, calisthenics, and sprinting and running for overall conditioning. In police work, time is in short supply. Tailor workouts to last about 50 minutes. Exercising at or near maximum capability will make the workout effective. Using a heart rate monitor[48] will ensure the operator is not over training or under training. Exceeding one's comfort zone develops a higher level of fitness.

However, people do not participate long in activities hated. For any fitness program to work two things must occur. First, the person must work the program. Second, the program must work for the person.[49] See fitness as a priority.[50] There are people who despise lifting free weights and others who cringe at the thought of running. The key is to find a blend of exercises that work for the individual. An operator's negative attitude about a particular exercise may change as his or her level of fitness improves.

There also needs to be a baseline measurement for fitness. The state agency that regulates law enforcement credentials will typically have a baseline or a physical agility test for police officers. Military physical fitness tests tend to emphasize the long distant running not applicable to most assignments in law enforcement. A distance of 1.5 miles (2.4 kilometers) is adequate to test cardiovascular fitness of police officers.[51] The distance should be ran and not jogged. Other informational sources are available from fitness research facilities that specialize in studies involving law enforcement.[52] National government agencies may also provide useful resources such as the Federal Bureau of Investigation's Special Agent Physical Fitness Test.

Special Agent Physical Fitness Test[53] *(maximum effort is required on each exercise)*

Pull-ups[54]	10 repetitions
Sit-ups	50 repetitions or more (1minute)
*Push-ups[55]	50 repetitions or more (not timed)
**Dips	15 repetitions
300 Meter Sprint	45 seconds or less
1.5 Mile Run	10:30 minutes:seconds

*The FBI does not time the push-up event, but push-ups can be completed in 1-minute to test upper body power as well as strength. ** The Special Agent Physical Fitness Test does not evaluate dips, but the exercise strengthens muscles used for climbing over a wall or fence.

The special agent fitness standards are about midrange scores for a male. These midrange standards are high for the average police officer. It is unlikely the average police officer could perform 10 pull-ups or run a 7-minute mile (1.6-kilometer) pace. The main point is to compare a person's fitness level to a baseline. Such a baseline would provide the necessary feedback for evaluating personal fitness. To add variety, use the test once or twice a month in place of a regular workout. The operator needs to push past his or her comfort zone on each exercise to reach a higher level of fitness. The fitness test did provide the author with a measure of assurance about his level of fitness before attending an antiterrorism combat course in Israel.

A basic requirement for operational survival is the ability for operators to handle the weight of their own body. Operators can improve handling their body weight by performing pull-ups, push-ups, body rows, and dips. Low strength and excessive body fat have a negative effect on the ability to push and pull body weight. Operators that are not willing or capable of maintaining an acceptable level of fitness for operational survival should move on to a new endeavor.[56]

Workout Program

A healthy workout program will be sustainable over a lifetime with adjustments made for additional recovery time required because of aging. Avoid workout programs that can damage the body. An example is the prolong use of heavy weights that eventually damages the body's joints. Excessive physical activity can also damage the heart. There is a balance between what is healthy and unhealthy. Know the difference and seek professional advice.

Flexible workout programs allow for changes according to how the operator feels. An example is an operator experiencing excessive muscle soreness may want to swap a scheduled weight lifting workout with a session of freestyle exercising. Freestyle is various exercises performed in no particular order. A freestyle session is also an excellent opportunity to work on weak areas.

Some operators lifting weights may prefer dumbbells to barbells. Dumbbells do employ muscles required for lateral stability of the weight. Fixed dumbbells can also reduce workout time, as there is no need to remove and replace weights. A home weight lifting gym can be as simple as several pairs of fixed dumbbells, weight bench, and pull-up bar. Many large retail stores sell modest priced dumbbells. To stay physically fit there is no need to spend a large amount of money on fitness equipment or a gym membership. Minimum equipment allows an operator to perform weight resistance training at home.

An excellent total body barbell lifting routine consists of five exercises performed two times weekly: (1) squat, (2) deadlift, (3) bench press, (4) chin up or body row, and (5) overhead press. Complete each exercise while performing 1 to 3 sets of 10 to 12 repetitions. Use enough weight so no more than the specified repetitions can be performed. After reaching 12 repetitions, add enough weight to perform only 10 repetitions. "For most people, a single set of 12 repetitions with the proper weight can build strength just as efficiently as can 3 sets of the same exercise."[57] The twelfth repetition should be the maximum repetition the operator can perform. A great exercise to complete the workout is the farmer's walk as described in the next section.

Others exercise routines may combine calisthenics with resistance weight training.[58] It is important to perform the exercises properly. Proper form requires discipline, especially on the final repetition. An operator needs to stay disciplined at all times, including while exercising. The operator must be mentally committed to physically performing the sets until the body cannot continue (muscle failure), but doing so without causing an injury.

When beginning a workout program, it is important to stay committed. This is especially true for operators over the age of 40. When a 2- to 4-week layoff occurs, it is difficult if not impossible to resume the program at the same level as when stopping. Whatever amount of time taken off, it will likely take two to three times that amount to return to the previous fitness level. Therefore, make every effort to continue working out. Exercising first thing in the morning stops the preoccupation throughout the day of having to exercise later. That preoccupation can cause stress because of the possibility of missing an afternoon workout. Make sure the workout is scheduled daily just as any other important commitment.

Realize that it could take several years to reach a healthy weight depending on the amount of fat that must be lost. The success of a workout program is as much a mental accomplishment as it is physical. What must *not* occur is allowing the body to dictate to the mind. The mind must maintain control over the body forcing it to respond. There is a vast difference between being in pain (muscle ache) and being injured (physical damage). Pain is associative of muscle ache "…caused by the rupture of microscopic muscle fibers or the connective tissue between the muscle and the tendon."[59] The difference between what is muscle soreness and pain caused by an injury should be recognizable. One of the most notable signs is that muscle soreness begins 1 or 2 days after the activity and diminishes within about 6 days.[60] It is likely that pain associated with an injury will not decrease during this same time and would likely get worse.

Stretching will help to alleviate injuries and maintain the body's symmetry. Each week set aside 1 day to perform about 50 minutes of stretching. Stretching reduces muscle resistance through its range of motion that results in less physical effort for the movement. It is easy to overlook stretching in a fitness program, but is a critical component of overall functional conditioning. However, any *combat* workout program dependent on stretching before performing the task is not realistic. A police officer cannot ask for 5 minutes to stretch before beginning a foot chase. The police officer has to be 100 percent capable of job related physical activity in a split second. This is why stretching is a vital part of the *fitness* program, but not the *combat* program.

An example of a combat program is showing up at the range and running an obstacle course. Police officers need to maintain adequate flexibility to perform job related functions on demand. Improve flexibility by stretching before and after fitness training. A partner can enhance the training experience. Partners can encourage and motivate each other, especially on difficult days. When a workout partner is the operator's spouse, their relationship can benefit from the physical and emotional intimacy of working out together. Working out with a like-minded person of the opposite sex other than a spouse can create problems and possibly result in an extramarital affair. Careful consideration is called for when making such workout choices and agreed on by *all* parties.

Strength Training for Combat Shooting

The inability to control a pistol can sometimes be traced to low strength in the hands, wrists, arms, and upper body. Operators whether male or female need to realize the importance of having adequate strength to shoot a pistol. Only after the operator is convinced of such importance would he or she be motivated to start and continue a strength building program designed to improve combat shooting. Each hand should be equally as strong and capable of firing the pistol. The non-dominant arm would become the firing arm in the event of a dominant arm injury.

Exercising both hands provides the means for an operator to have equal strength in each hand. Stronger hands provide a more stable grip and better recoil control with all other things equal.[61] Grip strength is what keeps the pistol from moving around in the hands.[62] Operators are encouraged to warm up to reduce the chance of injury before beginning any strenuous exercise program. Although some of the exercises may not seem strenuous to some operators a warm up is still advisable.

The recommended exercises are based on a gradual building process beginning with lighter resistance and low repetitions and increasing both as improvement occurs. Performing recommended exercises for the hands, wrists, arms, and overall body will increase strength required for combat shooting. Issuing a *hand exerciser* and a *hand gripper tool* to recruits for use at the beginning of an academy will improve their hand strength throughout the training cycle. Follow the manufacturer's recommendations for proper use unless otherwise directed by a healthcare professional.

Hand Exerciser: The hand exerciser is ideal for an operator wanting to develop individual finger strength.[63] The fingers operate by a separate system of muscles and tendons in the hand, wrist, and forearm. The hand exerciser has springs allowing each finger to work independently. The hand exerciser is available in four color-coded models ranging from 3 pounds (1.36 kilograms) up to 9 pounds (4.08 kilograms) of individual finger resistance. The hand exerciser allows maintaining a shooting grip while strengthening the trigger finger and improving the speed of pulling a trigger. (Figure 1-2)

To use the hand exerciser, hold it vertically with the resistance buttons toward the fingers and the hook (tang) of the ergonomic palm bar positioned in the same place as the back strap of a pistol. Extend the arm in front of the body as when firing a pistol. Grip the buttons with the middle, ring, and little finger. Compress and hold the lower three springs for 3 to 5 seconds while isolating the index or trigger finger. Compress and release the top button *quickly* with the index finger as if pulling a trigger. Breathe throughout the exercise.

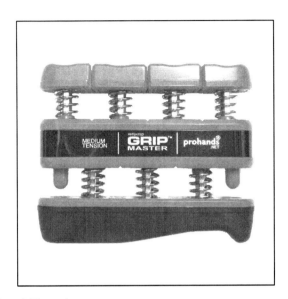

Figure 1-2 *Hand Exerciser*

Hand Gripper Tool: An excellent way to build overall hand strength is to use a heavy-duty hand gripper tool.[64] (Figure 1-3) The hand gripper tool is available from 60 pounds (27.21 kilograms) up to 365 pounds (165.56 kilograms) of resistance. The trainer 100-pound (45.35-kilogram) hand gripper tool is a general recommendation for civilians, police officers, and military operators serious about grip training. [65] Small stature operators may require a hand gripper tool with lighter poundage. Randall J. Strossen, Ph.D., wrote on the principles of effective training with the hand gripper tool in his book titled, *Captains of Crush Grippers.*[66]

To use the hand gripper tool, place one handle in the palm where the back strap of a pistol rests, wrap the fingers over the other handle, and extend the arm as if firing a pistol. Compress the gripper tool from the front straight to the rear. Exhale on the squeeze and inhale on the return. This works the *crush grip* (fingers toward palm) pressure of the hand. The exercise can also be performed with the elbow bent as when holding a pistol in the join position of the draw. The crush grip is the same force generated with the firing hand gripping a pistol front to back and the non-firing hand gripping side to side.

Figure 1-3 Hand Gripper Tool

Farmer's Walk: The farmer's walk is one of the best exercises an operator can do for his or her grip strength and overall body conditioning. The exercise builds strength in the hands, wrists, forearms, biceps, shoulders, neck, back, and legs. What may look like a simple exercise is in reality a test of the mind and body when performed with heavy weights and walking at a fast pace.

To perform the exercise pick up a barbell plate, dumbbell, kettlebell, ammunition can, bucket of sand or water, etc., in each hand. (Figure 1-4) Quickly walk 50 yards (45.72 meters) and return to the starting position. Rest for 60 seconds and complete the walk again for a total of 200 yards (182.88 meters). The weights are carried in the same manner as suitcases. The amount of weight carried will vary according to the operator's ability. However, the operator should strive to increase to the maximum amount of weight his or her grip can hold while covering the distance.

WARNING: Wear proper fitting footwear and walk on a stable surface free of debris when performing the farmer's walk to help prevent an ankle injury.

Figure 1-4 *Farmer's Walk Exercise*

Eating to Live

Overweight people in restaurants tend to have a mound of food on their plates. Some Americans eat much more food than necessary for good health. Being overweight contributes to and may even cause some serious health problems. Obesity is a form of self-destruction and fad diets do *not* work. What will work are correct portions of healthy foods eaten at proper intervals to sustain the body. Proper intervals include the *midmorning* and *afternoon* snacks. These snacks prevent excessive hunger that results in overeating at lunch and dinner. Not eating until being hungry is going too long without food. Periodically consume healthy snacks even when not hungry. This will keep hunger in check and prevent the urge to overeat.

A lifestyle change will not occur until the person makes up his or her mind to lose fat and keep it off. In the beginning, it may be a daily struggle not to overeat. It might even be an hourly struggle. Identify the *reasons* for overeating. Is the overeating because of boredom, stress, or compulsion? As an example, staying up late at night and eating when the person should be sleeping. Be assured the answer to an emotional problem is *not* in a refrigerator. By eating large amounts of comfort food, the problem will only get worse. Identify the problem and find a healthy means to avert the desire to overeat.

Engineering out human error will also increase the chance of success. This means not having unhealthy food in the home or at the office. According to Brown University researchers, a person will eat what is available: "The biggest influence on junk food intake appeared to be the amount people kept in their house."[67] A cabinet full of junk food is too tempting for most people. Just having junk food in the home can create stress. This occurs from having to resist the temptation to eat or worse giving in to the temptation. When temptation strikes ask yourself, "Will what I am about to eat bring me closer or take me farther away from my goal?"

Fat loss will *not* occur while eating desserts, candies, and junk food daily. This important fact must be *mentally* accepted so *physically* fat loss can occur. Will it kill a person to stop eating junk food? Obviously the answer is "no." However, eating junk food daily can cause health problems leading to a person's premature death. The label of "junk food" is fitting in that it is "rubbish" making little or no contribution to a healthy lifestyle. A healthy lifestyle begins by making decisions that promote good health—eat to live, not live to eat.

Clean out the junk food and stock cabinets with nutritious foods. Accept there may be setbacks. A setback can come in the form of bingeing on a favorite sweet for several days. Do not give up! There is always the choice of throwing away the binge food. This may occur from a self-realization of the extra calories are not worth the temporary pleasure of eating them. It takes about a year to have a sustainable lifestyle change. The difference between failure and success is commitment. Commitment is that ability to have a setback, but return to the program. Eventually the setbacks will be fewer and fewer and the program will evolve into a lifestyle. It will become second nature to eat proper portions. The previous mounds of food will cause feelings of revulsion. The ability to calculate calories and make a decision will be reactive—just another survival skill.

NOTE: To admit going on a diet eventually leads to going off the diet. Going off the diet will likely lead to gaining the previous weight back and then some more. Eating right is *not* a short-term diet. Eating right is a long-term lifestyle change.

Total calories and fat intake are equally important in the quest to lose fat. A study at Cornell University revealed that limiting fat intake to about 25 percent of daily calories might reduce a person's body weight by 10 percent in a year.[68] However, to reduce the risk of heart disease some experts believe that saturated fat intake must be limited to 10 percent of daily calories.[69] Losing fat is not only about fat intake. The body runs on calories and the *total* amount consumed is equally important to losing fat. Keep fat intake to about 20 percent of total calories while burning more calories than consumed and the body loses fat efficiently. The average person needs only 2,000 calories to remain healthy.

Most people do not realize how many calories they consume daily and the *small* amount of food it takes to reach 2,000 calories. The 2,000 calories is for a 24-hour period, *not* 8 hours. The *Nutrition Facts* label on packages will provide total calories and calories from fat. The 2,000 calories also includes *beverages*. Keep a food and beverage consumption log to discover the total calories and calories from fat consumed in a week. This is a crucial component for realizing the number of calories consumed. Read the labels for a calorie count per serving and be honest in the *number* of servings consumed.

To establish what is a serving size use measuring cups. As an example, 1 cup (236 milliliters) is a serving size for many beverages. Pour water into a measuring cup and then pour that amount into a glass commonly used during mealtime. The amount will likely fill only half the glass, but it is a serving size. Pouring a full glass would probably be two servings. Do the same for cereals, vegetables, etc. Know what a serving size looks like in the dishware used in the home and workplace. There are Internet sites than can provide serving size and calorie information for most foods. This includes fast foods. Below is an example of an approximate 1,500-calorie meal plan for 24 hours.[70]

Breakfast: Cereal – 385 calories
1.5 ounces (43 grams) whole grain low fat cereal (165)
1 cup (236 milliliters) 1% milk (110)
1cup (236 milliliters) orange juice (110)
Noncaloric beverage (recommend water)

Lunch: Sandwich – 265 calories
2 slices whole wheat bread (140)
1teaspoon (5 milliliters) mustard (0)
2 ounces (57 grams) white meat (about 8 thin slices), chicken or turkey (80)
1 ounce (28 grams) ultra thin sliced cheese (1slice) (45)
Noncaloric beverage (recommend water)

Dinner: Steak Dinner – 731 calories (men) 561 calories (women)
3 ounces (85 grams) lean sirloin, broiled (176)
½ cup (118 milliliters) green beans, canned, no salt added (55)
2½ - 3 inches (66 – 76 millimeters) in diameter baked potato (160)
2 teaspoons (10 milliliters) butter (60)
1 cup (236 milliliters) 1% milk (110)
Noncaloric beverage (recommend water)
Men add:
2 slices whole wheat bread (140)
1 teaspoon (5 milliliters) butter (30)

Snacks: Mid-morning and Mid-afternoon – 200 calories (100 calories snack each)
1 large banana 8¾ inches (222 millimeters) long (100)
1 apple 3-inch (76-millimeter) diameter (100)
½ cantaloupe 5-inch (127-millimeter) diameter (94)
3 plums (90)
1 ounce 2 small ½-ounce (14-gram) raisins boxes (82)
1 cup (236 milliliters) light, nonfat, flavored yogurt (100)

　　The meal plan is 1,581 calories for men and 1,411 calories for women for 24-hours. The 1,581- and 1,411-calorie plans also include 200 calories for snacks. Some may find it necessary to add a third 100-

calorie snack about 2 hours after dinner. Obviously not everyone is going to like every food listed in the sample meal plan. Just substitute the undesirable foods for something comparable in nutritional value and calories. Maintain a structured meal plan and keep impromptu meals to a minimum. Impromptu meals many times provide opportunities to eat unhealthy foods. Water is also a crucial component of the meal plan.

The above recommendations are based on an average person eating a 2,000-calorie diet, but the actual number of calories required based on the person's desired weight, sex, and age are easily computed. As people age they do not need as many calories because after the age of 20 their metabolism slows down 2 percent each decade.[71] An easy formula to figure how many calories are needed is to take the desired weight and multiply it by 11 for a *female* and 12 for a *male*. Then subtract the 2 percent for every 10 years after the age of 20 and add 10 percent to provide needed calories for daily life functions. The final number is the minimum daily calorie intake.

As an example, a 30-year-old *female* whose ideal body weight is 130 pounds (58.9 kilograms) would calculate her Basal Metabolic Rate (BMR) as follows:[72]

Desired weight = 130 pounds (58.9 kilograms)
130 x 11 = 1,430
1430 – 1(1,430 x 0.02) = 1401
1,401 + 140 = 1,541 calories per 24 hours

As an example, a 50-year-old *male* whose ideal body weight is 175 pounds (79.3 kilograms) would calculate his BMR as follows:

Desired weight = 175 pounds (79.3 kilograms)
175 x 12 = 2,100
2100 – 3(2,100 x 0.02) = 1,974
1,974 + 197 = 2,171 calories per 24 hours

NOTE: The calories burned during a daily workout are *not* included and may need adding to the BMR *if* losing fat is not the goal.

Operators might consider taking vitamin supplements along with eating the correct number of calories. A healthcare professional should be consulted before beginning a vitamin supplement program. Vitamins are generally taken *with* food. Some operators may find a convenient time to take vitamin supplements is in the morning with an 8-ounce (236.58-milliliter) glass of water after eating a balanced breakfast. Vitamins *supplement* the nutrients found in food, but are not a replacement for wholesome food. Taking prepackaged vitamins in plastic packs specifically gender formulated may be an option.[73] It is common in the United States for retail drugstores to put vitamins on sale. Taking advantage of a sale can reduce the expense of buying vitamins.

Typically, when a male reaches 40 years of age his androgen level declines and when a female reaches 40 years old her estrogen level declines. Taking dehydroepiandrosterone (DHEA) may help increase androgens and estrogen levels. A typical daily oral dosage is 50 milligrams.[74] A blend of glucosamine and chondroitin may help maintain comfort, mobility, and flexibility in the joints.[75] The androgen, estrogen, and joint care supplements are *not* normally included in the single plastic packets, but can be purchased separately. Do *not* take vitamins in excess as it can cause health problems.

WARNING: Check with a health care provider before beginning any nutritional program or taking vitamins. Keep vitamins out of the reach of children and read the warning label printed on the containers.

The Secret to Losing Fat

As seen in the previous section it takes a small amount of *food* and *beverage* to reach the 1,500-calorie mark. Here is how to lose fat: It takes a deficiency of 3,500 calories to burn 1 pound (0.45 kilogram) of fat. Eating 1,500 calories produces a 500-calorie deficient with a 2,000-calorie diet. Doing that for 7 days will equal a 3,500-calorie deficient (500 x 7 = 3,500). The person has burned 1 pound (0.45 kilogram) of fat in 7 days. Exercising 5 days a week while burning 350 calories in each workout will equal 1,750 additional calories burned (350 x 5 = 1,750). This will burn an additional half-pound (0.22 kilogram) of fat for the week.

The facts are a person normally requiring a 2000 calorie per day diet can consume 1,500 calories per day, burn 1,750 calories in 5 workouts and lose 1.5 pounds (.68 kilograms) of fat per week. Consider this level of fat loss as healthy and sustainable. In a 4-week period, 6 pounds (2.7 kilograms) of fat will be loss. In a 52-week period, 78 pounds (35.3 kilograms) of fat will be loss. Obviously as fat is loss and lean muscle increases the metabolic rate will increase. All other things equal this will result in fat being burn at a greater rate in the same period.

NOTE: Use the meal plan to control body fat and a workout program to sustain fitness. An injury that prevents working out requires a reduction in caloric intake to prevent gaining fat.

Dietary guidelines consist of 60 percent carbohydrates, 20 percent protein, and 20 percent fat.[76] This will provide a healthy diet for most people. As an example, consume no more than 400 calories from fat when using a daily 2,000-calorie meal plan. The *total fat percentage* is on the *Nutrition Facts* label on food packages. Eat foods mainly that contain 20 percent or less fat while eliminating *trans fat* from the diet.[77] To increase success use the additional suggestions that follow.

Sleeping for 8 hours and not drinking fluids dehydrates the body. Keep a pitcher of water in the refrigerator. First thing in the morning, drink 16 ounces (473 milliliters) of chilled water. This will jump-start the body's metabolism for the next 90 minutes.[78] Drink 2 quarts or 8 cups (1.8 liters) of water throughout a 12-hour day. Consider doubling the amount if physically active.[79] Some foods have a high concentration of water and count toward the 2-quart (1.8-liter) goal. One of the easiest ways to get the required fluid intake is to replace sugary beverages with water.

The body has also been without food for 8 hours after a night's sleep. Eating breakfast is crucial to a wellness program, but a person is not going to lose fat eating a 1,400 to 1,500 calorie breakfast. To lose fat eat a healthy 300 to 500 calorie breakfast. While eating breakfast, review weight loss goals established in a *written* plan. Written goals reviewed often have a greater chance of success. Take personal responsibility of successes and failures. Pack a 300-calorie lunch and include two 100-calorie fruit servings for the morning and afternoon snacks. Stay clear of vending machines and eat what is in the packed lunch. Get an average of 8 hours of rest nightly. Between 10:00 p.m. and 6:00 a.m. is the ideal time for an adult to sleep.[80] Sleeping provides time for the body's muscles to heal and hormones to function properly to burn fat.

NOTE: A Stanford University study found that "…the secretion of leptin, a hormone that regulates appetite, decreased significantly during the period of *sleep deprivation*. Decreases in leptin levels are associated with increased appetite and possibly weight gain."[81]

A preoccupied mind is detrimental to a good night's sleep. Review your goals and "Things to Do" list before going to bed. Write down any necessary changes. This may prevent lying awake thinking and worrying about the next day's activities. Do not go to bed mad at someone—especially a spouse. Unresolved anger will wreak havoc on the body and may result in a restless night. Having a loving supporting spouse is medicine to the body. A spouse should be treated with at least the same amount of respect as a supervisor. Think about it. Do employees normally yell, scream, and curse at their supervisors? Not for long and work there! Then can an operator not treat the person he or she supposably loves more than any other with that same level of respect?

Helpful Hints to Losing Fat

The hints provided in this section will help an operator to maintain optimal weight. Limit desserts to once a week. The author and his wife go out every Friday night—their date night. They have dessert, but split it dividing the calories. Neither one of them are consuming an excessive amount of calories from fat. Find out the portion size when ordering a meal. The so-called single portion in a restaurant can be two or more times the recommended portion size. In such cases order one plate of food and split it with your spouse. When dining alone ask for a carryout box with the meal and immediately divide the portions. Another advantage is getting two meals for the price of one. Another option may be to order a smaller portion from the kids menu or seniors menu. When ordering a steak, choose the healthier smaller size and leaner cut. Some restaurants may also offer grilled vegetables that have a nice flavor and are healthy.

Try not to eat after 7:00 p.m., this will provide adequate time for the body to burn dinner calories before morning. Abstain or drink colas in moderation. Colas are nothing but empty calories. Sixteen ounces (473 milliliters) of cola has about 200 calories. Drink mostly water and 100 percent fruit juice. Eat whole wheat bread to include hamburger and hotdog buns. Seldom eat food made from processed (white) flour and sugar. Begin a meal by first eating some vegetables to get a feeling of fullness. A variety of bright color vegetables and fruits are desirable. Eat until the feeling of hunger is satisfied, but *not* to the point of being stuffed. Read the Nutrition Facts label to determine the serving size and the number of calories. Knowing how to count calories and how many to eat is no different from knowing how to count money and how much to spend.

Drink water while working out, *not* a sports drink. Sports drinks are for people that have minimum body fat and the extra calories are necessary to sustain the workout. The point of working out for the average person is to burn excess calories (body fat). Drinking 48 ounces (1419 milliliters) of a sports drink equals to about 300 calories. A 30-minute calisthenics workout would burn about 300 calories—300 sports drink calories—with little or no fat loss occurring from the workout. As a rule, abstain from drinking calories. Consume calories from nutritious foods and not sugary liquids.

Water can help a person lose fat in two ways.[82] First, water can reduce the effects of craving food. What a person may interpret as being hungry can be nothing more than thirst. Drinking sips of 3 to 4 ounces (88 to 118 milliliters) of water throughout the day can help stop the feeling of hunger. Second, calories must be burned to warm the ice-cold water back to body temperature. The body will burn about 226 calories to warm a gallon of 40-degree Fahrenheit (4.4-degree Celsius) water to a body temperature of 98.6 degrees Fahrenheit (37 degrees Celsius).[83]

Prepare in advance for upcoming engagements (birthdays, anniversaries, and holidays) that serve rich fatty foods. Contrary to what some may think—holiday calories do count! Two weeks before the engagement follow a strict meal plan. In the same 2 weeks, include additional fat burning workouts. This will cause a further reduction in body fat before the engagement and minimize the effects of indulging in desserts. Going on a binge and eating irresponsibly for 2 weeks can take 2 months of strict meal planning to lose the excess fat.

Those that have gone on and off fad diets might begin a lifestyle change by eating one healthy meal per day. The makeup of the remaining meals continues as they have been in the past. What the operator will likely realize in taking this small step is that one healthy meal will turn into two and then three healthy meals. Begin the one meal change with a healthy breakfast as it sets the tone for the daily meal plan.

Losing fat is not a mystery. It is a matter of education and developing healthy eating habits. Performing thousands of crunches will not reveal six-pack abs under a layer of fat. If fat is initially lost, but the pounds begin to creep back. Simply review these recommendations and fix the problem. Think and act like a thin person to stay thin!

The Mental Aspect of Losing Fat

A person may not be in a position to eat a scheduled meal because of unforeseen circumstances. Mentally accept the meal is missed, but it is not the end of the world. A healthy person is not going to starve to death from missing a meal. Take control mentally and make a conscious decision when to eat the next available meal and what type of food. Do not allow a mind-set of overeating to creep in just because of one missed meal. Stick to a nutritious meal plan and do *not* think because of one missed meal that a double portion is acceptable for the next meal.

Most people have a threshold for tolerating a certain amount of fat. That threshold is a *mental* breaking point. Sometimes the threshold is reached only because of a traumatic event and the person hits rock bottom. Such occurrences may be an operation to correct a medical problem caused by excessive fat or the embarrassment of not being able to sit in a single seat on an airplane. The threshold is a matter of making a decision that fat will not be tolerated beyond a specified amount (whether physical size or actual weight).

Set the threshold at a point that provides an enjoyable quality of life. Quality of life not only includes the individual, but also a spouse, children, extended family members, and even friends. Obesity is not only a personal problem, but it affects others as well. Spouses generally have the same eating habits—good or bad. One spouse may have to take the lead on establishing a healthy lifestyle, not only for the other spouse, but also for other family members. Parents can pass the problem of obesity to their children. It is likely that until a lifestyle change occurs a cycle of obesity will continue into the next generation.

TRAINING AND TACTICS

Training needs to be considerably more difficult than operational requirements.[84] Pushing operators to their mental and physical limits during training helps them to operate effectively in an adversarial environment. Training should include a simple, but effective method to push operators. Operational survival skills must be carried out while under stress and in low light environments. Respond to stress with aggression to improve operational survival. To learn the skills use a strict sequence of drills[85] applied during courses of fire.[86]

The training philosophy of "simple is better" applies.[87] The creator of SEAL Team Six, listed Ten Commandments of Special Warfare, and number seven on the list commands to "keep it simple."[88] One reliable method to accomplish a task is better than two or three methods that can create indecision and confusion. Multiple options in the decision-making process will slow down response time. "Studies of reaction time indicate that when the number of possible responses increases from one to two, reaction time increases 58 percent."[89] The theory of "another tool in the toolbox" can quickly become a "cluttered toolbox" which is counterproductive to operational survival.[90] When failure occurs during training—operational failure is the next logical outcome. For armed civilians: fail in training—fail in the community. For police officers: fail in training—fail on the street. For military operators: fail in training— fail on the battlefield.

Seamless Training Integration

A shooting system and its related tactics must seamlessly progress through dry fire, marking cartridges or airsoft, range live fire, shoot house, and the operational area. This seamless integration must be accomplished with little or no changes to the shooting system or tactics. When a student keeps hearing the words from an instructor, "Do it this way here, but in the field you will do it like this." Find another instructor. Training time is a precious commodity. Why waste it on a system that cannot be live fired? When the system does not allow live firing more than likely the system is too complicated. Bringing the operational environment to the range forces realistic live fire training.

NOTE: Reality begins on the range, trainers must allow for real-life handling of the pistol. Know the differences between the range, an operational environment, and Hollywood. Movies are for entertainment—*not* training purposes!

Think of it like this. A system that will *not* work in a controlled environment (flat range) is certainly not going to work in a chaotic environment (gunfight). An operator confused and indecisive in training because of complicated techniques and tactics will be even more so in combat. There are a variety of tactics that could be taught in training. However, does the instructor teaching those tactics wear the same type of equipment worn by the students or required operationally? Equipment can vary greatly between an armed civilian, undercover police officer, uniform police officer, Special Weapons and Tactics (SWAT) officer, and military operator. Students wearing a full ensemble of gear must train to a tactical level of competency required by the operation. Anything short of this is a waste of resources.

Operational requirements must dictate training and tactics. This is the first and foremost factor. There must be real-life reasons for suggested training and tactics. When political concerns and other such factors take precedence over operational requirements—substandard training or injury and death to personnel are likely outcomes. In the training chain of command, there should be a person with enough rank or political influence to curtail negative outside interference.

Procedural Memory Training

The vast majority of equipment and firearms manipulation problems are because of the operator *not* acquiring procedural memory. *Procedural memory* is the gradual, incremental learning of motor and cognitive skills.[91] It is also defined as "…involving the recall of learned skills."[92] Simply stated, a person has learned and now can remember how to do things (ride a bicycle, swim, type on a keyboard, etc.).[93] These procedural memories tend to persist although not used for many years.[94] As an example, do we forget how to ride a bicycle? To fight with a pistol an operator needs to go through a learning progression to acquire necessary skills carried out *without* conscious thought, i.e., *procedurally memorized.*[95] Procedural memory provides long-term subconscious motor function skills best developed by correct *repetitious* practice.

Shooting deficiencies occur many times because of the operator not performing the necessary repetitions to acquire motor function, i.e., physical skill. A former Special Operations soldier stated that he dry fired his weapon for 8 hours a day for a 2-week period before ever firing the first shot during Special Operations training.[96] The author's observation as a firearms instructor is that 90 percent of necessary skills for fighting with a firearm can be initially taught and subsequently maintained without live firing. The remaining 10 percent of skill necessary for fighting with a pistol is acquired by live fire and centered on recoil control.

Below is a list of 10 requirements for fighting with a firearm. Obliviously the list is *not* all-inclusive, but covers the major requirements of fighting with a firearm. Recoil control requires live fire exercises to *confirm* the skill is acquired. The remaining skills use dry fire and can be taught and practiced without firing a live round.

1. Equipment (placement and manipulation)
2. Fighting Stance
3. Grip
4. Drawing (static and dynamic)
5. Sight Alignment
6. Sight Picture
7. Trigger Control
8. Loading / Unloading / Reloading
9. Clearing Stoppages
10. Recoil Control (live fire)

The above results at first glance may seem surprising. However, a common problem for an operator is nothing more than *not* being comfortable with his or her pistol, equipment, or both. Inadequate recoil control is an example of being uncomfortable caused by a lack of a proper grip. While firing a pistol the problem is readily identifiable with the constant resetting of the non-firing hand or in some cases both hands. Accurate and consistent shooting will never occur until an operator can *subconsciously* obtain a comfortable solid grip to control the pistol.

The sense of being uncomfortable is similar to driving an automobile for the first time. The awkwardness of not knowing how much force to use when pressing the gas or brake pedals, how quick to let out on the clutch pedal, or how close to get to an object before possibly striking it with the vehicle. These acts are difficult in the beginning, but after performing many repetitions, driving becomes a subconscious skill. This is the same goal when firing a pistol. The operator performs the mechanics of shooting on a subconscious level. Performing subconsciously frees the conscious mind to process other information necessary for making decisions and survival.[97] The operator must be aggressive, but feel comfortable with the pistol to maximize its potential.

It is a challenge to obtain that level of comfortableness with limited training time. This problem is especially true for law enforcement. Spend what training time is available on performing procedures in the same manner as in real-life. Preferably, there are no distinctions between *administrative* procedures and *combat* procedures. The adage "train as you will fight" applies here.[98] The operator should feel comfortable performing the procedure during dry firing, while on the range, and in the operational environment.

Use an *inert* or *solid plastic pistol* for firearms training in a classroom.[99] Some of the *classroom* training sessions are as follows: (1) fitting a pistol to the hands, (2) assuming a fighting stance, drawing and presenting the pistol, (3) obtaining a sight picture, (4) turning, (5) assume various firing positions, and (6) use of cover and concealment. Students experience less fatigue because of the inert pistol's lighter weight. Instructors can also freely move among students without fear of a negligent discharge. Use a practice pistol or a pistol that has an inert solid plastic barrel or a chamber blocker installed to teach how to pull the trigger properly.

Taking the time to teach the required skills using correct repetition will build procedural memory. Recruits should be taught firearms handling skills at the beginning of the police academy. This will ensure during simulation training and defensive tactics that recruits correctly handle their firearms. Teach reloading skills using a practice pistol or a pistol with an inert solid plastic barrel or chamber blocker along with inert solid plastic blue magazines. Teach stoppage clearance skills using inert cartridges. Glock makes orange magazine floor plates for identifying magazines used for training and *not* operationally.[100] The orange floor plates permit range personnel to confirm the insertion of a magazine in the pistol.[101]

NOTE: When using functional firearms with *dummy rounds* or *dummy cartridges*[102] conduct training drills at a range. This ensures any live round mistakenly mixed with dummy rounds and inadvertently fired will be contained *if* the operator follows the Four Rules for Firearms Handling.

Training with a pistol that fires a marking cartridge can further develop firearms skills. The pistol has a light recoil and low noise signature. This will allow the operator to concentrate on the mechanics of shooting without the distraction of loud noise and recoil. The instructor can correct operator problems without fear of a negligent discharge from a lethal weapon. The pistols are ideal for force-on-force training in sensitive environmental situations (schools, hospitals, churches, etc.).[103] The Glock training pistols are restricted to law enforcement.[104]

A more economical method of non-lethal training than marking cartridges is using airsoft technology. An airsoft pistol fires a plastic BB at a low velocity. Make sure the airsoft pistol will automatically cycle the slide with each pull of the trigger. Having to rack the slide manually after each trigger pull will build procedural memory counterproductive to shooting a semiautomatic pistol. Most models of pistols used in law enforcement and military operations are available in airsoft. Operators trained with marking cartridges or airsoft BBs will likely perform better when live firing. The time spent training with a marking cartridge or an airsoft pistol will also likely reduce the amount of ammunition required during live fire training. A logistical advantage with marking cartridges and airsoft is that training can be conducted almost anywhere—day or night.

Training with a Pistol for Survival

Base the survival training for armed civilians, police officers, and military operators using a pistol on the criteria as follows:

1. Have the mind-set to identify and immediately react to a threat by quickly drawing and firing within required accuracy.[105]

2. A shooting method enhanced by the body's physiological reaction under stress[106] at various distances to a threat.

3. Train in environments closely related to actual deadly force encounters[107] while enforcing round accountability.

The *first* criterion is the mind-set to react to a deadly force encounter where the measurable outcome is in hundredths of a second. The armed civilian, police officer, and military operator can react and have a chance of surviving or hesitate resulting in the likely outcome of dying.[108] The choice to react begins with realistic training to prepare the operator. The operator must be capable of moving, drawing, and hitting the adversary.

Target Focused Sighted Shooting (TFSS)[109] is an effective method of shooting for training and deadly force encounters. The operator focuses[110] on the target, brings his or her firearm into the line of sight while simultaneously applying pressure to the trigger, sees[111] the aligned sights, and breaks the shot. This allows fast delivery of shots, but within required accuracy. Such accuracy is necessary to protect the female depicted in Figure 1-5.

Figure 1-5 *Hostage Situation*

Joan N. Vickers, Ph.D., and William Lewinski, Ph.D., in their study documented the effectiveness of shooting "...that establishes the line of gaze on the target from the outset, followed by alignment of the sights of the weapon to the line of gaze."[112] This method of shooting leads to a longer *quite eye*[113] duration on the target or adversary prior to pulling the trigger and should improve decision making and operational survival performance.[114]

Another study by William Lewinski, Ph.D., revealed that with the trigger finger on the receiver it is 0.09 second faster focusing on the target and firing than having to acquire a sight picture before firing.[115] Target Focused Sighted Shooting overcomes this issue by teaching the operator to fixate on the target or adversary, but be aware of the sights.[116] There is no loss of time because the operator does *not* have to change his or her visual focus from the target back to the sights. When confronted by an adversary an operator will likely focus on and squarely face the threat.[117]

Any method of combat shooting should conform to the natural survival instincts of the body—not the natural survival instincts of the body conform to a method of shooting. Incidentally, the Combat Shooting Phase 1 chapter explains how focusing on the front sight with both eyes open will create two target images. The operator cannot afford such visual confusion because the entire encounter will probably be over in a matter of seconds. In the same chapter, detailed information is available on the TFSS method and it working with the body's *alarm reaction.*

NOTE: The alarm reaction is also called *sympathetic stress reaction* or *fight-or-flight* reaction.[118]

The *second* criterion is utilizing the body's natural physiological reaction to stress. In all likelihood, an operator will not have time to assume nor would want to assume an upright standing position while focusing on the front sight. The operator will likely assume a crouched fighting stance while focusing on the adversary—see an image of aligned sights and then fire. A former British Special Air Service (SAS) soldier in his course manual explained the difference between aiming *technically* and in *reality.*[119]

"Technically: With both eyes open focus from the rear sight to the front sight, hold the focus on [the] front sight making the target a slight blur."

"Reality: When in a "lethal force action" your total focus will be on the weapon in the suspects' hands. The sights will both be a slight blur, *but* enough to align and take the shot."

The *third* criterion is to train in environments that are as close to actual deadly force encounters as possible. Using airsoft or marking cartridge guns during simulation training allows shooting at a live adversary replicating real-life conditions. [120] This crucial element exposes operators to simulated circumstances found in deadly force encounters.

Another example is the flash of a muzzle. Firing blanks in a dark environment at a distance recommended by the blank manufacturer provides operators with a realistic experience of a muzzle flash.[121] The exercise teaches what a muzzle flash signature looks like. Facing the flash, it is generally a round shape and when perpendicular to the flash it is a teardrop shape.[122] That knowledge could be crucial in determining what direction an adversary is shooting. Enforce minimum shooting distances with any training ammunition such as blanks, plastic BBs, or marking cartridges.

Finally, employ live fire target discrimination training on a range and in a shoot house. [123] *Target discrimination* is the act of quickly distinguishing between threat and no-threat targets and firing only at deadly threats.[124] There are operators that have excellent shooting skills, but those skills can quickly deteriorate when target discrimination is thrown into the mix. [125] Being able to discriminate quickly *if* an individual is an adversary can be the difference in an operator living or dying.

DANGER: Using a *functional* firearm for simulation training is a tragedy waiting to happen. Only use firearms for simulation exercises that *cannot* fire live ammunition. Replace the real barrel with an inert solid plastic barrel or use a chamber blocker to make the pistol nonfunctional.

While attending the Police Assessment, Selection, and Training Program (PAST) before the author's deployment to Afghanistan there were two students that violated the safe minimum distance rule for shooting marking cartridges at a person. The safety briefing provided two pieces of critical information: The minimum shooting distance, and none of the simulations would require shots within the minimum distance. Nevertheless, the students made a decision to use deadly force and engage perceived threats violating the previously announced safety rules. The students should have remembered that none of the shooting scenarios would require shots within the minimum safe distance. It was the last scenario on the final day of training and both students were dismissed from the selection program.

Target and Video Feedback

Paste the holes in targets often or replace targets to provide accurate feedback on effective accuracy. In addition, use a video camera to improve shooting skills. This form of self-correction is even more useful when combined with an experienced instructor. It provides the operator an opportunity to see exactly what is occurring while moving, drawing, reloading, etc. The video camera is suitable for dry fire and live fire training sessions. The operator from a side view should be centered in the frame of the picture. In addition, the upper body and hands can be videoed close up to see exactly what the operator is doing.

The video recording can be reviewed at the range using the camera's built-in display. This will allow the operator to make on the spot corrections. What may provide the greatest benefit is to connect the camera to a large screen television and review the shooting session. The large screen will allow the operator to see small details otherwise gone unnoticed. The video can be slowed down or paused. Operators can identify their weaknesses and work to transform them into strengths. The shooter's personal camera phone can also be used to record his or her performance for reviewing later.

Principles of Learning

Adults learn best by doing or hands-on experience as opposed to lectures. Instructors would do well to remember this point when developing lesson plans. The instructor at the beginning of a training course should explain the amount of lecture time in comparison to practical exercises. Explaining time allocation reduces the mental preoccupation of operators thinking, "When is the lecture going to end, and the practical exercises begin?" An instructor seeing operators yawning from boredom during a lecture should question the effectiveness of the material presented. An instructor should provide students ample rest periods. A training session will normally last 50 minutes with a 10-minute break.

Adult learners also do better with training that outlines the objectives. Lesson plans for police training developed by a certified general or specialized instructor in North Carolina have clear objectives. The instructor should not only explain *what* and *how* something is done, but also *why* it is done. Training begins with the fundamentals and proceeds to an efficient *application* of those fundamentals under difficult circumstances. Instructors should constantly strive to improve methods of instruction that are more effective and efficient. Review and update lesson plans annually.

Training objectives that are confusing or not results driven can frustrate operators. Frustration can quickly drain an operator's motivation to learn. Use a step-by-step process to reduce operator frustration when building skills. Combine individual skills into a group of skills to address real-life problems that operators face. An example is teaching first how to draw a pistol, but then combine it with moving off the line of attack, and return fire. Effective techniques accepted by the operator will produce desired results and in turn build self-confidence. Operators have a reluctance to use ineffective techniques. Techniques accepted as effective are also easier to learn and quickly retained. This learning process is a collaboration of the conscious and subconscious mind.

Memory and Physical Skills: The conscious mind controls short-term memory.[126] When learning new information or a task, short-term memory is used. The author's experience is that note taking helps to retain about 50 percent of information presented. Taking notes allows the studying, reviewing, and memorization of course material at the student's convenience. Such a convenience will improve the amount of information retained. The subconscious mind controls long-term memory.[127] Long-term memory processes already learned information as a reflexive skill. A reflexive skill is when the mind and body work together carrying out a motor function without conscious thought. One of the best methods to learn a physical skill until it becomes a reflex is by performing correct repetitions.[128]

The performance of physical skills is *simple* versus *complex*.[129] A simple skill is drawing a pistol. A complex skill has several steps involved such as clearing a double feed by locking the slide, clearing the pistol, and reloading. Under stress the small muscles (fine motor skills) deteriorate more so than large muscles (gross motor skills). An example of a fine motor skill is using the slide stop lever (not extended) on a Glock pistol to release the slide, especially while wearing gloves.[130] Gross motor skills in contrast are easier to perform under stress. An example is releasing the slide with an *underhand* technique.[131]

Captured on video from the dashboard camera was a police officer after being shot, using the underhand technique during a reload while moving backward in front of a rolling police car and still being shot at by a suspect with a .223-inch (5.56-millimeter) caliber rifle.[132] The police officer had also stripped the magazine from her pistol as the first step in performing the reload. This is an example of a police officer handling her pistol with rapidity of movement because of practice and training that brought all her movements under subconscious control.[133]

Motivation for Learning: One of the best ways to motivate an operator is to provide information and training based on real-life occurrences. Law enforcement statistics as an example bear out that training at distances of 20 feet (6 meters) and less with a pistol is realistic.[134] There needs to be an emphasis on speed when drawing and firing. The level of accuracy required is dependent on the immanency of the perceived threat versus the clarity of the sight image *superimposed*[135] on the adversary.

Effective accuracy of an 8-inch (203.2-millimeter) group according to the situation may do the job. However, in another situation a surgical 1-inch (25.4-millimeter) group may be required to save a life. Teach this spectrum of skill level using a *training and evaluation model* rather than a *qualifying model.*[136] Evaluate the operator first achieving proficiency while training and the target will take care of itself during qualification.

Demonstrations and Presentations: Instructors need to exercise caution when demonstrating the wrong way to perform a task. A student may miss that it is wrong and perform the task incorrectly. This also applies to visual training aids. Visual input will normally override audible input. Place the universal *no symbol* on any drawing, photo, etc. that depicts an incorrect method. While attending Sector Security

Reform (SSR) meetings in Afghanistan the author realized the effectiveness of a visual presentation in comparison to a lecture.

A new British Military Regiment arrived and changed the previous Regiment's format of the daily SSR meeting. The original format included a video presentation using graphical references accompanied by a verbal explanation. Without a graphical reference such as a *map* for the audience, the written locations provided in a slide presentation may be nothing more than numbers (meaningless). There is little if any advantage to announcing locations unfamiliar to an audience without having a visual reference of origin.

The graphical information in contrast was easy to follow and provided the correct spelling of names and places that may not have been familiar to attendees. The basis of the new format was a round table discussion. The round table format did not adequately present the technical and logistical aspects of daily incidents. The round table format lacked the visual learning experience that is effective for adults. The round table format did provide a question and answer session. The best of both worlds would have been a round table discussion combined with a video presentation using graphical references.

Descriptive Labels: Use *descriptive* labels (titles) and *not* obscure ones. Descriptive labels describe the associated task to speed the learning process. The label should reflect what action is occurring. The labels used in this book describe the tasks. As an example, the steps of the draw are *grip*, *join*, and *extend*, not *step one*, *step two*, and *step three*. The same thought process is applicable to teaching stoppage drills. Use the term *failed to fire* and not *type one stoppage*. Do not use the stoppage technique terms *immediate* action and *remedial* action. Use the terms *tap-rack-ready* and *lock-clear-reload* that describes the action.

As an example an instructor when teaching stoppage clearance drills would tell the operators that if the tap-rack-ready drill did not work then perform the lock-clear-reload—simple and easy to understand. As opposed to telling operators to do an *immediate action drill* and if that does not work, then perform a *remedial action drill*. Using obscure labels requires the operator to mentally translate or convert the verbiage—something that takes time. Time is a valued commodity during stressful situations. In Table 1-1 is a list of descriptive labels an instructor may consider using in a training program. Nearly all the descriptive labels will work with either a pistol or carbine providing uniformity of training.

Descriptive Labels

Verbal Communication
Moving
Move
Cover
Covering
Ready
Up
Contact Right
Contact Left
Contact Front
Contact Rear

Firearms Discharges
Justified
Negligent
Accidental

Firing Positions
Fighting Stance
Kneeling
Prone
Rollover Prone
Reverse Rollover Prone
Squatting
Sitting
Retention

Flashlight Activations
Proper
Improper
Accidental

Flashlight Positions
Shoulder
Offset
Side-by-side
Syringe
Inverted-L

Pistol Condition
Slide Forward
Slide Back

Firearms Handling
Low Ready
High Ready
Compressed Ready
Carry Position

Reloads
Drop Reload
Save Reload

Stoppages
Tap-Rack-Ready
Lock-Clear-Reload

Tactics
Priority of Fire
Close the Distance
Move to Contact
Triangulate
Flank
Break Contact

Table 1-1 Descriptive Labels

NOTE: An operator in a stressful situation may recall the words of an instructor. Those words should lead to actions that help and *not* hinder the operator's survival.

Scanning for Threats

An operational area has different planes of view depending on the body position of the operator. An operator standing will have a different view of the operational area than when in a prone position. Each plane of view will provide the operator with a different perspective because of the changing field of vision. For these reasons, it is imperative the operator scan the operational area from each firing position (prone, kneeling, etc.) *before* moving to another position.

Scanning on the firing line using slow robotic movements with the head is unrealistic. Even worse is doing it while holding a pistol with its slide locked back.[137] To appreciate the scanning technique, first put it in perspective. The scanning technique is searching for additional *dangerous* adversaries after stopping one or more. Is it likely or unlikely that an operator would slowly turn his or her head? Snap the head quickly to each area to search for other adversaries.[138]

When startled, snapping the head occurs naturally.[139] Quickly snap the head during training and actually *see* what is going on in the training environment. Seeing is *not* only looking at something, but also mentally determining its significance (friend or foe). Locate adversaries by using *target indicators* such as shape, sound, and movement.[140] When on the firing line take the opportunity to see what other operators are doing and identify any safety violations that require a cease-fire. Effective training improves physical skills as well as situational awareness skills.

NOTE: The sights dropping out of the operator's line of sight should be a visual stimulus to scan the area automatically. The operator goes from a narrow field of vision (engaging the adversary) to a broad field of vision (scanning the environment).[141] An operator that does not train to break the narrow field of vision will be incapable of efficiently assessing his or her environment in combat.

Shoot, Move, and Communicate

From the time recruits enter an academy, they are taught a dispatcher is a lifeline. This is certainly true when calling for help. However, there are incidents in which police officers are pressing the transmit button on a radio when they should be pulling the trigger on a firearm. This fact is *regrettably*, but vividly evident in the murder of a deputy.[142] The deputy yelled to the suspect, "Step away from your vehicle—put the gun down!" The next thing the deputy did was transmit over his radio, "I got a man with a gun, I need help." The deputy before firing gave *four* separate verbal commands for the suspect to drop his gun.

The use of deadly force when required is imminent—immediate action required.[143] This is not the time to yell on the radio, "I am being shot at!" or "I need help!" Such an encounter is a time to deploy a weapon system and handle the situation. The police officer needs to cease verbal commands and aggressively and without hesitation employ a weapon until the adversary is no longer a threat. Those in law enforcement that are depending on other officers to arrive in time to assist in a gunfight are being unrealistic. The average gunfight is over in a matter of seconds. Compare that to the time it takes for the first police officer to arrive on scene *after* the transmission of an assist officer call.

Operators should embrace the tactical response of *shoot, move, and communicate*.[144] The three actions according to the circumstances may be executed separately or nearly simultaneous. *Shooting* requires effective hits on an adversary. *Moving* is used to improve the current position to gain the tactical advantage in relation to the adversary. Moving off the line of attack quickly while deploying a firearm is a necessary survival skill. Captured on video from the dashboard camera was this type of movement.[145] *Communicating* encompasses the ability to think, make proper decisions, and express those decisions while experiencing stress. That expression might be verbal communication, hand signal, slap or squeeze on the shoulder, colored smoke, flare, radio transmission, or phone call. Gunfire is not widely thought of as a form of communication, but it can convey an operator is offensively engaging an adversary or defensively breaking contact using a bounding maneuver. Gunfire from that perspective *is* a form of communication.

The operator *if* possible should change positions to prevent being a stationary target after firing at the adversary—especially at night because of the muzzle flash indicator.[146]

NOTE: The phrase *shoot, move, and communicate* needs to be burned into an operator's mind, practiced during training, and carried out when the next adversary makes that fatal decision to fight.

Shooting vs. Gunfight

Being in a shooting is different from being in a gunfight. In the context of operational survival, a *shooting* is an operator firing at an adversary. A *gunfight* is an exchange of gunfire between an operator and an adversary. Being in a shooting instead of a gunfight will likely depend on the operator's ability to "...read danger cues early on and anticipate..."[147] the adversary's actions before they are carried out. Preferably, there are more operators than adversaries. This provides additional eyes and ears to read danger cues. If a shooting does occur, the more operators effectively firing at the adversary the quicker the fight ends.[148] An operator must be ready to react to another operator's actions. When a partner quickly turns and presents a firearm, then the other operator had better be doing the same thing. It is unlikely that an armed civilian would have the assistance of other private citizens. Consider this fact before voluntarily getting involved in a dangerous situation.

In a close range shooting do not underestimate the tactical advantage of firing the first shot. The adversary may have sensory overload for about 2 seconds even if the shot misses by a narrow margin.[149] The adversary during those 2 seconds will likely try to recover mentally. The adversary's ability to shoot accurately will likely suffer under the circumstances. This is *not* a declaration to shoot haphazardly! The operator is responsible for every bullet he or she fires in a community or operational area.[150] Just be aware the person who fires first may have a momentary tactical advantage.

Effective fire normally results in the person retreating. The ideal situation is a one-sided affair in which the operator is doing the shooting and delivering effective hits on the adversary. Unfortunately, according to a Federal Bureau of Investigation study, only 15 percent of the officers killed had fired their weapons.[151] In another Federal Bureau of Investigation study 64 percent of officers assaulted were not aware the attack was about to occur.[152] There are indictors that most of the officers killed and those assaulted were surprised. When failing to recognize the onset of an attack even a skilled operator is inept in the eyes of an adversary. Maintaining situational awareness combined with effective tactics will improve the chances of being involved in a shooting versus a gunfight.

NOTE: An operator should be honest in assessing his or her performance involving the last life-threatening situation. Did the operator do well because of his or her superior skills or was the adversary incompetent?

Tactics Used by Criminals

The tactics that criminals use against police officers have changed little in the past 100 years. A police officer will likely face multiple criminals moving in the dark at close range. The criminal's subtle or sudden hand movement may be the cue that begins the attack.[153] Sixty-eight percent of the time the distance between the police officer and criminal will occur at a range from contact to 10 feet (3 meters).[154] There is a chance when a criminal discharges a firearm at such a close range the police officer will experience a blinding muzzle flash followed by a deafening boom.

NOTE: Some officers, including the author, have reported a gunshot sound as a muffled *pop* or not heard.[155] An untrained civilian female that had no handgun experience before taking a Smith & Wesson revolver from a would-be rapist and shooting him reported the same auditory exclusion phenomenon.[156]

The above description of tactics used by criminals is the reality of many police involved gunfights. It is not an exaggeration of circumstances to induce fear, but an accurate account to motivate competence. What will prepare a police officer to defeat the tactics used by criminals? Is it recreational shooting? Is it an annual qualification? The answer to such violent encounters involving criminals is for police officers to receive realistic firearms training. Training developed to defeat tactics used by criminals.

The Federal Bureau of Investigation produces an annual publication called Law Enforcement Officers Killed and Assaulted. The publication includes summaries of the tactics used by criminals who killed police officers. Using the summaries can provide themes for police training. Ultimately, it is the *individual* police officer's responsibility to ensure his or her safety by defeating the criminal's tactics.

Concealed Carry Tactics

Criminal laws govern the actions of operators carrying a concealed pistol by regulating the carrying of the pistol and under what circumstances the pistol should be used. The author has heard several instructors in the introduction of teaching the *law* portion of a concealed carry class explain that it will be dry and boring. The instructors were acting irresponsibly for making such statements. The law portion is arguably the *most* important. An operator with a concealed carry permit should have a thorough understanding of the laws that govern the use of deadly force. Without understanding the laws and their application, it would be difficult to know with certainty when to use deadly force. Having an understanding *of* the law, allows the operator to work *within* the law.

An operator with a concealed carry permit is either an *asset* or a *liability* to society. There is no in between. It is that operator's responsibility to get the proper training and become an asset. An operator's skill level is validated during training and in a time of crisis relied on. Just as police officers and military operators train, armed civilians must regularly train to maintain their survival skills. However, an armed civilian should be *reluctant* to get involved in any situation *not* a matter of life-and-death. The reason is the civilian is armed and what was a simple argument might end with the use of deadly force. Likewise, an armed civilian should *not* brandish his or her pistol.

According to some laws, it is even unlawful to fail to conceal a pistol intentionally.[157] Dress in a manner that hides the pistol, but allows for immediate access. Dark colored clothing tends to hide the print of a pistol (outline). *Immediate access* is the operator firing the first shot within 2 seconds of reacting to a life-and-death situation.[158] The reason for 2 seconds is that it generally takes an operator 0.25 second to realize a problem exists and another 0.25 second to act and about 1.5 seconds to draw and fire the pistol.[159]

A reduction in time is possible by combining multiple tasks into one action.[160] An operator caught in a life-threatening situation may get only one chance to draw a pistol. Even if the draw is fumbled, continue to get the pistol out as quick as possible. A fumbled draw can occur from not releasing the retention device, cloth caught between the firing hand and pistol, or snagging the pistol on clothing. In a deadly force encounter an operator must *not* stop.

The holster on the waist near the dominant side hip provides an efficient method to draw. Another method is to wear an inside the waistband holster between the hip and centerline of the body on the dominant side. This is called an *appendage* carry. A holster is vital for securing the pistol after being involved in a shooting and prior to the police arriving. An inside the pants holster that is not rigid can make holstering difficult. Arriving police officers will take at gunpoint an unknown person holding a pistol. Even worse, the incident might end with the police shooting an operator mistakenly.

Be aware of the firing hand side when carrying a concealed pistol and walking with others. It is usually best to keep the firing side free in case of drawing the pistol. An example would be walking with the family and keeping control of a small child. Use the *non-firing* hand to push or pull a family member out of harm's way while drawing. Carry at least one spare magazine for the pistol and a flashlight in a combination magazine and flashlight pouch. Another choice is a double magazine pouch and a small flashlight in a pocket.

An operator could also be in a public place when a takeover robbery occurs. The robbers will use violence of action and intimidation to keep control of their victims. The last thing an operator needs is to raise both arms and expose a pistol. Likewise, a police officer would not want to expose a badge or pistol. An operator caught in this situation should try to keep the elbows down and the hands near the ears.[161] (Figure 1-6) When forced to put the hands behind the head do *not* interlock the fingers. Keep the firing hand lightly on the back of the non-firing hand. This is to prevent trapping the firing hand between the non-firing hand and the back of the head.

Keeping the arms down also applies when prone on the ground. Stretching the arms overhead would likely expose the pistol or badge. The operator must not fidget because the eyes pick up movement first and any movement would draw the robber's attention. Operators during training need to use an electronic timer to verify how quick they can draw and fire from the kneeling and prone positions that are common during hostage situations. Operators need to also practice while moving from a kneeling position into the fighting stance or a prone position, and vice versa. The operator's capabilities validated in training provide an account of available options for use in a real-life hostage situation.

The fastest method of drawing is to move the hand in a straight line to the pistol. Keep the firing hand as close to and in line with the edge of the cover garment to reach down and sweep it for the draw. The operator can quickly stand back up as the situation allows. Practice drills will help operators realize their limitations during training and *not* when caught in a real-life situation. The drills can also be practiced using airsoft guns during simulation training. No live *weapons* (firearms, knives, batons, pepper spray, etc.) or *ammunition* can be in the simulation training area—no exceptions!

Figure 1-6 *A seemingly submissive position that actually puts the operator's hands in grabbing distance of the pistol.*

NOTE: Do *not* carry a pistol in violation of the law. An operator wanting to carry a concealed pistol, but lives in a state that does *not* allow it can rally to change the law or move to a state that does allow concealed carry.

In a Restroom: A restroom is a socially accepted place of privacy, but to a criminal it can be a location of opportunity. The attacker's intent may be a robbery, rape, or assault. The attack may begin when the victim is most vulnerable—sitting on a toilet. There are psychological and tactical advantages for the criminal to attack a person sitting on a toilet. Grabbing the victim's feet and violently pulling him or her from under a stall is a psychological distraction that would induce fear. The victim's naked body is exposed and at a time of expelling bodily waste.

The victim would be at a tactical disadvantage. The victim's underwear would likely be around the legs limiting the ability to fight or flee. The victim may be mortified and have a feeling of helplessness.[162] Likewise, from an adjoining stall an attacker could peer over the top and using a weapon to threaten the unsuspecting victim. The way to defeat such attacks is to maintain situational awareness and be prepared to stop the attacker. The issue of responding with a firearm while sitting on a toilet is no different from any other position. The pistol must be in the operator's control at all times and immediately accessible. This eliminates the options of hanging the pistol on a stall hook, placing on a toilet tank, etc.,[163] which could result in the operator walking off and leaving it in the stall. Keep the pistol in its holster *if* possible because that is where it belongs.

To use the toilet with a belt carry, unzip the zipper, and unfasten the belt. Control the holstered pistol with one hand by grasping the belt and pants just in front of the pistol. Lower the pants to mid-thigh and sit on the toilet. Buckle the belt around the knees loosely *if* necessary to keep the pistol above the lower edge of the stall.[164] Keep the feet back and away from the edge of the stall to prevent being grabbed by an attacker. Complete necessary hygienic care. When finished, unbuckle the belt grabbing it and the pants on each side, stand, and pull up the pants. One hand keeps control on the pants and belt just in front of the pistol. The other hand if necessary tucks the shirttail. Fasten the pants along with the belt and zip up. Make necessary attire adjustments before leaving the stall.

An off the body carry such as a holster purse or fanny pack can be hung around the neck.[165] Likewise, a female operator carrying a purse, but wearing a pistol on the *waist* can still hang the purse around her neck.

Whatever holster device is used the operator with an *inert* or *unloaded* pistol needs to practice the procedure to work out issues and become proficient. Practice includes simulation training of retrieving the pistol and dry firing. Dry firing practice can be conducted in the privacy of the operator's home with an *unloaded* or *inert* pistol.

Male operators using a urinal need to look over their shoulders periodically to maintain situational awareness. Use the reflections from mirrors, chrome-plated pipes, shiny fixtures, and even tiles on the walls to see what is going on.[166] To reduce the chance of an attack when using the restroom chose a location that affords the best view of the restroom and offers a close escape route. Any feelings of uneasiness after entering a restroom demands a high level of situational awareness or better yet find another restroom.

Physically Disabled Operator: A physically disable operator (PDO) to the best of his or her mental and physical ability has a moral obligation to defend themself and family members. There are challenges to overcome for the PDO that carries a concealed pistol for protection. However, such a person is use to overcoming life's challenges and will likely have the *mettle* to do so. The physical disability may have existed from birth or sustained from a work related injury (civilian employment, law enforcement, or military operation). Likewise, a vehicle collision may be the cause of the injury. This section addresses how the PDO who uses a wheelchair can conceal a pistol for the protection of self and others.

The concealed pistol must be immediately accessible while remaining in the PDO's control and the muzzle pointed in the appropriate direction. This prerequisite applied to a wheelchair-user eliminates the option of concealing the pistol on the wheelchair. There is also the possibility that during an attack the PDO might be separated from his or her wheelchair. Carrying a pistol behind the hip or in the small of the back could make it difficult to get a hand between the body and the side of the wheelchair to draw quickly.

Examined are four options for a wheelchair-user: (1) fanny pack, (2) cross-draw, (3) shoulder, and (4) ankle carry. The fanny pack may be the most efficient and inconspicuous solution.[167] Some fanny packs are made to hold either a small or large frame pistol. Bystanders do not give a second thought to a fanny pack worn by a wheelchair-user. The fanny pack does not hang down as when standing, but lays flat on the lap. Wear the fanny pack on the non-dominant side to make the pistol easily accessible with the dominant hand. The fanny pack that separates on three sides exposes the pistol for efficient drawing. An internal holster that adjusts vertically helps prevent the pistol from falling out when ripping the fanny pack open. Make sure the pull device used to open the fanny pack is easily accessible. Logistically the fanny pack has the advantage of multiple compartments allowing for storage of wallet, keys, currency, cell phone, flashlight, pepper spray, knife, spare ammunition, etc.

A holster for a wheelchair-user can be difficult to put on and take off. This fact may discourage the PDO from going armed when running a quick errand. However, a cross-draw holster worn in front of the hip is easier to put on than a hip holster and allows for a speedy draw. Wheelchair-users have a tendency to hold their hands in their laps. This location is already near the concealed pistol. The non-dominant hand lifts the cover garment and the dominant hand accesses the pistol.

A shoulder holster is another option for a wheelchair-user. The horizontal shoulder holster is more user friendly than the vertical holster. The horizontal shoulder holster allows for a more natural draw, but the muzzle points directly to the rear. Shooting ranges will likely prohibit the use of a horizontal shoulder holster. This is an important issue when deciding on a carry method. Be sure to choose a method of carry that is allowed on the range.

The ankle or calf carry requires wearing the holster under loose fitting clothing. A wheelchair user can wear the pistol on the *outside* of the leg on the dominant hand side. This closely resembles the firing side hip carry. To access the pistol the non-dominant hand grabs the pants leg at the knee and pulls it up quickly. This allows the pants leg to ride over the pistol. The muzzle travels from the holster straight to the target or adversary when drawing the pistol.[168] When drawing from the holster in any of the carry positions (waist belt, shoulder, etc.) the muzzle must not point at the PDO's body or others. The carry method and draw should allow the muzzle to go safely from the holster to the target or adversary.

There are tactical considerations that apply specifically to a wheelchair-user. The most prominent is the loss of mobility. The wheelchair-user cannot move to cover quickly or maneuver over obstacles. This fact needs to be addressed so the PDO will understand and mentally accept personal limitations. The PDO will likely be in the open and for all practical purposes; cover will be effective hits on the adversary. The PDO must have the capability to draw and place rapid hits. Quickly stopping the adversary is crucial for the PDO *not* to be injured or killed. The steps of the draw are *access*, *grip*, *join*, and *extend*. The PDO needs to also practice firing from the retention position. The wheelchair-user does not have the luxury of crouching, kneeling, or going prone. Most gunfights end quick with only a few rounds fired. However, the PDO could be involved in an extended fight and should carry spare ammunition.

A wheelchair-user getting in and out of a vehicle might unknowingly depress an exposed or extended magazine catch. The magazine catch depressed would cause the magazine to release. A Glock pistol would fire only one time and some pistols with a magazine disconnect would *not* fire. Obvious a magazine not seated would be disastrous in a gunfight. The holster should prevent the inadvertent pressing of the magazine catch, but periodically check to make sure the magazine is seated. Checking the magazine does not require removing the pistol from its holster or fanny pack. Push on the area where the magazine floor plate is located. Feeling the click or hearing it means the magazine is unseated. Identify and resolve the problem that caused the magazine to release.

Discussed in this section were wheelchair-users, but other PDOs with various disabilities can seek out professional advice related to carrying a concealed pistol.[169]

Interaction with the Police: An operator carrying a concealed pistol needs to know how to interact with the police during a vehicle stop. To the police officer a *traffic* stop is an unknown-risk stop.[170] An *unknown-risk* stop is one the police officer is uncertain about the risks. A *known-risk* stop is one the police officer is certain about the risks (stolen vehicle, robbery suspect, sexual assault suspect, etc.). More police officers die from unknown-risk stops than known-risk stops.[171]

There are things an operator carrying a concealed pistol can do to put the police officer at ease allowing the unknown-risk stop go as smooth as possible. The violator seeing the police lights should immediately turn on the turn signal. This will alert the police officer to the violator's acknowledgment of the stop. Once stopped, roll down the window halfway, turn off the engine, and place both hands on the steering wheel. If it is dark, turn on all available interior lighting. The police officer should identify him or herself, explain the reason for the traffic stop, and ask if they is any reason for the violation. The violator should explain that he or she is carrying a concealed pistol, where it is located, and the reason *if* any for the violation. These actions demonstrate the violator's willingness to comply with the police officer.

The police officer should tell the violator what to do next. The violator should *not* do anything until told to do so. The police officer will likely instruct the violator to provide his or her concealed carry permit and other necessary documents to complete the traffic stop. The police officer has a great deal of latitude when interacting with a violator that is armed. The police officer may ask to take possession of the pistol during the traffic stop. A police officer should give careful consideration before disarming a citizen that is *lawfully* carrying a concealed pistol.

There are also safety and liability issues when disarming a citizen. Does the police officer allow the citizen to handle the pistol? On the other hand, does the officer try to retrieve the pistol from its holster? It is likely the pistol and holster will be unfamiliar to the police officer. What if there is a negligent discharge from handling the firearm by the violator or police officer? Law enforcement agencies need to have standard operating procedures (SOPs) governing contact with people that are lawfully carrying a concealed pistol. The author has stopped numerous individuals who were carrying a concealed pistol. The violators were respectful and polite and he never felt a need to take their pistol during the traffic stops.

Police Officers Tactics Recorded on Video

One of the best sources to observe people's behavior in deadly force encounters are the videos from the dashboard cameras of police vehicles. There are also other video sources such as surveillance recordings from stores, banks, parking lots, etc. What is seen many times on these videos is a sudden explosive attack on the police officer. The startled police officer is in a lag time situation from mentally processing that an attack has occurred. In a 10-year period, over half of the attacks on police officers occurred in the dark.[172] In the same 10-year period, murderers used handguns to kill police officers about 67 percent of the time.[173]

Since people were 2-years-old, they have been hiding behind something or somebody they thought would protect them. It is a natural response to a deadly threat to hide behind the pistol and pull the trigger. The anticipation or actual occurrence of a bullet passing by a police officer's head provides plenty of motivation to crouch and get behind a pistol.[174] A state of hypervigilance[175] will probably be present because of the police officer mentally anticipating a deadly force encounter or maybe from pursuing a suspect on foot. The police officer in such a state will also tightly grip his or her pistol.

Encountering worst-case scenarios in training helps to minimize surprises during deadly force encounters. Training programs must harness the natural responses of the body as seen in the videos from police dashboard cameras. Combining the body's natural responses with controlled aggression[176] and effective tactics is a tactical formula to defeat criminals.

EQUIPMENT AND WEAPONS

A person is either an actor in the world or a person being acted on when facing a disaster or its aftermath. Sometimes the equipment and weapons carried distinguishes the difference. Equipment the author carried assisted him in saving a vehicle collision victim from being burned alive. The estimated speed of 106.47 mph (171.34 kph) caused the vehicle to be airborne 120.5 feet (36.72 meters).[177] The overturned vehicle had caught fire with the driver pinned inside while upside down. The author used a backup flashlight to assess the situation, a steel baton to rake the window, and a serrated knife to cut the seat belt. He dragged the victim clear of the vehicle and with a military type bandage treated a gapping head wound. The author had the necessary equipment for the situation and fortunately was able to save the driver's life.

First Aid Equipment

No mentally sound person desires to be inadvertently shot or blown up. Unfortunately, in operational environments injuries do occur. Police officers and military operators must not depend solely on others for medical assistance. A police officer shot in the leg used his shoes laces as makeshift tourniquets to stop the bleeding. The police officer's self-treatment saved his life.[178] A deputy shot in his forearm while answering a domestic disturbance call nearly bled to death because of *not* having the proper resources to self-treat. An assisting deputy used a flex-cuff as a makeshift tourniquet to save the wounded deputy.[179] Police advisers and military operators in Afghanistan routinely carried two tourniquets.

Self-treatment is "...critical to a positive combat mind-set and individual survival."[180] Police officers can carry on their soft body armor at least one lightweight nylon tourniquet that can be put on with one hand. Being able to self-treat may also prevent others from having to expose themselves to danger to reach fallen colleagues.[181] An armed civilian should also have basic knowledge of first aid for gunshots. There may be a need to self-treat or treat others that are injured. An Individual First Aid Kit (IFAK, pronounced eye-fack) used by operators should be *gunshot* injury specific. It could take an extended amount of time for medical assistance to arrive or allowed to enter a shooting scene. Operators need to consider how to layer their equipment not only for tactical engagements, but also for medical emergencies. First aid equipment should be accessible using either hand.

A basic IFAK contains the items as follows: powder free nitrile gloves, trauma shears, permanent marker, tourniquet, trauma dressing, dual-purpose hemostatic gauze, compressed gauze, chest seals, nasopharyngeal airway, and sterile water-soluble lubricating jelly.[182] (Figure 1-7) Operators may want to have a primary tourniquet accessible without going into the IFAK. A second tourniquet could be strapped to an IFAK pouch[183] or *if* room permitting stored inside. The IFAK should be positioned in the same place on each operator's body of the same organization to ensure speedy retrieval under stressful conditions.

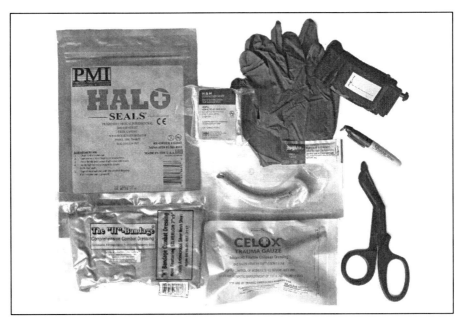

Figure 1-7 *Individual First Aid Kit (IFAK)*

The powder free nitrile gloves protect against blood and other bodily fluids. The 7.5-inch (190.5 millimeter) black trauma shears can quickly cut clothing allowing treatment of injuries. The permanent marker is used to record the time a tourniquet was applied. The tourniquet is quick to deploy, easy to use, and the first line of defense against an extremity hemorrhage that is life-threatening. The trauma dressing is a hemostat for arterial bleeding and hemorrhaging in limbs and deployable using one hand under stressful conditions. The dual-purpose hemostatic gauze is composed of chitosan chemistry (not impregnated or coated) and has the ability to control traumatic bleeding and to help cool and protect first and second degree burns. The compressed gauze packed into a small package allows additional packing material over the dual-purpose hemostatic gauze when treating moderate to severe wounds involving heavy bleeding. The chest seals are occlusive dressings for treating penetrating chest wounds along with securing other wound dressings even in severe conditions. The nasopharyngeal airway is for single use made of sterile, pliant material with rounded edges and a fixed flange for maintaining an airway. The sterile water-soluble lubricating jelly is for lubricating the nasopharyngeal airway for ease of insertion.

The IFAK does not have a tension pneumothorax decompression needle because its proper use is an advanced practice skill. An operator not certified and lacking the skill in performing a chest decompression could further injure the victim. However, an operator with the proper training *should* carry a decompression needle.[184] (Figure 1-8) First aid kits that are gunshot specific should also be kept in the home and available at the firearms range. Equipment alone is not enough. Training must accompany the equipment to ensure its proper use in a timely manner under stressful conditions.

Figure 1-8 *Tension Pneumothorax Needle*

Training should also include operators live firing on a range and treating a simulated injury. This may include shooting a reactive or moving target, and while it is down or stopped the operator applies a tourniquet to himself, herself, or another person. The target may appear or move again during the application of the tourniquet and have to be immediately engaged. [185] This drill forces the operator to maintain situational awareness—even when treating an injury. Nobody will be able to receive help from an operator that has bled to death. The operator's goals should be to stop the bleeding and have a functioning firearm to stay in the fight. Operators that can self-treat, maintain a functioning firearm, and communicate they are all right can reduce the chaos of other operators responding to the location.

Effective Equipment

The needs of the operation will dictate the type of equipment carried. Equipment that allows manipulation in low light conditions is usually the most effective. There is a great deal of tactical equipment available for purchase. Buy quality equipment so the purchase will only have to be made once. Common sense dictates what equipment is required and carried to accomplish the mission. The New York City Police Department reported during *adversarial* conflicts 20 percent of police officers fired 1 shot and 68 percent fired 5 or less shots. [186] Statistics confirm carrying two spare magazines is adequate for most operations in law enforcement.

However, there are operational environments that extended capacity magazines are the better choice. Glock makes a 33 round magazine for the 9x19mm and a 22 round magazine for the .40 S&W. (Figure 1-9) The extended magazines will fit and function in the subcompact, compact, and standard pistols. The extended magazine fulfills a specialized role. An armed civilian, police officer, or for that matter a military operator would not normally carry an extended magazine in a pistol. Extended magazines would likely be stored in an equipment bag (active killer bag, go bag, etc.). This is *not* to say that extended magazines cannot be carried on an equipment vest or in a magazine pouch, especially a drop pouch. However, comfortably carrying the extended magazine may present a challenge.

Equipment to be comfortable must fit properly. Equipment that fits poorly will be a burden to the operator. The author while in Afghanistan tried different holster configurations before settling on one that would work with his hard body armor plates and equipment. There was the issue of getting in and out of armored vehicles, helicopters, and fixed wing aircraft under normal and emergency conditions. The pistol mounted on the front of his equipment vest interfered with him shooting in the prone position. Moreover, if he had taken a round in the center of his body armor the pistol would have been struck, turning it into flying shrapnel. The holster mounted directly in front of his thigh rubbed against the steering wheel. The dominant side carry with a drop thigh holster worn forward of the hip resolved the issues. Sometimes trial and error is the only means to getting equipment sorted out.

Figure 1-9 Glock extended 33 round 9x19mm magazine on the left and the extended 22 round .40 S&W magazine on the right.

Equipment and Weapon Ergonomics

Ergonomics is the "...applied science of equipment design, as for the workplace, intended to maximize productivity by reducing operator fatigue and discomfort."[187] Ergonomics is also called biotechnology, human engineering, and human factors engineering. Any operator selecting equipment or a weapon must first look at the manufacturer's intended design. The operator should select equipment and weapons that reduce fatigue and discomfort. Equipment and weapons that do *not* fit the operator's body will accelerate fatigue and be uncomfortable. One sure way to reduce fatigue is to use lightweight equipment and weapons that fit the operator's body size and shape.

Regrettably, female operators in particular are sometimes forced to use equipment or weapons designed for the average size male operator. This can be troublesome when gripping a pistol, drawing from a holster, and firing ammunition with a high chamber pressure. The pistol must fit the operator's hand if she is going to properly hold and control it during recoil. A belt and holster needs to fit the contour of the female waist and body shape. A holster riding too high prevents a proper draw reducing the female operator's ability of self-protection. Ammunition with a high chamber pressure can greatly reduce some female operator's ability to recover from the recoil for quicker follow-up shots. Controlling the pistol during recoil can be improved with a proper fitted pistol and the operator performing hand and arm exercises regularly to increase strength.

Operators should seek out the assistance of manufacturers when selecting equipment. The manufacturer may have an entire line of equipment for the female operator. Whether male or female an operator should *not* be seen as troublesome because of an expectation that equipment and weapons fit comfortably. The operator should have an expectation that if equipment or weapon issues arise they will be resolved. Not resolving such issues and allowing the operator go operational is putting him or her and others at risk unnecessarily. Some operators that have been labeled as "problem shooters" are in reality suffering from attempts to overcome the poor ergonomics of their equipment and weapon.

Another issue with some so-called problem shooters may *not* be the equipment or firearm, but pain caused by injuries acquired during extended training. An example is a recruit attending a week of firearms training at a police range. The recruit's hands early on may have multiple blisters from loading magazines and shooting. The recruit's progress throughout the week might diminish not because of poor fundamentals, but because of pain. To prevent blisters, apply strips of "duct tape," also called "rigger's tape," or "100-mph tape" to the areas on the hands that are prone to blistering, and use a speed loader. When in pain it is difficult to learn and perform as expected. The pain can get so bad that the only thing going through an operator's mind is to get through the training.

Personal Layered Protection with Weapons

Personal layered protection is a system of self-protection. For police officers the first line of protection because of the nature of the job is normally a pistol. The second would be an edged weapon (knife). The third would be non-lethal weapons: baton, electronic control device, and pepper spray. The forth are personal weapons: hands, elbows, feet, knees, teeth, etc. Utilization of the layers is according to the situation and the response needed to stop an adversary. It is to the police officer's advantage to have a long gun available when responding to a known risk situation that has the propensity for violence. The long gun would become the first layer of protection with the handgun second and so forth.

NOTE: Woven within the personal layered protection is *improvised* weapons found in the operational environment. Do not hesitate to use whatever object is at hand as a weapon for self-protection or to protect the life of another.

The appropriate police response would be an *edged* weapon during a hand-to-hand fight that justifies deadly force and no firearm is available. The police officer would continuously cut or stab the suspect to stop the attack.[188] In the Federal Bureau of Investigation's *Violent Encounters* study, it revealed when unarmed suspects removed service weapons from law enforcement officers, in *every* instance the suspects tried to shoot or had shot the officers.[189] Utilizing a personal layered protection system hardens the target (operator) against such attacks. The fact is predators do not like to hunt professionals that hunt predators.[190]

The above example would be for a police officer. However, applying the same approach to a military operator will yield similar results. Some of the weapons are more powerful and may involve explosives. The first weapon may be a squad automatic weapon (SAW), the second a rifle, the third hand grenades, the fourth a pistol, the fifth a bayonet, the sixth a combat knife, the seventh improvised weapons (striking with a ballistic helmet), and finally personal weapons. A military operator may also carry some type of anti-armor rocket. The weapon system deployed is dependent on the distance from the military operator to the adversary. It is preferred to fight at the farthest distance and not allow the adversary to close that distance. However, every military operator must be prepared to fight hand-to-hand.

NOTE: The offensive deployment of weapons continues until threats no longer exist—take the fight to the adversary.[191]

SUMMARY

Operational survival is an individual responsibility that requires continuous self-evaluation. The operator must be honest and admit personal shortcomings. A person may not have the mind-set to take a human life or the fitness level required for operational survival. These two things are foundational elements necessary to continue with training and the implementation of tactics. The firearms training program must teach armed civilians, police officers, and military operators that not only does an attack demand a response, but also the threat of an attack. Use the most recent and best equipment available along with a simple, but effective weapon system that provides superior firepower. It is an integration of mind-set, fitness, training, tactics, equipment, and weapons that maximize the operator's fighting capability. Operators carrying a first aid kit to self-treat may save their own life and prevent others from having to expose themselves to danger to reach injured operators. The so-called problem shooter may be suffering from an attempt to overcome the poor ergonomics of their equipment, weapon, or pain from injuries rather than poor shooting skills. Personal layered protection is a system of self-protection that includes, but is not limited to personal weapons, edged weapons, firearms, and improvised weapons.

DISCUSSION QUESTIONS

1. Define operational survival.
2. What are the names of the three sides of the operational survival triad?
3. Which London University professor developed the idea for the flight-or-flight theory and described it in his book? What year was the book published?
4. Which Harvard University professor in his book popularized the fight-or-flight condition? What year was the book published?
5. Explain what is the fight-or-flight reaction and how it affects the

body?

6. What maneuver can two or more operators use to break contact with one of more adversaries?

7. What are the three levels of situational awareness? Give examples of each level as related to your operational environment.

8. Explain the three viewpoints that an operator's actions will be judged and how it can affect his or her personal and professional life.

9. What is stress and some of its causes? Give an example of stress in your life.

10. Explain the importance of functional conditioning.

11. Discuss how grip strength can be improved for combat shooting.

12. What is procedural memory and its importance to operational survival?

13. Describe the three criteria for training with a pistol for survival.

14. Why is Target Focused Sighted Shooting suited for operational survival?

15. Describe how adults learn best. What is an effective motivator?

16. What are descriptive labels? Give an example of an effective label and an example of an ineffective label.

17. Explain how to scan an area for threats and the importance of scanning on each different plane of view.

18. What are some of the advantages of moving, shooting, and communicating?

19. How can communicating be a disadvantage in a life-threatening situation?

20. What is the difference between a shooting and a gunfight?

21. Describe the common tactics used by adversaries during a gunfight that law enforcement officers have faced for the past 100 years.

22. What are some of the tactics to consider when carrying a concealed handgun? Do you employ such tactics? If not, why?

23. Explain how to keep control of a pistol when using the toilet.

24. What is one of the best sources to observe a person's behavior in a deadly force environment?

25. What are two disadvantages of wearing a pistol on the front of the chest?

26. What are two advantages to medical self-aid?

27. When should an operator carry a decompression needle?

28. What two things can be done to help prevent blisters on the hands during extended firearms training?

29. Explain how layered protection hardens the individual operator against attacks.

ENDNOTES

[1] *American Heritage Dictionary of the English Language Online*, 4th ed., s.v. "mind-set," http://www.thefreedictionary.com/mind-set (accessed September 22, 2012).

[2] Itay Gil and Dan Baron, *The Citizen's Guide to Stopping Suicide Attackers* (Boulder, CO: Paladin Press, 2004), 3.

[3] Zahava Solomon, *Combat Stress Reaction* (New York, NY: Plenum Press, 1993), 40-41.

[4] Force Science Institute, LTD., "Mind Traps That Can Trick You and Those Who Judge Your Actions," *Force Science News* #160, (October 8, 2010), http://www.forcescience.org/fsinews/2010/10/force-science-news-160-%e2%80%9cmind-traps%e2%80%9d-that-can-trick-you-and-those-who-judge-your-actions/ (accessed September 22, 2012).

[5] Institute for International Sport, "Sportsmanship Quotes, Coach Paul "Bear" Bryant," *National Sportsman Day* (2006), http://www.internationalsport.org/nsd/sportsmanship-quotes.cfm (accessed September 22, 2012).

[6] Federal Bureau of Investigation, "Law Enforcement Officers Killed and Assaulted," *Table 12 – Victim Officer's Use of Weapon During Incident, 2001–2010*, (October 2011), http://www.fbi.gov/about-us/cjis/ucr/leoka/leoka-2010/tables/table12-leok-feloniously-victim-use-of-weapon-01-10.xls (accessed September 22, 2012).

[7] Thomas D. Petrowski, J.D., "Use-of-Force Policies and Training," *FBI Law Enforcement Bulletin*, (November 2002): 25-27.

[8] Itay Gil and Dan Baron, *The Citizen's Guide to Stopping Suicide Attackers* (Boulder, CO: Paladin Press, 2004), 3.

[9] U.S. Department of Justice, Federal Bureau of Investigation, Firearms Training Unit, *FBI Academy, Handgun Wounding Factors and Effectiveness* (Quantico, VA, July 14, 1989), 2.

National Rifle Association, *NRA Guide to the Basics of Personal Protection Outside the Home* (Fairfax, VA: National Rifle Association of America, 2006), 148.

[10] U.S. Department of Justice, Federal Bureau of Investigation, Firearms Training Unit, *Wound Ballistic Workshop "9mm vs. .45 auto"* (Quantico, VA, September 15-17, 1987), 19.

[11] National Rifle Association, *NRA Guide to Basics of Personal Protection Outside the Home* (Fairfax, VA: National Rifle Association of America, 2006), 35-36.

[12] Melissa Soalt, *Fierce and Female*, (Boulder, CO: Paladin Press, 2000): DVD Part Two.

[13] Random House Dictionary, s.v. "fight-or-flight reaction" http://dictionary.reference.com/browse/fight+or+flight+re+action's (accessed: September 22, 2012).

[14] Random House Dictionary, s.v. "fight-or-flight reaction" http://dictionary.reference.com/browse/fight+or+flight+re+action's (accessed: September 22, 2012).

[15] William McDougall, *Introduction to Social Psychology*, (London: 1908), 49, 59.

[16] Walter B. Cannon, *Bodily Changes in Pain, Hunger, Fear and Rage* (D. Appleton and Company: 1915), 187.

[17] Walter B. Cannon, *Bodily Changes in Pain, Hunger, Fear and Rage* (D. Appleton and Company: 1915), 211.

[18] Walter B. Cannon, *Bodily Changes in Pain, Hunger, Fear and Rage* (D. Appleton and Company: 1915), 212.

[19] Kathleen D. Vonk, "Police Performance Under Stress," (Belleville, MI: *Louka Tactical*, 2007), http://loukatactical.com/articles/Heart_Rate_and_Performance_Under_Stress_Article_t o.pdf (accessed January 17, 2012).

[20] Kathleen D. Vonk, "Police Performance Under Stress," (Belleville, MI: *Louka Tactical*, 2007), http://loukatactical.com/articles/Heart_Rate_and_Performance_Under_Stress_Article_t o.pdf (accessed September 22, 2012).

[21] Department of the Army, *Leader's Manual for Combat Stress Control* (Washington, DC: FM 22-51, September 29, 1994), 2-8.

[22] National Rifle Association, *NRA Guide to the Basics of Personal Protection Outside the Home* (Fairfax, VA: National Rifle Association of America, 2006), 49-52.

[23] "If contact is likely, then the patrol should move by bounds. Moving by bounds, with one element overwatching another element, is used in urban terrain just as in rural terrain." An element can be a single operator, team, squad, etc. and bounding can be used for offensive forward movement (ingress) or defensive disengagement (egress). See Department of the Army, *Tactics in Counterinsurgency FM 3-24.2* (Washington, DC: Headquarters, 2009), 5-34.

[24] "The cornering of an animal when in the headlong flight of fear may suddenly turn the fear to fury and the flight to a fighting in which all the strength of desperation is displayed." See Walter B. Cannon, Bodily Changes in Pain, Hunger, Fear and Rage (D. Appleton and Company: 1915), 275.

[25] National Rifle Association, Refuse to Be a Victim Instructor's Manual (Fairfax, VA: National Rifle Association, October 2009), 7.

[26] "The autonomic nervous system has two major branches; the parasympathetic and sympathetic. Generally speaking, the sympathetic nervous system prepares the body for direct action and confrontation by increasing heart pulse rate and bringing increased blood supply to large muscle groups. Also, ocular pupil diameter increases, and the ciliary muscle relaxes, forcing a person to focus the eyes at far distance, perhaps to be behaviorally better prepared for a perceived on-coming threat. Looking towards infinity has the tendency of allowing the observer to process a relatively greater volume of peripheral space.

The parasympathetic nervous system allows one to maintain a more relaxed, balanced state of readiness by slowing an accelerated heart rate, decreasing pupil size, and allowing the eye's accommodative system to focus at closer distances. The parasympathetic nervous system aims to bring neural physiology back to a state of balance or relative homeostasis." See Edward C. Godnig, O.D., "Body Alarm Reaction and Sports Vision," *Journal of Behavioral Optometry* (2001, Vol. 12, No. 1): 3.

[27] National Rifle Association, Refuse to Be a Victim Instructor's Manual (Fairfax, VA: National Rifle Association, October 2009), 7.

[28] Timothy D. Blakeley, "Personal notes from the Gathering Information Session," *Antiterrorism Combat Course*, (Tel Aviv, Israel: 2008): 8.

[29] "Even though the attack came as a complete surprise, the officer later reported: "I'm thinking to myself, I'm not gonna die here; I'm not gonna let this guy get me." See U.S. Department of Justice, *Violent Encounters*, 2006, (Washington, DC: FBI, 2006), 21.

"The officers did not receive any physical injuries in this incident. Both stated that they were surprised when the offender initiated the attack." See U.S. Department of Justice, *Violent Encounters*, 2006, (Washington, DC: FBI, 2006), 97.

"After he initially stabbed me, I was caught off guard. I was surprised." See U.S. Department of Justice, *Violent Encounters*, 2006, (Washington, DC: FBI, 2006), 107.

Even the offenders that attacked officers noted some of the officers were surprised. "When asked to assess the officers' demeanor at the time of the confrontation, 31 percent of the offenders were of the opinion that the officer was surprised by the attack." See U.S. Department of Justice, *In the Line of Fire*, 1997, (Washington, DC: FBI, 1997), 30.

[30] Glock Inc., *Glock Pistol Transitional Instructor Workshop Course Outline*, (Smyrna, GA: 2012): 3.

[31] Joe Navarro, and Marvin Karlins, Ph.D., *What Every Body Is Saying* (New York, NY: HarperCollins, 2008), 4.

[32] Anthony J. Pinizzotto, Ph.D., Harry A. Kern, M.Ed., and Edward F. Davis, M.S., "One-Shot Drops," *FBI Law Enforcement Bulletin*, (October 2004): 17.

[33] "At the time of their deaths, 81 percent of the study victims were in uniform." See U.S. Department of Justice, *Killed in the Line of Duty*, 1992, (Washington, DC: FBI, 1992), 31.

[34] "For police officers, who may need to use deadly force on the job, any hesitation could prove fatal. To overcome the human aversion to killing, police academies condition their officers to meet force with force." See George T. Williams, "Reluctance to Use Deadly Force," *FBI Law Enforcement Bulletin*, (October 1999): 4.

Suspects that actively resist require greater force by the police officer to overcome the resistance. See Mayard v. Hopwood, 105 F. 3d 1226 (8th Cir. 1997).

Referencing the Mayard v. Hopwood case, John C. Hall, J.D., wrote: "Obviously, an officer may require higher levels of force to overcome a suspect engaged in active arrest resistance." See John C. Hall, J.D., "Police Use of Nondeadly Force to Arrest," *FBI Law Enforcement Bulletin*, (October 1997).

"Rossi observes, "At the moment of your possible demise," you must be able to "will yourself to become a bigger predator than the one trying to take your life away." That means striking back ruthlessly, taking full advantage of any of his [or her] weaknesses, with an unbending commitment to winning the contest for your survival." See Charles Remsberg, *Blood Lessons* (San Francisco, CA: Calibre Press, 2008), 28.

[35] *American Heritage Dictionary of the English Language Online,* 4th ed., s.v. "stress," http://www.thefreedictionary.com/stress (accessed September 22, 2012).

[36] Fred Travis, Ph.D., "Brain Functioning as the Ground for Spiritual Experiences and Ethical Behavior," *FBI Law Enforcement Bulletin*, (May 2009): 28.

[37] Men's Health Magazine, *How a Man Stays Young* (Emmaus, PA: Rodale Press, 1993), 183.

[38] Zahava Solomon, *Combat Stress Reaction* (New York, NY: Plenum Press, 1993), 30.

[39] Zahava Solomon, *Combat Stress Reaction* (New York, NY: Plenum Press, 1993), 30.

[40] American Heart Association, "Stress and Heart Health," (Dallas, TX: *Conditions)*, http://www.heart.org/HEARTORG/Conditions/More/MyHeartandStrokeNews/Stress-and-Heart-Health_UCM_437370_Article.jsp (accessed September 22, 2012).

[41] National Law Enforcement Officers Memorial Fund, "Causes of Law Enforcement Deaths," *Over the Past Decade (2002-2011)*, (April 2012), http://www.nleomf.org/facts/officer-fatalities-data/causes.html (accessed September 22, 2012).

[42] Charles Remsberg, *Blood Lessons* (San Francisco, CA: Calibre Press, 2008), 13.

Men's Health Magazine, *How a Man Stays Young* (Emmaus, PA: Rodale Press, 1993), 83-85.

[43] Department of Health and Human Services, "Centers for Disease Control and Prevention," *Overweight and Obesity*, (revised May 24, 2012), http://www.cdc.gov/nccdphp/dnpa/obesity/ (accessed September 22, 2012).

[44] Daniel E. Shell, "Physical Fitness," *FBI Law Enforcement Bulletin*, (May 2005): 28.

[45] Velcro: "A trademark used for a fastening tape consisting of a strip of nylon with a surface of minute hooks that fasten to a corresponding strip with a surface of uncut pile. This trademark sometimes occurs in print in lowercase." See *American Heritage Dictionary of the English Language Online*, 4th ed., s.v. "Velcro," http://www.thefreedictionary.com/velcro (accessed September 22, 2012).

[46] Daniel E. Shell, "Physical Fitness," *FBI Law Enforcement Bulletin*, (May 2005): 29.

[47] Rory Miller, *Meditations on Violence* (Wolfeboro, NH: YMAA Publication Center Inc., 2008), 6.

[48] Polar Electro Inc., "Products," (Aurora, IL: *Polar Electro*, 2011), http://www.polarusa.com/us-en/products (accessed September 22, 2012).

[49] Daniel E. Shell, "Physical Fitness," *FBI Law Enforcement Bulletin*, (May 2005): 30.

[50] Charles Remsberg, *Blood Lessons* (San Francisco, CA: Calibre Press, 2008), 23.

[51] The Cooper Institute, "Commonly Ask Questions," *Common Questions Regarding Physical Fitness Tests, Standards and Programs for Public Safety,* (2010), http://www.cooperinstitute.org/education/law_enforcement/documents/LAWCommonlyAskedQuestions.pdf (accessed September 22, 2012).

[52] The Cooper Institute, "Home," (2010), http://www.cooperinstitute.org/ (accessed September 22, 2012).

[53] Federal Bureau of Investigation, "Special Agents Becoming One of America's Finest," *FBI Special Agent Physical Fitness Test Scoring Scale*, (2012), http://www.fbijobs.gov/11131.asp (accessed September 22, 2012).

[54] Federal Bureau of Investigation, "Special Agents Becoming One of America's Finest," *FBI Special Agent Physical Fitness Requirements – Standard Pull-ups,* (2012), http://www.fbijobs.gov/11133.asp (accessed September 22, 2012).

[55] The push-up is considered by some as the one best exercise for the body. See Men's Health Magazine, *How a Man Stays Young* (Emmaus, PA: Rodale Press, 1993), 239.

[56] Timothy D. Blakeley, "Personal notes from the Antiterrorism Combat Fitness session," *Antiterrorism Combat Course*, (Tel Aviv, Israel: 2008): 6.

[57] Mayo Clinic, "Fitness," *Weight Training: Do's and Don'ts of Proper Technique*, (November 21, 2009), http://www.mayoclinic.com/health/weight-training/SM00028 (accessed September 22, 2012).

[58]   Beachbody,   "P90X,"   *P90X*,   (2012) http://www.beachbody.com/product/fitness_programs/p90x.do?code=BBHOME_CON TROL_P90X (accessed September 22, 2012).

[59] Colonel David Ben-Asher, *Fighting Fit: The Israel Defense Forces Guide to Physical Fitness and Self-Defense* (New York, NY: The Putnam Publishing Group, 1983), 219.

[60] Colonel David Ben-Asher, *Fighting Fit: The Israel Defense Forces Guide to Physical Fitness and Self-Defense* (New York, NY: The Putnam Publishing Group, 1983), 219.

[61] Robert Vogel, *Make Ready with Bob Vogel: Building World Class Pistol Skills* (Columbia, SC: Panteao Productions, 2010): Hand Strength, DVD.

[62] Bill Rogers, *Make Ready with Bill Rogers: Reactive Pistol Shooting* (Columbia, SC: Panteao Productions, 2010): Dominant Eye, Grip, and Stance, DVD.

[63]   Accu-Net,   LLC,   "Handgun,"   *GripMaster*,   (2011), http://prohands.net/who/sports/handgun/ (accessed September 22, 2012).

[64] IronMind Enterprises, Inc., "Product Info," *Captains of Crush Grippers*, (2012), http://ironmind.com/ironmind/opencms/Main/captainsofcrush.html   (accessed September 22, 2012).

[65] "No. 1250 CoC Trainer c. 100 lb. For everyone who is ready for serious grip training: athletes, public safety & military personnel." See IronMind Enterprises, Inc., "Product   Info,"   *Captains   of   Crush   Grippers*,   (2012), http://ironmind.com/ironmind/opencms/Main/captainsofcrush.html   (accessed September 22, 2012).

[66] Randall J. Strossen, Ph.D., J.B. Kinney, and Nathan Holle, *Captains of Crush Grippers: What They Are and How to Close Them* (Nevada City, CA: IronMind Enterprises, Inc., 2009).

[67] Hollie A. Raynor, Ph.D., and Rena R. Wing, Ph.D., "Effect of Limiting Snack Food Variety Across Days on Hedonics and Consumption," *Appetite*, (March 2006, Volume 46, Issue 2): 168-176.

[68] Men's Health Magazine, *How a Man Stays Young* (Emmaus, PA: Rodale Press, 1993), 244-246.

[69] "Limit saturated fat to no more than 10 percent of your total calories. Limit to 7 percent to further reduce your risk of heart disease. Based on a 2,000-calorie-a-day diet, a 10 percent limit amounts to about 22 grams of saturated fat a day, while 7 percent is about 15 grams. Saturated fat intake counts toward your total daily allowance of fat."

See Mayo Clinic, "Nutrition and Healthy Eating," *Dietary Fats: Know Which Types to Choose*, (February 15, 2011), http://www.mayoclinic.com/health/fat/NU00262 (accessed September 22, 2012).

[70] The meal plan recommendation is a modified version of the Fast Fat Loss Now! See Ellington Darden, Ph.D, "Fast Fat Loss Now," *Bowflex Xtreme2 Owner's Manual and Fitness Guide* (May 2004): 57-65.

[71] Stefan Aschan, "The Fastest Way to Burn Body Fat," in abc*news.go.com*, (January 24, 2007), http://abcnews.go.com/Health/Exercise/story?id=2817212&page=1 (accessed September 22, 2012).

[72] Stefan Aschan, "The Fastest Way to Burn Body Fat," in abc*news.go.com*, (January 24, 2007), http://abcnews.go.com/Health/Exercise/story?id=2817212&page=1 (accessed September 22, 2012).

[73] Nature's Bounty, "Prescriptive Formulas Men's Optimal Vitamin Packs," *Prescriptive Formulas Optimal Men's # 030010*, http://www.naturesbounty.com/product/030010 (accessed September 22, 2012).

Nature's Bounty, "Prescriptive Formulas Women's Optimal Vitamin Packs," *Prescriptive Formulas Optimal Women's # 030000*, http://www.naturesbounty.com/product/030000 (accessed September 22, 2012).

[74] "A substantial amount of work has been done in both elderly subjects and hypoadrenal subjects to determine the optimal dose to restore DHEA levels to those seen in young adults; 50 mg/d is sufficient to increase DHEA levels into the reference range of age-matched young adults." See Ketan K. Dhatariya, MBBS, MRCP (UK), MSc, and K. Sreekumaran Nair, MD, Ph.D., "Dehydroepiandrosterone: Is There a Role for Replacement?," (*Mayo Clinic Proceedings*, October 2003 vol. 78 no. 10 1257-1273), http://download.journals.elsevierhealth.com/pdfs/journals/0025-6196/PIIS0025619611628486.pdf (accessed September 22, 2012).

Nature's Bounty, "Product," *DHEA 25 mg. # 003421*, http://www.naturesbounty.com/product/003421 (accessed September 22, 2012).

[75] Nature's Bounty, "Product," *Flex-a-min Complete Product No. 014856*, http://www.naturesbounty.com/product/014856 (accessed September 22, 2012).

[76] These guidelines are published every 5 years. See U.S. Department of Health and Human Services, "Dietary Guidelines," (Washington, DC: *Dietary Guidelines for Americans, 2010*), http://www.health.gov/dietaryguidelines/dga2010/DietaryGuidelines2010.pdf (accessed September 22, 2012).

[77] "Trans fat is made by adding hydrogen to vegetable oil through a process called hydrogenation, which makes the oil less likely to spoil. Using trans fats in the manufacturing of foods helps foods stay fresh longer, have a longer shelf life and have

a less greasy feel...Commercial baked goods — such as crackers, cookies and cakes — and many fried foods, such as doughnuts and french fries — may contain trans fats. Shortenings and some margarines can be high in trans fat." See Mayo Clinic, "Hight Cholesterol," *Trans fat is Double Trouble for Your Heart Health*, http://www.mayoclinic.com/health/trans-fat/CL00032 (accessed September 22, 2012).

[78] Michael Boschmann, Jochen Steiniger, Uta Hille, Jens Tank, Frauke Adams, Arya M. Sharma, Susanne Klaus, Friedrich C. Luft and Jens Jordan, "Water-Induced Thermogenesis," *The Journal of Clinical Endocrinology & Metabolism Vol. 88, No. 12 6015-6019*, http://jcem.endojournals.org/cgi/content/full/88/12/6015 (accessed September 22, 2012).

[79] Men's Health Magazine, *How a Man Stays Young* (Emmaus, PA: Rodale Press, 1993), 29.

[80] MedicineNet, "Health Feature," *How To Get a Good Night's Sleep*, (January 30, 2005) http://www.medicinenet.com/script/main/art.asp?articlekey=50595 (accessed September 22, 2012).

[81] Stanford University School of Medicine, "News Releases" *Stanford Researchers Identify Best Hours for Shut-Eye When Sleep Must be Limited*, (May 29, 2003) http://med.stanford.edu/news_releases/2003/may/sleep.html (accessed September 22, 2012).

[82] Men's Health Magazine, *How a Man Stays Young* (Emmaus, PA: Rodale Press, 1993), 246-247.

[83] Men's Health Magazine, *How a Man Stays Young* (Emmaus, PA: Rodale Press, 1993), 247.

[84] "If you train people properly, they won't be able to tell a drill from the real thing. If anything, the real thing will be easier." See Richard Marcinko, Leadership Secrets of the Rogue Warrior: A Commando's Guide to Success (New York, NY: Pocket Books, 1996), 60.

[85] Drill: "A disciplined exercise or a systematic regimen of prescribed operations designed to instill specific skills though repetitive practice. Firearms drills may be a unit of a manual of arms (teaching safe handling or proficiency in the various mechanical operations of a firearm), marksmanship exercises, or elements of training in the tactical deployment of firearms and threat management. A drill may consist of a complex course of fire or a stage or element thereof. For a variety of tactical firearms training drills and courses of fire, a useful reference is the IALEFI *Tactical Firearms Handbook* (Laconia NH: IALEFI Inc.)." See International Association of Law Enforcement Firearms Instructors, *Standards & Practices Reference Guide for Law Enforcement Firearms Instructors*, (January 1995): 252.

[86] Course of Fire: "Prescribed positions, number of shots, distance and time." See International Association of Law Enforcement Firearms Instructors, *Standards & Practices Reference Guide for Law Enforcement Firearms Instructors*, (January 1995): 250.

[87] "The more complex any system or strategy is, the more likely it will be to fail." See Richard Marcinko, Leadership Secrets of the Rogue Warrior: A Commando's Guide to Success (New York, NY: Pocket Books, 1996), 98.

[88] "7. Thou shalt Keep It Simple, Stupid." See Richard Marcinko, Leadership Secrets of the Rogue Warrior: A Commando's Guide to Success (New York, NY: Pocket Books, 1996), front matter.

[89] Dean T. Olson, "Improving Deadly Force Decision Making," *FBI Law Enforcement Bulletin*, (February 1998): 7.

[90] Paul R. Howe, *The Tactical Trainer* (Bloomington, IN: AuthorHouse, 2009), 30.

[91] Neal J. Cohen and Howard Eichenbaum, *Memory, Amnesia, and the Hippocampal System* (Cambridge, MA: 1994), 49-50.

[92] *Columbia Encyclopedia*, s.v. "procedural memory," http://education.yahoo.com/reference/encyclopedia/?s=procedural+memory (accessed September 22, 2012).

[93] "...procedural memory refers to knowledge that underlies motor and cognitive skills, many of them automatized (such as speech, typing, bicycle riding, and possibly certain types of tacit knowledge, such as how a system works or a game is played)." See Daniel Druckman and John A. Swets, *Enhancing Human Performance: Issues, Theories, and Techniques* (Washington D.C.: National Academy Press, 1988), 41.

[94] "...procedural memory, also referred to as skill memory. Procedural memory means knowing how to do things. You have learned and now "remember" how to ride a bicycle, how to swim or swing a bat, how to type, how to turn on the lights, and how to drive a car. Procedural memories tend to persist even when we have not used them for many years. (Do we ever forget how to ride a bicycle?)" See Spencer A. Rathus, *Psychology in the New Millennium* (Orlando, FL: 1999), 284.

[95] David Hartman, MSW and Diane Zimberoff, M.A., "Memory Access to our Earliest Influences," *Journal of Heart-Centered Therapies*, Vol. 5, No. 2 (2002): 22.

[96] Paul R. Howe, *The Tactical Trainer* (Bloomington, IN: AuthorHouse, 2009), 62.

[97] "A gun is a tool, and officers need to be so practiced with it that the mechanics of using it become automatic and unconscious. That frees up more time and attention for decision-making and for concentration on the adversary's behavior." See Force Science Institute, LTD., "Point Shooting Clarification," *Force Science News* #135 (October 23, 2009), http://www.forcescience.org/fsinews/2009/10/force-science-news-135-%e2%80%9cpoint-shooting%e2%80%9d-clarification%e2%80%a6plus-what-

new-gaze-pattern-findings-mean-for-your-training-more/ (accessed September 22, 2012).

"To be effective in combat, the Marine must train to perfect the physical skills of shooting so they become second nature. The more physical skills that can be performed automatically, the more concentration that can be given to the mental side of target engagement." See Headquarters United States Marine Corps, *Pistol Marksmanship MCRP 3-01 B* (Department of the Navy, Washington, D.C., 25 November 2003), 2-18.

[98] Department of the Army, *Training for Full Spectrum Operations* (Washington, D.C.: Headquarters, December 12, 2008) 2-5.

[99] International Association of Law Enforcement Firearms Instructors, *IALEFI Guidelines for Simulation Training Safety*, (2004): 18.

[100] Glock Inc., *Armorer's Manual*, (Smyrna, GA: 2009): 62.

[101] Glock Inc., "Original Accessories," *Glock Autopistols 2012*, (New York, NY: Harris Publications Inc., 2012): 104.

[102] Dummy Cartridge: "Also: dummy. A cartridge without powder or primer...An inert cartridge or simulation of a cartridge which cannot be fired, used for demonstration or training purposes or for testing the actions of firearms." See Enforcement Firearms Instructors, *Standards & Practices Reference Guide for Law Enforcement Firearms Instructors*, (January 1995): 164.

[103] Glock Inc., "Original Accessories," *Glock Autopistols 2012*, (New York, NY: Harris Publications Inc., 2012): 103.

[104] Glock Inc., *Glock Buyer's Guide Professional Edition*, (Smyrna, GA: Glock Inc., 2012): 30.

[105] George T. Williams, "Reluctance to Use Deadly Force," *FBI Law Enforcement Bulletin*, (October 1999): 2.

[106] Department of the Army, *Combat Training with Pistols, M9 and M11* (Washington, DC June 2003), 2-11.

[107] Dean T. Olson, "Improving Deadly Force Decision Making," *FBI Law Enforcement Bulletin*, (February 1998): 5-6.

[108] George T. Williams, "Reluctance to Use Deadly Force," *FBI Law Enforcement Bulletin*, (October 1999): 4.

[109] Target Focused Sighted Shooting: The shooter focuses on the target, brings his or her firearm into the line of sight while simultaneously applying pressure to the trigger, sees the aligned sights, and breaks the shot.

[110] Focus: "To render (an object or image) in clear outline or sharp detail by adjustment of one's vision or an optical device; bring into focus." See *American Heritage Dictionary of the English Language Online*, 4th ed., s.v. "focus," http://www.thefreedictionary.com/focus (accessed September 22, 2012).

[111] See: "To perceive with the eye." See *American Heritage Dictionary of the English Language Online*, 4th ed., s.v. "see," http://www.thefreedictionary.com/see (accessed September 22, 2012).

[112] Joan N Vickers, and William Lewinski, "Performing under Pressure: Gaze Control, Decision Making and Shooting Performance of Elite and Rookie Police Officers." *Human Movement Science* (2012, 31, No. 1): 102-117.

[113] "The quite eye is a final fixation or tracking gaze that is located on a specific location or object in the visuomotor workspace within 3° of visual angle (or less) for a minimum of 100 ms. The onset of the quite eye occurs prior to the final movement of the task, and the offset occurs naturally when the gaze deviates off the location or object by more than 3° of visual angle for a minimum of 100 ms. Since elite performers exhibit an optimal control of the quite eye relative to the final movement, the quiet eye may be viewed as an objective measure of optimal perceptual-motor coordination." See Joan N. Vickers, *Perception, Cognition, and Decision Training: The Quiet Eye in Action* (Champaign, IL: Human Kinetics, 2007) 11.

[114] Joan N Vickers, and William Lewinski, "Performing under Pressure: Gaze Control, Decision Making and Shooting Performance of Elite and Rookie Police Officers." *Human Movement Science* (2012, 31, No. 1): 114-115.

[115] "3. Finger on frame – simple, unsighted, reaction time - .45" "4. Finger on frame with a sight picture, reaction time - .54." (.54 - .45 = .09 reaction time difference) See Bill Lewinski, Ph.D., "Biomechanics of Lethal Force Encounters," *The Police Marksman* (November/December 2002): 19.

[116] "Some marksmen [and markswomen] can maintain visual awareness of the front sight even though the eye's focusing system is drawn toward infinity during the BAR." See Edward C. Godnig, O.D., "Body Alarm Reaction and Sports Vision," *Journal of Behavioral Optometry* (2001, Vol. 12, No. 1): 4.

[117] Dean T. Olson, "Improving Deadly Force Decision Making," *FBI Law Enforcement Bulletin*, (February 1998): 4.

U.S. Department of Justice, *Violent Encounters*, 2006, (Washington, DC: FBI, 2006), 70.

"When confronted with a target, the natural physical reaction is to face the target and push out with the arms." See Headquarters United States Marine Corps, *Pistol Marksmanship MCRP 3-01 B* (Department of the Navy, Washington, D.C., 25 November 2003), 4-5.

[118] *Miller-Keane Encyclopedia and Dictionary of Medicine, Nursing, and Allied Health*, 7th ed., s.v. "alarm reaction," http://medical-dictionary.thefreedictionary.com/fight-or-flight+reaction (accessed September 22, 2012).

[119] Phil Singleton, *3 Day Tactical Pistol for Hostage Rescue, High Risk Warrant and Drugs Raids,* (Warrenton, VA: Singleton International): 12.

[120] Dean T. Olson, "Improving Deadly Force Decision Making," *FBI Law Enforcement Bulletin*, (February 1998): 5.

[121] International Association of Law Enforcement Firearms Instructors, *IALEFI Guidelines for Simulation Training Safety*, (2004): 17.

[122] J. Henry FitzGerald, *Shooting* (Boulder, CO: Paladin Press, 2007), 364. Originally published in 1930 by J. Henry FitzGerald.

[123] Live Fire House: "A structure or training facility with safe backstops or ballistic barriers that allow live fire in more than one direction for the purpose of realistically simulating dynamic, close-quarter combat situations in such settings as multi-room buildings, stairwells, hallways, closets, alleys and other locations." See International Association of Law Enforcement Firearms Instructors, *Standards & Practices Reference Guide for Law Enforcement Firearms Instructors*, (January 1995): 237-238.

[124] "Target discrimination is the act of quickly distinguishing between combatant and noncombatant personnel and engaging only the combatants." See Department of the Army, *Combine Arms Operations in Urban Terrain* (Washington, DC 25 February 2002), 3-24.

[125] Robert K. Taubert, *Rattenkrieg! The Art and Science of Close Quarters Battle Pistol* (North Reading, MA: Saber Press, 2012), 139.

[126] Glock Inc., *Glock Pistol Transitional Instructor Workshop Course Outline*, (Smyrna, GA: 2012): 3.

[127] Glock Inc., *Glock Pistol Transitional Instructor Workshop Course Outline*, (Smyrna, GA: 2012): 3.

[128] Glock Inc., *Glock Pistol Transitional Instructor Workshop Course Outline*, (Smyrna, GA: 2012): 3.

Anthony J. Pinizzotto, Ph.D., Harry A. Kern, M.Ed., and Edward F. Davis, M.S., "One-Shot Drops," FBI *Law Enforcement Bulletin*, (October 2004): 18.

[129] Glock Inc., *Glock Pistol Transitional Instructor Workshop Course Outline*, (Smyrna, GA: 2012): 3.

[130] Glock Inc., *Glock Pistol Transitional Instructor Workshop Course Outline*, (Smyrna, GA: 2012): 3.

[131] Underhand Technique: The pistol in an upright position is rotated 45 degrees toward the ground and the non-firing hand's pad and fingertips grasp the slide pulling rearward until the slide is stripped from the non-firing hand.

[132] Patrol Officer Stephanie Bellis of the Brentwood Police Department. See In the Line of Duty, "Brentwood (TN) Bank Robbery and Shootout," *Volume 8 Program 3*: Video Recording.

[133] Ed McGivern, *Ed McGivern's Book of Fast and Fancy Revolver Shooting* (New York, NY: Skyhorse Publishing, Inc., 2007): 223.

[134] In a 10-year period in which law enforcement officers were feloniously killed, about 50 percent of the time the offender was between contact and 5 feet from the officer. About 80 percent of the time, the offender was between contact and 20 feet from the officer. See Federal Bureau of Investigation, "Law Enforcement Officers Killed and Assaulted," *Table 36 – Distance Between Victim Officer and Offender, 2001–2010*), http://www.fbi.gov/about-us/cjis/ucr/leoka/leoka-2010/tables/table36leok-feloniously-with-firearms-distance-victim-offender-01-10.xls (accessed September 22, 2012).

Glock Inc., *Glock Pistol Transitional Instructor Workshop Course Outline*, (Smyrna, GA: 2012): 3.

[135] XS Sight Systems Inc., *XS Sight Systems 2009 Catalog*, (Fort Worth, TX: 2009), 15.

Bruce N. Eimer, Ph.D., "Armed Senior Citizen," *Concealed Carry Magazine*, (July 2006): 37.

[136] Glock Inc., *Glock Pistol Transitional Instructor Workshop Course Outline*, (Smyrna, GA: 2012): 3.

[137] This occurred as witnessed by the author while attending the Glock Pistol Transitional Instructor Workshop course on February 3-5, 2010 held at Glock Inc., in Smyrna, Georgia.

[138] "Make quick glances at specific points throughout the area, rather than just sweeping the eyes across the terrain in one continuous panoramic view." See Department of the Army, *Rifle Marksmanship M16-/M4-Series Weapons* (Washington, DC August 2008), 6-2.

[139] Lori Hartman Gervasi, *Fight Like a Girl... and Win* (New York, NY: St. Martin's Griffin, 2007): 182.

[140] "A target indicator is anything that a Soldier (friendly or enemy) does or fails to do that reveals his position." See Department of the Army, *Rifle Marksmanship M16-/M4-Series Weapons* (Washington, DC August 2008), 6-3.

[141] Jeff Gonzales, *Combative Fundamentals, an Unconventional Approach* (Cedar Park, TX: Trident Concepts, LLC, 2002), 38.

[142] Kyle Dinkheller, a professional law enforcement officer murdered while protecting and serving the citizens of Laurens County, Georgia. See In the Line of Duty, *Murder of a Georgia Deputy*, (Saint Louis, MO): VHS Volume 7 Program 2.

U.S. Department of Justice, *In the Line of Fire*, 1997, (Washington, DC: FBI, 1997), 64.

[143] National Rifle Association, *NRA Guide to Basics of Personal Protection Outside the Home* (Fairfax, VA: National Rifle Association of America, 2006), 147.

[144] The U.S. Army uses the doctrine of shoot, move, and communicate as necessary skills for combat. See Department of the Army, *Soldier's Manual of Common Tasks Warrior Skills Level 1* (Washington, DC: September 11, 2012), 3-1 through 3-154.

[145] The video shows on Friday, January 6, 2012, Deputy Jeff Nichols and Reserve Deputy Jeremy Conley of Kalamazoo Sheriff's Office in Michigan stopping a vehicle on East Michigan Avenue after it ran a traffic light. When Deputy Nichols approached the driver's side window, shots are fired at him. See Jeff Nichols and Jeremy Conley, *Cop Gets Shot at on Traffic Stop*, YouTube video, uploaded January 19, 2012, http://www.youtube.com/watch?v=w9JbdwHvRZo (accessed September 22, 2012).

[146] J. Henry FitzGerald, *Shooting* (Boulder, CO: Paladin Press, 2007), 364. Originally published in 1930 by J. Henry FitzGerald.

[147] Force Science Institute, LTD., "Point Shooting Clarification," *Force Science News* #135 (October 23, 2009), http://www.forcescience.org/fsinews/2009/10/force-science-news-135-%e2%80%9cpoint-shooting%e2%80%9d-clarification%e2%80%a6plus-what-new-gaze-pattern-findings-mean-for-your-training-more/ (accessed September 22, 2012).

[148] Paul R. Howe, *Leadership and Training for the Fight* (New York, NY: Skyhorse Publishing, 2011), 151.

[149] W.E. Fairbairn and E.A. Sykes, *Shooting to Live* (Boulder, CO: Paladin Press, 1987), 45. Originally published in 1942 by W.E. Fairbairn and E.A. Sykes.

[150] Robert K. Taubert, *Rattenkrieg! The Art and Science of Close Quarters Battle Pistol* (North Reading, MA: Saber Press, 2012), 235.

[151] U.S. Department of Justice, *Violent Encounters*, 2006, (Washington, DC: FBI, 2006), 48.

[152] U.S. Department of Justice, *In the Line of Fire*, 1997, (Washington, DC: FBI, 1997), 17.

[153] In the Line of Duty, "Trooper Coates Shooting," *Volume 1 Program 4 Duty Sheet and Lesson Plan*.

U.S. Department of Justice, *In the Line of Fire*, 1997, (Washington, DC: FBI, 1997), 64.

[154] In a 10-year period in which law enforcement officers were feloniously killed, about 50 percent of the time the offender was between contact and 5 feet from the officer. About 80 percent of the time, the offender was between contact and 20 feet from the officer. See Federal Bureau of Investigation, "Law Enforcement Officers Killed and Assaulted," (Clarksburg, WV: *Table 36 – Distance Between Victim Officer*

and   Offender,   2001–2010),   http://www.fbi.gov/about-us/cjis/ucr/leoka/leoka-2010/tables/table36leok-feloniously-with-firearms-distance-victim-offender-01-10.xls (accessed September 22, 2012).

[155] Urey W. Patrick, and John C. Hall, *In Defense of Self and Others* (Durham, NC: Carolina Academic Press, 2010), 143.

[156] Melissa O'Connell awoke in her bed by a convicted rapist with a gun. O'Connel fought hand-to-hand with the rapist eventually taking his gun. O'Connel shot the rapist three times killing him. See Calibre Press, *Ultimate Survivors II*, (Carrollton, TX: 2005): DVD.

[157] Texas Constitution and Statutes, "Sec. 46.035. UNLAWFUL CARRYING OF HANDGUN BY LICENSE HOLDER. (a) A license holder commits an offense if the license holder carries a handgun on or about the license holder's person under the authority of Subchapter H, Chapter 411, Government Code, and intentionally fails to conceal   the   handgun.", http://www.statutes.legis.state.tx.us/Docs/PE/htm/PE.46.htm#46.035   (accessed September 22, 2012).

[158] J. Henry FitzGerald, *Shooting* (Boulder, CO: Paladin Press, 2007), 394. Originally published in 1930 by J. Henry FitzGerald.

[159] North Carolina Justice Academy, "SWAT Operator," *Firearms Use in Tactical Operations* (Salemburg, NC: January 2008): 14.

[160] Bill Rogers, *Be Fast, Be Accurate, Be the Best* (Rogers Shooting School Publications: Jacksonville, FL, 2010), 66.

[161] Itay Gil and Dan Baron, *The Citizen's Guide to Stopping Suicide Attackers* (Boulder, CO: Paladin Press, 2004), 73-74.

[162] National Rifle Association, *NRA Guide to Basics of Personal Protection Outside the Home* (Fairfax, VA: National Rifle Association of America, 2006), 142.

[163] National Rifle Association, *Law Enforcement Handgun Instructor Manual* (Fairfax, VA: Off-Duty Firearm Safety, Edition 6.1, 2006), 3.

[164] Kathy Jackson, *The Cornered Cat: A Woman's Guide to Concealed Carry* (White Feather Press, 2010), 85.

[165] National Rifle Association, *Law Enforcement Handgun Instructor Manual* (Fairfax, VA: Off-Duty Firearm Safety, Edition 6.1, 2006), 3.

[166] National Rifle Association, *NRA Guide to Basics of Personal Protection Outside the Home* (Fairfax, VA: National Rifle Association of America, 2006), 143.

[167] Bruce N. Eimer, Ph.D., "Bear Arms in a Wheelchair," *Concealed Carry Magazine* (Volume 02 - Issue 08): 28.

[168] This method of carry for a wheelchair-user is favored by the National Rifle Association of America. See National Rifle Association, *NRA Guide to Basics of*

Personal Protection Outside the Home (Fairfax, VA: National Rifle Association of America, 2006), 137-138.

[169] For additional information or advice on concealed carry for people with physical disabilities contact Manager, Disabled Shooting Services, Competitive Shooting Division, National Rifle Association of America at 703-267-1495 or online at www.NRA.org.

[170] North Carolina Justice Academy, *Officer Safety and Readiness Instructor Training* (Edneyville, NC: July 2004), Vehicle Stop Tactics – Instructor, 14.

[171] North Carolina Justice Academy, *Officer Safety and Readiness Instructor Training* (Edneyville, NC: July 2004), Vehicle Stop Tactics – Instructor, 14.

[172] From 8:00 p.m. to 6:00 a.m. See Federal Bureau of Investigation, "Law Enforcement Officers Killed and Assaulted," (Clarksburg, WV: *Table 3 – Time of Incident, 2001–2010*), http://www.fbi.gov/about-us/cjis/ucr/leoka/leoka-2010/tables/table03-leok-feloniously-time-of-incident-01-10.xls (accessed September 22, 2012).

[173] Federal Bureau of Investigation, "Law Enforcement Officers Killed and Assaulted," (Clarksburg, WV: *Table 27 – Type of Weapon, 2001–2010*), http://www.fbi.gov/about-us/cjis/ucr/leoka/leoka-2010/tables/table27-leok-feloniously-type-of-weapon-01-10.xls (accessed September 22, 2012).

[174] U.S. Department of Justice, *Violent Encounters*, 2006, (Washington, DC: FBI, 2006), 70.

The Grant-Taylor Manual, *The Palestine Police Force Close Quarter Battle* (Boulder, CO: Paladin Press, 2008), 26. Originally published in 1943. Reprinted by Paladin Press in 2008.

[175] Hypervigilance: "abnormally increased arousal, responsiveness to stimuli, and scanning of the environment for threats." See *Dorland's Medical Dictionary for Health Consumers Online,* 2007 ed., s.v. "hypervigilance" http://medical-dictionary.thefreedictionary.com/Hypervigilance (accessed September 22, 2012).

Dean T. Olson, "Improving Deadly Force Decision Making," *FBI Law Enforcement Bulletin*, (February 1998): 5.

[176] Paul R. Howe, *Leadership and Training for the Fight* (New York, NY: Skyhorse Publishing, 2011), 12.

[177] Lancaster Police Department, *Texas Peace Officer's Accident Report #95025806*, September 24, 1995, (Lancaster, TX: Lancaster Police Department, 1995).

Douglas Holt, *Crash Kills 1; Officer Saves 2nd Man* (Dallas, TX: Dallas Morning News, 1995).

[178] U.S. Department of Justice, *In the Line of Fire*, 1997, (Washington, DC: FBI, 1997), 42.

[179] Charles Remsberg, *Blood Lessons* (San Francisco, CA: Calibre Press, 2008), 85.

[180] Paul R. Howe, *The Tactical Trainer* (Bloomington, IN: AuthorHouse, 2009), 54.

[181] Campbell, John E., Lawrence E. Heiskell, Jim Smith, and E. John Wipfler III, *Tactical Medicine Essentials* (Sudbury, MA: Jones & Bartlett Learning, 2012), 208.

[182] Chinook Medical Gear, Inc., (www.chinookmed.com) as of this writing is an excellent source for operators to obtain medical supplies for combat operations and the items that follow should serve an operator well for a basic Individual First Aid Kit (IFAK): Martac EMT Combat Shears; SOF Tactical Tourniquet Wide (1.5 inch); Tactical Defender Nitrile Gloves; Halo Chest Seal; Nasopharyngeal Airway 28Fr; Surgilube; Silver "H" Compression Bandage; CELOX Trauma Gauze; and PriMed Compressed Gauze Bandage. A well designed IFAK pouch made by Original S.O.E. Gear is the Compact Tear-Off Med Pouch and comes in either vertical or horizontal orientation.

[183] A well-made IFAK pouch made by Original S.O.E. Gear (www.originalsoegear.com) is the Compact Tear-Off Med Pouch and comes in either a vertical or a horizontal orientation.

[184] Campbell, John E., Lawrence E. Heiskell, Jim Smith, and E. John Wipfler III, *Tactical Medicine Essentials* (Sudbury, MA: Jones & Bartlett Learning, 2012), 56.

[185] Paul Howe, *Make Ready with Paul Howe: Advanced Tac Pistol/Rifle Operator* (Columbia, SC: Panteao Productions, 2010): Concealed Carry & Tactical Follow-up, DVD.

[186] New York City Police Department, "New York City Police Department Annual Firearms Discharge Report 2007," (New York, NY: *Incident Details*, 2007), http://www.nyc.gov/html/nypd/downloads/pdf/public_information/2007_firearms_disc harge_report.pdf (accessed September 22, 2012).

[187] *American Heritage Dictionary of the English Language Online*, 4th ed., s.v. "ergonomics," http://www.thefreedictionary.com/ergonomics (accessed September 22, 2012).

[188] U.S. Department of Justice, *Violent Encounters*, 2006, (Washington, DC: FBI, 2006), 110-111.

[189] U.S. Department of Justice, *Violent Encounters*, 2006, (Washington, DC: FBI, 2006), 50.

[190] Eugene Sockut, *Secrets of Street Survival Israeli Style* (Boulder, CO: Paladin Press, 1995), 12.

[191] David G. Bolgiano, *Combat Self-Defense: Saving America's Warriors from Risk-Averse Commanders and Their Lawyers* (Little White Wolf Books: 2007), 79.

U.S. Department of Justice, Federal Bureau of Investigation, Firearms Training Unit, *Wound Ballistic Workshop "9mm vs. .45 auto"* (Quantico, VA, September 15-17, 1987), 24.

PERSONAL EQUIPMENT

Police officers and military operators will normally carry equipment approved by their organizations. Civilians have the latitude within the law to choose whatever equipment they believe is necessary for personal protection. Any equipment selected must be of the highest quality and suitable for operational requirements. An operator not current with the right equipment is not at the top of his or her game. It goes without saying, "Take care of your equipment, and it will take care of you."

Training can cause wear and tear on equipment. An operator may want to consider having dedicated training equipment. Training equipment must be the same type as used operationally and carried in the same configuration. The most common example is having dedicated training magazines. Glock magazines used for training should have orange floor plates.[1] The author qualifies with his duty magazines, but uses other magazines with orange floor plates for training courses. This allows him to train realistically (drop magazines on concrete, gravel, etc.), while keeping his duty magazines in pristine condition. There have been times he used his duty magazines for training, but he has never used his training magazines on duty.

Operators sometimes while training realize their equipment or the manner in which it is set up does not work. Equipment may fall out or be difficult if not impossible to retrieve or return to its holder. Operators at some point during training need to wear the same equipment carried operationally. The safe way to test equipment effectiveness and proper set up is in a training environment.[2]

Training might not always teach something new, but simply reinforce what is already known. Training should validate that operational equipment is functional and effective. Ineffective equipment can undermine an operator's sense of security and strength.[3] Equipment must *not* prevent the operator from fighting effectively. The equipment itself is not the only issue. The operator carrying the equipment must accept responsibility and acknowledge when something does not work. Operators that live in denial and avoid responsibility may at times make excuses for inferior equipment or its improper placement.

The author was getting his haircut in a small town located in the eastern United States and a local police officer walked in the barbershop. He noticed the police officer wore a combination handcuff/magazine pouch that held only one magazine. The author spoke to the police officer about the tactical disadvantage of carrying one spare magazine for his semiautomatic pistol. The police officer responded, "You might only have to use that [spare magazine] once in a lifetime." The police officer did not take responsibility for his lacking equipment. He did not see an extended gunfight as something *real* requiring two spare magazines. The police officer chose to believe such occurrence was possible, but unlikely. Such an attitude is *not* conducive to operational survival. In contrast to a police officer that answered a domestic disturbance call and was involved in a gunfight that lasted 12 minutes. What was that officer's main concern? The police officer said, "My biggest fear was running out of ammunition."[4]

The author also noticed the police officer's magazine pouch was located on his non-firing side mounted horizontally on his duty belt with the flap closure toward the firing side. He asked the police officer how he could remove the magazine from its pouch using economy of motion. The police officer gladly and proudly demonstrated how easy it was to withdraw the magazine and simulated inserting it in a pistol. The police officer twisted his hand while flipping the magazine. What it looked like from the author's perspective was a slight of hand act.

The author introduced himself as a law enforcement firearms instructor and in a tone of humbleness explained to the police officer that his horizontal pouch's flap closure should be turned toward the non-firing side and not away from it. He went on to say with the flap closure pointing toward the non-firing side that a magazine could be withdrawn and inserted into the pistol using economy of motion. What was the police officer's response to the author's suggestion? The police officer said, "Well, that is what they issued us." Regrettably, some people do not readily accept constructive criticism and many times dismiss suggestions for improvement.

NOTE: People have to accept what they do not know, to accept what they need to know or "...they are unlikely to take steps to improve their ability."[5]

HOLSTER

The most important piece of equipment for a pistol is a quality holster. A properly designed holster allows the magazine catch to be uncovered,[6] but also protects it so the magazine is not accidently released. This is especially critical for pistols with an *extended* magazine catch or for left-handed operators with the magazine catch on the left side. The design also allows the exchanging of magazines while the pistol is in the holster. Give careful consideration before selecting and purchasing a holster. (Figure 2-1) Holsters are made from leather, nylon, synthetic, and plastic. A pistol shoved inside the waistband is *not* secured.

Figure 2-1 *Right-hand holster with dual tension adjustment screws.*[7]

The *rise* which is how high or low the holster sits on the belt can affect draw speed. Using the thigh holster as an example, it should be worn just low enough to prevent interference with the body armor, but not so low that it slows down the draw speed. Some manufactures make a drop mount holster for females. The contoured drop mount (belt loop adapter) fits the female waist and hip. The drop mount allows the holster to sit parallel to the body and lowers the pistol about 1.5 inches (38.1 millimeters) below the waistline permitting a natural draw. The *drop mount* designed for female operators solves a couple of problems: The pistol riding under the armpit, and the painful experience of the holster at an excessive angle pressing against the body. Some male operators may find the lower sitting holster more comfortable and quicker to draw. Normally the inside of the elbow touches the butt of the pistol. This provides a physical indicator of the pistol's location and mental reassurance of its availability.

Retention versus Readiness

When selecting a holster, consider retention versus readiness. *Retention* is the manner in which the holster secures the pistol. Are there multiple snaps to release and the pistol move in a certain direction? Does the thumb push a locking device in a particular direction and then an actuator? Does the index finger push an actuator in a particular direction? These types of retention devices are built-in to various holsters. All the devices have one thing in common. Before drawing the pistol, each device must be released. Retention ratings for *security holsters* are *Level 1, Level 2,* and *Level 3*. The *least* secure being one and the *most* secure being three. Security holsters do require a higher level of training.[8]

Readiness is accessibility of the pistol coupled with the effort expended to complete the steps to remove it from the holster. There is no arguing a pistol in its holster needs to be secure. However, an operator must be able to draw the pistol from a holster quickly. Any holster can be manipulated in a stress-free environment. Adding stress to the training environment ensures a holster can be manipulated under less than ideal conditions. The holster must also allow removal of the pistol while using only one hand (dominant or non-dominant) while under stress. Preferably, using a downward motion with the thumb releases the retention device and the pistol pulled from the holster. This is the natural movement of the hand when establishing the grip position.

DANGER: A deputy after placing a cell phone in front of his holster could not remove the pistol. The cell phone prevented the holster's hood from rotating forward.[9] Fortunately, for the deputy this occurred at his home and not during a life-threatening situation.

A video from the dashboard camera captured the brutal attack on a Columbia, Missouri police officer while she made a traffic stop.[10] The police officer wore a triple retention security holster. The police officer could not release the retention device and she pulled on the handgun relentlessly until being shot.[11] The police officer made a valiant effort to stay in the fight, but died of her injuries about 1 month after the attack. The tragic death of the police officer is an example for the necessity of efficient equipment manipulation and its importance to operational survival.

The decision of retention versus readiness can be a matter of life-and-death for an operator. The butt of the pistol normally protrudes from the holster allowing the hand to get high on the back strap with one quick motion. However, holsters used by some militaries have a flap that covers the butt of the pistol. The flap is needed to prevent damage to the pistol from the steel interior of an armored vehicle. The flap has to be released to grip the back strap. This is a tradeoff of readiness versus protecting the pistol. It is slower to draw the pistol, but seen by some as necessary when inside armored vehicles.

It is common for military operators to wear a coiled[12] or straight lanyard to prevent accidental loss and aid in retention of the pistol.[13] (Figure 2-2) Operators that repel, board watercraft, climb ladders, etc., and have to handle a pistol should consider using a lanyard. The lanyard hooks in the opening in the back of the frame and the other end attaches to a waist belt. The coiled lanyard is available in black, tan, green, and brown.[14]

There are several methods used to secure a pistol in the holster. The holster may have a top strap with a snap, a rotating hood, or a locking or pinching mechanism that engages the trigger guard. Already discussed is the holster flap. Because of procedural memory it is preferable that an *on duty* and *off duty* holster use the same type of securing mechanism.[15] This will prevent the operator from having to acquire procedural memory for two different securing mechanisms. The mechanics of drawing a pistol should *not* be a decision making process. The operator will have to make an informed decision balancing the importance of retention versus readiness when purchasing a holster.

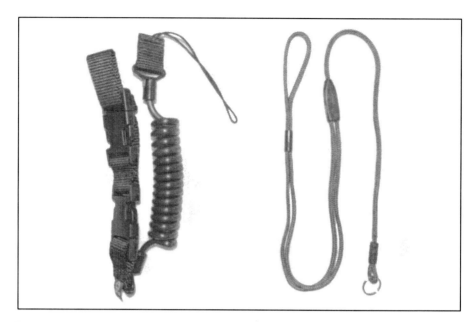

Figure 2-2 *Lanyards*

NOTE: Holsters that have the top strap attached with a hook-and-loop fastener may present a problem. A hook-and-loop fastener will become ineffective when exposed to dirt and the retention strap can pull loose from the holster. To prevent this problem have a local upholstery shop sew the top strap to the holster.

The bottom side of the holster is normally open to allow the evaporation of moisture. The holster should cover the slide down to the muzzle. This will prevent the muzzle from catching on the arm of a chair as the operator sits down. A pistol pushed out of its holster and hitting the floor in a public place may result in a criminal charge. To check how well a holster will retain a pistol begin by *unloading* the pistol and installing a *chamber blocker*. This ensures a live round cannot be chambered. Insert a full magazine into the pistol and place it in the holster. Hold the holster upside-down over a soft surface such as a bed and shake the holster. The pistol should remain secured, *if* not make necessary adjustments until it is secure. Those adjustments may include tightening a tension screw or having to buy a new holster. *Never* perform this test holding the pistol over a hard surface or with a round in the chamber.

Positioning and Securing the Holster

Where is the best place to wear a holster? That depends on the physical capability of the operator and operational environment. An operator with a shoulder injury may not be capable of rotating the elbow back to draw a pistol from a holster carried on the hip. It is popular in law enforcement for a patrol officer to wear the pistol on the hip of the side of the dominant eye. The officer can draw and shoot with speed, but also protect the pistol using his or her hand and forearm. The author as a police adviser in Afghanistan wore a pistol in a thigh holster positioned forward of his hip. As previously discussed, wearing the holster directly on the hip interfered with getting in and out of armored vehicles and aircraft.

It is a common practice for armed civilians to wear their concealed handgun attached to the waist belt on the dominant eye side. This is also true for plainclothes officers. The waist belt not only provides the foundation for the holster, but it is also used for racking the slide with one hand. Purchase a belt engineered to support the weight of the pistol and spare magazines. A flimsy belt does not provide a foundation for the holster or the means to rack the slide. A flimsy belt will have a tendency to move upward when the pistol is drawn. The holster needs to provide internal resistance against the pistol to prevent it from accidentally falling out. Only the pistol should move up when drawing and *not* the holster.

The belt's width needs be the same as the holster's loophole for the belt. Wear a holster with 1.5-inch (38.1-millimeter) wide loops on a 1.5-inch (38.1-millmeter) wide belt. The belt must be sturdy enough to prevent an adversary from tearing the holster and pistol off the operator's body. An excellent belt for concealed carry that provides holster retention is made of nylon with a five-stitch pattern. The belt is 1.5 inches (38.1 millimeters) wide with 5 stitch lines along the length significantly stiffening it for enhanced load bearing. The belt's vertical rigidity is similar to a leather equipment belt, but flexible horizontally and rotationally for comfort. A slightly thicker version of the belt is also available with polyethylene insert increasing vertical rigidity. The buckle is made of titanium (aerospace-grade Ti6Al-4V alloy) making it nearly 50 percent lighter than a steel buckle. The belt is available in black, olive drab, tan, and is commonly called an *instructor belt*.[16]

The adversary violently pulling on the police officer's pistol during a gun takeaway can cause his or her equipment belt to rotate on the waist. This can be disorienting to a police officer—especially in low light or the dark. The police officer must orient to the pistol's new location and react. The police officer may be able to draw and fire from the pistol's new location or have to pull it violently back to the original location.

An operator may ask, "How much money should I spend on a holster?" The answer is to buy the best holster the operator can afford. Do *not* settle on a poorly constructed holster. Such a holster could contribute to the operator being injured or killed. Take the time to research and gather information on what holster options are available for specific needs. It is more economical and tactically sound to buy one high quality holster than several inferior quality holsters.

The type of pistol purchased influences the method of carry. With the exception of police and the military it is *not* normally recommended to openly carry a pistol in public. Some may prefer a shoulder or ankle holster in comparison to a waist belt. A paddle holster worn on the waist belt is convenient for removing and putting back on without first removing the pistol. The operator can remove the paddle holster before entering a location that prohibits firearms. A *small-of-the-back* holster places the pistol in the center of the back. A small-of-the-back holster provides concealment from the front, but it might be seen *if* the operator bends over. The small-of-the-back holster can be uncomfortable, especially against hard-backed chair. In addition, a rearward fall might result in a back injury.

There are three types of shoulder holsters: *upside-down, horizontal,* and *vertical.* The upside-down holster holds the pistol vertical with the muzzle pointing up at the armpit. Horizontal shoulder holster holds the pistol horizontal with the muzzle pointing to the rear. The vertical shoulder holster holds the pistol vertical with the muzzle pointing down. Shoulder holsters are worn on the non-dominant side of the body. There are firearms ranges that do not allow any shoulder holsters and this is a consideration when wanting to live fire practice using a holster.

An *ankle holster* must remain securely fastened on the leg and the pistol secured in its holster. The ankle holster worn on the *inside* of the leg is less susceptible to banging into objects while walking or running. The ankle holster is worn on the non-dominant side leg. To access the pistol, the head remains up (situational awareness) while bending down, *not* over. The non-dominant hand grabs the pant leg below the knee and pulls it up quickly. This allows the pant leg to ride over the pistol and it gripped with the dominant hand.

It would be beneficial to visit a reputable gun store and try on different holsters. This allows the operator an opportunity to make an informed decision about the holster purchase. Clothing and weather will play a role in carrying the pistol and choosing a holster. Another factor in choosing a holster is the cant or angle of the pistol. The hand must quickly reach the back strap of the pistol for a fast draw. A study involving police officers revealed, "...the greatest factor in the speed or the draw is the amount of time the officer spends practicing with that holster."[17]

DANGER: When putting on or taking off a holster, keep the muzzle pointed at the ground. Do not allow the muzzle to point at the body. This mistake is especially prone to occur when twisting a paddle holster loose from the waist belt.

Other Carry Methods

In a hot environment where tee shirts and shorts are worn, a carry option may be the fanny pack. A fanny pack is a small bag that on the inside contains a holster for the pistol. Pulling on a string attached to a zipper or pulling apart a hook-and-loop fastener opens the fanny pack. Female operators may choose an off-the-body carry with the pistol in a holster purse designed for concealed carry.[18] (Figure 2-3) To maximize the pistol's potential it must be immediately accessible. (Figure 2-4) This should be the underlying goal when choosing a method of carry for a pistol used for self-protection.

An efficient draw begins with the pistol positioned properly in the handgun compartment. A quick fix to make drawing and holstering a pistol easier from a holster purse is to fasten a hard plastic holster in the handgun compartment using a hook-and-loop fastener. A hard plastic holster with the paddle or belt faster removed will work. Apply the self-adhesive hook-and-loop fastener on the outside of the holster and position it inside the handgun compartment of the purse. The hook-and-loop fastener will hold the holster in place and the purse will not collapse around the holster. This will speed up drawing and holstering the pistol.

Initially positioning the holster inside the handgun compartment can be difficult. This is because of the hook-and-loop fastener grabbing between the handgun compartment and the holster. A simple fix is to cut a piece of stiff paper (file folder, card stock, etc.) the width and length of the holster. The paper must be long enough to fold over both sides of the holster with the *unloaded* pistol inserted. The fold of the paper is on the back strap of the pistol. Insert the paper and holster assembly into the handgun compartment and position as desired. Simply pull the paper out and press on the side of the handgun compartment securing the hook-and-loop fastener on each side of the holster.

Figure 2-3 Holster Purse

One of the worst things an operator can do is buy a pistol and holster and never practice drawing. At a restaurant, a police officer off duty saw a robber display a pistol in his waistband. The police officer tried to draw his pistol from a new holster received as a present. The police officer said, "I pulled and pulled, and the gun wouldn't come out of the holster. When it finally did come out, the whole holster came with it. By then, I had already been shot twice. I dropped the gun and it fell onto the floor, still contained in the holster."[19] Unfamiliarly with the holster nearly cost the police officer his life.

Figure 2-4 Handgun Compartment

The police officer learned that a new holster does not automatically turn a person into a quick-draw expert. Only proper practice and plenty of it will. Take it slow to begin with. Practice in front of a mirror[20] with an *unloaded* pistol or better yet an *inert* pistol.[21] Work toward drawing and accurately firing in about 1.5 seconds. Avoid people that without reason dislike a particular holster. As an example, a person may have distain for a shoulder holster. It is likely that person never had to sit on an aircraft or in the confined interior of a heavily armored vehicle. The physical limitations of the operator or the operational environment dictate how the pistol is carried. Sometimes creative thinking is required to meet the operational needs of the mission.

Operational Constraints

The author had a female undercover police officer that needed to be armed during controlled drug buys. However, it was hot humid weather and she would be sitting in a vehicle. He insisted the officer keep a pistol on her body in case drug dealers dragged her from the vehicle. The solution was for the police officer to wear a tank top shirt tucked in the waist with an elastic bellyband over the shirt and the pistol positioned under her left breast. (Figures 2-5 and 2-6)

The right-handed police officer wore a loose fitting tee shirt over the rig. The tee shirt draped from her breasts concealing the subcompact pistol inside the elastic bellyband. The draw of the pistol was completed by taking the non-dominant hand pulling up the tee shirt and drawing the pistol with the dominant hand. The police officer sitting in a vehicle or being dragged from a vehicle could quickly draw her pistol.

 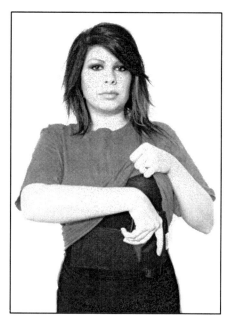

Figure 2-5 *Elastic Bellyband (carry)*   ***Figure 2-6*** *Elastic Bellyband (draw)*

On a range, the author did physically drag the police officer from the vehicle and she had to draw and accurately fire at multiple targets. Until the police officer drew the handgun, it was secure in the elastic bellyband. This is an example of overcoming operational constraints by taking the time and expending the energy to ensure the police officer could defend her life. After working with the police officer on the range the author was convinced that any drug dealer that pulled her from a vehicle would make the mistake of a lifetime—probably a short-lived lifetime.

MAGAZINE POUCH

There are two types of magazine pouches: (1) open top, and (2) flap covered. The open top does not have a flap and the pouch itself creates tension on the magazine body to hold it in place. The flap covered magazine pouch has a flap that goes across the top of the magazine to retain it in the pouch. The pouches may also have a tension device (screw) to assist in retaining the magazine. A hook-and-loop fastener or a snap may secure the loose end of the flap to the body of the magazine pouch.

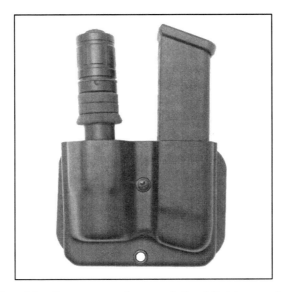

Figure 2-7 Combination magazine and flashlight pouch worn on the right side for a left-handed operator.

Do not mix the open top and flap covered magazine pouches on an equipment vest or waist belt. Doing so is inhibitive to procedural memory. The conscious mind should not be making decisions on how to access one particular magazine in comparison to another. An example would be having a double open top magazine pouch, but also wearing a single flap covered magazine pouch.[22] Accessing magazine pouches should be based on procedural memory and performed subconsciously. Use the same type of magazine pouches for pistol magazines and carbine magazines to reinforce procedural memory.

The pouches come in single, double, and triple magazine capacity.

Like holsters, magazine pouches are made from leather, nylon, synthetic and plastic. For uniform appearances, manufacturers will make magazine pouches in the same finish as holsters. That finish may include plain black, basket weave, or high-gloss. Agency regulations dictate the finish and style of magazine pouches for police officers and military operators. An armed civilian has the latitude of choosing the desired style and finish. Some pouches hold one magazine and a flashlight. (Figure 2-7) This pouch is a compromise between carrying one spare magazine and having a flashlight available.

Positioning the Magazine Pouch

Position the magazine pouch so the magazine is immediately accessible. The magazine needs to protrude from its pouch with significant height to allow a secure grip. This instant access is required for efficient reloading. There is a saying that goes, "How long do you have to reload?" The answer is, "The rest of your life." The length of that life may depend on how quick the reload is accomplished. This is the reason that a simple and reliable method of reloading is necessary.

Position the magazine pouch vertically on the non-dominant side of the body for a vertical carry with the nose of the bullets facing toward the dominant side. The magazine pouch can be centered, behind, or forward of the hip. Position the magazine pouch horizontally for a horizontal carry with the nose of the bullets pointing up and the floor plate facing the non-dominant side of the body.[23] Patrol officers normally wear the magazine pouch on the opposite side of their pistol. The patrol officer may want to wear his or her off duty magazine pouch in about the same position as when on duty. This will prevent the off duty police officer from mistakenly grasping in the wrong location for a magazine.

Military operators have a lot of latitude in positioning equipment on a vest. Position magazines on the equipment vest for easy retrieval. The situation is probably critical if a military operator or police adviser working in a combat zone had to transition to his or her pistol, and on top of that perform a reload. The reason is that military operators and police advisers use a rifle as a primary weapon. The use of a pistol signals the operator may be out of rifle ammunition, a stoppage occurred, a mechanical failure occurred, or the fastest reload is transitioning to the pistol. All are indicators that life-and-death issues are at stake.

KNIFE

A pistol is a machine and at any given moment can have a mechanical failure. The worst possible time would be during a life-threatening situation at close range. What may have begun as a gunfight can quickly turn into hand-to-hand combat. It is a tactical advantage to have a knife accessible with either hand and available for immediate use. If accessibility with both hands is not possible at least carry a pistol on one side of the body and a knife on the other side. This negates the problem of carrying both on the same side because *if* one were not accessible then both would not be accessible.

A double-edged knife provides several advantages over a single edge. The double-edged knife provides cutting in two directions. The operator in a low light environment does not have to index the edged side of the knife to the adversary. The knife only has to be deployed—either side will suffice for cutting and slashing. When stabbing, there are two edges cutting, and penetrating the flesh. A fixed blade knife is preferred for hand-to-hand combat. Deployment is more reliable under stressful conditions and likely faster than a folding knife.

NOTE: Usually there are no restrictions for military and police to carry a double-edged knife in an official capacity. However, it may be a criminal offense for a civilian to carry a double-edged knife. Check with applicable regulating authorities before carrying a double-edged knife.

A police officer counterattacking a criminal with a knife is not something readily expected, but it has happened.[24] In one incident, a female police officer off duty stabbed a robber that was armed with a pistol. The off duty officer's boyfriend, also a police officer was fighting with the robber. After being stabbed, the robber dropped his pistol. In a second incident, a police officer on duty slashed a suspect's neck. The suspect took the officer's service pistol and fired 1 round at him. The police officer grabbed the suspect's hand holding the pistol. The police officer using his knife slashed the suspect's neck. The police officer regained control of his pistol, stepped back, and shot the suspect in the forehead. Both wounds were fatal. Keep the *primary* purpose in mind when selecting and buying a knife—self-protection. A knife may also need to perform rescue duties, such as cutting through a seat belt. A knife is a vital part of the personal layered protection system.

FLASHLIGHTS AND HANDCUFFS

Flashlights: A flashlight is used to identify, search, and gain a tactical advantage. Various companies build quality handheld flashlights that are recommended for operational survival.[25] The flashlight must withstand a drop from about 6 feet (1.82 meters). Flashlights suited for operational survival are usually constructed from Type Mil-Spec aircraft aluminum that is abrasion and corrosion-resistant or a polymer. Make sure the flashlight has an O-ring or other appropriate seal to keep out dust and moisture. A rubber tailcap switch allows turning on and off the light with the thumb efficiently even in stressful situations. Some flashlights also have a head-mounted switch, but it can be difficult to locate when under stress. Switches designed for tactical operations can have a momentary-on and constant-on setting. A shatter resistant lens is desirable to protect the lamp.

Flashlights generally have two types of lamps: LED (light-emitting diode) and incandescent bulb. The LED lights are available in white, blue, red, green, and infrared (IR). The LED has the advantage of no glass or filament to break. LEDs will normally last the life cycle of the illumination tool (flashlight). Some flashlights are available with variable illumination from dual lamps, LED sources, or a rotating selector switch. Dependent on the manufacturer and the flashlight model the body is available in black, olive drab (OD) green, yellow, orange, gray, and tan.

Lithium, alkaline, or rechargeable batteries power flashlights. Rechargeable lights are promoted as being more cost-effective. The cost factor for an operator may not be an issue *if* the employer supplies the batteries. Run time for batteries is dependent on the quality of the battery and if the flashlight is equipped with an LED or an incandescent bulb. The LED flashlight will have substantial longer run time than a flashlight with an incandescent bulb. Flashlights used for self-protection have a crenellated bezel and scalloped tailcap to strike an adversary.[26] (Figure 2-8)

NOTE: The primary flashlight is normally worn on the non-dominant side. An operator can access the flashlight while keeping the firing hand free. A *backup* flashlight should be accessible with either hand.

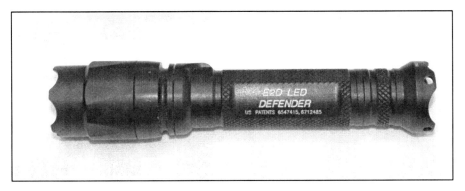

Figure 2-8 *A flashlight that can be used for self-protection.*

Handcuffs: Police officers on duty predominately used metal handcuffs. However, police officers off duty may consider carrying a flex-cuff folded up in a pocket. Not only is this a personal safety issue, but a legal issue as well. Using a flex-cuff to restrain a suspect may reduce the need for the continued use of force. Flex-cuffs are much lighter in weight than steel handcuffs. Some handcuffs are made of polymer and aluminum to reduce weight. Handcuffs either come in a chain or hinge design.

Proper training is necessary for any piece of equipment carried. The availability of proper training is another consideration regarding the decision to carry a restraint device. Military operators in a combat area should carry disposable flex-cuffs. Use restraining devices designed and engineer for restraining humans. Do not use plastic ties designed for industrial maintenance. Those ties have sharp edges than can cut the skin. Moreover, such ties do not have the tensile strength required for securing humans. Armed civilians should *not* physically secure an adversary.[27] Withstanding exigent circumstances wait for the police and they will secure the adversary.

BALLISTIC VEST

Uniform patrol officers working full or part-time should wear a ballistic vest. It is preferable that military operators in combat zones also wear ballistic vests. Police officers or military operators *not* wearing a ballistic vest and involved in deadly force encounters are dramatically reducing the chance of survival. A foreign concept should be wearing a police uniform without a ballistic vest. Think of the ballistic vest as a part of the uniform and *not* apart from the uniform. The two should be inseparable.

Even when not working in uniform still consider wearing protective body armor. A plainclothes task force officer left a convenience store and while walking to his car was attacked by two men. The officer struggled with his attackers, but received a gunshot in the abdomen.[28] After several surgeries, regrettably the officer died of his injuries.[29] The day the officer was sworn in he had promised to wear his vest, according to his mother.[30] The officer had used his vehicle radio to broadcast the shooting. Lying on the vehicle's seat was the officer's ballistic vest.[31] A piece of equipment that would have saved the officer's life and sadly may be the last thing he ever saw.

The ballistic vest not only protects from gunshots, but some vests can protect from edged weapon attacks and to some degree automobile collisions.[32] A ballistic vest to protect must be worn. It is common practice for the media to use the incorrect term *bulletproof vest* when describing body armor. Body armor is rated for its ability to stop specific bullets. "Unfortunately, there is no such thing as bulletproof armor."[33] The media should use the correct term *body armor*.

NOTE: An excellent resource of tactical and firearms terms and their definitions is the International Association of Law Enforcement Firearms Instructors manual called *Standards & Practices Reference Guide for Law Enforcement Firearms Instructors* available at www.ialefi.com.

HEADGEAR

Headgear worn must not interfere with the ability to see while in any of the firing positions. Headgear would include a baseball cap, trooper style hat commonly worn in the United States by State police, ballistic helmet, etc. The practice of removing or adjusting headgear on a range is unrealistic. An adversary will not allow an operator time to make headgear adjustments. The basis of agency headgear selection is operational effectiveness. Headgear is operationally *ineffective* that requires removal or turning backward before an operator can shoot. Select headgear that does *not* require such adjustments. Required headgear on duty should also be worn during simulation training, firearms qualification, and combat shooting. Requiring headgear may be unnecessary or undesirable in some operational areas. The Dallas Police Department (Texas) which is one of the largest law enforcement agencies in the United States does *not* require police officers to wear a hat during normal patrol duties.

SUMMARY

Issue equipment based on operational necessity. Discard equipment not suitable for an operation. Any organization not using the most technology advanced equipment is already behind the curve. The proper placement of equipment is just as important as the equipment itself. Equipment is of little value *if* inaccessible in the heat of the battle. Sort out equipment issues while training and *not* during an operation. Administrators need to accept that one size may not fit everyone.[34] Test and evaluate equipment on a small scale before deploying agency wide. The effectiveness of layered protection is directly dependent on the quality and type of equipment selected. Equipment is double-edged and can contribute to saving or costing an operator his or her life. Preparation will likely make that determination.

DISCUSSION QUESTIONS

1. Discuss how ineffective equipment can affect the operator.
2. What is the most important piece of equipment for a pistol?
3. Discuss holster retention versus readiness.
4. What are some of the dangers with not practicing with a holster before using it operationally?
5. How do operational constraints dictate the pistol's method of carried?
6. Which holster is susceptible to causing a back injury if an operator falls backwards?
7. What is a quick fix to make drawing and holstering a pistol easier from a holster purse?
8. Discuss what is one of the worst things an operator can do after buying a pistol and holster?
9. Why should a knife and pistol be carried on separate sides of the body?
10. Discuss the advantage of carrying a double-edged knife for self-

protection.

11. How is the primary flashlight and backup flashlight normally worn and why?
12. Flashlights with a crenellated bezel and scalloped tailcap can be used for what?
13. What device for restraining adversaries should military operators carry?
14. Describe the difference between bulletproof versus bullet resistant as related to a ballistic vest.
15. What is the reason for choosing headgear?

ENDNOTES

[1] Glock Inc., "Original Accessories," *Glock Autopistols 2012*, (New York, NY: Harris Publications Inc., 2012): 104.

[2] Paul R. Howe, *Leadership and Training for the Fight* (New York, NY: Skyhorse Publishing, 2011), 201-202.

[3] Zahava Solomon, *Combat Stress Reaction* (New York, NY: Plenum Press, 1993), 41.

[4] U.S. Department of Justice, *Violent Encounters*, 2006, (Washington, DC: FBI, 2006), 104.

[5] Force Science Institute, LTD., "Force Science News #160," (Mankato, MN: *"Mind traps" that can trick you and those who judge your actions*, October 9, 2010).

[6] National Rifle Association, *Law Enforcement Handgun Instructor Manual* (Fairfax, VA: Equipment and Ammunition, Edition 2.1, 2006), 3.

Chad A. Kaestle, and Jon H. Buehler, "Selecting a Duty-Issue Handgun," *FBI Law Enforcement Bulletin*, (January 2005): 5.

[7] Blade-Tech Industries, "OEB Belt Holsters," *SRB (Sting Ray Belt Holster,) IDPA Approved*), http://www.blade-tech.com/SRB-Sting-Ray-Belt-Holster-IDPA-Approved-pr-939.html#product_images (accessed September 22, 2012).

[8] National Rifle Association, *Law Enforcement Handgun Instructor Manual* (Fairfax, VA: Equipment and Ammunition, Edition 2.1, 2006), 2.

Chad A. Kaestle, and Jon H. Buehler, "Selecting a Duty-Issue Handgun," *FBI Law Enforcement Bulletin*, (January 2005): 5.

[9] A password is required to access this link. See PoliceOne.com News, "Make Sure Your Cell Phone Doesn't Compromise Your Safety," (San Francisco, CA: *Submitted by: Mike Holt, Charles County Sheriff, Maryland*, 2011), http://www.policeone.com/Officer-Safety/tips/3385021-Make-sure-your-cell-phone-doesnt-compromise-your-safety/ (accessed September 22, 2012).

[10] Molly Suzan Thomas-Bowden, a professional police officer that lost her life protecting and serving the citizens of Columbia, Missouri.

[11] Federal Bureau of Investigation, "Law Enforcement Officers Killed and Assaulted," (Clarksburg, WV: *Summaries of Officer Felonious Killed –Missouri*, 2005), http://www.fbi.gov/about-us/cjis/ucr/leoka/2005 (accessed September 22, 2012).

Deputy Chief Tom Dresner of the Columbia Police Department in Missouri by telephone with author, July7, 2009, confirmed the circumstances of the shooting.

[12] Gemtech, "TRL Lanyards," *TRL Tactical Retention Lanyards*, http://www.gem-tech.com/store/pc/Tactical-Retention-Lanyard-26p144.htm (accessed September 22, 2012).

[13] Glock Inc., *Glock Buyer's Guide Professional Edition*, (Smyrna, GA: Glock Inc., 2012): 54.

[14] Gemtech, "TRL Lanyards," *TRL Tactical Retention Lanyards*, http://www.gemtech.com/store/pc/Tactical-Retention-Lanyard-26p144.htm (accessed September 22, 2012).

[15] National Rifle Association, *Law Enforcement Handgun Instructor Manual* (Fairfax, VA: Off-Duty Firearm Safety, Edition 6.1, 2006), 7.

[16] Wilderness Tactical Products, LLC, "Tactical Belts," *Titanium Instructor Belt*, http://www.thewilderness.com/storepinnacle/index.php?p=product&id=1585&parent=0 (accessed September 22, 2012).

[17] "3. Finger on frame – simple, unsighted, reaction time - .45" "4. Finger on frame with a sight picture, reaction time - .54." (.54 - .45 = .09 reaction time difference) See Bill Lewinski, Ph.D., "Biomechanics of Lethal Force Encounters," *The Police Marksman* (November/December 2002): 20.

[18] The Concealment Shop Inc., "Feminine Protection Handbags," http://www.theconcealmentshop.com/index.php (accessed September 22, 2012).

[19] U.S. Department of Justice, *Violent Encounters*, 2006, (Washington, DC: FBI, 2006), 126.

[20] The Grant-Taylor Manual, *The Palestine Police Force Close Quarter Battle* (Boulder, CO: Paladin Press, 2008), 27. Originally published in 1943. Reprinted by Paladin Press in 2008.

[21] A pistol can be made inert by replacing the barrel with a solid filled plastic barrel or inserting a chamber blocker. Moreover, an option is to use a solid plastic training pistol.

[22] The author saw a police officer with a double open top magazine pouch and a single flap covered magazine pouch on his duty belt while attending the Glock Pistol Transitional Instructor Workshop course held February 3-5, 2010 at Glock Inc., in Smyrna, Georgia.

[23] National Rifle Association, *Law Enforcement Handgun Instructor Manual* (Fairfax, VA: Equipment and Ammunition, Edition 2.1, 2006), 4.

[24] U.S. Department of Justice, *Violent Encounters*, 2006, (Washington, DC: FBI, 2006), 109-111.

[25] Insight Operations, 9 Akira Way, Londonderry, NH 03053, USA, Toll-free: 866-509-2040, www.InsightTechnology.com.

Leapers, Inc., 32700 Capitol Street, Livonia, MI 48150, USA, Phone: 734-542-1500, Fax: 734-542-7095, www.Leapers.com

Streamlight Inc., 30 Eagleville Road, Eagleville, Pa. 19403, USA, Toll-free: 800-523-7488, Fax: 800-220-7007, www.streamlight.com.

SureFire, LLC, 18300 Mount Baldy Circle, Fountain Valley, CA 92708, USA, Toll-free: 800-828-8809, Fax: (714) 545-9537, www.SureFire.com.

[26] SureFire, LLC, "Flashlights," *E2D LED Defender*, http://www.surefire.com/E2DL (accessed September 22, 2012).

[27] National Rifle Association, *NRA Guide to Basics of Personal Protection Outside the Home* (Fairfax, VA: National Rifle Association of America, 2006), 67.

[28] United States Drug Enforcement Administration, " Wall of Honor," *Task Force Officer Jay Balchunas*, http://www.justice.gov/dea/about/wall-honor/wall-of-honor_bios.shtml#balchunas (accessed September 22, 2012).

[29] John "Jay" Balchunas, a professional law enforcement officer that lost his life protecting and serving the citizens of the State of Wisconsin.

[30] Charles Remsberg, *Blood Lessons* (San Francisco, CA: Calibre Press, 2008), 120-121.

[31] Charles Remsberg, *Blood Lessons* (San Francisco, CA: Calibre Press, 2008), 122.

[32] Frank Hernandez while wearing a ballistic vest had a 2x6 board impale his chest while driving a law enforcement vehicle. The ballistic vest helped to save Frank's life, a truly amazing story. See Calibre Press, *Ultimate Survivors II*, (Carrollton, TX: 2005): DVD.

[33] National Institute of Justice, "Technology and Tools," *Body Armor*, http://www.nij.gov/topics/technology/body-armor/welcome.htm (accessed September 22, 2012).

[34] Tim Blakeley, "Overcoming Lateral Transfer Training Issues," *The Police Chief*, (December 2005): 95.

Chad A. Kaestle, and Jon H. Buehler, "Selecting a Duty-Issue Handgun," *FBI Law Enforcement Bulletin*, (January 2005): 6.

PISTOLS AND AMMUNITION

A *pistol* is a semiautomatic handgun, normally short barreled, designed to hold and fire with one hand. [1] Some refer to the semiautomatic pistol as an automatic pistol. In that sense, the pistol with each pull of the trigger will fire and automatically load the next round from the magazine into the chamber until the magazine is empty.[2] The only true *automatic pistols* that Glock makes are models 18 and 18C (compensated) called machine pistols. Glock models 18 and 18C with one pull of the trigger (held to the rear) will continuously fire all the ammunition in the magazine. Glock pistols with the exception of the model 18 are *semiautomatic* recoiled operated, locked breech with a removable magazine that feeds the chamber.

When buying a pistol for self-protection, make sure it is a quality firearm. A low price must not be the motivation for buying a pistol. Resolve the issue of not having enough money to buy a quality pistol by delaying the purchase until obtaining the necessary funds. It will be well worth the wait in the end. A Glock Gen4 pistol set with the Modular Back Strap (MBS) comes with a pistol (short trigger housing pin initially installed in the pistol without a back strap), +2mm back strap, +4mm back strap, trigger housing pin (long), MBS tool, 2 magazines (law enforcement kit may have 3 magazines), magazine speed loader, cleaning set (bore brush and cleaning rod), Instructions for Use Glock Safe Action Pistols All Models manual, cable lock, and pistol case.[3] (Figure 3-1)

Glock brand pistols have an advanced technological design that results in ease of operation, extreme reliability, simple function, minimal maintenance, durability, and lightweight.[4] However, there are *other* reliable pistols successfully used by civilians, police officers, and military operators. It is beyond the scope of this book to cover each brand of pistol.

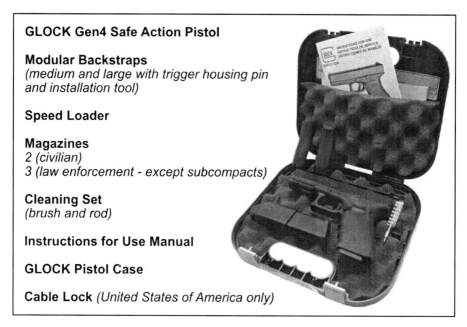

GLOCK Gen4 Safe Action Pistol

Modular Backstraps
(medium and large with trigger housing pin and installation tool)

Speed Loader

Magazines
2 (civilian)
3 (law enforcement - except subcompacts)

Cleaning Set
(brush and rod)

Instructions for Use Manual

GLOCK Pistol Case

Cable Lock *(United States of America only)*

Figure 3-1 *Glock Model 17 Gen4 Pistol Set*

Consult the instruction manual for guidance on the operation and maintenance of a particular pistol. The *fundamentals* of firearms handling in this book will work for other brands of pistols as well as Glock pistols. Operators have asked since the invention of the pistol, "Which is the best pistol?" The answer is obvious, "The one in the operator's hand."

DEVELOPMENT OF THE GLOCK PISTOL

Gaston Glock assembled a panel of firearms experts in the hope of developing a near perfect combat handgun. Soon after that emerged the Glock 17 pistol in a 9x19mm. In 1980, the Austrian Army held trials to replace their service pistol.[5] The Glock pistol won the contract. The Austrian Army in 1982 adopted the pistol and called it the P80.[6] Early on a rumor surfaced that a Glock pistol could defeat x-ray machines by being invisible.[7] This is simply *not* the case as Figure 3-2 shows. A Glock pistol is constructed with over a pound (0.45 kilogram) of metal and *is* detectable by metal detection machines.[8]

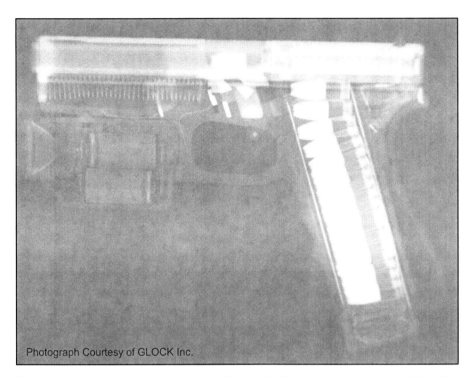

Photograph Courtesy of GLOCK Inc.

Figure 3-2 X-ray view of loaded Glock 9x19mm pistol, model 17 with a plus two magazine and Glock Tactical light.[9]

The features desirable for a pistol used in combat were incorporated in the design. The ergonomics of the pistol came from research Gaston Glock conducted by taking hand measurements from military personnel. The grip angle of 105 degrees[10] provides natural pointing of the pistol without the muzzle dipping down when the arms are extended. The low bore axis design helps to reduce felt recoil by diverting forces straight back into the hand. [11] The large magazine capacity provides an ammunition availability advantage without frequent reloading. The locked breach provides a complete locking of the barrel and slide.[12] The trigger requires a single weight pull that finalizes the cocking and releasing of the firing pin.

Glock labeled the first generation as Gen1 and each successive generation is sequentially numbered. Gen1 pistols were available in the United States beginning in the mid-1980s and commonly referred to as a pebble frame.[13] In March 1989, Glock introduced the Gen2 pistols with a checkered frame.[14] In early 1998, Glock introduced the Gen3 pistols with finger grooves and the accessory rail (FGR).[15] In 2009 Glock added a rough textured frame 2 (RTF2) with *spikes* (miniature pyramids)[16] to select model Gen3 pistols. In January 2010, Glock introduced the Gen4 pistols with a scientifically designed rough textured frame (RTF) in a short frame (SF), two replaceable modular back straps, a reversible magazine catch, larger dual coil recoil spring assembly, and retain the accessory rail for accessory attachments such as a light.[17] The magazine catch is three times larger than the previous one and extends to the rear providing an easier reach.[18] The design changes make the pistol nearly adaptable to any adult hand size and operational requirements.

Magazines designed for Gen4 pistols equipped with a *reversible magazine catch* will work with *all* types of magazine catches (reversible and ambidextrous).[19] The magazine has two *notches* for the reversible magazine catch and a *recess* in the center for the ambidextrous magazine catch. (Figure 3-3) A magazine designed for a pistol with the magazine catch on the left side *only* will work in the Gen4 receiver *if* the magazine catch remains on the left side (right-handed position).[20] The magazines designed for a pistol with the magazine catch only on the left side will *not* work in a Gen4 receiver when the magazine catch is changed to the right side for a left-handed operator.

Figure 3-3 *Magazine with single notch (left) and Gen4 magazine with a recess and two notches (right).*[21]

PISTOL ENGRAVING SERVICE

Glock offers an engraving service for its pistols.[22] A person can express their passion by having a Glock pistol personalized with special engravings. Glock employs a group of engravers that can likely meet any request. Engravings range from a simple name to an official symbol of an agency to artistic golden ornamental engravings.

TECHNICAL BULLETIN INFORMATION

Glock to improve its pistols has made minor changes.[23] The magazines are full metal lined with reshaped lips. The slide near the breech face went from a 90-degree cut to a 15-degree cut. The firing pin had an upgrade. The extractor had a debris channel added. The firing pin safety had an upgrade along with a stronger safety spring. The spring loaded bearing had an upgrade. The trigger bar upright had an upgrade. Return a pistol eligible for product upgrades to the address as follows:

Glock Inc.
6000 Highlands Parkway
Smyrna, GA 30082

Glock no longer sells older style parts. Pistols in the serial number ranges shown below are eligible for product upgrades.[24]

Glock 17 Pistols — Alphabetical Prefix up to and including XG
Glock 19 Pistols — Alphabetical Prefix up to and including XK
Glock 20 Pistols — Alphabetical Prefix up to and including WX
Glock 21 Pistols — Alphabetical Prefix up to and including ALD
Glock 22 Pistols — Alphabetical Prefix up to and including YB
Glock 23 Pistols — Alphabetical Prefix up to and including SL

The pistol models with a three-letter prefix already have the upgraded part system except for the G21. A G21 model pistol (.45 Auto) *before* serial number ALD qualifies for slide modifications: "...pickup rail is reduced and the right rear edge of the ejection port is angled."[25] For more questions contact Glock Inc., or consult with a certified Glock armorer.

PURPOSE OF A PISTOL

When buying a pistol know its purpose. A target pistol in .22 Long Rifle is great for plinking, but a poor choice for self-protection. This is because of the lack of penetration and the ability to cause a large *permanent* wound channel. A situation that warrants a pistol when it comes to personal protection is likely a matter of life-and-death. At such a time, it would be disastrous to second-guess the pistol's quality or stopping power. A pistol used for self-preservation is a weapon of combat and must be accurate, reliable, and easy to operate. An operator may carry a rifle as a primary weapon, but a stoppage or being out of ammunition can quickly move the pistol into the primary role.

Operators are fortunate today in that most manufacturers offer standard and compact size pistols. Glock also offers the competition and subcompact pistols. Increasing accuracy for target engagement was the primary reason for the competition pistol also known as *tactical/practical*.[26] Some SWAT teams use the competition pistol and it is popular among recreational shooters. The subcompact pistol is an excellent choice for carrying undercover or off duty. However, because of the subcompact's shorter barrel length and smaller magazine capacity it would not be a suitable choice as the primary pistol for uniformed patrol. A *compact* pistol can be used as a primary firearm or a backup pistol.

The recommended minimum pistol caliber for self-protection is a 9x19mm or larger,[27] but the .380 Auto has also been successfully used.[28] Shot placement is critical because of the low energy developed by the .380 Auto.[29] Even with proper shot placement the .380 Auto bullet may *not* have enough energy to penetrate to vital organs. An operator does not have to compromise compactness for stopping power with Glock pistols. The 9x19mm is available in the same size pistol as the .380 Auto. A certain caliber in a Glock pistol may not be available in all countries. Contact a local representative of Glock for availability. See Figure 3-4 for a size comparison of the pistols.

With the various barrel lengths available, one may believe that a shorter barrel offers a quicker draw. This is not the case. The draw used for combat shooting emphasizes bringing the pistol well above the holster and rotating the pistol ninety degrees onto the target. This method allows either a 3.5- or 6-inch (88.9- or 152.4-millimeter) barrel to clear the holster in the same amount of time. The extended trigger guard makes an allowance for gloves during cold weather operations. This guard allows adequate room for the trigger finger to transition from the receiver onto the trigger.

Competition   Standard   Compact   Subcompact

Figure 3-4 *Pistol Sizes*

Some agency managers allow only one model for their agency.[30] Uniformed police officers normally use the *standard* pistol because of its longer barrel and additional ammunition capacity. Ideally, plainclothes officers should have an option to carry a *compact* pistol and narcotics officers a *subcompact* pistol.[31] A patrol officer should not have to give up the longer barrel length and extra ammunition for the sake of uniformity. Likewise, a plainclothes officer should not have to give up compactness and concealment.

Although some agency managers may not like the idea of having to buy two or possibly three different models for their agency—tactically it is the *ideal* solution. Some law enforcement agencies welcome ideal solutions and have the logistics to implement a plan.[32] A policy of a *single model* for the sake of having such a policy should not be the driving factor when choosing a pistol. Agency managers need to accept the advantages that each pistol size can offer and make accommodations whenever possible. (Table 3-1)

An agency because of financial constraints or logistics that chooses to adopt a single model would do well with the Glock Gen4 *compact* pistol. The compact pistols are comparable in size and weight to small .38 Special revolvers, but offer more firepower and are easier to rapid fire.[33] The Glock compact model 19 in 9x19mm is the preferred pistol of the New York City Police Department and is the standard firearm of the United Nations security personnel.[34] The model 19 is also used for executive protection worldwide. Although the model 19 is a compact pistol, it delivers close to full-size performance.

Glock Pistol Barrel Length and Magazine Table[35]

Glock Pistol Model	Approximate Barrel Length in Inches	Magazines Supplied with Law Enforcement Pistols
9x19mm Caliber Pistols		
Glock 17 standard	4.5"	(3) 17-rd mags
Glock 17C standard	4.5" ported	(3) 17-rd mags
Glock 17L long-slide	6.0"	(3) 17-rd mags
Glock 19 compact	4.0"	(3) 15-rd mags
Glock 19C compact	4.0" ported	(3) 15-rd mags
Glock 26 subcompact	3.5"	(2) 10-rd mags
Glock 34 competition	5.3"	(3) 17-rd mags
.357 SIG Caliber Pistols		
Glock 31 standard	4.5"	(3) 15-rd mags
Glock 31C standard	4.5" ported	(3) 15-rd mags
Glock 32 compact	4.0"	(3) 13-rd mags
Glock 32C compact	4.0" ported	(3) 13-rd mags
Glock 33 subcompact	3.5"	(2) 9-rd mags
.40 S&W Caliber Pistols		
Glock 22 standard	4.5"	(3) 15-rd mags
Glock 22C standard	4.5" ported	(3) 15-rd mags
Glock 23 compact	4.0"	(3) 13-rd mags
Glock 23C compact	4.0" ported	(3) 13-rd mags
Glock 24 long-slide	6.0"	(3) 15-rd mags
Glock 24C long-slide	6.0" ported	(3) 15-rd mags
Glock 35 competition	5.3"	(3) 15-rd mags
Glock 27 subcompact	3.5"	(2) 9-rd mags
.45 G.A.P. Caliber Pistols		
Glock 37 standard	4.5"	(3) 10-rd mags
Glock 38 compact	4.0"	(3) 8-rd mags
Glock 39 subcompact	3.5"	(2) 6-rd mags

Glock Pistol Barrel Length and Magazine Chart		
Glock Pistol Model	**Approximate Barrel Length in Inches**	**Magazines Supplied with Law Enforcement Pistols**
.45 Auto Caliber Pistols		
Glock 21 standard	4.6"	(3) 13-rd mags
Glock 21C standard	4.6" ported	(3) 13-rd mags
Glock 30 subcompact	3.8"	(2) 10-rd mags
Glock 36 slim-line	3.8"	(2) 6-rd mags
10mm Auto Caliber Pistols		
Glock 20 standard	4.6"	(3) 15-rd mags
Glock 20C standard	4.6" ported	(3) 15-rd mags
Glock 29 subcompact	3.8"	(2) 10-rd mags

Table 3-1 Glock Pistol Barrel Length and Magazine Chart

PISTOL RELIABILITY

Several technological breakthroughs make Glock pistols reliable. The barrels and slides are treated with a *Nitration* finishing process.[36] The surface treatment process optimizes the molecular structure of the metal surfaces resulting in a hardness approaching that of a diamond. The scratch resistant surface treatment also maximizes corrosion resistance—even in saltwater. The surface treatment is a matte black finish that minimizes light reflection offering a tactical advantage.[37] The polymer receiver's unsurpassed breaking strength in the cold is obtainable because it does *not* contain glass fiber reinforcement.[38] The polymer receiver provides a 90 percent weight savings, minimum thermal conductivity, and characteristics that are ergonomically ideal while continuously firing.

The barrel is easy to clean and maintains precision even after firing a high number of rounds. This is because the barrels are solid cold-hammered in conjunction with the surface treatment. The barrels have rounded (hexagonal or octagonal) interior profiles. These profiles offer the advantages of not having corners and edges as with a lands and grooves profile. The rounded interior profile reduces deposits and provides a better ballistic yield.[39] A better bullet to barrel fit and gas seal improves ballistic yield in comparison to conventional rifling.[40]

NOTE: Glock barrels known as the "Miami Barrel" are available with micro-etched grooves for law enforcement agencies only.[41] The micro-etched barrel is unique to that firearm. An agency can fire control bullets to keep as a reference to maintain accountability for rounds fired by its agency's personnel.[42]

Information provided by a police officer vividly describes the durability of a Glock pistol.[43] The officer at the request of his sergeant tested the Glock pistol. The evaluator *intentionally* tried to break the pistol. The pistol was thrown from a motorcycle traveling at 40 MPH (64 KPH), soaked in saltwater, fired underwater, and thrown from a five-story building onto concrete. After the pistol had 57,000 rounds fired through it, the evaluator stopped keeping count! The evaluator later shot 3000 rounds in 45 minutes damaging the guide rod, but the pistol continued working. Years later after the testing and firing thousands of rounds of +P+ type 9x19mm ammunition and over a dozen over-proof loads did the pistol finally break. The slide cracked below the ejection port.

Glock made several changes in the Gen4 model to continue improving its reliability.[44] The most notable change internally is the larger dual recoil spring assembly. As an example the recoil spring assemblies for the Gen4 models 17 and 19 (standard and compact) look like longer versions of the Gen3 model 26 (subcompact). The design change doubles the rated service life of the larger dual recoil spring assembly over the earlier smaller spring. Because of the larger dual recoil spring assembly, the slide has a larger guide ring hole and inside the front of the receiver has a deeper cut. (Figure 3-5)

The trigger with trigger bar underwent two changes: First, the extension where the trigger spring connects has a straighter angle along with the hole's radius groove to reduce spring breakage. Second, the vertical extension that disengages the firing pin safety has a raised dimple to keep the extension centered on the firing pin safety. The .40 S&W follower has a wider *shelf* for the slide stop lever to contact. The wider shelf increases reliability when the reversible magazine catch is on the right for a left-handed operator. The Gen4 slide, receiver, dual recoil spring assembly, short frame trigger mechanism housing, trigger housing pin, and magazine catch are *not* interchangeable with previous versions.

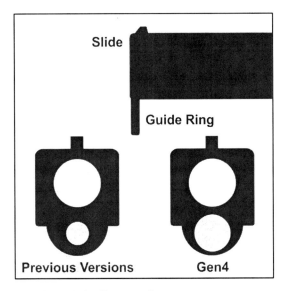

Figure 3-5 *Guide Ring Hole Comparison*

NOTE: After releasing the Gen4 model, Glock developed a new design for the recoil spring assemblies to replace several Gen4 variations *excluding* models 26 and 27.[45] The connector and extractor were also changed after the release. Contact Glock to verify if a Gen4 pistol has the correct recoil spring assembly, connector, and ejector installed.

Glock includes the same technological advancements into each pistol, making reliability identical between the subcompact, compact, standard, and competition pistols. Each of the pistols can be placed in mud, sand, etc., retrieved, and function properly.[46] This is important because the pistols are exposed to many different environments. One distinct advantage of the standard pistol over its smaller counterparts is the ability to absorb recoil. Although it may not be that noticeable between a compact and standard, it is when compared to a subcompact and standard. Any Glock pistol selected can be an effective tool for self-protection.

NOTE: To preserve Glock's standard of reliability use only Glock magazincs in Glock pistols and service as recommended.

PISTOL SIGHTS

When selecting pistol sights, keep in mind what are the operational requirements. A mission in which close quarters combat is likely requires sights designed and built for such fighting. Various manufactures make quality aftermarket combat sights.[47] The combat sights need to be visible against any color and in the dark. The pistol used for personal protection would do well to have self-luminous sights. Green appears brighter in darkness than other colors[48] and used for self-luminous sights. Self-luminous sights used in the dark can assist indexing the pistol while in a ready position providing assurance of aligned sights.

Self-luminous sights also allow an operator in his or her bedroom to locate the pistol without turning on the light and creating a backlight situation. Self-luminous sights are a technological advancement in combat shooting worthy of consideration. Sights have to be rugged to handle the harsh conditions found in various operational environments. Adjustable pistol sights are too fragile for combat and *not* generally recommended.[49] The design of the rear sight must allow bracing it against an object to rack the slide. A snag free sight is not designed to rack the slide. Eliminate any sight from consideration not durable enough to rack the slide or designed to do so. The slide may have to be racked by holding the rear sight against a heel, holster, belt, pocket, doorframe, table, chair, etc.

Combat Sights

Some sights are more suited for combat shooting than other sights. An encircled white ring on the front sight is excellent for combat shooting. The white color is one of the quickest colors for the eye to acquire.[50] A white ring reflects ambient light for excellent half-light sight acquisition. Half-light is the"…soft, subdued light seen at dusk or dawn or in dimly lit interiors."[51] The white front ring should resist powder residue and cleaners/degreasers. The rear notch should be of sufficient width to pick up light around the front sight for quicker acquisition. Some operators may prefer an encircled ring other than white.

A tritium-filled glass lamp in the front sight and two in the rear sight will illuminate in the dark.[52] Double tritium lamps that have black rings on the rear sight help draw the operator's attention to the encircled white ring on the front sight. Sometimes a front green with yellow rear tritium lamps are advocated as preventing sight misalignment in the dark. The theory is the same color front tritium lamp could be positioned to the left or right of one of the rear tritium lamps. The front tritium lamp would then erroneously appear to be one of the rear tritium lamps. Doing this would cause the pistol to be grossly misaligned in the hand with little or no semblance of a natural index. Such misalignment would likely have to be forced to occur and would feel unnatural to a trained operator. The advantage in having two colors is the operator's attention drawn from the rear sight to the front sight. [53]

An operator wanting a more readily visible sight picture in the dark should consider using the brighter green tritium lamps for the front and rear sights. Glock makes steel sights with green three-dot tritium lamps (night sight) that are available on new pistols or ordered separately.[54] (Figure 3-6) Glock also makes in *polymer* and *steel* a white "U" outline rear sight with a corresponding white dot on the front blade sight.[55] (Figure 3-7) The U outline polymer sights come standard on Glock pistols unless otherwise specified. A legendary shooter in his book recommended a white outline rear sight as being useful to some people.[56] The distinctive U outline sights align quickly and superimposes easily as a single sight image on a target. The steel rear sights can be pressed against an object to rack the slide.

Figure 3-6 *Tritium Sight*

Figure 3-7 *U Outline Sight*

NOTE: The tritium lamps sit below the top edge of the sights. Aligning the front tritium lamp with top edge of the rear sight will cause shots to hit high.[57] However, if the tritium lamps are horizontally aligned and symmetrical, and the front lamp is placed on the aim point, the shot will hit about 1/16 inch (1.58 millimeter) higher than when using the top edge of the sights.

Zeroing Glock Sights

When zeroing a pistol use the ammunition that will be carried operationally. Check pistol sights for a proper zero at two distances. First, shoot from the 5-yard (4.57-meter) line. The operator in a fighting stance fires 5 rounds and maintains a 1-inch (25.4-millimeter) group. Second, shoot from the 25-yard (22.86-meter) line. The operator from a *supported* position fires 5 rounds and maintains a 3- to 6-inch (76.2- to 152.4-millimeter) group. The grouping needs to be centered around the aim point.

If the operator is shooting tight groups, but the grouping is other than at the aim point, adjust the sights. The rear sight can be adjusted left or right to correct horizontal impact. Replace the rear sight to correct elevation. Each incremental change of the rear sight height will result in a point of impact shift of about 1.97 inches (50 millimeters) at 27 yards (25 meters).[58] (Table 3-2) Fire a 3-round group from the 5-yard (4.57-meter) and 25-yard (22.86-meter) line to confirm after making the final adjustment.

Normally there are no issues from the factory with Glock pistol sights. Glock pistols are test fired for accuracy before shipping.[59] Removing and replacing sights without understanding Glock's height specifications creates problems. As an example, a customer buys a previously owned 9x19mm model 19 pistol. What the customer did not know is the previous owner had the gun store remove the expensive custom sights leaving the pistol bare. The gun store happened to have a used set of Glock factory sights with a 6.9 height rear sight. An unsuspecting customer buys the model 19 with the 6.9 height rear sight. The new owner takes the model 19 to the range, but does not understand why it shoots nearly 2 inches (50.8 millimeters) high at the 25-yard (22.86-meter) line. The answer is simple. Look at the *Glock Rear Sight Ballistic Table at 25 Meters* and find 9x19mm, go across and find the number zero. A 6.5 height rear sight is required for the pistol to be zeroed (point of aim, point of impact) at about 27 yards (25 meters). A 6.9 height rear sight will make the Glock Model 19 shoot nearly 2 inches (50.8 millimeters) high at about 27 yards (25 meters). To correct the problem a 6.5 height rear sight would need to be installed.

Glock Rear Sight Ballistic Table at 25 Meters (27 Yards)				
Caliber	*Sight Marking & Height*			
	6.1	6.5	6.9	7.3
.380 Auto	-3.94 in.	-1.97 in.	0	+1.97 in.
9x19mm	-1.97 in.	0	+1.97 in.	+3.94 in.
9x19mm* *(17L)*	0	+1.97 in.	+3.94 in.	+5.91
.357 SIG	-3.94 in.	-1.97 in.	0	+1.97 in.
.357 SIG** *(33)*	-1.97 in.	0	+1.97 in.	+3.94 in.
.40 S&W	-1.97 in.	0	+1.97 in.	+3.94 in.
.45 G.A.P.	-1.97 in.	0	+1.97 in.	+3.94 in.
.45 Auto	-3.94 in.	-1.97 in.	0	+1.97 in.
10mm Auto	-3.94 in.	-1.97 in.	0	+1.97 in.
1.97 inches = 50 millimeters				
NOTE: The **6.5** height is the standard rear sight on 40 S&W, .45 G.A.P., and 9x19mm **except** the Model 17L (long-slide) that uses a 6.1. The **6.9** height is the standard rear sight on .45 Auto, 10mm Auto, and .357 SIG **except** the **Model 33 that uses a 6.5. Sight markings are stamped on the right side of the sight.				

Table 3-2 *Rear Sight Ballistic Chart*

Figure 3-8 illustrates an example of a Glock factory rear sight moved excessively to the right. A police officer carried the pistol. The rear sight had been adjusted by a state certified law enforcement firearms instructor to correct so-called shooter error. The firearms instructor had pushed the rear sight too far to the right. The police officer attended the firearms instructor's course mandated by the state and the lead firearms instructor discovered the problem. The firearms instructor immediately moved the sight back to the center position and corrected the officer's shooting deficiencies. Make sure it is not operator error before moving or replacing sights. An operator that cannot consistently shoot a tight group (barring any mechanical issues with the pistol) must accept it is operator error and not the sights.

Figure 3-8 *Rear sight moved excessively to the right in an attempt to correct operator error.*

Glock Sights Installation[60]

Sights[61] and pins[62] *remove* from left to right and *install* right to left with the pistol seen from the shooter's perspective. When in doubt, check the Glock Armorer's Manual. Glock uses polymer and steel for front and rear sights from the factory. Use steel sights on a pistol carried for self-protection. Suffering a debilitating arm injury can require cycling the slide against a surface using the rear sight. This requirement eliminates for combat use the low profile snag resistant rear sight.[63] Front sights may be staked on (discontinued by Glock) or secured with a screw.

WARNING: Make sure the pistol is *unloaded* before fieldstripping to install the sights. Thoroughly read and understand the sights' installation instructions before beginning the installation process.

Screw-On Front Sight: A front sight mounting tool (Glock factory) with a *magnetic* insert is used to remove and install screws in a screw-on front sight.[64] (Figure 3-9) To remove a front sight secured with a screw, place the front sight tool's 3/16 inch (4.7 millimeter) hex on the screw head and turn counterclockwise. Remove the sight. Use a cleaner/degreaser to leave the surface free of lubricant residue. Clean both sides of the slide where the front sight mounts and the sight mounting screw fits. Mock fit the front sight to the slide to ensure a proper fit and the sight does not protrude past the inside edge of the slide. Remove the sight and place the screw's hex head squarely in the installation tool.

Figure 3-9 Front Sight Tool

NOTE: According to the manufacturer, blue threadlocker "...is designed for the locking and sealing of threaded fasteners which require normal disassembly with standard hand tools." [65]

Place *blue* threadlocker on the sight's base and one drop on the *side* of the screw's threads.[66] Placing threadlocker on top of the screw can break the tritium capsule.[67] This occurs because the threadlocker places hydraulic force on the capsule. Position the front sight on top of the slide, insert the screw through the bottom side of the slide into the front sight, and turn the screw clockwise until snug. Using parallel jaw pliers straighten the front sight *if* necessary and finish tightening the screw. Excessively tightening the screw can damage the front sight threads or screw. Wipe away any excess threadlocker compound.

CAUTION: According to the manufacturer, red threadlocker "...is designed for the permanent locking and sealing of threaded fasteners...It is only removable once cured by heating up parts to 500°F (260°C)."[68]

Stake-On Front Sight:[69] Use only screw-on front sights made from *steel* for pistols carried for self-protection. No instructions are provided in this book for *installing* or *maintaining* a stake-on front sight. To remove a staked on front sight, take a 1/16 inch (1.5 millimeters) punch and from the inside of the slide—drive the front sight out.

Rear Sight: An installation tool (not Glock factory) that has a robust machined aluminum body to remove and install standard height rear sights without damaging them can be used.[70] (Figure 3-10) Make sure to use the shim under the slide clamp *if* needed to raise certain slides up closer to the pusher block, but check the clearance when doing so.

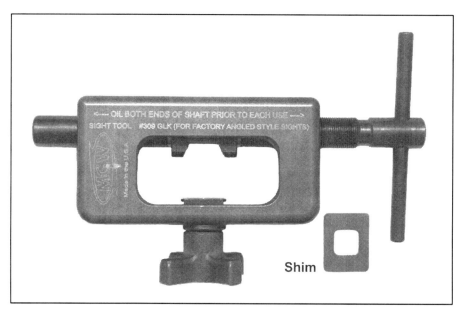

Figure 3-10 *Rear Sight Tool*

To begin removing the rear sight (metal or polymer) hold the rear sight tool with the t-handle pointing to the left.[71] Insert the rear of the slide into the frame with the muzzle end pointed away from the operator. Position the rear sight in the center of the pusher block. Do this by loosening the star knob and inserting the back of the slide's rail cuts into the frame. Tighten star knob securing the slide. Turn the t-handle clockwise removing the rear sight from the dovetail on the right side of the slide. Remove the sight, unclamp the slide and move it toward the operator far enough to insert the new rear sight (*hand interference fit*) into the *right* side of the dovetail at *least* 1/8 inch (3.1 millimeters). Tritium-filled glass lamps face to the rear. Center the sight in the pusher block and clamp the slide using the star knob. Install the rear sight by *pulling* it from right to left.[72] Turn the handle counterclockwise until the rear sight is centered on the slide. Remove the sight tool.

CAUTION: A rear sight that will not slide into the dovetail by hand at least 1/8 inch (3.1 millimeters) requires metal removal from the bottom of the sight.[73] Remove metal by laying the bottom on the sight on a flat file and carefully and incrementally shaving away metal. Check the dovetail fit often until acquiring the 1/8-inch (3.1-millimeters) hand fit interference.

An alternative method to removing the rear sight is to use a *no marring* punch. Drive the sight out from left to right. Driving out self-luminous sights with tritium-filled glass lamps can cause the lamps to break. "Attempting to push an oversized rear sight into the slide may result in damage to the slide, sight, and/or sight tool. This is why proper knowledge of how to fit gun sights is required when using a sight tool"[74]

PISTOL GRIP[75]

Glock pistols are well suited for operators working in harsh environments. A standard feature of the Glock pistol is the finger grooves molded into the receiver to aid in a secure grip.[76] Operators that prefer a more aggressive grip surface than on previous Gen3 models have a choice of Glock's Rough Textured Frame (RTF) on the Gen4 models.

Rough Textured Frame: The RTF has small polymer *squares* that are more aggressive than the previous surfaces, but not as aggressive as the RTF2.[77] The RTF will *not* damage clothing making it suitable for concealed carry. The RTF cubids are on the front, rear, sides, but not on the thumb rests. The RTF is an excellent grip surface and improved especially for sweaty, wet, or blood soaked hands. The RTF is the best all-around texture and well worth the upgrade.

Rough Textured Frame 2: Glock has *discontinued* the Rough Textured Frame 2 (RTF2) for the United States market.[78] Glock designed the RTF2 using feedback from United States Special Operations Command (USSOCOM). The RTF2 has small polymer *spikes* shaped like pyramids on the front, rear, sides, and thumb rests.[79] The RTF2 was suited for hot, dusty, or cold environments where military operators may encounter sweat, sand, snow, etc. The RTF2 surface frayed clothing and was *not* suitable for carrying concealed every day. While the author attended a personal protection course, he witnessed a female attendee shooting a Glock pistol with the RTF2 suffer an abrasion on the palm of her firing hand. She had fired about 100 rounds. The RTF2 grip surface was too aggressive for the attendee's bare hands.

Textured Adhesive Grips: Textured adhesive grips (commonly called *grip tape*) in a sand or rubber finish can be added on Glock pistols.[80] The grip tape's sand surface may be *unsuitable* for concealed carry because of potential damage to clothing. Clothing damage is *not* an issue with the rubber finish. Grip tape offers a superior bond between the hand and pistol in harsh environments (sweat, rain, snow, heat, humidity, mud, or saltwater). Make sure the surface is clean before installing grip tape. Do not touch the adhesive as it can reduce adherence to the surface. Cleaning a pistol using solvents excessively may dissolve adhesive backing.

CAUTION: Grip tape can shift on the receiver (improper installation or adhesive deterioration) and interfere with the magazine catch.

Rubberized Grip Sleeve: Some operators prefer a rubberized grip. The *rubberized grip sleeve* has a special contoured shape that hugs the contours of the Glock pistol.[81] The sleeve has a special shape superior to a simple *tube* sleeve. The grip sleeve has proportioned finger grooves with a cobblestone texture. Inside the grip sleeve are recesses allowing a tight fit between the sleeve and finger grooves.

The installation of the grip sleeve is simple. Spray the grip of the pistol and the grip sleeve with a cleaner/degreaser formulated for *firearms*. Slide the grip sleeve onto the pistol grip and position correctly. Once the cleaner/degreaser evaporates, the grip sleeve is firmly in place.

Remove the grip sleeve by using the same cleaner/degreaser technique. A pistol with a grip sleeve may no longer settle in the hand as it did with the factory texture. The sleeve could also shift affecting the operator's shooting index or interfere with the magazine catch.

Finger Groove Extension: Gripping a subcompact pistol with two fingers may feel uncomfortable to some operators. The issue is resolved by installing an *aftermarket* magazine floor plate. The floor plate has a finger groove extension to aid in recoil management.[82] (Figure 3-11) The finger groove extension lengthens the subcompact's grip allowing the use of three fingers instead of two. The extension protruding below the magazine well also helps with seating and removing the magazine.

Figure 3-11 *Finger Groove Extension*

Lanyard Hole: Militaries from around the world use lanyards on pistols to prevent loss. On many of the Glock pistols is a small hole located at the bottom rear of the pistol grip. The hole is for attaching a lanyard.[83] Near the lanyard hole is also large opening at the bottom of the grip. The large opening allows debris to fall free and water to drain.

Allowing debris and water to expel improves the pistol's reliability.

Beavertail Back Strap: The slide as it cycles can sometimes contact the web of the hand (commonly referred to as slide bite). This may happen to operators with larger hands that grip high into the back strap. The Glock back strap with the extended beavertail reduces the chance of the slide contacting the web of the hand. The back strap comes in +2mm and +4mm sizes that fit the Gen4 pistol. The back strap is held in place using the long trigger housing pin. Some operators may find the beavertail back strap improves recoil control.

PISTOL TRIGGER

There are several different types of triggers: double-action (DA), single action (SA), and double-action/single action (DA/SA). The DA trigger is a single pull of the trigger that both cocks and releases the hammer.[84] The SA is manually cocking the hammer of a firearm before pulling the trigger.[85] The DA/SA is a single pull of the trigger that both cocks and releases the hammer. The first pull of the trigger is double-action and subsequent shots are fired single action. The rearward movement of the slide automatically cocks the hammer after the first shot.

An operator using a DA/SA pistol would not normally use the thumb to cock the hammer before firing. There is limited tactical use (hostage situation) for cocking the hammer on the first shot. The technique is also slower than using a DA trigger pull. Gunfights with a pistol do not normally allow enough time to cock the hammer and make a precise shot. Practice shooting using a continuous trigger pull and accuracy should not suffer.

Glock Trigger: A trigger with the same action on the first and subsequent shots is easier to master.[86] The Glock pistol uses its proprietary Safe Action design that works similar to a constant double-action.[87] The firing mechanism is a striker design. With the trigger in a forward position the firing pin is partially cocked and under spring tension. Pulling the trigger moves the firing pin rearward until fully cocked. The trigger bar will move downward releasing the firing pin striking the cartridge primer making the pistol fire.[88] A conventional semiautomatic pistol has a hammer that strikes the firing pin. A striker fired pistol does not have a hammer, but uses spring pressure combined with the inertia of the firing pin to fire.

There are three distinct advantages to the Safe Action design.[89] First, the trigger is the single control for the operation of the pistol. Second, there are no external levers requiring manipulation for the state of safe or fire. Third, cocking does not occur until pulling the trigger to the rear. In addition, the Safe Action design has three automatic safeties:[90] (1) built-in trigger safety that disengages when the trigger is pulled, (2) firing pin block safety, and 3) drop safety. Pulling or releasing the trigger makes the three safeties work sequentially.[91]

The trigger pull weight in a Glock pistol is changed by replacing either the connector or the trigger spring or both.[92] In the Glock Parts Order Form, there are four connectors listed that vary in weights from 4.5 pounds (2 kilograms) to 8 pounds (3.5 kilograms).[93] The 4.5-pound (2-kilogram) connector is marked with a minus sign (-) and is available only to law enforcement via letterhead from ranking official of the agency. The standard 5.5-pound (2.5-kilogram) connector is unmarked. The 8-pound (3.5-kilogram) connector is marked with a plus sign (+). Glock makes a Gen4 connector marked with a dot (•). The dot connector in a Gen4 pistol produces a 5.5-pound (2.5-kilogram) trigger pull weight and feels similar to the Gen3 pistol. The dot connector is available only to law enforcement via letterhead from the ranking official of the agency or as a *replacement* part with a required serial number of the Gen4 pistol printed on the Parts Order Form.[94]

Glock makes a coil trigger spring, and two New York trigger springs. The coil spring has a battleship-gray coating. The New York trigger springs come in two colors: olive (NY 1), and orange (NY 2). The NY 1 olive housing with a silver spring attached increases the trigger pull weight by about 3 pounds (1.5 kilograms) over the normal pull weight associated with that connector. The NY 2 orange housing with a black spring attached increases the trigger pull weight by about 5 pounds (2.5 kilograms) over the normal pull weight associated with that connector. "The New York trigger spring is an alternative to the standard coil trigger spring and gives a more "revolver-type" feel to the trigger pull."[95]

CAUTION: Install a New York spring with either the 4.5-pound (2-kilogram) connector marked with a minus (-) or 5.5-pound (2.5-kilogram) connector unmarked, *never* with the 8-pound (3.5-kilogram) connecter marked with a plus (+).[96]

Most Glock pistols from the factory generally have a 5.5-pound (2.4-kilogram) trigger pull. The pull weight is significant to allow the operator's trigger finger to remain in contact with the trigger as the pistol moves forward when extending the arms. A lighter trigger could contribute to a premature discharge, especially while wearing gloves. It is preferred the operator's pistol and carbine have about the same trigger pull weight.[97]

PISTOL SAFETIES

Ideally, a pistol used for self-protection will *not* have a manual safety.[98] Reducing the number of devices on a pistol that requires manipulation simplifies its operation and lessens the amount of time needed for training. The Glock Safe Action pistol fits this criterion and favored by many law enforcement agencies worldwide. When the trigger is in the forward position, the safeties activate.[99] When the trigger is pulled, the safeties deactivate.[100]

Time is of the essence when responding to a sudden deadly attack. The fewer things the mind has to process[101] the quicker the body's response.[102] The loss of learned patterns can many times be seen during training at the range. A police officer will step to the firing line, draw, forget to disengage the safety, and pull the trigger. The failure of the pistol discharging is usually followed by the police officer having a dumbfounded to embarrassed look. What the police officer should have is a sick feeling cause by a self-realization of incompetence to defend his or her life. This may sound harsh, but the truth can sometimes be that way. What follows in the rest of this section is information about different types of pistol safeties other than Glock's Safe Action.

Manual Safety: A *manual safety* desired as a personal preference or required by agency policy needs to be *ambidextrous* and preferably released by a downward motion of the thumb.[103] Pistols without an ambidextrous manual safety are not well suited for left-handed operators.[104] The downward motion is a gross movement in which the length of the thumb rakes down against the safety lever. It is more natural for the thumb to make a downward motion during the draw. Keep the thumb on the safety lever to prevent it from accidently getting pushed on safe.[105] When carrying the pistol in its holster, keep the safety in place according to the manufacturer's recommendation.[106] Do not tamper with or disable safety devices in any manner as it could result in an injury, death, or legal consequences.

An operator carrying a pistol with a manual safety lever must receive specific training on properly operating the safety. Training provides guidance on what stage of the draw the safety is disengaged and engaged when holstering. Sweep the safety off with the firing hand thumb after pulling the pistol from its holster and rotating 90 degrees.[107] This allows firing the pistol from the retention position. Stressful simulation training is desirable while having to disengage and engage the safety according to the operator's situational awareness. This type of training helps to ensure operator competence.

Rotating Safety/Decocking Lever: A pistol equipped with a slide mounted *rotating safety/decocking lever* may be inadvertently placed on safe. This can occur when reloading or clearing stoppages because of the operator's fingers pulling back on the slide near the safety/decocking lever. Using the *overhand* technique[108] to rack or release the slide increases the likelihood of the occurrence. Using the *underhand* technique helps to alleviate the problem. Use the thumb and index finger to grab forward and below the safety/decocking lever when pulling the slide back. This allows the pulling up motion of the safety/decocking lever to the fire position and provides a secure grip.[109] The range command after firing is "decock and scan." Cycle the safety/decocking lever from *safe* back to the *fire* position decocking the pistol. Place the pistol back on safe before holstering.

Frame Mounted Decocking Lever: A right-handed operator with the firing hand thumb operates the *frame mounted decocking lever* on the left side. A left-handed operator uses the trigger finger to operate the decocking lever on the left side. The pistol can still be operated with one hand even with a debilitating arm injury.

Grip Safety: A *grip safety* prevents the pistol from firing unless a grip is established. Use a tight grip to seat the back strap of the pistol into the palm of the firing hand. This ensures the grip safety is depressed. Some one-hand stoppage clearing techniques will not work with a grip safety because it prevents the slide from cycling.[110] As an example, it is *not* an option while kneeling to use the technique of reversing the pistol and placing its grip between the calf and back of the knee to lock the slide back. However, instead of placing the grip between the calf and back of the knee, place the pistol's grip in a front pocket. Push forward on the slide and the edge of the pocket will depress the grip safety allowing the slide to be locked back using one hand. This technique requires an accessible large sturdy pocket common to military and tactical pants.

Passive Safety: An option in lieu of the *manual safety* is to carry a pistol that does *not* have one. [111] Many firearms instructors after a negligent discharge occurred can attest to hearing the words, "I thought the safety was on." A *passive safety* provides greater tactical deployment reliability. This is because of the pistol being in a ready state *without* additional manipulation. The operator uses the Universal Cover Mode (UCM) rather than transitioning from safe to fire. [112] A pistol without a manual safety is better suited for training and ease of operation. [113]

BACKUP PISTOL

A *backup* pistol is a second pistol carried by an operator. Why carry a backup pistol? As stated earlier, a pistol is a machine and like any machine is subject to break. The primary pistol may be dropped, damaged when struck by gunfire, or taken by an adversary. These are valid reasons to carry a backup pistol. A backup pistol acts as a readily accessible replacement. The backup pistol when deployed becomes the primary pistol. The backup pistol needs to be of sufficient size and caliber that it could be used confidently on duty and off duty.

Some people *expect* a police officer to carry a backup pistol. It may be surprising to find out who is one of those individuals. A police officer searched an arrestee and found a gun in the front of his waistband. The police officer admitted to being *shocked* to find a second gun in the waistband in the back. The arrestee's response when questioned by the police officer for carrying two guns: "You carry a backup gun right?"[114] It could be argued that some criminals have a higher expectation of officers and related survival tactics than the officers themselves do.

NOTE: When a carbine is carried, it is referred to as *primary.* When a pistol is carried, it is referred to as the *secondary.* [115] The pistol is referred to as the *primary pistol* and the second pistol is referred to as a *backup pistol* when a carbine is not carried. Law enforcement also refers to a primary pistol as a *duty pistol.* The backup pistol may perform double-duty as an *off duty pistol* and in law enforcement is sometimes referred to by the same name.

Guidelines for Choosing

To prevent any confusion it is assumed a carbine is *not* carried and the term *primary pistol* will be used. Use the guidelines that follow to assist in making a decision on what pistol to carry as a *backup*:

1. The backup pistol should have the same handling characteristics as the primary pistol.

2. The backup pistol should be the same caliber as the primary pistol and accept its magazines.

3. The backup pistol should have the same type of sights as the primary pistol.

4. The backup pistol should have the same type of trigger as the primary pistol.

The above guidelines apply to any of the Glock pistols in the same caliber, except the model 36.[116] The model 36 as of this writing uses a single-stack magazine that is not shared with any subcompact or standard pistol. As a sample guideline, a 9x19mm caliber, model 17 pistol with a smooth face trigger, and self-luminous sights installed would be carried as a primary pistol. The pistol magazine will hold 17 rounds of ammunition with one in the chamber bringing the total to 18 rounds of ammunition. Carrying the two spare magazines provide 34 rounds of spare ammunition. The total number of rounds available for use is 52.

To complement the model 17 there are two preferred choices for a backup pistol: models 19 and 26. Both models have the same handling characteristics and functionality as the model 17. Both models are a 9x19mm caliber and available with self-luminous sights. The models 19 and 26 likely come with *grooved triggers*. The grooved trigger with trigger bar in a Glock 19 or 26 can be replaced with a *smooth trigger with trigger bar* used in a Glock model 17. This enables the backup pistol to meet the criterion of having the same trigger as the primary pistol. A Glock certified armorer can install the inexpensive trigger with trigger bar.

It is preferred the primary pistol and back-up pistol receivers be of the same generation and have the same trigger distance. This will provide optimal handling and pointing characteristics when transitioning from one pistol to the other. Changing the size of the back strap on Gen4 pistols adjust the trigger distance. As an example, the model 17 Gen4 pistol without a back strap has a trigger distance of 2.76 inches (70 millimeters). With a +2 mm back strap the trigger distance is 2.83 inches (72 millimeters). With a +4 mm back strap the trigger distance is of 2.91 inches (74 millimeters).[117]

NOTE: Glock triggers come in a smooth and grooved surface. The Bureau of Alcohol, Tobacco, Firearms, and Explosives (ATF) considers the grooved trigger a target trigger. The grooved trigger adds required points that allow importing the pistol to the United States.

The magazine capacity of the model 19 is 15 rounds of ammunition and the model 26 is 10 rounds. The model 19 has 16 rounds and the model 26 has 11 rounds when fully loaded. This provides a police officer with either 68 rounds of ammunition (models 17 and 19) or 63 rounds (models 17 and 26) between the primary pistol, the backup pistol and two spare model 17 magazines. Another option is to carry two model 19 pistols, one as the primary pistol and the other as the backup pistol.[118]

The magazines for the model 17 will fit into the model 19 or 26 and fire. This is an important consideration when choosing a backup pistol. Being able to use spare ammunition is a tactical advantage. The model 17 magazine will protrude from the *magazine well* [119] (also called magazine shaft) [120] of the model 19 and 26. This will not affect functionality of either pistol. An operator that thinks this is going to the extreme and it is not necessary should try to mentally picture what it would be like in a gunfight with either a broken pistol or no pistol at all (lost or taken). That no doubt would be a sickening feeling.

WARNING: Some operators when firing a *subcompact* pistol and using *standard* size magazines *may* experience the firing hand pinched between the protruding magazine and the grip of the pistol. The painful experience can be mentally distracting. In an alarm reaction state, it is likely the pinch would not be noticed *if* it occurred.

CONCEALED CARRY PISTOL

In the United States, there are states that allow its citizenry to carry a concealed pistol. Many of the citizens do carry a pistol for self-protection. Like most endeavors in life, there are advantages and disadvantages. Some of the *advantages*: The person has a device to use for self-protection and the protection of others. Carrying a concealed pistol can give a person a sense of confidence of not becoming prey for an attacker. Some of the *disadvantages*: The person may experience stress from having to maintain a higher level of situational awareness. This can be mentally draining. Carrying a pistol can be uncomfortable and physically tiring. There will be moral and legal ramifications to contend with if someone is injured or killed.

A concealed carry pistol that is a smaller version of a standard size pistol maximizes familiarity. The operator may own only one pistol for concealed carry and it has to perform double-duty as a home defense firearm. Extremely small pistols (commonly called pocket pistols) are not as efficient to manipulate as subcompact, compact or standard pistols. When shooting a pocket pistol using the thumbs forward grip, the non-firing hand thumb may have to be held down to prevent it from extending past the muzzle. It is unlikely an operator would remember to tuck the thumb down when firing the pocket pistol if a standard size pistol is normally carried. This is especially true when under duress. A pistol used for home defense would do well to have a light attached. Pocket pistols as a rule do not have the option to mount a light.

Do not use an inferior quality pistol for self-protection. Such pistols do not have consistent tolerances from the manufacturer that would ensure the reliability necessary for self-protection. Choose a quality 9x19mm or larger caliber pistol and train regularly to become proficient. Read the instruction manual to learn how to operate and clean the pistol.

PISTOL MAGAZINE IDENTIFICATION

Magazines can be marked with *sequential numbers* and the pistol's *serial number*. (Figure 3-12) A law enforcement agency may also want their name and badge or seal engraved. Have an engraving company engrave the desired information on each of the magazines. However, because of logistics and cost an agency may choose not to use an engraving company. A handheld electric engraver is another option for engraving magazines.

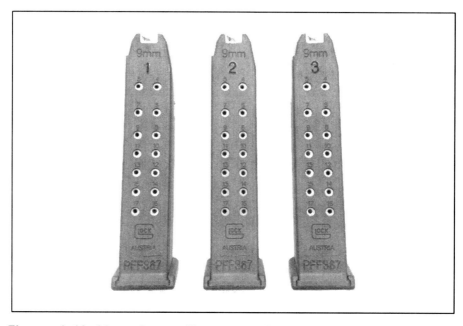

Figure 3-12 *Magazines with engraved sequential (top) and serial numbers (bottom).*

The reasons that police magazines should be marked are as follows:

1. The agency name and the pistol serial number show ownership.

2. A dropped magazine on the ground establishes the police officer's location in a shooting.

3. Location of the police officer could be important in a criminal or civil trial.

4. Damaged magazines are identifiable and can be discarded.

Magazine identification is as follows:

1. The magazine in the pistol is marked with a "1." The magazine in its pouch closest to the pistol is marked with a "2." The

remaining magazine in the pouch is marked with a "3."

2. The magazine in the backup pistol is marked with a "1." A backup spare magazine *if* carried is marked with a "2."

NOTE: Plus 2 rounds extended floor plates and inserts are available for standard frame models in calibers 9x19mm, .357 SIG, .40 S&W, and .45 G.A.P.[121] (Figure 3-13) Magazine capacity is increased by 2 rounds with the added benefit of easier seating and removal of the magazine.[122] The magazine spring may have to be replaced in some models when using the plus 2 rounds extension.[123] Contact Glock Inc., for more information about specific models and using the plus 2 rounds extension.

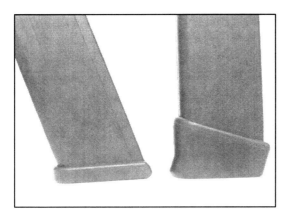

Figure 3-13 *Standard floor plate on left and plus two floor plate on right.*

NOTE: On the body of a new Glock magazine, there may be a decal. After reading the decal, peel it off. This is to prevent the decal from inadvertency peeling up and interfering with the insertion or removal of the magazine.

AMMUNITION TYPES AND COMPONENTS

The two types of cartridges are *rimfire* and *centerfire*. The rimfire cartridge has its priming mixture enclosed in a cavity at the rim of the head of the case.[124] A .22 Long Rifle is a rimfire cartridge. A centerfire cartridge has its primer located in the center of the base of the case.[125] The .380 Auto, 9x19mm, .357 SIG, .40 S&W, .45 G.A.P., .45 Auto, and

10mm Auto are centerfire cartridges. A cartridge has four basic components.[126] (1) The cartridge *case* houses the components. (2) The *primer* is the source of ignition. (3) The *powder* is the propellant charge that thrusts the bullet. (4) The *bullet* also called projectile is what travels through the barrel and strikes the target or adversary.

AMMUNITION STOPPING POWER

The subject of *stopping power*[127] of pistols in the firearms training community is plagued with controversy. On one side of the argument is the belief that a large slow moving bullet is the most effective means of stopping the human threat. On the other side of the argument is the belief not bullet size, but placement is what stops a human threat. The answer would seem to be what happens in actual shootings with particular calibers. This too does not provide definitive answers to the quest of the ideal pistol caliber. Definitive answers can sometimes be illusive and due in part to the number of variables involved in stopping an adversary.

Those variables are the adversary's state of mind, stamina, size, and blood alcohol or drug content. Alcohol and drugs can dramatically modify an adversary's tolerance to pain resulting in an almost *superhuman* level of strength in some cases. There are also firearms and environmental related variables that include the pistol's barrel length, bullet impact velocity, ammunition design, serviceable condition, and barriers the bullet would have to go through to hit the adversary. Most importantly is the path a bullet takes from entry to exit and the tissue damaged along the way. Two bullets can take nearly identical paths, but the one that hits a major artery or the upper spine can produce a vastly different result. Therefore, the best advice in the hope of definitive answers is to read on and accept what the facts reveal.

NOTE: The willingness to use deadly force is more important than either the pistol or ammunition carried.

Pistol Calibers

There are calibers that are *not* well suited to penetrate the flesh and destroy bone causing a permanent wound channel with rapid blood loss. The small calibers (.22, .25, and .32) will not be considered for incapacitating a human quickly. The larger 9x19mm, .357 SIG, .40 S&W, .45 G.A.P and .45 Auto calibers for a semiautomatic pistol will be examined. These represent the most popular calibers used by police officers [128] and capable of immediately stopping a human threat. [129] Operators are mentally handicapping themselves before the fight begins by doubting that any of the calibers used in law enforcement are not capable of incapacitating an adversary.

Action movies have portrayed that large caliber bullets can knock people off their feet. This is utter nonsense and confirmed by the basic principles of physics. [130] Training programs can counter this fallacy by providing realistic training combined with accurate ballistic information. [131] An adversary when shot will most likely bend forward and fall. Video from the dashboard cameras have captured such behavior. [132] The fact is "…a bullet simply cannot knock a man [or woman] down. If it had the energy to do so, the equal energy would be applied against the shooter and he [or she] too would be knocked down." [133]

Some advocate the answer to stopping a human threat is the "knock down power" of the large heavy bullet traveling at subsonic speed. Advocates of the large caliber see it as capable of stopping the human threat. Others believe that a lighter bullet traveling at high rate of speed will have a "shock effect" on the body. Some tout the "temporary cavity" as a major factor in stopping effectiveness. The fact is that "…temporary cavity is frequently, and grossly, overrated as a wounding factor when analyzing wounds." [134] "Temporary cavitation is nothing more than a stretch of the tissues, generally no larger than 10 times the bullet diameter (in handgun calibers), and elastic tissues sustain little, if any, residual damage." [135] "Kinetic energy does not wound. The temporary cavity does not wound. The "shock" of a bullet impact is a fable and "knock down" power is a myth. The critical element is penetration." [136]

Ammunition technology has nearly perfected the hollow point (HP) [137] bullet. Many manufacturers produce a HP bullet that after striking flesh expands reliably, but more importantly *penetrates* to vital organs. The bullet does exactly as designed—expands uniformly on impact—penetrates the central nervous system (CNS) or areas causing *significant blood loss* (SBL). Significant blood loss is people losing about "…20 percent of the volume of their blood, which can take 8 to 10 seconds to accomplish." [138]

The law enforcement community having apprehension regarding

over penetration is a responsible concern. However, "the risk of over-penetration (exit) is exaggerated, given the burst strength characteristics of the skin as the bullet exits."[139] Experiments have revealed that skin on the exit side of the body is tough, flexible and about the same resistance to a bullet passing through 4 inches (101.6 millimeters) of muscle tissue.[140] The fact is that bullets manufactured for civilian and law enforcement self-protection are not likely to over penetrate *if* they expand as designed. A police officer dying because his or her bullet over penetrated an adversary is unlikely, but there are police officers killed because of under penetration.[141]

Nevertheless, a full metal jacket (FMJ)[142] bullet *is* more likely to over penetrate[143] than a HP. The same can be said for a total metal jacket (TMJ).[144] There are better choices than the FMJ and TMJ bullets for self-protection. The FMJ and TMJ are suited for training, practice, and commonly referred to as *practice ammunition*. The Hague Convention of 1899 does *not* allow expanding bullets such as HPs in the theater of military combat.[145] The larger and heavier FMJ bullet is the likely reason that some people favor the .45 Auto over the 9x19mm in the area of battlefield stopping capability. The .45 Auto and .45 G.A.P. cartridges have nearly identical ballistic specifications.[146]

The weakness of a HP bullet is its hollow cavity being plugged with barrier material (cloth, sheetrock, etc.) resulting in over penetration from the required hydraulics for expansion *not* occurring.[147] The weaknesses of a FMJ bullet are over penetration and its inability to expand to create a larger permanent wound. The *expanding full metal jacket* (EFMJ) solves each of these problems. The EFMJ does *not* have a hollow cavity that could be plugged with barrier material. The EFMJ does have expanding characteristics similar to HP bullets. The EFMJ design is a patented synthetic rubber core for *consistent* expansion required for self-protection.[148]

There are stopping power stories that contradict one another. There are stories that depict the .45 Auto as the one-shot stop. However, a police officer firing a 230 grain .45 Auto hollow-point bullet shot a knife wielding suspect 5 times in the chest. Only after the fifth round did the suspect drop the knife. The suspect *never* fell to the ground. The suspect said, "The wounds felt like bee stings."[149] Then there are instances of the 9x19mm stopping the person with one hit,[150] and another story of the same caliber in which a person had been hit 33 times[151] before being stopped. To add further confusion to the topic, there is the case in which a suspect with a .22 caliber revolver killed a state trooper after the trooper had shot the suspect five times with a .357 Magnum revolver.[152]

Two other cases represent the opposite ends of the stopping power spectrum. The first case is a police shooting where the suspect instantly drops after being shot with a .380 Auto. The bullet penetrated from front to back stopping near the spine, but in a few moments, the suspect got back to his feet.[153] Hunters have experienced this same phenomenon when their shot narrowly missed the animal's central nervous system (spine). In the second case, a young male at a range of 2 to 3 feet (0.60 to 0.91 meter) was shot in the chest with a 12-gauge shotgun *shredding* apart his heart. The male turned and ran from the location for 65 feet (19.81 meters), according to the medical examiner.[154] How is it that a .380 Auto caliber *instantly* dropped a suspect, but a 12-gauge shotgun blast to the heart did not?

NOTE: "Thus, the brain can cause you to lift your hand and fire a gun even if you have no heart."[155] If the electrical system works and blood pressure is up (oxygen to the brain), the person is a potential threat.

Examining the actual shootings involving various calibers will *not* settle the argument of which is the best caliber for self-protection. The answer only to a certain degree applies to the caliber of the bullet. There is also the physiological (anatomy) and psychological elements (mental state) of the human. Obviously, the caliber has to have enough velocity and mass to *penetrate* flesh and bone to disrupt the central nervous system or quickly cause significant blood loss.[156] Significant blood loss is "...sufficient to drop blood pressure or the brain is deprived of oxygen."[157] "Any bullet that will not reliably penetrate a *minimum* of 10 to 12 inches [254 to 304.8 millimeters] of soft tissue is inadequate."[158]

NOTE: Consider choosing *one* bullet that meets all the operational requirements for self-protection.[159] Examples of such requirements are shooting through a vehicle's windshield from the outside toward inside or inside toward outside, penetrating household sheetrock, or heavy winter clothing, etc. Bonded bullets virtually eliminate *fragmenting* caused by core jacket separations when obstructed by bone or other real-life shooting barriers.[160]

Stopping a Determined Adversary

Do not advocate a predetermined numbers of shots—shoot until the adversary stops. The *burst fire*[161] shooting technique of multiple shots into the adversary will multiply the effectiveness of any caliber. Any emergency room trauma surgeon can attest to the devastation of wounds caused by multiple gunshots. Advocated *is* a pistol that can deliver a large volume of fire with a high capacity to curtail the need to reload frequently. During a deadly force encounter an operator who can make a pistol resemble a machine gun while maintaining effective accuracy will likely end the adversary's attack.

The Federal Bureau of Investigation's publication on handgun wounding factors and effectiveness clarifies the point of stopping a determined adversary:

"Physiologically, a determined adversary can be stopped reliably and immediately only by a shot that disrupts the brain or upper spinal cord. Failing a hit to the central nervous system, massive bleeding from holes in the heart or major blood vessels of the torso causing circulatory collapse is the only other way to force incapacitation upon an adversary, and this takes time. For example, there is sufficient oxygen within the brain to support full, voluntary action for 10-15 seconds after the heart has been destroyed."[162]

According to the shooter's skill level, semiautomatic pistols are capable of 4 rounds per second.[163] A determined adversary can massacre a large number of people in 10 to 15 seconds. The importance of immediately incapacitating an adversary cannot be overstated. The goal of an operator *is* the immediate incapacitation of an adversary.[164] In addition, pain caused by a gunshot *cannot* be relied on to stop a determined adversary:

"Pain is irrelevant to survival and is commonly suppressed until sometime later. In order to be a factor, pain must first be perceived, and second must cause an emotional response. In many individuals, pain is ignored even when perceived, or the response is anger and increased resistance, not surrender."[165]

The author while in Afghanistan had the opportunity to discuss with a military doctor the effects of gunshots on the human body. During that conversation, he learned the problem of *over penetration* might not be only in the bullet, but also the lungs. Think of the chest cavity having two balloons inside. A layer of flesh, muscle, and bones cover the lungs. A shot that hits the lung area is passing through a good portion of air. There is also the question about the *under penetration* of the trooper's .357 Magnum revolver. The suspect weighed about 300 pounds (136 kilograms) and was 5 feet 7 inches (170.18 centimeters) tall. The .357 Magnum revolver was loaded with .357 Magnum 145-grain bullets that struck a thick layer of fat and failed to penetrate to the central nervous system or major arteries.[166] What is the answer in both of these cases?

Train for the most effective result against the most determined drug induced or psychotic adversary. That means shooting in an area of the body that will disrupt the central nervous system (CNS) or cause significant blood loss. That region is the area located between the forehead and the bottom of the sternum called *high center mass*. (Figure 3-14) The high center mass is not susceptible to amassing fat that can become a natural protective layer against bullets. It is preferred to shoot the head for an instantaneous incapacitation. When the head is *not* a viable target, shoot the high center mass if possible.[167]

NOTE: A former U.S. Navy SEAL described combat accuracy as hitting 8 inches (203.2 millimeters) in the thoracic cavity and 4 inches (101.6 millimeters) in the ocular-cranial cavity at whatever distance the operator may be from the adversary.[168]

Obtain a sight picture in the high center mass area and fire multiple rounds until the adversary stops posing a threat.[169] Rounds shot high may hit the neck or head. Rounds shot low may hit the liver or stomach. The high center mass area will provide the best possible results short of shooting the adversary in the head. The shoulders are usually the widest portion of the upper body and a shot to the left or right would likely disable that shoulder or arm. A round in the throat would likely prevent the adversary from shouting, using a radio, or cell phone. There are also tactical advantages of aiming in the high center mass area.

Figure 3-14 *Combat Qualification Target*

Body armor does not usually cover the area just below the neck. In addition, it is unlikely a high center mass shot would hit the vest of a suicide bomber. A shot to the lower torso of a suicide bomber is a different situation. A small group of Israeli soldiers had overpowered a would-be suicide bomber.[170] There would not have been any issues, except for an armed civilian shooting the suicide bomber in the stomach resulting in the vest exploding killing three Israelis and the bomber. The correct tactical option would have been to shoot the suicide bomber in the head. That is the combat doctrine stressed in Israel for stopping a suicide bomber.[171]

Do *not* think of the head as a separate unobtainable target, but view it as part of the high center mass. An added benefit is a terrorist or criminal will probably raise the firearm to this same general area. Use the technique of allowing the eyes to find the center of the perceived target area. The *center* of two objects is the same size. The size of the object can change, but the center is the center. An operator frequently *focuses* on and shoots at the adversary's firearm or the muzzle flash. The operator before shooting at a muzzle flash *must* know (positive identification) it is the adversary and *not* another operator.[172]

Once a threat is identified, do not become fixated on the whole person. Focus on the *center* of high center mass if a full torso area is offered.[173] This forces a mental zooming in on the upper torso in an attempt to keep rounds in that area. The high center mass is the preferred target area, but the operator may have to shoot the center of any exposed mass.[174] Operators in a life-threatening situation must *not* wait for a full frontal and unobstructed torso shot reminiscent of a target used during firearms qualification when some other part of the adversary's anatomy is presented.[175] There may not be time or opportunity for a better shot to stop a determined adversary. Operators during training must be taught that shooting *any* exposed area may stop the adversary's mental or physical ability to fight.[176]

Statistically, police officers killed in the line of duty are shot in the head about half the time.[177] If a criminal can make a head shot—an armed civilian, police officer, or military operator can do the same. A police officer about 18 feet (5.48 meters) away shot a suspect three times in the chest and three times in the face as he wielded a knife.[178] In another incident, a deputy shot a kidnapper that held a pistol to her child's head.[179] The deputy fired a single shot at the kidnapper striking her in the head. View the head as a viable and obtainable target, especially at *close* range.[180] The head is a part of the high center mass that provides a greater chance of immediate incapacitation.[181] When shooting the head from a frontal view aim for the *mouth*. Aiming for the mouth provides a lesser margin of error under stress in comparison to a quick upward transition from the torso that may cause shots to hit high.[182]

NOTE: "Immediate incapacitation is defined as the sudden physical or mental inability to pose any further risk or injury to others."[183]

A suspect during an arrest using a .32-caliber revolver at close range killed two North Carolina police officers wearing body armor. The suspect during a fight with the police officers fired five shots striking each officer in the side of the head.[184] This tragedy is an example of the ability of a determined attacker who was willing to take a head shot not against one, but two police officers.

When an adversary is shot by an operator, sometimes he or she does not know if the bullets struck the intended aim point. The operator has a couple of options *if* the initial shots do not stop the adversary: First, shoot another burst into the high center mass area. Second, change the visual focus to the head (close quarters) or pelvic area and fire. The pelvis is a basin-shaped structure that includes the hips and groin area (inverted triangle). The aim point is between the waist and the groin and called the *low center mass* area. The *pelvic area* is a viable *secondary target* and when broken will cause an adversary to fall.[185] The fallen adversary will likely have use of his or her hands and additional shots may be required.

Well documented in law enforcement publications is the bullet performance of the suggested calibers in this section.[186] As the reader now knows the argument of which caliber is the best involves more factors than just the cartridge. Another crucial factor not previously discussed in this section is the operator. The pistol must properly fit the operator's hand. In addition, the operator must be able to control the pistol's recoil.[187] A large caliber pistol is of little use if the recoil is unmanageable resulting in ineffective hits.

A recap of this section reveals there is ample proof that various firearms may not perform as expected. Some of the preconceived ideas and misnomers should now be clearer. After examining many police involved shootings, there is one definite truth. The *human factor* and *bullet placement* with *sufficient penetration* have more to do with stopping an adversary than the caliber of the pistol used.[188] A battle hardened, demented or drug induced person will likely endure a great deal more damage than the untrained, mentally sound, or sober individual. Moreover, the only control the operator truly has is bullet placement.

NOTE: There are instructors that will tell students it makes no difference whether one bullet hits the upper chest and the other bullet hits the lower abdomen. The fact is that shot placement in the *high center mass* (specific area) is crucial to *quickly* stopping an adversary.[189]

The technological advances in bonded bullet design provide optimum bullet expansion and penetration performance. In a wound ballistic test[190] in *bare gelatin* the 9x19mm +P expanded to 0.75 inch (19.0 millimeters) and penetrated 13.25 inches (336.55 millimeters); the .40 S&W expanded to 0.69 inch (17.52 millimeters) and penetrated 13.5 inches (342.9 millimeters); and the .45 Auto expanded to 0.75 inch (19.0 millimeters) and penetrated to 13.5 inches (342.9 millimeters). The bullet penetration and mass of each caliber is sufficient to incapacitate an adversary.

NOTE: "If a .45 and 9mm expand to the same diameter and at the same *rate* and reach the same *depth*, they will produce identical injury. If they do not expand, the .45 produces more injury at the same depth than does the 9mm."[191]

One-Shot Stop

Advice for the operator looking for the *pistol* cartridge guaranteeing a one-shot stop—it does not exist.[192] The closest thing to the one-shot stop is to disrupt the brain or sever the upper spinal column.[193] However, ammunition and pistols manufactured of the highest quality exist and when combined with a competent operator will likely send an adversary to one of three places: (1) *jail*, (2) *hospital*, or (3) *morgue*.

AGENCY WIDE CONSIDERATIONS

Reliability must be at the top of the list when choosing a pistol for agency wide distribution. Likewise, evaluate a pistol on the number of parts it has and the ease of maintenance for the operator and armorer. Pistols across different brands may have a close resemblance on the exterior, but the interior can be dramatically different. As an example the Glock pistol *with* the magazine has about 36 parts (model dependent) whereas another pistol may have over twice that many.[194] The Glock pistol has about 31 parts without a magazine.

Having fewer parts simplifies spare parts logistics and reduces the susceptibility for administrative errors and overall maintenance cost.[195] There is also the consideration of how many parts will interchange within different models of the same brand. Glock Inc., has achieved 76 percent parts compatibility across its pistol line.[196] A pistol brand and particular model must *never* be adopted agency wide without vetting by the armorer section.

A pistol with the versatility to be custom fitted to various hand sizes is desirable. A modular back strap system fulfills this role. Back straps that change the size of the pistol grip along its full-length are ideal. The full back strap assures the pistol's pointing characteristics will remain the same. Another preferred option is to have a reversible magazine catch. The reversible magazine catch allows uniform training among left- and right-handed operators. The magazine catch is configurable for operation by the right or left firing hand thumb. This will allow left- and right-handed operators to perform the common task of reloading in the same consistent manner.

The pistol must be user-friendly for a left- and right-handed operator. Glock pistols are easy to manipulate with the left or right hand using proper techniques. The operator can pull the trigger, load, unload, reload, clear stoppages, lock open and release the slide, and disassemble and reassemble the pistol.[197] Use caution with a magazine catch on the left side of the pistol when worn on the left hip. An inadvertent bump against the exposed magazine catch could release the magazine. The problem worsens with an extended magazine catch. This issue is resolve with the reversible magazine catch on the right side of the pistol when worn on the left hip.

It is preferable the pistol model also be available in a training pistol, and practice pistol for training purposes. *Training* pistols used for simulation exercises fire non-lethal ammunition. *Practice* pistols allow inserting and removing magazines, sight alignment, trigger pull and reset, and fieldstripping. The practice pistol should be the same size as a real pistol with the same weight and feel. The practice pistol must *not* be capable of discharging live ammunition. Glock training and practice pistols meet these requirements.[198]

NOTE: To prevent any chance of a negligent discharge in a classroom, there should be enough practice pistols and magazines with corresponding color floor plates, and inert cartridges (dummy rounds) for recruits when conducting an introductory pistol course (nomenclature, disassembly, etc.).[199]

Agency wide distribution of multiple calibers of ammunition poses special challenges that are not applicable to the solo operator. The allowance of multiple calibers has it strengths, but also weaknesses. The greatest strength is a tailored caliber size that an operator can manage the recoil. There is also a psychological advantage of having confidence in a personally chosen caliber. The downside for multiple calibers can be cost, stocking logistics, and training. There can be significant price differences between common and uncommon calibers. This may have a negative influence on an agency's budget. Each caliber adopted will have to be stored in its own section of the storage facility. Trainers have to ensure each operator receives the correct caliber ammunition and documents the information.

The most important issue is *safety.* Chambering the *wrong* caliber ammunition can cause a barrel to bulge or worse—rupture. An example would be firing a .40 S&W round in a .45 Auto pistol.[200] In addition, the wrong size caliber ammunition may unknowingly be loaded in a magazine and cause a stoppage. Agency wide adoption of a single caliber reduces or eliminates many of these problems. Operators can hand off ammunition to one another without concern over caliber size in exigent circumstances.

NOTE: Pulling a trigger before fieldstripping a pistol may seem to some as a reason not to select the Glock pistol. There may be fear of a negligent discharge in the cleaning room. This issue is easily resolved: After training or qualification, unload the pistol on the firing line and remove the slide. Place the receiver in the holster and hand carry the slide assembly to the cleaning room.

GENERAL RECOMMENDATIONS

Purchase a pistol model comfortable to carry, fits the hand well, simple to operate, reliable, shoots accurately, and uses affordable ammunition allowing for frequent practice. A 9x19mm or larger caliber is preferred.[201]

Quarterly live fire practice is important for operators if they are going to maintain their operational survival skills.[202] An agency may not require quarterly live fire training, but that does not negate an operator's responsibility of proficiency. An operator who thinks of ammunition as being expensive would probably not shoot quarterly. In the operator's mind—it would be unaffordable. It does little good for an operator or an agency for that matter to purchase a pistol caliber that ammunition is so expensive regular practice is unaffordable. Using common calibers allows operators to purchase reasonably priced ammunition readily available from large retail stores.

NOTE: Any caliber of pistol commonly used in law enforcement in conjunction with brand name ammunition designed for stopping a human is well suited for the task of self-protection.

SPECIAL PISTOL MODELS

The designation for Glock special model pistols have the model number with an associated letter or name that follows. The designated letter or name signifies the purpose of the pistol. Consult the current Glock Buyer's Guide or contact Glock Inc., for availability of special model pistols.

C Models[203]

Glock intended for its *compensated pistols* to be used for recreational shooting. The compensator integrated in the barrel allows the pistol when fired rapidly to be more controllable by keeping the muzzle down. [204] The integrated compensator is made by cutting two longitudinal openings in the barrel and slide in a V-position arrangement.

The V-position design reduces blackening of the front sight even though the integrated compensator is located on top and near the front of the slide. The compensated pistol is available in compact and standard sizes.

WARNING: Significant muzzle blast and particulate released out the ports of a compensated pistol can seriously injure the operator when fired from a retention position.[205] Do *not* fire compensated pistols from the retention position!

Cut Models[206]

A Glock *cutaway pistol* is for technical firearms training. The cutaway pistol allows the operator to see the interaction of the three safeties. The cutaway pistol also allows a clear view of the trigger assembly. The cutaway pistol is an excellent training tool to help operators understand why the Glock pistol is one of the safest pistols on the market. The cutaway pistol is available in *subcompact* (G26 Cut), *compact* (G19 Cut and G23 Cut), and *standard* sizes (G17 Cut, G20 Cut, G21 Cut, and G22 Cut), but available only to law enforcement agencies.[207] Some models may not be available in the United States, contact Glock Inc., for availability.

T Models[208]

Glock *training pistols* benefit Police, SWAT, Military, and Special Operations that conduct realistic simulation training. Training pistols have a straight blow back system that fires marking ammo of different colors (FX or UTM specific) and special rubber bullets.[209] The training pistol has a *blue* receiver signifying a training instrument. The magazines supplied also have a blue floor plate identifying them for use in the training pistol. The training pistol is available in *subcompact* (G26T), *compact* (G19T), and *standard* sizes (G17T), but available only to law enforcement.[210] Some models may not be available in the United States, contact Glock Inc., for availability.

P Models[211]

Use Glock *practice pistols* for dry fire practice of loading and unloading, trigger operation, manual operation of the slide, and fieldstripping and disassembly.[212] Also, use the pistols for hand-to-hand combat training. The practice models have a *red* receiver, plugged barrel and a solid breech face.[213] The magazines supplied also have a red floor plate[214] identifying them for the practice pistol. The pistols are safe to use in a classroom environment. The pistols have the same weight and feel as functioning pistols, but will *not* chamber dummy rounds (plugged barrel). The red receiver designates the pistol is a training instrument.[215] The practice pistol is available in *subcompact* (G26P), *compact* (G19P and G23P), and *standard* sizes (G17P and G22P), but available only to law enforcement.[216] Some models may not be available in the United States, contact Glock Inc., for availability.

DANGER: It *is* possible to install a functioning slide on a red receiver. Make sure the red receiver has an *inert* slide and barrel installed!

R Models[217]

Use Glock *reset pistols* with shooting simulators to provide safe and practical training. The reset models have a *red* receiver and the barrel allows the installation of an aftermarket laser impulse generator. When pulling the trigger the firing pin activates the impulse generator and the simulator screen displays the hits. The reset pistol offers the advantage of after every shot the trigger automatically resets to the forward position without having to rack the slide. The reset pistol also has a solid breech face, but the barrel *will* chamber dummy rounds. The magazines supplied also have a red floor plate[218] identifying them for the reset pistol. The reset model has a *red* receiver and is available in *compact* (G19R) and *standard* (G17R) sizes, but available only to law enforcement.[219] The G19R may not be available in the United States, contact Glock Inc., for availability.

ALTERNATIVE TO A PISTOL

Some people have no desire to train with a pistol. However, the same person may feel comfortable with a long gun. The person as a child could have hunted with a parent or received rifle training in the military. In such cases, the carbine with a 16-inch (406.4-millimeter) barrel may be a better home defense solution. These types of carbines are easy to operate, have good pointing characteristics, and excellent stopping power. The carbine needs to have an optic sight, mounted light, sling, and at minimum a flash hider. A suppressor is preferred for home defense to reduce noise and muzzle flash. The carbine can be stored with the safety *on* with a round in the chamber and 28 rounds in the magazine. A shotgun in 20- or 12-gauge with an 18-inch (457.2-millimeter) barrel may also be an option.

Store the carbine or shotgun with its muzzle down when not in use in a cabinet or safe approved for firearms. Muzzle down storage allows grabbing the carbine or shotgun with the muzzle indexed toward the ground. The homeowner not willing to exert the needed energy and money to get proper equipment and training should consider other means to feel safe in the home. This could mean purchasing a home security system with a panic alert and have a large barking dog. Moreover, the armed homeowner's lack of dedication to training and unsafe firearms handling would put family members at more risk than any criminal.[220]

SUMMARY

For personal protection use a quality pistol that is easy to operate and comfortable to shoot. Base the purchase or issuance of a pistol on the needs of an operation. Sights on a pistol need to be visible in any lighting condition. A 9x19mm or larger caliber is preferred for self-protection. Aim the shots in the high center mass area to stop a determined adversary. The head is a viable target and when penetrated with a bullet and has the greatest probability to stop an adversary immediately.[221] Continue shooting until an adversary no longer poses a deadly threat. *Shot placement* combined with *sufficient penetration* to disrupt the central nervous system (CNS) or cause *significant blood loss* (SBL) is the most important aspect of stopping an adversary. Agency wide deployment of pistols should be based on reliability, simplicity, ease of maintenance, and operator comfort. Special pistol models provide capabilities to fulfill specific needs resulting in safer and more efficient training. Not every person may feel comfortable using a pistol for home defense. Examine other considerations, such as a carbine, shotgun, alarm system, dog, etc.

DISCUSSION QUESTIONS

1. What is the difference between a semiautomatic and automatic pistol?
2. Discuss the difference between ambidextrous and reversible magazine catches.
3. What is a disadvantage of a grip safety that prevents the slide from being manually operated during a one-hand stoppage drill?
4. An operator may carry a carbine as a primary weapon, but a pistol is an important secondary weapon, why?
5. What are the four guidelines that assist in making a decision on what type of pistol to carry as a backup?
6. Discuss the advantages of marking law enforcement magazines with sequential numbers and the pistol's serial number.
7. Using a pistol, what is the most critical element to stop a human?
8. Discuss the belief that stopping a determined adversary immediately and reliably is only possible with a shot that disrupts the brain or upper spinal cord. How do you train to take advantage of this belief?
9. Describe the high center mass area and why shooting there is effective for stopping an adversary.
10. What percentage of police officers killed in the line of duty are shot in the head?
11. Discuss why the human factor and bullet placement with sufficient penetration has more to do with stopping an adversary than the caliber of the pistol used.
12. What does immediate incapacitation mean?
13. What is the closest thing to the one-shot stop?
14. Describe some agency wide considerations when selecting a pistol.
15. What danger exists for the operator when firing a compensated pistol from the retention position?
16. Discuss special model pistols and their uses.
17. What are reasons a person would chose a carbine or shotgun over a pistol for home defense?
18. What makes a homeowner with a firearm more dangerous than a criminal?

ENDNOTES

[1] International Association of Law Enforcement Firearms Instructors, *Standards & Practices Reference Guide for Law Enforcement Firearms Instructors*, (January 1995): 70.

[2] Glock Inc., *Instructions for Use Glock Safe Action Pistols All Models*, (Smyrna, GA: March 2011), 3.

[3] Items included in the author's law enforcement purchase of a Glock 17Gen4 on March 5, 2010.

[4] Glock Inc., *Armorer's Manual*, (Smyrna, GA: 2009): 7.

Glock Inc., *Instructions for Use Glock Safe Action Pistols All Models*, (Smyrna, GA: March 2011), 3.

[5] Gaston Glock, "Annual Message from the Founder," *Glock Autopistols 2010*, (New York, NY: Harris Publications Inc., 2009): 4.

[6] Glock Inc., *Glock Buyer's Guide Professional Edition*, (Smyrna, GA: Glock Inc., 2012): 25.

[7] Photograph courtesy of Glock Inc. See Glock Inc., *Glock Professional LE*, (Smyrna, GA: 2010): DVD PowerPoint Slide 6.

[8] Photograph courtesy of Glock Inc. See Glock Inc., *Glock Professional LE*, (Smyrna, GA: 2010): DVD PowerPoint Slide 6.

[9] Photograph courtesy of Glock Inc. See Glock Inc., *Glock Professional LE*, (Smyrna, GA: 2010): DVD PowerPoint Slide 6.

[10] Glock Inc., "Glock Advantage," *Handy Shape*, http://www.glock.com/english/pistols_adv10.htm (accessed September 22, 2012).

[11] Robert K. Taubert, *Rattenkrieg! The Art and Science of Close Quarters Battle Pistol* (North Reading, MA: Saber Press, 2012), 67.

[12] Glock Inc., *Armorer's Manual*, (Smyrna, GA: 2009): 85.

[13] Glock Inc., "Glock Gen4 Models Introduced," *The Glock Report 2010 Reference Edition*, (Smyrna, GA: Glock Inc., 2010): 1 and 4.

[14] Glock Inc., "Glock Gen4 Models Introduced," *The Glock Report 2010 Reference Edition*, (Smyrna, GA: Glock Inc., 2010): 1 and 4.

[15] Glock Inc., "Glock Gen4 Models Introduced," *The Glock Report 2010 Reference Edition*, (Smyrna, GA: Glock Inc., 2010): 1 and 4.

[16] Glock Inc., *Glock Buyer's Guide Professional Edition*, (Smyrna, GA: Glock Inc., 2012): 29.

[17] Glock Inc., "Gen4: The Next Generation Glock," *Glock Autopistols 2010*, (New York, NY: Harris Publications Inc., 2010): 81.

[18] Glock Inc., *Attachment Sheet Gen4 Armorer's Manual*, (Smyrna, GA: 2012): 1.

[19] Glock Inc., "Gen4 Next Generation of Perfection," (Smyrna, GA: 2010): 4.

[20] Glock Inc., *Attachment Sheet Gen4 Armorer's Manual*, (Smyrna, GA: 2012): 10.

[21] Glock Inc., "Gen4 Next Generation of Perfection," (Smyrna, GA: 2010): 4.

[22] Glock Inc., *Glock Buyer's Guide Professional Edition*, (Smyrna, GA: Glock Inc., 2012): 24.

[23] Glock Inc., *Armorer's Manual*, (Smyrna, GA: 2009): 90-93.

[24] Glock Inc., *Armorer's Manual U.S. Addendum*, (Smyrna, GA: 2012): 2.

[25] Glock Inc., *Armorer's Manual U.S. Addendum*, (Smyrna, GA: 2012): 2.

[26] Glock Inc., *Glock Buyer's Guide Professional Edition*, (Smyrna, GA: Glock Inc., 2012): 9.

[27] National Rifle Association, *NRA Basics of Personal Protection Outside the Home Course: Course Outline and Lesson Plans*, (Fairfax, VA: April 2009), 9.

[28] National Rifle Association, *NRA Basic Personal Protection in the Home Course: Course Outline and Lesson Plans*, (Fairfax, VA: May 2009), V-4 and V-6.

[29] National Rifle Association, *NRA Basic Personal Protection in the Home Course: Course Outline and Lesson Plans*, (Fairfax, VA: May 2009), V-4 and V-6.

[30] Chad A. Kaestle, and Jon H. Buehler, "Selecting a Duty-Issue Handgun," *FBI Law Enforcement Bulletin*, (January 2005): 6.

[31] Chad A. Kaestle, and Jon H. Buehler, "Selecting a Duty-Issue Handgun," *FBI Law Enforcement Bulletin*, (January 2005): 7.

[32] "Uniform officers were issued the full-size Glock 17 while plainclothes and undercover officers were issued the compact Glock 19." See Christian Shepherd, "Glock On Duty: Virginia Beach P.D.," *Glock Autopistols 2011*, (New York, NY: Harris Publications Inc., 2011): 28.

[33] Glock Inc., "Buyer's Guide," *Glock Autopistols 2012*, (New York, NY: Harris Publications Inc., 2012): 85.

[34] Glock Inc., "Buyer's Guide," *Glock Autopistols 2012*, (New York, NY: Harris Publications Inc., 2012): 85.

[35] Glock Inc., *Armorer's Manual U.S. Addendum*, (Smyrna, GA: 2012): 1.

[36] Glock Inc., *Glock Professional*, (Smyrna, GA: 2012): DVD PowerPoint Slide 41. Glock Inc., "Glock Technology Built Into Every Single Firearm," *Nitrite Treatment*, http://us.glock.com/products/technology (accessed September 22, 2012).

[37] Glock Inc., "Technology," *Engineering, Surface Treatment*, http://us.glock.com/technology (accessed September 22, 2012).

[38] Glock Inc., *Glock Buyer's Guide Professional Edition*, (Smyrna, GA: Glock Inc., 2012): 15.

[39] Glock Inc., *Glock Buyer's Guide Professional Edition*, (Smyrna, GA: Glock Inc., 2012): 16.

[40] Glock Inc., *Armorer's Manual*, (Smyrna, GA: 2009): 23.

[41] "In 2003, Glock introduced the Enhanced Bullet Identification System that has become known as the "Miami Barrel." See Thomas Fadul, "The Miami Barrel," *The Police Chief* (Alexandria, VA: September 2009): 56.

[42] Glock Inc., "Glock Storms the Beach," *Glock Autopistols 2010*, (New York, NY: Harris Publications Inc., 2010): 25.

[43] Robin Taylor, Bobby Carver, and Mark Passamaneck, *The Glock in Competition*, (Bellingham, WA: Taylor Press, 2010): 228-229.

[44] Glock Inc., *Attachment Sheet Gen4 Armorer's Manual*, (Smyrna, GA: 2012): 1.

[45] Glock Inc., "Recoil Spring Exchange Program," (2011), http://www.teamglock.com/customer-service/recoil-spring-exchange (accessed September 22, 2012).

[46] Glock Inc., *Glock Buyer's Guide Professional Edition*, (Smyrna, GA: Glock Inc., 2012): 23.

[47] AmeriGlo LLC, 5579B Chamblee Dunwoody Road, Suite 214 Atlanta, Georgia 30338 USA, Phone: 770-390-0554, Fax: 770-390-9781, www.AmeriGlo.com

Trijicon, Inc., 49385 Shafer Avenue, P. O. Box 930059, Wixom, Michigan 48393 USA, Toll-free: 800-338-0563, Phone: 248-960-7700, Fax: 248-960-7725, www.Trijicon.com

Truglo, Inc., 710 Presidential Drive, Richardson, TX 75081USA, Toll-free: 888-887-8456, Phone for Dealers: 972-774-0300, Fax: 972-774-0323, www.Truglo.com

XS Sight Systems Inc., 2401 Ludelle, Fort Worth, TX 76105 USA, Toll-free: 888-744-4880, Phone: 817-536-0136, Fax: 800-734-7939, www.XsSights.com

[48] Department of the Army, *Rifle Marksmanship M16-/M4-Series Weapons* (Washington, DC August 2008), C-3.

[49] Robert K. Taubert, *Rattenkrieg! The Art and Science of Close Quarters Battle Pistol* (North Reading, MA: Saber Press, 2012), 49.

[50] Jeff Gonzales, *Combative Fundamentals, an Unconventional Approach* (Cedar Park, TX: Trident Concepts, LLC, 2002), 47.

[51] *American Heritage Dictionary of the English Language Online*, 4th ed., s.v. "half-light," http://www.thefreedictionary.com/half-light (accessed September 22, 2012).

[52] Jeff Gonzales, *Combative Fundamentals, an Unconventional Approach* (Cedar Park, TX: Trident Concepts, LLC, 2002), 47.

[53] Jeff Gonzales, *Combative Fundamentals, an Unconventional Approach* (Cedar Park, TX: Trident Concepts, LLC, 2002), 48.

[54] Glock Inc., *Glock Buyer's Guide Professional Edition*, (Smyrna, GA: Glock Inc., 2012): 38.

[55] Glock Inc., *Glock Buyer's Guide Professional Edition*, (Smyrna, GA: Glock Inc., 2012): 39.

[56] Ed McGivern, *Ed McGivern's Book of Fast and Fancy Revolver Shooting* (New York, NY: Skyhorse Publishing, Inc., 2007): 83.

[57] Phil Singleton, *3 Day Tactical Pistol for Hostage Rescue, High Risk Warrant and Drugs Raids,* (Warrenton, VA: Singleton International): 12.

[58] Glock Inc., *Glock Buyer's Guide Professional Edition*, (Smyrna, GA: Glock Inc., 2012): 38.

[59] Glock Inc., *Glock Buyer's Guide Professional Edition*, (Smyrna, GA: Glock Inc., 2012): 22.

[60] Glock Inc., *Armorer's Manual*, (Smyrna, GA: 2009): 69-74.

[61] Glock Inc., *Armorer's Manual*, (Smyrna, GA: 2009): 70.

MGW, Precision Inc., *Instructions for MGW Rear Sight Installation and Adjustment Tool*, (Augusta, GA), 1.

[62] Glock Inc., *Armorer's Manual*, (Smyrna, GA: 2009): 38.

[63] Jeff Gonzales, *Combative Fundamentals, an Unconventional Approach* (Cedar Park, TX: Trident Concepts, LLC, 2002), 47-48.

[64] Glock Inc., *Armorer's Manual*, (Smyrna, GA: 2009): 72.

[65] "Loctite® Threadlocker Blue 242® is designed for the locking and sealing of threaded fasteners which require normal disassembly with standard hand tools. The product cures when confined in the absence of air between close fitting metal surfaces. It protects threads from rust and corrosion and prevents loosening from shock and vibration. Loctite® Threadlocker Blue 242® is particularly suited for applications on less active substrates such as stainless steel and plated surfaces, where disassembly is required for servicing." See Loctite Brand, "Products," *Loctite Threadlocker Blue 242*, (2012), http://www.loctiteproducts.com/p/t_lkr_blue/overview/Loctite-Threadlocker-Blue-242.htm (accessed September 22, 2012).

[66] Glock Inc., *Armorer's Manual*, (Smyrna, GA: 2009): 74.

[67] "Use only a very small drop of Loctite on the end of the threads of the screw for the front blade. The amount of Loctite should not be more than will fill the threads. It is important that no excess Loctite remain on the end of the screw. Excess Loctite in the hole could cause a force to be placed on the capsule inside which could break it. Hand tighten the screw securely into the threaded front sight." See Trijicon, Inc., *Installation Instructions for Glock Pistols* (Wixom, MI: April 2008).

[68] "Loctite® Threadlocker Red 271™ is designed for the permanent locking and sealing of threaded fasteners. The product cures when confined in the absence of air between close fitting metal surfaces. It protects threads from rust and corrosion and

prevents loosening from shock and vibration. It is only removable once cured by heating up parts to 500°F (260°C)." See Loctite Brand, "Products," *Loctite Threadlocker   Red   271,   (2010),* http://www.loctiteproducts.com/p/10/15/t_lkr_red/overview/Loctite-Threadlocker-Red-271.htm (accessed September 22, 2012).

[69] Glock Inc., *Armorer's Manual*, (Smyrna, GA: 2009): 74.

[70] MGW Precision Inc., *MGW Rear Sight Installation and Adjustment Tool*, http://www.mgwltd.com (accessed September 22, 2012).

[71] MGW, Precision Inc., *Instructions for MGW Rear Sight Installation and Adjustment Tool*, (Augusta, GA), 1.

[72] MGW, Precision Inc., *Instructions for MGW Rear Sight Installation and Adjustment Tool*, (Augusta, GA), 1

[73] MGW, Precision Inc., *Instructions for MGW Rear Sight Installation and Adjustment Tool*, (Augusta, GA), 1

[74] MGW, Precision Inc., *Instructions for MGW Rear Sight Installation and Adjustment Tool*, (Augusta, GA), 1.

[75] Grip: "The portion of a firearm designed to be grasped by the shooting hand in normal operation. In handguns: the handle for holding the weapon in the shooting hand [firing hand]; also, a panel or covering attached to or enveloping the grip frame." See International Association of Law Enforcement Firearms Instructors, *Standards & Practices Reference Guide for Law Enforcement Firearms Instructors*, (January 1995): 50.

[76]   Glock   Inc.,   "Glock   Advantage,"   *Handy   Shape*, http://www.glock.com/english/pistols_adv10.htm (accessed September 22, 2012).

[77] Dennis Adler, "The New Glocks," *Glock Autopistols 2011*, (New York, NY: Harris Publications Inc., 2011): 8.

[78] Glock Inc., *Glock Buyer's Guide Professional Edition*, (Smyrna, GA: Glock Inc., 2012): 29.

[79] Dennis Adler, "Tweaking Perfection Glock's G22 RTF2," *Glock Autopistols 2010*, (New York, NY: Harris Publications Inc., 2010): 13.

[80]   TractionGrips,   "Store   Page: Buy   Here,   *Tractiongrips*, http://www.tractiongrips.com/id47.html (accessed September 22, 2012).

[81]   Hogue   Inc.,   "Products,"   *HandAll   Universal   Grip*, http://www.getgrip.com/main/overview/handall.html (accessed September 22, 2012).

[82] Pearce Grip Inc., "Products," *Glock Model 26 Shown with PG-26 Installed*, http://www.pearcegrip.com/Products/GLOCK/PG-26 (accessed September 22, 2012).

[83] Glock Inc., *Glock Buyer's Guide Professional Edition*, (Smyrna, GA: Glock Inc., 2012): 54.

[84] International Association of Law Enforcement Firearms Instructors, *Standards & Practices Reference Guide for Law Enforcement Firearms Instructors*, (January 1995): 42.

[85] International Association of Law Enforcement Firearms Instructors, *Standards & Practices Reference Guide for Law Enforcement Firearms Instructors*, (January 1995): 85.

[86] Chad A. Kaestle, and Jon H. Buehler, "Selecting a Duty-Issue Handgun," *FBI Law Enforcement Bulletin*, (January 2005): 2.

[87] Glock Inc., *Armorer's Manual*, (Smyrna, GA: 2002): 4.

[88] Glock Inc., *Armorer's Manual*, (Smyrna, GA: 2002): 10.

[89] Glock Inc., *Armorer's Manual*, (Smyrna, GA: 2002): 4.

[90] Glock Inc., *Armorer's Manual*, (Smyrna, GA: 2002): 4.

[91] Glock Inc., *Glock Buyer's Guide Professional Edition*, (Smyrna, GA: Glock Inc., 2012): 9.

[92] Glock Inc., *Armorer's Manual*, (Smyrna, GA: 2009): 44.

[93] Glock Inc., *Armorer's Manual U.S. Addendum*, (Smyrna, GA: 2012): 9.

[94] Glock Inc., *Armorer's Manual U.S. Addendum*, (Smyrna, GA: 2012): 9.

[95] Glock Inc., *Armorer's Manual*, (Smyrna, GA: 2009): 44.

[96] Glock Inc., *Armorer's Manual*, (Smyrna, GA: 2009): 44.

[97] Kyle E. Lamb, *Green Eyes and Black Rifles*, (Trample and Hurdle Publishers, 2008), 25.

[98] U.S. Department of Justice, Federal Bureau of Investigation, Firearms Training Unit, *Weapons Workshop* (Quantico, VA, May 16-19, 1988), 6.

[99] Glock Inc., *Instructions for Use Glock Safe Action Pistols All Models*, (Smyrna, GA: March 2011), 21.

[100] Glock Inc., *Instructions for Use Glock Safe Action Pistols All Models*, (Smyrna, GA: March 2011), 21.

[101] Glock Inc., *Glock Buyer's Guide Professional Edition*, (Smyrna, GA: Glock Inc., 2012): 13.

[102] Jeff Gonzales, *Combative Fundamentals, an Unconventional Approach* (Cedar Park, TX: Trident Concepts, LLC, 2002), 34.

[103] National Rifle Association, *Law Enforcement Handgun Instructor Manual* (Fairfax, VA: Handgun Training Tips, Edition 4.1, 2006), 2.

Chad A. Kaestle, and Jon H. Buehler, "Selecting a Duty-Issue Handgun," *FBI Law Enforcement Bulletin*, (January 2005): 5.

[104] National Rifle Association, *Law Enforcement Handgun Instructor Manual* (Fairfax, VA: Handgun Training Tips, Edition 4.1, 2006), 2.

[105] Kyle E. Lamb, *Stay in the Fight*, (Trample and Hurdle Publishers, 2011), 24-25.

[106] J. Henry FitzGerald, *Shooting* (Boulder, CO: Paladin Press, 2007), 353. Originally published in 1930 by J. Henry FitzGerald.

[107] National Rifle Association, *Law Enforcement Handgun Instructor Manual* (Fairfax, VA: Handgun Training Tips, Edition 4.1, 2006), 2-3.

[108] "In the Overhand method, the Support Hand's four finger wrap over the top of the slide with the ejection port facing away from the body." See National Rifle Association, *Law Enforcement Handgun Instructor Manual* (Fairfax, VA: Handgun Handling Techniques, Edition 6.1, 2006), 16.

[109] National Rifle Association, *Law Enforcement Handgun Instructor Manual* (Fairfax, VA: Handgun Training Tips, Edition 4.1, 2006), 3.

[110] National Rifle Association, *Law Enforcement Handgun Instructor Manual* (Fairfax, VA: Handgun Training Tips, Edition 4.1, 2006), 6.

[111] Glock Inc., *Glock Buyer's Guide Professional Edition*, (Smyrna, GA: Glock Inc., 2012): 13.

[112] The Universal Cover Mode (UCM): "…Muzzle below center mass, at a ready position where the suspect's hands are clearly visible; finger securely registered outside the trigger guard, until you are on target and have made the decision to shoot." See International Association of Law Enforcement Firearms Instructors, *Standards & Practices Reference Guide for Law Enforcement Firearms Instructors*, (January 1995): 310.

[113] Chad A. Kaestle, and Jon H. Buehler, "Selecting a Duty-Issue Handgun," *FBI Law Enforcement Bulletin*, (January 2005): 2.

Glock Inc., *Glock Buyer's Guide Professional Edition*, (Smyrna, GA: Glock Inc., 2012): 13.

[114] Charles Remsberg, *Blood Lessons* (San Francisco, CA: Calibre Press, 2008), 132.

[115] Jeff Gonzales, Combative Fundamentals, an Unconventional Approach (Cedar Park, TX: Trident Concepts, LLC, 2002), 250-252.

[116] Glock Inc., *Armorer's Manual*, (Smyrna, GA: 2009): 59.

[117] Glock Inc., "Buyer's Guide," *Glock Autopistols 2012*, (New York, NY: Harris Publications Inc., 2012): 84.

[118] Eugene Sockut, *Secrets of Street Survival Israeli Style* (Boulder, CO: Paladin Press, 1995), 168.

[119] Magazine Well: "The opening in a firearm's frame or receiver which receives a detachable magazine." See International Association of Law Enforcement Firearms

Instructors, *Standards & Practices Reference Guide for Law Enforcement Firearms Instructors*, (January 1995): 63.

[120] Glock Inc., *Instructions for Use Glock Safe Action Pistols All Models*, (Smyrna, GA: March 2011), 23.

[121] Glock Inc., *Armorer's Manual U.S. Addendum*, (Smyrna, GA: 2012): 10.

[122] Glock Inc., *Armorer's Manual*, (Smyrna, GA: 2009): 62.

[123] Glock part number SP 02551; Magazine Spring, G17, G18, G34, 19-round magazines only (17-round magazine with SP 07151 floor plates and SP 07165 insert). See Glock Inc., *Armorer's Manual U.S. Addendum*, (Smyrna, GA: 2012): 11.

[124] International Association of Law Enforcement Firearms Instructors, *Standards & Practices Reference Guide for Law Enforcement Firearms Instructors*, (January 1995): 178.

[125] International Association of Law Enforcement Firearms Instructors, *Standards & Practices Reference Guide for Law Enforcement Firearms Instructors*, (January 1995): 162.

[126] International Association of Law Enforcement Firearms Instructors, *Standards & Practices Reference Guide for Law Enforcement Firearms Instructors*, (January 1995): 157.

[127] Stopping Power: "Roughly speaking, for practical purposes, stopping power is the ability of a specific ammunition (or, more precisely, a specific ammunition-firearm combination) to incapacitate a person or animal or to stop some action by a person or animal quickly, when that person has been shot with that ammunition (or ammunition-firearm combination)." See International Association of Law Enforcement Firearms Instructors, *Standards & Practices Reference Guide for Law Enforcement Firearms Instructors*, (January 1995): 199.

[128] Chad A. Kaestle, and Jon H. Buehler, "Selecting a Duty-Issue Handgun," *FBI Law Enforcement Bulletin*, (January 2005): 3.

[129] Anthony J. Pinizzotto, Ph.D., Harry A. Kern, M.Ed., and Edward F. Davis, M.S., "One-Shot Drops," *FBI Law Enforcement Bulletin*, (October 2004): 15.

[130] U.S. Department of Justice, Federal Bureau of Investigation, Firearms Training Unit, *FBI Academy, Handgun Wounding Factors and Effectiveness* (Quantico, VA, July 14, 1989), 9.

Itay Gil and Dan Baron, *The Citizen's Guide to Stopping Suicide Attackers* (Boulder, CO: Paladin Press, 2004), 72.

[131] Anthony J. Pinizzotto, Ph.D., Harry A. Kern, M.Ed., and Edward F. Davis, M.S., "One-Shot Drops," *FBI Law Enforcement Bulletin*, (October 2004): 16.

[132] In the Line of Duty, "Homicide Suspect Suicide," *Volume 4 Program 2 Video*.

Ronald J. Adams, Thomas M. McTernan, and Charles Remsberg, *Street Survival*, (Northbrook, IL: Calibre Press, 1980), 209.

[133] U.S. Department of Justice, Federal Bureau of Investigation, Firearms Training Unit, *FBI Academy, Handgun Wounding Factors and Effectiveness* (Quantico, VA, July 14, 1989), 9.

[134] U.S. Department of Justice, Federal Bureau of Investigation, Firearms Training Unit, *FBI Academy, Handgun Wounding Factors and Effectiveness* (Quantico, VA, July 14, 1989), 5.

[135] U.S. Department of Justice, Federal Bureau of Investigation, Firearms Training Unit, *FBI Academy, Handgun Wounding Factors and Effectiveness* (Quantico, VA, July 14, 1989), 7.

[136] U.S. Department of Justice, Federal Bureau of Investigation, Firearms Training Unit, *FBI Academy, Handgun Wounding Factors and Effectiveness* (Quantico, VA, July 14, 1989), 16.

[137] Hollow Point: "Also: hollowpoint. A projectile with an open cavity in its point; intended to aid expansion on impact, especially in animal tissue." See International Association of Law Enforcement Firearms Instructors, *Standards & Practices Reference Guide for Law Enforcement Firearms Instructors*, (January 1995): 167.

[138] Anthony J. Pinizzotto, Ph.D., Edward F. Davis, M.A., Shannon Bohrer, M.B.A., and Robert Cheney "Law Enforcement Perspective on the Use of Force," *FBI Law Enforcement Bulletin*, (April 2009): 18.

[139] U.S. Department of Justice, Federal Bureau of Investigation, Firearms Training Unit, *Wound Ballistic Workshop "9mm vs. .45 auto"* (Quantico, VA, September 15-17, 1987), 24.

[140] U.S. Department of Justice, Federal Bureau of Investigation, Firearms Training Unit, *FBI Academy, Handgun Wounding Factors and Effectiveness* (Quantico, VA, July 14, 1989), 12.

[141] "Five shots struck home, but the attacker's extraordinary fat just sucked them up before they could penetrate to vital organs." See Charles Remsberg, *Tactics for Criminal Patrol* (Northbrook, IL: Calibre Press, 1995), 239-240.

In the Line of Duty, "Trooper Coates Shooting," *Volume 1 Program 4*: DVD.

"This was the above cited "non-survivable" wound inflicted on Platt. Over the course of the next several minutes, Platt continued to move and fight, killing Special Agents Grogan and Dove over three minutes later. By the end of the shoot-out, Platt had lost essentially half his blood volume from this and other wounds. The bullet performed exactly as it was designed to do—expand violently and penetrate no more than 6-7 inches. It was a failure." See Urey W. Patrick, and John C. Hall, *In Defense of Self and Others* (Durham, NC: Carolina Academic Press, 2010), 96.

"Penetration less than 12 inches is too little, and, in the words of two of the participants in the 1987 FBI Wound Ballistics Workshop, "too little penetration will get you killed." See Urey W. Patrick, and John C. Hall, *In Defense of Self and Others* (Durham, NC: Carolina Academic Press, 2010), 95.

[142] Full Metal Jacket: "Also: full jacketed bullet, full metal case bullet, full patch bullet. A projectile in which the bullet jacket encloses the core, usually with the exception of the base." See International Association of Law Enforcement Firearms Instructors, *Standards & Practices Reference Guide for Law Enforcement Firearms Instructors*, (January 1995): 151.

[143] U.S. Department of Justice, Federal Bureau of Investigation, Firearms Training Unit, *Wound Ballistic Workshop "9mm vs. .45 auto"* (Quantico, VA, September 15-17, 1987), 2.

[144] Total Metal Jacket: "A bullet on which a metal jacket encloses the whole bullet (the nose, the core, and the base), as opposed to a full metal jacket bullet which does not envelope the base. Totally jacketed bullets are useful components of so-called "lead free" ammunition, which is designed to minimize direct exposure to, and accumulation of, lead contamination on shooting ranges." See International Association of Law Enforcement Firearms Instructors, *Standards & Practices Reference Guide for Law Enforcement Firearms Instructors*, (January 1995): 155.

[145] "The Contracting Parties agree to abstain from the use of bullets which expand or flatten easily in the human body, such as bullets with a hard envelope which does not entirely cover the core or is pierced with incisions." Declaration (IV, 3) concerning Expanding Bullets. The Hague, 29 July 1899.

Expanding Bullet: "...the Hague Convention of 1899 (not the Geneva Convention of 1925, as commonly thought, which largely dealt with gas warfare) prohibited future use of such bullets in warfare." See International Association of Law Enforcement Firearms Instructors, *Standards & Practices Reference Guide for Law Enforcement Firearms Instructors*, (January 1995): 150-151.

[146] Glock Inc., *Glock Professional*, (Smyrna, GA: 2012): DVD PowerPoint Slide 18.

[147] Federal Premium, "Resources," *Technical Bulletins, EFMJ Brochure*, http://le.atk.com/downloads/technical_bulletins/EFMJBrochure.pdf   (accessed September 22, 2012).

[148] Federal Premium, "Resources," *Technical Bulletins, EFMJ Brochure*, http://le.atk.com/downloads/technical_bulletins/EFMJBrochure.pdf   (accessed September 22, 2012).

[149] Anthony J. Pinizzotto, Ph.D., Harry A. Kern, M.Ed., and Edward F. Davis, M.S., "One-Shot Drops," *FBI Law Enforcement Bulletin*, (October 2004): 16.

[150] Special Agent John "Jay" Balchunas was shot once by an adversary with a 9mm pistol. "The slug tore through his liver, exited his back, and caught into his clothing." Agent Balchunas died a week later from his injuries. See Charles Remsberg, *Blood Lessons* (San Francisco, CA: Calibre Press, 2008), 119-120.

[151] Ronald J. Adams, Thomas M. McTernan, and Charles Remsberg, *Street Survival*, (Northbrook, IL: Calibre Press, 1980), 215.

[152] Trooper Mark Coates a professional law enforcement officer that was murdered while protecting and serving the citizens of the South Carolina. See In the Line of Duty, "Trooper Coates Shooting," *Volume 1 Program 4 Duty Sheet and Lesson Plan.*

Trooper Coates fired a .357 Magnum 145-grain Winchester Silvertip cartridge from his .357 Magnum revolver, according to a representative of the South Carolina State Police. Interview with representative of the South Carolina State Police, February 2009.

[153] W.E. Fairbairn and E.A. Sykes, *Shooting to Live* (Boulder, CO: Paladin Press, 1987), 74-75. Originally published in 1942 by W.E. Fairbairn and E.A. Sykes.

[154] U.S. Department of Justice, Federal Bureau of Investigation, Firearms Training Unit, *Wound Ballistic Workshop "9mm vs. .45 auto"* (Quantico, VA, September 15-17, 1987), 5.

[155] U.S. Department of Justice, Federal Bureau of Investigation, Firearms Training Unit, *Wound Ballistic Workshop "9mm vs. .45 auto"* (Quantico, VA, September 15-17, 1987), 5.

[156] U.S. Department of Justice, Federal Bureau of Investigation, Firearms Training Unit, *FBI Academy, Handgun Wounding Factors and Effectiveness* (Quantico, VA, July 14, 1989),3-10.

[157] U.S. Department of Justice, Federal Bureau of Investigation, Firearms Training Unit, *FBI Academy, Handgun Wounding Factors and Effectiveness* (Quantico, VA, July 14, 1989), 8.

[158] U.S. Department of Justice, Federal Bureau of Investigation, Firearms Training Unit, *Wound Ballistic Workshop "9mm vs. .45 auto"* (Quantico, VA, September 15-17, 1987), 2.

[159] Paul Howe, *Make Ready with Paul Howe: Advanced Tac Pistol/Rifle Operator* (Columbia, SC: Panteao Productions, 2010): Vehicle as Cover, DVD.

[160] ATK, "Gold Dot Duty Ammunition," *Law Enforcement Ammunition 2012 Catalog*, 2012, 4.

[161] Burst: "2. A metaphorical term for a string of shots fired in rapid succession from a single firearm (as in "He let fly a withering burst of shots from his revolver") as distinct from a volley of shots fired in rapid succession from a number of weapons." See International Association of Law Enforcement Firearms Instructors, *Standards &*

Practices Reference Guide for Law Enforcement Firearms Instructors, (January 1995): 32.

[162] U.S. Department of Justice, Federal Bureau of Investigation, Firearms Training Unit, *FBI Academy, Handgun Wounding Factors and Effectiveness* (Quantico, VA, July 14, 1989), 8.

[163] North Carolina Justice Academy, "SWAT Operator," *Firearms Use in Tactical Operations* (Salemburg, NC: January 2008): 9.

[164] U.S. Department of Justice, Federal Bureau of Investigation, Firearms Training Unit, *FBI Academy, Handgun Wounding Factors and Effectiveness* (Quantico, VA, July 14, 1989), 2.

[165] U.S. Department of Justice, Federal Bureau of Investigation, Firearms Training Unit, *FBI Academy, Handgun Wounding Factors and Effectiveness* (Quantico, VA, July 14, 1989), 8.

[166] Charles Remsberg, *Tactics for Criminal Patrol* (Northbrook, IL: Calibre Press, 1995), 239-240.

Trooper Coates fired a .357 Magnum 145-grain Winchester Silvertip cartridge from his .357 Magnum revolver, according to a representative of the South Carolina State Police. Interview with representative of the South Carolina State Police, February 2009.

[167] National Rifle Association, *Law Enforcement Handgun Instructor Manual* (Fairfax, VA: Section C, The Fundamentals of Handgun Marksmanship , Edition 6.1, 2006), 12.

After Trooper Mark Coates' murder, the South Carolina Highway Patrol began teaching to shoot the upper torso and head. See In the Line of Duty, "Trooper Coates Shooting," *Volume 1 Program 4 Duty Sheet and Lesson Plan.*

[168] Jeff Gonzales, *Combative Fundamentals, an Unconventional Approach* (Cedar Park, TX: Trident Concepts, LLC, 2002), 45.

[169] U.S. Department of Justice, Federal Bureau of Investigation, Firearms Training Unit, *Wound Ballistic Workshop "9mm vs. .45 auto"* (Quantico, VA, September 15-17, 1987), 3.

[170] Itay Gil and Dan Baron, *The Citizen's Guide to Stopping Suicide Attackers* (Boulder, CO: Paladin Press, 2004), 52.

[171] While training in Israel the author was taught the combat doctrine of using a pistol to shoot the terrorist in the head during close quarters combat. Timothy D. Blakeley, "Personal notes from the Antiterrorism Combat Shooting session," *Antiterrorism Combat Course*, (Tel Aviv, Israel: 2008): 7.

Itay Gil, author of Citizen's Guide to Stopping Suicide Attackers, also confirmed the Israeli combat doctrine of shooting terrorists in the head, by telephone with author, March 9, 2010.

[172] J. Henry FitzGerald, *Shooting* (Boulder, CO: Paladin Press, 2007), 364. Originally published in 1930 by J. Henry FitzGerald.

[173] National Rifle Association, *Law Enforcement Handgun Instructor Manual* (Fairfax, VA: Section C, The Fundamentals of Handgun Marksmanship , Edition 6.1, 2006), 12.

[174] J. Henry FitzGerald, *Shooting* (Boulder, CO: Paladin Press, 2007), 318. Originally published in 1930 by J. Henry FitzGerald.

[175] Urey W. Patrick, and John C. Hall, *In Defense of Self and Others* (Durham, NC: Carolina Academic Press, 2010), 159.

[176] Robert K. Taubert, *Rattenkrieg! The Art and Science of Close Quarters Battle Pistol* (North Reading, MA: Saber Press, 2012), 130.

[177] Federal Bureau of Investigation, "Law Enforcement Officers Killed and Assaulted," (Clarksburg, WV: *Table 38 - Location of Fatal Firearm Wound, and Number of Victim Officers Wearing Body Armor*, 2001–2010), http://www.fbi.gov/about-us/cjis/ucr/leoka/leoka-2010/tables/table38-leok-feloniously-location-wound-wearing-bodyarmor-01-10.xls (accessed September 22, 2012).

[178] U.S. Department of Justice, *Violent Encounters*, 2006, (Washington, DC: FBI, 2006), 104-105.

[179] In the Line of Duty, "DeKalb County (TN) Deputy Shooting," *Volume 9 Program 1*: Video Recording.

[180] Itay Gil and Dan Baron, *The Citizen's Guide to Stopping Suicide Attackers* (Boulder, CO: Paladin Press, 2004), 52.

[181] U.S. Department of Justice, Federal Bureau of Investigation, Firearms Training Unit, *FBI Academy, Handgun Wounding Factors and Effectiveness* (Quantico, VA, July 14, 1989), 8.

The International Association of Chiefs of Police, Training Key #582, *Suicide (Homicide) Bombers: Part II* (Alexandria, VA, 2005) 2.

Itay Gil and Dan Baron, *The Citizen's Guide to Stopping Suicide Attackers* (Boulder, CO: Paladin Press, 2004), 52.

[182] Phil Singleton, *3 Day Tactical Pistol for Hostage Rescue, High Risk Warrant and Drugs Raids,* (Warrenton, VA: Singleton International): 46.

[183] U.S. Department of Justice, Federal Bureau of Investigation, Firearms Training Unit, *FBI Academy, Handgun Wounding Factors and Effectiveness* (Quantico, VA, July 14, 1989), 2.

[184] Federal Bureau of Investigation, "Law Enforcement Officers Killed and Assaulted," (Clarksburg, WV: *Summaries of Officer Felonious Killed – North Carolina,* 2007), http://www.fbi.gov/about-us/cjis/ucr/leoka/2007 (accessed September 22, 2012).

[185] Department of the Army, *Combat Training with Pistols, M9 and M11* (Washington, DC June 2003), 2-15.

[186] Anthony J. Pinizzotto, Ph.D., Harry A. Kern, M.Ed., and Edward F. Davis, M.S., "One-Shot Drops," *FBI Law Enforcement Bulletin*, (October 2004): 14-21.

Federal Bureau of Investigation, "FBI Ammunition Testing," *National Firearms Program Unit Ballistic Research Facility*, (revised December 3, 2002).

U.S. Department of Justice, Federal Bureau of Investigation, Firearms Training Unit, *Wound Ballistic Workshop "9mm vs. .45 auto"* (Quantico, VA, September 15-17, 1987), 1-21.

[187] Chad A. Kaestle, and Jon H. Buehler, "Selecting a Duty-Issue Handgun," *FBI Law Enforcement Bulletin*, (January 2005): 7.

[188] U.S. Department of Justice, Federal Bureau of Investigation, Firearms Training Unit, *Wound Ballistic Workshop "9mm vs. .45 auto"* (Quantico, VA, September 15-17, 1987), 22-25.

[189] Anthony J. Pinizzotto, Ph.D., Harry A. Kern, M.Ed., and Edward F. Davis, M.S., "One-Shot Drops: Surviving the Myths," *FBI Law Enforcement Bulletin*, (October 2004): 21.

[190] This is only one example and there are many other manufacturers that design and produce similar quality ammunition. Speer bonded pistol ammunition: 53617 124gr. (9mm +P), 53962 180gr. (.40 S&W) and 53966 230gr. (.45 Auto). See ATK, "Wound Ballistics Workshop," *Host Agency: Ft. Collins Police Department*, June 26, 2008, 7 (marked as 1 of 3).

[191] U.S. Department of Justice, Federal Bureau of Investigation, Firearms Training Unit, *Wound Ballistic Workshop "9mm vs. .45 auto"* (Quantico, VA, September 15-17, 1987), 24.

[192] U.S. Department of Justice, Federal Bureau of Investigation, Firearms Training Unit, *Wound Ballistic Workshop "9mm vs. .45 auto"* (Quantico, VA, September 15-17, 1987), 22.

[193] Anthony J. Pinizzotto, Ph.D., Harry A. Kern, M.Ed., and Edward F. Davis, M.S., "One-Shot Drops," *FBI Law Enforcement Bulletin*, (October 2004): 16.

U.S. Department of Justice, Federal Bureau of Investigation, Firearms Training Unit, *Wound Ballistic Workshop "9mm vs. .45 auto"* (Quantico, VA, September 15-17, 1987), 22.

[194] Glock Inc., *Glock Professional LE*, (Smyrna, GA: 2010): DVD PowerPoint Slide 31.

[195] Glock Inc., *Glock Buyer's Guide Professional Edition*, (Smyrna, GA: Glock Inc., 2012): 35.

[196] Glock Inc., *Glock Buyer's Guide Professional Edition*, (Smyrna, GA: Glock Inc., 2012): 35.

[197] Glock Inc., *Armorer's Manual*, (Smyrna, GA: 2009): 75.

[198] Glock Inc., *Glock Buyer's Guide Professional Edition*, (Smyrna, GA: Glock Inc., 2012): 30.

[199] When the Florida Highway Patrol purchased Glock pistols, the organization also purchased practice pistols for issuing to academy recruits. See Massad Ayoob, "FL Troopers Shoot the G.A.P.," *Glock Autopistols 2011*, (New York, NY: Harris Publications Inc., 2011): 25.

[200] Alan Ramsey, Director of Training for Glock provided the information during the Advance Armorer's course held at Glock Inc., in Smyrna, Georgia, in a face-to-face conversation with the author, January 26-27, 2010.

[201] National Rifle Association, *NRA Basics of Personal Protection Outside the Home Course: Course Outline and Lesson Plans*, (Fairfax, VA: April 2009), 9.

[202] International Association of Law Enforcement Firearms Instructors, *Firearms Training Standards for Law Enforcement Personnel*, (2004): 14.10.

[203] Glock Inc., *Glock Buyer's Guide Professional Edition*, (Smyrna, GA: Glock Inc., 2012): 32.

[204] Glock Inc., *Armorer's Manual*, (Smyrna, GA: 2009): 12.

[205] Glock Inc., Glock *Pistol Transitional Instructor Workshop Course Outline*, (Smyrna, GA: 2012): 12.

[206] Glock Inc., *Glock Buyer's Guide Professional Edition*, (Smyrna, GA: Glock Inc., 2012): 32.

[207] Glock Inc., *Glock Buyer's Guide Professional Edition*, (Smyrna, GA: Glock Inc., 2012): 32.

[208] Glock Inc., *Glock Buyer's Guide Professional Edition*, (Smyrna, GA: Glock Inc., 2012): 30.

[209] Glock Inc., "Buyer's Guide," *Glock Autopistols 2012*, (New York, NY: Harris Publications Inc., 2012): 103.

[210] Glock Inc., *Glock Buyer's Guide Professional Edition*, (Smyrna, GA: Glock Inc., 2012): 30.

[211] Glock Inc., *Glock Buyer's Guide Professional Edition*, (Smyrna, GA: Glock Inc., 2012): 31.

[212] Glock Inc., "Buyer's Guide," *Glock Autopistols 2012*, (New York, NY: Harris Publications Inc., 2012): 103.

[213] Breech Face: "That part of the breechblock or breech bolt which is against the head of the cartridge case or shotshell during firing." See International Association of Law Enforcement Firearms Instructors, *Standards & Practices Reference Guide for Law Enforcement Firearms Instructors*, (January 1995): 30.

[214] Floor Plate: "The base or bottom of a magazine, which may be either detachable or non-detachable." See International Association of Law Enforcement Firearms Instructors, *Standards & Practices Reference Guide for Law Enforcement Firearms Instructors*, (January 1995): 44.
Glock Inc., *Armorer's Manual*, (Smyrna, GA: 2009): 62.

[215] Glock Inc., "Buyer's Guide," *Glock Autopistols 2012*, (New York, NY: Harris Publications Inc., 2012): 103.

[216] Glock Inc., *Glock Buyer's Guide Professional Edition*, (Smyrna, GA: Glock Inc., 2012): 31.

[217] Glock Inc., *Glock Buyer's Guide Professional Edition*, (Smyrna, GA: Glock Inc., 2012): 31.

[218] Glock Inc., *Armorer's Manual*, (Smyrna, GA: 2009): 62.

[219] Glock Inc., *Glock Buyer's Guide Professional Edition*, (Smyrna, GA: Glock Inc., 2012): 31.

[220] J. Henry FitzGerald, *Shooting* (Boulder, CO: Paladin Press, 2007), 407. Originally published in 1930 by J. Henry FitzGerald.

[221] Department of the Army, *Rifle Marksmanship M16-/M4-Series Weapons* (Washington, DC August 2008), 7-46.

SAFETY

4

Anyone contemplating owning or using a firearm needs to accept firearms are inherently *dangerous* devices[1] and viewed as such by the courts.[2] A bullet from the muzzle of a pistol can travel up to 1.5 miles[3] (2.4 kilometers) and can be coined a *liability*. Working with this realization and getting proper training can lessen the danger and liability. Even with the risks—each year while training—civilians, police officers, and military operators fire thousands of rounds safely. Since 1904, the accidental gun death rate has declined by 94 percent.[4] The decline occurred amid an estimated 45 percent of American households keeping one or more firearms.[5] However, if a person does not know how to use a pistol they should do themselves, their family, and the police a favor and leave it locked up until acquiring proper training.

DANGER: Nobody has ever been shot with an *unloaded* firearm, but many have been shot with a firearm *thought* to be unloaded.

For a pistol to discharge and a person get injured or killed, there are five factors that must occur: (1) the pistol loaded, (2) the pistol handled, (3) the pistol functional, (4) the pistol pointed at a person, and (5) the pistol fired.[6] The person handling the firearm has a moral responsibility of realizing the importance of proper training to prevent a tragedy. Training is especially important for pistols. The pistol's compact size makes it susceptible to pointing in an inappropriate direction. The mistake can happen easily when a person or event draws the operator's attention. The operator turns to speak to the person or looks at what just occurred and inadvertently points the muzzle in an inappropriate direction. Keeping the pistol in its holster when not in use will alleviate much of the issue.[7] After a firearm related tragedy occurs, it provides little comfort to say what needed to be done.

The prevention of a firearm related tragedy is in direct proportion to the operator's adherence to instructions. While training a group of police officers, the author gave the command, "Unload and show clear." One of the officers pulled the trigger—bang! The first words the police officer said, "I thought it was unloaded." The police officer violated the rule that firearms are considered loaded until *proven* empty. The police officer had *not* proven her pistol empty. The police officer only *thought* the pistol was empty. Fortunately, the police officer had adhered to the rule of keeping the muzzle pointed in the appropriate direction—the backstop. The inappropriate handling of a firearm can end an operator's career, but even worse can end the life of an innocent person.

Every operator and trainer should read the International Association of Law Enforcement Firearms Instructors (IALEFI) publication titled, "IALEFI Guidelines for Simulation Training Safety" paying particular attention to the section called, "Background – Compendium of Training Accidents."[8] This section is a reality check for any *operator, trainer, supervisor,* or *administrator* on the dangers of firearms in a training environment. Below is 1 of 25 examples listed in the IALEFI publication:

"(15) December 25, 1993: An Orange County, California sheriff's deputy was accidentally shot to death during a traffic stop training exercise. The county afterwards settled a lawsuit by the deputy's widow for $5 million."

NOTE: A so-called *friendly fire* or a *self-inflicted* gunshot wound causes the same injury or death as when inflicted by an adversary.[9]

FIREARMS DISCHARGES

There are three classifications of firearm discharges: (1) *justified*, (2) *negligent*, and (3) *accidental*. Each type of discharge has defining elements that warrants the classification. Operators that use firearms for self-protection need to understand what differentiates the three discharges.

Justified Discharge (JD)

The *justified discharge* of a firearm is the operator firing when reasonable in view of the circumstances. Adhering to the Four Rules for Firearms Handling establishes the probability of success when deploying or discharging a firearm.

Negligent Discharge (ND)

The *negligent discharge* of a firearm is the operator's failure to adhere to the Four Rules for Firearms Handling. The operator *neglected* to do one or more of the following: (1) proved the firearm empty, (2) kept the muzzle pointed in the appropriate direction, (3) kept the trigger finger on the receiver, or (4) fired when reasonable in view of the circumstances. The *unintentional* act of property damage, personal injury, or death is usually from a negligent discharge, *not* an accidental discharge.

Accidental Discharge (AD)

The *accidental discharge* of a firearm is unforeseen circumstances *not* humanly anticipated, such as a mechanical failure or parts breakage causing the *unintentional* firing of the firearm. In reality, there are few accidental discharges. However, adhering to the Four Rules for Firearms Handling reduces or eliminates the probability of an injury.

FIREARMS HANDLING

NOTE: The terms indicating *direction* in this book are indexed to the pistol as held in the operator's hand: left and right, front (muzzle) and rear, top and bottom, up and down, and forward and backward.

It would be impossible to write separate rules for each situation related to the use of firearms. The proper use and storage of firearms is an *individual's* responsibility. Much of firearms safety is common sense. The person in control of the firearm must consciously be aware of the firearm and its condition. Is the firearm loaded or unloaded? What direction is the muzzle pointed? Is the trigger finger on the receiver? These requirements apply equally to armed civilians, police officers, and military operators.

Anytime a pistol is handled, the first thing to do is prove its condition (loaded or unloaded). Operators that are unfamiliar with how to manipulate a particular pistol's mechanical devices should *not* attempt to experiment. Obtain familiarity by reading and understanding the instruction manual,[10] consulting another operator familiar with the pistol, or seeking assistance from a firearms instructor.

While attending training courses operators should *not* manipulate their pistols unless told to do so by an instructor. Not only is it irritating to an instructor while addressing a group to hear the unauthorized manipulation of a firearm, but it is also a *safety* violation. Such violations can get the guilty operator removed from the range. Instructors must *not* compromise on enforcing the Four Rules for Firearms Handling.

In American law enforcement, negligent discharges with firearms are the *second* most common causation for civil litigation.[11] Adhering to the Four Rules for Firearms Handling will prevent a negligent discharge. Firearms can provide a great deal of security when *safety* is viewed as the most important step in the learning process. The loudest sound in a gunfight is a click! The loudest sound in a classroom is a bang! An operator that shows little interest in firearms safety or is careless with a firearm will likely be the same in other crucial areas of operational survival.[12]

DANGER: Never jokingly point a firearm whether it is thought to be unloaded or not at any person. Never joke about shooting a person. Doing either may result in loss of employment, criminal charges filed, or the death of an innocent person.

Four Rules for Firearms Handling

The Four Rules for Firearms Handling begin by outlining the topic of that particular rule and ending with the desired outcome. For ease of memorization, the rules are brief. The four rules should be so ingrained in an operator that adherence is a subconscious action. The ingraining of the rules result in a *safety reflex* in which an operator cannot make him or herself violate any of the rules.[13] It is a person's responsibility to learn and adhere to the Four Rules for Firearms Handling. Think of the rules not *only* as firearms handling, but also as lifesaving rules. The International Association of Law Enforcement Firearms Instructors (IALEFI) in their professional journal (The Firearms Instructor) published the author's article on the Four Rules for Firearms Handling.[14]

Four Rules for Firearms Handling

1. Firearms are considered loaded until proven empty.

2. Keep the muzzle pointed in the appropriate direction.

3. Keep the trigger finger on the receiver unless firing.

4. Fire when reasonable in view of the circumstances.

The first rule says, "Firearms are considered loaded until proven empty." That means when a firearm transfers from one person to another it is the receiving person's responsibility to ensure the firearm is unloaded. This requirement places the responsibility on each person that handles that firearm. The rule assumes the condition of the firearm is loaded until the receiving person proves it unloaded.[15] Only after proving the firearm's condition can the person make a decision how it will be used (dry or live fire).

The second rule says, "Keep the muzzle pointed in the appropriate direction." What is the appropriate direction? That depends on the operator's task and the environment. The appropriate direction while unloading or loading a firearm within a secured compound is a clearing barrel. It is the backstop on a range. It is the ground when a police officer is about to make entry on a structure. It is normally at the ground just in front of a felony suspect (not at flesh) when taking him or her at gunpoint. The appropriate direction can quickly change according to the environmental conditions and the operator's situational perspective. It is the operator's responsibility to acknowledge those changes and make any necessary adjustments.

The third rule says, "Keep the trigger finger on the receiver unless firing." This provides a single criterion to meet before placing the trigger finger on the trigger. The operator must be in the process of firing.[16] The rule also explains where to keep the trigger finger until meeting that criterion—on the receiver. The *receiver* is also called the *frame*. Place the trigger finger on the receiver parallel with the slide. The trigger finger should *not* be on the slide, as it can get hot. This is especially true for a machine pistol *(selective fire pistol)*. Likewise, do *not* keep the trigger finger on the trigger guard. This practice can result in the trigger finger inadvertently slipping past the trigger guard onto the trigger. That would likely cause a negligent discharge. The trigger finger of a small stature operator may not be long enough to contact the front of the trigger guard.

An involuntary contraction can occur for several reasons: postural disturbance (lost balance), startled response (loud noise), and sympathetic response. The sympathetic response of the firing hand can occur when the non-firing hand grasps an object. An example is grabbing a person while having a drawn pistol. The pulling or pushing against the operator's non-firing hand might cause an involuntary contraction of the firing hand resulting in a negligent discharge. Trigger affirmation can also contribute to a negligent discharge. *Trigger affirmation* is the trigger finger moving from the receiver onto the trigger briefly and back to the receiver.[17] Trigger affirmation normally occurs subconsciously during high levels of stress whether the operator is training or operational.

The fourth rule says, "Fire when reasonable in view of the circumstances." While at the range the circumstances for an operator is a controlled environment with designated targets to shoot and a backstop to contain the bullets. An operator's action of shooting under those circumstances is reasonable.

Applying reasonableness to a hypothetical traffic stop provides further clarification. The violator shoots at the police officer during the traffic stop and a foot chase ensues. The suspect stops in front of a brick wall and exchanges gunfire with the police officer. The suspect takes off running again through a park. In the park there are children playing. The suspect stops in front of the children and shoots again at the police officer. The police officer is in the open with no cover immediately available. Will it make a bad situation worse if the police officer shoots back at the suspect? The police officer has to assess the situation quickly and take reasonable action at that point.

The police officer may create more of a hazard for the children by shooting at the suspect than quickly moving to cover. Even if that cover is somewhat far away. However, what would happen if the suspect started executing the children? The police officer would have to recognize the circumstances of the situation changed dramatically. The children are now living targets being murdered by the suspect. Not taking action *guarantees* many deaths will occur. A *reasonable* course of action in view of the new circumstances would be for the police officer to engage the *active killer* immediately and stopping the murderous spree.[18] The police officer shooting at the suspect might do so without being sure what is behind him, but the officer's actions would still be reasonable in view of the circumstances.

A person's handling and use of a firearm must be reasonable. Reasonableness is the only standard to use in determining the moral and legal correctness of a police officer's action. Being reasonable is the only standard required by the U.S. Supreme Court.[19] Police officers do not operate in a utopian environment where easily adhering to absolutes is possible. As the Supreme Court noted, police officers operate "...in circumstances that are tense, uncertain and rapidly evolving."[20]

A standard of reasonableness concerning a person's action is probably more widespread than many would think. The author while working as a police adviser in Afghanistan was held to a standard of reasonableness. Military operators should also be held to a standard of reasonableness when responding to a hostile act or demonstrated hostile intent.[21] However, the standard of reasonableness to fire does not apply with a force or group *declared* as hostile or enemy combatants by the United States government and the fire is directed at the enemy.[22] Whatever standard of reasonableness is adopted by any organization it should never limit an operator's inherit right to self-defense.[23]

It is reasonable to require operators to adhere to the Four Rules for Firearms Handling and instructors must set the example while enforcing the standard. The instructor must deal with violations decisively. This may mean an on the spot correction or stopping the training and addressing the group or applying physical motivation (push-ups, sit-ups, etc.).[24] Physical motivation is the *least* desirable method for correction except for military training.[25] This is especially true for armed civilians and police officers. Such correction may breed resentment among operators and actually reduce their desire to learn. A course description should clearly state if physical motivation is a method of correction and will be used during training.

A serious violation may call for live fire training to stop and simulation training to reenact the violation showing what could have happened. This change will require live weapons (pepper sprays, electronic control devices, batons, knives, and firearms) to be secured and the training area transformed to a simulation forum. There may also be additional consequences for those operators that violate firearms handling rules. The consequences can be verbal or written counseling, removal from the training program, and in severe cases termination from the organization. Proper firearms handling is ultimately an *individual* responsibility.

NOTE: Operators legally carrying a loaded pistol to a recreational shooting competition that runs a *cold* range (unloaded firearms, except on the firing line) should immediately on arrival contact a Range Safety Officer (RSO) for instructions on what the procedure is for unloading.

Firearms Handling for CQC

Close Quarters Combat (CQC) is fighting that brings an operator in personal contact with an adversary at ranges sometimes consisting of only a few yards (meters).[26] The Glock pistol is well suited for CQC, but requires adhering to the Four Rules for Firearms Handling. The *trigger finger* during CQC training remains on the receiver while the pistol is in a ready position. Only after making the decision to engage and the muzzle is pointing toward the adversary is the trigger finger placed on the trigger. The *trigger finger* must be on the receiver *before* an operator moves to another area and after the clear signal (audible or physical) is given.

NOTE: An appropriate method for CQC using pistols equipped with a manual *safety lever* is to place it on *safe* anytime the operator is on the move or a clear signal given and on *fire* after making the decision to engage and the muzzle is pointed toward the adversary.[27]

An operator in the most forward position of the team has *priority of fire*. It is irresponsible for an operator to shoot past another team member. Such practice will eventually result in one team member shooting another one. An operator must also guard against moving laterally in front of another operator's muzzle. An operator should *not* move behind a target during CQC training. Moving behind a target is a safety violation with a high probability for an injury or death. The operator must not shoot *if* there is any doubt. As one former Special Operations soldier said, "When in doubt, don't pull the trigger."[28]

The operator's trigger finger must be on the receiver before physically handling any person. It does not matter if the person handled is another operator, civilian, or adversary. It makes no difference if the person handled is receiving first aid or physically restrained. The operator's trigger finger remains on the receiver. The best practice is for another operator with a firearm to cover an operator taking an adversary into custody. Make certain an injured operator's firearm is on safe (if equipped) and properly secured before giving first aid.

DANGER: Take the firearms of an *incoherent* operator to prevent any chance of friendly fire causalities (fratricide).

Handing a Pistol to Someone

Unless an instructor directs otherwise remove the magazine and lock the slide to the rear before giving a pistol to someone.[29] Nevertheless, it may be necessary to hand a loaded pistol to another person. This would probably occur on a hot range (weapons remain loaded). An example would be a firearms instructor that shoots a student's pistol and afterwards hands it back. The two most important elements for the giver is to keep the muzzle pointed at the ground or a backstop and allow the receiving person to get control of the pistol by acquiring a secure grip. The handling procedure outlined below will seamlessly transform from the range to an operational environment. The muzzle normally points at the ground in an operational area.

WARNING: The giver should not grasp a *hot* pistol by its slide. Doing so could result in a burn injury. This is especially true when firing the Glock 18 machine pistol in automatic mode.

Standing Side-by-side: The receiving person and giver are standing side by side. The muzzle points toward the backstop or ground. The slide is grasped over the top between the fingertips and palm of the hand.[30] Keep the fingers clear of the muzzle. Keep the hand clear of the ejection port *if* the slide is locked open. The giver will wrap four fingers over the top of the slide and keep the thumb against the index finger. This method exposes the pistol's grip and allows the receiving person to obtain a normal grip and take control. When standing on a firing line on the *left* side of the receiving person, the giver will use the *left hand* to present the pistol. (Figure 4-1) When standing on the *right* side of the receiving person, the giver will use the *right hand* to present the pistol. (Figure 4-2)

Standing In Front: The grip is modified when a receiving person is standing in front of the giver. The *non-firing* hand thumb and fingers grasp the pistol with its muzzle down and the back strap against the web of the hand. The fingers wrap over the bottom of the trigger guard. Keep the fingers clear of the muzzle. Keep the hand clear of the ejection port *if* the slide is locked open. Present the butt of the pistol to the receiver. (Figure 4-3)

Figure 4-1 *Handing pistol to the left.*   **Figure 4-2** *Handing pistol to the right.*   **Figure 4-3** *Handing pistol to the front.*

Picking Up a Dropped Pistol

An operator during a deadly force encounter may sustain a fall or injury that results in a dropped pistol. The non-dominant hand becomes the firing hand *if* the dominant arm is injured. This is an example of needing to train for a worst-case scenario. Train using one hand (left and right) to pick up the pistol. An operator will instinctively want to pick up the pistol by its grip. The priority is to get the back strap into the vee of the hand without dropping the pistol again. The pistol grip can be in a less than ideal position on the ground. Overcome this by grabbing the grip regardless of its position and brace the front of the receiver against the ground *if* necessary to get a normal grip. (Figures 4-5 through 4-7)

Figure 4-5 Start   **Figure 4-6** Grip and   **Figure 4-7** End
Brace

The operator in a kneeling position needs to keep his or her head up as much as circumstances allow when picking up the pistol. The operator's survival could depend on a speedy response from that position. The operator from the kneeling position can continue fighting the moment a normal grip is established *if* the pistol is functional. A pistol with an *extended* magazine catch and falling to a hard surface is more susceptible to releasing the magazine. The operator should perform a tap-rack-ready to ensure the pistol is functional *if* circumstances allow.

LOADING AND UNLOADING MAGAZINES AND PISTOLS

WARNING: It is recommended that inexperienced personnel use *dummy* rounds to perform the loading and unloading procedures prior to using live ammunition. No live ammunition can be in the dry fire training area.

Loading a Magazine

To prevent damage to the pistol magazine it must be loaded and unloaded properly. Loading a magazine means filling it with cartridges. To load the empty magazine grasp the cartridge in the firing hand, press the rim of the cartridge down against the magazine follower while sliding the cartridge rearward and under the inward curved lips of the magazine. (Figures 4-8 and 4-9) Repeat the process until the magazine is full. (Figure 4-10) Forcing the cartridge straight down past the lips will *damage* the magazine by deforming the feed lips. Slap the rear of the magazine against the palm of the opposite hand to ensure all cartridges are positioned to the back of the magazine.[31]

 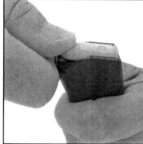 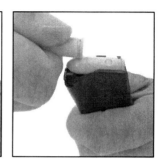

Figure 4-8 Depress *Figure   4-9*   Slide *Figure 4-10* Repeat
Follower   Under Curved Lips   the Process

Another option to load magazines is to use a Glock speed loader or a universal magazine loader. Both loaders are an efficient method to load magazines. The loaders will prevent finger injuries because of the repeated manual forcing of cartridges under the lips of the magazine. Instructors need to encourage the use of the loaders not only to prevent injuries, but also to reduce the amount of time required to load magazines resulting in a more efficient use of training time. How to use the two loaders are explained in the next two sections.

How to Use the Glock Speed Loader

Glock makes its speed loader to assist in loading cartridges more efficiently.[32] Most will find the non-dominant hand works best operating the speed loader and the dominant hand inserts the cartridges. To use the speed loader slide it over the top of the magazine (fits one way) with the thumb placed on top of the speed loader. (Figure 4-11) With the base of the magazine floor plate supported on a solid surface, push down with the thumb to move the follower down into the magazine. With the other hand insert the rim of the cartridge under the lips of the magazine and allow the speed loader to move upward about 0.75 inch (19 millimeters) while simultaneously pushing rearward on the cartridge. (Figure 4-12) The cartridge will move rearward fully seating in the magazine. Lift the speed loader up and repeat the process to fill the magazine.

It can be difficult with new magazines to load the last several rounds. Just hold pressure down on the speed loader and using the thumb of the other hand push the nose of the bullet down. Another method is to let off the pressure on the cartridges and push the speed loader down again.

Figure 4-11 *Speed Loader (up)*

Figure 4-12 *Speed Loader (down)*

CAUTION: To prevent damaging the magazine spring, *never* load magazines beyond the specified capacity. View round capacity through the magazine's windows.[33] The windows are small holes at the back of the magazine with a corresponding number. As an example, a Glock 17 magazine holds 17 rounds, but forcing 18 rounds into the magazine *might* be possible. Once a cartridge appears in the seventeenth window—do *not* load the magazine with any more rounds.

How to Use a Universal Magazine Loader

There is a military-grade universal magazine loader designed for loading single and double stack pistol magazines of various manufacturers in 9x19mm up to .45 Auto.[34] The universal loader may load other magazines including some .380 Auto. The universal loader is easy to use and works reliably. The universal loader does not require inserts, spacers, or adjustments.

The universal loader protects the operator's fingers and the magazine. The cartridges drop in for easy loading without pushing or pressing of the fingers. An operator can load hundreds of rounds painlessly. With a minimum of practice, an operator can load 1 round per second which is about 1/3 of the time it takes to load by hand. The durable universal loader easily fits in a cargo pocket and weighs only 2.3 ounces (66 grams). The universal loader has a lock that holds it in the compressed position for compactness while in transport or storage.

CAUTION: Use only quality ammunition and count the rounds while loading to prevent overfilling a magazine. Immediately stop loading if there is excessive resistance from the beak, press, or the magazine is full or jammed.[35]

To use the universal loader slide it over the top of the magazine so the beak points toward the front (bullet side of the magazine). Support the base of the magazine floor plate on a solid surface. Wrap the fingers around the front of the universal loader's press and the thumb over the top. The rear of the universal loader fits in the web of the hand. (Figure 4-13) Squeeze the press while pushing down forcing the follower or cartridge down in the magazine. Insert the rim of the cartridge over the beak and under the lips of the magazine using the other hand. (Figure 4-14) Simultaneously raise the universal loader about 0.75 inch (19 millimeters) and open the press to release the beak from the magazine. Repeat the squeezing of the press while pushing down and sliding new cartridge over the beak to fill the magazine.

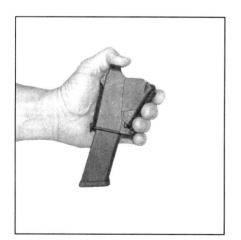 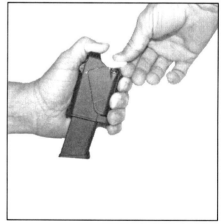

Figure 4-13 *Universal Loader (up)*   **Figure 4-14** *Universal Loader (down)*

The universal loader does *not* load the magazines as follows: Where there is less than 8 millimeters between the magazine lips. A Glock G36 six-round .45 Auto single stack magazine (beak will not come out of magazine). A Smith & Wesson 7-round 9x19mm single stack magazine (beak too wide, does not enter between lips).[36] In addition, the universal loader may not load the last round in a few other magazines. Maintain the universal loader by oiling metal parts to prevent corrosion.

Unloading a Magazine

To unload the magazine hold it in the non-dominant hand while using the thumb to press forward against the rim of the uppermost cartridge ejecting each one until empty. Use the other hand or a container to catch the cartridges.

Loading a Pistol

Loading a pistol is filling it with cartridges. This includes loading an empty magazine, inserting it into the magazine well, and chambering a round. To load a pistol no special techniques are advocated such as locking the slide back and then inserting the magazine. Loading a pistol uses the same technique as reloading and vice versa.[37] The methodology assists in building the operator's procedural memory. Maintain the muzzle in the appropriate direction during the loading process. Do not as a matter of practice drop a round in the chamber and let the slide slam forward. The extractor can chip when forced to jump over the rim of the case.[38]

To load the pistol, stand holding the pistol just under the line of sight with the trigger finger on the receiver. Bend the firing arm at a 90-degree angle, or slightly less, between the forearm and upper arm with the upper arm *naturally* resting on or near the body. (Figure 4-15) Insert the magazine into the magazine well using either the finger index or thumb index technique.

Use the *finger* index technique by maintaining a tight grip on the magazine with its front against the palm of the non-firing hand and the index finger positioned along the front of the magazine. Contact the upper *rear* portion of the magazine at a slight angle against the *rear* portion of the magazine well (back-to-back) pivoting the magazine upward and straight into the magazine well.

Use the *thumb* index technique by maintaining a tight grip on the magazine with its front against the palm of the non-firing hand and the thumb positioned along the side of the magazine. Contact the upper *front* portion of the magazine at a slight angle against the *front* portion of the magazine well (front-to-front) pivoting the magazine upward and straight into the magazine well. With either of the index techniques—use the heel of the hand with one smooth continuous motion to firmly press against the magazine floor plate seating the magazine into the pistol. (Figure 4-16)

Figure 4-15 *Loading (arm 90 degrees)*

Figure 4-16 *Loading (seating magazine)*

Figure 4-17 *Loading (racking slide)*

Figure 4-18 *Loading (join and extend)*

Load a round in the chamber by rotating the top of the pistol about 45 degrees toward the ground. With the non-firing hand, grab the serrated rear portion of the slide between the pad and the fingertips. Pull rearward with the non-firing hand until the slide reaches rear full extension. The slide at full extension strips from the grip of the non-firing hand. (Figure 4-17) The slide slams forward picking up the magazine's top cartridge forcing it into the chamber.

The firing hand rotates back upright while extending the arm to a naturally locked position. The arms are in a push-compress state with fingers on fingers and the firing hand thumb on top of non-firing hand's first knuckle of the thumb. The pistol is ready to fire. (Figure 4-18) Some operators after chambering a round like to perform a visual or physical inspection commonly referred to as a chamber check. A chamber check is explained in the *Loading Live Ammunition for Operational Carry* section in the Combat Shooting Phase 1 chapter.

WARNING: Do *not* attempt to ride the slide forward with the non-firing hand. This might pinch the hand or cause the barrel *not* to lock in place.

Unloading a Pistol

To unload a pistol hold it just under the line of sight and keep the muzzle pointed in the appropriate direction throughout the process. An appropriate direction is one that in the event of a negligent discharge *no* personal injury would occur and *minimum* or *no* property damage. Keep the trigger finger on the receiver unless instructed otherwise.

The firing arm bends at a 90-degree angle, or slightly less, between the forearm and the upper arm with the upper arm *naturally* resting on or near the body. (Figure 4-19) Press in on the *left* side magazine catch with the firing hand thumb (right-handed operator) or with the trigger finger (left-handed operator). A *reversible magazine catch* on the *right* side uses the firing hand thumb to press (left-handed operator). The non-firing hand strips the magazine (source of ammunition) from the magazine well. Drop the magazine on the ground or store it in a pouch or pocket.

Figure 4-19 *Magazine Removal*

Figure 4-20 *Racking the Slide*

Figure 4-21 *Visual Check*

Figure 4-22 *Pulling the Trigger*

Extend the firing arm and rotate the top of the pistol about 45 degrees toward the ground. (Figure 4-20) Watch the ejection port to see a round eject, but do *not* try to catch it. Grab the serrated rear portion of the slide with the non-firing hand between the pad (just below the thumb joint nearest the wrist) and the fingertips. Make sure *not* to cover the ejection port with the thumb or fingers. Hold the pistol stationary with the firing hand and aggressively pull rearward with the non-firing hand until the slide is fully to the rear stripping it loose from the non-firing hand. Repeat the process racking the slide three distinct times.[39] Lock the slide open by holding it fully to the rear and pushing the slide stop lever up.[40] Push the slide stop lever up with the thumb of the *firing* hand for a *right-handed* operator and with the thumb of the *non-firing* hand for a *left-handed* operator while easing the slide forward allowing the slide stop lever to engage the slide stop lever *notch*.

Look through the ejection port ensuring *no* magazine is in the magazine well and *no* round in the chamber. (Figure 4-21)

With the pistol pointed in an *appropriate* direction, use the underhand technique to release the slide allowing it to spring forward, and pull the trigger to the rear. (Figure 4-22) The pistol is unloaded. The operator could also assume a fighting stance before pulling the trigger to reinforce the fundamentals of shooting.

WARNING: Covering the ejection port with the non-firing hand and catching the live round is dangerous. The ejector may strike the primer igniting the gunpowder and rupturing the case resulting in an *ejector fire*.[41] The gas pressure of a rupture case can cause a severe injury to the non-firing hand.

Locking the Slide to the Rear: It is safer to rack the slide three times and eject a round from the chamber as opposed to locking the slide to the rear on the first racking of the slide. Small stature operators may find it difficult to hold the slide stop lever up while pulling the slide to the rear. Combining these two actions can cause the trigger finger to move inadvertently from the receiver onto the trigger. Whereas performing only one action (racking the slide) allows maintaining the grip on the pistol. Ejecting the chambered round first by racking the slide before locking it eliminates the chance of a negligent discharge. Using one unloading method will build procedural memory ensuring consistency.

In addition, racking the slide three distinct times acts as an indicator *if* the magazine (source of ammunition) remained in the pistol.[42] Three rounds being ejected are a visual and most likely an audible indicator according to the landing surface, i.e., concrete, gravel, etc. The indicators are not only for the operator, but also for bystanders. The bystanders should immediately tell the operator the source of ammunition is in the pistol. Racking the slide three times is also for clearing stoppages, which reinforces the lock-clear-reload skill.

WARNING: Do *not* put a finger between the barrel breach and the slide with it *locked* back to physically check for an empty chamber.[43] An injury can result from the slide unexpectedly slamming forward, hang fire[44] occurring, or touching hot metal. A bore light can be used *if* a visual and physical inspection of the chamber is required.

Visual Inspection: Removing the source of ammunition and visually inspecting the chamber is a sufficient method to verify whether a round is in the chamber or not. This method of checking the chamber is applicable to handguns and long guns. To reduce human error and provide consistent training it is recommended to use one method of checking the chamber for handguns that will also be used for long guns—visual inspection.

Loaded Chamber Indicator: Current Glock pistols have a square raised area on the extractor that acts as a *loaded chamber indicator* (LCI).[45] (Figure 4-23) The raised square extends above the slide surface indicating that a round is in the chamber. The eyes can see or a finger can feel the loaded chamber indicator. Use the loaded chamber indicator as a *secondary* confirmation the chamber is loaded or empty. Do *not* rely solely on the loaded chamber indicator. A Glock pistol that is extremely dirty with debris under the extractor can give a *false* indicator that a round is in the chamber.[46]

WARNING: "Glock users must not rely only upon a protruding extractor to confirm that a round is in the chamber. In addition, Glock users must not rely only upon the fact that the extractor is not protruding from the slide to confirm an empty chamber to the exclusion of manually checking the chamber."[47]

The author as a chief of police in a small gang and drug-ridden community was tasked with dismantling a criminal operation. While conducting covert antidrug operations there were many occasions in which known violent criminals would come to the location to deliver drugs. The confidential informants were in one room, the author and another officer were in the adjoining room. On several occasions tempers flared between the confidential informants and the dealers. Although he knew his pistol was loaded, in the dark room he performed a *secondary* confirmation. He pressed his thumb against the protruding loaded chamber indicator knowing at that moment his pistol was in a state of readiness.

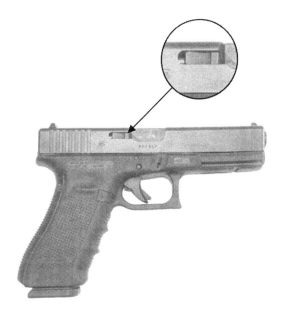

Figure 4-23 *Loaded Chamber Indicator*

GENERAL PRECAUTIONS

This section addresses topics that are sometimes overlook in the firearms training program. For additional information on any of the topics examined, please seek assistance from an appropriate instructor, public official, or organization.

Read the Instruction Manual

Whether a pistol is purchased by an individual or issued by an organization—read the instruction manual thoroughly. [48] Even experienced operators that get a new pistol still need to read the instruction manual. [49] The manufacturer might have made design changes that would affect the handling or care of the pistol. The operator needs to be aware of such changes. If the pistol did not come with an instruction manual one can be obtained by contacting the manufacturer. When selling a pistol include the instruction manual that goes with it to the new owner.[50]

NOTE: When developing a lesson plan for firearms training a starting point is the manufacturer's instruction manual.

Trigger Safety

The design of the *trigger safety* prevents the pistol from discharging when dropped on the rear of the slide or subjected to lateral pressure.[51]

DANGER: Danger of an accidental discharge exists *if* a Glock trigger safety is determined not to work as specified. The pistol must be immediately *unloaded* and *not* used until repaired.[52] Glock Inc., or a Glock certified armorer should perform the repair. Do *not* use the pistol until repaired.

Checking for Barrel Obstructions

Check the barrel for obstructions before firing a pistol.[53] A barrel with obstructions such as mud, excessive lubricant, or rust can cause higher than normal chamber pressures. The higher pressures can potentially bulge or rupture the barrel.

WARNING: A damaged pistol with a bulged or ruptured barrel can cause serious bodily injury to the operator or bystanders. Return a damaged pistol for repair or replacement to Glock Inc.

Use Only Recommended Ammunition

The slides, barrels, and magazines of Glock pistols come stamped with the caliber designation.[54] As an example, the designation stamps may be as follows: .380 Auto, 9x19, .357, .40, .45 Auto, .45 G.A.P., or 10mm Auto. The number represents the diameter of the barrel. The 9x19 barrel diameter is 9mm. The .357 barrel diameter is 0.357 inch. The .40 barrel diameter is 0.40 inch. The .45 Auto and .45 G.A.P. barrel diameters are 0.45 inch. The 10mm Auto barrel diameter is 10mm. Letters that follow a caliber designation represent the company that designed the cartridge. Common designations are as follows: .357 SIG

(Sig Sauer), .40 S&W (Smith & Wesson), .45 ACP (Automatic Colt Pistol), and .45 G.A.P. (Glock Automatic Pistol). Ammunition will have the caliber designation stamped into the head of the cartridge (headstamp)[55] and printed on its container.

Be aware that a cartridge that fits into the pistol does not necessarily mean that it is safe to fire. Keep in mind the earlier discussion about the excessive pressures. A firearm develops pressure when the primer ignites the gunpowder and the bullet pushes through the barrel. The cartridge case withstands the pressure because it is enclosed in the chamber. The precise amount of gunpowder in the cartridge determines the amount of pressure with other factors being normal, i.e., no barrel obstructions. Glock designs, manufactures, and tests its pistols to fire ammunition specified by the Sporting Arms and Ammunition Manufacturers Institute (SAAMI), and the North Atlantic Treaty Organization (NATO). [56] Shooting hand-loaded ammunition, also commonly called reloads[57] will *void* the warranty on a Glock pistol.[58]

WARNING: A *squib load* is the cartridge partially or totally missing its powder charge or a sufficient amount did not properly ignite.[59] This is recognizable by *reduced recoil* or a *pop sound* or both. Do *not* attempt to fire the pistol without first inspecting the bore and removing any obstructed bullet. If it pops—stop!

Do not fall into a trap of purchasing or shooting ammunition someone else has reloaded.[60] Such ammunition could result in chamber pressures that exceed the rating of the pistol. That reload may destroy the pistol and could result in a serious injury or death to the shooter or bystanders. It is not worth the risk. Another advantage to shooting factory ammunition is that manufacturers carry liability insurance. There is a venue to seek financial compensation if an accident occurs because of faulty ammunition. Give careful consideration before purchasing ammunition manufactured outside the operator's country of residency. It would take an enormous amount of effort and time to recover financial compensation *if* ever from an overseas ammunition manufacturer.

Ammunition Storage

Store ammunition in a *locked* container separated from any firearms.

Ammunition is best stored in a cool dry area to prevent corrosion and out of direct sunlight.[61] Live ammunition needs to be stored *away* from flammable liquids or materials. Store blank ammunition in clearly marked containers separated from live ammunition. This is to prevent the inadvertent mixing of live cartridges with blank cartridges.

A British military firearms instructor was training young cadets on a range. The cadets were firing blank ammunition. One of the cadets presented a live rifle round to an instructor. The instructor concerned for the safety of the cadets called a cease-fire. The cadet had obtained his equipment vest from a military operator who had returned from Iraq. The live round had been lodge in an obscure pocket in the vest. At that point, all of the cadets' pockets were checked. Fortunately, for everyone involved, the cadet did the right thing and immediately reported the safety violation.[62]

Rotate the ammunition at least annually. Fire the ammunition in the pistol and any spare magazines then obtain new replacement ammunition.

Wear Eye and Ear Protection

Shooting a pistol can be a scary venture. The pistol is loud, kicks, spits fire, and can kill! Safety equipment is crucial when firing a pistol. (Figure-4-24) The noise of gunfire can permanently damage unprotected hearing.[63] Hearing loss can occur not only from loud noise entering the ear canal, but also from the base of the ear. For this reason, earmuffs are preferred to earplugs and combining the two offers additional hearing protection and may reduce flinching. Electronic earmuffs provide the ability for weak sounds to be amplified and loud noises reduced. This allows the operator to hear a normal tone of voice, but at the same time provides protection against sudden impulsive noise. There are also custom molded electronic earplugs to fit the individual operator and work similar to electronic earmuffs.

The electronic earmuffs with a low profile earcup design provide clearance for a firearm stock. The electronic earmuffs also fit under a military helmet and are an excellent choice for shooting.[64] An automatic 4-hour shut off increases battery life and the external compartment allows for easy access to the AAA batteries. The auxiliary jack connects to radios, scanners, and MP3 players. There is one power and volume control knob for convenience. The unit is water resistant and has a convenient folding design for easy storage. Make sure the seal on the earmuffs fit snug around the ears without any gaps. Earmuffs worn loose around the ears will not protect the operator's hearing.

CAUTION: When installing batteries turn off the electronic earmuffs to prevent damage and make sure the batteries are positioned correctly.

Figure 4-24 *Eye and Ear Protection*

Although earmuffs are preferred, earplugs are small and convenient to carry in a combat zone. The author while in Afghanistan mainly wore noise activated earplugs. The earplugs allowed him to hear low-level sounds (conversation, footsteps, vehicles, etc.), but provided assurance that his hearing would be protected from sound of gunfire and to some degree an IED explosion[65] (according to proximity). The earplugs have a dual-ended design with a yellow end (weapons fire) and green end (steady noises). Pulling the ear up and outward allows an easier insertion of the earplugs in the ear canal. (Figure 4-25) Follow the manufacturer's instructions for use and cleaning. Another option is custom molded earplugs that mold directly into the operator's ear for a custom fit.[66] The custom molded earplugs are made from a nontoxic hypoallergenic silicone that provides all-day comfort.

NOTE: Wearing hearing protection during firearms training duplicates the *pop* sound associated with auditory exclusion.

Not only is hearing at risk *if* unprotected, but also eyesight. Operators need to wear safety glasses with side protection that wrap around the face. [67] This is to protect against ejected casings and backsplash of foreign materials such as bullet splatter from shooting steel targets. A shard of bullet can be invisible to the operator, but it tends to have sharp edges.[68] Edges are so sharp they can slice through the human eye. The best procedure is to put on safety glasses immediately after arriving at the range.

Figure 4-25 *Insertion of earplug.*

Operators have a tendency to pull safety glasses that are fogging up away from their face. This allows air circulation and reduces fogging. However, eye protection is reduced and it can lead to a hot case being trapped behind the glasses. Wear a billed cap to prevent an ejected case from being trapped between the face and glasses. The author witnessed a hot case get lodged behind an officer's safety glasses. The police officer chose *not* to wear a ball cap. Fortunately, the police officer received only a minor burn to her face and not an eye injury. Coating the safety glasses with an antifog solution should help prevent fogging and lessening the need to pull them away from the face.[69]

Safety eyewear that is an excellent choice for shooting will meet some of the highest impact protection standards.[70] The safety glasses meet the..."ANSI Z87.1-2003 (High Impact) and military V0 ballistic impact test (protection against impact energies 7x higher than ANSI requirements)." The elastomer browguard diffuses and deflects impacts. The safety glasses also have a factory bonded protective coating to the lens that offers triple protection: (1) *antifog* to reduce clouded vision from fogging, (2) *anti-scratch* to resist scratches from everyday use providing longer lens life, and (3) *anti-static* to help repel abrasive dust particles allowing for a longer lens life.[71]

The safety glasses come in three primary colors for shooting: (1) *gray*, (2) *amber* (yellow) and (3) *clear*.[72] The color of the lens may enhance the eyesight in an operational environment. The gray lens reduces the sun's visible brightness and glare from reflected sunlight. The amber lens reduces glare and haze without reducing the brightness of the sun. Because of the eye's increased sensitivity to amber, visual acuity sharpens and contrast enhances. A clear lens works well for areas the sun's glare and brightness are *not* an issue and when working indoors.

Not only is eye protection required while shooting, but also recommended when disassembling and cleaning a pistol. Safety glasses will protect the eyes from the impact of uncontrolled springs during disassembly and assembly. There is also the issue of splatter from aerosol cleaning agents. A priority of combat shooting is the care and protection of an operator's hearing and eyesight.

Range Clothing

The operator needs to dress appropriately when shooting a firearm. This is especially critical when attending a training course and multiple operators are on the line firing. Hot ejected cases flying through the air are capable of burning the skin. This is especially true for a female operator if a hot case is trapped in her bra (brassiere) against the breasts or in the waist gap at the back of low-rise jeans against the buttocks. Some shirts have a tendency for the opening at the neck to fold into a funnel shape when the arms are extended while shooting. Shirts with an open collar are not a good choice for shooting. Long sleeve crewneck shirts tucked in are a better choice for the range. Mock turtlenecks offer even more protection.

The long sleeve shirt acts as barrier against hot ejected cases. A secondary benefit is protection from the elements. The greater danger of a hot ejected case going down an operator's shirt is not necessarily a burn injury, but the possibly of a negligent discharge resulting in a serious injury or death. The priority is for the operator's muzzle to remain pointed at the backstop if a hot case touches the skin. The operator shooting from a fighting stance simulates a hot case going down her shirt. (Figure 4-26) The operator bends over at the waist and pulls the shirt away from her body to minimize a burn injury.

Figure 4-26 *Hot Case Response*

When bending over, do *not* extend the head past any muzzle. This may mean taking a half step back before being over. The shirt is held away from the body until the hot case cools and can be retrieved. Do *not* try to holster the pistol while bending over. Holster from the standing position. Always wear closed-toe footwear on the range to protect the feet from burn injuries caused by sun exposure or hot cases.

Acceptable safety protocols must also reflect operational requirements. Some organizations may require the shooting position to be maintained and for the operator to ignore the pain of being burned. This prepares the operator for a real-life operation where taking the time to remove a hot case could prove fatal.

NOTE: Train and qualify in cold weather clothing and rain gear *if* worn operationally.

Cease-fire on the Range

On a firearms range use the word "cease-fire," *not* the word "stop." This will prevent operators from thinking the word stop is being used as a verbal command. Every person on a range acts in the capacity of a Range Safety Officer (RSO) and can call a cease-fire.[73] Every person on a range has a *moral* obligation to call a cease-fire when recognizing a safety violation. When a cease-fire is called, operators need to stop what they are doing, remain in place, and wait for instructions.[74] This allows the range safety personnel an opportunity to resolve the safety issue.

Minimizing Lead Exposure

Overexposure to lead (heavy metal) is a safety concern that regrettably can be easily overlooked by an operator, instructor, and organization. It is not only lead that is dangerous, but also other metals. Some of those metals are barium, antimony, copper, and arsenic.[75] Lead can enter the body by inhalation, ingestion, or skin absorption. The lungs can remove lead from the air and put it in the bloodstream just as efficient as oxygen. Lead can be swallowed and absorbed in the intestines. Lead can be absorbed through the sweat ducts and hair follicles in the skin.

There are a number of ways that an operator can get high blood lead levels: (1) shooting on an indoor range that is inadequately ventilated, (2) shooting ammunition with lead bullets or primers, (3) handling and loading cartridges with exposed lead bullets, (4) touching the eyes, nose, or mouth while on the range, (5) picking up fired casings or other materials, especially near the backstop without using disposable gloves, (6) using clothing or headgear to collect fired casings, (7) drinking or eating on the range, (8) not washing the hands and face thoroughly before drinking, eating, or leaving the range, (9) washing the hands and face with hot water (opens pores in skin) instead of cool water, (10) not changing clothes and showering immediately after arriving at home, (11) and not wearing disposable gloves when cleaning firearms.

There are ways to minimize lead from entering the body: (1) shoot on an indoor range that has plenty of ventilation or an outdoor range, (2) shoot lead-free ammunition, (3) do not handle or load cartridges with exposed lead bullets, (4) avoid touching the eyes, nose, or mouth while on the range, (5) wear disposable gloves when picking up fired casings and other materials, (6) use an approved container and not clothing or headgear to collect fired casings, (7) refrain from drinking and eating on the range, but when necessary do wash hands and face thoroughly, (8) use a hand soap that removes heavy metal dusts, lead, and contaminants from the skin and hands,[76] (9) wash with cool water to prevent opening the pores in the skin, (10) shower at the earliest opportunity and keep range clothing and footwear separate from other apparel, and (11) wear disposable gloves when cleaning firearms.

One company examined the effects of personal hygiene on blood lead levels at a lead processing facility. The study showed there is a strong correlation between the lead levels in the blood and the presence of lead on the hands.[77] Those with high levels of skin contamination also had the highest blood lead levels. The importance of hygiene cannot be overstated. Lead exposure is dangerous to adults, but even more so to children.

Although there are serious health risks for overexposure to lead, there are also serious financial consequences. As an example, the Department of Labor's Occupational Safety and Health Administration (OSHA) in the United States cited a company responsible for cleaning shooting ranges and reclaiming the lead.[78] The alleged violation was for the company knowingly neglecting to protect workers from overexposure to lead. The proposed fines total $480,000.00. To avoid health and financial repercussions follow all agency, local, state, and federal recommendations for minimizing exposure to lead.

Alcohol, Drugs, and Firearms

Gunpowder and alcohol do *not* mix! Handling a pistol requires the operator's complete attention. Do *not* handle firearms if under the influence of drugs or alcohol.[79] A lapse in judgment can cost a human life and that is too high of a price to pay for indulging in alcohol or drugs while shooting. Especially those drugs that can cause drowsiness, slow reflexes, and impair decision-making.

Sleep Deprivation and Firearms

Do *not* dry or live fire a pistol when suffering from fatigue. Sleep deprivation can have mental and physical impairing effects.[80] Impairing effects from fatigue can be similar as with alcohol or drugs. Remaining awake for 19 hours results in impairments that are similar to having a blood alcohol concentration (BAC) of 0.05 percent. Moreover, after 24 hours without sleep it is comparable to having a BAC of 0.10 percent. Those extra 5 hours without sleep doubled the BAC effect.[81]

Pregnant and Nursing Women

There are safety issues for women who are pregnant or breastfeeding and considering shooting or cleaning firearms. The safety concerns are exposure to *lead, noise,* and *chemicals.* All three can have a negative effect on a woman pregnant and her unborn baby. Exposure to lead and chemicals can also have a negative effect on a woman breastfeeding. Noise is not an issue for a woman that breastfeeds *if* she is wearing hearing protection while shooting. A mother that breastfeeds—given the choice—obviously would *not* expose her newborn baby to the noise of gunfire. Other issues are heavy metals (beyond lead). Specifically, the U.S. Air Force found "concerning" levels (maybe not toxic, but beyond their permissible thresholds) of copper in ranges where lead-free ammo was used.[82]

Exposure to Lead: Pregnant and nursing women should avoid exposure to lead. Current research suggests that there is no safe lead exposure threshold for children, infants, or unborn babies. The mother can transmit lead via the placenta to the unborn baby. Exposure to lead during pregnancy has been attributed to spontaneous abortion, premature membrane rupture, preeclampsia, and pregnancy hypertension. Breast milk is another excretion route for lead and the amount of lead is associated with the concentration in the mother's blood.

Exposure to Noise: The safe threshold of noise exposure during pregnancy is unknown. Pregnant women should avoid exposure to the sound of gunfire. Loud noise is considered detrimental during a pregnancy. Rimfire rifles produce about 125 to 140 decibels. Rimfire pistols produce 140 to 150 decibels. Centerfire rifles, pistols, and shotguns produce about 150 to 160 decibels. Intrauterine (within the womb) measurements revealed an unborn baby was not protected against such loud noises. Exposure to noise while pregnant has been associated with miscarriage, intrauterine growth retardation, preterm delivery, and altered immune response in the unborn baby. Combining noise and lead exposure increases toxicity associated with heart lesions, which did not occur from noise or lead alone.

Exposure to Chemicals: Pregnant and nursing women should avoid exposure to chemicals used to clean and maintain firearms. Training with firearms may expose women to metals other than lead, including barium, antimony, copper, and arsenic. These metals too could be toxic depending on the concentration. A safe level has *not* been assessed for pregnant women. Organic solvents contained in firearms cleaning products are another source of chemical hazards and are known to be teratogenic (cause malformations of an unborn baby).

Pregnant women should *not* shoot firearms (except in the case of self-protection) and avoid exposure to firearms ranges. Women who are breastfeeding should shoot only lead-fee ammunition. Except in the case of self-protection a mother would never expose a newborn baby to the dangers of shooting—an unborn baby should be afforded that same level of care. Much of the information in this section is from the *excellent* work of Fabrice Czarnecki, M.D., M.A., M.P.H., and is available from the Police Policies Study Council,[83] and the American College of Occupational and Environmental Medicine.[84]

Firearms Storage and Children

Common sense dictates that a child must *not* have unsupervised access to a firearm.[85] Federal law under the Youth Handgun Safety Act dictates that it is unlawful, except in certain limited circumstances for any person who is a juvenile to knowingly possess a handgun or its ammunition.[86] States may also have laws regulating the storage of firearms to protect minors.[87] There are tragic stories of children who were able to get access to a loaded firearm. Unknowingly the child would shoot the firearm causing a self-inflicted gunshot or shoot another person. The outcome many times is the same—death of an innocent child. Gun owners that experienced such tragedy will forever live with the guilt of not securing their firearm. Such pain is something that no person should have to endure. The *greatest* pain is the loss of an innocent child.

Do not be naive and think that a child does not have the hand strength to pull a trigger. A child will use both of his or her index fingers to pull the trigger.[88] A child could also point the muzzle at him or herself and use both thumbs to pull the trigger. A method to prevent tragedies involving children is to store firearms unloaded in a locked container with the ammunition stored in a separate locked container. Those who purchase a firearm for home protection may choose a firearms safe that opens by releasing a mechanical or electronic locking device. This is a means to have a firearm secure, but still readily accessible. It is preferable to mount the safe in a location *inaccessible* to children. Choose a *safe* designed for securing firearms that can be opened only by an adult.

NOTE: Do not carry or store an unloaded pistol with an empty magazine in the magazine well. Removing the magazine (source of ammunition) is part of the unloading process. It contradicts the unloading process to leave even an empty magazine in the pistol.

Animals and Firearms

The sound of gunfire can startle untrained animals resulting in property damage, injury, or death. Do *not* shoot firearms near untrained animals.

Glock Safety Lock

The safety lock *if* equipped is located in the back of the grip on a Glock pistol.[89] Pistols with the safety lock ship in a locked condition.[90] The pistol cannot be used or disassembled with the safety lock engaged. In the back strap an indicator stud signifies the condition of the pistol as locked or unlocked. The key incorporates a hierarchical technology readily adaptable to the group key requirements of law enforcement agencies. The key fits the pistol and security case. State of the art technology also allows each key to be unique.

Transporting Firearms

Federal, state, and local laws regulate the transportation of firearms.[91] There are states with concealed carry laws that permit civilians to travel with loaded firearms. As a rule, when transporting firearms make sure they are unloaded and locked in a container designed for that purpose. It is important to remember that laws vary from state to state. It is the gun owner's responsibility before traveling to check on applicable laws to ensure a safe and pleasant trip.

INERT EQUIPMENT AND THE TRAINING ENVIRONMENT

Recommended are three inert firearms training aids to purchase along with a pistol. The first training aid is a detailed *replica* of the pistol.[92] (Figure 4-27) The blue pistol replica is nonfunctioning and made of impact resistant polyurethane. Use the nonfunctioning replica to practice drawing and moving. The mounting rails if equipped will accept a handgun mounted light.

Figure 4-27 *Blue training replicas of Glock models 26, 17 and 19.*

The second training aid is *dummy rounds*. There are two types of *orange* dummy rounds examined. (Figure 4-28) Both are highly visible making them easy to identify. The first dummy round is a one-piece design made of a durable synthetic material.[93] The advantage of the one-piece design is its cheaper cost, but rim breakage can occur.[94] The second dummy round is made with a metal case and filled with an orange Acrylonitrile Butadiene Styrene (ABS) plastic insert.[95] The advantage of the metal case is that rim breakage is reduced and it is better suited to diagnose mechanical issues with the pistol.

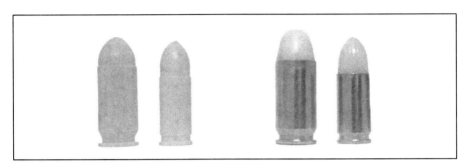

Figure 4-28 One-piece orange plastic design on left and metal case design on right.

Use the dummy rounds for loading and stoppage drills. The orange color reduces the risk of mixing live ammunition and dummy rounds. The orange color also aids in locating rounds on the range after each shooting drill or course of fire. At the conclusion of a training day a couple of things must occur. Magazines emptied to negate the chance of dummy rounds mixed with live ammunition, especially ammunition for operational carry. Any pistol used with dummy rounds needs to be fieldstripped, inspected for small plastic chips, and function tested. This is to ensure no plastic chips are interfering with the pistol's action preventing firing.[96] Discard damaged dummy rounds.

NOTE: Store the agency training magazines vertically in a container with the followers pointing up.[97] This allows the instructor to inspect each magazine for live rounds before and after training.

The third training aid is a yellow *inert barrel*. replacement.[98] (Figure 4-29) The inert barrel allows the pistol to be dry fired. However, because the barrel is a solid piece of plastic it is impossible to chamber live ammunition. By eliminating the firearms ability to chamber live ammunition there is no chance of a negligent discharge. This allows the conducting of realistic, but safe firearms handling in a classroom. The slide functions properly other than not being able to chamber a round. This allows the trigger to function and to perform a tap-rack-ready drill. Reloading drills can be performed safely using the yellow plastic barrel in conjunction with inert blue magazines. (Figure 4-30) The training barrel also allows the operator to practice getting sight picture when presenting the pistol on a target without fear of a negligent discharge.

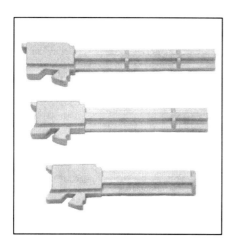

Figure 4-29 Yellow inert barrels for Glock models 17, 19, and 26.

Figure 4-30 Blue inert magazines for Glock models 17, 19, and 26.

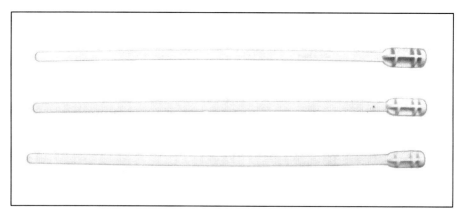

Figure 4-31 Chamber Blockers

An alternative to replacing the barrel is to use a chamber blocking device. The *chamber blocker* fills the chamber with a plastic plug that has a flexible yellow plastic strip that extends from the barrel.[99] (Figure 4-31) This provides a visual indication the pistol is empty. Installation of the chamber blocker does not require any disassembly or alterations to the pistol. The device allows the functioning of the pistol minus the capability of loading a round in the chamber. The device is specific to the caliber of pistol.

Simulation Training Environment

Functional pistols must be *deactivated* (incapable of firing live ammunition) before conducting simulation training.[100] Use a chamber blocking device or inert barrel to deactivate a functional pistol. Use a triple-check procedure[101] to verify the pistol is *unloaded*. The procedure consists of an inspection of the pistol by the operator, two students (on the left and right), and the instructor. The inspection must occur *before* an instructor installs a chamber blocking device and *afterwards*. Once the blocking device is installed and confirmed, the pistol is considered deactivated.

Physically search students for live ammunition before simulation training begins. Students also cannot have any live weapons (knives, pepper spray, batons, etc.) on their person or in the training area.[102] Students that leave the area during simulation training and return are searched again and their pistol inspected. Visitors with live weapons are *not* allowed in the training area.[103] Post signs stating that simulation training is being conducted and warning of no live (functioning) weapons. Search vehicles used for simulation training. No functional weapons are stored in a vehicle's interior, console, glove box, etc.[104]

Make sure the scenario is applicable to the operator's operational environment when conducting simulation training. The training of civilians requires a concealed carry scenario, police officers a law enforcement scenario, and military operators a combat mission scenario. Simulation training needs to induce stress on the operator and include target discrimination. Allow operators to use their same communication devices as deployed in the operational areas. This includes radios, mobile data computers, cell phones, verbal commands, hand signals, smoke devices, flares, or distraction devices.

ELECTRONIC TIMER FOR FIREARMS TRAINING

A police officer failed the annual qualification, but vowed that it would never happen again. The police officer failed to fire the required number of rounds within the prescribed time limit as outlined in the qualification course. Afterwards the police officer completed remedial firearms training and passed the qualification course. The agency issued the police officer 50 rounds of ammunition per month for practice as part of the remedial program. The police officer also bought 50 extra rounds each month. The police officer fired about 1200 rounds of ammunition during the year. When the next annual qualification arrived, the police officer was confident of qualifying, but again failed the course. What was the reason for the police officer failing?

The police officer failed the second time for the same reason as the first. Shooting too slow and not firing the required number of rounds within the prescribed time limits. The police officer had a problem of perception. What seemed as shooting fast was actually slow. Using an electronic timer during practice sessions would have revealed the problem of shooting too slow. (Figure 4-32) To the police officer, perception was reality. In actuality, only the facts are reality. The electronic timer tells the facts. Using an *electronic timer* transforms perception into reality—good or bad.

A handheld electronic timer[105] will allow an operator to practice live fire on the range, but also dry fire in a convenient area. The *start delay* can be set between 0.5 second and 9.9 seconds for either fixed or random. The factory set time delay will be 1 to 4 seconds. This feature allows the operator to press the start button resulting in a random start time between the set parameters. The *par time* feature, also known as the *second beep* notifies the operator when the maximum time is reached. As an example, the operator desires to practice drawing from the holster to the target. The timer is set with a random start time and a par time of 1.5 seconds. The timer will randomly beep the first time between the set limits and a second beep will sound at exactly 1.5 seconds later. The draw begins on the first beep and completed before the second beep.

Use the electronic timer to dry fire segments of a qualification course to ensure an operator can physically accomplish the movements within the designated time. An operator at the 25-yard (22.86-meter) line may have 60 seconds from behind a barricade to draw from the standing, assume the prone fire 6 rounds, reload in the kneeling, stand, and fire 6 rounds.[106] An electronic timer can determine whether the operator within the specified time can draw, go to the prone position and dry fire 6 rounds, come to a kneeling position, perform a reload, stand, and dry fire 6 rounds. An operator that cannot *dry fire* the course within the prescribed time limit will probably fail during *live fire* qualification.

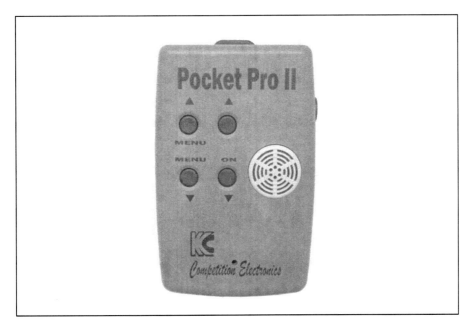

Figure 4-32 *Electronic Timer*

An electronic timer can also be used to test an operator's reflexes safely in a *classroom*. The only equipment needed is an electronic timer that has a spring loaded belt clip. The instructor sets the electronic timer to random start. The instructor holding the electronic timer allows operator using the index finger and thumb to grab the belt clip and pull it away from the case. The operator releases the belt clip when the buzzer randomly sounds. The belt clip will pop against the case and the reaction time records. The operator's reaction time can also be tested using *live fire* on a range. The operator stands with the muzzle pointed at the backstop and the trigger finger on the trigger with the slack taken out. Pull the trigger when the buzzer sounds. The reaction time records on the sound of the shot. The operator needs to respond instantly to the buzzer just as the sound begins.

FIREARMS INVENTORY AND TRAINING NOTEBOOK

A firearms inventory and training notebook can be a valuable resource for an operator. The notebook should have five sections as follows:

1. *Legal Representation and Insurance:* Contact information for legal representation available 24 hours a day. Contact information of the insurance carrier and copies of any liability and medical insurance policies.

2. *Firearms Laws and Regulations:* A summary of applicable state and federal laws governing use of force.

3. *Firearms Inventory:* A written inventory of each firearm owned. The inventory list needs to include the manufacturer, model, serial number, caliber, person, or company purchased from, date purchased and cost.

4. *Training Courses and Certifications:* A chronological list of tactical and firearms courses completed and copies of the course lesson plan and qualification scorecard.

5. *Firearms Instruction Manual:* An instruction manual for every firearm owned. This includes firearms used privately or professionally.

SUMMARY

Firearms are inherently dangerous devices. Training is required for the proper operation of firearms. There are three classifications of discharges: (1) *justified,* (2) n*egligent, and* (3) *accidental.* Most negligent discharges are cause by *not* following the Four Rules for Firearms Handling. It is an individual's responsibility to adhere to the Four Rules for Firearms Handling. Tolerating violations of the Four

Rules for Firearms Handling in training encourages those same negligent practices in real-life operations.[107] Not adhering to the Four Rules for Firearms Handling will probably result in damaged property, an injury, or a death. Firearms must *not* be accessible to unsupervised children. Wear eye and hearing protection while shooting firearms during training. Wear safety glasses when cleaning firearms. Use an electronic timer to verify an operator's ability to shoot a course of fire or a drill in a prescribed time. A firearms training and inventory notebook provides a convenient place for information on legal representation and insurance, firearms laws and regulations, firearms inventory, training courses and certifications, and firearms instruction manuals.

DISCUSSION QUESTIONS

1. What term describes a bullet after it has left the muzzle of a firearm? Why is the term fitting?
2. Discuss why people are shot with so-called unloaded firearms.
3. Name the three types of firearms discharges.
4. List the Four Rules for Firearms Handling.
5. Discuss the difference in firing when reasonable in view of the circumstances in comparison to being sure of the target and what is around and behind it.
6. Which team member has priority of fire in a CQC environment?
7. The operator with a firearm presented, but performing the contact operator role needs to do what before physically handling another person?
8. An incoherent operator must have what taken from him or her to prevent any chance of friendly fire causalities?
9. Explain what is an ejector fire and how it occurs? What is the danger of an ejector fire to an operator?
10. Explain the procedure of unloading a Glock pistol.
11. What is a loaded chamber indicator (LCI) and can it be solely depended on?
12. Describe how to give back a loaded firearm to a shooter on the firing line.
13. Describe how to pick up a dropped pistol.
14. Why is it important to read the instruction manual thoroughly before firing a pistol for the first time?
15. Explain how to determine the correct ammunition for a pistol.

16. What does the phrase "If it pops—stop!" mean. What should an operator do?
17. Discuss the proper storage method for live and blank ammunition.
18. What two pieces of safety equipment are crucial when firing a pistol during training?
19. Describe how to reduce the chance of a burn injury when a hot case goes down the front of an operator's shirt.
20. Each operator has a moral obligation to call a cease-fire after recognizing what?
21. Discuss some of the ways an operator is exposed to lead?
22. Discuss some of the ways an operator can reduce the exposure to lead?
23. Why is it important not to handle firearms when under the influence of drugs or alcohol?
24. Explain the hazards of shooting or cleaning firearms for women that are pregnant or breastfeeding?
25. When is the only time a pregnant woman should shoot a firearm?
26. Discuss how to prevent children from gaining access to a firearm.
27. Name the three inert firearms training aids recommended to purchase along with a pistol.
28. Describe how to deactivate (incapable of firing live ammunition) functional firearms before conducting simulation training.
29. When an electronic timer is used perception immediately transforms to what?
30. List the information that needs to be included in a firearms inventory and training notebook.

ENDNOTES

[1] Glock Inc., *Instructions for Use Glock Safe Action Pistols All Models*, (Smyrna, GA: March 2011), 1.

[2] John C. Hall, J.D., "Firearms Training and Liability," *FBI Law Enforcement Bulletin*, (January 1993): 28.

[3] Glock Inc., *Instructions for Use Glock Safe Action Pistols All Models*, (Smyrna, GA: March 2011), 6.

[4] National Rifle Association, "Articles," *Firearms Fact Card 2012*, http://www.nraila.org/gun-laws/articles/2012/nra-ila-firearms-fact-card-2012.aspx?s=Firearms+Fact+Card&st=&ps= (accessed September 22, 2012).

[5] National Rifle Association, "Articles," *Firearms Fact Card 2012*, http://www.nraila.org/gun-laws/articles/2012/nra-ila-firearms-fact-card-2012.aspx?s=Firearms+Fact+Card&st=&ps= (accessed September 22, 2012). "Today over 70 million Americans own and use firearms, and the Federal Government estimates that firearms are kept in over half the households in this country." See Glock Inc., *The Basic Rules of Firearm Safety*, (Smyrna, GA: 2005): 1.

[6] National Rifle Association, *Law Enforcement Handgun Instructor Manual* (Fairfax, VA: Off-Duty Firearm Safety, Edition 6.1, 2006), 6.

[7] National Rifle Association, *Law Enforcement Handgun Instructor Manual* (Fairfax, VA: Firearm Safety and Range Organization, Edition 6.1, 2006), 4.

[8] International Association of Law Enforcement Firearms Instructors, *IALEFI Guidelines for Simulation Training Safety*, (2004): 10-14.

[9] Paul R. Howe, *Leadership and Training for the Fight* (New York, NY: Skyhorse Publishing, 2011), 369.

[10] Glock Inc., *Instructions for Use Glock Safe Action Pistols All Models*, (Smyrna, GA: March 2011), 1.

[11] North Carolina Justice Academy, "Specialized Firearms Instructor Training," *Civil Liability: Firearms Training* (Salemburg, NC: Summer 2005): 25.

[12] J. Henry FitzGerald, *Shooting* (Boulder, CO: Paladin Press, 2007), 346. Originally published in 1930 by J. Henry FitzGerald.

[13] National Rifle Association, *Law Enforcement Handgun Instructor Manual* (Fairfax, VA: Firearm Safety and Range Organization, Edition 6.1, 2006), 2.

[14] Tim Blakeley, "Rethinking the Rules of Firearms Handling," *The Firearms Instructor*, volume 39 (2005): 48-51.

[15] Department of the Army, *Combat Training with Pistols, M9 and M11* (Washington, DC June 2003), 2-30

Glock Inc., *Instructions for Use Glock Safe Action Pistols All Models*, (Smyrna, GA: March 2011), 5.

[16] Glock Inc., *Instructions for Use Glock Safe Action Pistols All Models*, (Smyrna, GA: March 2011), 5.

[17] "That is that the trigger finger leaves its properly indexed position, touches the trigger briefly, then returns to the properly indexed position." See Bert DuVernay, "Covering Suspects," (Spofford, NH: *The Police Policies Study Council*, November 11, 2002),   http://www.theppsc.org/Staff_Views/DuVernay/covering%20suspects.htm (accessed September 22, 2012).

[18] North Carolina Justice Academy, "Rapid Deployment Instructor Training," *Rapid Deployment: Immediate Response to the Active Shooter* (August 2001): 11.

[19] U.S. Supreme Court, *Graham v. Connor*, 490 U.S. 386 (1989).

[20] U.S. Supreme Court, *Graham v. Connor*, 490 U.S. 386 (1989).

[21] David G. Bolgiano, *Combat Self-Defense: Saving America's Warriors from Risk-Averse Commanders and Their Lawyers* (Little White Wolf Books: 2007), 95-103.

[22] "In a full up, force on force war with declared hostiles, there is no concern for when a serviceman fires, how long or how often he fires, so long as it is directed at the enemy." See David G. Bolgiano, *Combat Self-Defense: Saving America's Warriors from Risk-Averse Commanders and Their Lawyers* (Little White Wolf Books: 2007), 61.

[23] David G. Bolgiano, *Combat Self-Defense: Saving America's Warriors from Risk-Averse Commanders and Their Lawyers* (Little White Wolf Books: 2007), 11-17.

[24] Paul Howe, "Firearms Safety Rules," *Combat Shooting and Tactics PowerPoint Presentation*, (Combat Shooting and Tactics, Nacogdoches, TX: 2009): slide 23.

[25] R.E. Parham III, *Firearms Instructor's Manual* (Springfield, IL: Charles C. Thomas Publisher, LTD, 1999), 9.

[26] The terms Close Quarters Combat and Close Quarters Battle are used interchangeably. See David G. Bolgiano, J.D., "Military Support of Domestic Law Enforcement Operations: Working Within Posse Comitatus," *FBI Law Enforcement Bulletin*, (December 2001): 21.

The Grant-Taylor Manual, *The Palestine Police Force Close Quarter Battle* (Boulder, CO: Paladin Press, 2008), 11. Originally published in 1943. Reprinted by Paladin Press in 2008.

[27] Paul R. Howe, *Leadership and Training for the Fight* (New York, NY: Skyhorse Publishing, 2011), 375.

[28] Paul R. Howe, *Leadership and Training for the Fight* (New York, NY: Skyhorse Publishing, 2011), 377-379.

[29] National Rifle Association, *Law Enforcement Handgun Instructor Manual* (Fairfax, VA: Firearm Safety and Range Organization, Edition 6.1, 2006), 5.

[30] Erik Lawrence, *Tactical Pistol Shooting*, (Lola, WI: Gun Digest Books, 2005), 140.

[31] National Rifle Association of America, *NRA Guide to the Basics of Pistol Shooting* (Fairfax, VA: The National Rifle Association of America, 2009), 48.

[32] Glock Inc., *Glock Buyer's Guide Professional Edition*, (Smyrna, GA: Glock Inc., 2012): 54.

[33] Glock Inc., *Armorer's Manual*, (Smyrna, GA: 2009): 62.

[34] Maglula Ltd., "Pistol Mag Loaders," *UpLULA™ - 9mm to 45ACP*, http://www.maglula.com/PistolMagLoaders/UpLULA9mmto45ACPmags.aspx (accessed September 22, 2012).

[35] Maglula Ltd, Operating Instructions, (Rosh Ha'aylin, Israel: *Item Number 24222*, 2007-2010) maglula p/n UP60B.

[36] Maglula Ltd., "Pistol Mag Loaders," *UpLULA™ - 9mm to 45ACP*, http://www.maglula.com/PistolMagLoaders/UpLULA9mmto45ACPmags.aspx (accessed September 22, 2012).

[37] Erik Lawrence, *Tactical Pistol Shooting*, (Lola, WI: Gun Digest Books, 2005), 93.

[38] Glock Inc., *Glock Professional*, (Smyrna, GA: 2012): DVD PowerPoint Slide 112.

[39] Timothy D. Blakeley, "Personal Notes from the Firearms Training Session," *U.S. Marshals Fugitive Investigator's Course,* (Federal Law Enforcement Training Center, Brunswick, GA: 2005): 6.

Glock Inc., *Glock Pistol Transitional Instructor Workshop Course Outline*, (Smyrna, GA: 2012): 6.

Phil Singleton, *3 Day Tactical Pistol for Hostage Rescue, High Risk Warrant and Drugs Raids,* (Warrenton, VA: Singleton International): 28.

[40] Glock Inc., *Instructions for Use Glock Safe Action Pistols All Models*, (Smyrna, GA: March 2011), 11.

[41] National Rifle Association, *Law Enforcement Handgun Instructor Manual* (Fairfax, VA: Handgun Handling Techniques, Edition 6.1, 2006), 11.

[42] Phil Singleton, *3 Day Tactical Pistol for Hostage Rescue, High Risk Warrant and Drugs Raids,* (Warrenton, VA: Singleton International): 28.

[43] Glock Inc., *Instructions for Use Glock Safe Action Pistols All Models*, (Smyrna, GA: March 2011), 15.

[44] Hang fire: "A brief delay in the ignition and firing of a round of ammunition after being struck by the hammer, firing pin, or striker or being subjected to other

igniting action. The ignition delay is most often a few tenths of a second or less, but in rare instances can be as long as several seconds." See International Association of Law Enforcement Firearms Instructors, *Standards & Practices Reference Guide for Law Enforcement Firearms Instructors*, (January 1995): 166.

[45] Glock Inc., *Glock Buyer's Guide Professional Edition*, (Smyrna, GA: Glock Inc., 2012): 17.

[46] Kyle E. Lamb, *Stay in the Fight*, (Trample and Hurdle Publishers, 2011), 101.

[47] Glock Inc., *Instructions for Use Glock Safe Action Pistols All Models*, (Smyrna, GA: March 2011), 21.

[48] Glock Inc., *The Basic Rules of Firearm Safety*, (Smyrna, GA: 2005): 4.

[49] Glock Inc., *Instructions for Use Glock Safe Action Pistols All Models*, (Smyrna, GA: March 2011), 3.

[50] Glock Inc., *Instructions for Use Glock Safe Action Pistols All Models*, (Smyrna, GA: March 2011), 29.

[51] Glock Inc., *Armorer's Manual*, (Smyrna, GA: 2009): 14.

[52] Glock Inc., *Instructions for Use Glock Safe Action Pistols All Models*, (Smyrna, GA: March 2011), 5.

[53] Glock Inc., *The Basic Rules of Firearm Safety*, (Smyrna, GA: 2005): 5.

[54] Glock Inc., *The Basic Rules of Firearm Safety*, (Smyrna, GA: 2005): 5-6.

[55] Headstamp: "Numerals, letters, and symbols (or combination thereof) stamped into the head of a cartridge case or shotshell to identify the manufacturer, caliber, gauge or give additional information." See International Association of Law Enforcement Firearms Instructors, *Standards & Practices Reference Guide for Law Enforcement Firearms Instructors*, (January 1995): 166.

[56] Glock Inc., *Instructions for Use Glock Safe Action Pistols All Models*, (Smyrna, GA: March 2011), 15.

[57] Reload: "A fired cartridge case which has been reassembled with a new primer, powder, projectile(s) or other components." See International Association of Law Enforcement Firearms Instructors, *Standards & Practices Reference Guide for Law Enforcement Firearms Instructors*, (January 1995): 178.

[58] Glock Inc., *Instructions for Use Glock Safe Action Pistols All Models*, (Smyrna, GA: March 2011), 15.

[59] International Association of Law Enforcement Firearms Instructors, *Standards & Practices Reference Guide for Law Enforcement Firearms Instructors*, (January 1995): 169-170.

[60] Kathy Jackson, *The Cornered Cat: A Woman's Guide to Concealed Carry* (White Feather Press, 2010), 222-223.

[61] Federal Premium, "Federal FAQ," *What is the shelf life of ammo and storage?* http://www.federalpremium.com/resources/faqs.aspx (accessed September 22, 2012).

[62] Corporal Mark Jones of the British Army (United Kingdom) while in Afghanistan conveyed the story in a face-to-face conversation with the author in 2008.

[63] Glock Inc., *Instructions for Use Glock Safe Action Pistols All Models*, (Smyrna, GA: March 2011), 13.

[64] Howard Leight by Sperian Hearing Protection, LLC, "Consumer Products," *Impact Sport*, http://www.howardleight.com/ear-muffs/impact-sport--2 (accessed September 22, 2012).

[65] Peltor Inc., "Combat Arms Earplugs," *More Than a Hearing Protector* (February 2006) 318-00218 Instructions for Use.

[66] Radians Inc., "Products," *Radians Custom Molded Earplugs*, http://www.radians.com/radsite/index.php/products/industrial-safety-products/hearing-protection/item/radians-custom-molded-earplugs?category_id=8 (accessed September 22, 2012).

[67] Glock Inc., *The Basic Rules of Firearm Safety*, (Smyrna, GA: 2005): 6.

[68] Julie Golob, *Shoot: Your Guide to Shooting and Competition* (New York, NY: Skyhorse Publishing, 2012), 3.

[69] McNett Corporation, "Product Info," *Op Drops Antifog Lens Cleaning System*, http://www.mcnett.com/Op-Drops-Anti-Fog-Lens-Cleaning-System-P329C94.aspx (accessed September 22, 2012).

[70] Sperian Protection Americas, Inc., "Product Configuration," *Safety Eyewear Genesis XC* (Smithfield, RI: 2012), http://www.uvex.us/uploadedFiles/ProductConfiguration/ProductLiterature/Uvex_Genesis_XC_Brochure.pdf (accessed September 22, 2012).

[71] Sperian Protection Americas, Inc., "Product Configuration," *Safety Eyewear Genesis XC* (Smithfield, RI: 2012), http://www.uvex.us/uploadedFiles/ProductConfiguration/ProductLiterature/Uvex_Genesis_XC_Brochure.pdf (accessed September 22, 2012).

[72] Howard Leight by Honeywell, "Consumer Products," *Genesis XC Kit*, http://www.howardleight.com/ear-muffs/genesis-xc (accessed September 22, 2012).

[73] Glock Inc., *Glock Pistol Transitional Instructor Workshop Course Outline*, (Smyrna, GA: 2012): 3.

[74] National Rifle Association, *Law Enforcement Handgun Instructor Manual* (Fairfax, VA: Firearm Safety and Range Organization, Edition 6.1, 2006), 4.

[75] Elizabeth Kennedy and Fabrice Czarnecki, M.D., *Shooting While Pregnant: Dangerous or Not?*, (Association for Women's Self-defense Advancement),

http://www.awsda.org/index.php?option=com_content&view=article&id=59%3Ashoot
ing&catid=25&Itemid=18 (accessed September 22, 2012).

[76] Esca Tech, Inc., "Products," *Skin Cleaning D-Lead Hand Soap*, (2012),
https://www.esca-tech.com/ProductDetail.php?category=1000&productnum=4222ES
(accessed September 22, 2012).

[77] Daniel P. Askin and Mark Volkmann, "Effect of Personal Hygiene on Blood
Lead Levels of Workers at a Lead Processing Facility," *American Industrial Hygiene
Association Journal* 58, (1997), 752-753.

[78] Occupational Safety and Health Administration, *Welch Group Environmental
Fined $480,000* [paragraph one], (United State Department of Labor),
http://www.osha.gov/pls/oshaweb/owadisp.show_document?p_table=NEWS_RELEAS
ES&p_id=21627 (accessed September 22, 2012).

[79] Glock Inc., *The Basic Rules of Firearm Safety*, (Smyrna, GA: 2005): 7.

[80] Men's Health Magazine, *How a Man Stays Young* (Emmaus, PA: Rodale Press,
1993), 284.

[81] Bryan Vila, Ph.D., "Sleep Deprivation," *Law Enforcement Coordinating
Committee News*, (May/June/July 2009): 4.

[82] Moran, Michael P., Major, USAF, BSC and Ott, Darrin K., Major, USAF, BSC,
*Lead Free Frangible Ammunition Exposure at United States Air Force Small Arms
Firing Ranges, 2005 – 2007* (Brooks City-Base, TX: Air Force Institute for Operational
Health, May 2008).

[83] Fabrice Czarnecki, M.D., "Staff Views," *The Pregnant Officer,* (August 2003),
http://www.theppsc.org/Staff_Views/Czarnecki/pregnant_officer.htm   (accessed
January 22, 2012).

[84] American College of Occupational and Environmental Medicine, "Knowledge
Centers," *ACOEM Guidance for the Medical Evaluation of Law Enforcement Officers*,
http://www.acoem.org/LEOGuidelines.aspx (accessed September 22, 2012).

[85] Glock Inc., *The Basic Rules of Firearm Safety*, (Smyrna, GA: 2005): 7.

[86] Glock Inc., *Instructions for Use Glock Safe Action Pistols All Models*, (Smyrna,
GA: March 2011), 49.

[87] North Carolina General Statute, § 14‑315.1. Storage of Firearms to Protect
Minors.

[88] Robert K. Taubert, *Rattenkrieg! The Art and Science of Close Quarters Battle
Pistol* (North Reading, MA: Saber Press, 2012), 80.

[89] Glock Inc., "Glock Internal Key Locking System," *Glock Autopistols 2010*,
(New York, NY: Harris Publications Inc., 2010): 104.

[90] Glock Inc., *Instructions for Use Glock Safe Action Pistols All Models*, (Smyrna,
GA: March 2011), 53.

[91] Glock Inc., *The Basic Rules of Firearm Safety*, (Smyrna, GA: 2005): 8.

[92]   Ring's   Manufacturing,   '"Home,"   *Blueguns,* http://www.blueguns.com/default.asp? (accessed September 22, 2012).

[93]   Precision   Gun   Specialties,   "Product   Overview,"   *Saf-T-Trainers,* http://www.precisiongunspecialties.com/strainer-main.html (accessed September 22, 2012).

[94] Randy L. Smith, "Can Dummy Rounds be Dangerous?," *The Firearms Instructor*, (Issue 48 2010): 7.

[95]   S.T.   Action   Pro,   "Home,"   *Action   Trainer   Dummy   Rounds,* http://www.stactionpro.com/action-trainer-dummy-rounds-c-1.html   (accessed September 22, 2012).

[96] Randy L. Smith, "Can Dummy Rounds be Dangerous?," *The Firearms Instructor*, (Issue 48 2010): 7.

[97] Timothy D. Blakeley, "Personal Notes from the Firearms Training Session," *U.S. Marshals Fugitive Investigator's Course,* (Federal Law Enforcement Training Center, Brunswick, GA: 2005): 6.

[98] Blade-Tech Industries, "Training Accessories" *The Blade-Tech Training Barrel,* http://www.blade-tech.com/Training-Barrel-pr-1018.html (accessed September 22, 2012).

[99]   Ammo-Safe   Inc.,   "Home,"   *Ammo-Safe,*   http://www.ammo-safe.com/ammosafe/index.html (accessed September 22, 2012).

[100] International Association of Law Enforcement Firearms Instructors, *IALEFI Guidelines for Simulation Training Safety*, (2004): 19.

[101] International Association of Law Enforcement Firearms Instructors, *IALEFI Guidelines for Simulation Training Safety*, (2004): 21.

[102] International Association of Law Enforcement Firearms Instructors, *IALEFI Guidelines for Simulation Training Safety*, (2004): 21.

[103] International Association of Law Enforcement Firearms Instructors, *IALEFI Guidelines for Simulation Training Safety*, (2004): 21.

[104] International Association of Law Enforcement Firearms Instructors, *IALEFI Guidelines for Simulation Training Safety*, (2004): 18.

[105] Competition Electronics Inc., "View Shooting Products," *Pocket Pro II,* https://www.competitionelectronics.com/view-shooting-products.html?page=shop.product_details&flypage=flypage.tpl&product_id=28&category_id=7 (accessed September 22, 2012).

[106] North Carolina Justice Academy, *In-Service Firearms Qualification Manual* (Salemburg, NC: November 2009), BLET 2000 Handgun Qualification Course – 50 Rounds, Stage 4.

[107] Paul Howe, "Firearms Safety Rules," *Combat Shooting and Tactics PowerPoint Presentation*, (Combat Shooting and Tactics, Nacogdoches, TX: 2009): slide 28.

MAINTENANCE

Pistols are mechanical devices that require maintenance and can break, but proper maintenance reduces the likelihood of a mechanical failure. Properly maintained pistols are also more reliable, accurate, and have a higher resale value.[1] This chapter explains how to fieldstrip, clean, lubricate, inspect, and function test a Glock pistol. Much of the information on maintenance is applicable to other pistols as well.

Read the *Instructions for Use Glock Safe Action Pistols All Models* manual before performing preventive maintenance. Put down a protective barrier made from paper, plastic, cardboard, or cloth. After performing preventive maintenance and function testing the pistol, do not reload it immediately. Instead, leave the slide locked back and put the pistol in a secure place. Take a few minutes and dispose of used cleaning materials, clean and organize the cleaning area, and put back the cleaning kit.

Mentally accept that maintenance on the pistol is complete and retrieve ammunition for the pistol. Load the magazines and then load the pistol. While loading the pistol repeat aloud, "This firearm is loaded…This firearm is loaded…This firearm is loaded."[2] This forces the mind to focus consciously on the changed status of the pistol. An operator should never load a firearm after cleaning it until mentally changing focus from a maintenance mindset to an operational mindset.

An operator should be familiar with the pistol's nomenclature. (Figure 5-1) Nomenclature[3] is the correct name for each of the pistol's components. Knowing the name of the components helps the operator to understand the information provided in the Instructions for Use Glock Safe Action Pistols All Models manual. Likewise, when taking a training course the operator will know the component and its purpose *if* referred to by an instructor.

1. Front Sight
2. Slide
3. Slide Lock
4. Slide Stop Lever
5. Rear Sight
6. Back Strap
7. Grip Panel

8. Magazine
9. Front Strap
10. Magazine Catch
11. Trigger
12. Trigger Safety
13. Trigger Guard
14. Accessory Rail

15. Receiver/ Frame
16. Slide Cover Plate
17. Ejection Port
18. Muzzle (barrel)
19. Thumb Rest

Figure 5-1 Glock Safe Action Pistol Nomenclature

NOTE: As a rule, replacement parts are interchangeable within the *same* model of Glock pistols. There is no need, nor is it recommended to hand fit, file, or polish the parts.[4]

FUNCTIONS OF THE PISTOL

Proper maintenance will help ensure the four basic functions of the pistol occur as designed. The four basic functions of the pistol are as follows: (1) fire, (2) extract, (3) eject, and (4) feed. The entire function of the Glock pistol is as follows: (1) fire, (2) unlock, (3) extract, (4) eject (compression, recoil spring), (5) reset action, (6) feed, (7) chamber, (8) lock into battery, and (9) lock open (last shot).[5] However, an operator that understands the four functions will have the basic knowledge of how a pistol cycles.

The cycle begins once an operator pulls the trigger with a live round in the chamber and the firing pin strikes a primer causing the pistol to fire. The slide is forced back compressing the recoil spring assembly and the extractor is hooked on the rim of the case pulling it from the chamber. The slide continues to move rearward and the case strikes the ejector ejecting the case through the ejection port. The slide begins to move forward uncompressing the recoil spring assembly picking up a new round from the magazine feeding the round into the chamber. The cycle repeats until the magazine is empty.

When the magazine is empty, its follower will push upward against the slide stop lever causing the slide stop lever to engage the slide stop lever *notch* locking the slide to the rear.

Four Basic Functions

1. *Fire:* This occurs when the firing pin strikes the primer causing the powder charge to ignite.

2. *Extract:* The extractor hooks the rim of the case pulling it from the chamber.

3. *Eject:* The head of the case strikes the ejector ejecting the case through the ejection port.

4. *Feed:* The breech face contacts the uppermost round in the magazine pushing it into the chamber.

SERVICE INTERVALS

Following a regularly scheduled maintenance program will help ensure reliable pistol operation. This is especially important to those who carry a pistol for self-protection. Glock builds its pistols to resist harsh environmental conditions. However, cleaning and lubricating is required to prevent accumulated dirt and debris from interfering with the proper functioning of the pistol.

There may be people who boast about infrequent cleaning of their pistols. Boasting about *not* maintaining a firearm is merely expressing publicly a person's ignorance of responsible gun ownership. The operator's life or someone else's life could depend on the maintenance of a pistol. There are particular events that prompt the fieldstripping, cleaning, lubricating, and function testing of a Glock pistol.[6] Some of those events are as follows:

1. At the factory 2 rounds are fired and before firing the pistol again, perform maintenance.[7] Although the 2 rounds leave only a small amount of powder residue, clean and lubricate the pistol anyway.[8] Burnt gunpowder on the pistol can be a major issue during an investigation questioning whether the operator fired or not. Leave the factory lubricating grease in place to assist during the break-in period when cleaning a new pistol.

2. As needed to remove perspiration, saltwater, dirt, dust, etc.[9] Maintenance is particularly important for uniform police officers or military operators that work in adverse conditions (rain, snow, dust storms, mud, etc.). Clean and inspect a pistol for defects anytime it is dropped. Have the pistol inspected by a certified armorer if there is any doubt about its proper functioning. Patrol officers may be less than enthusiastic about cleaning their pistols after working a long tiring shift in the rain. Even less appealing is the thought of an inoperable pistol in a gunfight.

3. Clean and lubricate the pistol after each shooting session.[10] The proper functioning of the pistol is not the only reason. A pistol

used in a shooting resulting in a criminal investigation will be examined for gunpowder residue. The amount of residue on the pistol helps to establish the number of shots fired. A pistol not cleaned and used in a shooting poses a physical evidence problem (excessive residue in comparison to the number of shots allegedly fired).

4. Clean and lubricate the pistol monthly.[11] A monthly maintenance program ensures not only the proper functioning, but provides a specific time about the location and condition of the pistol. How many times have police officers answered a call involving a stolen firearm and the owner could not remember for sure the last time he or she saw the firearm?

5. Annually have a certified armorer perform an inspection of the pistol[12] and ensure that serial numbers of the components match. Take care in not mixing components of disassembled pistols when in a cleaning room. The pistol's serial number is stamped in the receiver, slide, and barrel. It is the responsibility of each operator to ensure they assemble their pistol with the correct components.

Proper pistol maintenance cannot be overstated. The desire to have a functioning firearm should outweigh any distain for cleaning a pistol. Neglecting the maintenance of a firearm is comparable to driving a vehicle and not regularly changing the oil or replacing worn and defective parts. The fact is cleaning a pistol is not a hard or complicated process. An assortment of cleaning supplies is required. These can be purchased in a cleaning kit from gun stores, some department stores, and online.

Cleaning and Lubrication Kits

To clean the bore an aluminum rod, stainless steel rod,[13] plastic coated steel rod,[14] or Glock's polymer cleaning rod (included in the locking pistol case) will do the job. Some cleaning rods have a guard to prevent damage to the barrel, and a rotating handle that allows the brush to track in the bore providing precise cleaning. The rod will have a threaded end to screw on attachments. The attachments are a ribbed jag, slotted jag, phosphor bronze straight bristle brush, or nylon bristle brush (included in Glock's locking pistol case). For most users the phosphor bronze brush is the preferable choice because of its rigidity.[15] A *ribbed jag* through the barrel provides a more consistent cleaning than the slotted jag. Purchase the jag separately if not included in the cleaning kit.[16] Also needed are cloth patches (caliber specific), cleaner/degreaser agent, oil, grease, and a plastic bristled brush with a handle. Purchase a complete cleaning kit to takeout the guesswork. (Figure 5-2)

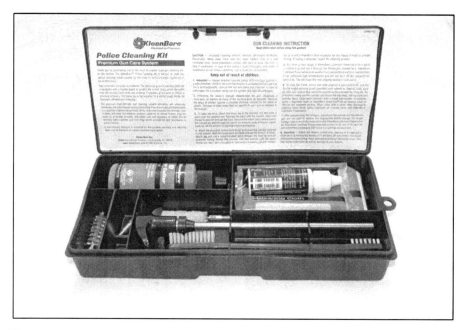

Figure 5-2 *Pistol Cleaning Kit*

Assemble a more environmentally friendly cleaning kit by substituting a solvent-based cleaner with a water-based enzymatic synthetic cleaner/degreaser and a petroleum-based lubricant with an extreme performance synthetic lubricant. A *refillable* 0.5-fluid ounce (14.78-milliliter) oil bottle made for the United States military that fits into most commercial cleaning kits is National Stock Number (NSN) 1005-00-242-5687.[17] The shape of the tip of the bottle is excellent for placing a drop of oil under the connector hook on a Glock pistol. (Figure 5-3)

Figure 5-3 *Refillable Oil Bottle*

Cleaning and Lubrication Products

Not all cleaning products for firearms perform equally. Most will do the job, but some are better. One of the best products to *clean* a firearm with is water-based, environmentally safe non-toxic formula that breaks down gun lubricants, powder residue, and other debris. (Figure 5-4) This non-toxic *cleaner/degreaser* leaves the surface of firearms free of lubricant residue providing an ideal surface for application of extreme performance lubricant.[18] The cleaner/degreaser also has a mild scent making cleaning firearms a more enjoyable experience.

One of the best product lines to *lubricate* a firearm with is a synthetic-based lubricant that penetrates the pores of metal surfaces while creating a roller bearing smooth surface. The lubricant is designed for extreme pressure and heavy load bearing conditions. The lubricant is available in grease[19] with the viscosity of a cold cream and in oil[20] with a thin viscosity. (Figure 5-5)

NOTE: Shake the tube of grease and oil bottle well before using. For the syringe applicator, pull the plunger back some and then shake.

Figure 5-4 *Non-toxic Cleaner/Degreaser*

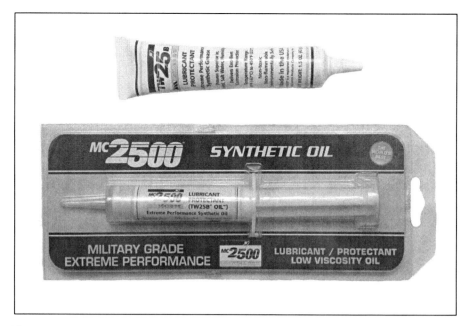

Figure 5-5 *Synthetic Lubricants*

The lubricant will perform reliably in temperatures from a minus 90 to 450-degrees Fahrenheit (minus 67.7 to 232.2-degrees Celsius).[21] The lubricant provides protection for not only wear parts, but the bore as well. Proper application will reduce galling, short-cycling, and may improve bore accuracy.[22] The lubricant also works well for long-term firearm storage and maintaining weapons in a ready condition. The non-toxic *synthetic* lubricant is approved for use on Glock pistols.[23]

CAUTION: Use cleaner/degreasers and lubricants in ventilated areas.[24] "Keep out of the reach of children. Avoid ingestion, inhalation, and eye contact."[25]

PREVENTIVE MAINTENANCE

WARNING: It is advisable to wear disposable nitrile *gloves*[26] and *safety glasses*[27] when cleaning a pistol. The disposable gloves are to prevent the skin from absorbing the cleaner, lubricant, and heavy metals. The safety glasses will help prevent eye injuries from uncontrolled spring-loaded parts, cleaner splatter, or lubricant splatter.[28] A clamp on *cleaning shield* that catches bore splatter from brushes and patches can be used to reduce airborne lead.[29]

Unloading the Pistol for Fieldstripping

Fieldstripping is the disassembling of a pistol at the operator level to perform normal maintenance (cleaning and lubrication).[30] There are no tools required and the pistol disassembles into four main components. The first step in fieldstripping is to ensure the pistol is *unloaded*. To unload the pistol, see the "Unloading Procedure" section in the Safety chapter.

CAUTION: When the slide is *locked back* on a Glock pistol or it is *fieldstripped*, do *not* reset the trigger to the forward position and pull it. Doing so can damage the trigger safety.[31]

Fieldstripping the Pistol

Review the Instructions for Use Glock Safe Action Pistols All Models manual on how to fieldstrip the pistol safely before performing maintenance. Many manufacturers have their instruction manuals online for downloading and viewing. Glock pistols require the slide to be forward and the trigger pulled before fieldstripping. The operator must make sure the pistol is *unloaded* and no ammunition is in the immediate area.[32]

DANGER: Remove all ammunition from the cleaning area!

The fieldstripping process can begin after having verified the pistol is *unloaded*. Carefully lay out each of the pistol's parts during the disassembly. A dissembled pistol will have a receiver (frame), slide, barrel, and recoil spring assembly (rod and spring). These are the four basic components. (Figure 5-6)

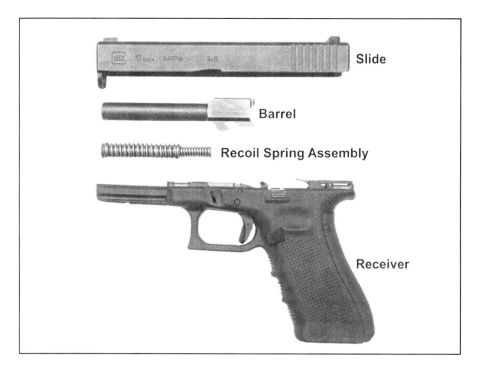

Figure 5-6 User/Operator Level Disassembly (fieldstripped)

Slide Removal:[33] The slide *cannot* be removed without the trigger being in the rear position. The trigger must be pulled to release the firing pin to remove the slide. Make sure the pistol *is* unloaded! A pistol equipped with a New York (NY) trigger spring may require a second pull of the trigger to remove the slide. Either hand can hold the pistol, but it may be easier to use the firing hand. Keep the muzzle pointed away from the body. The four fingers wrap over and grip the top of the slide with the thumb placed under the back strap. (Figure 5-7)

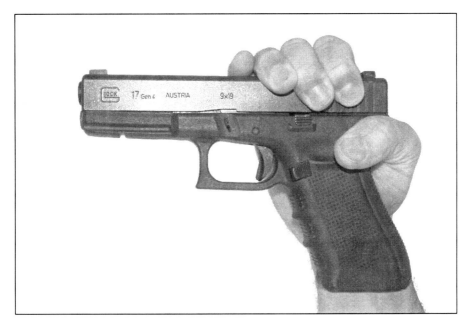

Figure 5-7 *Fingers wrapped over slide and thumb under the back strap.*

Using the four fingers, pull back about 1/8 inch (3.1 millimeters)[34] on the slide and hold. (Figure 5-8) The slide lock is disengaged from the barrel and the lock can be pulled down.

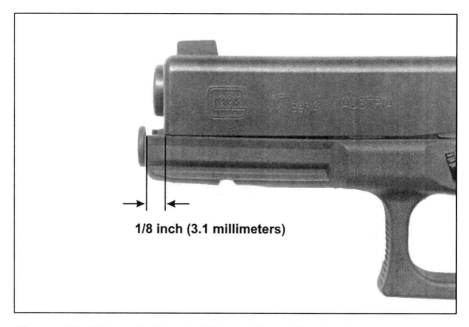

1/8 inch (3.1 millimeters)

Figure 5-8 Slide pulled back 1/8 inch (3.1 millimeters).

NOTE: Pulling the slide back too far will reset action and the trigger moves to the forward position. If this occurs, repeat the unloading procedure, keep the pistol pointed in the *appropriate direction*, pull the trigger to the rearward position, and repeat the slide removal steps.

While holding the slide back 1/8 inch (3.1 millimeters), simultaneously from underneath the receiver pull down and hold both sides of the slide lock using the thumb and index finger of the free hand. (Figure 5-9) With the slide slightly retracted and both sides of the slide lock held down, slightly push forward on the slide. (Figure 5-10) Rotate the pistol 90 degrees toward the centerline of the body and push the slide forward to separate it from the receiver. (Figure 5-11)

WARNING: The recoil spring assembly is under tension! Do not allow the recoil spring assembly to spring loose. Maintain control of the recoil spring assembly after removing the slide.

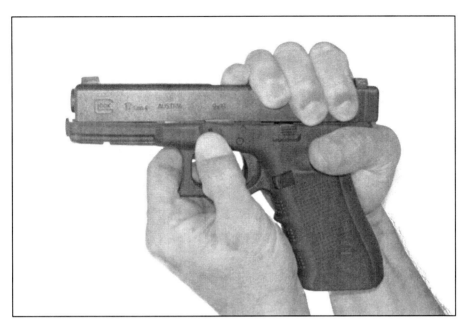

Figure 5-9 *Slide pulled back 1/8 inch (3.1 millimeters) while both sides of the slide locked is held down.*

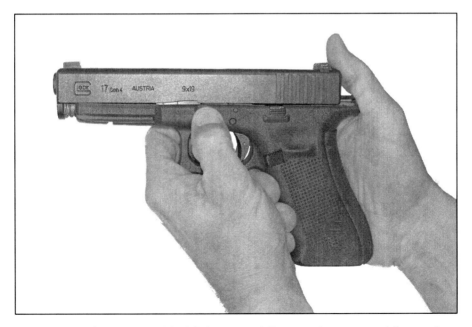

Figure 5-10 *Slide locked held down and the receiver moved forward.*

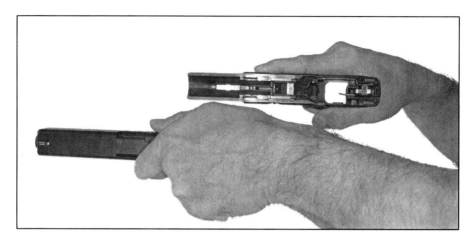

Figure 5-11 *Move slide forward until it separates from the receiver.*

Barrel Removal:[35] Grasp the back of the recoil spring assembly and push it slightly forward lifting it up and away from the barrel. (Figure 5-12)

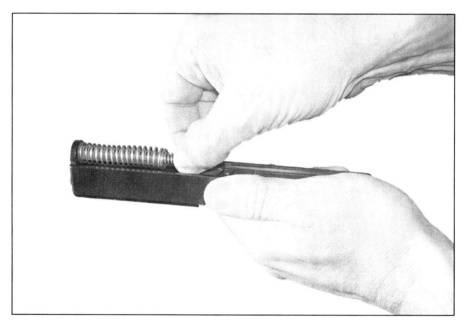

Figure 5-12 *Grasp the back of recoil spring assembly to remove.*

CAUTION: Since 1991, a one-piece recoil spring assembly superseded the recoil spring/recoil spring guide. Do *not* attempt to disassemble the recoil spring assembly.[36]

Remove the recoil spring assembly. (Figure 5-13) Grasp the barrel lug and lift the barrel from the slide. (Figure 5-14) Be careful *not* to drop the fieldstripped slide as an impact on a hard surface can crack or bend the guide ring or damage the rear of the rails.[37]

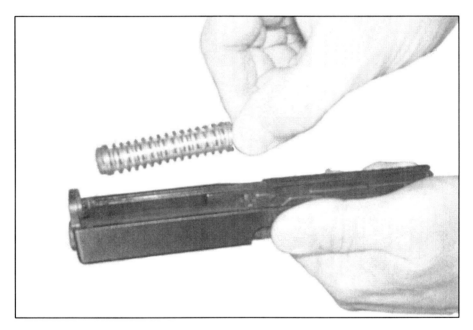

Figure 5-13 *Lift spring up and out.*

CAUTION: Further disassembly by the user is *not* required nor recommended. Only a certified Glock armorer should disassemble the pistol beyond fieldstripping.

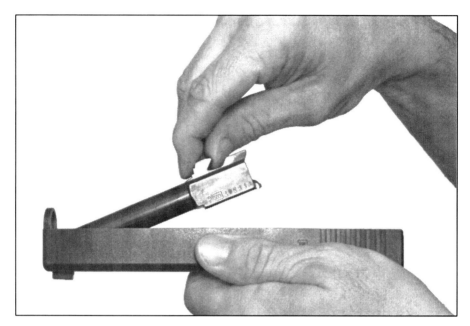

Figure 5-14 *Grasp barrel lug and lift to remove.*

Cleaning the Fieldstripped Pistol[38]

Make sure the fieldstripped pistol is free of cleaner/degreaser, especially from the firing pin channel, barrel chamber, and magazine body.[39] The cleaner/degreaser prepares the appropriate metal surfaces for treatment with the lubricant. The lubricant will not penetrate the metal pores unless the cleaner/degreaser is removed. The cleaner/degreaser is either sprayed onto the surfaces or wiped on with a soft cloth saturated with the solution. All surfaces are brushed or wiped thoroughly until clean. Finish by wiping the clean surfaces with a clean, dry cloth. The treated surfaces will be free of residue.

CAUTION: Do *not* dip the bronze brush or patches in the cleaner/degreaser to prevent contaminating the bottle.

Barrel: When a pistol is fieldstripped, the barrel and chamber are easily cleaned. Place a patch soaked with cleaner/degreaser on the ribbed jag and run it through the barrel a couple of times. Screw the bronze brush on the cleaning rod, wet the brush with cleaner/degreaser and push the bronze brush from the *chamber end* until it comes out the muzzle.

Now pull it back through and out of the chamber. Do this about 10 times. Changing direction inside the barrel with a brush will *damage* it. Place a patch soaked with cleaner/degreaser on the ribbed jag and run it through the barrel. Repeat until there is no debris on a patch. Finish the job with a couple of dry patches. The final patch should not have any fouling. When holding the barrel up to the light and looking through the bore there should not be any fouling visible.

CAUTION: Glock does *not* recommend to fire bullets without a metal jacket.[40] The lead can build up quickly causing enormous chamber pressure when firing.[41] Glock recommends using only metal jacket bullets to prevent the premature build up.

Recoil Spring Assembly: With a plastic bristle brush and cleaner/degreaser, clean the recoil spring assembly. With a clean soft cloth, wipe off the recoil spring assembly. It is not necessary to lubricate the recoil spring assembly.

Slide: Using a soft cloth wipe off the slide. Use a patch on a plastic brush and clean the rail cuts. On areas of the slide of a *new* Glock pistol, there may be a copper color lubricant.[42] The lubricant operates from minus 20 to 1800 degrees Fahrenheit (minus 29 to 982.2 degrees Celsius).[43] Do not remove the lubricant until it has dissipated as it provides lubrication during the break-in process.[44] The lubricant will dissipate under normal use. Turn the slide with the firing pin hole pointing down and brush the breech face and the extractor hook. Holding the slide in this manner *prevents* debris and lubricants from entering the firing pin channel. Remove the debris present and wipe the slide off with a cloth.

Receiver: Apply a cleaner/degreaser directly to the receiver as needed and scrub with a *plastic* bristle brush. Using a clean cloth dampened with a firearm cleaner/degreaser wipe off the receiver. Do *not* use harsh solvents such as nitrate-based on the outside or inside of the polymer receiver. Using a nitrate-based solvent to clean metal parts in the receiver will *damage* the plating.[45] Use a patch on the small end of a plastic brush and clean inside the receiver. Use caution when cleaning the receiver. Pulling out a cleaning cloth tangled with components in the receiver can damage the pistol. Small *cotton swabs* built for the rigors or firearms cleaning work well for reaching recessed areas in the receiver.[46]

Do *not* leave oil or grease on the receiver. Wipe the parts free of any cleaner/degreaser leaving them clean and dry.

NOTE: The four critical areas to clean are as follows: (1) breech face, (2) extractor hook, (3) slide rails, and (4) chamber/barrel.[47]

Inspecting the Fieldstripped Pistol[48]

A pistol fieldstripped and inspected at regular intervals will help ensure proper functioning. A function check that fails and cannot be resolved with proper cleaning warrants an examination of the pistol by Glock Inc., or a Glock certified armorer.

External Inspection: Inspect the pistol for dirt, corrosion, and physical damage. Look carefully at the sights, trigger, trigger safety, slide stop lever, slide lock, magazine catch, and extractor.

Barrel Inspection: Inspect the barrel for dirt, bulges, and cracks. Use the large hole in the front of the slide as a barrel inspection gauge. Slide the barrel muzzle first from the front of the slide into the large hole. (Figure 5-15) A barrel bulged will bind in the hole at the bulge. A barrel without a bulge will freely slide until stopped by the barrel hood. Inspect the barrel bore for build up or obstructions.

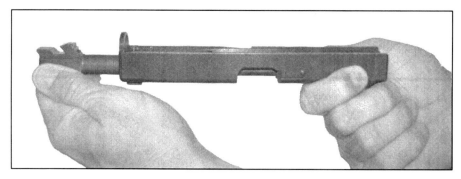

Figure 5-15 *Slide used as a gauge to check for bulged barrel.*

WARNING: A pistol that has a barrel with a crack, bulge, or obstruction in the bore should be returned to Glock Inc., for repair.

Slide Inspection: Glock pistols can develop wear marks in two places on the bottom of the slide. (Figure 5-16) This is called *slide peening.* The wear marks have *no* effect on the pistol's reliability or accuracy. Slide peening may be more noticeable on .40 S&W caliber pistols.[49] The two areas will wear some and then stop. A Glock armorer using a diamond file can smooth the edges *if* they are too sharp.

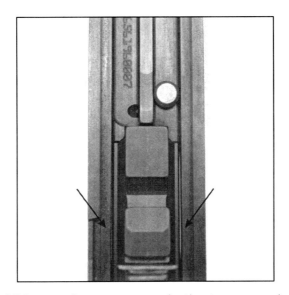

Figure 5-16 *Slide peening can occur in the two area depicted by the arrows.*

DANGER: A pistol most likely has a cracked slide if the shot group at 7 yards (6.4 meters) suddenly moves 12 inches (304.8 millimeters) to the left of the point of aim.[50] The crack will probably be near the ejection port.[51] To inspect for a crack use both hands to flex the slide on the ejection port side in a convex direction. (Figure 5-17) Do *not* fire the pistol until inspected and repaired by Glock Inc.

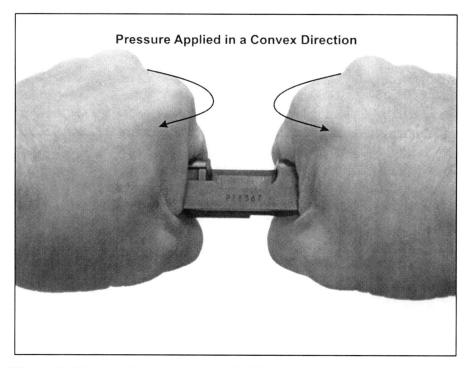

Figure 5-17 Inspecting for a cracked slide.

Firing Pin Safety Check: With the barrel and recoil assembly removed from the slide, pull the firing pin lug rearward until it stops. Maintain control of the lug. Now ease the firing pin forward until making contact with the firing pin safety.

CAUTION: Damage can occur to the firing pin or firing pin safety if the firing pin snaps forward slamming against the firing pin safety instead of allowing the firing pin to ease forward resting against the firing pin safety.

Push the firing pin forward with the thumb using about 5 to 8 pounds (2.2 to 3.6 kilograms) of pressure.[52] (Figure 5-18) The firing pin safety should block the firing pin and it should *not* protrude from the breech face of the slide.

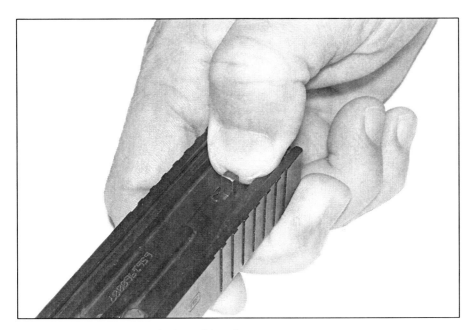

Figure 5-18 *Firing Pin Safety Check*

Firing Pin: Hold the slide muzzle end down and with a finger press in on the firing pin safety. The firing pin should move down with its tip protruding from the breech face. Make sure the tip of the firing pin is *not* chipped or blunted.

NOTE: A new pistol may require light finger pressure applied to the firing pin lug to assist the firing pin in moving downward.

Firing Pin Channel: Hold the slide while using a finger to press in on the firing pin safety and vigorously shake the slide end to end. There should be an audible rattle of the firing pin moving freely back and forth in the firing pin channel. Not hearing the rattle indicates there is a problem and a Glock armorer at minimum will need to clean the firing pin and firing pin channel.

NOTE: A new pistol may require several hundred rounds fired before the firing pin will move freely in the firing pin channel.

Extractor: The extractor claw should *not* be chipped or broken. Hold the slide, front sight end down. Look across the breech face inspecting for cleanliness and a damaged extractor. The extractor *should* be under heavy spring pressure with the chamber indicator flush with the slide.

CAUTION: A chipped extractor is usually a result of dropping a round directly in the chamber and allowing the slide to go forward.[53] The extractor has to jump the rim of the case. Load a Glock pistol from the magazine and a chipped extractor should not be a problem.

Ejector: The ejector in the receiver of the pistol should *not* be bent or broken.

Slide Stop Lever Test: The slide stop lever is spring loaded. Pull up on the slide stop lever and release. The slide stop lever should snap sharply down into the receiver. A slide stop lever properly cleaned, but is sluggish or remains in the up position is defective. Have the pistol repaired by Glock Inc., or a certified Glock armorer.

Lubricating the Fieldstripped Pistol[54]

Lubricating the Glock pistol is a simple matter and best accomplished using oil and grease. Use oil under the connector hook because the lubricant must migrate between the trigger bar and the connector. The oil has the same performance properties as grease in the same product line of lubricants.[55] Use grease for other areas requiring lubrication because of its resistance to debris adhesion in adverse conditions (sand, mud, water, etc.). The synthetic grease according to the manufacturer may last up to 10 times longer than other lubricants.[56] Oil can be used in the place of grease by wiping the components with a patch slightly dampened with oil in the same areas as when using grease. The lubricating procedures using oil are also in the Instructions for Use Glock Safe Action Pistols All Models manual.[57]

Lubricate the pistol with grease by putting it on a patch and run it from the breach end through the barrel. This will apply a light coat of white grease (not visible) inside the barrel. Make sure to wrap a clean dry patch around a small brush and dry the chamber. The chamber must remain free of lubricant. Using a clean patch dampened with grease, wipe a light coat of white grease on the outside of the barrel and barrel hood and lugs. (Figure 5-19) Wipe a light coat of white grease on inside of the slide at the top forward of the ejection port where during operation the hood rubs. Wipe a light coat of white grease around the opening the barrel slides though in front of the slide.

Figure 5-19 *Barrel lubrication is depicted by the black outline.*

Spread a moderate layer of white grease (slightly visible) along each of the rail cuts and the face of the offset ramp where the connector hook makes contact. (Figure 5-20) A small cotton swab works well for spreading the grease. Most important is to put a drop of *oil* under the connector hook located on the right rear corner of the receiver where the rear end of the trigger bar and the connector meet.[58] (Figure 5-21) Tilt the receiver to the left at a 45-degree angle when placing the drop of oil under the connector hook. The angle will assist in placing the oil and it migrating between the trigger bar and the connector. A symptom of little or no lubricant is a *hard* trigger pull that can lead to the trigger bar or connector being damaged.[59]

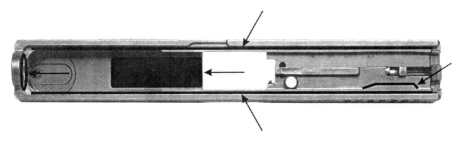

Figure 5-20 *Lubricate slide where depicted by arrows.*

The stated lubricating regiment will also work well for a pistol stored for an extended period. Do *not* store a pistol in a leather holster. Leather will absorb moisture and when in contact with metal causes rust to accumulate.

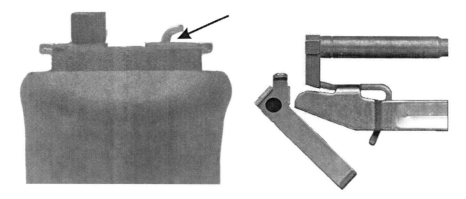

Figure 5-21 *Connector lubrication under the hook is depicted by the arrow and where the oil migrates is shown by the black dot on the connector.*

CAUTION: The hole near the extractor is visible with the bottom of the slide facing up. This hole has been *mistaken* as a lubrication point. This hole is *not* for lubrication![60] The hole *is* a channel for debris to fall out. Putting lubricant in the hole will cause carbon to build up into a paste negating the engineered purpose of the channel. The carbon paste buildup will cause the firing pin *not* to freely travel back and forth.[61] Keep the firing pin channel clean and dry. (Figure 5-22)

No Lubrication!

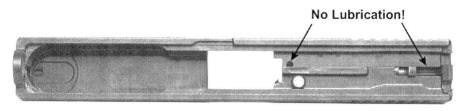

Figure 5-22 *Do not lubricate the two areas depicted by the arrows!*

One of the most common mistakes of firearms maintenance is applying too much lubricant. A pistol lubricated excessively when fired may inadvertently splatter the operator. The excessive application of lubricant has no benefit to the pistol's operation. The design of the Glock pistol allows it to operate properly with minimal lubrication. Excessive lubricant will attract unburned powder and foreign residue that can interfere with the proper operation. Do not over lubricate.[62]

Reassembling the Fieldstripped Pistol

Pick up the barrel by its bottom lug and insert into the slide.[63] (Figure 5-23) Place the recoil spring assembly small end into the guide ring and use the thumb to push against larger end compressing the spring. (Figure 5-24) Make certain the larger end seats in the semicircular cut located in the bottom of the front barrel lug.[64] (Figure 5-25) The recoil spring assembly must be centered, and parallel with the barrel.[65] This is especially critical for a Gen4 pistol.

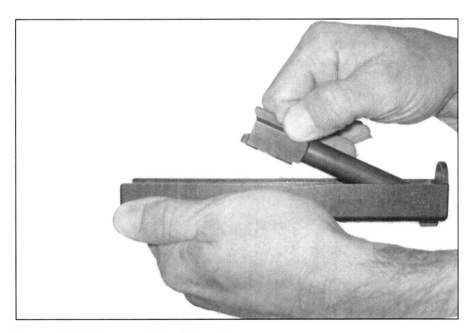

Figure 5-23 Reassembly of Barrel

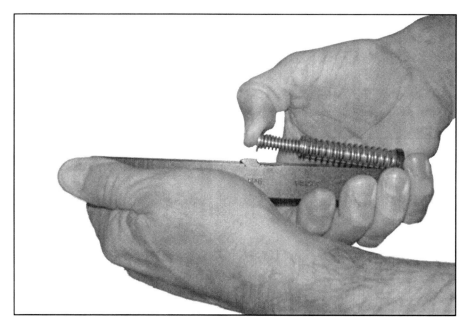

Figure 5-24 *Reassembly of Recoil Spring Assembly*

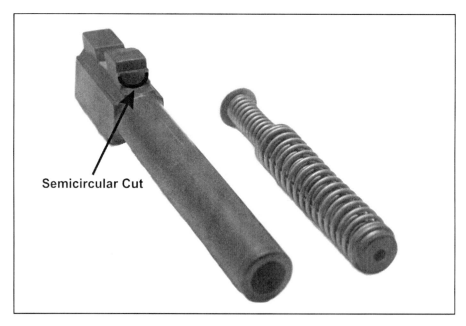

Semicircular Cut

Figure 5-25 *Semicircular cut in the bottom of the barrel lug.*

Rotate the *slide* in the hand where the back of it is facing to the rear. Rotate the receiver 90 degrees lining up the slide grooves with the four frame rails and pull the slide onto the receiver all the way to the rear. (Figure 5-26) Abnormal resistance means the recoil spring assembly is *not* seated, centered, and parallel.[66] Once seated, centered, and parallel, pull the slide to the rear and release allowing it to cycle forward. Using this technique eliminates the step of manually resetting the *trigger with trigger bar* to its forward position before installing the slide on the receiver of a Gen4 pistol in an attempt to make the installation easier.

NOTE: The receiver is rotated 90 degrees to help prevent jumping the slide over the rear frame rails by allowing the two parts to push toward each other naturally. To correct a pistol with the rear rails jumped make sure the trigger is in the rear position. Move the slide back 1/8 inch (3.1 millimeters) and hold down on the slide lock with the non-firing hand thumb and index finger. Use firing hand thumb push the slide forward and off the jumped rear frame rails. Reassemble the slide and receiver according to the previous paragraph.

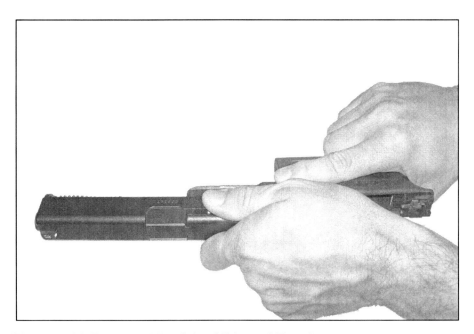

Figure 5-26 *Reassembly of the Slide and Receiver*

Inspecting the Reassembled Pistol[67]

With the pistol reassembled as outlined in the "Reassembling the Fieldstripped Pistol" section—inspect the *unloaded* pistol.

Slide Lock Test: With the pistol *unloaded* and the slide forward, use the thumb and index finger to pull down on the slide lock. The *slide lock* not moving means the slide is forward and locked in battery. Pull back on the slide 1/8 inch (3.1 millimeters) while pulling down on the slide lock and release. This verifies the spring is working and the slide lock will unlock.[68]

Trigger Safety Check: Rack the slide to reset the trigger to the forward position. Point the *unloaded* pistol in an appropriate direction, without touching or depressing the trigger safety and using the index finger and thumb, grasp the sides of the trigger and attempt to move the trigger rearward. The trigger's built in safety (trigger safety) should prevent the trigger from moving rearward. The pistol should *not* dry fire.

WARNING: A *failure* of the trigger safety allowing the trigger to move rearward and dry fire demands an immediate inspection and repair by Glock Inc., or a Glock certified armorer. Do *not* load or attempt to fire the pistol!

Trigger Reset Test: Point the *unloaded* pistol in an appropriate direction, pull the trigger, and hold it to the rear. There should be a click heard and felt from the firing pin falling. Do not let the trigger reset, continue to hold the trigger to the rear. Pull back on the slide and let it snap forward. Do *not* ride the slide forward. Let it snap forward under the pressure of the recoil spring. Release the trigger to allow it to reset to the forward position. Repeat the test three times.

Firing Pin Safety Release (free movement): Pulling the trigger allows the firing pin safety to move upward to clear the firing pin channel allowing the firing pin to strike the primer. Pull the trigger on an *unloaded* pistol to the rear and hold it to the rear while shaking the pistol back and forth. The noise of the firing pin moving back and forth should be heard. This means the firing pin channel is unobstructed and the firing pin safety moved enough for the firing pin to move freely.[69]

Recoil Spring/Guide Rod Assembly: Hold the *unloaded* pistol muzzle up at a 45-degree angle and pull the trigger. Hold the trigger to the rear. While holding the trigger to the rear pull the slide back and release it slowly. The recoil spring should push the slide forward into battery verifying that under less than ideal circumstances the ammunition should chamber.[70]

Magazine Inspection: Inspect the *empty* magazines for dirt and physical damage. Look carefully for spread or damaged feed lips or a broken magazine follower. With a fingertip press the follower down and release. A proper functioning follower will spring fully upward without sticking or sluggish movement inside the magazine tube.

Slide Lock-open Test: Make sure the magazine is clean and *empty.* Insert an empty magazine in the pistol. Aggressively pull the slide to the rear. The slide should lock back and remain open. This verifies the magazine spring is strong enough to feed the ammunition reliably and can move the slide stop lever up to lock the slide back on an empty magazine. With each empty magazine, repeat the process.

After inspecting the reassembled *unloaded* pistol, perform one final wipe with a clean cloth of the entire outer surfaces. Do not leave any fingerprints on the outer metal surfaces as body oils can cause corrosion. Make sure the slide is forward and the trigger is to the rear when storing an *unloaded* Glock pistol.

MAGAZINE MAINTENANCE

Glock makes a full metal lined[71] magazine commonly referred to as *drop free.* The four sides of the magazine are lined with metal. The magazine at the top rear has a square shape cutout with the middle angled. This magazine has *windows* (holes marked with numbers) to view cartridges indicating the number rounds. The older Glock magazines (non-full metal lined)[72] were metal lined on three sides and commonly referred to as *non-drop free.* This magazine at the top rear has a circular shape cutout. The non-drop free was designed to swell to prevent the loss of a magazine (military applications) in the advent the magazine catch was inadvertently activated.[73]

Magazine disassembly and cleaning is *not* normally required each time the Glock pistol is cleaned. However, clean magazines every 3 to 4 months.[74] Magazines that are exposed to dirt, mud, sand, etc., require a thorough cleaning.

CAUTION: Unload the magazines and store the ammunition in a container. Place the container of ammunition in an area other than the cleaning area. This practice reduces the chance of a negligent discharge and prevents cleaners and lubricants from contaminating the ammunition.[75] Exposing ammunition to cleaners and lubricants may cause a failure to fire stoppage. This is because of the primer or powder of the cartridge becoming soaked with cleaner or lubricant.

To disassemble a Glock magazine the floor plate must be removed. The three types of magazines are as follows: (1) magazine floor plate with an insert, (2) standard magazine with a 10 round capacity, and (3) early style magazine without an insert.[76] Each magazine type disassembles differently.

CAUTION: "The magazine spring, follower, and inner floor plate are under spring tension, and can cause eye or other injury if not controlled during removal. Wear protective safety glasses to reduce the risk of eye injuries. Be sure to maintain downward pressure on the magazine spring, with your thumb, while disassembling."[77]

Standard Magazine Disassembly[78]

The magazine disassembles into five components. (Figure 5-27) To remove the floor plate, push a pin punch into the hole of the floor plate disengaging the magazine insert.[79] (Figure 5-28) With the pin punch inserted, pull the floor plate forward while simultaneously with the thumb and index finger *squeezing* the sides of the magazine together near its base. This disengages the retaining tabs from the notches in the floor plate and it will slide forward. Remove the pin punch from the floor plate. The magazine spring is under tension! Use the thumb to cover the bottom of the magazine tube *controlling* the magazine spring (Figure 5-29). Failure to control the spring could result in an injury. Slide the magazine floor plate from the magazine tube. Remove the insert, spring, and follower.

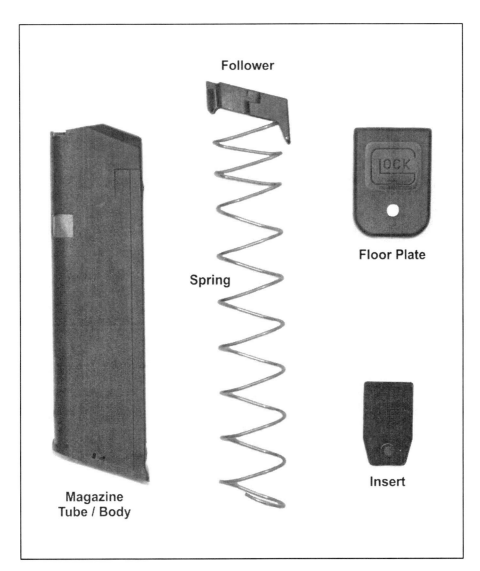

Figure 5-27 *Magazine Components*

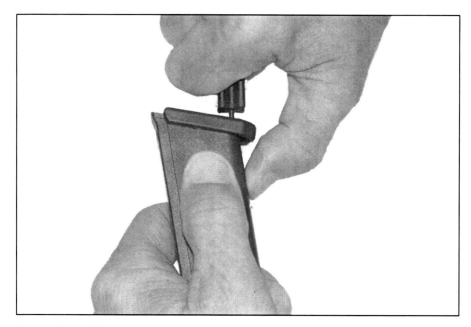

Figure 5-28 Magazine Disassembly

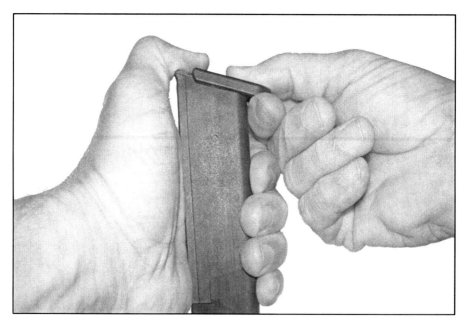

Figure 5-29 Magazine spring controlled.

Ten Round Standard Magazine Disassembly

Use a thin bladed screwdriver to unlock the floor plate. To remove the floor plate, slightly push down the insert and pull the floor plate forward. The magazine spring is under tension! Use the thumb to cover the bottom of the magazine tube to control the magazine spring. Failure to control the spring could result in an injury. Slide the magazine floor plate from the magazine tube and remove the magazine spring and follower.

Early Style Magazine Disassembly

To remove the floor plate, grasp the bottom of the magazine with the thumb and index finger, squeeze the sides together to disengage the retaining tabs from the notches in the floor plate. Holding both sides together, press a rear corner of the floor plate against a solid surface (tabletop, etc.) and dislodge about 1/8 inch (3.1 millimeters) toward the front of the magazine tube. The magazine is under tension! Use the thumb to cover the bottom of the magazine tube to control the magazine spring. Failure to control the spring could result in an injury. Slide the magazine floor plate from the magazine tube and remove the magazine spring and follower.

Magazine Maintenance[80]

Use a dry brush to brush out a disassembled magazine. Wipe off the spring with a soft dry cloth. Brush the follower clean and wipe with a soft dry cloth. Wipe off any cleaner or lubricant from the magazine parts to prevent contamination of ammunition. Contamination can result in a failure to fire. Do *not* use harsh solvents on the magazine or attempt to lubricate any of its components.

Fraying can occur around the catch notch on Glock magazines. Use a razor knife and cut away any fraying flush with the magazine body. The magazine spring should protrude two to three coils above the bottom edge of the magazine body.[81] Replace any spring protruding lower than two coils. Consult Glock Inc., or a Glock Parts Order Form for specific models and the required magazine springs. After assembling the magazine, perform a *slide lock-open* test.[82] With the slide forward on an empty pistol, insert an *empty* magazine into the magazine well. Pull the slide to the rear using an underhand technique. The slide should lock open. Repeat using each empty magazine.

Not the pistol, but a damaged magazine is frequently the cause of stoppages. The feed lips can get bent deforming the original shape. The damaged magazine will likely not retain the cartridges as designed. As the top cartridge is stripped, the next cartridge may pop free during the feeding cycle causing double feed stoppage. Inspect the magazine feed lips for cracks or deformation. A damaged magazine does *not* allow the rounds to feed into the chamber automatically and can convert a semiautomatic pistol into a single shot firearm. Something an operator does *not* want in a gunfight. Do *not* attempt to straighten deformed lips of a magazine. Dispose of damaged magazines.

FIELD REPAIR KIT

There are remote locations that would make it difficult to obtain spare parts for a Glock pistol. An operator going to such a location would do well to take three tools and some spare parts. The tools are as follows: (1) front sight mounting tool, (2) Glock 3/32 inch (2.5 millimeter) pin punch disassembly tool,[83] and (3) 90-degree dental pick. The spare parts are as follows:

1. Assembled Firing Pin Unit (firing pin, spacer sleeve, firing pin spring, and spring cups)
2. Extractor
3. Front Sight & Mounting Screw (inadvertently torn off)
4. Pin Set (trigger pin, locking block pin, and trigger housing pin)
5. Recoil Spring Assembly
6. Slide Lock (slide lock can fall out if the spring breaks)
7. Slide Lock Spring
8. Slide Stop Lever & Spring (one assembly)
9. Trigger Spring

CAUTION: Remove a broken slide lock spring without damaging the receiver by applying pressure with the pointed tip of the dental pick to the broken portion and flicking it out of the frame.[84]

SCHEDULED REPLACEMENT PARTS[85]

Periodically inspect Glock pistols heavily used or exposed to harsh environments. Although usage and operational conditions will dictate inspection intervals, a good rule of thumb is an *annual inspection* by a certified Glock armorer. Replace worn or defective parts. Replace *wearable* parts to reduce the chance of a future mechanical failure. "Wearable parts are those that by their nature will not maintain absolute factory specifications forever and will need to be monitored periodically for satisfactory function."[86] Utilizing periodic field inspections may reveal potential problems.

Springs

The proper cycle of operation for the pistol depends on springs that are not weak or damaged. Worn, damaged, or broken springs will lead to unsatisfactory performance. The list below is of springs in a Glock pistol and magazine that may require attention.

1. Extractor Depressor Plunger Spring
2. Firing Pin Safety Spring
3. Firing Pin Spring
4. Magazine Catch Spring
5. Magazine Spring
6. Recoil Spring Assembly
7. Slide Lock Spring
8. Slide Stop Spring (attached to the slide stop lever—not a separate part, sold as a unit)
9. Trigger Spring

Extractor

The extractor tip should not have any chipping. The extractor should be clean and have proper tension. A worn or damaged extractor can cause feeding and extraction problems.

Firing Pin/Firing Pin Safety

The firing pin safety is engaged by the front of the firing pin and wear can occur in these areas.

Magazine Followers

The magazine followers hold rounds at the proper angle for reliable feeding and place upward pressure on the slide stop lever to lock the slide back on an empty magazine. Periodically check the follower for serviceability.

Magazine Bodies

The lips of the magazine body assist with proper feeding of a round into the chamber. The lips can be *damaged* by improper cleaning, i.e., pulling a cloth through the body out the lips forcing them apart. The magazine catch to operate properly engages either the front recess (ambidextrous) or side notches (reversible) on the magazine body. These cuts can build up polymer burrs, frequently check cut areas. Remove the burrs using a razor knife.[87]

SUMMARY

How to maintain a Glock pistol is in the Instructions for Use Glock Safe Action Pistols All Models manual. Proper maintenance helps to ensure the pistol will function as designed. Properly maintained pistols generally have a higher resale value. Only a certified Glock armorer should disassemble a Glock pistol beyond fieldstripping. A serial number is stamped on the major components of a pistol. Do not mix components between pistols. Always wear safety glasses when cleaning a pistol. Clean a pistol as required or at least monthly. Have a Glock pistol inspected annually by a certified Glock armorer. Know how to function test a pistol to ensure it is operating properly. The pistol may be the *only* available weapon capable of preventing the death of an operator or innocent person. Engraving magazines with the pistol's serial number is an effective method to establish agency or private ownership.

DISCUSSION QUESTIONS

1. A pistol is what type of device that can break and requires maintenance?
2. Before performing preventative maintenance on a particular brand and model of pistol, what needs to be first read and thoroughly understood?
3. Why does Glock Inc., recommend not to hand fit, file, or polish the parts of a Glock pistol?
4. List the four basic functions of a pistol.
5. Discuss the events that prompt the fieldstripping, cleaning, lubricating, and function testing of a pistol.
6. What type of jag provides a more consistent cleaning of the barrel than the slotted jag?
7. What is the operator level disassembly of a pistol to perform normal maintenance (cleaning and lubrication) called?
8. Why should the magazines be unloaded, and the ammunition stored in a container before performing maintenance of a pistol?
9. Why is it recommended to wear rubber gloves and safety glasses when cleaning a pistol?
10. Discuss how to fieldstrip, clean, inspect, lubricate, assemble and function check a Glock pistol.
11. How often should Glock magazines be cleaned?
12. Describe how to disassemble, clean, inspect, and assemble Glock magazines.
13. List the field repair kit recommended parts for a Glock pistol.
14. Describe the parts in a Glock pistol that are wearable due to normal use.
15. Why is it important to replace the wearable parts in a Glock pistol?

ENDNOTES

[1] National Rifle Association, *NRA Guide to the Basics of Personal Protection Outside the Home* (Fairfax, VA: National Rifle Association of America, 2006), 329.

[2] Kathy Jackson, *The Cornered Cat: A Woman's Guide to Concealed Carry* (White Feather Press, 2010), 252.

[3] Nomenclature: "A system of names used in an art or science: the nomenclature of mineralogy." See *The American Heritage Dictionary of the English Language Online*, 4th ed., s.v. "nomenclature," http://www.thefreedictionary.com/nomenclature (accessed September 22, 2012).

[4] Glock Inc., *Armorer's Manual*, (Smyrna, GA: 2002): 4.

[5] Glock Inc., *Glock Pistol Transitional Instructor Workshop Course Outline*, (Smyrna, GA: 2012): 4.

[6] Glock Inc., *Instructions for Use Glock Safe Action Pistols All Models*, (Smyrna, GA: March 2011), 42.

[7] Glock Inc., *Preventative Maintenance of the Glock Semiautomatic "Safe Action" Pistol*, (Smyrna, GA: 2003): 1.

[8] Glock Inc., *Glock Advanced Armorer's Manual*, (Smyrna, GA: 2008): 3.

[9] Glock Inc., *Preventative Maintenance of the Glock Semiautomatic "Safe Action" Pistol*, (Smyrna, GA: 2003): 1.

[10] Glock Inc., *Preventative Maintenance of the Glock Semiautomatic "Safe Action" Pistol*, (Smyrna, GA: 2003): 1.

[11] Glock Inc., *Preventative Maintenance of the Glock Semiautomatic "Safe Action" Pistol*, (Smyrna, GA: 2003): 1.

[12] Glock Inc., *Instructions for Use Glock Safe Action Pistols All Models*, (Smyrna, GA: March 2011), 48.

[13] Kleen-Bore Inc., "Our Products," *Law Enforcement Kits*, http://store.safariland.com/kleen-bore/lawkits.html (accessed September 22, 2012).

[14] Kleen-Bore Inc., "Our Products," *Saf-T-Clad Cleaning Kit*, http://store.safariland.com/kleen-bore/saftcladkits.html (accessed September 22, 2012).

[15] Kleen-Bore Inc., "FAQs," *What Brush Material Should I Use for Bore Cleaning?* http://www.kleen-bore.com/faq.html (accessed September 22, 2012).

[16] Kleen-Bore Inc., "Jags – Bore Cleaning," *Cleaning Jags*, http://store.safariland.com/kleen-bore/jags.html (accessed September 22, 2012).

[17] "National Stock Number. Indicates the National stock number assigned to the item and will be used for requisitioning purposes." See Departments of the Army, Navy, Air Force, Commandants, Marine Corps and Coast Guard, *Operator's Manual Pistol, Semiautomatic, 9mm, M9 (1005-01-118-2640*, (Washington, DC: July 31, 1985), B-2.

[18] Mil-Comm Products Company Inc., *Basic Application Instructions*, MC25® Cleaner/Degreaser, (East Rutherford, NJ: February 2006).

[19] Mil-Comm Products Company Inc., "Weapon Lubricants Gun Care," *TW25B Light Grease Lubricant/Protectant*, http://www.mil-comm.com/index.php?page=shop.product_details&flypage=shop.flypage&product_id= 6&category_id=5&manufacturer_id=0&option=com_virtuemart&Itemid=65 (accessed September 22, 2012).

[20] Mil-Comm Products Company Inc., "Weapon Lubricants Gun Care," *MC2500 Oil Lubricant/Protectant*, http://www.mil-comm.com/index.php?page=shop.product_details&flypage=shop.flypage&product_id= 1&category_id=1&manufacturer_id=0&option=com_virtuemart&Itemid=65 (accessed September 22, 2012).

[21] Mil-Comm Products Company Inc., "For Military and Law Enforcement Security Hardware Marine Markets and Manufacturing," *FAQs*, http://www.mil-comm.com/index.php?option=com_content&task=view&id=29&Itemid=43 (accessed September 22, 2012).

[22] Gall: "To damage or break the surface of by or as if by friction; abrade…" See *The American Heritage Dictionary of the English Language Online*, 4th ed., s.v. "gall," http://www.thefreedictionary.com/gall (accessed September 22, 2012).

[23] "Other leading firearms manufacturers serving the law enforcement community also specify or approve TW25B® for use, among them: Glock, FN, ArmaLite, DPMS and Knight's Armament." See Mil-Comm Products Company Inc., "For Military and Law Enforcement," *Law Enforcement*, http://www.mil-comm.com/index.php?option=com_content&task=view&id=45&Itemid=63 (accessed September 22, 2012).

[24] Glock Inc., *Glock Advanced Armorer's Manual*, (Smyrna, GA: 2008): 3.

[25] Caution label used on TW25B products. See Mil-Comm Products Company Inc., *Material Safety Data Sheet (M.S.D.S.) TW25B HMIS Code: 211B*, (East Rutherford, NJ: June 2010).

[26] National Rifle Association, *NRA Guide to Basics of Personal Protection Outside the Home* (Fairfax, VA: National Rifle Association of America, 2006), 329.

[27] Glock Inc., *Armorer's Manual*, (Smyrna, GA: 2009): 19.

Glock Inc., *Instructions for Use Glock Safe Action Pistols All Models*, (Smyrna, GA: March 2011), 43.

[28] Glock Inc., *Instructions for Use Glock Safe Action Pistols All Models*, (Smyrna, GA: March 2011), 43.

[29] Accu-Fire Inc., "Home," *Muzzlemate*, http://www.accufireproducts.com/ (accessed September 22, 2012).

[30] Glock Inc., *Armorer's Manual*, (Smyrna, GA: 2009): 19.

Glock Inc., *Instructions for Use Glock Safe Action Pistols All Models*, (Smyrna, GA: March 2011), 42.

[31] Glock Inc., *Instructions for Use Glock Safe Action Pistols All Models*, (Smyrna, GA: March 2011), 31.

[32] Glock Inc., *Armorer's Manual*, (Smyrna, GA: 2009): 19.

Glock Inc., *Instructions for Use Glock Safe Action Pistols All Models*, (Smyrna, GA: March 2011), 43.

[33] Glock Inc., *Preventative Maintenance of the Glock Semiautomatic "Safe Action" Pistol*, (Smyrna, GA: 2003): 4.

[34] Glock Inc., *Armorer's Manual*, (Smyrna, GA: 2009): 21.

Glock Inc., *Instructions for Use Glock Safe Action Pistols All Models*, (Smyrna, GA: March 2011), 43.

[35] Glock Inc., *Instructions for Use Glock Safe Action Pistols All Models*, (Smyrna, GA: March 2011), 44.

[36] Glock Inc., *Instructions for Use Glock Safe Action Pistols All Models*, (Smyrna, GA: March 2011), 15.

[37] Glock Inc., *Armorer's Manual*, (Smyrna, GA: 2009): 23.

[38] Glock Inc., *Preventative Maintenance of the Glock Semiautomatic "Safe Action" Pistol*, (Smyrna, GA: 2003): 11.

[39] Glock Inc., *Glock Advanced Armorer's Manual*, (Smyrna, GA: 2008): 3.

[40] Glock Inc., *Instructions for Use Glock Safe Action Pistols All Models*, (Smyrna, GA: March 2011), 15.

[41] Robin Taylor, Bobby Carver, and Mark Passamaneck, *The Glock in Competition*, (Bellingham, WA: Taylor Press, 2010): 65-76.

[42] Loctite Brand, "Industrial," *Loctite C5-A Copper Anti-Seize*, http://www.henkelna.com/cps/rde/xchg/henkel_us/hs.xsl/product-search-1554.htm?iname=Loctite+C5-A+Copper+Anti-Seize&countryCode=us&BU=industrial&parentredDotUID=productfinder&redDotUID=0000000I5D (accessed September 22, 2012).

[43] Loctite Brand, "Loctite C5-A Copper Anti-Seize," (Westlake, OH: September 2009), https://tds.us.henkel.com//NA/UT/HNAUTTDS.nsf/web/7506CCBCD9CC920E882571870000D92C/$File/C5-ACBAS-EN.pdf (accessed September 22, 2012).

[44] Glock Inc., *Armorer's Manual*, (Smyrna, GA: 2009): 79.

[45] "Exercise care when using any nitrate-based solvent as it can adversely affect some types of finishes (including nickel plating)." See Glock Inc., *Glock Advanced Armorer's Manual*, (Smyrna, GA: 2008): 3.

[46] Bear Metal Gun Cleaning Supplies, Inc., "Gun Cleaning Supplies," *G-tip Gun Cleaning Swabs,* http://www.bearmetalclean.com/ (accessed September 22, 2012).

[47] Glock Inc., "Law Enforcement," (Smyrna, GA: *2010 General Information*): DVD, PowerPoint Slide 92.

[48] Glock Inc., *Preventative Maintenance of the Glock Semiautomatic "Safe Action" Pistol*, (Smyrna, GA: 2003): 13-16.

[49] Robin Taylor, Bobby Carver, and Mark Passamaneck, *The Glock in Competition*, (Bellingham, WA: Taylor Press, 2010): 100.

[50] Alan Ramsey, Director of Training for Glock provided the information during the Advance Armorer's course held at Glock Inc., in Smyrna, Georgia, in a face-to-face conversation with the author, January 26-27, 2010.

A police officer had a slide crack below the ejection port on a Glock pistol that underwent a torture test. The rounds did impact to the left, but the pistol continued to function. See Robin Taylor, Bobby Carver, and Mark Passamaneck, *The Glock in Competition*, (Bellingham, WA: Taylor Press, 2010): 228-229.

[51] Glock Inc., *Glock Advanced Armorer's Manual*, (Smyrna, GA: 2008): 5.

[52] Glock Inc., *Instructions for Use Glock Safe Action Pistols All Models*, (Smyrna, GA: March 2011), 47.

[53] Robin Taylor, Bobby Carver, and Mark Passamaneck, *The Glock in Competition*, (Bellingham, WA: Taylor Press, 2010): 105.

[54] Glock Inc., *Preventative Maintenance of the Glock Semiautomatic "Safe Action" Pistol*, (Smyrna, GA: 2003): 11-13.

[55] Mil-Comm Products Company Inc., "For Military and Law Enforcement," *FAQs*, http://www.mil-comm.com/index.php?option=com_content&task=view&id=29&Itemid=43 (accessed September 22, 2012).

[56] Mil-Comm Products Company Inc., "Weapon Lubricants Gun Care," *TW25B Light Grease Lubricant/Protectant,* http://www.mil-comm.com/index.php?page=shop.product_details&flypage=shop.flypage&product_id=6&category_id=5&manufacturer_id=0&option=com_virtuemart&Itemid=65 (accessed September 22, 2012).

[57] Glock Inc., *Instructions for Use Glock Safe Action Pistols All Models*, (Smyrna, GA: March 2011), 46-47.

[58] Glock Inc., *Instructions for Use Glock Safe Action Pistols All Models*, (Smyrna, GA: March 2011), 46.

[59] Glock Inc., *Armorer's Manual*, (Smyrna, GA: 2009): 78.

[60] Glock Inc., "Law Enforcement," (Smyrna, GA: *2010 General Information*): DVD, PowerPoint Slide 98.

[61] Robin Taylor, Bobby Carver, and Mark Passamaneck, *The Glock in Competition*, (Bellingham, WA: Taylor Press, 2010): 109.

[62] Glock Inc., *Armorer's Manual*, (Smyrna, GA: 2009): 78.

[63] Glock Inc., *Armorer's Manual*, (Smyrna, GA: 2009): 25.

[64] Glock Inc., *Armorer's Manual*, (Smyrna, GA: 2009): 25.

[65] Glock Inc., *Armorer's Manual*, (Smyrna, GA: 2009): 25.

[66] Glock Inc., *Armorer's Manual*, (Smyrna, GA: 2009): 25.

[67] Glock Inc., *Preventative Maintenance of the Glock Semiautomatic "Safe Action" Pistol*, (Smyrna, GA: 2003): 13-16.

[68] Glock Inc., *Armorer's Manual*, (Smyrna, GA: 2009): 63.

[69] Glock Inc., *Armorer's Manual*, (Smyrna, GA: 2009): 64.

[70] Glock Inc., *Armorer's Manual*, (Smyrna, GA: 2009): 63.

[71] Glock Inc., *Armorer's Manual*, (Smyrna, GA: 2009): 93.

[72] Glock Inc., *Armorer's Manual*, (Smyrna, GA: 2009): 93.

[73] Robin Taylor, Bobby Carver, and Mark Passamaneck, *The Glock in Competition*, (Bellingham, WA: Taylor Press, 2010): 83.

[74] Glock Inc., *Instructions for Use Glock Safe Action Pistols All Models*, (Smyrna, GA: March 2011), 45.

[75] Glock Inc., *Instructions for Use Glock Safe Action Pistols All Models*, (Smyrna, GA: March 2011), 43.

[76] Glock Inc., *Armorer's Manual*, (Smyrna, GA: 2009): 60.

[77] Glock Inc., *Instructions for Use Glock Safe Action Pistols All Models*, (Smyrna, GA: March 2011), 45.

[78] Glock Inc., *Preventative Maintenance of the Glock Semiautomatic "Safe Action" Pistol*, (Smyrna, GA: 2003): 13-16.

[79] Magazine Insert: "The magazine insert serves to lock the floor plate to the magazine body." See Glock Inc., *Armorer's Manual*, (Smyrna, GA: 2009): 62.

[80] Glock Inc., *Preventative Maintenance of the Glock Semiautomatic "Safe Action" Pistol*, (Smyrna, GA: 2003): 8-10.

[81] Alan Ramsey, Director of Training for Glock provided the information during the Advance Armorer's course held at Glock Inc., in Smyrna, Georgia, in a face-to-face conversation with the author, January 26-27, 2010.

[82] Glock Inc., *Instructions for Use Glock Safe Action Pistols All Models*, (Smyrna, GA: March 2011), 48.

[83] Glock Inc., *Armorer's Manual*, (Smyrna, GA: 2009): 26.

[84] Alan Ramsey, Director of Training for Glock provided the information during the Glock 18 (18C) Select-Fire Familiarization Workshop course held at Glock Inc., in Smyrna, Georgia, in a face-to-face conversation with the author, January 28, 2010.

[85] Glock Inc., *Armorer's Manual*, (Smyrna, GA: 2009): 80-81.

[86] Glock Inc., *Armorer's Manual*, (Smyrna, GA: 2009): 80.

[87] Glock Inc., *Glock Advanced Armorer's Manual*, (Smyrna, GA: 2008): 4.

COMBAT SHOOTING PHASE 1

6

Combat shooting for the purpose of this book is an operator subconsciously discharging a pistol quickly and accurately at one or more adversaries that may appear only briefly. The ability to discharge a pistol subconsciously comes from repetitious practice of handling and firing in training until becoming a part of the operator's procedural memory. Accuracy is the operator's ally and must be required during training. The thought process while firing in combat is twofold: Am I hitting the adversary? Is it working? A "no" answer to either one of the questions means an immediate adjustment is necessary until both answers are "yes."

Combat shooting is *not* firing in the operator's own time frame, but within the time frame the adversary is exposed. Combat shooting is *not* expending large amounts of ammunition just for the sake of firing. A bad situation is being in a gunfight with an empty pistol and no more ammunition. Combat shooting will enable an armed civilian, police officer, or military operator to best utilize a pistol for self-protection. The deployment of a pistol usually signifies a probable or actual life-and-death situation. An operator in such situations had better have the solution to the problem and not be a part of the problem, i.e., poor combat shooting skills.

Precision shooting conversely is a conscious application of the fundamentals of marksmanship: getting into a comfortable shooting position, obtaining a sight picture, controlling the natural respiratory pause, reducing the wobble area to an acceptable degree, applying pressure to the trigger until the break occurs, and the shot fires.[1] Precision shooting is beneficial for a sniper as the effects of an alarm reaction are usually not an issue and the adversary may be 100 yards (91.44 meters) or more away. Precision shooting is also used for zeroing firearms, which is a skill every operator should possess.

The mechanics of precision shooting will *not* work in close quarters combat. The operator does *not* have time to get into a shooting position, raise the pistol, get a sight picture, control the breathing, reduce the wobble area, and apply pressure to the trigger until the pistol fires. All these things occur nearly simultaneous in combat. Precision shooting is exemplified by techniques used in bull's-eye competition as the shooter controls the time of the shot.[2] A back-to-back comparison of the two shooting disciplines at a target 10 yards (9.14 meters) away will prove combat shooting is sufficiently accurate and quicker than precision shooting.

Combat shooting should be taught before precision shooting.[3] The most important and applicable shooting skills for self-protection in close quarters combat are the priority. Teaching precision shooting first can be counterproductive to self-protection by providing an operator with a false sense of security. An operator trained only in precision shooting is at a disadvantage in a combat environment. As closely and realistically as possible bring the combat environment to the range.

NOTE: With the exception of warfare, it is morally and legally preferable *not* to shoot a human. Sometimes just presenting a pistol *without* firing is sufficient to stop or deter an adversary.[4] However, an operator should *never* put his or her life in danger for the sake of not shooting an adversary when deadly force is reasonable.

Depicted in this book are Glock pistols, but the principles of fighting with a pistol apply to *any* brand. Glock pistols do not have an external lever required to render the condition of safe or fire.[5] Not having an external lever simplifies learning how to fight with a pistol. Although Glock pistols do not have a manual safety lever it is not necessary.[6] The Glock pistol has three automatic safeties: (1) trigger safety, (2) firing pin safety, and (3) drop safety.[7] Pulling the trigger causes each of the safeties to deactivate. Releasing the trigger activates the three safeties.

There are other semiautomatic pistols on the market and each with its own particular design features. Being familiar with a pistol's features and the use of a manual safety (if equipped) is the operator's responsibility. Operators need to read and understand the operation manual of their particular pistol before attending training courses. To cover all the popular pistols used for combat would only create an unnecessary maze of information in this book. The basics of handling and firing are similar enough that one brand is adequate to provide instruction in how to fight with a pistol.

Ample dry firing practice will build trigger control proficiency. Dry fire practice is especially important because of two different trigger pulls for pistols that are first shot double-action (DA) with subsequent single-action (SA) shots. Glock pistols use the same trigger pull for the first shot as well as subsequent shots. The simplified trigger design regarding trigger control minimizes operator frustration and reduces training time. Glock pistols can be dry fired[8] without expectation of causing damage to the firearm.[9]

CARRY CONDITION

A pistol could be in one of three conditions for carry: (1) unloaded with a magazine on the operator's person, (2) magazine in the pistol with an empty chamber, or (3) magazine in the pistol and a round in the chamber. It has been recommended for American police officers to carry their semiautomatic pistols with a round in the chamber since at least 1930.[10] Today it is standard practice. The pistol is carried with a round in the chamber during military combat operations. American civilians who have a concealed carry permit will likely have a round in the chamber. However, Glock does not recommend that civilians carry a round in the chamber.

WARNING: Glock states, "Do not carry the pistol in the ready to fire condition. This is not the recommended safe-carrying method for civilian use."[11]

The recommendation has mistakenly led some to believe a Glock pistol is not safe to carry with a round in the chamber. A Glock pistol is safe to carry with a round in the chamber. The deciding factor to carry the pistol with a round in the chamber or empty is *not* the pistol, but the operator's level of training. Glock specifically mentions a higher level of preparedness pertaining to law enforcement and military personnel, but common sense would dictate the same standard applies to trained civilians. A properly trained civilian can carry a Glock pistol with a round in the chamber as safely as a police officer or military operator.

WARNING: Glock states, "The higher level of preparedness required of law enforcement and military personnel may override several of the following safety instructions. To provide safety while operating at a higher level of preparedness, proper initial combat oriented training and a reasonable amount of periodic training, which stresses safe tactical procedures, is recommended."[12]

COMBAT SHOOTING VS. RECREATIONAL SHOOTING

The two basic purposes for a pistol are recreational shooting and combat shooting. Recreational shooting is the use of firearms for pleasure or during a contest where people are scored, timed, awarded prizes, and ranked on performance. Recreational shooters vary from amateurs at local matches to paid professionals at international matches. Recreational shooting competitions can benefit operators learning combat shooting.[13] This benefit is realized only when the operator accepts the significant *physiological*[14] and *tactical*[15] differences between combat shooting and recreational shooting. Notably combat shooting occurs in a dangerous environment for the protection of self and others.

It would be irresponsible to say that recreational shooting has no combat value. Recreational shooting is not used to build tactics, but it can be a tactical skill builder. Recreational shooters have to make split-second decisions between hostile and friendly targets, which improve discrimination skills. Target discrimination is one of the most critical skills an operator can possess. Recreational shooters are also held to rigid safety standards regarding the use and firing of their pistols.[16] Furthermore, many have expended a great deal of dedication in pursuit of their chosen sport. Such dedication should be respected.

Physiological Differences

Although a fight-or-flight reaction (alarm reaction) can occur in a recreational event, it will *not* be to the same degree of intensity as in a life-and-death situation.[17] A fight-or-flight reaction can drive the blood out of the vegetative organs of the body to provide more blood for the heart, lungs, brain, and major muscle groups.[18] This diversion can sometimes have the negative effect of trembling muscles reducing dexterity.[19] The positive effect is that muscle strength is increased and a much higher tolerance for pain occurs because of the adrenal production of epinephrine.[20] The body is prepared to fight or flee.[21] Other effects are beneficial to maximize visual input for self-preservation, but can override the operator's desire to shoot with one eye closed.

"Among these other beneficial effects, the sympathetic nervous system causes the upper eyelids to elevate. Therefore, both eyes are forced by the situation (and the sympathetic nervous system) to be wide open. If this same suddenly intense combat situation requires marksmanship, both eyes are likely to be involved, even if monocularity[22] were the preferred method of aiming a weapon."[23]

Recreational shooters during competition can squint or close their non-dominant eye at will. The operator in a combat environment must have a method of shooting that works when the fight-or-flight reaction occurs. The method of shooting must work for the average armed civilian, police officer, and military operator. Average people do not get to shoot 50,000 rounds of ammunition annually as some professional competitive shooters do.[24] Shooting techniques that will *not* work during a fight-or-flight reaction are discouraged—such as closing the non-dominant eye.

The shooting techniques advocated in this book are based on specific physiological traits of the human body while in a fight-or-flight reaction under the worst of conditions. Those conditions often include the operator thinking, "I may die."

Tactical Differences

Combat shooting is based on sound tactics performed at a tempo to ensure operator survival and adversarial defeat. Moving hastily during a search would likely result in an adversary being overlooked. Some recreational shooting events[25] by design have competitors running and overexposing their bodies in contradiction to what would occur in real-life tactical situations. A recreational shooter stopping in the front of windows and doors while shooting *paper people*[26] is acceptable during competition. The practice of stopping in the front of windows and doors while shooting is obviously *not* acceptable for an armed civilian, police officer, or military operator.

Recreational shooters routinely shoot a predetermined number of rounds and transition to the next target. Stopping the adversary determines the speed of the fight in combat. Stopping an adversary is dependent on disrupting the central nervous system or causing significant blood loss. It could take 1 to 3 rounds or more to stop a determined adversary.[27] An operator must be prepared to shoot as many rounds as needed.[28] The operator should quickly neutralize the greatest threat first before moving on to other threats. There needs to be a thought process of who or what can hurt or kill me. The operator remains in that mind-set until no more threats exist and the area of responsibility is dominated.

Recreational shooters use a *relaxed* technique of standing up straight while drawing and presenting a pistol. No body movement is advocated other than the arms and hands.[29] Combat shooting encourages lowering the body into an *aggressive* fighting position while drawing and presenting a pistol. An operator being shot at will certainly *not* be relaxed. Likewise, standing up straight and not moving with the potential of bullets passing by is not natural and conflicts with the fight-or-flight response. The operator should practice the fighting stance (crouching) in training, because it is a natural reaction in combat.[30]

Many recreational shooters when firing with one hand will make a fist with their non-firing hand and place it over the heart against the chest. This keeps the non-firing arm from influencing the stability of the body. The theory is holding the arm down at the side acts as a pendulum destabilizing the body.[31] This technique is problematic for some operators because it puts flesh and bone directly in front of their body armor. Body armor is a piece of safety equipment commonly worn during law enforcement and military operations. A hand held against the chest has a higher probability of being struck by an adversary's bullet.

An operator maintaining a correct *survival* mind-set and adhering to *tactical* procedures can maximize the benefits of practical self-protection shooting competitions.[32] Police agencies should encourage their officers to get involved in practical self-protection shooting. The author has shot in competitions that featured various realistic shooting scenarios: shooting from inside of a vehicle, sitting in the vehicle, getting out, moving behind cover to shoot, fighting to cover, and physically striking a dummy then shooting as well as other practical scenarios. Police officers would benefit from using their duty or backup pistol during a match to improve combat shooting skills. Police officers to get replacement practice ammunition from their agency should have to present the scorecard showing participation in the match.

Operators can also benefit from other shooting competitions that stress proper firearms handling, target discrimination, accuracy, and speed.[33] In addition, do not overlook firearms training courses and competitions offered by a manufacturer.[34] Operators must never think of range training as a game. A skewed perspective on the seriousness of training will likely be evident in the operator's mediocre firearms skills. People that want to learn how to *shoot* a firearm train until they get it right. Operators that want to learn how to *fight* with a firearm train until they cannot get it wrong.[35] Operators taught to fight with a pistol can subconsciously utilize their skills correctly even in hostile and chaotic environments.

COMBAT SHOOTING VS. QUALIFICATION SHOOTING

Combat shooting *techniques* and *tactics* must address law enforcement violent encounters *if* a reduction in the number of police officers killed is going to occur. It is by human nature that people do not readily accept change. Nevertheless, those in charge of training for police firearms programs must be at the forefront of this change.

Realistic training is required to improve the hit ratio on an adversary. A qualification course is *not* training, but an evaluation of fundamental skills in conjunction with a measure of limited civil liability protection for the agency. However, removing excessively long time limits for qualification courses is an improvement. Time is in short supply and stress is in abundance in combat. (Figure 6-1) Unfortunately, time is in abundance and stress is in short supply on many ranges.

Large amounts of stress within short time frames are necessary in the firearms training program to replicate as best as possible some of the conditions of a deadly force encounter. The adversary is certainly not going to shoot *slower* because of the operator's deficiencies caused by training with liberal time limits. A skilled operator that can function effectively during a professional firearms training course will have no issues with a qualification course. The qualification course is merely a confirmation of what the operator already knows and can do.

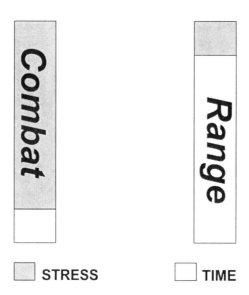

☐ STRESS   ☐ TIME

Figure 6-1 Stress versus time related to combat and the range.

According to some exhaustive testing by military Special Operations, even skilled operators can lose up to 30 percent of their proficiency when required to perform under extreme physical and emotional stress.[36] The way to minimize the effects of stress is to induce it in training, i.e., stress inoculation. Inoculation training does not eliminate stress, but rather teaches how to manage stress. How can stress be induced? Physical *anaerobic exertion* combined with *decision-making* can induce stress. An example is an operator breathing heavily and sweating, and having to fire multiple rounds quickly to engage only *threat* targets located among no-threat and friendly targets. Hits on the threat targets must be within effective accuracy.[37] Tolerating poor accuracy is not an option, because in an operational environment lives are at stake.

NOTE: The element of *decision making* is crucial to inducing stress. Physical exertion and shooting at known targets (no decision required) will *not* induce the stress desired in combat training.[38]

CORRECTING VISION FOR SHOOTING

The first step of combat shooting is to ensure the operator's eyesight has normal visual acuity (the clarity or sharpness of vision), also known as 20/20 vision.[39] The minimum acuity standard for an operator is 20/40. The 20/40 standard "...is the transition point for the performance decrease in both target discrimination and marksmanship ability."[40] Instructors can test the operator's visual acuity *unofficially* using a Snellen vision acuity chart at the correct distance of 20 feet (6 meters) which is optical infinity.[41] The test begins before the firearms course. The test is *not* a substitute for professional medical care. Operators identified with poor visual acuity would need to seek the services of a healthcare *professional* experienced in vision correction for the specific task of shooting firearms.

The operator must not only see the aligned sights, but also visually determine what action if any needs to be taken. Making that determination requires clearly focusing on the potential threat. An operator with blurred vision is already behind the survival curve. Blurred vision will also slow the operator's recognition of a sight picture. One solution for some operators is to have their eyesight corrected using *reverse monovision*.[42] This is especially true for operators age 40 and older who are affected by presbyopia. Presbyopia occurs as part of the aging process in which the eye's crystalline lens loses its ability to focus clearly on close objects.[43]

NOTE: An operator under bright and sunny conditions might try shooting with clear safety glasses in order to keep the pupils small providing a pinhole effect reducing some of the effects of presbyopia.

The traditional monovision treatment is the dominant eye corrected for *far* vision, and the non-dominant eye for *near* vision. The traditional method is the opposite of what is needed for operators shooting firearms. For operators shooting firearms, reverse monovision corrects the *dominant* eye for *near* vision, and the *non-dominant* eye for *far* vision.[44] This allows *focusing* clearly on the target or adversary with the non-dominant eye while *seeing* the aligned sights with the dominant eye creating a sight picture. Reverse monovision can be done with surgery, contacts, or glasses.

"When different images are presented to the left and right eyes, only a single, combined ''cyclopean'' image is perceived."[45] The brain's ability to combine two images can be proven with a red dot scope. Place the lens cap on the front of the scope and with both eyes open look though the scope.[46] A sight picture will form, but the aiming eye behind the scope is blocked from seeing far vision. The brain combines the red dot seen with the near vision and the eye opposite the scope seeing far vision into one image.

EYE DOMINANCE AND SHOOTING

The study on eye dominance began with Giovanni Battista della Porta in his book called *De Refractione* written in 1593.[47] Since then eye dominance has been widely studied and theorized. In one study, eye dominance is scored and classified not as simply right or left, but sighting, sensory, and acuity dominance.[48] The labels coincide with numerous tests used to evaluate eye dominance.[49] As Alistair P. Mapp, Ph.D., Hiroshi Ono, Ph.D., and Raphel Barbeito, Ph.D., pointed out in their study, eye dominance can also be a somewhat contentious topic with opinions varying widely.[50] Fortunately, the application of eye dominance for an operator is more narrowly driven by a shooting task rather than the expansiveness of clinical study. An operator's concern should be centered on which eye is preferred for aiming during combat conditions.[51]

Eye dominance,[52] also called *ocular dominance*[53] is the brain's unconscious preference for *visual input* from one eye compared to the other for certain purposes such as sighting through a telescopic sight. Target Focused Sighted Shooting encompasses the three forms of eye dominance—*sighting, sensory,* and *acuity*: Sighting dominance is the stronger visual input used to aim a firearm. Sensory dominance is the more vivid diplopic image of the sights. Acuity dominance is the superior appearance of the target. Eye dominance should not be minimized, but regarded as a crucial component of operational survival.

The dominant eye is sometimes referred to as the *sighting dominant eye,*[54] *sighting eye,*[55] or *shooting eye.*[56] Operators will likely find that one eye is more comfortable to shoot with than the other eye. The sighting dominant eye "...activates a larger area of the primary visual cortex than the non-dominant eye."[57] This asymmetry may be the reason for the stronger visual input when sighting with the dominant eye.[58]

Nonetheless, "...stimulation of any one eye reaches both cerebral hemispheres."[59] This is contrary to handedness or footedness that is controlled by the cerebral hemisphere opposite the hand or foot.[60]

It is believed that about 65 percent of people are right eye dominant, 32 percent are left eye dominant, and 3 percent do not demonstrate a consistent preference.[61] Eye dominance is possibly established around 4 years of age and is *not* based on heredity.[62] The dominant eye may *not* have the best visual acuity naturally.[63] Typically, a dominant eye lacking visual acuity would be corrected and then used for sighting. Eye dominance may reverse temporarily dependent on the horizontal gaze angle. In one study, the switch occurred at gaze angles of only 15.5 degrees from the center.[64] It is important to keep the upper body parallel to the target and the arms extended with the pistol in front of the dominant eye to help reduce the temporary reversal of eye dominance.

The brain receives an image from each eye and combines them into one cohesive image.[65] This is accomplished when the images of objects form on the fovea of the eyes.[66] The images fall on a *single* point midway between the two eyes as if there was an imaginary single eye in the middle of the forehead, i.e., a *cyclopean eye*.[67] An operator can focus on a finger in front of his or her eyes, close one eye and then the other, and see an object behind the finger move. The object moves from its position because the eyes are positioned 2.36 to 2.55 inches (60 to 65 millimeters) apart causing the world to be seen from two slightly different points.[68] The different perspectives create three-dimensional depth perception, which is an advantage of binocular vision known as *perceptual fusion* or *stereopsis*.[69]

A double image is created when an image falls on the outside of the *fovea* (F). When focusing with both eyes open on a far object (target), the nearer object (sights) in the line of sight will be imaged on the *temporal retina* (TR) of the eyes in non-corresponding points causing a double image known as *crossed diplopia*.[70] (Figure 6-2) Likewise, when focusing with both eyes open on a near object, the distant object in the line of sight will be imaged on the *nasal retina* (NR) of the eyes causing a double image known as *uncrossed diplopia*. The double image phenomenon is a natural occurrence of the sensory visual system[71] called *physiological diplopia*.[72]

An operator may ask the question, why he or she is not always aware of physiological diplopia? Humans from the time binocular vision is established become accustomed or conditioned to seeing with both eyes including physiological diplopia. Humans through a psychological process learn to disregard physiological diplopia because it is normally suppressed centrally preventing the unwanted visual impulses from entering consciousness. [73] Physiological diplopia is sometimes inadvertently discovered by a child who complains of double vision. Physiological diplopia should *not* be confused with *pathological diplopia*, which is an abnormality in the visual system requiring medical treatment.[74]

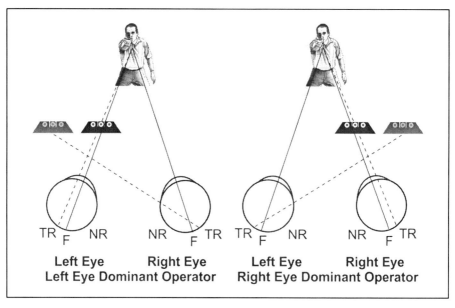

TR F   NR   NR   F TR   TR F   NR   NR   F TR

Left Eye   Right Eye   Left Eye   Right Eye
Left Eye Dominant Operator   Right Eye Dominant Operator

Figure 6-2 *Physiological Diplopia. The operator focuses on a distant target causing crossed diplopia.*

The suppression of the non-dominant eye image usually occurs subconsciously while aiming. The brain suppresses the diplopic sighting image from the non-dominant eye and attends to the diplopic sighting image of the dominant eye.[75] Therefore, with both eyes open the sights can be aligned between the dominant eye and the target. This is best accomplished by firing with the same hand on the same side as the dominant eye.[76] If an operator is right eye dominant, the right hand is used. If an operator is left eye dominant, the left hand is used. The natural dominance of a hand is immaterial as either hand can be trained until necessary procedural memory is acquired for combat shooting. The fact is people do some things with their right hand and some things with their left hand.

It has been suggested that eye dominance in some sense may be stronger than hand dominance as demonstrated "...when a left-eyed man [or woman] is right handed but prefers to shoot a gun from the left shoulder, his [or her] eyedness being stronger than his [or her] handedness in that one situation at least."[77] Conversely, "...in sighting down a rifle, the pressure to have the dominant hand on the trigger might be stronger than the pressure to have the dominant eye aligned with the sights."[78] To negate such contradictions when testing eye dominance perform the test as described in the next section.

Operators who have a dominant eye opposite the dominant hand are referred to as *cross-dominant*. [79] Cross-dominance examples are a dominant *left* hand in conjunction with a dominant *right* eye or a dominant *right* hand in conjunction with a dominant *left* eye. Some people are *ambiocular*, which means they do not have a strong dominance for either eye.[80] The operator that is ambiocular may be capable of using either eye to shoot with, but one eye will probably be preferred over the other one.

Checking for Eye Dominance

What makes one eye preferable over the other for aiming? The choice of using one eye over the other is dependent on *vision performance*. Vision performance for shooting is the quickness in which an eye can develop and sustain a sight picture. Developing a sight picture is based on the operator with both eyes open focusing on the target, bringing the firearm into his or her line of sight, and seeing aligned sights on the target.[81] The operator will be able to see the sights *quicker* with both eyes in comparison to one or the other.[82] Keeping both eyes open increases the overall reaction time by approximately 6 percent over the *dominant* eye and approximately 10 percent over the *non-dominant* eye.[83] The dominant eye is motorically superior to the non-dominant eye[84] and provides better visual performance for shooting.[85] This is especially evident when rapid firing and the *dominant* eye tracks the sights continuously as the pistol recoils up and back down on the target. The sights may seem to disappear when rapid firing and aiming with the *non-dominant* eye. An operator can shoot only as fast as he or she can see the sights. The fastest way to see is with both eyes open and using the dominant eye to establish a sight picture.

The tests in which the dominant eye is commonly identified vary greatly with outcomes not necessarily the same.[86] Gordon L. Walls, Sc.D., compiled a list of 25 different criteria of eye dominance described in his article entitled "A Theory of Ocular Dominance."[87] As an example, one of those criterions is based on the hole-in-card test.[88] The hole-in-card test is a forced choice sighting test that results in a dominant left eye or right eye. The test does *not* quantitatively evaluate eye dominance.[89] The test forces the operator "…under abnormal and non-physiologic conditions to choose between one eye or the other when determining ocular dominance."[90] Forced choice tests as a rule do *not* preserve objectivity for determining the dominant eye used in shooting. Objectivity is preserved by allowing *simultaneous* use of both eyes under the conditions of using a firearm. Daniel M. Laby, M.D., and David G. Kirschen, O.D., Ph.D., in their article titled, "Thoughts on Ocular Dominance—Is It Actually a Preference?" provided guidance on how to measure eye dominance:

> "To properly measure eye dominance, and if we are to assume we are measuring a property as is normally used, we must test that property under normal conditions. Tests of eye dominance that do not allow the subjects to maintain their normal state of binocular cooperation therefore do not accurately assess eye dominance under those conditions. Tests that do not meet this criterion, therefore, should not be used when attempting to explore the relationship between eye dominance and sporting performance, normally performed binocularly."[91]

It is clear their recommendations for an operator that keeps both eyes open while shooting a firearm is to perform an eye dominance test under the conditions found in the operational environment, i.e., doing so with both eyes open. Any test that cannot meet these specified criterion should be disregarded.

The *perceptual eye dominance test* is accurate because of its simultaneous interaction of the eyes, body, firearm, and environment. The goal of the perceptual eye dominance test is to evaluate the three forms of eye dominance by determining which eye has the stronger visual input used to aim a firearm, a more vivid diplopic image of the sights, and a superior appearance of the target. Studies have shown the dominant eye as being phenomenally clearer with greater color saturation than the non-dominant eye.[92] In particular, the dominant eye shows a greater perceptual stability than the non-dominant eye in that the sights presented to it are more resistant to fading.[93]

Physiological diplopia to some degree will occur when focusing on the *target* creating one image of the target and two images of the handgun. Likewise, focusing on the *sights* creates one image of the handgun and two images of the target. An operator's concern for combat shooting is to *focus* on the target or threat visually while maintaining mental *attention* on the sights in the line of sight to establish a sight picture.[94] Endogenous attention may increase the apparent contrast of the sights when viewed by the dominant eye, thereby reducing fading of the sights when aiming.[95]

Operators when performing the perceptual eye dominance test should use the right or left fighting stance associated with the right or left firing hand, or firing side shoulder. This allows the firearm when presented to the right and left side of the sagittal plane[96] to be an equal distance from each fovea. Having the finger on the trigger during testing encompasses handedness that can affect the test results of eye dominance.[97] This method provides uniformity and consistency for back-to-back test comparisons. When performing the test an operator's concentration must be on the overall performance of each eye in the back-to-back comparison, and not on the awkwardness of holding a firearm with the non-dominant hand versus the dominant hand.

Handgun with Iron Sights: Conduct the perceptual eye dominance test using an *unloaded* handgun or preferably an *inert* handgun while assuming a two-hand fighting stance. Keep the muzzle pointed in an appropriate direction. Hold the handgun in the *right* hand just below the line of sight. Focus on a target at least 20 feet (6 meters) away and raise the handgun into the line of sight of the *right* eye with the trigger finger on the trigger. Maintain focus on the target, but be mentally attentive of the handgun's aligned sights. Do *not* try to focus on the sights visually, but just be mentally aware of their presence. There should be two images of the handgun. Are the sights of the *left* handgun image stable with good contrast or are the sights fading in and out? Lower and raise the handgun in the line of sight several times taking notice if the sights are stable or fading. Do the same thing again, except use the *left* hand and raise the handgun in front of the *left* eye. This time the image of the handgun on the *right* will be evaluated. Which eye produced the image with the best contrast and most stability—right or left? The preferred sighting eye will be the one with the more vivid stable image.

The perceptual eye dominance test can also be performed using a long gun with iron sights or a telescopic sight.

Long Gun with Iron Sights: Conduct the perceptual eye dominance test using an *unloaded* long gun or preferably an *inert* long gun with *iron sights* by assuming a fighting stance. Keep the muzzle pointed in an appropriate direction. Mount the long gun on the right shoulder with the muzzle just below the line of sight. Focus on a target at least 20 feet (6 meters) away and raise the long gun into the line of sight of the *right* eye with the finger on the trigger. Maintain focus on the target, but be mentally attentive of the aligned sights. With both eyes open, look through the rear sight to the front sight to the target using the right eye. Do *not* try to focus on the sights visually, but just be aware of their presence. There should be two images of the long gun. Are the sights stable with good contrast on the left long gun image or are the sights fading in and out? Lower and raise the long gun in the line of sight several times taking notice *if* the sights are stable or fading. Do the same thing again, except mount the long gun on the *left* shoulder and raise it in front of the *left* eye. This time the image of the long gun on the *right* will be evaluated. Which eye produced the best contrast and most stability—right or left? The preferred sighting eye will be the one with the more vivid stable image.

Long Gun with a Telescopic Sight: Conduct the perceptual eye dominance test using an *unloaded* long gun or preferably an *inert* long gun with a telescopic sight by assuming a fighting stance. Keep the muzzle pointed in an appropriate direction. Mount the long gun on the *right* shoulder and with both eyes open look through the scope with the *right* eye. Is the image of the scope clear without the contents of the field of view from the *left* eye superimposed in the scope's field of view? Do the same thing again, except mount the long gun on the *left* shoulder and with both eyes open look through the scope with the *left* eye. Again, is the image of the scope clear without the contents of the field of view from the *right* eye superimposed in the scope's field of view? Trying to use the non-dominant eye behind the scope will cause the contents of the field of view of the dominant eye to superimpose in the scope's field of view that cannot be ignored and seem to interfere with good observation through the scope. The non-dominant eye is the easier eye to suppress allowing quicker aiming of the scope.[98] The preferred sighting eye will be the one with the more vivid stable image and *without* the contents of the field of view from the *non-sighting* eye superimposed in the scope's field of view when viewing through the scope. This includes traversing the long gun back and forth to scan across an area with the scope.

General Observations: The perceptual eye dominance test is a *subjective* test in regards to the self-reporting of the operator's perception of his or her iron sights or telescopic sight. However, the operator's perception *is* what matters. The test is *objective* in the fact it is comparing each eye under the same circumstances with equal opportunity to be the dominant sighting eye. The perceptual eye dominance tests can also be performed in a classroom setting by using a nonfunctioning blue handgun or long gun replica made of impact resistant polyurethane. The telescopic sight can be mounted on a replica long gun that has a mounting rail.

An operator will find the *dominant* eye is more capable of seeing the sights and focusing on the target as a single image without it separating into two images while establishing a sight picture than the *non-dominant* eye.[99] The operator may also find the best indicator of eye dominance is the ability to look through the telescopic sight with both eyes open *without* the contents of the field of view from the *non-sighting* eye superimposed in the scope's field of view.[100] Everyone will have a preferred eye for sighting a firearm whether it is equipped with iron sights or a telescopic sight. The integrity of the perceptual eye dominance test depends on the operator having normal visual acuity either by nature or by ocular correction.

Improving Moderate Eye Dominance

Some operators shooting with both eyes open have trouble clearly distinguishing the image of the pistol used for sighting. This usually occurs because of moderate eye dominance. Placing a piece of frosted tape on the safety glasses' lens in front of the *non-dominant* eye will help strengthen and train the moderate dominant eye.[101] This training technique can be used with live or dry fire drills.

Use a piece of frosted tape about 1 inch (25.4 millimeters) in diameter. While in a fighting stance and looking at a target, place the tape directly in front of the pupil of the *non-dominant* eye. This will allow maximum use of the dominant eye while retaining *peripheral* vision.[102] As the dominate eye gains strength the size of the tape can be reduced and eventually eliminated.

The goal is to increase the dominance of the *dominant* eye to see superimposed aligned sights on the target. As an example, a *right-handed* operator moderately *right* eye dominant will place the tape on the left side of the safety glasses. The brain with continued training accepts the *right eye* is used to establish a sight picture. Discontinue the use of the tape at the earliest possible time. Do not confuse the practice of improving the strength of a moderate dominant eye with the *ill-advised* practice of a cross-dominant operator trying to shift his or her eye dominance permanently.

Cross-Dominance

Eye dominance can affect some cross-dominant operators more so than others regarding the bullet's point of impact when shooting with *both* eyes open. Some operators that are *right-handed* and *left* eye dominant have a tendency to align a pistol subconsciously with the muzzle pointing slightly to the left. The shots impact to the *left* of the aim point. The opposite is true if the operator is *left-handed* and *right* eye dominant. The shots usually impact to the *right* of the aim point.[103] A cross-dominant operator shooting with both eyes open while attending to the sights and aiming with the *non-dominant* eye will find that targets are more susceptible to splitting into double images. This is especially true for targets that appear small.

The most important reason to fire with the hand on the dominant eye side is to *maximize* an operator's ability to protect him or herself. A cross-dominant operator firing with the hand opposite the dominant eye begins the fight with a built-in physiological disadvantage. Some people may consider it morally irresponsible for an organization to send a cross-dominant operator into an operational area knowing that with both eyes open the rounds may hit to the left or right of the aim point. Both eyes will likely remain open during an alarm reaction.

There can also be civil ramifications from allegations of disparate training. The cross-dominant operator could argue that he or she received inferior training as compared to an operator who shoots with both eyes open and fires his or her pistol with the dominant hand on the same side as the dominant eye. The firing hand and dominant eye do work together more *efficiently* when on the same side of the body.[104]

Shooting a firearm does *not* have analogs[105] with other sports dependent on handedness or footedness for throwing or kicking a ball. Pointing a firearm and pulling the trigger is a motor skill that either hand can perform regardless of handedness. Footedness is not a factor because shooting is done mainly from the waist up. Changing the firing hand to the same side as the dominant eye is a *solution* to cross-dominance.

There seems to be little resistance by instructors to change an operator to shoot a long gun on the same side as the dominant eye. However, when a handgun is involved there seems to be an innate reluctance to make the change. With repetitious practice, a cross-dominant operator will build *procedural memory* resulting in the ability to shoot a pistol on the same side as the dominant eye. Starting over may not be appealing to the cross-dominant operator, but it is certainly better than firing and routinely missing the aim point. Below are questions and answers addressing some of the issues regarding cross-dominance.

Can a cross-dominant operator change or shift his or her eye dominance? Research provides limited and conflicting information. One study suggests that eye dominance can be change with vision training.[106] In the study there were 157 right-hand and 23 left-hand cross-dominant test subjects. None of those test subjects were identified as adults and the average age was 7 years and 8 months. The fact is that not one cross-dominant *adult* showed a marked improvement. Even with the malleable placidity of the young brain, it still took an average of 7 months of vision training to see the first marked improvement. The fact is that extensive vision training is necessary to achieve any measureable change of weakening eye dominance and to produce any shifts in eye dominance.[107]

There is a consensus among ophthalmological and optometric sources that eye dominance is *not* susceptible to change and tampering with the dominance relationship often leads to discomfort to the person participating.[108] Likewise, forcing a shift in eye dominance by wearing frosted tape on safety glasses is *not* a recommended option for combat shooting.[109] The tape blocking the central vision[110] of the *dominant eye* will negatively affect depth perception.[111] The operator may suffer from headaches caused by eyestrain.

Can the operator squint or close the dominant eye just before firing the shot? This too will probably *not* work. With intense combat conditions "…the sympathetic nervous system drives both eyes wide open."[112] It is unlikely while experiencing an alarm reaction the eye could be closed. In addition, some operators under normal conditions might not be able to close one eye—ever see the person that could not wink. An interesting, but not necessarily a reliable indicator of the dominant eye is the one that is more difficult to wink or cannot be winked without some lowering of the opposite eyelid.[113]

Can the *cross-dominant* operator efficiently present the pistol in front of the dominant eye? An operator experiencing an alarm reaction will likely keep both eyes open and rapidly push the pistol forward toward the threat.[114] The presentation of the pistol can occur with one or two hands. The two-hand forward movement of the pistol with the firing hand *opposite* of the dominant eye breaks the wrist to the outside (back of the hand toward the forearm). An operator, especially of small stature may experience issues with recoil management and the slide short cycling. The situation would worsen with sweat, dirt, or fresh blood on the hands. The best method of keeping the hand centered with the arm (vertical and horizontal planes) is to fire with the hand on the same side of the body as the dominant eye. Operators must be able to shoot accurately even after physical exertion or an injury that can greatly reduce arm and hand strength.

There is also the preferred method of transitioning from a carbine to a pistol. A right-handed operator will move the sling equipped carbine to the left and draw the pistol. A left-handed operator will move the carbine to the right and draw the pistol. A cross-dominant operator that shoots a pistol with the one hand and a carbine with the other during a transition would likely move the carbine on top of the pistol creating an accessibility issue. Some may suggest not moving the carbine over, but allow it to hang straight down. This could be a painful experience if the operator had to run. Moreover, a fall could drive the muzzle into the ground and the stock into the operator's face. Keep in mind any method advocated should provide the *best* possible outcome.

Organizationally speaking there needs to be one standard for operators. Barring any documented medical limitations of using the dominant eye or marked improvements of the non-dominant eye because of vision therapy—cross-dominant operators should change to the hand on the side of their dominant eye. It is easier for the operator to use repetitious training to build procedural memory than to continuously struggle with the cross-dominant issue. Shooting a *pistol* and *carbine* on the side of the dominant eye side maximizes procedural memory and can reduce overall training time. The cross-dominant operator that makes the shift to the hand on the side of the dominant eye and shoots with both eyes open without blinking will probably obtain *speed* and *accuracy* previously not thought possible.

The author's experience when converting cross-dominant operators is that they have a feeling of *comfortableness* with drawing and obtaining a sight picture within about 2 hours of practicing. The skills after about 5 to 6 hours of training should start to become a part of the operator's procedural memory.[115] Changing the firing hand from the *dominant* hand to the *non-dominant* hand in the beginning will probably feel unnatural. The converted operator because of past procedural memory will have a tendency to draw the pistol and align it in front of the non-dominant eye. The operator's head may move around in an attempt to locate the sights. These things are normal and part of the learning curve.

The operator needs to keep his or her head still, keep both eyes open, and practice slowly drawing an *inert* or *unloaded* pistol and presenting it in the dominant eye's line of sight. This will build *new* procedural memory overwriting the old procedural memory. In front of a mirror perform each step of the draw (grip, join, and extend) slowly and perfectly. The steps in the beginning are a conscious thought process, but drawing becomes subconscious and speed increases automatically as procedural memory builds. The goal when live firing on a range is to draw and consistently place one shot on the aim point. After achieving one shot, fire two, three, and so on.

Training the Non-dominant Hand to Become Dominant

Using the non-dominant hand to shoot a pistol on the same side of the body as the dominant eye is not difficult. Operators in less than a day will find bringing the pistol in front of the dominant eye is natural resulting in improved speed and accuracy. The fact is each person goes through his or her day and does some things with the right hand and some things with the left hand regardless of hand dominance. There are things an operator can do to speed the process of learning to use the hand on the same side of the body as the dominant eye.

A cross-dominant operator to train the non-dominant hand to become dominant for combat shooting can use the suggestions as follows: (1) change all equipment to work efficiently with the firing hand (holster, magazine pouch, long gun sling, etc.), (2) wear the equipment in the safety of the operator's residence for extended periods to get comfortable with the placement, (3) dry fire to build procedural memory (drawing, loading, unloading, reloading, firing positions, etc.), (4) practice gripping the pistol in each hand comparing how the back strap feels tight against the palm until both hands feel the same, (5) improve dexterity by using a magazine loader with the non-firing hand and place the rounds in the magazine loader with the firing hand, (6) place loose rounds in the pocket on the firing hand side and load magazines manually using the firing hand (improves hand strength and dexterity), (7) pick up the pistol using the firing hand to prevent switching hands, (8) when physically exercising begin with the firing side of the body to build procedural memory, (9) when practicing hand-to-hand training preform techniques left and right side beginning with the firing side, and (10) shoot a long gun with an appropriate length stock on the same side as the dominant eye. A cross-dominant operator making a conscious effort to use the hand on the same side as the dominant eye will activate the opposite hemisphere of his or her brain.

NOTE: Once an operator changes using his or her hand on the *same* side as the dominant eye—that hand is referred to as the dominant hand for the purposes of shooting. A *cross-dominant* operator may be naturally right-handed, but his or her *left* hand will be referred to as the *dominant* hand. A *cross-dominant* operator may be naturally left-handed, but his or her *right* hand will be referred to as the *dominant* hand.

SHOOTING WITH BOTH EYES OPEN

An operator should not visually fight between the threat and the front sight. A couple of problems emerge when keeping both eyes open and *focusing* on the front sight. First is the creation of double target images. An operator cannot afford the *visual confusion* of seeing multiple images of the same adversary. Second, is blurring of the target or adversary.[116] In reality, an operator must be capable of clearly distinguishing the target or actions of an adversary.

Shooting with both eyes open and focusing on the threat can eliminate visual confusion. This section breaks down the complexities of shooting with both eyes open. Such as the complexity of each eye seeing from a different perspective creating two images—one *sighting* and one *non-sighting.* Explained are drills that enable an operator to understand which eye is creating the sighting image and which one is creating the non-sighting image. The number of pistol images or target images (single or double) an operator sees is an *objective* test to determine if the target or front sight is being focused on.

Shooting with both eyes open maximizes *speed, accuracy,* and *peripheral vision.* Having full peripheral vision [117] is crucial to identifying threats and maintaining overall situational awareness. [118] Closing one eye reduces overall vision and the nose partially blocks (blind spot) the peripheral vision of the other eye. With both eyes open the blind spots are eliminated allowing about a 200-degree field of view with a 120-degree overlap. [119] Maximizing the field of view in the operational area enhances personal survival. Although many operators do shoot with both eyes open there seems to be a void in explaining how it is accomplished. The information that follows will provide the guidance needed to shoot with both eyes open.

NOTE: Make sure the pistol used in the following drills is *unloaded* or *inert* (plastic barrel replacement or a chamber blocker).

Human Eye Limitations

A critical element of combat readiness is accepting the "...eye can *focus* on only one object at a time at different distances."[120] This is proven by extending one arm with the thumb pointing up and holding the other thumb near the extended arm's elbow.[121] (Figure 6-3) Try to focus on both thumbs. It is impossible to do so. However, an operator with the appropriate degree of attention, skill, and practice, "...can maintain visual awareness of the front sight even though the eye's focusing system is drawn toward infinity."[122] Joan N. Vickers, Ph.D., in her book, Perception, Cognition, and Decision Training: The Quiet Eye in Action, explained the ability as *covert attention* in which the "...gaze is located on one object or location and the attention on another."[123]

Focusing in regards to combat shooting is the operator fixated on the target or threat (infinity) while paying attention (attending) to the aligned sights.[124] Focusing in regards to the mechanics of the eye "...is used to describe the action of the eye required to make a target clear."[125] An operator with practice has the ability to focus on the target or threat visually while attending to the aligned sights to form a sight picture by the hand pointing a pistol at the aim point.[126] It has been documented in one study that some international elite pistol shooters use an aiming method of fixating on the target first and do not visually deviate from the target as the pistol is raised into their line of sight.[127]

Figure 6-3 *Eye Focus Test*

Looking Through the Rear Sight

A pistol has an unusual rear sight because it is held at arm's length from the eye. On the other hand, many carbines designed for self-protection have a rear *iron* sight held close to the eye. It can be thought of as the pistol having a *far* rear sight and the carbine having a *near* rear sight. The near rear sight is usually seen with only one eye. There are some exceptions such as the AK-47 rifle that has its rear iron sight mounted forward of the receiver. With both eyes open and looking through the near rear iron sight the sight picture does not change. This is because the sight is close to the face and only one eye sees through the rear sight. Nevertheless, proper practice allows keeping both eyes open and shooting a pistol or carbine with a far rear sight. Aim by fixating on the target and as the firearm enters into the line of sight look through the rear sight to the front sight to the target.

Focusing on the Front Sight

With both eyes open, point an *inert* or *unloaded* pistol at a target that is 20 feet (6 meters) or farther. Focusing on the *front* sight will cause two targets to appear. (Figure 6-4) Hold the pistol in the other hand—focus on the front sight—the target will again split into two images. It does not matter which hand holds the pistol the images will split. Focusing on the front sight creates the *two* target images. Continue to focus on the front sight and move the pistol sideways back and forth between the two target images. Both images remain. Close the left eye and the left target image will disappear. Close the right eye and the right target image will disappear. While holding the pistol in the right hand and focusing on the front sight, the right eye would aim at the right target image. While holding the pistol in the left hand and focusing on the front sight, the left eye would aim at the left target image.

Left Eye Image / Right Eye Image

Figure 6-4 *Focusing on the front sight.*

In a combat environment with both eyes open and trying to *focus* on the front sight is problematic. There is usually not a single stationary defined adversary separated from the other adversaries and innocent people. Stationary defined targets are common in recreational shooting, police qualifications, and military qualifications. A combat environment is a mixture of different shapes, sizes, colors, and movement. Try to imagine an adversary standing among a group of people. The operator with both eyes open focusing on the front sight sees two of everybody in the group! Induce movement within the crowd in a low light setting and the situation only gets worse. The fallacy of keeping both eyes open and *focusing* on the front sight while in a combat environment should be overwhelmingly apparent.

When an operator enters into an alarm reaction "…an inevitable series of neural and biochemical reactions cascade into action. From a visual perspective, the accommodation system loses its ability to maintain clear focus on close targets."[128] This occurs because the "…ocular pupil diameter increases, and the ciliary muscle relaxes, forcing a person to focus the eyes at far distance, perhaps to be behaviorally better prepared for a perceived on-coming threat."[129]

Focusing on the Target

Hold an *unloaded* pistol within the line of sight of the dominant eye and *focus* on the target at least 20 feet (6 meters) away. Two sets of sights appear. (Figure 6-5) Not only should the two sets of sights appear, but also two complete pistols. One of the images is used for sighting and the other image is a non-sighting image and will need to be ignored. Likewise, in darkness while focusing in the distance a pistol with self-luminous sights will appear as two sets of glowing dots. One set of the dots is the sighting image and one set is the non-sighting image. The exercises that follow will identify the images and their role in the aiming process.

Hold the unloaded pistol in the *right* hand, focus on a target, and aim with the *left* image of the pistol. Do not focus on the pistol, but see the image of the sights superimposed on the target. Close the left eye and the right pistol image will disappear. The right pistol image that disappeared is the *non-sighting* image. Close the right eye and the left pistol image with disappear. The left image that disappeared is the *sighting* image. This is the interesting part. The pistol image on the *left* is connected to the *right* eye and the pistol image on the *right* is connected to the *left* eye (crossed diplopia). This is why the left pistol image in front of the right eye is considered the sighting image for an operator with a dominant right eye.

Hold an *unloaded* pistol in the *left* hand, focus on the target, and aim with the *right* image of the pistol. Do not focus on the pistol, but see the image of the sights superimposed on the target. Close the right eye and the left pistol image will disappear. The left pistol image that disappeared is the *non-sighting* image. Close the left eye and the right pistol image will disappear. The right pistol image that disappeared is the *sighting* image. Again, the pistol image on the *left* is connected to the *right* eye and the pistol image on the *right* is connected to the *left* eye. This is why the right pistol image in front of the left eye is considered the sighting image for an operator with a dominant left eye.

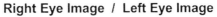

Right Eye Image / Left Eye Image

Figure 6-5 *Focusing on the target.*

An alternate method to using an unloaded pistol for the drill is to use an ink pen. The ink pen works well for a classroom setting. The tip of the ink pen acts as the front sight. Hold the ink pen in the *right hand* at arm's length. Hold the tip of the ink pen at the bottom of an object such as a light switch. The operator should be 20 feet (6 meters) from the light switch. Begin by focusing on the light switch and actually see its fine details. Now there are two images of the ink pen. Do *not* focus on the ink pen. This will cause the two images to collapse or converge.

Continue to focus on the light switch to see the two ink pens. While continuing to focus on the light switch, move the ink pen side to side. Place the image on the left at the bottom of the light switch and close the left eye. The image on the right that disappeared is the non-sighting image. The image on the left is the sighting image. Hold the ink pen in the *left hand* at arm's length and place the image on the right at the bottom of the light switch. Close the right eye. The image on the left that disappeared is the non-sighting image. The image on the right is the sighting image.

An operator that can *suppress* (mentally ignore) the non-sighting image will gain the maximum benefit of shooting with both eyes open. Mentally suppressing the non-sighting image allows seeing the sights as one superimposed image while focusing on the target. It is the equivalent of shutting the non-dominant eye, but without the drawback of giving up half of visual capability. Cross-dominant operators trying to shoot with their dominant hand and non-dominant eye will likely find it impossible to suppress the non-sighting image created by the stronger dominant eye.

As an example, a *right-handed* operator has a *left* dominant eye. The pistol is raised in the line of sight, but the *left* image generated by the *right* eye (non-dominant) is not clear enough to shoot with. The choice is to squint or close the dominant left eye or change the firing hand to the left side. The *preferred* method for the operator is to change the firing hand to the left side allowing the left dominant eye to be used for sighting. A renowned firearms instructor stated that no one should be allowed to start training using the hand *opposite* the dominant eye.[130] The instructor went on to say irrespective of how uncoordinated the operator thinks he or she is with the non-dominant hand—training should *not* begin in a cross-dominant situation. In reality, the operator's coordination will quickly develop from proper repetitious practice that builds procedural memory.

Keep the Head Centered

Hold an *unloaded* pistol in the firing hand within the line of sight and point at a target. While *focusing* on a target turn the head side to side. The images of the pistol will appear to move off the target. It is best to leave the head centered over the body and facing directly forward in combat shooting. This will assist in maintaining a line of sight from the dominant eye through the pistol's sights to the target. Turning the head will change the line of sight. To obtain effective hits on a target it is important to assume a fighting stance and visually *maintain* the aim point as the pistol's sights enter the line of sight. The drill can also be performed using an ink pen instead of an unloaded pistol. Turning the head side to side causes the tip of the ink pen to move off the target.

Application of Both Eyes Open

A *right-handed* operator focusing on the target and holding the pistol in front of the *right* eye should aim with the image of the pistol on the *left*. A *left-handed* operator focusing on the target and holding the pistol in front of the *left* eye should aim with the image of the pistol on the *right*. Remember the sighting image of the pistol used by the dominant eye is closest to the centerline of the body. Alignment of the sighting image of the pistol between the dominate eye and target is accentuated because of the natural point of aim while in the fighting stance. This is sometimes called the *body index*.[131] The stance helps to ensure the dominant eye uses the pistol image closes to the body centerline. The operator will use the hand for firing on the same side of the body as the dominant eye. A right-eye dominate operator uses his or her right hand to shoot. A left-eye dominate operator uses his or her left hand to shoot.

NOTE: The goal for the operator is to leave both eyes open while *mentally* suppressing the non-dominant eye thus *reducing* or *eliminating* the visual presence of the non-sighting image and in conjunction will clarify the sighting image in front of the dominant eye.

The operator is *focusing* on the target, but *seeing* an image of the aligned sights superimposed on the target when shooting.[132] (Figures 6-6 and 6-7) That is why the term Target Focused Sighted Shooting is used. The variables of *distance* to the threat, threat *immanency*, and the operator's ability to suppress the non-dominant eye will affect the *clarity* of the superimposed image of aligned sights. The operator sees the aligned sights break the line of sight creating a sight picture, but remains focused on the threat. The operator is instantly looking *through* the rear sight to the front sight to the target. The moment a sight picture is acquired the trigger is pulled. There can be no hesitation.

Hesitation can cause the superimposed sight image to disappear within the line of sight. This occurs when suppression of the non-dominant eye is lost. The operator may need to blink both eyes or manually suppress the non-dominant eye by squinting or closing it momentarily to see the sight picture. Squinting or closing the non-dominant eye momentarily will only occur *if* the operator is physically capable and is *not* experiencing the onset of an alarm reaction. The more distance between the adversary and the operator the greater likelihood of a perception that he or she has enough time to squint or close the non-dominant eye—barring no physical limitations. With proper training and practice many operators will be able to leave both eyes open and shoot at the maximum effective range of the pistol. The next drill can improve suppression of the non-sighting image.

Left-Hand Operator
Right Eye Image / Left Eye Image

Right-Hand Operator
Right Eye Image / Left Eye Image

*Figure **6-6** Left hand operator focusing on the target while seeing superimposed sights.*

*Figure **6-7** Right hand operator focusing on the target while seeing superimposed sights.*

Improving Non-sighting Image Suppression

Get in a fighting stance using a two-hand grip and hold an *unloaded* pistol at arm's length. Point the unloaded pistol at a target 20 feet (6 meters) or more away. Keep the trigger finger on the receiver. Focus on the aim point of the target. Maintain a proper hand/arm position with the sights in the line of sight. See the aligned sights, but do *not* focus on them. Focusing on the sights will cause the target to split into two images. The non-dominant eye may have to be squinted and opened in cycles to aid in suppressing the non-sighting image. The dominant eye will probably tear up from straining and this is normal. Maintain the position until the eye tears up, rest, and repeat. The dominant eye is working hard to maintain focus on the target and simultaneously see the aligned sights.

Train to leave both eyes open looking through the rear sight to the front sight to the target. Focus on the target and see the aligned sights while mentally suppressing the non-sighting image of the pistol to the point of automaticity. Automaticity is the operator's ability "...to invoke a learned visual skill without any conscious awareness and effort."[133] Practice the drill also in low light conditions. Mentally suppressing the non-sighting image of the pistol is easier for operators with a strong dominant eye. In the beginning when live firing it may help to squint or close the non-dominant eye to get a sight picture. Remain focused on the target, but see the aligned sights.[134] Take the slack out of the trigger and open the non-dominant eye just before taking the shot. Increase the time between closing or squinting the non-dominant eye and taking the shot until it is no longer necessary.

FUNDAMENTALS OF COMBAT MARKSMANSHIP

The seven fundamentals of combat marksmanship are as follows:

1. Fighting Stance
2. Grip
3. Sight Alignment
4. Sight Picture
5. Breath Control
6. Trigger Control
7. Follow-through

There are seven fundamentals listed. However, an operator that can immediately and aggressively assume an effective firing position, see a sight picture, and utilize trigger control should perform well in combat. Although not all operators may be able to quote the seven fundamentals of combat shooting, they should be able to state the three most important: (1) *fighting stance*, (2) *sight picture*, and (3) *trigger control*.

Fighting Stance

The primary firing position is the *fighting stance.*[135] The fighting stance is the same as the *crouch position* used by the U.S. Army when shooting a pistol under conditions of stress found in combat.[136] The fighting stance can also be used whether the operator is unarmed, armed with a knife, pistol, or carbine.[137] It does not matter which weapon system is used. The fighting stance will work with adjustments for the transference of body weight. The design of the fighting stance allows it to work with the body's *natural* reaction to dangerous situations.[138] During an alarm reaction, the body instinctively lowers by bending at the knees and lowering the chin to protect the neck. Sometimes an alarm reaction causes the hands to come up and protect the face.

NOTE: A deputy was captured on a video from the dashboard camera during a traffic stop with his hand on a holstered handgun. The deputy when shot at removed the hand from his handgun for a split-second to protect his face before drawing and firing.[139]

Humans are binocular[140] beings and instinctively face an adversary when fighting.[141] Practice the fighting stance by standing squared to a target. The feet are wider than shoulder width with the toes of the firing side foot aligned with the heel of the non-firing side foot.[142] This is referred to as *toe to heel*. The position allows operators, especially those of small stature better recoil control of a semiautomatic pistol, machine pistol, machine gun, carbine, or shotgun. The position is normally assumed by stepping forward and to the outside with the non-firing foot. However, dependent on the situation a side step can occur to either side. The knees bend while leaning forward at the hips. The chin drops lowering the head, but *not* to the point of looking through the edge of the eyelids.

Looking through the edge of the eyelids will cause visual distortion,[143] and reduce peripheral vision above eye level.[144] The chin dropping is a similar response as when fighting hand-to-hand. The head position should feel natural, *not* forced. Forcing the head to far forward (craning) causes an operator wearing safety glasses or ballistic goggles to have distorted vision. In extreme cases, an operator wearing a helmet may see its top edge, which is not desirable in combat when firing at an adversary.[145] Likewise, there are negative effects for keeping the head too upright.

An international competitive shooter in his book explained the *disadvantages* of keeping the head too upright.

"Keeping you head too upright is wrong. When you keep your head upright, the recoil pushes your head back and changes your eye position in relation to your sights. This makes sight recovery far more complex than necessary. In addition, if you head is driven back, even slightly, it tends to pull your shoulders back, and gradually, over multiple shots, your center of gravity shifts back. Recoil control then becomes impossible. You should always have your head slightly forward, in an aggressive stance." [146]

The ears are in front of shoulders and the shoulders are in front of hips. This is an aggressive stable fighting position and allows freedom of movement and quick follow up shots. (Figures 6-8 and 6-9) Everything is level—pistol with the eyes—hands and arms with the shoulders. In an alarm reaction situation, the pistol is driven aggressively toward the adversary and the shoulders roll forward naturally. [147] The shoulders in the natural position allow for better recoil control when shooting a pistol or carbine. The fighting stance has an advantage of the operator's body armor facing toward a threat. When the author attended the U.S. Marshals Fugitive Investigator's Course an instructor explained that his organization used the squared stance after interviewing marshals involved in shootings. [148] It was a matter of real-life experience dictating what is taught in training.

The fighting stance varies from a standing position common to recreational shooting. In comparison, recreational shooters typically stand with feet about shoulder width apart and slightly offset, knees slightly bent, slight forward bend at the waist, shoulders down, and the head is up. [149] However, the fighting stance closely resembles the instinctive reaction of the body during combat. The fighting stance also helps to harness the operator's natural point of aim.

NOTE: Teach the fighting stance before teaching the grip. This is to eliminate the individual's preoccupation of the pistol once it is in his or her hands. This may apply especially to people that have never fired a pistol or have reservations about doing so.

An operator standing 7 yards (6.4 meters) from a human silhouette target can check his or her *natural point of aim*. The operator grips an *unloaded* or *inert* pistol and while in the fighting stance aims at the target. The focus is on a specific aim point in the high center mass area.

While maintaining the grip and fighting stance, the operator closes his or her eyes for 3 to 5 seconds.[150] The operator then opens his or her eyes and checks for a sight picture. The sights should be superimposed on the same aim point previously focused on.[151] Continue the drill and make stance adjustments until achieving success. This drill and the one that follows can begin as a familiarization in which the operator is not wearing equipment, but should quickly progress to using operational equipment.

Figure 6-8 *Fighting Stance (female operator)*

Figure 6-9 *Fighting Stance (male operator)*

The natural point of aim can be further developed using an unloaded or inert pistol. The operator assumes a fighting stance 7 yards (6.4 meters) from a human silhouette target. Both eyes are open with the focus maintained on a specific aim point in the high center mass area. Extend both arms in a natural locked position while applying forward pressure and keeping the shoulders level. Align the sights on the aim point establishing the sight picture. Close the eyes and swing the pistol side to side at smaller and smaller movements until the pistol comes to rest. Open the eyes and the pistol should be pointing at the aim point. Adjust the stance if necessary and repeat.

Once the natural point of aim is established, with both eyes open maintain a visual *focus* on the target. The sights will wobble some, but try to keep it to a minimum. The wobble area is an *arc of movement*[152] shaped like an infinity sign or the number eight positioned sideways.

The trigger finger takes up the slack and applies pressure just before the trigger breaks. The operator remains in this position for four breaths and during the fifth breath, pulls the trigger directly to the rear without disturbing the sights. The operator racks the slide, comes to a standing position, and rests for five breaths. Repeat the drill until fatigued. This drill uses isometric muscle contraction to build procedural memory. The drill will also work well on a range using a pistol with live ammunition and reinforces the elements of combat shooting.

NOTE: Using a solid plastic inert training pistol for the drills is an option. Obviously, the trigger will not move, but the trigger finger can apply the appropriate amount of pressure straight to the rear without disturbing the sight picture.

The drill can be performed with one or two hands using the dominant hand and the non-dominant hand as the firing hand. Having a consistent natural point of aim (one- or two-hand firing) is crucial to establishing a fast sight picture. An operator cannot afford to be visually searching for the sights to complete the sight picture in a gunfight.[153] The pistol should consistently stop in the sweet spot[154] as the arms reach natural extension. The *sweet spot* in shooting is the small invisible area in which the pistol stops in the line of sight with the sights already aligned.[155] The ability to consistently and quickly have aligned sights within the line of sight as the arms reach a natural extension is a common ability among SWAT officers.[156]

Females have a lower *center of gravity* than males. When shooting a firearm the female's lower center of gravity has a tendency to cause her body to lean backward. Females need to plant their feet firmly, aggressively lean forward the same as their male counterparts while keeping the arms and wrists naturally locked. Keeping the firing side foot toes parallel with the heel of the non-firing side foot with both feet more than shoulder width apart will naturally force a forward fighting stance.

Leaning back can cause the pistol to short cycle. *Short cycling* is the slide not traveling fully rearward. The short cycle will not allow stripping of the round from the magazine or in the case of an empty magazine lock the slide to the rear. The pistol must have a rigid platform to work against to operate properly. Fortunately, during stressful encounters the arms and wrists have natural tendency to lock. The recoil of the pistol is absorbed in the body in the same matter as when firing a carbine or shotgun. The operator must control his or her firearm and *not* be controlled by the firearm.[157]

The arms and wrists when naturally locked also prevent fatigue when consecutively firing multiple magazines. Arms *unlocked* when firing multiple magazines have a tendency to move the pistol closer and closer toward the body, especially for smaller stature operators. The pistol in recoil will travel the path of least resistance and if the arms or wrists are unlocked, that path traveled will be those bends. The pistol with the arms or wrists unlocked will not recoil straight back in a consistent manner. Drive the pistol forward until the arms naturally lock from muscle contraction supported by the skeletal structure.

The author and other attendees during an Israeli antiterror combat course were taught to use an aggressive fighting stance. Doing so made the body and firearm operate as one unit. The fighting stance for combat shooting should provide the operator a foundation in which to fire accurately one round after the other about every 0.25 second.[158] The operator should first learn to fire 1 round, then 2, 3, 4, and advance to 5 or more rounds. Firing multiple rounds with 0.25 second between shots tests the integrity of the grip and fighting stance. Another method commonly used by instructors to check stance integrity is to push rearward on the operator's extended hands. However, pushing *only* rearward is a deficient test for checking the integrity of the stance.

Operators must be able to keep their balance while being pushed in *any* direction. Another team member on the move or a victim fleeing danger could inadvertently bump an operator. Lowering the body into a fighting stance by bending the knees and having one foot forward allows the body to maintain the best possible balance. The back foot provides the explosive power to move quickly forward or laterally. The body automatically lowers itself with the expectation of bullets flying. The body position reflects the situation at hand. Further explanation will drive home the point.

The author while in Afghanistan was about 109 yards (100 meters) from a suicide bomber when he detonated. The author was moving on foot with a British Military Unit led by a Special Air Service (SAS) team leader (TL). Each person on the team immediately crouched when the explosion went off. The team took small arms fire on the street and we continued to crouch while looking for attackers.[159] The author has been a part of or witnessed the crouching behavior from police officers on the streets in Dallas, Texas to military operators and police advisers in Afghanistan. Instructors should *not* stop operators on a range from crouching. Such behavior to the contrary needs to be required as a part of the fighting stance.

NOTE: Body armor may prevent an operator from shooting with the arms naturally extended. The width and stiffness of a ballistic vest can cause the arms to be more noticeably bent.

The fighting stance when combined with aggression and yelling is intimidating. The author while working at the Dallas Police Department began using the fighting stance. Most suspects he took at gunpoint would mentally lock-up (freeze). He interviewed several of the suspects and asked why they did not immediately follow his directions. The answer every time: "I thought you were going to shoot me! I was scared and couldn't move!" The fact criminals are afraid of armed police officers is a good way to ensure the officers survival.[160] A police officer must be willing and capable of shooting a criminal at any moment. The criminal's *perception* should be a *reflection* of the police officer's mind-set.

DANGER: An excessively angled shooting stance makes the body more susceptible to a gunshot injury. One shot through the side can hit a lung, heart, and second lung. Utilizing an excessively angled shooting stance would *not* maximize the frontal body armor protection or allow for dynamic movement. Humans do not normally walk fast or run while sideways.[161]

Grip

The one- and two-hand grip advocated for combat must work with a small or large stature operator. The grip must also work in adverse conditions (cold, sweaty, or blood soaked hands) and not just ideal conditions (warm, dry hands). Operators do *not* have the luxury of custom molded pistol grips[162] or using liquid grip enhancers[163] as do some recreational shooters. The hands losing contact with each other while shooing is unacceptable regardless of the conditions. An operator must be able to maintain the integrity of his or her grip to ensure hits on an adversary. To shoot a pistol accurate and fast the pistol has to be bonded solidly to the body. The grip establishes that bond and allows the pistol to become a natural extension of the body.[164]

NOTE: Wetting the hands with water or soapy water can replicate sweat or fresh blood, and dipping the hands in ice water for about a minute diminishes normal blood flow. Doing these things will quickly identify weaknesses in an operator's grip and will prove the methods in this section as valid.

Wearing rings, especially large thick ones can also prevent a good bond between the hands and a pistol. A general recommendation is *not* to wear any rings, but certainly wear no more than a wedding set on one hand and one ring on the other hand. There is also the tactical consideration of a ring entangled with an object and the finger being torn off. This is a real danger for police officers that wear rings and climb over chain link fences, especially during a foot pursuit. Long fingernails are another issue that can negatively affect the shooting grip. The fingernails of the firing hand can cut into the palm of the non-firing hand when shooting thumbs forward. A recommendation is for the fingernails *not* to extend past the fingertips, but certainly not more than 1/8 inch (3.1 millimeters).

At best without a consistent tight grip on the pistol recoil control is haphazard and the pistol will never be managed the same from shot to shot. Trigger control is incorrectly blamed many times for misses when in fact a lose grip is the cause. A *tight grip* for combat shooting keeps the hands securely in contact with the pistol while firing quickly and accurately. To build a tight grip there needs to be an understanding of the forces generated when firing a pistol and the effect on the hands. Firing a pistol causes the slide to move back and the muzzle up resulting in *muzzle flip*.[165]

When firing with two hands the pistol receiver is gripped from front to rear (firing hand) and side to side (non-firing hand). Unfortunately, applying more pressure in these two directions *alone* will do little to keep the muzzle from lifting off the target during recoil.[166] To reduce muzzle flip get the firing hand high on the back strap and apply forward pressure. The forward pressure in conjunction with locked wrists will minimize muzzle flip and allow the muzzle to return consistently to the starting position before the next shot.

The forward pressure technique practiced in training may in a real-life encounter become even stronger. The hand muscles in response to an imminent threat (stressful situation) tighten around an object being held. This is the reason while training a tight grip is advocated, i.e., clamp down on the pistol with both hands. This is an example of a technique forced in training, but will come natural in combat. A tight grip with the firing hand reduces muzzle movement as the non-firing hand applies side to side pressure. A tight grip is also recommended for shooting a carbine.[167] A tight grip is essential for maintaining a bond between the pistol and the hands while wearing gloves. Gloves if worn operationally should also be worn during training. Gloves may degrade operator skill by 10 to 20 percent when shooting a pistol.[168]

One-Hand: An operator using one hand must be able to consistently present a pistol with sights aligned and fire while controlling the recoil. This accomplishment begins with fitting the proper size pistol to the hand. A pistol with a grip circumference too large for the operator's hand creates a feeling of *not* having control resulting in diminished self-confidence. Physical control and self-confidence will naturally occur with proper practice using a pistol that properly fits the operator's hand. A pistol with a modular back strap frame provides adjustment capability for operators with small or large hands.[169]

There are three frame size options for Glock Gen4 pistols. The first is the *short frame* (SF) that does *not* have any optional back straps installed. The *short* trigger housing pin is installed in the frame. The second is a medium back strap installed on the SF resulting in a *standard* frame. The third is a large back strap installed on the SF resulting in a *large* frame. The medium and large back straps use the *long* trigger housing pin in the frame. The back strap size markings are located on the inner side. The medium (M) is a +2mm and the large (L) is a +4mm. Utilizing the frame size option includes the removal and reinsertion of the trigger housing pin. Changing the back strap alters the grip circumference.

NOTE: The grip angle does *not* change from the full-length back strap modifications. This ensures the operator will not fire low or high when changing back straps or when transitioning from one Glock pistol to another.[170]

To install the modular back strap remove the trigger housing pin using the provided disassembly tool or a Glock armorer's 3/32 inch (2.5 millimeter) pin punch disassembly tool. (Figures 6-10 and 6-11) To change the size of the grip, remove the back strap if mounted, chose the different frame size option or the pistol can remain without a modular back strap. To install a modular back strap hook it to the lower backside of the frame. Use the flat side of the disassembly tool to install the corresponding trigger housing pin. A correctly installed trigger pin will be centered and not protruding from either side of the receiver.

Figure 6-10 *Disassembly Tool (provided with Gen4 pistol)*

Figure 6-11 *Disassembly Tool (pin punch with chamfered end)*

WARNING:[171] Using the *long* size trigger housing pin in a pistol *without* a modular back strap installed can result in the protruding pin bruising the operator's hand. Using the *short* size trigger housing pin in a pistol *with* a modular back strap installed can result in the strap coming loose.

The pistol grip circumference is correct if the thumb and middle finger can touch or overlap and the back strap is pulled tight against the palm. Allowing the thumb and middle finger to nearly touch or touch is a natural part of the one-hand grip. The trigger finger somewhere between the middle of its pad to the first joint nearest the fingertip (distal interphalangeal joint) is on the trigger. The circumference is too *large* if the trigger finger barely reaches the trigger. The circumference is too *small* if the thumb and fingers overlap without pulling the back strap tightly against the palm or the trigger finger is too far in on the trigger. Too far in occurs when the first joint passes the face of the trigger. The trigger finger past the first joint would require more finger movement to pull and reset the trigger.

To establish a one-hand shooting grip place the pistol in the vee of the hand with the web high and firm on the back strap, but not so high to interfere with the slide's operation.[172] There should *not* be a gap between the web of the hand and the upper back strap. However, this is not always possible because of the operator's hand size in relation to the size of the pistol.

Having the web of the hand high into the upper back strap allows the bore axis of the pistol to sit as close as possible to the hand and in line with the forearm. This provides an advantage in shot-to-shot accuracy by reducing muzzle flip and recovery time. When the hand is high into the back strap a wrinkle (fold of skin) appears in the web of the hand. Wrap the lower three fingers around the grip. Do *not* grip using circular pressure. The three fingers are *each* gripping tightly and evenly from front to rear driving the vee of the hand high into the back strap. The back strap is tight against the palm with the wrist and elbow locked.[173] (Figure 6-12)

There is no gap between the middle finger and the bottom of the trigger guard. The bottom rear of Glock's trigger guard is relieved (notched) allowing the firing hand more natural angle and relieves pressure on the middle finger.[174] Allow the thumb to *naturally* curve down while lying in the thumb rest. The amount of curve in the thumb will vary according to the hand size in relation to the pistol. The thumb lying in the thumb rest prevents interference with the slide stop lever. The trigger finger somewhere between the middle of the pad to the first joint is on the trigger. (Figure 6-13)

NOTE: Grip pressure applied to the pistol must be equal to or more than the pressure required to pull the trigger to the rear.[175] Not having sufficient grip pressure to *overcome* the pressure required to pull the trigger (trigger pull weight) will cause misalignment of the sights. This can be a significant problem for a small stature operator required to carry a pistol with a heavy trigger pull.

Figure 6-12 One-Hand Grip

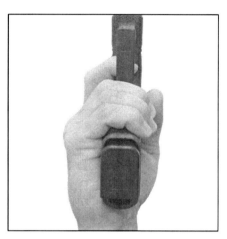

Figure 6-13 Trigger Finger Placement

Establish a *tight grip* using one hand by applying pressure with the three fingers front to rear until the hand begins to tremble, relax until the trembling stops.[176] The pistol's back strap remains pulled tight against the palm throughout the firing cycle. *Heeling* is tightening the large muscle in the heel of the hand just before pulling the trigger.[177] Heeling can occur when an operator attempts to stop a trigger jerk by tightening the bottom of the hand usually resulting in a heeled shot. Heeling causes the bullet to impact high on the firing side of the target. An operator can prevent most shooting errors by maintaining a *tight grip* while moving the *trigger finger* straight to the rear.

NOTE: The subcompact pistol is gripped with two fingers and the little finger curls under and against the magazine floor plate.

Two-Hand: A two-hand grip offers the greatest control of the pistol. This is especially true if the operator is breathing heavy from a foot pursuit or running from one position of cover to another.[178] When establishing a solid two-hand grip it is important to maintain contact of *both* hands with each other (one piece) and maximize flesh against the pistol's grip panels (friction). Accomplish this by using a *thumbs forward* grip.[179] Having the thumbs forward creates a cam effect that forces the non-firing wrist downward.[180] The cam effect helps to return the pistol after the muzzle lifts for faster follow-up shots. Another advantage of the cam effect is the reduction of muzzle flip through the biomechanics of the body and not pressure.[181] The thumbs forward grip must not interfere with the slide or slide stop lever.

Any interference with a pistol's controls caused by the thumbs forward grip must be remedied. Although *not* preferred, an operator may have to use the thumbs crossed grip. The thumbs crossed grip is the same as the thumbs forward grip with one exception. The non-firing hand thumb crosses over the top of the firing hand thumb. When shooting a Glock pistol use the thumbs forward grip *unless* an operator's physical disability *or* interference with the slide stop lever prevents it. The *thumbs forward* grip maximizes lateral and vertical control of the pistol. The two hands are indexed properly if the firing hand's index finger alongside the receiver is about even with the non-firing hand's thumb.[182]

To establish a two-hand shooting grip for *demonstration* purposes only—first obtain the one-hand grip as described in the previous section. Hold the *firing* arm straight in front of the body. Hold the *non-firing* arm parallel to the firing arm with the thumb parallel to the ground and the fingers at a 45-degree angle. (Figure 6-14) With both arms held straight in front of the body, bring the hands together. Allow the firing hand thumb to exert light pressure and rest at the base of the non-firing hand thumb just behind its second joint (nearest to the wrist). (Figure 6-15) Exerting heavy pressure with the firing hand thumb will break apart the grip. The non-firing hand fingers wrap over the firing hand fingers making contact. The hands of a *right-handed* operator will fit together at the *left* rear of the pistol like two pieces of a puzzle making total hand-to-hand contact.[183] The hands of a *left-handed* operator will fit together at the *right* rear of the pistol like two pieces of a puzzle making total hand-to-hand contact.

An operator with small hands or gripping a large frame pistol may *not* be able to fit the hands together at the rear of the pistol. It is more important for the middle joint of the non-firing hand fingers to interlock over the middle joint of firing hand fingers and the pad of the non-firing hand lay flat against the grip panel. Place the fingers of the non-firing hand in the grooves created by the fingers of the firing hand.[184] The fingers fit together and remain in contact. The non-firing hand index finger is tight against the bottom of the trigger guard (no gap) and wraps over the firing hand's middle finger. The non-firing hand middle and ring fingers are in the top and bottom grooves of the firing hand's ring finger. The non-firing hand little finger wraps over the firing hand's little finger. The *non-firing* hand thumb is straight and *rests* on the receiver, never on the slide.[185] Forward pressure of the firing arm presses the fingers firmly into the grooves of the non-firing hand's fingers bonding the hands together allowing the cammed non-firing wrist to maintain *downward* force. The non-firing hand fingers firmly compress the firing hand's fingers with side to side pressure. Perform the *push-compress* with enough pressure to keep the hands bonded together while firing, but *not* enough to cause the hands to tremble. More on this topic is included later in this section.

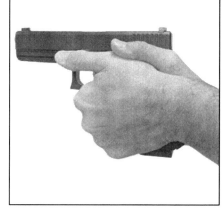

Figure 6-14 *Establishing Two-hand Grip*   **Figure 6-15** *Two-hand Grip*

WARNING: Do *not* place the non-firing hand thumb behind the pistol across the base of the firing hand thumb (commonly referred to as a revolver grip).[186] The slide moving rearward can strike the non-firing hand thumb causing an injury.[187]

Rest the firing hand thumb at the base of the non-firing hand thumb.[188] Keep the firing hand thumb as close to the receiver as possible *without* touching the slide stop lever. This aids in centering the pistol in the hand and is *crucial* for controlling recoil. The firing hand thumb (right-handed operator) *if* allowed to make contact with the slide stop lever can cause it to be held down and the slide cycle on an empty magazine. The thumb if pushed up against the slide stop lever can cause the slide to lock back on a partially filled magazine. This is especially true with pistols equipped with an extended slide stop lever. The Glock *extended* slide stop lever has a protruding rest for the thumb to depress to release the slide.[189] There is not a slide stop lever on the right side of a Glock pistol so interference is *not* an issue when shooting left-handed.

NOTE: The *recurved* design that Glock uses on the front of a trigger guard was specified in the Joint Service Operational Requirement (JSOR) for a Personal Defense Weapon (PDW) Standard Service Sidearm document dated May 6, 1980. The JSOR stated the recurved trigger guard was for the purpose of support of the non-firing hand.[190] The support technique is explained in two manuals from the Department of the Army: (1) Combat Training with Pistols, M9 and M11[191] and (2) Soldier's Manual of Common Tasks Warrior Skills Level 1.[192] This ill-advised technique *reduces* the compress effect diminishing the ability to control recoil and muzzle flip.[193] The index finger would also have to be controlled independently from the other fingers.[194] A more practical use of the trigger guard is to brace the front of it against cover to steady the firing position as advocated in the U.S. Marine Corps Pistol Marksmanship publication.[195]

Get a tight grip on the pistol each time when training. Just how much pressure is applied to the pistol when using a tight grip? It is common for the pistol's frame (receiver) texture pattern to be imprinted on the operator's hand after using a tight grip.[196] A tight grip settles the pistol in the hands providing consistent pointing of the muzzle and returning it to the starting position after firing. The pistol should recoil straight up and straight back down (neutral return).

The trigger finger remains parallel and indexed on the receiver when presenting the pistol and *not* firing. Do *not* place the trigger finger high on the slide. It is not a natural position and an extremely hot slide (Glock 18) can burn the trigger finger. A left-handed operator with the trigger finger positioned high on the slide would cover the slide stop lever *not* allowing it to be pushed up with the thumb of the non-firing hand when locking the slide to the rear. The trigger finger naturally wants to curve when the pistol is gripped. The trigger finger does *not* have to lay flat against the receiver. The trigger finger should not exert side pressure against the receiver. It is more comfortable and efficient to keep a slight bend in the trigger finger with its pad touching the receiver.

The topic of how much pressure each hand applies to the pistol is an extensively debated topic in the shooting community. Gripping a pistol should not be a mathematical equation.[197] Arguably, the most accomplished pistol shooter in modern times sees developing a grip based on percentages as problematic. He admitted when shooting fast he could not say what the percentages are other than 100 percent of his ability to grip the pistol. His advice for shooting a pistol fast and accurate is applying maximum pressure with the firing hand without limiting the ability to pull the trigger and maximum pressure with non-firing hand without causing a tremor.[198]

Generally, the fingers of both hands grip with even pressure.[199] Each hand will grasp items using the same amount of pressure, especially when the body is in an alarm state. As an example, a driver using both hands keeps a light grip on the steering wheel under normal driving conditions. However, when that driver is in a near collision situation each hand spontaneously tightens around the steering wheel. An operator shooting recreationally can control the amount of pressure each hand applies to the pistol, but during an alarm reaction, both hands will subconsciously exert maximum pressure equally. One of the most accomplished female shooters in modern times also recommended gripping the pistol as strongly a possible while still being able to move the trigger finger freely.[200]

The amount of bend in the elbows is another topic discussed extensively in the shooting community. Naturally locked arms with a slight bend provides better recoil control and assists the hands in moving together and not breaking apart during recoil. Do *not* hyperextend the elbows and shoot, it stresses the joints from the repeated jolts of the pistol's recoil and can lead to an injury.[201] Establish the correct amount of bend in the elbows by momentarily locking them out (hyperextending) until feeling pain in the joints and then unlock the elbows until the pain stops.[202] This is the natural locked position. The elbows should be raised slightly and *not* point toward the ground or be exaggerated out to the side.[203] Raising the elbows slightly activates the lower and upper muscles of the forearms. The hands apply inboard pressure against the pistol when the elbows are raised slightly.[204] The muscles in the forearms do the work. This is an important part of building a tight grip to control recoil.

The bend of the elbow is the same as when performing everyday tasks, such as picking up a bucket full of water and carrying it.[205] The amount of bend in the arms should feel comfortable and be a natural stopping place.[206] The pistol can be moved slowly forward and rearward using a two-hand grip to find the position that *maximizes* grip pressure between the hands and what feels natural. Keeping the arms naturally bent may reduce the angle between the pistol and hands providing better recoil control. Forcing the arms beyond their natural locked position causes the non-firing hand fingers to slip off the back of the firing hand and reduces the side to side grip pressure on the pistol.[207]

Push-compress is the *biomechanical* [208] technique of applying forward pressure with the firing hand through the back strap of the pistol into the non-firing hand resulting in forward pressure of both arms while compressing the fingers of the firing hand with side to side pressure of the non-firing hand fingers locking the pistol in a vise like state. The non-firing arm is pushed forward, but *not* pulling back. Although the firing arm is pushing forward, it is *not* intentionally bent or straightened any more than the non-firing arm. Both arms remain about the same length and have the same slight bend at the elbow. This can be checked in front of a mirror from the standing firing position by lowering both arms to a 45-degree angle. Both arms from the wrists to the shoulders should be nearly mirror images. Applying equal pressure from the front strap to the back strap and side to side produces a neutral grip allowing the muzzle to remain undisturbed. The technique is simple and consistent.

NOTE: The forward pressure technique is demonstrated by interlocking the fingers palm to palm with the thumbs parallel and extending the arms in a shooting position. The firing arm pushing forward also pushes the non-firing arm forward. This is what is meant by forward pressure.

Using the *same* amount of pressure front-to-back, forward, and side to side is what makes the technique work. The correct amount of pressure is applied when the muscles tremble, then relax until the trembling stops. The step-by-step method to teach the correct grip pressure with maximum recoil control is as follows: (1) the firing hand fingers apply pressure front to back until the muscles tremble, then relax until the trembling stops, (2) continue to maintain the pressure as described in one while the firing hand applies forward pressure against the non-firing hand until the muscles tremble, then relax until the trembling stops, and (3) continue to maintain the pressure as described in one and two while the non-firing hand fingers apply side to side pressure until the muscles tremble, then relax until the trembling stops.

The pressure applied with both hands is the maximum amount without creating trembling. This is probably the strongest grip that an operator can produce and still shoot accurate and fast. Although the two-hand grip is taught in three steps: when nearing the end of the extension pressure is applied in each direction almost simultaneously. The hands breaking apart while firing indicate the grip is not tight enough.[209] Maintaining a tight grip that keeps the pistol under control, and not blinking while shooting should cure the problem of flinching.

An operator with a properly fitted pistol, stable fighting stance, and proficient with the grip technique, but still cannot control the recoil required for combat shooting may find it necessary to reduce the caliber size *if* it is an option. An accomplished competitive shooter admitted she could shoot a 9x19mm much faster than a .40 S&W and do so while dropping fewer points.[210] Matching the best caliber for a particular operator is yet another option to help ensure his or her survival in combat. Controlling the pistol's recoil is *not* just in the hands and arms. To some degree the entire body is involved, especially the upper body.[211]

NOTE: Some combat shooting doctrines advocate a push-pull technique—pushing forward with the firing hand and *pulling* rearward with the non-firing hand.[212] The same doctrine warns that both hands not exerting the same pressure could result in a missed target.[213] A competitive shooter and instructor wrote on the matter. He said, "Why should you pull on the gun when it is already going that way during recoil?"[214] The push-pull method is an ill-advised technique for combat shooting.

Thumbs Forward vs. Thumbs Crossed: The thumbs forward (two-hand) grip allows the pads of each hand to lay flat against the pistol's grip panels. This grip produces a bond between the hands and pistol grip. The thumbs crossed grip creates a hollow area between the non-firing hand and the pistol grip. To prove there is a hollow area an ink pen or pencil can be shoved between the web of the non-firing hand and the first joint of the thumb on the firing hand. (Figure 6-16) Recoil of the pistol is like water and will flow the path of least resistance.[215]

Figure 6-16 *Hollow area caused by using the thumbs crossed grip.*

There is *no* hollow area using the thumbs forward grip and the pencil *cannot* be shoved between the non-firing hand and the pistol's grip panel. The hollow area is empty space in which the pistol can move freely. Many times this movement is obvious from resetting the non-firing hand after the pistol fires. Another sign is the pistol recoiling off to one side (circling out) and not straight up and back down.[216] Sometimes both hands are reset which indicates the grip is not tight enough.[217] Shooting accuracy and speed is interdependent with a solid grip.

Sight Alignment

Most pistols have iron sights (non-optical) featuring a flat-topped front sight post and a square-cornered rear sight. Sight alignment is one component of aiming. Proper sight alignment is the sights even across the top with the front sight centered in the rear sight as viewed by the operator.[218] (Figure 6-17) This is also referred to as equal *height* and equal *light*. Self-luminous sights with three dots will be visible in the dark and need to be aligned horizontally and spaced equally vertically.

Figure 6-17 Sight Alignment

NOTE: *Aiming* consists of two stages: sight alignment, and sight picture.[219] Once an operator understands how to align sights, he or she can learn how to obtain a sight picture. It is impossible to have a correct sight picture without having the sights aligned.

Sight Picture

A *sight picture* is the appearance of the pistol's sights to the operator's eye as aligned against the target or adversary.[220] An efficient method to demonstrate how to align sights on the intended aim point begins with drawing an "X" on a piece of paper. The center where the lines cross is where the bullet should hit. Place the muzzle of an *unloaded* or *inert* pistol against the target. Put the top edge of the front sight in the center of the X to show where to place the front sight when aiming. (Figure 6-18) Take the pistol away and draw the *front* sight on the X. (Figure 6-19) Again, put the top edge of the front sight in the center of the X and see the sight against the X. Take the pistol away and draw the *rear* sight on the X. (Figure 6-20)

Figure 6-18 *Pistol Against Target* **Figure 6-19** *Front Sight Drawn* **Figure 6-20** *Rear Sight Drawn*

Again, put the top edge of the front sight in the center of the X and look through the rear sight to see the sights aligned. The non-dominant eye may have to be closed to see the sights aligned. Hang the paper on a wall and stand holding the muzzle against the paper while aiming the aligned sights at the X. Aim the top edge of the sights at the center of the X while fitting the sights onto the drawing as a piece in a puzzle.

An operator should train to see his or her sight picture while keeping both eyes open. Keeping both eyes open maximizes visual input improving situational awareness. [221] The training program from the beginning needs to include shooting with both eyes open.[222] With both eyes open, the sights are seen as one image *superimposed* on the target. (Figure 6-21)

The operator's focus is on the target, but he or she sees the sights in the line of sight. The *line of sight* is the imaginary line between the dominant eye, sights, and the aim point on the target. Using TFSS requires the operator to learn only one method of aiming. The method of sighting is effective within the capability of the firearm. It is the operator's responsibility to see the sight image with enough *clarity* to make the shot with certainty.

Unlike other methods of shooting the operator is not preoccupied with the decision to *focus* on the target and then *focus* back to the front sight. It has already been proven that keeping both eyes open and focusing on the front sight will create two blurred target images. The operator must clearly identify the adversary in combat. Seeing an adversary as a blurred double image is counterproductive. The operator's attention needs to be on the adversary combined with enough clarity of the superimposed sight image to ensure a hit.

Figure 6-21 *High Center Mass Sight Picture*

Components of a Sight Picture: The three components of the sight picture as explained in the International Association of Law Enforcement Firearms Instructors, *Standards & Practices Reference Guide for Law Enforcement Firearms Instructors* are as follows:[223]

1. *Sight Alignment:* "How the components of the sighting apparatus themselves are aligned with each other from the perspective of the shooting eye."

2. *Aim Point:* "The intended point of impact on a target with which the shooter aligns the sights."

3. *Point of Focus:* "The shooting eye's point of focus, whether the shooting eye is focused on some component of the sighting apparatus or on the aim point of the target."

To shoot fast and accurate the operator must employ the three components. A solid grip combined with a natural point of aim based on procedural memory will provide consistent sight alignment. Operators must be comfortable in any of the firing positions to maximize the natural point of aim. The more consistent the target and pistol are naturally in line *(natural point of aim)* the less movement is required to obtain a sight picture. The aim point can be a small reference point such as the adversary's muzzle.

The eyes naturally find the center of an area focused on.[224] In the case of a close quarters gunfight, many times the threat perceived is the muzzle. This fact is evident in the number of people (operators and adversaries) involved in gunfights that get their hand shot holding the firearm. The operator with both eyes open focuses on the aim point while superimposing aligned sights. The first sight picture is as accurate as the second, third, fourth and so on.

The goal of aiming is to focus with both eyes open on the *available* center mass of the target seeing superimposed sights and pulling the trigger. Speed in responding and seeing the sights are critical in any deadly force encounter. A *reflexive* response is required regardless of the distance to the target. Using short time exposures of the targets can reinforce this requirement. Immediate action on any exposed imminent threat is necessary for survival. The sight picture is what dictates the speed of pulling the trigger and shooting the target or adversary. A slow sight picture translates into a slow trigger pull resulting in a slow shot.

An operator to make a reflexive shot should *not* mentally or physically slow down, but speed up seeing the sights. Be *aggressive* at quickly seeing the sights. The front sight with a white dot and the "U" outlined rear sight works well with the superimposed sighting method. It is not necessary in every instance to use the top edge of the front sight to place the shot. An operator within 7 yards (6.4 meters) can *focus* on where the bullet needs to hit, align the dot, and the shot should be there.[225] The white dot placed on the target can be quicker for some operators, especially those with aging eyes, or less than perfect eyesight.

NOTE: With sights *aligned* there is about 1/16 inch (1.58 millimeter) from the top edge of the front sight to the center of the front sight dot. This means the bullet would impact the aim point about 1/16 inch (1.58 millimeter) higher using the center of the front sight dot versus the top edge of the sight.

Breath Control

The human body has a natural respiratory pause (NRP). The pause is between the exhale and the inhale. The pause affords the operator the least amount of body movement. The respiratory pause is at the bottom of the breathing cycle and provides the greatest breath control. *Breath control* is the method of breathing used to minimize body movement while aiming.[226] Under ideal conditions, it would be beneficial to obtain a sight picture and fire each shot on a respiratory pause. (Figure 6-22) Nevertheless, an adversary is not going to wait for the operator's NRP. The attack will likely be spontaneous causing the operator to breath heavy.

Situation permitting, such as running from one place of cover to another the operator on arrival may be able to use *combat breathing*.[227] Combat breathing is taking three to five deep breaths that are inhaled through the nose for a count of four, held for a count of four, and exhaled through the mouth for a count of four.[228] What the author has found to be more practical in stressful situations is *not* to hold the breath, but to take a few deep cleansing breaths exhaling forcefully and then continue with the task. Deep breathing has a calming effect on the body thus reducing the level of arousal.[229] A police officer attributed combat breathing to saving her life after receiving a gunshot to the head.[230] Controlling breathing is the mark of a seasoned operator and is beneficial in stressful situations.[231]

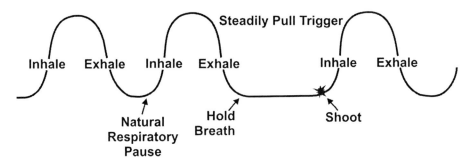

Figure 6-22 Breath control based on respiratory pause.

NOTE: Breathing is one of two autonomic nervous system actions that can be consciously controlled.

Under combat conditions, breathing will increase and the breath at times of exertion (mentally or physically) is often held subconsciously. This is vastly different from the NRP traditionally taught on the range. Combat shooting cannot depend on whether the breath is inhaled, paused, or exhaled. The shot must be taken in combat when required, but holding the breath only long enough to take the shot. (Figure 6-23)

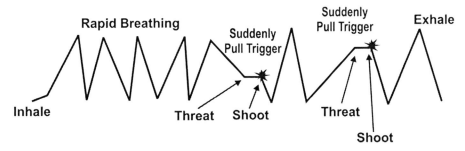

Figure 6-23 Breath control based on combat shooting.

Guard against holding the breath for more than 3 seconds when firing.[232] The level of blood oxygen dropping will affect eye muscles causing vision to deteriorate.[233] This fact is evident when shooting precise groups and holding the breath too long. The vision will blur and the mind responds by forcing the body to take a breath. The operator fighting in a dynamic combat environment will probably not be aware of his or her breathing. [234] Combat breathing at its lowest common denominator can be just remembering to breathe!

Trigger Control

Trigger control is the operator's ability to move the trigger rearward until the pistol discharges, without excessive movement of the pistol that would prevent accurate firing.[235] There are three views on controlling the trigger. The first is *riding the reset,* which is allowing the trigger forward just far enough to reset.[236] The second is *slapping the trigger reset,* which is the finger coming off the trigger after each shot allowing the trigger to reset.[237] The third is the *90-degree reset,* which is the finger moving forward about 90 degrees and staying in contact with the trigger allowing the trigger to reset. [238] A trigger control method advocated for combat shooting must work in a worst-case scenario while the operator is gripping the pistol tight and experiencing an alarm reaction.

NOTE: The body applying force to an object to cause or tend to cause motion *toward* the body is pulling, i.e., a rope is pulled. The body applying force to an object so as to cause or tend to cause motion *away* from the body is pressing, i.e., a button is pressed. Regarding shooting—a trigger is pulled—a magazine catch is pressed.[239] The two are different motions. The difficulty of a shot *does* affect the speed of pulling the trigger, but it is still a pull.

In a close quarters combat an operator would grip the pistol tight and likely pull the trigger as fast as humanly possible. The operator does not have the luxury of feeling something specific (pretravel, engagement, or overtravel)[240] because the entire encounter would probably be over in seconds. Accepting this fact raises questions. Should the natural movement of the finger conform to a method of controlling the trigger? On the other hand, should a method of controlling the trigger conform to the natural movement of the finger? Controlling a trigger by feel may be done in training and recreational shooting, but may not even be possible when experiencing an alarm reaction.

The diminished blood supply to the skin and the release of epinephrine in the bloodstream results in a loss of sensitivity during an alarm reaction. This allows the body to sustain injuries with little or no sense of pain, but it also hinders feeling the trigger. Because of a loss of feeling and the noise level when shooting, an operator should *not* train to be dependent on feeling or listening for the reset when shooting fast.[241] Even if the operator is *not* experiencing an alarm reaction—trying to reset the trigger by feel can inhibit shooting quickly.

Arguably, the most accomplished pistol shooter in modern times contends the trigger reset will *not* be felt when shooting quickly.[242] A method of trigger control not dependent on feeling the trigger and allows natural movement of the trigger finger is required for combat shooting. This can be especially important if the operator is experiencing an alarm reaction. The trigger moving forward into the pretravel stage is a by-product of a tight grip and shooting quickly. Corrective action is not necessary or desired *if* the operator is shooting quickly *and* the shots are accurate.[243]

NOTE: A tight grip in conjunction with the flexor muscles of the fingers being stronger than the extensor muscles limits the forward movement of the trigger finger to a natural 90-degree angle. Trying to force the trigger finger past the 90 degrees will cause a sympathetic release of the grip.[244]

There are advantages to the trigger finger moving into the pretravel stage. Moving the trigger into the pretravel stage ensures the trigger resets and prevents short stroking. [245] *Short stroking* occurs by *not* moving the trigger far enough forward to reset, which prevents firing with the next pull of the trigger. [246] Short stroking a trigger in competition can cost a few points. It can cost someone's life in combat. Why play on the edge of making the pistol function by precisely trying to reset the trigger? Another advantage is the prevention of a negligent discharge caused by putting too much pressure on the trigger after barely resetting it (riding the reset) resulting in an unaccounted for round. The operator is surprised when the round fires. This type of negligent discharge is preventable by removing pressure off the trigger to ensure it resets and reapply pressure only when intending to fire. The devastating effects of a negligent discharge can ruin an operator's professional and personal life. Limiting the natural movement of the trigger finger causes tension, hinders smooth movement, contributes to short stroking the trigger, and can result in a negligent discharge.

Combat shooting is a selective firearms skill based on being *responsible*. This means an operator must fire only when intending to do so and account for each round fired. Allowing the trigger finger to move forward until it is perpendicular to the receiver (90 degrees) should *reset the trigger* and build *procedural memory*. As the pistol recoils, take advantage of the time and reset the trigger by quickly releasing it forward. Once the shot is fired and instantly called, it is pointless to hold the trigger to the rear *unless* it is required by a specific drill when training. The operator resetting the trigger is not going to feel the reset or reset the trigger faster than the slide cycles.

The Glock trigger has slack that must be taken up before "...the trigger bar releases the firing pin by means of the connector...,"[247] "...resulting in two distinct stages: a lighter "take up" stage followed by a heavier "let off" stage..."[248] commonly referred to as a *two-stage* trigger. To understand how the two-stage trigger works, dry fire an *unloaded* Glock pistol. Rack the slide on an *empty* Glock pistol and move the trigger finger rearward directly in the centerline of the pistol pulling the trigger past the take up stage (pretravel) until feeling the resistance of the let off stage (engagement). Pull the trigger past the engagement stage until the trigger stops (overtravel) and hold it to the rear. Rack the slide and move the trigger forward into the pretravel stage, but keep the trigger finger in contact with the trigger. Immediately reapply pressure feeling the engagement stage. The pistol is ready to dry fire again.

The movement of the trigger finger is done in one smooth fast continuous motion when live firing quickly. The *difficultly* of the shot and the *skill* of the operator determines how fast the trigger is pulled. The Glock trigger has quite a bit of pretravel and even when shooting quickly the trigger finger can remain in contact with the trigger. Moving the trigger forward into the pretravel stage ensures the trigger resets and a negligent discharge would not occur from precisely trying to reset the trigger.[249]

The pistol's back strap for *combat shooting* is preferably centered in the vee of the hand with the trigger finger's first joint on the trigger. This is because the first joint provides more strength to pull the trigger. The first joint is sometimes referred to as the "power crease" and for combat shooting is the best compromise between precision (toward the fingertip) and strength (near the finger's base).[250] Centering the pistol's back strap in the vee of the hand is *not* an option *if* the trigger finger *barely* touches the trigger. The trigger finger must fall naturally on the trigger while having at *least* the center of the pad squarely on the trigger.[251] Doing so may require shifting the grip to a less than optimal position.

The trigger finger has a tendency to curl inward as the tight grip is applied. This is proven by holding an *unloaded* pistol loose in one hand with the trigger finger straight and just outside of the trigger guard. Squeeze the hand as hard as possible and watch what happens to the trigger finger. The trigger finger naturally curves inside the trigger guard in front of the trigger. The trigger finger between the center of the pad down to the first joint should fall somewhere on the trigger. The natural tendency for the trigger finger to curl inward will likely cause it to lie close or against the receiver from gripping the pistol tight. The trigger finger against the receiver of a properly fitted pistol will *not* move the muzzle when pulling the trigger *if* the pistol is gripped tight.[252]

Not having a gap between the trigger finger and the receiver is inconsequential.[253] Moving the trigger finger toward the tip to establish a gap between the trigger finger and the receiver will cause the grip to loosen. This is easily checked by gripping a pistol tightly letting the trigger finger fall naturally on the trigger and then moving the trigger finger out toward its tip. The grip loosens because the trigger finger is forced out of the grip and the others fingers try to follow sympathetically.[254] The same is true when the trigger finger moves in and naturally falls on the trigger. The other fingers try to follow sympathetically in the closed position enhancing the grip. The trigger finger's first joint positioned naturally on the trigger resulting from a tight grip provides a consistent index point under stress.

NOTE: Gripping the pistol tightly causing the sympathetic inward curling of the trigger finger is the reason for it feeling comfortable with a slight bend and not straight while resting on the receiver.

To summarize trigger control for combat shooting—hold the pistol tight and move the trigger finger straight to the rear in a smooth motion—without disturbing the pistol (sight picture). How fast the trigger is pulled is dependent on the difficultly of the shot and the operator's skill. The trigger is reset quickly while the pistol is in recoil after the shot is fired and the sequence is repeated. Gripping the pistol tight limits the forward movement of the trigger finger *naturally* to about 90 degrees while resetting the trigger. The trigger moves forward and into the pretravel stage. Pulling the trigger to the rear beginning from the pretravel stage is immaterial *if* the shots are accurate.

NOTE: Teaching an operator to have a surprise break as a method for combat shooting is tactically wrong. To maximize survival tactics an operator for all practical purposes had better know when his or her firearm is going to fire.[255] Instructors should stop teaching *front sight— press, press, press, surprise break,* and begin teaching, *sight picture— break the shot.*

Follow-through

Follow-through is the operator maintaining all the elements of firing such as position, sighting, trigger control, breathing, etc., for a period if only for fractions of a second after the shot.[256] That is to say, the operator will remain in a firing position, see the second sight picture, fire the shot if necessary, and repeat the process. To learn proper follow-through there must be a positive reinforcement, i.e., hitting the aim point.

As this positive reinforcement occurs the "…subconscious can form the mental trace, or neural pathway, of the entire event."[257] The operator by hitting the aim point forms the necessary procedural memory to repeat the process on demand. With proper practice the operator's follow-through will occur subconsciously which is desirable for combat. This is to confirm the incapacitation of the adversary before discontinuing the use of force against him or her and transitioning to the next potential threat.

DRAW

Lowering the body and facing the threat in a stressful situation allows the operator to react swiftly. Training programs for the sake of safety that only permit the operator to remain stationary and draw are inadequate for operational survival training. As one *suspect* said, "I can hit on the fly, on the draw; I can come from anywhere, on the ground. But, that was training I taught myself."[258] The suspect had fired 12 rounds at a police officer and struck him 3 times. The police officer fired 7 rounds, but none struck the suspect.

An operator would do well to adopt the suspect's training regimen of being able to move in any direction and draw simultaneously.[259] With practice an operator can simultaneously step to the side, draw, and fire in the same time frame as when standing still, drawing and firing.[260] The operator should not only practice stepping quickly to each side, but also diagonal, forward, and back. An operator that has the ability to move, draw, and shoot increases his or her chance of survival during a close quarters attack.

Likewise, practice drawing with the hands in different starting positions, not just from a common position. The draw speed never changes regardless of the distance to a target.[261] Draw as fast at 25 yards (22.86 meters) from a target as being 1-yard (0.91-meter) —there is no distinction. The only thing that changes is the time it takes to superimpose the aligned sights on the target. That time will depend on the distance to the target and how much of the target is exposed. Greater the distance to the target the smaller it will appear and smaller targets normally require additional time to aim.

When learning the draw an operator may find it beneficial to perform the draw slowly in reverse order to see each stage and how it interrelates with motor functions (muscle activity). The operator may also find it beneficial to isolate and practice each step of the draw. As an example, practice just the *grip* step of the draw to get accustomed to moving both hands quickly at the same time and pulling the pistol's back strap tight against the palm. Then add the join position and finally the extend position where it all comes together.

NOTE: The response of drawing and back-pedaling from an adversary can result in the operator falling backward.[262] The human body is *not* designed to move backward quickly, especially on unfamiliar terrain. Operational environments are *not* the same as flat, clean, sterile training areas. There is also the issue of withdrawing straight back that might keep the operator directly in the adversary's line of fire. Move backward *only* when there is no better option.

An operator must be able to draw quickly from the holster, fire, and consistently hit the aim point. An operator expecting the stimulus and already having identified the target to shoot in a training environment might be able to draw and fire in 1.25 to 1.5 seconds.[263] Some operators may be capable of drawing and shooting an 8-inch (203.2-millimeter) target at 10-yards (9.14 meters) in less than 1 second.[264] The less than 1-second draw is an outstanding goal to set and accomplish. The grip, join, and extend steps of the draw integrate seamlessly with the fighting stance.

Grip: The body quickly moves into a fighting stance with both arms moving in tandem. The body remains upright without leaning to one side and exhales during the exertion for explosive power. Continue to breathe throughout the draw to help conserve energy. The *non-firing* hand moves up at about chest height, but not against it with the palm canted and fingers forward and loosely spread.[265] Simultaneously the *firing* side elbow drives straight to the rear. The firing hand goes down releasing any holster retention devices while moving forward positioning the center of the web of the hand high on the center of the back strap. The middle finger contacts the underside of the trigger guard. The three fingers pull straight back sinking the back strap *solid* into the palm settling the pistol in the hand and establishing the grip. The elbow remains close to the body. (Figures 6-24 and 6-25) The down and up movement of the firing hand is similar to a bouncing motion as the pistol is snatched from its holster.[266]

CAUTION: Coming up from underneath the pistol to draw can result in a dropped pistol. This occurs when the three fingers contact the *front strap* first pulling the pistol free of the holster without the web of the hand against the back strap—flinging the pistol downrange.

Allowing the firing side elbow to stick out from the body will cause the pistol to twist and bind in the holster when drawing. Standing with the firing side shoulder lightly touching and perpendicular to a wall prevents the elbow from sticking out when drawing. Repetitively griping the holstered pistol in this position is an effective training method to teach keeping the elbow close to the body.

Figure 6-24 Grip (front view)   **Figure 6-25** Grip (side view)

Join: Pull the pistol straight up from the holster and rotate 90 degrees at about chest height.[267] The trigger finger is on the receiver with the muzzle parallel to the ground and perpendicular to the body. A manual safety at this point would be disengaged *if* equipped.[268] To keep the pistol settled and aligned in the hand it is imperative the back strap remain *tight* against the palm. The firing arm moves forward and the joining of the hands occur at or above chest level directly under the dominant eye. The fingers of the non-firing hand are spread and the index finger makes contact under the trigger guard against the middle finger of the firing hand as a reference point. The non-firing hand fingers wrap firmly over the fingers of the firing hand. Hold the firing hand thumb *close* to the receiver, but not touching the slide stop lever. (Figure 6-26 and 6-27) To take a shot, place the trigger finger on the trigger *after* the hands join. This allows the pistol to settle in the hands before applying pressure on the trigger.

NOTE: After pulling the pistol clear of the holster, do *not* move the pistol down below the holster and then back up (scooping) or up above the shoulder and then back down (lobbing). Both movements are unnecessary, inefficient, and waste valuable time.

Figure 6-26 *Join (front view)*   **Figure 6-27** *Join (side view)*

CAUTION: The non-firing hand cants inward naturally with the fingers loosely spread and pointing nearly straight before the hands join. This will prevent the fingers from accidentally colliding with the pistol. Allowing the non-firing hand finger tips to curve *excessively* inward can result in a painful strike against the side of the pistol or worse accidentally shoved inside the trigger guard resulting in a negligent discharge. The hands generally join at the same height as when clapping.[269]

Extend: The head remains stationary and eyes focused on the target. The pistol is pushed forward with the muzzle pointing at the target in case a shot is taken *before* reaching full extension. The arms extend rapidly while stopping *smoothly* at the end of the natural extension with the firing arm pushing the non-firing arm forward. The hands *compress* together as the arms reach full extension (push-compress). The non-firing hand's canted angle, locked wrist, and both elbows slightly raised assists in controlling the pistol. The sights remain within the line of sight between the dominant eye and the aim point. See the aligned sights as a single image *superimposed* on the target. Pull the trigger when the arms reach a natural locked position. (Figure 6-28 and 6-29) The shoulders remain in a natural forward position.

Figure 6-28 Extend (front view)   **Figure 6-29** Extend (side view)

The brain processes the *extend* command without preoccupation of stopping the arms at a self-imposed distance. The elbows are even when viewed from the side and the shoulders are level when viewed from the front resulting in a balanced body. Forcing the arms past the natural locked position (overextending) can result in pushing the muzzle to the side or excessive forward rolling of the shoulders.

Reference Lines: A visual training reference can be added after the correct hand position is established and the arms locked. A coach using a medium point marker can draw two reference lines spaced about 1 inch (25.4 millimeters) apart.[270] This will provide a visual reference for the operator to obtain a proper grip until it is mastered. (Figure 6-30)

WARNING: Make sure the operator does not have an allergy to ink and get his or her verbal or written permission (liability release) before drawing the two reference lines.

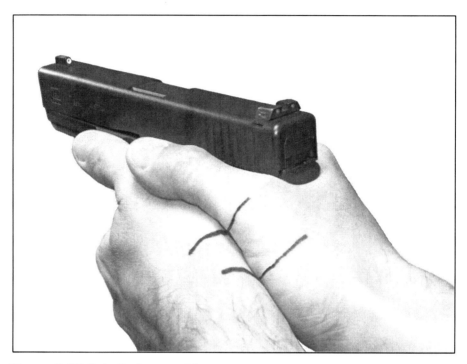

Figure 6-30 Grip Reference Lines

Drawing and Holstering: The draw is initially taught in three separate steps. The steps in the beginning can be performed *slowly* using *perfection* to build correct procedural memory. The draw is accomplished *aggressively* in one fluid motion after procedural memory is acquired.[271] The goal is to keep the pistol constantly pushing out.[272] The trigger finger will remain on the receiver while drawing and holstering. The non-firing hand must never cross in front of the muzzle.[273] Accomplish this by bringing the non-firing hand up close to the chest *clear* of the muzzle. The technique works with hip holster, shoulder holster,[274] or cross-draw[275] holster. Holster and secure the pistol using only the firing hand to prevent pointing the muzzle at the non-firing hand.

The muzzle should never point at the operator's own body. This includes *hunting the holster* with the muzzle. This occurs when the pistol is angled to put it in the holster and in doing so points the muzzle at the operator's body. This is a common mistake with police officers. A simple solution to holstering a pistol when encountering difficulty is to touch the outside upper edge of the holster with the slide near the muzzle then move the pistol up and over into the holster. (Figures 6-31 and 6-32) This method should work well for an operator wearing an equipment vest that may block his or her view of the holster when looking down. Likewise, a female operator's own breast may block the view of her holster when looking down even when not wearing an equipment vest.[276]

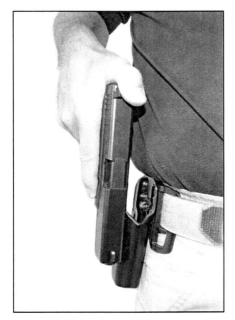 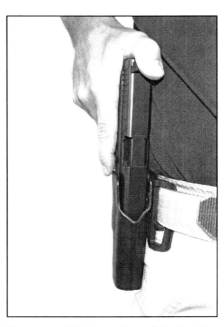

Figure 6-31 *Slide touches side of the holster.*   **Figure 6-32** *Inserting pistol in the holster.*

WARNING: It is possible when holstering a pistol for the top strap of some holsters to get tangled in the trigger. The pushing down motion of holstering combined with the entangled strap can push against the trigger causing the pistol to fire. The trigger finger on the receiver acts as a guide to help keep the strap of the holster clear of the trigger.

Looking down at the holster while holstering is a common *habit*, but it can also be a dangerous one. Operators without looking at the holster and using only their firing hand should be able to holster a pistol.[277] Keeping a visual focus on the target while holstering will prevent looking down at the holster. However, dependent on the circumstances a quick glance down may be necessary to holster efficiently.[278] An armed civilian after just having shot an attacker may need to holster his or her pistol as the police are arriving. A police officer may need to holster to transition to a different weapon or to handcuff a suspect. A military operator may need to holster and pick up a rifle on the battlefield.

Checking the Slide: One school of thought when holstering is for the firing hand thumb to be placed on the back of the slide.[279] This is to prevent the slide from coming *out of battery*[280] when the pistol is inserted into the holster forcefully. Use this method to push a pistol in an inside of the pants holster or elastic bellyband. In addition, the method provides a physical indicator if the operator were to inadvertently try to holster a pistol with the slide back. *Checking the slide* is placing the thumb on the back of the slide. (Figures 6-33 and 6-34) This technique requires the loss of the normal grip on the pistol, but if done properly is safe and tactically sound.

Figure 6-33 Checking the Slide (left hand)

Figure 6-34 Checking the Slide (right hand)

The author had been taught to place his thumb on the back of the slide, but while practicing in the rain had dropped his pistol. Only after attending an antiterrorism combat course in Israel did he learn the proper mechanics to the technique. The Israeli combat doctrine is about *aggression* and this technique is no different. The correct technique is to hold the thumb on the back of the slide *forcefully* while pulling directly to the rear with the three fingers wrapped around the pistol grip. The pistol is in a vise like state. The author after being in a vehicle pursuit at night had the driver at gunpoint. He had the suspect in a prone position on the ground. As he went to holster his pistol quickly, he could feel the slide moving back. The checking the slide technique prevented the pistol from coming out of battery possibly causing a stoppage.

Checking the slide can also be used to prevent the operator from scanning while holding a pistol with a slide locked back. After engaging a target or adversary, the pistol can be brought back into a two-hand compressed ready position with the firing hand thumb on the back of the slide. The ability to check the slide needs to be a subconscious act and this is especially important for an operator experiencing an alarm reaction or operating in low light conditions. The thumb cannot be placed on the back of a slide that is locked back. An operator in combat may or may not feel his or her slide lock back. This does not change the fact the operator has a responsibility to know the condition of his or her pistol. The fail-safe to ensure a pistol's condition is to perform a reload.

Actions After the Engagement: Immediately after a deadly force encounter, there needs to be a sense of holstering reluctantly.[281] There should *not* be thoughts of holstering quickly or immediately talking on a radio. Immediately talking on the radio after the initial gunfight was a contributing factor in a South Carolina trooper's murder.[282] The operator *if* possible should move to a position out of the adversary's line of sight, but keeping the adversary within the operator's line of sight. The entire area (360 degrees) must be quickly searched for additional threats using senses of the body applicable to the environment.

Search the surrounding area within 5 yards and then from 5 yards to 25 yards and then out from 25 yards. This check is called 5s-by-25s.[283] Operators that use the metric system can substitute meters for yards when performing the 5s-by-25s. Look for places at ground level and elevated heights that an adversary can hide and mount an attack. Looking is using only one element of the body's situational awareness. Look, listen, smell, and feel—be prepared to fight again.

NOTE: It is widely taught in law enforcement to have a pistol in the hand if the officer thinks it may be needed.[284] It is easier to put the pistol away if *not* needed than to suddenly need it urgently and have to draw from the holster.

Concealed Carry

One of the most common methods of concealing a pistol is to wear it under a cover garment. A favorite carry position is the pistol on a waist belt mounted behind the hip and on the same side as the dominant eye. This strong side position allows the elbow of the firing side arm to touch the pistol's grip. [285] The elbow touching the pistol's grip provides reassurance the pistol is where it should be and available for use. Concealed carry has the benefit of being low profile, but providing immediate access to a pistol without causing undue alarm to the public.

The smaller pistols are sometimes carried in the pants pocket. The drawback to this method is an operator having to draw while moving off the line of attack or breaking contact by running. It would be difficult if not impossible to draw a pistol from the pants pocket while moving. This major obstacle deserves serious consideration before adopting the carry method of a small pistol in the pants pocket.

An operator must not obsess over the pistol, but see it as *tool* that can become an extension of the body if circumstances dictate. There are risks to operators that choose to carry a concealed pistol. Risks not only come from confronting an adversary, but also the possibility of a self-inflicted gunshot.

A deputy who finished qualifying had holstered his pistol and was unaware the cord stopper on his raid jacket drawstring had lodged in the trigger guard.[286] This occurred when he moved the jacket back to holster the pistol trapping the stopper in the holster. The deputy removed his paddle holster with a Glock pistol still inside and the drawstring tightened engaging the trigger safety causing the pistol to discharge. (Figure 6-35) The deputy received a gunshot wound in the upper thigh.

A similar incident occurred with a pistol from a *different* manufacturer. A police officer while wearing a department issued rain jacket had drawn his pistol in the line of duty. A 2.25-inch (57.15-millimeter) cord attached to the zipper had lodged between the trigger and holster when the police officer holstered his pistol. The police officer unaware of the trapped cord pulled on his raincoat to free the zipper and the Smith & Wesson Sigma pistol discharged.[287] These two incidents involving two different brands of pistols are reason enough for an agency to provide awareness training on objects becoming lodged in the trigger guard—regardless of the brand of pistol carried.

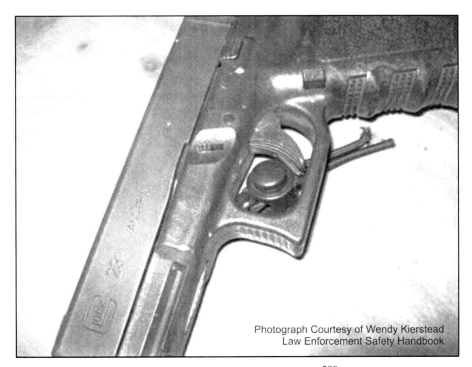

Photograph Courtesy of Wendy Kierstead
Law Enforcement Safety Handbook

Figure 6-35 *Cord stopper lodged in trigger guard.*[288]

DANGER: Examine outer clothing used operationally and remove any *drawstrings* and associated *attachments*. This includes any attachments connected to zippers.

Drawing from a Jacket

Neither the sights nor the pistol should have any sharp edges that could snag clothing while drawing. Drawing from a jacket uses all the previous steps for drawing except for of the firing hand sweeping the garment. Be aggressive when sweeping the jacket to access the pistol. With the four fingers of the firing hand grab the inside edge of the jacket about chest high. Move the elbow straight to the rear and quickly sweep the jacket back while curling the hand inside the jacket above and slightly behind the butt of the pistol. (Figure 6-36) Immediately come down high into the back strap with the web of the hand and grasp the grip of the pistol. (Figure 6-37) At this point, the operator will either complete the draw or discontinue if no action is required. An operator should *not* weight the pocket of a jacket to help move it out of the way when drawing. This method is a mere temporary fix in the place of learning how to access the pistol properly.

Figure 6-36 *Outer Garment (access)*

Figure 6-37 *Outer Garment (grip)*

To holster the pistol grasp it using the checking the slide technique. Catch the edge of the jacket to move it rearward using the tips of the three fingers around the pistol grip exposing the holster. Keep the firing arm elbow close to the body and rotate the pistol down inserting it into the holster. Secure any retaining devices. Maintaining good form while practicing will produce good results. Do *not* sacrifice form for speed. The speed will naturally come with proper *practice* combined with *aggression*.

NOTE: Wearing a pistol and spare magazines behind the hips may offer better concealment. However, police officers should wear their concealed pistol and magazines in about the same location as their duty pistol and magazines because of procedural memory.

Drawing from an Untucked Shirt

Draw a pistol using *two* hands while wearing an untucked shirt by grabbing the bottom of the shirt with the *non-firing* hand and pulling the shirt out away from the pistol and up to shoulder height. This exposes the pistol allowing access and the establishment of the grip. (Figures 6-38 and 6-39). At this point, the operator will either complete the draw or discontinue the draw if no action is required. Draw a pistol using *one* hand while wearing an untucked shirt by grabbing the bottom of the shirt with *firing* hand and pulling the shirt out and away from the pistol and up to the shoulder height. The firing hand goes down quickly on the pistol establishing a grip.

Figure 6-38 Shirt Not Tucked *(access)*   **Figure 6-39** Shirt Not Tucked *(grip)*

Pulling the shirt to the shoulder prevents the pistol and shirt from becoming entangled. Those operators that do not wish to expose their bare skin while training should wear an undershirt tucked in. The garment concealing the pistol is worn over the undershirt. This is especially applicable to females taking training and learning how to draw from an untucked shirt.[289] A good practice for an instructor teaching how to draw from an untucked shirt is to require *all* attendees to wear an undershirt.

A pistol should be in a holster designed to protect the trigger and worn either on the inside or outside of the waistband. Do *not* carry the pistol tucked inside of the waistband without a holster. A trigger unprotected might result in negligent discharge causing a person to be seriously injured or killed. The ability to holster a pistol safely is as important as drawing. Trying to cram a pistol into a waistband only increases the chance of a negligent discharge. A pistol stuck in the waistband is also susceptible to falling out during rigorous physical activity.

Drawing from a Holster Purse

The foundation of drawing from a holster purse begins with a quality product.[290] The holster purse should be ambidextrous in that it can be set-up for a right hand or left hand operator. Keep the holster purse in a state of readiness. This means not cramming it full of documents, makeup, sale advertisements, etc. The added weight and bulk will make drawing the pistol difficult. The compartments need to remain closed to prevent items from spilling when holding the purse diagonal to draw the pistol.

The holster purse is worn slung across the non-firing side shoulder. (Figure 6-40) Some operators may prefer to drape the strap around the neck and across the body. Just keep in mind the strap could be used to pull the operator to the ground. However, long guns as an accepted practice are slung in a similar manner. Maintaining situational awareness is the best deterrent to keeping adversaries out of reach of the purse and the operator. Whichever method of carry is chosen stick with it in order to build procedural memory.

DANGER: The purse must be in control of the owner at all times because of the pistol inside!

To draw, move into a fighting stance and simultaneously move the purse diagonal across to the front of the body with the handgun compartment up and the muzzle down. The angle of the hand and arm when drawing from the holster purse is about the same as the *carry position.* This downward angle helps to keep the muzzle pointed in the appropriate direction when drawing from the holster purse. Release the handgun compartment retention device (zipper, hook-and-loop fastener, etc.) to *access* the pistol. (Figure 6-41) Slip the firing hand inside the opening of the handgun compartment and *grip* the pistol. (Figure 6-42) Getting a tight grip is crucial because there is not time to adjust the grip during the draw. Pull the pistol straight out of the holster purse and release the grip on the purse. Be careful not to cross the non-firing hand in front of the muzzle.

NOTE: A zipper will be more difficult to manipulate under stress than ripping the handgun compartment open that is fastened with a magnetic closure or loop-and-hook fastener.

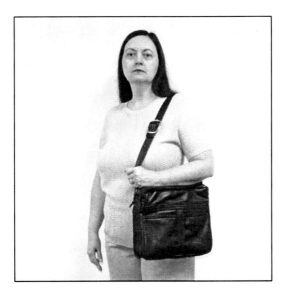

Figure 6-40 *Shoulder purse across non-firing side shoulder.*

NOTE: Moving the holster purse to a *diagonal* position in front of the body allows the same draw in training as in a real-life situation. On the street there is no downrange.

Figure 6-41 Holster Purse
(access)

Figure 6-42 Holster Purse
(grip)

Figure 6-43 Holster Purse
(join)

Figure 6-44 Holster Purse
(extend)

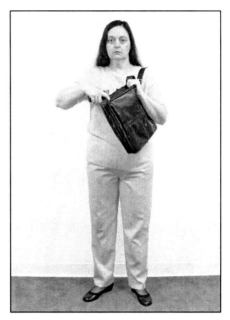

Figure 6-45 Holstering Pistol
(checking the slide)

Figure 6-46 Holstering Pistol
(separating the compartment)

Move the hands to the *join* position and then *extend*. (Figures 6-43 and 6-44) Acquire a superimposed sight picture and depending on the circumstances pull the trigger. Make sure to scan the area for other threats and take whatever action is necessary before putting the pistol back in the holster purse.

NOTE: There is no tactical advantage to slinging the holster purse to the rear after drawing the pistol. The holster purse shoulder strap will likely fall off the shoulder anyway. The rearward movement would only use time needed to win the fight.

To put the pistol back in the holster purse, grasp the shoulder strap and edge of the handgun compartment with the non-firing hand. (Figure 6-45) Use the firing hand index finger to separate the handgun compartment and slip the pistol inside. (Figure 6-46) Use the checking the slide technique to put the pistol in its handgun compartment. Release the grip, retract the hand from the holster purse, and secure the compartment retention device *if* applicable. An operator should be able to holster the pistol without looking.

Firing the pistol from inside the holster purse is an option under exigent circumstances. An operator would grip the pistol inside the holster purse—point it at the adversary and fire. The bullet will go through the purse. Use this method at contact or near contact distances from the adversary. There is a higher likelihood of missing the adversary when firing from inside the holster purse as opposed to drawing and using superimposed aligned sights. With a semiautomatic there is also the possibility of the slide not cycling and a stoppage occurring. A tap-rack-ready would be necessary before being able to shoot a second shot.

NOTE: Manufacturers may use steel cables sewn inside the shoulder strap or use other methods to make the shoulder strap slash resistant. This helps to prevent the shoulder strap from being cut and the holster purse stolen.

Drawing While Seated

Drawing while seated in a vehicle begins with the preparation of the cover garment. The seat belt secured over the cover garment will prevent accessing the pistol. When seated in a vehicle pull the cover garment away, fasten the seat belt, and put the garment back. Now the pistol is accessible. To draw the pistol while seated, lean the upper body forward, sweeping the garment out of the way then grip the pistol. (Figure 6-47) Bring the pistol out of the holster and up to chest level. (Figure 6-48)

Rotate the pistol 90 degrees at chest level *joining* both hands and then *extending*. (Figures 6-49 and 6-50) Bringing the pistol up high allows clearing the steering wheel and dashboard. This method works equally well when seated at a table. Starting to rotate the pistol before it has cleared a tabletop can result in snagging the front sight and possibly tearing it off. Hitting the table might also knock the pistol out of the operator's hand. Drawing and bringing the pistol up high to clear any obstructions helps to engineer out human error.

NOTE: Strive for one method of drawing that will work while standing, kneeling, or seated—simple and effective.

Figure 6-47 *Seated Drawing (access)*

Figure 6-48 *Seated Drawing (grip)*

Figure 6-49 *Seated Drawing (join)*

Figure 6-50 *Seated Drawing (extend)*

READY POSITIONS

There are tactics that require the pistol to remain in the hand ready for use. An advantage of a ready position is that it removes the chance of fumbling a draw. However, a ready position requires adherence to the Four Rules for Firearms Handling, especially rules two and three. Keep the muzzle pointed in the appropriate direction, and keep the trigger finger on the receiver unless firing. The appropriate direction is dependent on changing circumstances.

It is unacceptable for an operator to point a loaded pistol at him or herself, or an innocent person. Maintain an awareness of the pistol's muzzle in relation to the environment. In other words, know where the muzzle is being pointed and at what. It is an individual's responsibility to maintain the muzzle in the appropriate direction.

WARNING: The appropriate direction is a crucial element of a ready position and for the sake of safety cannot be overstated.

As the threat level increases, so should the operator's readiness to respond with deadly force. Ready positions are designed to place the operator in a state of increased readiness as circumstances change. There are three ready positions with the pistol: (1) *low ready*, (2) *high ready*, and (3) *compressed ready*. Law enforcement not only uses the three ready positions with a pistol, but so does the U.S. Marine Corps.[291] The ready positions permit an operator to challenge an adversary or respond with deadly force quickly when necessary.[292] The operator must be capable of moving seamlessly from one ready position to another or a firing position.

Uniformity of techniques across weapon systems improves operator combat efficiency. The U.S. Army and U.S. Marine Corps both use the *low ready* and *high ready* positions with a carbine.[293] The low and high ready positions work on the premise of the operator raising a lowered firearm with aligned sights into the line of sight whether a pistol or a carbine. Consistently having aligned sights is dependent on the operator's ability to bring the firearm into the line of sight stopping in the sweet spot. Two common attributes of any ready position are the muzzle pointed in the appropriate direction and the trigger finger on the receiver.[294]

NOTE: The three ready positions are part of a *ready continuum* based on the operator's perception of a threat and the environment. The pistol can be in any one of the positions or somewhere in between.

Low Ready

The low ready position is suited for searching inside of buildings especially when involving multiple operators. This is to prevent operators from pointing their muzzles at each other. An operator may find him or herself in the low ready position after shooting an adversary. The adversary after falling to the ground would require the operator to lower his or her pistol to reacquire a sight picture. The operator may have to continue to fire or move from the low ready position to engage another adversary.

To assume the *low ready* position use the steps as follows: With two hands or one hand, grasp the pistol grip firmly with the trigger finger on the receiver. Extend the arms or arm down at about a 45-degree angle to the body.[295] (Figure 6-51 and 6-52) Point the muzzle toward the target or in the likely direction of an adversary.

Figure 6-51 Low Ready Position (two-hand)

Figure 6-52 Low Ready Position (one-hand)

High Ready

The high ready position has been advocated as an option to hold an adversary at gunpoint while pointing the muzzle roughly at his or her pelvic area. This is to allow the operator to see the adversary's hands and postural movements.[296] Pointing a firearm at an adversary without the intention of firing is dependent on laws, rules of engagement, and the policies of the organization that employ the operator. The best practice *if* possible is to use the high ready, but *not* point the pistol at an adversary unless intending to fire. This practice will help prevent a negligent discharge that could result in an unintended injury or death. An electronic timer can be used to prove there is not any noticeable time different in pointing a pistol at the ground directly in front of an adversary as opposed to his or her pelvic area and bringing the pistol up into the line of sight to make a reactive shot.

Figure 6-53 High Ready Position (two-hand)   **Figure 6-54** High Ready Position (one-hand)

The high ready position can also be used for searching while keeping the pistol below the line of sight for a clear view of the area. The high ready position is favored by some operators for aircraft hostage rescue, and vehicle assaults were passengers are usually seated.[297] The high ready position can be physically tiring on the operator. To assume the *high ready* position use the steps as follows: Grip the pistol with two hands or one hand with the trigger finger on the receiver. Extend the arms or arm with the pistol just below eye level while keeping a clear field of view.[298] (Figure 6-53 and 6-54) Point the muzzle toward the target or in the likely direction of an adversary.

Compressed Ready

The compressed ready position is useful for searching in confined areas and when opening a door to search. The compressed ready position provides added weapon retention over the low and high ready positions. The compressed ready position is less tiring than the low and high ready positions and can provide physical relief during extended searches by resting the upper arms against the body.

To assume the *compressed ready* position use the steps as follows: Grip the pistol with two hands or one hand and the trigger finger on the receiver. Rest the upper arms against the body and the forearms or forearm down at about a 45-degree angle to the body.[299] (Figure 6-55 and 6-56) Point the muzzle toward the ground, target, or in the likely direction of an adversary.

Figure 6-55 Compressed Ready Position (two-hand)

Figure 6-56 Compressed Ready Position (one-hand)

NOTE: The ready positions may have to be performed with one hand. This can occur from having to use a cell phone, portable radio, flashlight, or to check on an injured person. The muzzle may need to be parallel to the ground when opening a door during a search to prevent pointing it at the non-firing hand.[300]

The ready positions advocated for fighting with a pistol allow keeping it locked out or compressed. The muzzle should point low enough to provide the operator with a clear field of view.[301] Each ready position is part of a *continuum* based on the operator's perception of the circumstances. How far the pistol is *lowered, raised, pushed out,* or *pulled back* can rapidly change and is dependent on the unfolding circumstances as perceived by the operator. There is no one ready position that will work for all situations.[302]

CARRY POSITION

There are times in which an operator cannot use a ready position, but still wants a pistol in hand. The *carry position* fulfills this requirement. The carry position will work on the range and equally well in an operational environment. The carry position with a pistol is essentially the same angle as for a carbine using a two-point sling. This is another example of using uniformity of techniques across weapon systems to improve combat efficiency. To avoid any confusion when training on a range, ready positions versus the carry position needs to be explained and demonstrated during the safety briefing. The carry position can be validated using an *inert* pistol equipped with a laser turned on. The laser should never intersect any part of the operator's body or an innocent person.

While kneeling or standing and using the carry position it allows the operator to turn 360 degrees without fear of pointing the pistol at another person. The author working for the Dallas Police Department began using the carry position when searching with multiple officers. There were times the close proximity prevented the use of a ready position. The author during those times used a one-hand carry position. It was a matter of using common sense and *not* pointing his muzzle at another police officer.

Assume the *one-hand* carry position by holding the pistol in one hand close to the body just in front of the holster with the muzzle pointing down. (Figure 6-57) The wrist remains straight and strong for weapon retention and the muzzle below the non-firing arm's work area. The one-hand carry position also works well when in a stack (linear formation) or moving through a crowd (weapon retention) in order to close the distance on an adversary. It is quick and efficient to assume a ready position from the one-hand carry position.

Figure 6-57 *Carry Position (one hand)*

Figure 6-58 *Carry Position (two hands)*

Assume a *two-hand* carry position by clasping the palm of the non-firing hand on the back of the firing hand. (Figure 6-58) Clasping the hands is a gross motor function that assists in controlling the pistol. The two-hand technique partially covers the drawn pistol lowering its profile. The holster is the preferred method to conceal and secure a pistol. However, the carry position in fast changing circumstances may be the appropriate option. To assume a *ready position* from the two-hand carry position, release the non-firing hand to its join position and rotate the pistol to bring the hands together.

NOTE: Whether the pistol is in the holster or in the hand is a matter of *retention* versus *readiness*. Retention is maintaining physical control of the pistol. Readiness is being able to deploy the pistol quickly.

DRY FIRE DRILLS

Unloaded or inert firearms are recommended for dry firing. The pistol should be pointed at an area (backstop) that no person would be injured *if* a live round discharged. It is the operator's responsibility when dry firing to ensure no person is injured or property damaged. Accomplish this by following the Four Rules for Firearms Handling in conjunction with using an inert barrel replacement, or a chamber blocking device in a functional firearm. It is also the operator's responsibility to place his or her target in an appropriate area to eliminate the chance of alarming bystanders.[303]

DANGER: No live ammunition is allowed in a dry fire training area!

The sights should be level across the top with equal spacing on each side of the front sight and the top edges centered on the target. An operator should be able to explain how to develop a sight picture. These dry fire drills will assist an operator in learning how to superimpose a sight picture quickly and pull the trigger while having both eyes open. The recoil control of a pistol is the only element of shooting that cannot be replicated while dry firing.[304]

The operator's focus is shifting to his or her sights *if* the target splits into two images. This occurs because the eyes pick up the movement of the sights coming into the line of sight. Keep the *focus* (fixate) on the target and *see* (attend to) the sights. Operators with a strong dominant eye will find it easier to focus on the target and maintain a single target image while also seeing the sights. Practice will strengthen the dominant eye to improve the operator's ability to aim quickly.

The first drill starts in the *high ready* position commonly used when taking adversaries at gunpoint. The second drill starts in the *join* position as when the hands join during the draw. The third drill is *drawing* from the holster, which is a necessary self-protection skill. Perform the drills in 5-repetition sets until quickly superimposing the sights on the center of the circle target—rest briefly between the sets. The body's core throughout the drills remains tight as if taking a punch to the stomach.

The circle target is 8 inches (203.2 millimeters) in diameter with a 0.25-inch (6.35-millimeter) black outline and white center. (Figure 6-59) The plain circle allows the eyes to find the center naturally for shooting quickly. Unlike a bull's-eye target that may cause the operator to shoot slower to make a precision shot. The circle target is easily printable on standard size office paper.

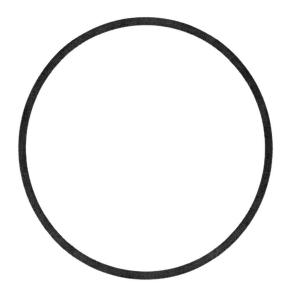

Figure 6-59 *Practice 8-Inch Circle Target*

Dry Fire: Sight Picture and Trigger Control

High Ready Position Drill: Assume the high ready position at a distance of 10 yards (9.14 meters) from a circle target hung about 5 feet (1.52 meters) from the ground. The trigger finger can have a small bend in it with the tip touching the receiver. Keep both eyes open while *focusing* on the center of the target.

Begin the drill with an electronic timer set on random start (first beep), and a 0.5-second par time (second beep). On the sound of the first beep, snap the pistol up while applying pressure to the trigger the instant the arms begin to move. Break the shot as the top edge of the sights are superimposed on the center of the circle target. The shot must break the *instant* the sights are superimposed on the circle target—*not* before or after. Hold the trigger to the rear while assessing the center of the circle target briefly. Place the trigger finger back on the receiver and rack the slide using the *underhand* technique. Return to the high ready position and repeat the drill. Practice until consistently establishing a sight picture and pulling the trigger in 0.5 second. The arms remain relaxed while in the high ready position and the muscles are flexed as the pistol is raised.

Join Position Drill: Assume the join position at a distance of 10 yards (9.14 meters) from a circle target hung about 5 feet (1.52 meters) from the ground. The trigger finger can have a small bend in it with the tip touching the receiver. Keep both eyes open while *focusing* on the center of the target.

Begin the drill with an electronic timer set on random start, and a 0.75-second par time. On the sound of the first beep, extend the pistol forward while applying pressure to the trigger. Break the shot as the arms reach full extension (naturally locked) and the top edge of the sights are superimposed on the center of the circle target. The shot must break the *instant* the sights are superimposed on the circle target. Hold the trigger to the rear while assessing the center of the circle target briefly. Place the trigger finger back on the receiver and rack the slide using the *underhand* technique. Return to the join position and repeat the drill. Practice until consistently establishing a sight picture and pulling the trigger in 0.75 second. The arms remain relaxed while in the join position and the muscles are flexed as the pistol is extended forward.

General Information: These drills condition the muscles to present the pistol consistently within the *sweet spot* with the sights aligned. Consciously aiming for the *center* of the circle and not the whole circle reduces the size of the sweet spot thereby enhancing accuracy. Having the muscle strength to keep the body and pistol movement to a minimum allows for quicker follow up shots when live firing. While practicing remember to *breathe* as there is a natural tendency to hold the breath. Maintain the integrity of the fighting stance throughout the practice.

The drills using an inert pistol are ideal for police academy training. An airsoft pistol and reactive targets could also be used to speed the learning process. Use appropriate *safety equipment* when training with airsoft guns. The recruit's procedural memory in an academy setting could be developed prior to arriving at the range. This would help to reduce the expenditure of ammunition during live fire training.

Dry Fire: Drawing, Sight Picture, and Trigger Control

Drawing Drill: Assume a fighting stance at a distance of 10 yards (9.14 meters) from a circle target hung about 5 feet (1.52 meters) from the ground. The hands are down by the sides and the arms relaxed. Keep both eyes open while *focusing* on the center of the target.

Begin the drill with an electronic timer set on random start and a 1.5-second par time. On the sound of the first beep, move both arms at the same time to complete the three-step draw process of *grip, join,* and *extend.* Stay focused on the center of the target while drawing. As the hands join and the pistol moves forward begin applying pressure to the trigger. Break the shot as the arms reach full extension (naturally locked) and the top edge of the sights are superimposed on the center of the circle target. The shot must break the *instant* the sights are superimposed on the circle target. Hold the trigger to the rear while assessing the center of the circle target briefly. Place the trigger finger back on the receiver and rack the slide using the *underhand* technique. Return the pistol to its holster and repeat the drill. Practice until consistently drawing, establishing a sight picture, and pulling the trigger in 1.5 seconds.

General Information: An operator in the beginning may need to practice step-by-step without the electronic timer, but eventually the steps of the draw should be combined in one continuous quick motion. A mirror is a low-tech training device that can be helpful for self-correcting when practicing. An operator dry firing in front of a mirror may be surprised at the amount of improvement that occurs in a short period. A video camera or cell phone camera is an option to record the practice session. Review the recorded session and make any necessary corrections.[305]

Operators wanting to shoot fast and accurate need to become proficient at the three previous dry fire drills. Those three drills build the foundational skills needed for the live fire drills. Operators should also accept the benefits of aligning a pistol within the dominant eye's line of sight. (Figure 6-60) The squared stance and the naturally locked arms and wrists assist in consistent sight alignment. The superimposed sight image technique is extremely reliable and effective within the capability of the pistol. Becoming proficient with this method of two-hand shooting is the basis for one-hand shooting techniques presented in the Combat Shooting Phase 2 chapter.

Figure 6-60 Pistol positioned in the line of sight.

RELOADING

The operator must appreciate the seriousness of a reload during combat. It will likely mean (barring a stoppage) the operator shot a full magazine or nearly a full magazine, but the adversary continued to fight! The seriousness of the situation demands absolute competence in the skill of reloading. The operator might be struggling with the effects of an alarm reaction resulting in heavy breathing and shaking hands.[306] An operator under life-and-death circumstances may do irrational things such as place magazines in the pistol backwards or insert an empty magazine back into the pistol.[307]

Overcome such issues by correctly placing equipment and use repetitious practice to achieve procedural memory. The operator should *not* have to think about how to reload and may not even remember performing one. This is the skill level necessary to perform a reload competently under stressful circumstances. Practice reloading in low light conditions, in various firing positions, and from behind different types of cover. The operator must train for the worst-case scenario.

NOTE: An external safety lever *if* equipped should be left in the fire position when reloading.[308] The reason is to train in the same manner as when performing a reload during a life-threatening situation. There is no time in such situations to place the safety lever from fire to safe and then back from safe to fire. Train responsibly, but also train realistically. Although a Glock pistol may not have an external safety lever there are many pistols used by armed civilians, police officers, and military operators that do.

Reloading Ideology: Reloading ideology is found in two instances. The *first* is the slide forward condition and the operator has the time and opportunity to reload and makes a conscious decision to do so. This can occur after an initial engagement and the operator wants to have a fully loaded pistol before moving from cover or pursuing the adversary. A fully loaded pistol allows the operator to continue the fight or break contact. The *second* is the slide back condition and the operator subconsciously does so. The operator ideally would feel the slide lock back and automatically perform a reload. An operator in combat may *not* feel the slide lock back, but will recognize the pistol did not fire. The goal of reloading during life-and-death circumstances is the subconscious manipulation of a pistol whether the slide is forward or back.

As one former British Special Air Service (SAS) soldier said, "A reload must be a consistent and identical action regardless of whether there are *rounds in the magazine or not*. A reload should be a reaction and not a decision making thought process."[309] (Figure 6-61) There should *not* be a distinction made between reloading a pistol with its slide forward or back. (Figure 6-62) After reloading the pistol with a magazine, simply rack the slide.[310] This method engineers out human error and ensures a round is in the chamber. Perform the reload quickly and work at maximum speed. Strip the magazine from the pistol using the non-firing hand dropping the magazine on the ground or placing it in a drop pouch or a pocket. Retrieve a magazine from its pouch, move the magazine quickly to the pistol, and insert it into the magazine well. Rack the slide chambering a new round.

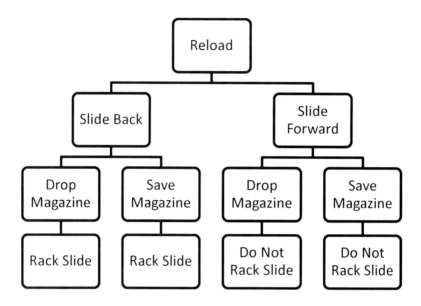

Figure 6-61 Complex Decision Making Process for Reloading

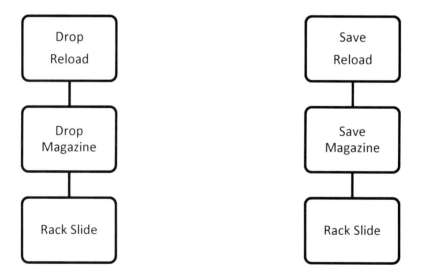

Figure 6-62 Simplified Decision Making Process for Reloading

Maintaining Control of the Pistol: The grip will likely have to be shifted to expose the magazine catch to perform a reload. This is especially true for a small stature operator. To keep control of the pistol and to have positive contact with the magazine catch use the non-firing hand to help support the pistol. It may take slightly longer than tossing and catching the pistol in the hand, but it ensures control of the pistol.[311] Such control is beneficial for releasing the magazine so it can be stripped from the magazine well. The technique works when the magazine catch is pressed with the thumb or index finger.

A pistol with a reversible magazine catch offers the advantage of switching the magazine catch to either side so the firing hand thumb can be used. From a two-hand grip position, bring the pistol back until the upper arms are close to or rest on the body. Allow the pistol to rotate on the bottom of its trigger guard against the middle joint of the index finger on the non-firing hand.[312] (Figure 6-63) Apply pressure to the magazine catch with the thumb and counterpressure with the index finger joint of the non-firing hand. Depress the magazine catch to release the magazine and strip it from the magazine well using the non-firing hand.

The left-handed operator manipulating a magazine catch on the *left side* uses the index finger (trigger finger) method. From a two-hand grip position, bring the pistol back until both upper arms are close to or rest on the body. Allow the pistol to rotate on the bottom of its trigger guard against the middle joint of the index finger on the non-firing hand. (Figure 6-64) With the index finger of the firing hand, apply pressure to the magazine catch, and counterpressure with the firing hand thumb and non-firing hand thumb against the side of the receiver. Depress the magazine catch releasing the magazine and strip it from the magazine well using the non-firing hand. Although not visible in illustration 6-64, the index finger is pressing the magazine catch.

The author first saw the method when he was training a small stature female police officer. The police officer was performing reloading drills with a Glock model 17 pistol. He questioned the police officer as for the reason of rotating the pistol on her non-firing hand's index finger. The police officer explained that she had never been taught the technique, but doing it provided a feeling of control over the pistol when pressing in on the magazine catch. The police officer went on to explain *not* doing it made her feel like she might drop the pistol.

This is an example of a police officer allowing her body to adapt naturally to accomplish a reload efficiently. The police officer is in good company as a former U.S. Navy SEAL advocates *not* tossing and catching the pistol in the hand, but to maintain control of the frame with the non-firing hand to ensure positive contact with the magazine catch.[313]

Figure 6-63 *Magazine Catch (right hand thumb pressing)*

Figure 6-64 *Magazine Catch (left hand index finger pressing)*

Stripping the Magazine: The author trained a police officer that questioned the usefulness of stripping the magazine from the magazine well versus pressing the magazine catch allowing the magazine to drop free. The police officer during combat training dropped a fully loaded magazine on the ground. The police officer reacted as could be expected in real-life and dropped to a kneeling position, grabbed the magazine off the ground, and quickly loaded it in her pistol. As the magazine entered the magazine well the author could hear the sand grinding! He knew there was no way that magazine was going to drop free. The police officer had to pull the magazine out and never again questioned the applicability of the technique.

Stripping the magazine first from the pistol ensures the magazine well is empty and ready for a fresh magazine. The reloading method is an example of simple is better. There is only one method to learn to retrieve magazines and reload. There is no *mental clutter* on the how to strip the magazine from the pistol or whether to rack the slide or the manipulation of two magazines at the same time. Trying to manipulate two magazines simultaneously during a life-and-death situation is a means to dropping one or both magazines. Such situations require one reloading system based on gross motor skills that work in low light, awkward positions, or while moving.

Stripping the magazine eliminates the dependence on *gravity* and *visual confirmation.* These can be important factors when reloading while lying on the ground or in the dark. When the magazine is stripped from the magazine well the operator knows the magazine well is empty. Trying to insert a replacement magazine into the magazine well still occupied with a stuck magazine can result in the replacement magazine being knocked out of the operator's hand. An operator should not stake his or her life on a magazine cooperating with gravity. The stripping technique applies equally to drop free magazines.[314]

Inserting the Magazine: Inserting the magazine efficiently begins with the placement of the magazine pouch. A vertical magazine pouch is favored because economy of motion is found many times in a straight line. The straight line is from the magazine pouch to the pistol's magazine well. A magazine pouch with flaps and positioned vertically should have the nose of the bullets facing toward the holster located on the firing hand side. This method allows the operator to rip the flap up, shove a thumb behind the magazine, and pull it out. The magazine will be indexed correctly for inserting into the magazine well. There are differences between the two techniques used for inserting the magazine. An operator should consider the differences before making a decision on which technique to use for fighting with a pistol.

The finger index requires the position of the tip of the index finger to be raised or lowered according to hand size and length of the magazine. Allowing the index finger to protrude over the top edge of the magazine can result in a painful collision with the pistol when reloading. The other fingers wrap around the magazine body while inserting it into the magazine well. This grip is *not* as secure as the thumb index because the index finger is not gripping the magazine. Releasing the fingers and losing the grip without the top of the magazine partially inserted with result in a fumbled reload and possibly a dropped magazine. This is an easy mistake to make when reloading quickly *if* the top edge of the magazine collides with the bottom edge of the magazine well. Operators should consider techniques that not only take into account when things go right, but also when things go wrong.

The thumb index *without* modifications works with magazines of various lengths. Unlike the finger index *technique* that requires the tip of the index finger placement to vary according to the length of the magazine. The fingers wrap around the magazine ensuring a secure grip while inserting the magazine into the magazine well. This grip is more secure than the finger index technique because the index finger also grips the magazine. The thumb index technique uses the same grip to load the magazine and strip it from the pistol providing a uniform method. The front-to-front method of inserting the magazine is *less* susceptible to the rim of the upper most cartridge catching on the rear edge of the magazine well. Operators may find the thumb index more reliable under stress as a greater portion of the magazine can be inserted into the magazine well before the fingers release and the hand pivots to seat the magazine. The front-to-front method transitions smoothly for many other firearms and is required for the AK-47 rifle.

Racking the Slide: Racking the slide after inserting a magazine develops procedural memory during training that carries over subconsciously into combat. The goal is *not* to eject a live round, but to ensure a live round is in the chamber. The possible ejection of a live round during the reload is a byproduct of making sure that a live round is in the chamber under *combat* conditions. Not racking a slide that is in the forward position would occur only *if* the operator had the time, cover, and presence of mind to perform a chamber check. An operator that racks the slide when reloading achieves a measure of assurance the firearm is in a state of readiness for combat.

A method for releasing the slide is to use the *underhand technique.*[315] There are reasons applicable to combat shooting for using the underhand technique to release the slide and not the slide stop lever. The most important reason is to prevent the slide from being released before the magazine is seated. This occurs because the slide stop lever is depressed a split second before the magazine is seated and the round is *not* stripped from the magazine and chambered. This results in an empty chamber and a click sound when the trigger is pulled. The author has seen this happen to competitive shooters, armed civilians, police officers, and military operators. Seating the magazine and racking the slide with the non-firing hand engineers out this human error. The sound of a click during a competition results in the loss of points—in combat it may result in the loss of a life. The underhand technique whether performed right- or left-handed rotates the ejection port toward the ground for clearing stoppages and keeps the muzzle pointing downrange.

NOTE: Another technique uses the non-firing hand thumb to depress the slide stop lever to release the slide after inserting the magazine. The technique does negate the issue of prematurely releasing the slide. Nonetheless, having fresh blood on the hands or pistol, or wearing gloves could make pressing the small slide stop lever difficult. The Glock extended slide stop lever does reduce the difficultly of depressing the slide stop lever.[316] However, the technique is still *not* applicable to the left-handed operator using a pistol with the slide stop lever only on the left side resulting in a *loss* of training consistency.

Releasing the slide with the non-firing hand will *not* allow the slide to go forward on an empty magazine. Using the slide stop lever *will* allow the slide to go forward on an empty magazine. An operator as an example in a low light environment strips an empty magazine dropping it on the ground. While reloading the replacement magazine, it is accidentally dropped, and lands near the empty magazine. Quickly, but mistakenly the operator picks up the empty magazine inserting it in the pistol and presses the slide stop lever sending the slide forward. The pistol failing to fire would prompt the operator to perform a tap-rack-ready and only after the slide locked back would the operator likely realize that an empty magazine had been inserted. The operator using the underhand technique in the same scenario would realize the magazine was empty because the slide would not go forward.

Reloading Technique: To reload a pistol from a firing position, bring the arms toward the body. Bend the arms so there is a 90-degree angle, or slightly less, between the forearm and upper arm and rest the upper arms *naturally* on or near the body.[317] (Figures 6-65 and 6-66)

The trigger finger remains on the receiver. Rotate the pistol in the hand if necessary to gain access to the magazine catch. Press in on the *left* side magazine catch with the firing hand thumb (right-handed operator) or with the index finger (left-handed operator). A *reversible magazine catch* on the *right* side can be pressed using the firing hand thumb (left-handed operator).

Strip the magazine from the pistol with the non-firing hand. (Figure 6-67) Drop the magazine on the ground or store it in a drop pouch or pocket. The non-firing hand continues to move down quickly to the magazine pouch. Rip open the flap on a covered magazine pouch. Drive the non-firing hand thumb behind the magazine and remove it while maintaining a tight grip. (Figure 6-68)

Figure 6-65 *Reloading (firing position)*

Figure 6-66 *Reloading (arms 90 degrees)*

Figure 6-67 *Reloading (strip magazine)*

Figure 6-68 *Reloading (grip magazine)*

Driving the non-firing hand thumb behind the magazine holds the flap up and out of the way and prevents the floor plate from snagging on the flap's snap *if* equipped. The index finger remains along the front of the magazine *if* using the finger index technique when removing the magazine from its pouch. The index finger curls around the magazine *if* using the thumb index technique when removing the magazine from its pouch as shown in Figure 6-68. Quickly move the magazine toward the magazine well, but pause an *instant* just before inserting it in the magazine well.[318] Pausing for an instant insures the insertion of the magazine using either technique.

NOTE: The upper arms may or may not contact the body or equipment vest when brought back at about a 90-degree angle according to the operator's build, flexibility, and equipment worn. The pistol is brought close to the body to facilitate control.[319] Control is critical, especially during an alarm reaction that results in trembling hands.

Finger Index Technique: The index finger should be centered on the front of the magazine body acting as a guide.[320] The tip of the index finger splits the centerline of the front strap of the pistol. Insert the magazine by contacting the upper *rear* portion of the magazine at a slight angle against the *rear* portion of the magazine well (back-to-back) pivoting the magazine upward and straight into the magazine well.[321] (Figure 6-69) Use the heel of the hand to firmly press against the magazine floor plate with one smooth continuous motion seating the magazine into the pistol. (Figure 6-71) The slight angle against the rear portion of the magazine well when wearing gloves helps prevent the tip of the glove on the index finger from being caught between the front of the magazine and magazine well.

Figure 6-69 *Reloading (insert magazine – finger index)*

Figure 6-70 *Reloading (insert magazine – thumb index)*

Thumb Index Technique: The thumb should be centered on the side of the magazine body acting as a guide. The tip of the thumb should split the centerline of the pistol grip. Insert the magazine by contacting the upper *front* portion of the magazine at a slight angle against the *front* portion of the magazine well (front-to-front) pivoting the magazine upward and straight into the magazine well. (Figure 6-70) Use the heel of the hand to firmly press against the magazine floor plate with one smooth continuous motion seating the magazine into the pistol. (Figure 6-71) The thumb index technique works well when wearing gloves.

NOTE: Attempting to precisely align a magazine (box) and insert it straight into a magazine well (box) is difficult to perform, especially while on the move or under stress. The slight angle method in the finger index and thumb index techniques increases reloading reliability.

Figure 6-71 *Reloading (seat magazine)*

NOTE: Make sure the magazine is started into the magazine well *before* releasing the grip and pressing the heel of the hand against the magazine floor plate. This is critical whether static or reloading on the move. Otherwise during a fumbled reload the magazine could be dropped.

Load a round in the chamber by rotating the top of the pistol about 45 degrees toward the ground. With the non-firing hand, grab the serrated rear portion of the slide between the pad and the fingertips. Pull rearward with the non-firing hand until the slide reaches rear full extension. (Figure 6-72) The slide at full extension strips from the non-firing hand's grip. The slide will slam forward picking up a round forcing it into the chamber. Rotate the firing hand upright while extending the arm to a naturally locked position. Fingers are on fingers with the firing hand thumb on top of the first knuckle of the thumb on the non-firing hand and the arms in a push-compress state. The pistol is ready to fire. (Figure 6-73) When learning to reload it may help to say the words "strip-insert-rack" while performing the steps.

NOTE: Keeping the *firing* arm relatively straight provides strong bone structure for racking the slide and keeps the pistol indexed in the hand.

Figure 6-72 Reloading (rack slide)

Figure 6-73 Reloading (extend)

Skill Building Reloading Techniques: An effective method to practice the insertion and removal phase of the magazine is to get in a fighting stance with arms extended. Quickly as humanly possible move the pistol back resting the upper arms on the body. Remove and reinsert the magazine just as quick. This is also an excellent drill to perform while running. It is preferred to use an inert solid plastic magazine[322] for this phase of training, but an empty magazine can be used. There must *not* be any ammunition or loaded magazines in the operator's possession or in the training area. Also, practice reloading while in the kneeling, prone, rollover prone, reverse rollover prone, and supine positions.

NOTE: Operators need to have the ability to run and reload at the same time. This is evident from an actual incident: "The offender pushed the first officer out of the way, threw the stove-piped service weapon at the third officer, picked up the butcher knives, and proceeded to chase the third officer, who was attempting to reload."[323]

Only in the early stages of training should the operator look at the magazine well. Discontinue the practice of looking at the magazine well after procedural memory is acquired. Procedural memory is *not* vision dependent. The problem with looking at the magazine well is the operator may work in low light conditions. Darkness especially when combined with exposure to muzzle flashes would make the ability to see the magazine well unlikely. The same is true if the vision is impaired because of dust, sand, pepper spray, fresh blood, etc. Do *not* reload at waist level, dropping the head causes a loss of situational awareness.[324] With proper practice, reloading becomes a reflexive movement. The magazine can be removed from a pouch and inserted into the magazine well by feel without looking.[325]

Operators during training should intentionally attempt to place (do *not* force) a magazine backwards into the magazine well. This is to expose the operator to what it feels like and immediately take corrective action. An example of this occurring might be from retrieving a magazine with the normal firing hand during an injured arm drill or in a real-life encounter.

Slamming the Magazine: Some operators to release the slide automatically use an *ill-advised* technique of slamming the magazine into the magazine well. The technique has several drawbacks. The most important is the technique is *not* 100 percent reliable. Next is the rounds may tumble inside of a partially filled magazine resulting in a stoppage. Finally, the operator must take the time to distinguish if the slide went forward or it still needs to be released manually. Making such a distinction requires conscious thinking—thinking better used for making tactical decisions.

Dry Fire: Reloading Drill

The *dry fire* drills listed in this section require using dummy rounds. The drills can be completed live fire at a proper facility. The coach is *not* required when using live ammunition because the slide will automatically function. The coach racks the slide acting in the place of live ammunition when the operator dry fires the pistol. An operator will begin slowly when learning how to strip and retrieve magazines, but should quickly work up to his or her maximum speed. The actions performed correctly when combined with aggression will develop speed.

Load 3 magazines with 2 dummy rounds. Place 2 magazines in their pouch and 1 magazine in the pistol. Chamber a dummy round and holster the pistol. Draw, acquire a sight picture, and pull the trigger. A coach will aggressively rack the slide, acquire a sight picture, and pull the trigger. A coach will aggressively rack the slide with a lock back occurring. Strip the magazine from the pistol and retrieve a magazine with 2 dummy rounds. The upper arms are close to or rest on the body (pistol held at eye level) and using the angle technique insert the magazine into the magazine well. Do *not* loosen the grip on the magazine until it enters the magazine well. With one smooth continuous motion, use the heel of the hand to firmly press against the magazine floor plate seating the magazine into the pistol.

NOTE: The arms resting (indexed) on the body provides a consistent position to reload even in low light conditions.

Rotate the top of the pistol about 45 degrees toward the ground and using an *underhand* technique release the slide. Obtain a sight picture and pull the trigger. With the exception of drawing, repeat the above steps.

NOTE: Rolling the pistol about 45 degrees provides a natural stopping point because of the biomechanics of the wrist and arm. The pistol stopping in the same spot provides a consistent index to release the slide. The firing arm pointing forward offers the greatest strength to release the slide, especially for the small stature operator. It also allows the body to remain squared to the target.

On slide lock of the second magazine, reload by inserting the third magazine into the magazine well. On slide lock of the third magazine, strip the magazine and verify the pistol is unloaded. Holster an unloaded pistol and set the drill up again if desired.

NOTE: Insert a magazine full of dummy rounds into an *unloaded* pistol to practice the underhand technique and build procedural memory. Assume a fighting stance with a two-hand grip and obtain a sight picture. Pull the trigger and place the trigger finger on the receiver. Quickly roll the top of the pistol about 45 degrees toward the ground and rack the slide. Rack the slide by stripping it out of the non-firing hand with a deliberate and aggressive rearward movement of the non-firing hand. Return the pistol quickly to its upright position and assume a tight two-hand grip. See a sight picture and pull the trigger. Repeat the process until the magazine is empty. Conduct the drill from other firing positions.

STOPPAGES

A police officer had his Glock pistol taken by a male about 7 feet (213.36 centimeters) tall and high on heroin, cocaine, and phencyclidine. The suspect shot a police sergeant two times in the chest and then put the pistol to the disarmed police officer's head and pulled the trigger. The pistol had a *failure to eject* stoppage and did not fire. A third police officer arrived and with his revolver shot the suspect six times in the chest. The suspect threw the Glock pistol at the police officer that had fired the shots. The disarmed police officer ran to the street, picked up the pistol and performed as he stated, "rip-and-work deal." The police officer now armed again shot the suspect six times. Three of the rounds struck the suspect in the face and he died at the scene.[326]

The priority for an operator experiencing a stoppage while being attacked is to get out of the line of the attack. That can mean taking one or several aggressive steps forward, sideways, diagonal, or back. The operator's feet will likely be farther apart after stopping than when in the fighting stance. This is because of the body's momentum from moving quickly. Maintaining the index of the upper body is more important than the position of the lower body. The lower body allows negotiation of the terrain. Maintaining the integrity of the upper body index allows acquiring the sights quickly and placing them on the adversary.

Operators must accept that a stoppage can occur at any time. A *stoppage* is the interruption of the firing cycle.[327] A stoppage is sometimes, but mistakenly referred to as a malfunction. Some view a stoppage as caused by the operator, out of ammunition, or poor maintenance. A malfunction is a mechanical failure of the pistol.[328] The correct term stoppage represents an interruption of the firing cycle *not* caused by a mechanical failure. The word *malfunction* represents a mechanical failure of the pistol.[329]

Stoppages can occur from operator error, defective ammunition, and poor maintenance. The most common stoppage is a failure to fire usually from *not* having a live round in the chamber.[330] A damaged magazine is common to a failure to feed stoppage. Short of a mechanical failure of the pistol (armorer required) or round stuck in the chamber (tool required) the operator should be able to immediately clear the stoppage. Some military operators carry a cleaning rod to knock a stuck case out of the chamber of their rifles. It would be reasonable for a police officer to strap a short length of rod to his or her ballistic vest for removing a stuck pistol cartridge. An operator must know what to do whether the pistol is working properly or has stopped working. Operators must be problem solvers whether related to tactics, equipment, or weapons—everything is solved. The four basic stoppages are as follows:

1. *Failure to Fire:* The cartridge does not fire. This can occur when a cartridge is not chambered *(most common occurrence)*, defective cartridge, gummed up firing pin spring, defective firing pin spring, or broken firing pin.

2. *Failure to Extract:* The cartridge may have fired or not, but remains in the chamber. Another cartridge may attempt to load in the occupied chamber *(the popular usage for the term double feed)*. This can occur when debris is under the extractor, defective rim on the case, or an extractor is broken.

3. *Failure to Eject:* The cartridge fires, but the spent case catches between the slide's breech face and the barrel's chamber *(stovepipe)*. This can occur from the wrists or elbows not locked, push-pull technique used, defective ammunition, or a defective ejector.

4. *Failure to Feed:* A cartridge does not chamber or two cartridges try to chamber simultaneously *(double feed)*. This can occur when the magazine is not seated, defective ammunition, or damaged magazine.

The above causes of stoppages are not all-inclusive. Any of the stoppages can include one or more of the factors listed or *not* listed. The acronym SAMM represents a logical process for isolating stoppages: *shooter, ammunition, maintenance,* and *mechanical.*[331] Stoppages can be reduced or eliminated by a tight grip on the pistol, locking the elbows naturally, a solid stance, quality ammunition, and maintaining the pistol and magazine properly. A tight grip high into the back strap with locked wrists will stop the "unlocked wrist" stoppages in a Glock pistol.[332] Unlock wrists will cause problems with the following: extraction, ejection, feeding, locking into battery, and locking open the slide on the last round.[333] For more information on stoppages and their causes, consult the specific model's instruction manual, a certified armorer, or the manufacturer.

The *problem* that caused the stoppage during training, qualification, or a real-life encounter needs to be identified. Finding the problem that caused the stoppage is an investigation after the fact: Did the agency receive a defective shipment of ammunition? Was it a damaged magazine? Was it operator error? Corrective action may be to contact the manufacturer to request an ammunition recall, replace the magazine, or provide training for the operator. Pistols or ammunition prone to stoppages or malfunctions must be immediately removed from service.

NOTE: Technically a *double feed*[334] is two cartridges trying to chamber simultaneously. The term double feed is widely accepted by civilians, police officers, and military operators to represent a round in the chamber (fired or live) with another round feeding. It could be argued that one round has already fed and the second one is trying to feed, i.e., a double feed. The term double feed in this book represents the technically correct former description, but also the more popular latter description. The term *feedway stoppage* is also acceptable.[335]

STOPPAGE DRILLS

The dry fire stoppage drills use *dummy rounds* and are performed mainly while in the fighting stance and kneeling position. However, dry fire stoppage drills can be performed from all firing positions. A coach racks the slide to indicate firing and *not* racking the slide represents a misfire. The first time the coach does not rack the slide causes the operator to perform a *tap-rack-ready* and fires. The successive second time of *not* racking the slide after the first signifies the tap-rack-ready did not work (failure to fire). The operator must perform a *lock-clear-reload*.

CAUTION: Damage to the trigger safety can occur by pulling the trigger when it is in a *forward position* and the slide is out of battery.[336]

The coach does *not* say, "click" to represent a misfire. The operator will not hear a click in a gunfight. The *physical* indicator of a stoppage will be the lack of felt recoil (slide not cycling to the rear) when the trigger is pulled. This is exactly what the coach induces to represent the stoppage—not racking the slide to the rear.

An additional failure to extract drill that does *not* require a coach can also be practiced. Make sure the pistol is *unloaded*. Rack the slide and pull the trigger. Lock the slide to the rear (the trigger will remain to the rear). Insert a dummy round in the chamber. Insert a magazine with a dummy round into the pistol and ease the slide forward. Assume a firing position (fighting stance, kneeling, etc.) and attempt to fire. Perform a tap-rack-ready and then a lock-clear-reload. Inspect the extractor for damage after completing training.

Another option to practice stoppage drills without the possibility of a discharge is to use an inert yellow plastic barrel, magazine loaded with 2 dummy rounds, and an inert blue magazine. Install the inert plastic barrel in an unloaded pistol with the trigger to the rear. The magazine is loaded with 2 dummy rounds and inserted in the pistol. Hold the trigger to the rear while pulling back on the slide and ease it forward. This allows the uppermost dummy round to contact the inert plastic barrel. The pistol has a double feed stoppage. The operator takes a firing position and attempts to fire the pistol and performs a tap-rack-ready. Immediately after the tap-rack-ready, performs a lock-clear-reload inserting the inert blue magazine. Assumes a firing position while superimposing the sights and pulls the trigger. Using this method is a safe means to practice stoppage drills in a classroom environment.

CAUTION: As the inert plastic barrel does not have a chamber, it prevents the extractor from having to jump the rim of the case as when using a live barrel and dummy rounds. *Chipping* of the extractor can occur from forcing it over the rim of the metal case. Use plastic dummy rounds to help reduce chances of chipping the extractor.

Analytical techniques to clear stoppages are usually ineffective in high stress situations.[337] This is also true for low light situations.[338] The operator may not be able to see what actually occurred. Working from this *worst-case* perspective there must be a method of clearing stoppages that is *not* normally dependent on visual examination of the pistol.[339] Nevertheless, an operator needs to take maximum advantage of the environment. That includes using available lighting to assess and solve a problem as quick as possible. An operator should also be able to clear a stoppage while moving. An operator clearing a stoppage out in the open and not moving is nothing more than a stationary target to an adversary.

CAUTION: A technique to force a slide that is out of battery back into battery is to strike the rear of the slide with the palm of the non-firing hand. This technique may make the stoppage worse by forcing a defective round deeper into the chamber.[340] The struck round would likely then have to be punched out with a rod.

The tap-rack-ready or lock-clear-reload will clear most stoppages. Technically, the slide does not have to be locked to the rear to strip out the magazine. However, clearing a double feed stoppage using only one hand would likely require locking the slide to the rear. The technique of locking the slide to the rear builds procedural memory equally transferable to many of the carbines used by civilians, police officers, and military operators, i.e., *lock-clear-reload*. Using the same stoppage clearing procedure *labels* for the pistol and carbine simplifies training and speeds the learning process.

Tap-rack-ready is used and *not* tap-rack-bang, because the situation may have changed since beginning the stoppage clearance procedure which may not justify a continuation of shooting.[341] The adversary may have fell and is incapable of continuing the assault. The adversary may have also surrendered or worse taken a hostage. The operator after performing a tap-rack-ready will need to come to a ready position and reassess the situation. An operator that automatically fires without reassessing the situation may only compound existing problems.

Any stoppage clearance procedure takes time. An adversary can cover a lot of ground depending on the time it takes to clear a stoppage and operators need to be aware of this fact. An exercise that drives home this point is to use an inert pistol with dummy rounds and a person in *good* health that is willing to run. The operator performs the various stoppage drills using two hands and one hand. The runner is standing next to the operator. The runner starts running when the operator begins a stoppage drill. The runner will stop when the operator finishes a stoppage drill and yells, "stop!" Repeat the drill for each stoppage drill. The exercise is enlightening and forces an operator to accept just how much distance an adversary can cover in the time it takes to clear different types of stoppages.

NOTE: An operator with only one magazine or not wanting to stow the magazine because of time constraints can place it between the ring finger and little finger of the firing hand when performing two-hand stoppage drills.[342] The magazine is reinserted in the pistol after clearing the stoppage. This method is dependent on the size of the operator's hand in relation to the size of the magazine.

Dry Fire: Tap-Rack-Ready

The tap-rack-ready takes under 2 seconds to complete.[343] To clear a failure to fire stoppage while in the fighting stance (Figure 6-74) or kneeling position use the steps as follows:

Tap: Make sure the trigger finger is on the receiver. Bring the pistol back to the same position as *if* reloading and with the palm of the non-firing hand tap the magazine's floor plate. (Figure 6-75)

Rack: Rotate the pistol in the opposite direction stopping at the 45-degree position as when the pistol is upright. Grab the serrated rear portion of the slide with the non-firing hand between the pad and the fingertips. Hold the pistol stationary and aggressively pull rearward with the non-firing hand until the slide is fully to the rear stripping it loose from the hand releasing the slide and chambering a dummy round. (Figure 6-76)

Ready: Rotate the pistol back to the upright position; establish a two-hand grip; extend the arms forward; and the pistol is ready to fire. (Figure 6-77) This is a *tap-rack-ready* drill.

Figure 6-74 *Firing Position*

Figure 6-75 *Tap*

Figure 6-76 *Rack*

Figure 6-77 *Ready*

NOTE: There are two reasons for tapping the magazine. First, tapping ensures the magazine is seated. Second, tapping dislodges a stuck magazine follower. The cartridges must be able to move freely up into the feed lips. The 45-degree position allows cartridges and casings to fall free from the ejection port.

Dry Fire: Lock-Clear-Reload

The tap-rack-ready failed to make the pistol operable. There is no advantage in trying a second tap-rack-ready. The lock-clear-reload takes from 5 to 8 seconds or more to complete.[344] While in the fighting stance or kneeling position, clear a failure to fire stoppage using the steps as follows:

Lock: Rotate the top of the pistol about 45 degrees toward the ground and lock the slide to the rear. (Figure 6-78)

Clear: Bring the pistol back to the same position as *if* reloading. Clear the ammunition from the pistol by removing the magazine (if last remaining magazine with rounds, do not discard) and aggressively rack the slide three distinct times using the underhand technique. Working the slide three times frees up and removes obstructions.[345] (Figure 6-79)

Reload: Perform a reload. The pistol is ready to fire. (Figures 6-80 and 6-81)

NOTE: A double feed can make it difficult to remove a magazine from the pistol without first locking the slide to the rear. Locking the slide removes the tension off the trapped rounds allowing removal of the magazine. Carbines also use the lock step for clearing a double feed stoppage promoting uniformity of training.

A *right-handed* operator can lock the slide to the rear by using the firing hand thumb to push up the slide stop lever while simultaneously pulling rearward with the non-firing hand. The slide is pulled to the rear by grasping the rear of the slide between the pad and the fingertips of the non-firing hand. Once the slide stop lever engages the slide notch, allow the slide to go slightly forward resting the slide notch against the slide stop lever.

Figure 6-78 Lock

Figure 6-79 Clear

Figure 6-80 Reload

Figure 6-81 Firing Position

A *left-handed* operator can lock the slide to the rear by using the non-firing hand to grasp the rear of the slide between the pad and the fingertips. The slide is pulled to the rear while simultaneously the thumb of the non-firing hand pushes up on the slide stop lever. Once the slide stop lever engages the slide notch, allow the slide to go slightly forward resting the slide notch against the slide stop lever.

DANGER: The *overhand* technique [346] combined with lower arm strength creates a tendency to rotate the muzzle parallel to the body. This can result in inadvertently pointing the muzzle at someone standing beside the operator. However, there are operators and instructors that do successfully use, train, and teach the overhand technique.

STUCK CASE REMOVAL

This drill drives home the point that not every stoppage can be cleared using tap-rack-ready or lock-clear-reload techniques. Make sure the pistol being used is *unloaded*. Sabotage a *dummy round* made of a synthetic material by clipping or grinding off the rim.[347] Then wrap a single layer of masking tape near the front of the dummy round where the case and bullet would meet. Load a dummy round in the magazine first, next the sabotaged dummy round, and then insert the magazine into a pistol. Rack the slide and chamber the sabotaged dummy round. Pull the trigger (simulated misfire) and perform a tap-rack-ready. The sabotage dummy round fails to extract causing a double feed stoppage. Perform a lock-clear-reload using a second magazine loaded with a dummy round. The dummy round from the second magazine will not feed. The extractor could *not* pull the sabotaged dummy round from the chamber creating another double feed. Lock the slide to the rear, remove the magazine, and use a cleaning rod to push out the stuck dummy round. Make sure there is *no* masking tape remaining in the chamber.

An operator needs to know what a stoppage feels like that cannot be cleared using a tap-rack-ready or lock-clear-reload. Knowing this can prevent the operator from panicking by repeatedly attempting a stoppage clearance drill that is ineffective. This type of stoppage can occur from a stuck case or cartridge in the chamber and requires a mechanical correction, i.e., some type of tool such as a cleaning rod.

INSPECTING AND LOADING LIVE AMMUNITION

Ammunition Inspection

Inspect each cartridge before loading it in a magazine.[348] Look at the cartridges in the factory box with bullets down and rim of the cases facing up. The cartridges should be the same overall height with no bullet pushed deeper in its case than any other. A bullet seated too deep in its case would result in *setback*.[349] (Figure 6-82) The primer should look flush with the case (not raised or sunk).[350] Remove cartridges from the box (pour onto a towel to prevent rolling off the workspace) and visually inspect at each cartridge for physical damage: bent case, deformed bullet, etc. Properly dispose of any damaged or deformed cartridges in accordance with the manufacturer's recommendations.[351]

Figure 6-82 *A normal cartridge on the left. The middle and right cartridges have bullets forced into their cases resulting in setback.*

Mark the container with the date the ammunition went into service as a reference. Replace ammunition at least annually and Glock recommends biannually.[352] Carrying ammunition indefinitely is *not* an option. An efficient method of rotating ammunition is to fire the rounds carried and replace those with new ammunition.

NOTE: The pistol can be fieldstripped and the barrel chamber used as a *quality control tool* to verify ammunition dimensions. With the fieldstripped barrel, drop each live round into the chamber. Did the round slide in without resistance? Is the rim of the case at the proper height? This method verifies the ammunition carried will chamber.

Loading Live Ammunition for Operational Carry

Operators need to perform a *top off* procedure for operational carry. This provides the operator with the pistol's maximum ammunition capacity. Follow the loading procedures in the *Safety* chapter under the *Loading a Pistol* subsection with the exception as described in the next paragraph.

After chambering the live round from a fully loaded magazine, remove the magazine and holster the pistol. This allows both hands to be free. With the pistol holstered, top off the magazine with 1 round. Draw the pistol and insert the topped off magazine in the magazine well. Pull on the floor plate to make sure the magazine is seated. Holster the fully loaded pistol as it is ready for duty carry. The extractor acts as a loaded chamber indicator and it protrudes above the surface of the slide when a round is in the chamber.

WARNING: When performing a chamber check make sure the muzzle does not cover the hand or fingers.

Some operators after chambering a round like to perform a visual or physical (also called tactile) inspection commonly referred to as a *chamber check*. A chamber check is unlocking the slide only far enough to visually or physically verify that a cartridge is in the chamber. The *physical verification* works in the dark. Bring the pistol into a compressed ready position to maintain control of the receiver and slide. With the non-firing hand's thumb and index finger from underneath the front of the slide, push it rearward about 0.375 inch (9.52 millimeters). Look in the ejection port to confirm visually a round is in the chamber. (Figures 6-83 and 6-85) Stick the index finger of the firing hand through the ejection port and touch the cartridge case to confirm physically a round is in the chamber. (Figures 6-84 and 6-86)

Figure 6-83 Visual Check (left-hand)

Figure 6-84 Tactile Check (left-hand)

The index finger is removed and the slide is allowed to go forward. Consistent training and procedural memory is developed from using the same method for a left- or right-handed operator to unlock the slide for a visual or physical chamber check.

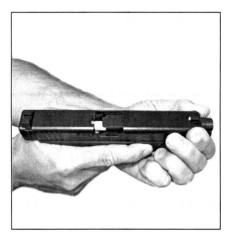

Figure 6-85 Visual Check (right-hand)

Figure 6-86 Tactile Check (right-hand)

Some agencies prefer *administrative loading*[353] which requires the pistol to remain in the holster *after* chambering the round. In other words, the pistol is not removed from the holster to insert the topped off magazine. With the pistol in the holster, insert the magazine into the magazine well until a click is felt. Using the fingertips pull on the front of the floor plate making sure it is seated. Sweep the thumb between the floor plate and clothing checking for pinched cloth. Glock refers to this as push, pull, and sweep.[354] The technique does *not* reinforce procedural memory used for reloading.

The allowance of administrative loading between courses of fire or drills reinforces there are no consequences for the failure to keep a fully loaded pistol. An example of a consequence is to perform the next drill with a partially loaded magazine and make necessary adjustments during the course of fire. Avoid training methods that are not conducive to operational survival.

WARNING: The repetitive loading and unloading of the same live round can push the bullet deeper into the case resulting in setback. "Do *not* chamber and eject the same round repeatedly!"[355]

LIVE FIRE DRILLS

In the Federal Bureau of Investigation study called *In the Line of Fire* it revealed the law enforcement officers studied were shot at 39 times and in 38 of the incidents the suspects fired first.[356] The average distance was *14 feet (4.26 meters)* between the officers and the suspects when they fired their pistols. The distance had increased to an average of *21 feet (6.4 meters)* when the *officer* returned fire. This increase occurred as the officer and suspect changed positions.

The suspect had the advantage of surprise and close distance resulting in a 91 percent hit rate. Even after being wounded and firing at a greater distance, officers still had a 41 percent hit rate. The law enforcement community must require that a police officer be able to move, quickly draw, and effectively hit a target at 7 yards (6.4 meters). This standard is equally applicable to the armed civilian and military operator. Segments of training need to be mentally and physically exhausting to best prepare operators for deadly force encounters. Operators must train to defeat known threats in their operational areas.

WARNING: When live fire training use a properly maintained pistol making sure the bore is unobstructed.

Live Fire: Learning Target Focused Sighted Shooting

The first obstacle an operator needs to overcome when live firing is flinching. *Flinching* is as a sudden spasmodic physical reaction caused by anticipating the *explosive sound* or *recoil* of the pistol.[357] However, there is a third part that causes flinching more so than the sound or recoil. It is the *concussion* from the muzzle blast.[358] The concussive pressure is the disturbing force that is detectable mainly through the eyes.[359] The subconscious does not like explosions and humans are predisposed to flinching when one occurs nearby. The dislike for explosions while firing is evident by an operator blinking and pushing the muzzle down away from his or her face. The farther the operator's face is from the source of the concussive pressure the more comfortable he or she will be.[360] This is another advantage to having the arms extended and naturally locked.

Blinking creates the problem of lost visual input of the pistol, which prevents follow-through.[361] Without follow-though a hit or miss cannot be called and here is the reason why: The operator establishes a sight picture, pulls the trigger, blinks, and pushes the pistol away just as the pistol fires, i.e., flinches. The pistol because of the operator's procedural memory returns to the original position used to establish the first sight picture. The operator saw the sight picture before the shot fired and afterwards, but missed and does not understand how. The answer occurred during the time the operator's eyes were closed—pushing the pistol away.

Blinking also causes an increase in time between shots (split time). This occurs because the operator cannot track the sights throughout the firing cycle to get back on target quickly. An operator pushing the pistol away from his or her face will likely cause the shots to hit low. Shooting right hand and pushing the muzzle down cause shots to hit low left. Shooting left hand and pushing the muzzle down cause shots to hit low right. Visual input from the pistol throughout the firing cycle allows proper follow-though that forms procedural memory needed for combat. An operator that experiences the success of *not* blinking while maintaining visual input of his or her pistol while firing multiple rounds with each hitting the intended aim point will never again accept anything less.

NOTE: An operator with a mild flinch that is consistent can shoot groups, but not at the aim point. It just becomes a group of misses.

Attempts to overcome flinching are using the *surprise break* technique of slowly pulling the trigger until the pistol fires surprising the operator or shooting a pistol with a *light* trigger pull. The problem is the conscious mind is saying, "front sight, press, press, press" which translates into "front sight, not yet…not yet…not yet, bang!" The term "surprise break" certainly fits, but the technique is the opposite of what is needed for combat shooting. Even the light trigger will fool the subconscious mind for only so long before it adapts resulting in a flinch response.[362]

How does an operator overcome flinching? The same way the operator learns to ride a bike, swim, touch-type on a keyboard, or drive a vehicle—through correct repetition until it becomes a *subconscious* act. With correct repetition, the subconscious mind accepts the explosion occurring about 24 inches (609.6 millimeters) in front of the face is *normal* and a *requirement* of combat shooting. The cognitive mind is motivated to practice as it reasons logically that combat shooting provides the operator with the greatest chance of survival in a gunfight. The operator should stop thinking, "do not flinch" and start thinking, "sight picture—break the shot."

Conversion Kit .22 Long Rifle: An operator that has an aversion to loud noise, felt recoil, and concussion of a 9x19mm or larger caliber will find it beneficial to practice with a .22 Long Rifle cartridge. The .22 Long Rifle in comparison to self-protection calibers is inexpensive to shoot. To build procedural memory the .22 Long Rifle is excellent for step-by-step drawing and firing practice. The .22 Long Rifle has little recoil and is accurate. Some Glock pistols are convertible to a .22 Long Rifle by replacing the slide and magazine.[363] (Figure 6-87) No tools or modifications are required. The conversion kit comes with a speed loader that operates like the Glock speed loader.

CAUTION: Certain .22 Long Rifle ammunition is *not* approved for the conversion kits. An approved list of ammunition for the conversion kits is provided by the manufacturer.[364]

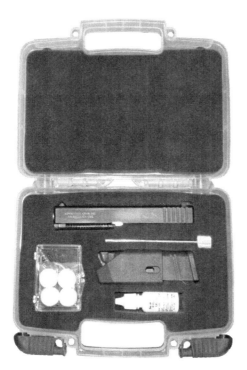

Figure 6-87 *Conversion Kit .22 Long Rifle*

Do *not* dry fire the .22 Long Rifle[365] conversion kit—except to remove the slide from the receiver.[366] To remove the .22 Long Rifle slide the pistol must be *unloaded.* Unload the pistol as outlined in the in the *Safety* chapter under the *Unloading a Pistol* subsection. The .22 Long Rifle conversion slide does *not* remove from the receiver in the same manner as a Glock slide. To remove the slide, press down on the receiver with the muzzle against a hard surface such as a tabletop. With the other hand pull and hold the slide lock down and with the firing hand thumb push the slide forward removing it from the receiver.

The .22 Long Rifle conversion kit should have the same sights installed as on the self-protection caliber slide. An empty magazine will activate the slide stop lever automatically locking the slide to the rear on the last shot. This ensures procedural memory is maintained. Transition back to the personal protection caliber only after achieving competence with the .22 Long Rifle.

Transitioning from the .22 Long Rifle to a 9x19mm caliber and then a .45 Auto with low chamber pressures may be helpful *before* transitioning to .40 S&W or .357 SIG with high chamber pressures. The felt recoil and concussion is less with the low-pressure calibers in comparison to the high-pressure calibers. This systematic desensitization allows the operator to build physical strength and his or her subconscious to become accustom to the increased concussion.[367] The worse thing for a new operator is to allow he or she to shoot a firearm that produces a great deal of recoil and concussion. One bad experience can teach the subconscious that it wants no part of the recoil or concussion ever again.[368]

NOTE: An operator struggling with being startled (flinching) from the concussion and sound of gunfire should use *safety glasses, earplugs,* and *earmuffs.* Doubling the hearing protection will reduce the noise of the gunshot helping to alleviate flinching. The operator can transition back to safety glasses and earmuffs when the flinching stops.

Handgun Control Drill: The operator to overcome flinching must feel he or she has control of the pistol. The foundation of control begins with a tight secure grip while firing. Pulling the trigger resulting in a spasmodic tightening of the hands (flinching) is an attempt to gain control. Flinching is a common problem while training, but *not* so much in combat. An operator in combat is more concerned about stopping the adversary. Ironically, the noise, recoil, and concussion of a firearm in combat are positive indicators the operator is still in the fight. The operator in training must be capable of controlling the pistol using a tight grip while accepting the noise, recoil, and concussion are harmless.

DANGER: Load 1 round into a magazine so the pistol is empty once it is fired *if* a person has little or no experience shooting a pistol. Repeat the loading and firing procedure making sure the shooter will not make any sudden movements that put him, her, or others in danger. Load the magazine to capacity only after the person is handling and firing the pistol properly.

In a fighting stance from the 3-yard (2.74-meter) line close the eyes and fire 1 round into the backstop.[369] Vary the position of the arms slightly on each shot to determine what position provides maximum gripping power to control the recoil. Make any necessary hand adjustments to establish a tight grip. Do this several times and then fire 2 to 3 rounds several times. A coach standing nearby can control the operator to ensure his or her pistol is pointed at the center of the backstop. The objective is to maintain a tight grip without the hands separating and feel the recoil pass through the body while mentally accepting that no harm occurs from the noise, recoil, or concussion.[370] Closing the eyes may help fool the subconscious mind in believing the eyes are protected from the concussive pressure.[371] Repeat the drill until achieving that acceptance.

Trigger Control Drill: Trigger control in this live fire drill is learned by feel, but only after maintaining a tight grip *and* accepting the noise, concussion, and recoil are harmless. The operator will perform the drill with his or her eyes closed. Closing the eyes and wearing double hearing protection forces the mind to depend on the sense of touch. Again, a coach standing nearby can control the operator to ensure his or her pistol is pointed at the center of the backstop. An operator first learning trigger control live fire should verbalize audibly "slack…pull…reset" while performing each action. This systematic process allows the operator to concentrate on each of the three steps of trigger control.

In a fighting stance from the 3-yard (2.74-meter) line, close the eyes. Say "slack" while taking up the slack from trigger. Say "pull" while pulling the trigger and holding it to the rear. Say "reset" while moving the trigger forward to the beginning of the free travel stage, but keeping the finger in contact with the trigger. Continue speeding up the three steps until the trigger is being controlled faster than the words are spoken. Rapid-fire about 5 rounds without saying the words. Repeat the drill until maintaining control of the trigger while rapid firing 5 or more rounds.

Eyes Open Drill: Keep both eyes *open* and in a fighting stance from the 3-yard (2.74-meter) line rapid-fire 5 rounds or more into the backstop.[372] Do not mentally count the rounds—just estimate the number fired—concentrate on seeing the movement of the pistol. The goal is *not* to blink.[373] Remember, blinking the eyes is a subconscious reaction (flinch response) to a pistol firing (concussion). An operator blinking will not be able to see the front sight lift out of the rear sight or the muzzle flash.[374] To shoot *accurate* and *fast* the operator has to see the sights and control the recoil. Sights should *not* be focused on, but seen within the line of sight.

NOTE: Blinking is one of two autonomic nervous system actions that can be consciously controlled.

Force the eyes to remain open and see the front sight move up and back down in the rear sight. It may help in the beginning to open the eyes so wide that it feels a little awkward and pull the trigger. Practice this until it is comfortable for the eyes *not* to blink. The focus remains on the backstop, but *not* at a particular spot. This allows the operator to concentrate solely on seeing the pistol move through its firing cycle. A coach can watch for blinking. Obviously, the coach must not blink in order to see *if* the operator is blinking. The operator should also fire 5 rounds slowly to confirm he or she can keep both eyes open on demand. Repeat the drills as necessary. There is not much more the operator can accomplish until he or she acquires the ability to keep both eyes open while firing.[375]

General Instructions: Drills are fired from the fighting stance. Load three magazines with 10 rounds each. Reloads are performed when the slide locks back. The drills are designed to shoot 10 rounds from each distance. This allows multiple repetitions of firing and reloading to build procedural memory. Fire the specified number of rounds from the 3-, 7-, and 10-yard (2.74-, 6.4-, and 9.14-meter) line and move back up to the 3-yard (2.74-meter) line and start over with the next higher specified number of rounds. (Table 6-1) After completing a drill, move to the next drill, and repeat the number of rounds and repetitions. To meet the time limits it may be necessary to begin with the .22 Long Rifle, and afterwards progress to a self-protection caliber.[376]

Use a white paper target with six 8-inch (203.2-millimeter) circles with a black 0.25-inch (6.35-millimeter) wide outline. Shoot the top circle from the 3-yard (2.74-meter) line; middle circle from the 7-yard (6.4-meter) line; and bottom circle from the 10-yard (9.14-meter) line. Each one of the three circles on the left and right corresponds to a firing line. The goal when firing is a balance of *speed* and *accuracy*. The operator shoots quickly while keeping his or her rounds inside the 8-inch circle. Keep the core tight and a tight grip on the pistol when firing. Keep both eyes open while focusing on the target, but superimpose aligned sights on the center of the target. Do *not* blink while firing. Use an electronic timer set to random start or use a coach to operate the timer verifying times.

Distance in Yards	Distance in Meters	Number of Rounds	Repetitions
3 / 7 / 10	2.74 / 6.4 / 9.14	1	10
3 / 7 / 10	2.74 / 6.4 / 9.14	2	5
3 / 7 / 10	2.74 / 6.4 / 9.14	5	2

Table 6-1 *Distance, Number of Rounds, and Repetitions*

Aimed Fire Drill: Focus on the center of the target superimposing aligned sights on the center. Apply pressure to the trigger past the pretravel (slack) until feeling the engagement stage. For a double action trigger apply pressure settling the trigger finger on the trigger, but do not make the hammer move. On the sound of the beep—instantly move the trigger finger straight back pulling the trigger and hold it to the rear. See a second sight picture resetting the trigger into the pretravel stage and then back to the engagement stage. This drill proves the trigger does *not* have to be pulled in a slow control manner for the shot to be accurate. The goal to fire the shot is 0.25 second. Follow the General Instructions and refer to Table 6-1 for number of rounds fired and the distance.

High Ready Position Drill: Hold the pistol in a *high ready* position pointing at the ground directly below the target. The trigger finger can have a small bend in it with the tip touching the receiver. While in the high ready position with both eyes open look at the sights to make sure they are aligned, and under the dominant eye. This allows the operator to build procedural memory of what the pistol feels like aligned in the high ready position. Keep both eyes open and *focus* on the center of a circle target. On the sound of the beep, from the high ready position raise the pistol until the top edge of the sights are superimposed on the center of a circle target. The instant the arms begin to move start applying pressure to the trigger. The shot must break the *instant* the sights are superimposed on a center of the circle target—*not* before or after. On the first 10 single shots hold the trigger to the rear, see a second sight picture, and reset the trigger. The goal is to fire the first shot within 0.5 second and a split time of 0.25 second thereafter.[377] Follow the General Instructions and refer to Table 6-1 for number of rounds fired and the distance.

NOTE: Trigger control is a *subconscious* pulling of the trigger as the pistol moves toward the target and the sights are superimposed on the target. Jerking the trigger is a *conscious* decision to slam the trigger to the rear in an attempt to catch the sight picture.[378]

Join Position Drill: This drill builds on the join position, which is the second stage of the draw. To fire the shot from the join position it takes about 0.25 second longer than the high ready position. The trigger finger can have a small bend in it with the tip touching the receiver. On the sound of the beep, aggressively push the pistol forward until the arms naturally lock and the top edge of the sights are superimposed on the middle of the circle target. The instant the arms begin to move, start applying pressure to the trigger. The trigger should break when the sights are superimposed on the target. On the first 10 single shots hold the trigger to the rear, see a second sight picture, and reset the trigger. The goal is to fire the first shot within 0.75 second and a split time of 0.25 second thereafter.[379] Follow the General Instructions and refer to Table 6-1 for number of rounds fired and the distance.

Drawing Drill: With all holster retention devices secured, on the beep, draw the pistol. Place the trigger finger on the trigger *after* the non-firing hand joins the firing hand. Apply pressure to the trigger as the arms move toward the target. Break the shot just as the arms reach full extension and the top edge of the sights are superimposed on the middle of the circle target. Some negligent discharges may occur (premature shots) while learning the technique. Slow down slightly and concentrate on prepping the trigger. With practice, prepping the trigger will become a subconscious act, and a part of the operator's procedural memory. Prepping the trigger during the extension phase is critical for a fast and accurate first shot.[380] On the first 10 *single* shots hold the trigger to the rear, see a second sight picture, and reset the trigger. The goal is to fire the first shot in 1.5 seconds and a split time of 0.25 second thereafter for multiple shots.[381] Follow the General Instructions and refer to Table 6-1 for number of rounds fired and the distance.

One-Hand Drill, Hand Opposite Dominant Eye Drill, and Low light Drill: After becoming competent live firing with two hands, use one-hand (left and right) and two-hands with the hand opposite the dominant eye (cant the pistol slightly and use the dominant eye). Use self-luminous sights and perform all the drills in a near *dark* environment if a low light range is available. On the first 10 single shots hold the trigger to the rear, see a second sight picture, and reset the trigger. Continue the drills until the shot is fired in 0.25 second for the Aimed Fire drill, 0.5 second for the High Ready drill, 0.75 second for the Join Position drill, and 1.5 seconds for one-hand drawing from the holster drill with a split time of 0.3 second thereafter. The additional 0.05 second added to the 0.25 second split time is because of the pistol moving more in recoil than when firing with two hands.[382] Follow the General Instructions and refer to Table 6-1 for number of rounds fired and the distance.

Dummy Round Drills: An operator having flinching issues can perform the two-hand high ready and join position drills again, but have a coach load 1 to 3 *live* rounds randomly mixed among a full magazine of *dummy* rounds. Dummy round drills commonly have 1 to 3 dummy rounds mixed among live rounds. However, the goal is to get the operator to overcome his or her flinch. Just shooting more ammunition will not solve the flinching problem. Shooting just live ammunition may condition an operator that is flinching—to flinch more.

Another option is to alternate a dummy round with a live round.[383] Maintain the time standards on each shot. On a misfire, perform a tap-rack-ready. Be sure to move the trigger finger onto the receiver *prior* to performing the tap-rack-ready.

An operator may need the practice pulling the trigger with the *possibility* of the pistol discharging to build a subconscious reaction of *not* flinching. The act of pulling the trigger so many times with the possibility of the pistol firing builds procedural memory useful for when the pistol does fire. As the operator overcomes the flinching, add more live rounds, and subtract dummy rounds. Continue to alternate more live rounds between each dummy round until firing only live rounds. The dummy rounds should be used in conjunction with eye protection and double hearing protection.

Live Fire: Moving Into the Fighting Stance While Drawing

The difference between these drills and the ones in the *Live Fire: Learning Target Focused Sighted Shooting* section is the operator instead of standing still and drawing while shooting at a circle target will now move into an *aggressive* fighting stance while drawing and shooting at a human silhouette target. Scoring lines on the target need to be subdued and not easily seen. This is to prevent the tendency to shoot slow using precision techniques.

NOTE: In a 10-year period when distances were reported, 85 percent of officers killed with firearms were 20 feet (6 meters) or less from their attackers.[384]

Perform the drills from a distance of *7 yards (6.4 meters)* and use a human silhouette target. The operator moves from a standing position to fighting stance, draws, and fires. With competence achieved from the previous drills, the size of the target and the close distance, the operator should maintain an 8-inch (203.2-millimeter) group. The target is large enough so the instructor can see the shot group and provide necessary correction to the operator.

The operator standing on the firing line with a loaded magazine will insert it in the pistol, chamber a round, and holster the pistol. The operator stands in a normal relaxed position for his or her operational environment. The operator keeps both eyes open, *focuses* on an aim point in the target's high center mass, moves into a fighting stance simultaneously draws acquiring a superimposed sight picture, fires 1 round and holds the trigger to the rear. The operator will remain in the fighting stance and holster *only* when directed by an instructor.

The sequence begins *slowly* performing each step perfectly to build procedural memory. As procedural memory develops, speed will automatically increase. Repeat the drill until being able to draw from the holster and fire in 2 seconds while maintaining an 8-inch (203.2-millimeter) group. The operator should strive to draw and fire in 1.5 seconds or less.

NOTE: Pull the trigger the *instant* there is a superimposed sight image on the target. A prolonged delay in firing may cause sight image deterioration or second-guessing by the operator.

The operator will draw and fire 2 shots. The operator needs to see the front sight lifting out of the rear sight and both sights return onto the target. This is a continuous sight picture. The second sight picture is part of the follow-through aspect of shooting. The operator will strive to fire a shot every .25 second while seeing a superimposed sight image on the target before pulling the trigger. The shots should remain within an 8-inch (203.2-millimeter) group in the high center mass area. The operator's failure point or shooting ability exceeded occurs when shots are no longer within the specified group. The operator will remain in the fighting stance after firing the second shot. This will further build procedural memory and provide the instructor an opportunity to correct deficiencies. The operator reloads as necessary and the instructor should correct any reloading deficiencies.

NOTE: The operator must train to a level of *calling the shot.*[385] Calling the shot is knowing with certainty the instant of pulling the trigger where the bullet struck according to the sight picture.[386] The exact moment the front sight lifts is where the bullet hits. Calling the shot is required for diagnosing what is done right and wrong. An operator that has the ability to call shots can transition between multiple steel targets without depending on the sound of a ping to verify a hit.[387] Shooting by sight is faster than shooting by hearing.

The instruction session must not be rushed. The instructor should explain the reason for any misses outside of the 8-inch (203.2-millimeter) group as the operator fires. The common mistakes are blinking, not maintaining a tight grip with the firing hand high in the back strap, not pulling the trigger finger straight back, and dipping the muzzle down. The likely reason for 2 shots widely apart is a loose grip. The instructor first evaluates the operator and then the target. The operator should be evaluated for a dominate eye, firing hand on same side as dominate eye, one- and two-hand grip, stance with natural point of aim, sight picture, trigger pull and reset, and second sight picture. A properly trained operator will be proficient and the target will either prove or disprove that proficiency.

NOTE: When rotating multiple firing orders operators not firing can gather 10 yards (9.14 meters) behind the firing line. This will provide operators watching an opportunity to learn from the successes and shortcomings of others. Talking among the observers is allowable as long as it does not disrupt the operators firing or the instructor teaching.

Perform the drill again, but fire a burst of 3 to 5 rounds until the pistol is empty. The operator will fire 3 full magazines.

The fighting stance is assumed while simultaneously drawing. Both eyes are kept opened *focusing* on the target and *seeing* the superimposed sight image on the target. The trigger finger at that moment moves straight back pulling the trigger. The pistol is seen recoiling up and settling back down with the superimposed sight image on the target and the trigger is pulled again. The operator maintains a focus on the target, but attends to the sights. The rate of fire is a 3- to 5-round burst with a 0.25 second split time until 3 magazines are empty. The operator as a rule is firing roughly 25 percent of the magazine's capacity during each succession of fire. The goal is to maintain an 8-inch (203.2-millimeter) group within the high center mass area of the target.

NOTE: Range training should include having operators after shooting to lower their pistols to reflect the target falling to the ground. This technique trains for a real-life encounter representing the adversary falling to the ground. Death can come quickly to an operator from *not* maintaining a clear field of view of the adversary's hands.[388] The adversary with a dying breath might raise a pistol and shoot an inattentive operator. The fight is *not* over until the operator overcomes the adversary's ability and will to fight.[389]

Live Fire: Reloading

NOTE: Glock intentionally designed the magazine catch *not* to be easily pressed when maintaining a proper shooting grip. The design attempts to force the operator to rotate the firing hand a few degrees to press the magazine catch.[390] This will prevent the trigger finger from accessing the trigger while removing a magazine.

Perform the drill at a distance of *7 yards (6.4 meters)* and use a human silhouette target. Load a magazine with 3 rounds, insert into pistol, chamber a round and holster. Load 2 magazines with 3 rounds and place in a magazine pouch. On command draw and fire until empty, reload and fire 1 round. Quickly perform a scan of the area (actually look 360 degrees and listen) and then holster.[391] Repeat the drill using the last magazine. Perform drills until proficiency is developed. One round can be placed in each magazine to conserve ammunition. The goal is to perform the reload in 3 seconds or less between the last shot of the first magazine and the first shot of the second magazine.[392]

An operator should practice experiencing the slide locking back. The experience can be acquired by repeatedly shooting 1 round and causing the slide to lock back. This practice not only teaches what it is like when the slide locks back, but also provides repetitions to build procedural memory for efficient reloading. Watch the targets while reloading. There is no need to look at the magazine pouch. Place equipment for immediate access. There should not be any grasping or fumbling for equipment. Reloading must be an automatic response without conscious thought and performed aggressively.[393]

Reloading drills were practiced during a Glock Pistol Transitional Instructor Workshop course the author attended. An operator had just finished performing slide back reloads and then was told to perform a save reload with the slide forward. The operator removed the pistol's magazine and dropped it on the floor. Quickly the operator grabbed another magazine inserted it into the magazine well and racked the slide ejecting a live round. The operator after the drill said, "I messed that up!" The fact is the operator did not mess up. He was working under the stress of getting the reload accomplished as quickly as possible. Why did the operator *not* stow the magazine, and *not* rack the slide? The slide after all was in the forward position. The *subconscious* mind made the decision to remove the magazine, insert the magazine, and rack the slide. This is an example of procedural memory taking over and is likely to occur under *combat* conditions.

Military operators and civilian operators in a combat zone are likely to carry a *drop pouch*.[394] The operator can perform a *save reload* by quickly dropping the empty or partially filled magazine in the pouch designed for that purpose. The magazines at the first opportunity are retrieved from the drop pouch and the remaining ammunition is consolidated to make fully loaded magazines. Those magazines are placed back in magazine pouches. This method of saving magazines is crucial to the military operator conducting combat operations in remote locations in which replacement magazines would not be readily available.

NOTE: The term *save reload* describes the action. First is saving the magazine and then reloading.

Armed civilians or police officers can also utilize the save reload. The magazine is placed in a *pocket*, instead of a drop pouch. A save reload would be performed by stripping the pistol of the partially filled or empty magazine and dropping it in a pocket. From the magazine pouch, retrieve a fully loaded magazine, and insert it in the pistol. The technique is applicable *if* an operator has the presence of mind to use it and there is no immediate threat.

The operator needs to perfect one method of reloading applicable to the operational environment. The operator as a habit should *not* switch from one method to the other. Either use the save reload in conjunction with a drop pouch or drop the magazine on the ground. It is unrealistic to expect an operator in the midst of a gunfight to make a *conscious* decision with two choices for storing a magazine. That determination should have already taken place on a *subconscious* level during realistic training.

However, it is *not* to say that an operator that has trained using the *save reload* may never drop a magazine on the ground or that an operator that has trained using the *drop reload* may never save a magazine in a pocket. An operator should *not* lose his or her life trying to pick up a partially filled or empty magazine off the ground. Do so only *if* time and opportunity allows. It is the combat tempo in the area of responsibility that dictates if an operator can look away to pick up a magazine.

NOTE: The procedure of saving a partially filled magazine in a uniform pocket is commonplace in law enforcement. Uncommon is requiring officers to *retrieve* those magazines and fire them. A magazine dropped in a pocket not retrievable is of no use in a subsequent engagement.

When reloading, yell a word or phrase that signifies to other team members a *reload* is occurring.[395] The operator reloading may kneel down or move to the side *if* tactically sound to do so and yell, "Cover!" The operator covering would yell "Covering!" When the operator kneeling is finished with the reload, he or she would yell "Ready!" and the covering operator would yell "Up!" The communication verbiage is useable whether an operator kneels, moves, or does neither. Do *not* yell the word "reloading" as the adversary may hear it and use the opportunity to close the distance on the operator. An adversary hearing an operator yell a word might think he or she is not working alone, but has a partner.

An adversary would likely interpret the words "cover or covering" as the operator having control of an area—the area is covered. Use the same language for a stoppage. It makes no tactical difference to use the same word for stoppage and reload. What matters is other team members know that an operator is not capable of firing. The words *cover, covering,* and *ready* coincide with the operators actions. The operator requests cover. Another operator provides cover. The operator that requested the cover is ready. Under stress, a single word is easier to remember than a phrase.

Live Fire: Clearing Stoppages

WARNING: Do not use live rounds in training to simulate a double feed stoppage. Use a dummy round in the chamber and the subsequent round.[396] A live chambered round can be detonated by the nose of the round trying to feed. A detonation can occur from a primer striking the ejector or extractor during the stoppage drill.[397] There is also an issue of the slide closing on a round forcing the bullet rearward into the case causing *setback*. Firing a round with setback can create dangerously high chamber pressures rupturing the firearm resulting in an injury.

There are combat doctrines that specify when clearing a stoppage *(circumstances permitting)* assume the kneeling position.[398] Carefully consider doctrines that dictate assuming a kneeling position automatically when clearing stoppages. There needs to be a reason that offers a tactical advantage for assuming a kneeling position. Some clearing procedures do not *require* the kneeling position. Not kneeling under certain circumstances may offer a tactical advantage. However, the kneeling position can be a visual indicator to other team members that a *stoppage* has occurred or a *reload* is taking place. In either case, the operator is not firing and other team members can provide assistance.

The kneeling position affords another operator (adhering to priority of fire) an option of firing in a wide field of view while standing next to the operator that is clearing a stoppage.[399] The kneeling operator may drop out of the view of other team members and this could be a disadvantage. The operator may also drop out of the view of the adversary which is something generally seen as advantageous. There is also a chance of another operator shooting the operator kneeling as he or she stands.

The operator kneeling when about to stand needs to shout a prearranged signal such as "Ready!" to alert other team members. The covering team member will yell, "Up!" and the kneeling operator will then stand. Team doctrines may also require the kneeling operator not to stand until *physically* pulled up by the covering operator. These methods should prevent the kneeling operator from standing up and interfering with a course of action occurring or about to occur.[400] These are some things to consider regarding close quarters combat.

NOTE: On the firing line, firearms instructors must *not* allow the *routine* raising of a hand to signify a stoppage has occurred. It is the operator's responsibility to identify and correct stoppages while continuing with the course of fire—stay in the fight.

Perform the drill at a distance of *7 yards (6.4 meters)* and use a human silhouette target. Load a magazine with 2 dummy rounds mixed among a full magazine (sabotaged). Load that magazine into the pistol. Load a second magazine with 2 dummy rounds side-by-side among live rounds and place in the pouch closest to the body centerline (first magazine to be used during reload). Load the final magazine same as the first and place in the last empty pouch. Even with an operator aware of the dummy rounds, any anticipation of the pistol firing will likely be evident from pushing the muzzle down.[401] Pushing the muzzle down is losing control of the pistol. To regain control of the pistol establish an aggressive fighting stance with a solid grip, establish a sight picture, and pull the trigger.

NOTE: A competent operator (one that shoots *fast* and *accurate*) may dip the muzzle when a dummy round is chambered, but it is because of *timing the pistol* to control recoil. Flinching occurs in essence *before* the bullet leaves the barrel and timing the pistol occurs *after* the bullet leaves the barrel. Hits or misses on a target determine which is occurring.

The operator using 3 magazines will fire 3 rounds within practical accuracy. The chambered dummy round will cause a failure to fire, also called a *misfire*. The operator will perform a failure to fire drill by immediately performing a tap-rack-ready and continuing to fire the next 3 rounds. On the second magazine, the tap-rack-ready will not clear the 2 dummy rounds side-by-side, the operator *may* go to a kneeling position, but should consider using available cover to perform a lock-clear-reload. The operator kneeling can stand or continue to fire from the kneeling position. On the final magazine perform a tap-rack-ready and fire the remaining rounds. The operator must maintain situational awareness to determine whether the kneeling position or using cover are appropriate actions.

NOTE: Magazines do not have to be fully loaded. Use fewer rounds in the magazines to reduce training cost. However, at some point in the training use a full magazine to ensure the operator has the physical endurance to perform stoppage drills while effectively firing all the rounds.

An alternative to the failure to fire drill is wrapping the magazine body with two or three wraps of masking tape.[402] The tape prevents the magazine from falling out of the magazine well. Press the magazine catch, unseating the magazine, and holster the pistol. Draw the pistol with a live round in the chamber and try to fire twice. When the failure to fire occurs, perform a tap-rack-ready, and continue to fire.

NOTE: A Glock pistol does not have a *magazine disconnect*.[403] A Glock pistol with the magazine removed, but has a live round in the chamber will fire.[404]

Time is of the essence when a stoppage occurs. How long does it take to get a pistol functional again? The answer is the rest of the operator's life. That life can be over in a split second. Perform stoppage drills without hesitation. The operator may perform a tap-rack-ready, lock-clear-reload, transition to a backup firearm, or have to break contact with the adversary. Seek cover when available and tactically practical. The operator must be able to clear stoppages while in any of the firing positions or on the move.

An operator's back exposed to an adversary is a risky venture. Turning and running might induce the predator response from the adversary. The adversary would view the operator as prey. When running, do so in a zigzag pattern (terrain permitting) and as fast as humanly possible. When running for cover do not stay exposed no more than 3 to 4 seconds. Any additional time would allow an adversary the opportunity to obtain a sight picture.[405] Not reaching cover within 3 to 4 seconds will likely result in the adversary shooting the operator. Operators must accept that exposing themselves for more than a few seconds to an adversary will probably end with a gunshot wound. At CQC distances (room clearing, traffic stop, etc.) the exposure time to the adversary is reduced dramatically and can be less than a second. This is why it is crucial for an operator at CQC distances to engage a deadly adversary immediately with overwhelming effective fire.

NOTE: A pistol equipped with a slide mounted *rotating safety/decocking lever* may be inadvertently placed on safe when racking the slide. After performing a tap-rack-ready and the pistol does not fire, check the safety by sweeping the thumb forward making sure the safety is *not* engaged before performing a lock-clear-reload.[406]

DRAWING AND TURNING

Adversaries do not always attack from the front. An attack can come from any direction. How an operator moves his or her body and turns depends on the perceived imminence. The operator's mind-set and job assignment can also determine movement. The body when startled will usually turn by moving the eyes, head, body, and then the feet. The entire movement takes less than a second. The movement done quickly can sometimes be more similar to a hop than a turn.

An operator must be capable of changing directions quickly to engage targets that are on either side or behind. To turn from one target to another rotate on the ball of the foot in the direction of the turn by pushing off with the other foot. The body will spin in the desired direction and stop when facing the threat. The trailing foot plants, and the operator stops in the fighting stance. The turning movement must *not* be complicated or difficult to perform. The movement as described below is an efficient method in which to turn and engage adversaries.

Moreover, it is a natural reaction.

The squaring of the body to the adversary is also natural and enables a pistol, carbine, submachine gun, or shotgun to remain in the line of sight for effective fire. The pistol does not come out of the holster until the operator is square to the adversary. Turning with the pistol out would likely cause it to sweep past the adversary. The pistol would then have to be brought back to the adversary wasting time. Drawing the pistol while squared to the adversary is more efficient because the body is in a natural fighting stance and the pistol is push directly toward the adversary.

DANGER: Operators on a firing line practicing turning and drawing must *not* point their pistol at other operators due to a premature draw.

Maintaining the fighting stance in conjunction with an aligned sight image within the line of sight causes the bullets to impact where the dominant eye is focusing. Not all situations will permit the operator to square up to the adversary. At close to contact distances a startled operator may flinch away, draw, and fire with one hand as explained in the Combat Shooting Phase 2 chapter.

NOTE: The steps for turning when described may seem robotic, but when performed should be *natural*, *explosive*, and *aggressive*.

Turning and moving forward is a display of aggression that takes the fight to the adversary. The down side is it puts the operator closer increasing the adversary's accuracy. [407] Stepping back can put the operator on the defensive and interpreted by the adversary as retreating. Moving backwards increases the chance of falling. There should be a tactical reason for moving backwards, such as gaining distance, or moving to cover. Moving backwards can also occur because of a flinch response during an alarm reaction. Stop any rearward movement at the earliest possible time, and go on the offense to stop the adversary.

Left and Right Turns

It is a natural response for the body to push off with the back leg when turning. The operator would likely tuck his or her body somewhat and turn on the leg closest to the threat or the direction desired. The operator should aggressively move his or her feet. Practice turning toward the right and left. (Figures 6-88 through 6-93)

Figure 6-88
Look to Identify
(left)

Figure 6-89
Turn to Face
(left)

Figure 6-90
Draw and Fire
(left)

Figure 6-91
Look to Identify
(right)

Figure 6-92
Turn to Face
(right)

Figure 6-93
Draw and Fire
(right)

Standing beside an obstruction may force which leg is used. Practice turns standing beside objects common to the operational area. As the body turns the draw begins, but allow the body to stabilize (fighting stance) before rotating the pistol horizontal to the ground. The arms extend naturally driving the muzzle toward the target acquiring a sight picture and the shot is taken.

Rear Turn

The rear turn is turning 180 degrees from the starting position. Practice turning to the rear from the right and left. (Figures 6-94 through 6-99)

DANGER: To prevent pointing the muzzle in an inappropriate direction it is imperative the body stabilize square to the target before rotating the pistol horizontal and driving the muzzle forward.

Figure 6-94
Look to Identify
(left rear)

Figure 6-95
Turn to Face
(left rear)

Figure 6-96
Draw and Fire
(left rear)

Figure 6-97
Look to Identify
(right rear)

Figure 6-98
Turn to Face
(right rear)

Figure 6-99
Draw and Fire
(right rear)

It is natural for the head to turn in the direction of a sound as interpreted by the brain. Usually a sound heard on the left will cause the head to turn left and when heard on the right will cause the head to turn right. The direction the head turns is the direction the body will turn. As the body turns the draw begins, but allow the body to stabilize (fighting stance) before rotating the pistol horizontal to the ground. The arms extend naturally driving the muzzle toward the target acquiring a sight picture and the shot is taken.

The rear turn is especially useful to police officers conducting traffic stops. The author's first phase Field Training Officer (FTO) at the Dallas Police Department taught the technique to provide rear security. The technique correctly performed will provide rear security while walking away from the violator's vehicle. The police officer turns to walk away, takes a step and quickly looks back over a shoulder, and continues to walk. The police officer is looking to make sure the violator is not mounting an ambush. The police officer will take several more steps and look again. The number of times the police officer looks is dependent on the circumstance and distance. While walking away the author has caught violators opening their vehicle doors. He would immediately turn and use whatever force option was appropriate. He also used the technique extensively in Afghanistan.

The author one night in south Dallas was looking for an armed robbery suspect that had fled on foot. While searching, he heard a sound behind him. The author thinking it was the armed robber quickly turned around 180 degrees. He stopped in a fighting stance with his pistol pointed toward a dog advancing quickly. He spontaneously yelled, "Stop!" The dog snarling and growling reluctantly gave in while turning away in the opposite direction. The turn allowed the author to quickly rotate in the opposite direction and challenge a threat. In a separate animal incident, he turned, fired, and shot a charging dog. The ability to turn in any direction is an effective means to engage threats quickly.

Turning 360 Degrees

An operator must have the ability to turn and engage adversaries in a 360-degree radius. The goal is to snap the head toward the target, turn quickly while simultaneously drawing, and aggressively assume a fighting stance facing the target directly. The drill is repeatable while using two or three targets.

Perform the same drill at a distance of *10 yards (9.14 meters)* and use a human silhouette target. The operator on each turn can fire a burst of 3 to 5 rounds.

Contact Left: Operator stands on firing line with *left* shoulder facing target. On command of *contact left* the operator snaps the head to the left looking at the target, pushes off with the right foot, turning on the *left* leg while simultaneously drawing, stops in a fighting stance facing the target, drives the muzzle to the target sees a sight picture, and fires.

Contact Right: Operator stands on firing line with *right* shoulder facing target. On command of *contact right* the operator snaps the head to the right looking at the target, pushes off with the left foot, turning on the *right* leg while simultaneously drawing, stops in a fighting stance facing the target, drives the muzzle to the target sees a sight picture and fires.

Contact Rear: Operator stands on firing line with *back* facing target. On command of *contact rear* the operator snaps his or her head over the right shoulder looking at the target, pushes off with the left foot, turns on the *right* leg while simultaneously drawing, stops in a fighting stance facing the target, drives the muzzle to the target, sees a sight picture, and fires. Repeat the drill with the operator looking over the left shoulder and turning to the *left*.

TRAINING FOR THE GUNFIGHT

Instructors during training can use short lectures as rest periods for operators while reemphasizing conditions likely encountered when using a pistol for self-protection. Much of the information has already been discussed in the Operational Survival chapter. However, the operator has to prepare for not only the gunfight where 3 to 5 rounds are fired at multiple adversaries in 3 to 5 seconds at 3 to 5 yards (2.74 to 4.57 meters) in low light conditions, but also the fight with multiple heavily armed adversaries in daylight that might last for 44 minutes or longer.[408] The adversary's actions in both cases force the operator's response.

NOTE: In real-life there is no warming up or practice sessions. The operator's skillset while cold is what will be used in a gunfight.[409]

The operator that understands the characteristics of gunfights will likely accept and apply training. An informed operator accepts that in *close quarters combat* the body will likely crouch. There is little or no time to *focus* on the front sight. The pistol is gripped tight as if the operator's life depended on it—because it does. The operator with aggression will drive the pistol into the line of sight *seeing* a superimposed sight image on the adversary and continuously fire until the threat no longer exists.

Seeing aligned sights on the adversary and pulling the trigger is the surest way of knowing (short of an immediate incapacitation) that bullets are hitting the adversary.[410] Unless at a distance of arm's reach from the adversary—simply pointing a pistol and firing does *not* necessarily mean that bullets are hitting the intended aim point. Using a sight picture with trigger control and follow-through is the only way to *know* that bullets are hitting the intended aim point as the shots are fired. Operators are doing a disservice to their self-preservation that train for anything less.

NOTE: The use of justified deadly force, also called perfect self-defense is *not* based on an adversary's race, sex, or age, but on the adversary's actions. Such actions in the State of North Carolina as an example include an imminent threat of death, great bodily harm, or sexual assault.[411]

SUMMARY

Target Focused Sighted Shooting allows the operator to *focus* on the adversary while *seeing* a superimposed sight image. The system works from 1 yard (0.91 meter) to the maximum effective range of the pistol. The fighting stance comes from the body's natural reaction to a dangerous situation. The fighting stance will work with personal weapons, knife, pistol, or carbine. The procedures of loading, unloading, and clearing stoppages use the same gross motor skills. Repetitious practice to engrain *procedural memory* is the best way to learn combat shooting skills. There is plenty of time and little stress on a range. There is plenty of stress and little time in combat. The first person that fires multiple rounds with *required accuracy* will likely win the encounter. Combat shooting is a survival endeavor, not a recreational sport.

DISCUSSION QUESTIONS

1. What is the instinctive movement of the human body under stress?
2. List the three automatic safeties built into the Glock pistol.
3. What is the standard carry condition of a pistol for American law enforcement officers?
4. There are significant physiological and tactical differences between combat shooting and what other type of shooting?
5. Discuss the physiological and tactical differences.
6. How can stress be induced on operators while training or qualifying on a range?
7. In layperson's terms describe eye dominance.
8. What is cross-dominance?
9. What is ambiocular?
10. What is a solution to cross-dominance for the operator involved in combat shooting?
11. Describe the first step in the journey of combat shooting.
12. Shooting with both eyes open maximizes speed, accuracy, and what else?
13. Describe what occurs when focusing with both eyes open on the front sight versus the target.
14. Explain the difference between breath control based on respiratory pause theory and breath control based on combat shooting theory.
15. Why is the fighting stance a universal fighting position?
16. Why do females have a tendency to lean backward when shooting a firearm?
17. To shoot a pistol fast and accurate it must bond to the body. What provides that bond?
18. Describe what is a tight grip for combat shooting with a pistol?
19. Glock fourth generation pistols have an add-on modular back strap that comes in what two sizes?
20. Discuss the advantages of a thumbs forward grip versus a thumbs crossed grip.
21. List the three steps of the draw?
22. Why is it important to remove drawstrings from garments when carrying a pistol?
23. Describe some of the differences between the ready positions and the carry position.
24. Discuss retention versus readiness in relation to having the pistol in

the hand versus the holster.

25. What are the three most important fundamentals of combat shooting?
26. Explain what is the fighting stance.
27. Explain what is a sight picture.
28. Explain what is trigger control.
29. Discuss the advantages of using a Glock speed loader or universal loader for loading magazines.
30. Explain why reloading should not be a decision making process.
31. What are the two types of reloads advocated for combat shooting?
32. Explain how to use the finger index technique when reloading.
33. Explain how to use the thumb index technique when reloading.
34. What is the difference between a stoppage and a malfunction?
35. What does the acronym SAMM mean and how is it applied to shooting?
36. Discuss why analytical techniques to clear stoppages are usually ineffective in high stress situations.
37. Explain when to use stoppage clearance techniques tap-rack-ready and lock-clear-reload.
38. What is setback as related to a cartridge and why is it dangerous?
39. Explain the procedure for loading live ammunition for duty carry.
40. Discuss the advantages of using a video camera to improve shooting skills.
41. Discuss the advantages of using a .22 Long Rifle pistol when teaching a shooter.
42. Explain how to turn in each direction from a fighting stance.
43. What are the characteristics of a close quarters gunfight?

ENDNOTES

[1] International Association of Law Enforcement Firearms Instructors, *Standards & Practices Reference Guide for Law Enforcement Firearms Instructors*, (January 1995): 275.

[2] International Association of Law Enforcement Firearms Instructors, *Standards & Practices Reference Guide for Law Enforcement Firearms Instructors*, (January 1995): 275.

[3] W.E. Fairbairn and E.A. Sykes, *Shooting to Live* (Boulder, CO: Paladin Press, 1987), 2. Originally published in 1942 by W.E. Fairbairn and E.A. Sykes.

Bill Rogers, *Be Fast, Be Accurate, Be the Best* (Rogers Shooting School Publications: Jacksonville, FL, 2010), 63.

[4] National Rifle Association, *NRA Guide to Basics of Personal Protection Outside the Home* (Fairfax, VA: National Rifle Association of America, 2006), 134.

[5] Glock Inc., *Armorer's Manual*, (Smyrna, GA: 2002): 4.

[6] U.S. Department of Justice, Federal Bureau of Investigation, Firearms Training Unit, *Weapons Workshop* (Quantico, VA, May 16-19, 1988), 6.

[7] Glock Inc., *Armorer's Manual*, (Smyrna, GA: 2009): 14-15.

[8] Dry Fire: "Also dry firing…Practice conducted with an assuredly unloaded firearm or a firearm loaded with dummy rounds only, intended to help the shooter become familiar with a new technique or to develop or maintain specific skills such as trigger control, proper grip, sight picture, etc." See International Association of Law Enforcement Firearms Instructors, *Standards & Practices Reference Guide for Law Enforcement Firearms Instructors*, (January 1995): 252.

[9] Glock Inc., *Armorer's Manual*, (Smyrna, GA: 2002): 16.

[10] J. Henry FitzGerald, *Shooting* (Boulder, CO: Paladin Press, 2007), 353-354. Originally published in 1930 by J. Henry FitzGerald.

[11] Glock Inc., *Instructions for Use Glock Safe Action Pistols All Models*, (Smyrna, GA: March 2011), 15.

[12] Glock Inc., *Instructions for Use Glock Safe Action Pistols All Models*, (Smyrna, GA: March 2011), 1.

[13] Chad Thompson, "Competition Shooting to Prepare for Survival on the Street" *The Firearms Instructor*, issue 50 (2011): 13-14.

[14] Edward C. Godnig, O.D., "Body Alarm Reaction and Sports Vision," *Journal of Behavioral Optometry* (2001, Vol. 12, No. 1): 3-6.

[15] Paul R. Howe, *The Tactical Trainer* (Bloomington, IN: AuthorHouse, 2009), 146.

[16] Chad Thompson, "Competition Shooting to Prepare for Survival on the Street" *The Firearms Instructor*, issue 50 (2011): 13-14.

[17] "In such terrific [life and death] fights as these, conducted in the extremes of rage and hate, the mechanisms for reinforcing the parts of the body which are of primary importance in the struggle are brought fully into action and are of utmost value in securing victory." See Walter B. Cannon, *Bodily Changes in Pain, Hunger, Fear and Rage* (D. Appleton and Company: 1915), 227.

[18] "In other words, at times of pain and excitement sympathetic discharges, probably aided by the adrenal secretion simultaneously liberated, will drive the blood out of the vegetative organs of the interior, which serve the routine needs of the body, into the skeletal muscles which have to meet by extra action the urgent demands of struggle or escape...Thus the absolutely and immediately essential organs—those the ancients called the "tripod of life"—the heart, the lungs, the brain (as well as its instruments, the skeletal muscles)—are in times of excitement abundantly supplied with blood taken from organs of less importance in critical moments." See Walter B. Cannon, *Bodily Changes in Pain, Hunger, Fear and Rage* (D. Appleton and Company: 1915), 108-109.

[19] "There are, of course, many surface manifestations of excitement. The contraction of blood vessels with resulting pallor, the pouring out of "cold sweat," the stopping of saliva-flow so that the "tongue cleaves to the roof of the mouth," the dilation of the pupils, the rising of the hairs, the rapid beating of the heart, the hurried respiration, the trembling and twitching of the muscles, especially those about the lips—all these bodily changes are well recognized accompaniments of pain and great emotional disturbance, such as fear, horror and deep disgust." See Walter B. Cannon, *Bodily Changes in Pain, Hunger, Fear and Rage* (D. Appleton and Company: 1915), 3.

[20] "Pain—and fighting is almost certain to involve pain would, if possible, call forth even greater muscular effort...The nervous impulses delivered to the muscles, furthermore, operate upon organs well supplied with energy-yielding material and well fortified by rapidly circulating blood and by secreted adrenin, against quick loss of power because of accumulating waste. Under such circumstances of excitement the performance of extraordinary feats of strength or endurance is natural enough." See Walter B. Cannon, Bodily Changes in Pain, Hunger, Fear and Rage (D. Appleton and Company: 1915), 189 and 218.

[21] "And the point was made that, since the fear emotion and the anger emotion are, in wild life, likely to be followed by activities (running or fighting) which require contraction of great muscular masses in supreme and prolonged struggle, a mobilization of sugar in the blood might be of signal service to the laboring muscles." See Walter B. Cannon, Bodily Changes in Pain, Hunger, Fear and Rage (D. Appleton and Company: 1915), 188-189.

[22] Monocular Vision: "Viewing with only one eye. When one eye is closed in taking sight with a gun, it is a case of monocular vision. Caveat: monocular vision compromises distance and depth perception." See International Association of Law Enforcement Firearms Instructors, *Standards & Practices Reference Guide for Law Enforcement Firearms Instructors*, (January 1995): 273.

[23] Eric S. Hussey, O.D., FCOVD, "Correcting Intermittent Central Suppression Improves Binocular Marksmanship," *Military Medicine*, April 2007): 414.

[24] Glock Inc., "Shoot Like a True Champion," *Glock Autopistols 2007*, (New York, NY: Harris Publications Inc., 2007): 53.

[25] Gun and run events are pure gamesmanship competitions with no tactical relevance in which the shooter will shoot targets with a predetermined number of shots as quickly as possible.

[26] The term *paper people* related to personal protection describes paper targets that obviously do not have the ability to shoot back, unlike real adversaries that do have the ability to shoot back. Tom Bullins, owner of Trigger Time, Carthage, North Carolina, used the term paper people while instructing a bodyguard training course in Monterrey, Mexico, in a face-to-face conversation with the author, January 16, 2010.

[27] National Rifle Association, *Law Enforcement Handgun Instructor Manual* (Fairfax, VA: Section C, The Fundamentals of Handgun Marksmanship , Edition 6.1, 2006), 12.

[28] Anthony J. Pinizzotto, Ph.D., Harry A. Kern, M.Ed., and Edward F. Davis, M.S., "One-Shot Drops," *FBI Law Enforcement Bulletin*, (October 2004): 20.

[29] Brian Enos, *Practical Shooting* (Clifton, CO: Zediker Publishing, 1991), 53.

[30] Department of the Army, *Combat Training with Pistols, M9 and M11* (Washington, DC June 2003), 2-11.

W. E. Fairbairn and E. A. Sykes, *Shooting to Live* (Boulder, CO: Paladin Press, 1987), 39. Originally published in 1942 by W.E. Fairbairn and E.A. Sykes.

Dean T. Olson, "Improving Deadly Force Decision Making," *FBI Law Enforcement Bulletin*, (February 1998): 4.

[31] Brian Enos, *Practical Shooting* (Clifton, CO: Zediker Publishing, 1991), 102.

[32] International Defensive Pistol Association, "Homepage," *Welcome to the Official IDPA Website,* http://www.idpa.com/ (accessed September 22, 2012).

[33] International Practical Shooting Confederation, "Homepage," *Welcome to IPSC,* http://www.ipsc.org/ (accessed September 22, 2012).

National Rifle Association Action Pistol: Competitive Shooting Division, "Competitive Shooting Programs," *NRA Action Pistol Competition*, https://www.nrahq.org/compete/dept-action.asp (accessed September 22, 2012).

United States Practical Shooting Association, "Homepage," *Experience the Thrill of Competition,* http://www.uspsa.org/ (accessed September 22, 2012).

[34] Glock Inc., "Welcome," *Training Division,* http://www.glocktraining.com (accessed September 22, 2012).

Glock Sport Shooting Foundation, "Homepage," *World of Glock,* http://www.gssfonline.com (accessed September 22, 2012).

[35] Quote: "Amateurs train until they get it right. Professionals train until they can't get it wrong."—Unknown

[36] Mike Pannone, *Glock Handbook* (Philippi, WV: Blackheart International, LLC, 2009), 46.

[37] Glock Inc., *Glock Pistol Transitional Instructor Workshop Course Outline,* (Smyrna, GA: 2012): 3.

[38] "It would be erroneous to use physical activity alone to elevate heart rate and blood pressure in order to simulate a highly stressful "psychological" encounter. Training under conditions of psychological/emotional stress will better prepare the brain to perform under those conditions when the need arises." See Valerie J. Atkins, M.S. and William A. Norris, Ph.D., Survival Score Research Project (Glynco, GA: Federal Law Enforcement Training Center, April 2004), 39.

[39] "20/20 vision is a term used to express normal visual acuity (the clarity or sharpness of vision) measured at a distance of 20 feet. If you have 20/20 vision, you can see clearly at 20 feet what should normally be seen at that distance. If you have 20/100 vision, it means that you must be as close as 20 feet to see what a person with normal vision can see at 100 feet." See American Optometric Association, "Glossary of All Eye & Vision Conditions," *Visual Acuity: What is 20/20 Vision?,* http://www.aoa.org/Visual-Acuity.xml (accessed September 22, 2012).

[40] Brian C. Hatch, David J. Hilber, James B. Elledge, James W. Stout, and Robyn B. Lee, "The Effects of Visual Acuity on Target Discrimination and Shooting Performance," *Optometry and Vision Science* (2009, Vol. 86, No. 12): E1366.

[41] "In optics, it is the region from which a point on an object sends rays of light which are considered to be parallel onto an optical system. Consequently it forms a clear image in the focal plane of that system. In clinical optometry, 6 metres is usually regarded as infinity." *Dictionary of Optometry and Visual Science,* 7th ed., s.v. "optical infinity," http://medical-dictionary.thefreedictionary.com/optical+infinity (accessed September 22, 2012).

[42] "Prescribing for pistol shooters – In general, the rule is to correct for the least amount of plus to clear the front sight in the dominant or shooting eye and, if necessary, the full distance prescription in the non-dominant eye (reverse monovision)." See Walter Potaznick, O.D., F.A.A.O, "American Optometric Association," *Prescribing for*

the   Aging   Shooter/Hunter,   http://www.aoa.org/impactwashingtondc/x6317.xml (accessed October 31, 2011).

[43] American Optometric Association, "Glossary of All Eye & Vision Conditions," *Presbyopia,* http://www.aoa.org/presbyopia.xml (accessed September 22, 2012).

[44] Walter Potaznick, O.D., F.A.A.O, "American Optometric Association," *Prescribing   for   the   Aging   Shooter/Hunter,* http://www.aoa.org/impactwashingtondc/x6317.xml (accessed October 31, 2011).

[45] Jian Ding and George Sperling, A Gain-control Theory of Binocular Combination, (Departments of *Cognitive Sciences and ‡Neurobiology and Behavior, and †Institute for Mathematical Behavioral Sciences, University of California, Irvine, CA   92697-5100),   http://www.pnas.org/content/103/4/1141.full.pdf   (accessed September 22, 2012).

[46] "If you have trouble shooting with both eyes open, we recommend this simple training exercise: Exercise No.2 Cover the front of your Aimpoint sight with the lens cover…Then bring your firearm into position while keeping both eyes focused on the target. The red dot will now be on the target." See Aimpoint Inc., "Products," *How to Improve Your Shooting & How to Shoot with a Red Dot Sight,* http://www.aimpoint.com/us/products/get-the-most-out-of-your-sight/how-to-improve-your-shooting-how-to-shoot-with-a-red-dot-sight/ (accessed September 22, 2012).

[47] Giovanni Battista della Porta, *De Refractione Optices Parte* (Libri Novem. 1593).

[48] Stanley Coren and C.P. Kaplan, "Patterns of Ocular Dominance," *American Journal of Optometry & Archives of American Academy of Optometry* (1973, 50): 283–292.

[49] Clare Porac, and Stanley Coren, "The Dominant Eye," *Psychological Bulletin* (1976, Vol. 83, No. 5): 883.

[50] Alistair P. Mapp, Hiroshi Ono, and Raphel Barbeito, "What Does the Dominant Eye Dominate?—A Brief and Somewhat Contentious Review," *Percept Psychophys* (2003, 65): 310-317.

[51] "We suggest here that the eye identified as the dominant one in a sighting task is determined by nothing more than the constraint of the sighting task that only one eye be used and the ease or the habit of using a particular eye to perform the task. We also suggest that other than being the "preferred" eye in some viewing situations, the sighting dominant eye has no special role for visual or oculomotor processes for the normal population." See Alistair P. Mapp, Hiroshi Ono, and Raphel Barbeito, "What Does the Dominant Eye Dominate?—A Brief and Somewhat Contentious Review," *Percept Psychophys* (2003, 65): 314.

"In summary, the functional significance of OD [ocular dominance] simply extends to identifying which of a pair of eyes will be used for monocular sighting tasks." See Jonathan S. Pointer, "Ocular Dominance within Binocular Vision," in *Binocular Vision: Development, Depth Perception, and Disorders*, ed. Jacques McCoun, and Lucien Reeves (Hauppauge, NY: Nova Science Publishers, 2009), 73.

[52] Eye Dominance: "an unconscious preference to use one eye rather than the other for certain purposes, such as sighting a rifle or looking through a telescope." See Mosby's Medical Dictionary, 8th ed., s.v. "eye dominance" http://medical-dictionary.thefreedictionary.com/eye+dominance (accessed September 22, 2012).

[53] Ocular Dominance: "The superiority of one eye whose visual function predominates over the other eye. It is that eye (called the dominant eye) which is relied upon more than the other in binocular vision. It is not necessarily the eye with the best acuity. The lack of ocular dominance is referred to as ambiocularity and such a person is ambiocular." See *Dictionary of Optometry and Visual Science*, 7th ed., s.v. "ocular dominance" http://medical-dictionary.thefreedictionary.com/ocular+dominance (accessed September 22, 2012).

[54] Clare Porac, and Stanley Coren, "Suppressive Processes in Binocular Vision: Ocular Dominance and Amblyopia," American Journal of Optometry and Physiological Optics (1975, Vol. 52): 652.

[55] Hiroshi Ono, and Raphael Barbeito, "The Cyclopean Eye vs. The Sighting-dominant Eye as the Center of Visual Direction," *Perception Psychophysics* (1982, 32): 201.

[56] Shooting Eye: "The dominant or "master" eye, the one used by a shooter to align his[/her] sights. The dominant eye may be identified by holding a finger at arm's length and with both eyes open lining it up with a distant object. If the finger appears to remain stationary when one eye is then closed, it is the open eye that is dominant." See International Association of Law Enforcement Firearms Instructors, *Standards & Practices Reference Guide for Law Enforcement Firearms Instructors*, (January 1995): 277.

[57] Serge A.R.B. Rombouts, Frederik Barkhof, Michiel Sprenger, Japp Valk, and Philip Scheltens, The Functional Basis of Ocular Dominance: Functional MRI (fMRI) Findings, *Neuroscience Letters 221* (1996): 4.

[58] Alistair P. Mapp, Hiroshi Ono, and Raphel Barbeito, "What Does the Dominant Eye Dominate?—A Brief and Somewhat Contentious Review," *Percept Psychophys* (2003, 65): 311.

[59] Clare Porac, and Stanley Coren, "The Dominant Eye," *Psychological Bulletin* (1976, Vol. 83, No. 5): 886.

[60] Clare Porac, and Stanley Coren, "The Dominant Eye," *Psychological Bulletin* (1976, Vol. 83, No. 5): 886.

[61] See Jonathan S. Pointer, "Ocular Dominance within Binocular Vision," in *Binocular Vision: Development, Depth Perception, and Disorders*, ed. Jacques McCoun, and Lucien Reeves (Hauppauge, NY: Nova Science Publishers, 2009), 66-67.

[62] See Jonathan S. Pointer, "Ocular Dominance within Binocular Vision," in *Binocular Vision: Development, Depth Perception, and Disorders*, ed. Jacques McCoun, and Lucien Reeves (Hauppauge, NY: Nova Science Publishers, 2009), 66.

[63] Clare Porac, and Stanley Coren, "The Dominant Eye," *Psychological Bulletin* (1976, Vol. 83, No. 5): 885.

"The contention that the sighting-dominant eye is usually or always the subject's better eye, i. e., his [or her] more sharply seeing eye, has been disproved again and again, but it will not die out of the textbook literature." See Gordon L. Walls, "A Theory of Ocular Dominance," *American Medical Association Archives Ophthalmology* (1951, 45): 395.

[64] Aarlenn Z. Khan, and J. Douglas Crawford, "Ocular Dominance Reverses as a Function of Horizontal Gaze Angle," *Vision Research*, (2001, 41): 1743-1748.

[65] Joan N. Vickers, *Perception, Cognition, and Decision Training: The Quiet Eye in Action* (Champaign, IL: Human Kinetics, 2007) 22.

[66] Fovea: "The base of the fovea centralis with a diameter of about 0.35 mm (or about 1° of the visual field). The image of the point of fixation is formed on the foveola in the normal eye. The foveola contains cone cells only (rod-free area). The foveal avascular zone is slightly larger (about 0.5 mm in diameter) (Fig. F9). Syn. fovea (term often used by clinicians)." See *Dictionary of Optometry and Visual Science*, 7th ed., s.v. "fovea" http://medical-dictionary.thefreedictionary.com/fovea (accessed September 22, 2012).

[67] Hiroshi Ono, and Raphael Barbeito, "The Cyclopean Eye vs. The Sighting-dominant Eye as the Center of Visual Direction," *Perception Psychophysics* (1982, 32): 201.

[68] See Ken Asakawa and Hitoshi Ishikawa, "Binocular Vision and Depth Perception: Development and Disorders," in *Binocular Vision: Development, Depth Perception, and Disorders*, ed. Jacques McCoun, and Lucien Reeves (Hauppauge, NY: Nova Science Publishers, 2009), 140.

[69] See Burkhart Fischer, "Development of Saccade Control," in *Binocular Vision: Development, Depth Perception, and Disorders*, ed. Jacques McCoun, and Lucien Reeves (Hauppauge, NY: Nova Science Publishers, 2009), 217.

[70] See Ken Asakawa and Hitoshi Ishikawa, "Binocular Vision and Depth Perception: Development and Disorders," in *Binocular Vision: Development, Depth*

Perception, and Disorders, ed. Jacques McCoun, and Lucien Reeves (Hauppauge, NY: Nova Science Publishers, 2009), 141.

[71] See Ken Asakawa and Hitoshi Ishikawa, "Binocular Vision and Depth Perception: Development and Disorders," in *Binocular Vision: Development, Depth Perception, and Disorders*, ed. Jacques McCoun, and Lucien Reeves (Hauppauge, NY: Nova Science Publishers, 2009), 140-141.

[72] Physiological Diplopia: "Normal phenomenon which occurs in binocular vision for non-fixated objects whose images fall on disparate retinal points. It is easily demonstrated to persons with normal binocular vision: fixate binocularly a distant object and place a pencil vertically some 25 cm in front of your nose. You should see two rather blurred pencils. The observation of physiological diplopia has been found to be useful in the management of eso or exo deviations, suppression, abnormal retinal correspondence, etc." See *Dictionary of Optometry and Visual Science Online*, s.v. "physiological   diplopia,"   http://medical-dictionary.thefreedictionary.com/physiological+astigmatism (accessed September 22, 2012).

[73] Suppression: "The process by which the brain inhibits the retinal image (or part of it) of one eye, when both eyes are simultaneously stimulated. This occurs to avoid diplopia as in strabismus, in uncorrected anisometropia, in retinal rivalry, etc." See *Dictionary of Optometry and Visual Science*, 7th ed., s.v. "suppression" http://medical-dictionary.thefreedictionary.com/suppression (accessed September 22, 2012).

[74] Pathological Diplopia "Any diplopia due to an eye disease (e.g. proptosis), an anomaly of binocular vision (e.g. strabismus), a variation in the refractive index of the media of the eye (e.g. cataract), a subluxation of the crystalline lens, or to a general disease (e.g. multiple sclerosis, myasthenia gravis)." See *Dictionary of Optometry and Visual Science*, 7th ed., s.v. "diplopia" http://medical-dictionary.thefreedictionary.com/diplopia (accessed September 22, 2012).

[75] "When we point at an object at a distance with one finger, we suppress the image of the non-dominating eye and we observe the finger with the dominating eye. When we close the dominating eye, the finger becomes suddenly visible to the eye which had been suppressed." See M.A. Breedjk, and M.F. Hoogesteger, "Physiological Suppression and Attention," Documenta Ophthalmologica (1989, 72): 400.

"It is the combination of attention to the sighting eye and suppression of the nonsighting eye that allows such alignment (sighting) tasks to be completed without visual confusion from doubled images." See Stanley Coren, and Clare Porac, "Central and Peripheral Sensitivity to Temporally Modulated Stimuli Presented to the Sighting and Nonsighting Eyes," *Optometry & Vision Science* (1989, Vol. 66, No. 7): 450.

"From this observation one can infer that one monocular view has been suppressed to eliminate the double vision inherent in such a task. The eye whose input is used in these situations has been referred to as the sighting dominant eye or simply the dominant eye. Eye dominance is an example of a suppressive process which is a part of normal visual coordinations." See Clare Porac, and Stanley Coren, "Suppressive Processes in Binocular Vision: Ocular Dominance and Amblyopia," *American Journal of Optometry and Physiological Optics* (1975, Vol. 52): 652.

[76] L.F. Jones, J.G. Classe, and M. Hester, "Association Between Eye Dominance and Training for Rifle Marksmanship: A Pilot Study," *Journal of the American Optometric Association* (1996, Vol. 67, No. 2): 73-76.

Bill Rogers, *Be Fast, Be Accurate, Be the Best* (Rogers Shooting School Publications: Jacksonville, FL, 2010), 76.

[77] Gordon L. Walls, "A Theory of Ocular Dominance," *American Medical Association Archives Ophthalmology* (1951, 45): 393.

[78] Clare Porac, and Stanley Coren, "The Dominant Eye," *Psychological Bulletin* (1976, Vol. 83, No. 5): 881.

[79] Clare Porac, and Stanley Coren, "The Dominant Eye," *Psychological Bulletin* (1976, Vol. 83, No. 5): 888.

[80] "The lack of ocular dominance is referred to as ambiocularity and such a person is ambiocular." See *Dictionary of Optometry and Visual Science*, 7th ed., s.v. "ocular dominance"   http://medical-dictionary.thefreedictionary.com/ocular+dominance (accessed September 22, 2012).

[81] A study from the Force Science Institute Ltd., study "...suggest that firearms training should change from a process that inadvertently teaches novices to fixate the sights of their own weapon first and the target second, to a type of training that establishes the line of gaze on the target from the outset, followed by alignment of the sights of the weapon to the line of gaze." Joan N Vickers, and William Lewinski, "Performing under Pressure: Gaze Control, Decision Making and Shooting Performance of Elite and Rookie Police Officers." *Human Movement Science* (2012, 31, No. 1): 102-117.

[82] Clare Porac, and Stanley Coren, "The Relationship between Sighting Dominance and the Fading of a Stabilized Retinal Image," *Perception & Psychophysics* (1982, 32): 572.

[83] Patricia Kelsey Minucci and Mary M. Connors, "Reaction Time Under Three Viewing Conditions: Binocular, Dominant Eye and Non-dominant Eye," *Journal at Experimental Psychology* (1964, Vol. 67, No. 3): 271.

[84] Clare Porac, and Stanley Coren, "The Dominant Eye," *Psychological Bulletin* (1976, Vol. 83, No. 5): 890.

[85] Stanley Coren, Sensorimotor Performance as a Function of Eye Dominance and Handedness," *Perceptual Motor Skills* (1999, 88): 424.

Gordon L. Walls, "A Theory of Ocular Dominance," *American Medical Association Archives Ophthalmology* (1951, 45): 404.

[86] Alistair P. Mapp, Hiroshi Ono, and Raphel Barbeito, "What Does the Dominant Eye Dominate?—A Brief and Somewhat Contentious Review," *Percept Psychophys* (2003, 65): 310-311.

Melissa L.Rice, David A. Leske, Christina E. Smestad, and Jonathan M. Holmes, "Results of Ocular Dominance Testing Depend on Assessment Method," *Journal of American Association for Pediatric Ophthalmology and Strabismus* (2008, 12, No. 4): 365-369.

[87] Gordon L. Walls, "A Theory of Ocular Dominance," *American Medical Association Archives Ophthalmology* (1951, 45): 390-391.

[88] A.C. Durand, M.D. and George M. Gould, M.D., "A Method of Determining Ocular Dominance," *Journal of the American Medical Association* (1910, 55): 369–370.

[89] "Clinically, eye dominance evaluated by a hole-in-card test for sighting eye dominance is the most facile investigative tool of eye dominance. However, this test is unable to quantitatively evaluate eye dominance." See Tomoya Handa, Kazuo Mukuno, Hiroshi Uozato, Takahiro Niida, Nobuyuki Shoji, and Kimiya Shimizu, "Effects of Dominant and Nondominant Eyes in Binocular Rivalry," *Optometry & Vision Science* (2004, Vol. 81, Issue 5): 378.

[90] Daniel M. Laby and David G. Kirschen, "Thoughts on Ocular Dominance—Is It Actually a Preference?" *Eye Contact Lens* (May 2011, Vol. 37, No. 3): 141.

[91] Daniel M. Laby and David G. Kirschen, "Thoughts on Ocular Dominance—Is It Actually a Preference?" *Eye Contact Lens* (May 2011, Vol. 37, No. 3): 141.

[92] Clare Porac, and Stanley Coren, "The Relationship between Sighting Dominance and the Fading of a Stabilized Retinal Image," *Perception & Psychophysics* (1982, 32): 572.

[93] Clare Porac, and Stanley Coren, "The Relationship between Sighting Dominance and the Fading of a Stabilized Retinal Image," *Perception & Psychophysics* (1982, 32): 574.

[94] "Now if one is able to maintain mental attention on the front sight, [he or] she will always 'see' the front sight although it will not be in clear focus. See Edward C. Godnig, O.D., "Body Alarm Reaction and Sports Vision," *Journal of Behavioral Optometry* (2001, Vol. 12, No. 1): 4.

[95] Sang Chul Chong, Duje Tadin, and Randolph Blake, "Endogenous Attention Prolongs Dominance Durations in Binocular Rivalry," *Journal of Vision* (2005, 5): 1004-12.

[96] Sagittal Plane: "A longitudinal plane that divides the body of a bilaterally symmetrical animal into right and left sections." See *The American Heritage Dictionary of the English Language Online*, 4th ed., s.v. "sagittal plane," http://www.thefreedictionary.com/sagittal+plane (accessed September 22, 2012).

[97] Clare Porac, and Stanley Coren, "The Dominant Eye," *Psychological Bulletin* (1976, Vol. 83, No. 5): 881.

[98] Gordon L. Walls, "A Theory of Ocular Dominance," *American Medical Association Archives Ophthalmology* (1951, 45): 404.

[99] Gordon L. Walls, "A Theory of Ocular Dominance," *American Medical Association Archives Ophthalmology* (1951, 45): 404.

[100] Gordon L. Walls, "A Theory of Ocular Dominance," *American Medical Association Archives Ophthalmology* (1951, 45): 404.

[101] Dave Anderson, "Two Eyes Good," *American Handgunner*, (March/April 2000): 38.

[102] Peripheral Vision: "Vision produced by light rays falling on areas of the retina beyond the macula. Also called indirect vision." See *The American Heritage Medical Dictionary Online,* s.v. "peripheral vision," http://medical-dictionary.thefreedictionary.com/peripheral+vision (accessed September 22, 2012).

[103] Matt Seibert and Sherrie Seibert, "Insight to Eye Dominance," *The Firearms Instructor*, (2008, Vol. 44): 32.

[104] Clare Porac, and Stanley Coren, "The Dominant Eye," *Psychological Bulletin* (1976, Vol. 83, No. 5): 888.

[105] Analog or Analogue: "An organ or structure that is similar in function to one in another kind of organism but is of dissimilar evolutionary origin. The wings of birds and the wings of insects are analogs." See *The American Heritage Medical Dictionary Online,* s.v. "analog," http://www.thefreedictionary.com/analog (accessed September 22, 2012).

[106] George E. Berner, and Dorothy E. Berner, "Relation of Ocular Dominance, Handedness, and the Controlling Eye in Binocular Vision," *American Medical Association Archives Ophthalmology* (1953, 50): 603-608.

[107] Clare Porac, and Stanley Coren, "The Dominant Eye," *Psychological Bulletin* (1976, Vol. 83, No. 5): 891-892.

[108] Clare Porac, and Stanley Coren, "The Dominant Eye," *Psychological Bulletin* (1976, Vol. 83, No. 5): 891-892.

[109] Brian Enos, *Practical Shooting* (Clifton, CO: Zediker Publishing, 1991), 82.

[110] Central Vision: "Vision produced by light rays falling directly on the fovea centralis of the eye. Also called direct vision." See *The American Heritage Medical Dictionary Online,* s.v. "central vision," http://medical-dictionary.thefreedictionary.com/central+vision (accessed September 22, 2012).

[111] Gordon L. Walls, "A Theory of Ocular Dominance," *American Medical Association Archives Ophthalmology* (1951, 45): 404.

[112] Eric S. Hussey, O.D., FCOVD, "Correcting Intermittent Central Suppression Improves Binocular Marksmanship," *Military Medicine,* (April 2007): 417.

[113] Clare Porac, and Stanley Coren, "The Dominant Eye," *Psychological Bulletin* (1976, Vol. 83, No. 5): 882.

[114] "When confronted with a target, the natural physical reaction is to face the target and push out with the arms." See Headquarters United States Marine Corps, *Pistol Marksmanship MCRP 3-01 B* (Department of the Navy, Washington, D.C., 25 November 2003), 4-5.

[115] "In motor skills learning, research performed at Johns Hopkins University determined that within the first 5-6 hours of practicing a new motor skill, the brain shifts the new instructions into long-term memory." See Valerie J. Atkins, M.S. and William A. Norris, Ph.D., *Survival Score Research Project* (Glynco, GA: Federal Law Enforcement Training Center, April 2004), 15.

[116] National Rifle Association, *Law Enforcement Handgun Instructor Manual* (Fairfax, VA: Section C, The Fundamentals of Handgun Marksmanship , Edition 6.1, 2006), 11.

[117] "Many superior athletes have reported a visual ability of maintaining an awareness of a central target while simultaneously being aware a vast amount of the peripheral visual field. This delicate balance and interplay between central and peripheral awareness is crucial to high level performance in many athletic skills." See See Edward C. Godnig, O.D., "Body Alarm Reaction and Sports Vision," *Journal of Behavioral Optometry* (2001, Vol. 12, No. 1): 3.

[118] National Rifle Association, *Law Enforcement Handgun Instructor Manual* (Fairfax, VA: Section C, The Fundamentals of Handgun Marksmanship , Edition 6.1, 2006), 13.

[119] See Ken Asakawa and Hitoshi Ishikawa, "Binocular Vision and Depth Perception: Development and Disorders," in *Binocular Vision: Development, Depth Perception, and Disorders*, ed. Jacques McCoun, and Lucien Reeves (Hauppauge, NY: Nova Science Publishers, 2009), 140.

[120] Department of the Army, *Combat Training with Pistols, M9 and M11* (Washington, DC June 2003), 2-5.

[121] See Burkhart Fischer, "Development of Saccade Control," in *Binocular Vision: Development, Depth Perception, and Disorders*, ed. Jacques McCoun, and Lucien Reeves (Hauppauge, NY: Nova Science Publishers, 2009), 221.

[122] See Edward C. Godnig, O.D., "Body Alarm Reaction and Sports Vision," *Journal of Behavioral Optometry* (2001, Vol. 12, No. 1): 4.

[123] Joan N. Vickers, *Perception, Cognition, and Decision Training: The Quiet Eye in Action* (Champaign, IL: Human Kinetics, 2007) 57.

[124] "Some marksmen can maintain visual awareness of the front sight even though the eye's focusing system is drawn toward infinity during the BAR." See Edward C. Godnig, O.D., "Body Alarm Reaction and Sports Vision," *Journal of Behavioral Optometry* (2001, Vol. 12, No. 1): 4.

"Now if one is able to maintain mental attention on the front sight, [he or] she will always 'see' the front sight although it will not be in clear focus. See Edward C. Godnig, O.D., "Body Alarm Reaction and Sports Vision," *Journal of Behavioral Optometry* (2001, Vol. 12, No. 1): 4.

"Reality: When in a "lethal force action" your total focus will be on the weapon in the suspects' hands. The sights will both be a slight blur, *but* enough to align and take the shot." See Phil Singleton, *3 Day Tactical Pistol for Hostage Rescue, High Risk Warrant and Drugs Raids,* (Warrenton, VA: Singleton International): 12.

[125] Kevin Loopeker, O.D., FCOVD, e-mail message to author, August 14, 2009.

[126] "The concurrent awareness of the front sight…is possible because of a learned eye-hand-mind coordination relationship. The coordination of the eye, hand, and mind to organize where you are in visual space in relation to other objects develops more strongly as one learns to fine tune these sensory-motor coordinating systems. Experiences in moving through the three dimensional world causes a feedback loop between where your eyes are focusing, where your mind is attending, and where your hand is pointing or touching." See Edward C. Godnig, O.D., "Body Alarm Reaction and Sports Vision," *Journal of Behavioral Optometry* (2001, Vol. 12, No. 1): 4-5.

[127] H. Ripoll, J.P. Papin, J.Y. Guezennec, J.P. Verdy, and M. Philip, Analysis of Visual Scanning Patterns of Pistol Shooters, *Journal of Sports Sciences* (1985, 3): 93-101.

[128] Edward C. Godnig, O.D., "Body Alarm Reaction and Sports Vision," *Journal of Behavioral Optometry* (2001, Vol. 12, No. 1): 3.

[129] Edward C. Godnig, O.D., "Body Alarm Reaction and Sports Vision," *Journal of Behavioral Optometry* (2001, Vol. 12, No. 1): 3.

[130] Bill Rogers, *Be Fast, Be Accurate, Be the Best* (Rogers Shooting School Publications: Jacksonville, FL, 2010), 76.

[131] International Association of Law Enforcement Firearms Instructors, *Standards & Practices Reference Guide for Law Enforcement Firearms Instructors*, (January 1995): 278.

[132] "Some marksmen can maintain visual awareness of the front sight even though the eye's focusing system is drawn toward infinity during the BAR." See Edward C. Godnig, O.D., "Body Alarm Reaction and Sports Vision," *Journal of Behavioral Optometry* (2001, Vol. 12, No. 1): 4.

[133] Edward C. Godnig, O.D., "Body Alarm Reaction and Sports Vision," *Journal of Behavioral Optometry* (2001, Vol. 12, No. 1): 5.

[134] "Assume a shooting posture, visually focus monocularly on where an imaginary front sight would be located (or focus on one fingernail at arm's length straight in front of your line of sight). Then change your fixation and focus to an object more than twenty feet away. Your mind may be aware that your fingernail is located at a distance approximating the end of your arm even though your sight picture is clearly focused on the distant target." See Edward C. Godnig, O.D., "Body Alarm Reaction and Sports Vision," *Journal of Behavioral Optometry* (2001, Vol. 12, No. 1): 5.

[135] Robert K. Taubert, *Rattenkrieg! The Art and Science of Close Quarters Battle Pistol* (North Reading, MA: Saber Press, 2012), 94-97.

[136] Department of the Army, *Combat Training with Pistols, M9 and M11* (Washington, DC June 2003), 2-11.

[137] Paul R. Howe, *The Tactical Trainer* (Bloomington, IN: AuthorHouse, 2009), 27-28.

[138] Department of the Army, *Combat Training with Pistols, M9 and M11* (Washington, DC June 2003), 2-11.

[139] The video shows on Friday, January 6, 2012, Deputy Jeff Nichols and Reserve Deputy Jeremy Conley of Kalamazoo Sheriff's Office in Michigan stopping a vehicle on East Michigan Avenue after it ran a traffic light. When Deputy Nichols approached the driver's side window, shots are fired at him. See Jeff Nichols and Jeremy Conley, *Cop Gets Shot at on Traffic Stop*, YouTube video, uploaded January 19, 2012, http://www.youtube.com/watch?v=w9JbdwHvRZo (accessed September 22, 2012).

[140] Binocular Vision: "Sighting or viewing with both eyes." See International Association of Law Enforcement Firearms Instructors, *Standards & Practices Reference Guide for Law Enforcement Firearms Instructors*, (January 1995): 264.

[141] Dean T. Olson, "Improving Deadly Force Decision Making," *FBI Law Enforcement Bulletin*, (February 1998): 4.

[142] "Many instructors teach a shooting stance with feet shoulder width apart. I prefer an even wider stance with my strong side foot (right foot for me) back so that the toes on my right foot are even with the back of my left heel. This helps me lower my

center of gravity and create a very stable platform while still allowing me to twist at the waist." See Julie Goloski, "The International Association of Defensive Pistol," (Berryville, AR: *Women's Perspective*, Volume 12, Issue 1), http://www.idpa.com/tj.asp?ID=177 (accessed September 22, 2012).

"e) Dynamic Stance[:] The dynamic stance is typically taught for subgun operation but also works well for handguns or shotguns...(3) Strong foot should be slightly back, toe of the strong foot is in line with the heel of the support foot." Endnote: Singleton International, Hostage Rescue Pistol Course, July 1995. See North Carolina Justice Academy, "Specialized Firearms Instructor Training," *Service Handgun: Operation and Use* (Salemburg, NC: July 2010): 27.

"(b) The strong foot should be dropped back slightly, no farther than the toe of the strong side foot aligned with the heel of the support side foot." See North Carolina Justice Academy, "SWAT Operator," *Firearms Use in Tactical Operations* (Salemburg, NC: January 2008): 11

[143] Saul Kirsch, *Thinking Practical Shooting* (ISBN 90-808805-3-1: Double-Alpha Academy, 2005), 21.

[144] Kyle E. Lamb, *Stay in the Fight*, (Trample and Hurdle Publishers, 2011), 24-25.

[145] Kyle E. Lamb, *Stay in the Fight*, (Trample and Hurdle Publishers, 2011), 24-25.

[146] Saul Kirsch, *Thinking Practical Shooting* (ISBN 90-808805-3-1: Double-Alpha Academy, 2005), 21.

[147] Travis Haley, *Make Ready with Travis Haley: Adaptive Handgun* (Columbia, SC: Panteao Productions, 2010): Fundamental 1, Feel, DVD.

[148] Timothy D. Blakeley, "Personal Notes from the Firearms Training Session," *U.S. Marshals Fugitive Investigator's Course*, (Federal Law Enforcement Training Center, Brunswick, GA: 2005): 6.

[149] Brian Enos, *Practical Shooting* (Clifton, CO: Zediker Publishing, 1991), 45-46.

[150] Department of the Army, *Combat Training with Pistols, M9 and M11* (Washington, DC June 2003), 2-4.

[151] Department of the Army, *Combat Training with Pistols, M9 and M11* (Washington, DC June 2003), 2-4.

Brian Enos, *Practical Shooting* (Clifton, CO: Zediker Publishing, 1991), 171.

[152] Arc of Movement: "Also: arc of error. The amount the weapon continues to move while the shooter is attempting to hold it motionless." See International Association of Law Enforcement Firearms Instructors, *Standards & Practices Reference Guide for Law Enforcement Firearms Instructors*, (January 1995): 263.

[153] Force Science Institute, LTD., "Force Science News #134," (Mankato, MN: *How Your Eyes can Cast Your Fate in a Gunfight*, October 9, 2009), http://www.forcescience.org/fsinews/2009/10/force-science-news-134-major-new-

study-how-your-eyes-can-cast-your-fate-in-a-gunfight-part-1/ (accessed September 22, 2012).

[154] Sweet Spot: "The place on a bat, club, racket, or paddle, where it is most effective to hit a ball." See *The American Heritage Dictionary of the English Language Online*, 4th ed., s.v. "sweet spot," http://www.thefreedictionary.com/Sweet+Spot (accessed September 22, 2012).

[155] Lenny Magil Productions, "How to Shoot Fast and Accurately," (San Diego, CA: GunVideo, 1997), *Item #P0001D DVD Video*.

[156] Force Science Institute, LTD., "Point Shooting Clarification," *Force Science News* #135 (October 23, 2009), http://www.forcescience.org/fsinews/2009/10/force-science-news-135-%e2%80%9cpoint-shooting%e2%80%9d-clarification%e2%80%a6plus-what-new-gaze-pattern-findings-mean-for-your-training-more/ (accessed September 22, 2012).

[157] Robert K. Taubert, *Rattenkrieg! The Art and Science of Close Quarters Battle Pistol* (North Reading, MA: Saber Press, 2012), 96.

[158] Bill Rogers, *Be Fast, Be Accurate, Be the Best* (Rogers Shooting School Publications: Jacksonville, FL, 2010), 92.

[159] The Gereshk Chief of Police quoted in the Helmand Messenger, a public newsletter condemned the attack that occurred on 17 March 2008. Haji Abdul Manaf, Chief of Police, Statement Made by District Chief of Gereshk on 18 March 2008, *Helmand Messenger*, Issue 3, page 4.

[160] Eugene Sockut, *Secrets of Street Survival Israeli Style* (Boulder, CO: Paladin Press, 1995), 12.

[161] Robert K. Taubert, *Rattenkrieg! The Art and Science of Close Quarters Battle Pistol* (North Reading, MA: Saber Press, 2012), 96.

[162] Saul Kirsch, *Thinking Practical Shooting* (ISBN 90-808805-3-1: Double-Alpha Academy, 2005), 23.

[163] Kyle E. Lamb, *Stay in the Fight*, (Trample and Hurdle Publishers, 2011), 32.

[164] Douglas A. Knight, "Perfect Practice Makes Perfect," *FBI Law Enforcement Bulletin*, (June 2007): 2.

[165] Muzzle Flip: "Also: barrel whip; muzzle rise is typical directional variety of muzzle flip (which can be in other directions). Movement of the barrel during the projectile's passage through it, caused by the forces of the propelling gas and the kinetic energy developed by the projectile." See International Association of Law Enforcement Firearms Instructors, *Standards & Practices Reference Guide for Law Enforcement Firearms Instructors*, (January 1995): 66.

[166] Saul Kirsch, *Thinking Practical Shooting* (ISBN 90-808805-3-1: Double-Alpha Academy, 2005), 22.

[167] Travis Haley, *Make Ready with Travis Haley: Adaptive Carbine* (Columbia, SC: Panteao Productions, 2010): Intro to Adaptive Shooting, DVD.

[168] Paul Howe, *Make Ready with Paul Howe: Advanced Tac Pistol/Rifle Operator* (Columbia, SC: Panteao Productions, 2010): Dry Fire Practice, DVD.

[169] Glock Inc., *Glock Back Straps*, (Smyrna, GA: 2009): 2.

[170] Glock Inc., "Glock Safe Action Gen4 Pistols," (Smyrna, GA: 2010), http://www.glock.com/downloads/GLOCK_Gen4_en.pdf (accessed September 22, 2012).

[171] Glock Inc., *Glock Back Straps*, (Smyrna, GA: 2009): 2.

[172] Glock Inc., *Glock Pistol Transitional Instructor Workshop Course Outline*, (Smyrna, GA: 2012): 5.

[173] National Rifle Association, *Law Enforcement Handgun Instructor Manual* (Fairfax, VA: Section C, The Fundamentals of Handgun Marksmanship , Edition 6.1, 2006), 5.

[174] Matt Burkett, *Practical Shooting Manual* (Scottsdale, AZ: Hotshots Publishing, 1995), VII-3.

[175] Headquarters United States Marine Corps, *Pistol Marksmanship MCRP 3-01 B* (Department of the Navy, Washington, D.C., 25 November 2003), 3-2.

[176] Department of the Army, *Combat Training with Pistols, M9 and M11* (Washington, DC June 2003), 2-1.

[177] Department of the Army, *Combat Training with Pistols, M9 and M11* (Washington, DC June 2003), 2-8.

[178] J. Henry FitzGerald, *Shooting* (Boulder, CO: Paladin Press, 2007), 362. Originally published in 1930 by J. Henry FitzGerald.

[179] Brian Enos, *Practical Shooting* (Clifton, CO: Zediker Publishing, 1991), 39-43.

[180] Brian Enos, *Practical Shooting* (Clifton, CO: Zediker Publishing, 1991), 42. Robert K. Taubert, *Rattenkrieg! The Art and Science of Close Quarters Battle Pistol* (North Reading, MA: Saber Press, 2012), 69.

[181] Brian Enos, *Practical Shooting* (Clifton, CO: Zediker Publishing, 1991), 43.

[182] Robert K. Taubert, *Rattenkrieg! The Art and Science of Close Quarters Battle Pistol* (North Reading, MA: Saber Press, 2012), 69.

[183] Matt Burkett, *Practical Shooting Manual* (Scottsdale, AZ: Hotshots Publishing, 1995), VII-3. Bill Rogers, *Be Fast, Be Accurate, Be the Best* (Rogers Shooting School Publications: Jacksonville, FL, 2010), 75.

[184] National Rifle Association, *Law Enforcement Handgun Instructor Manual* (Fairfax, VA: Section C, The Fundamentals of Handgun Marksmanship , Edition 6.1, 2006), 6.

[185] Bill Rogers, *Be Fast, Be Accurate, Be the Best* (Rogers Shooting School Publications: Jacksonville, FL, 2010), 75.

[186] Glock Inc., *Instructions for Use Glock Safe Action Pistols All Models*, (Smyrna, GA: March 2011), 1 and 13.

[187] Glock Inc., *Glock Pistol Transitional Instructor Workshop Course Outline*, (Smyrna, GA: 2012): 5.

[188] Bill Rogers, *Be Fast, Be Accurate, Be the Best* (Rogers Shooting School Publications: Jacksonville, FL, 2010), 75.

[189] Glock Inc., *Glock Buyer's Guide Professional Edition*, (Smyrna, GA: Glock Inc., 2012): 39.

[190] "(15) Trigger Guard: The trigger guard shall be large enough to permit firing (double or single action) while wearing heavy gloves or outer gloves and liners, and shall have a recurved front for support by non-firing hand." See Joint Service Small Arms Program, "Study of Issues Concerning the Standardization of Service Handguns," *United States Department of Defense* (June 5, 1980): 6.

[191] "Depending upon the individual firer, he may chose to place the index finger of his non-firing hand on the front of the trigger guard since M9 and M11 pistols have a recurved trigger guard designed for this purpose." See Department of the Army, *Combat Training with Pistols, M9 and M11* (Washington, DC: June 25, 2003), 2-2.

[192] "Note: The M9 pistol has a recurved trigger guard, which allows you to place the index finger of your non-firing hand on the front of the trigger guard if you wish." See Department of the Army, Soldier's Manual of Common Tasks Warrior Skills Level 1 (Washington, DC: June 18, 2009), 3-531.

[193] "The placement of the weak hand in the freestyle grip is where most people make mistakes. First, the fingers should all be under the trigger guard. Your weak hand index finger should never be on the front of the trigger guard." See Matt Burkett, *Practical Shooting Manual* (Scottsdale, AZ: Hotshots Publishing, 1995), VII-3.

"There should be no gaps in the fingers of either hand, and while some shooters like to extend the support hand's index finger to wrap around the front of the trigger guard, I don't think this technique offer as strong a grip. The thumb and index finger are the strongest part of your grip, and when you put on of them up on the trigger guard you've split them apart." Brian Enos, *Practical Shooting* (Clifton, CO: Zediker Publishing, 1991), 42.

"Placing the non-shooting trigger forward to ride on the front of the trigger guard accomplishes nothing. It improves neither recoil control, nor strength, nor accuracy. It lessens the gripping strength of you non-shooting hand, which in turn weakens your entire grip." See Kathy Jackson, *The Cornered Cat: A Woman's Guide to Concealed Carry* (White Feather Press, 2010), 258.

"The index finger of the support hand does NOT wrap around the front of the trigger guard "Hollywood Style" This reduces the available side-to-side grip pressure on the gun, resulting in less control during recoil." See National Rifle Association, *Law Enforcement Handgun Instructor Manual* (Fairfax, VA: Section C, The Fundamentals of Handgun Marksmanship , Edition 6.1, 2006), 4.

"The index finger of the support hand should NOT be placed on the trigger guard." See North Carolina Justice Academy, *Private Protective Services Firearms Training Manual Student 5th Edition* (Salemburg, NC: Module 4 Marksmanship Fundamentals, 1998), 4.

"The forefinger provides much of that grip strength and should be used to increase the clamp pressure on the handgun grip, and not out on the trigger guard." See Bill Rogers, *Be Fast, Be Accurate, Be the Best* (Rogers Shooting School Publications: Jacksonville, FL, 2010), 75.

"While several prominent competitive shooters warp their index finger around the forward edge of the trigger guard, I do not recommend this technique for most people because 1) when the fingers are spread the hand is weak, and 2) there is a tendency for many to "shoot the gun with the support hand," when the only thing that should move is the trigger finger." See Robert K. Taubert, *Rattenkrieg! The Art and Science of Close Quarters Battle Pistol* (North Reading, MA: Saber Press, 2012), 69.

[194] Brian Enos, *Practical Shooting* (Clifton, CO: Zediker Publishing, 1991), 41.

[195] Headquarters United States Marine Corps, *Pistol Marksmanship MCRP 3-01 B* (Department of the Navy, Washington, D.C., 25 November 2003), 5-4.

[196] Phil Motzer, *Kelly McCann's Crucible High-risk Environment Training Volume Five: Exploding Handgun Myths*, (Boulder, CO: Paladin Press, 2009): Grip, DVD.

Bill Rogers, *Make Ready with Bill Rogers: Reactive Pistol Shooting* (Columbia, SC: Panteao Productions, 2010): Dominant Eye, Grip, and Stance, DVD.

[197] Phil Motzer, *Kelly McCann's Crucible High-risk Environment Training Volume Five: Exploding Handgun Myths*, (Boulder, CO: Paladin Press, 2009): Grip, DVD.

[198] Rob Leatham, *Rob Leatham on Pistol Shooting*, interviewed by a representative from GunsForSale.com, YouTube video, uploaded May 20, 2011, http://www.youtube.com/watch?v=CqqhSSiU_j8, (accessed September 22, 2012).

[199] "Neutrality is both pressure and position in your hands." See Brian Enos, *Practical Shooting* (Clifton, CO: Zediker Publishing, 1991), 43.

"Both hands contribute equally to holding the firearm securely. Although many target and competition shooters have discovered that keeping the firing hand relaxed improves precision accuracy, you want to mimic the type of muscle tension produced under extreme stress." See Kathy Jackson, *The Cornered Cat: A Woman's Guide to Concealed Carry* (White Feather Press, 2010), 257.

"I know a 100 percent and a 100 percent works for me," said Travis Haley. See Magpul Dynamics, *The Art of the Dynamic Handgun* (Columbia, SC: Panteao Productions, 2009): Disc 1, Chapter 6, Seven Fundamentals, Grip, DVD.

"Rely on the brain's default mechanisms and stop making things so complicated. I was told, some years ago, to apply a 70/30 support and strong hand grip ration to my pistol. 'Huh?' What if I've got a 60/40? Will I be a soup sandwich? Just grip it to control the recoil would you please." See Patrick McNamara, *T.A.P.S. Tactical Application of Practical Shooting* (Bloomington, IN: iUniverse), 7.

"If you have applied equal force to the handgun with each hand and arm, the handgun will recoil in a uniform pattern." See Bill Rogers, *Be Fast, Be Accurate, Be the Best* (Rogers Shooting School Publications: Jacksonville, FL, 2010), 93.

[200] Julie Golob, *Shoot: Your Guide to Shooting and Competition* (New York, NY: Skyhorse Publishing, 2012), 174.

[201] "Some have found that locking their elbows straight while shooting helps them to control recoil. Though it may work for these shooters, I strongly discourage it because of the stress it places on the elbow joints, and in turn may lead to injury." See Julie Goloski, "The International Association of Defensive Pistol," (Berryville, AR: *Women's Perspective*, Volume 12, Issue 1), http://www.idpa.com/tj.asp?ID=177 (accessed September 22, 2012).

[202] Magpul Dynamics, *The Art of the Dynamic Handgun* (Columbia, SC: Panteao Productions, 2009): Disc 1, Chapter 6, Seven Fundamentals, Grip, DVD.

[203] Travis Haley, *Make Ready with Travis Haley: Adaptive Handgun* (Columbia, SC: Panteao Productions, 2010): The Fundamental 3, Feel, DVD.

[204] Robert Vogel, *Make Ready with Bob Vogel: Building World Class Pistol Skills* (Columbia, SC: Panteao Productions, 2010): Grip, DVD.

[205] Brian Enos, *Practical Shooting* (Clifton, CO: Zediker Publishing, 1991), 44-45.

[206] Brian Enos, *Practical Shooting* (Clifton, CO: Zediker Publishing, 1991), 45.

[207] Kyle E. Lamb, *Stay in the Fight*, (Trample and Hurdle Publishers, 2011), 19.

[208] Biomechanics: "The study of the mechanics of a living body, especially of the forces exerted by muscles and gravity on the skeletal structure." See *The American Heritage Dictionary of the English Language Online*, s.v. "biomechanics," http://www.thefreedictionary.com/Biomechanics (accessed September 22, 2012).

[209] Robert K. Taubert, *Rattenkrieg! The Art and Science of Close Quarters Battle Pistol* (North Reading, MA: Saber Press, 2012), 72.

[210] Julie Goloski said, "I shoot 9mm so much faster than I can shoot a .40, and I drop a lot fewer points." See Robin Taylor, Bobby Carver, and Mark Passamaneck, *The Glock in Competition*, (Bellingham, WA: Taylor Press, 2010): 238.

[211] Magpul Dynamics, *The Art of the Dynamic Handgun* (Columbia, SC: Panteao Productions, 2009): Disc 1, Chapter 6, Seven Fundamentals, Stance, DVD.

[212] Department of the Army, *Combat Training with Pistols, M9 and M11* (Washington, DC June 2003), 2-4.

Rex Applegate, *Kill or Get Killed* (Boulder CO: Paladin Press, 1976), 145.

[213] Department of the Army, *Combat Training with Pistols, M9 and M11* (Washington, DC June 2003), 2-4.

[214] Matt Burkett, *Practical Shooting Manual* (Scottsdale, AZ: Hotshots Publishing, 1995), VII-4.

[215] Phil Motzer, *Kelly McCann's Crucible High-risk Environment Training Volume Five: Exploding Handgun Myths*, (Boulder, CO: Paladin Press, 2009): Grip, DVD.

[216] Phil Motzer, *Kelly McCann's Crucible High-risk Environment Training Volume Five: Exploding Handgun Myths*, (Boulder, CO: Paladin Press, 2009): Grip, DVD.

[217] National Rifle Association, *Law Enforcement Handgun Instructor Manual* (Fairfax, VA: Section C, The Fundamentals of Handgun Marksmanship , Edition 6.1, 2006), 5.

Robert K. Taubert, *Rattenkrieg! The Art and Science of Close Quarters Battle Pistol* (North Reading, MA: Saber Press, 2012), 72.

[218] International Association of Law Enforcement Firearms Instructors, *Standards & Practices Reference Guide for Law Enforcement Firearms Instructors*, (January 1995): 282-283.

[219] National Rifle Association of America, *NRA Guide to the Basics of Pistol Shooting* (Fairfax, VA: The National Rifle Association of America, 2009), 66.

[220] Sight Picture: "The appearance of a firearm's sight or sights to the shooter's eye as aligned against a target; the picture formed in the shooter's conscious visual field by the sights as aligned against the background of an intended target." See International Association of Law Enforcement Firearms Instructors, *Standards & Practices Reference Guide for Law Enforcement Firearms Instructors*, (January 1995): 283.

[221] National Rifle Association, *Law Enforcement Handgun Instructor Manual* (Fairfax, VA: Section C, The Fundamentals of Handgun Marksmanship , Edition 6.1, 2006), 13.

[222] Erik Lawrence, *Tactical Pistol Shooting*, (Lola, WI: Gun Digest Books, 2005), 59.

[223] International Association of Law Enforcement Firearms Instructors, *Standards & Practices Reference Guide for Law Enforcement Firearms Instructors*, (January 1995): 283.

[224] Department of the Army, *Combat Training with Pistols, M9 and M11* (Washington, DC June 2003), 2-14.

[225] Robin Taylor, Bobby Carver, and Mark Passamaneck, *The Glock in Competition*, (Bellingham, WA: Taylor Press, 2010): 229-230.

[226] Breath Control: "Also: breathing control. To exercise proper control of the breath during the aiming and firing process, so as to minimize disturbance of aim." See International Association of Law Enforcement Firearms Instructors, *Standards & Practices Reference Guide for Law Enforcement Firearms Instructors*, (January 1995): 264.

National Rifle Association of America, *NRA Guide to the Basics of Pistol Shooting* (Fairfax, VA: The National Rifle Association of America, 2009), 67.

[227] Alexis Artwohl, Ph.D., "Perceptual and Memory Distortion During Officer-Involved Shootings," *FBI Law Enforcement Bulletin*, (October 2002): 23.

Dean T. Olson, "Improving Deadly Force Decision Making," *FBI Law Enforcement Bulletin*, (February 1998): 8.

[228] Navy and Marine Corps Public Health Center, "Combat Breathing," (Portsmouth, VA: *Combat Breathing*), http://www.nmcphc.med.navy.mil/downloads/stress/Combat_Breathing.ppt (accessed September 22, 2012).

[229] See Edward C. Godnig, O.D., "Body Alarm Reaction and Sports Vision," *Journal of Behavioral Optometry* (2001, Vol. 12, No. 1): 5.

[230] PoliceOne.com News, "How Combat Breathing Saved My Life," (San Francisco, CA: *Submitted by: Tricia Kennedy, Greenwich Police Department, Greenwich, CT,* 2011), http://www.policemag.com/Blog/Women-in-Law-Enforcement/Story/2011/03/Combat-Breathing-Saved-My-Life.aspx?ref=OnTarget-Thursday-20110310 (accessed September 22, 2012).

[231] Jeff Gonzales, *Combative Fundamentals, an Unconventional Approach* (Cedar Park, TX: Trident Concepts, LLC, 2002), 198.

[232] Magpul Dynamics, *The Art of the Dynamic Handgun* (Columbia, SC: Panteao Productions, 2009): Disc 1, Chapter 6, Seven Fundamentals, Breathing, DVD.

[233] Saul Kirsch, *Thinking Practical Shooting* (ISBN 90-808805-3-1: Double-Alpha Academy, 2005), 14.

[234] Magpul Dynamics, *The Art of the Dynamic Handgun* (Columbia, SC: Panteao Productions, 2009): Disc 1, Chapter 6, Seven Fundamentals, Breathing, DVD.

[235] International Association of Law Enforcement Firearms Instructors, *Standards & Practices Reference Guide for Law Enforcement Firearms Instructors*, (January 1995): 293.

[236] Dave Sevigny said, "One method is to come off the front of the trigger face after each shot, otherwise known as 'slapping' the trigger. The second way brings the trigger just far enough forward to reset the trigger. For optimum trigger speed and

accuracy, I prefer the reset technique." See Dave Anderson, "Glocken Triggers and Sevigny's Secrets," *American Handgunner*, May/June 2005, 38.

[237] "The 'slap' is most used by Rob Leatham. If you watch a video of Rob you will notice his finger coming completely off the trigger then smacking back against the trigger in one smooth motion." See Matt Burkett, *Practical Shooting Manual* (Scottsdale, AZ: Hotshots Publishing, 1995), VII-24.

[238] "Release to about a 90...you are not going to feel or hear that click people talk about." See Phil Motzer, *Crucible High-risk Environment Training II Volume 4: Combat Handgun*, (Boulder, CO: Paladin Press, 2010): Trigger Manipulation, DVD.

[239] "It is designed to fire one round each time the trigger is pulled." See Headquarters United States Marine Corps, *Pistol Marksmanship MCRP 3-01 B* (Department of the Navy, Washington, D.C., 25 November 2003), 1-1.

"Press the magazine release button and let the empty magazine fall to the deck." See Headquarters United States Marine Corps, *Pistol Marksmanship MCRP 3-01 B* (Department of the Navy, Washington, D.C., 25 November 2003), 2-9.

[240] A Glock trigger has an initial springy feel (slack) that is referred to as pretravel. Then it hits an engagement (trigger bar in contact with the firing pin lug) where there is resistance, which is overcome with some pressure. Overtravel is the rearward motion after the firing pin is released.

[241] Timothy D. Blakeley, "Personal Notes from the Firearms Training Session," *U.S. Marshals Fugitive Investigator's Course* Center, Brunswick, GA: 2005): 6.

[242] "Because if you're shooting really quick, you're never going to feel that trigger reset." See Rob Leatham, *Rob Leatham on Pistol Shooting*, interviewed by a representative from GunsForSale.com, YouTube video, uploaded May 20, 2011, http://www.youtube.com/watch?v=CqqhSSiU_j8, (accessed September 22, 2012).

[243] "What you do with your trigger does not matter as long as you don't disturb gun alignment." See Robert K. Taubert, *Rattenkrieg! The Art and Science of Close Quarters Battle Pistol* (North Reading, MA: Saber Press, 2012), 78.

[244] Phil Motzer, *Crucible High-risk Environment Training II Volume 4: Combat Handgun*, (Boulder, CO: Paladin Press, 2010): Fire, DVD 1.

[245] "Those of us that come off the trigger on fast shots do so without trying. The focus is not to come off the trigger, but to ensure that the trigger has reset." See Rob Leatham, "Questions and Answers," (Mesa, AZ: *Shooting Mechanics*, September 10, 2004), http://www.robleatham.com/answers040910.htm#top (accessed March 2010).

[246] National Rifle Association, *Law Enforcement Handgun Instructor Manual* (Fairfax, VA: 2006), Section C, The Fundamentals of Handgun Marksmanship, Edition 6.1, 16.

[247] Glock Inc., *Instructions for Use Glock Safe Action Pistols All Models*, (Smyrna, GA: March 2011), 11.

[248] International Association of Law Enforcement Firearms Instructors, *Standards & Practices Reference Guide for Law Enforcement Firearms Instructors*, (January 1995): 95.

[249] "Again, I don't want to lose the trigger. I want to stay in contact. At my school, I teach a full reset, which means I don't do a short reset on that trigger. That short reset is perishable and I see a lot of folks doing a double-tap—losing a round. So I do a full reset." See Paul Howe, *Make Ready with Paul Howe: Advanced Tac Pistol/Rifle Operator* (Columbia, SC: Panteao Productions, 2010): Line Drill, DVD.

[250] Kathy Jackson, *The Cornered Cat: A Woman's Guide to Concealed Carry* (White Feather Press, 2010), 254.

[251] "Your finger will fall on the trigger where it will. There is no perfect position. The position that will work best for you depends partially on your grip and the length of your finger." See Brian Enos, *Practical Shooting* (Clifton, CO: Zediker Publishing, 1991), 43.

"Placement of the finger should be natural and allow free movement of the trigger finger. A natural trigger finger placement allows the trigger to be moved straight to the rear while maintaining sight alignment." See U.S. Marine Corps, *Pistol Marksmanship* (Albany, GA: November 2003), 3-3.

[252] Phil Motzer, *Kelly McCann's Crucible High-risk Environment Training Volume Five: Exploding Handgun Myths*, (Boulder, CO: Paladin Press, 2009): Trigger Manipulation, DVD.

[253] "I have always taught students to have a little daylight between the frame of the gun and your finger, so they will not apply lateral pressure to the gun when the[y] function the trigger. However, Rob Leatham disputes that and says it does not really matter." See Robert K. Taubert, *Rattenkrieg! The Art and Science of Close Quarters Battle Pistol* (North Reading, MA: Saber Press, 2012), 78.

[254] Phil Motzer, *Kelly McCann's Crucible High-risk Environment Training Volume Five: Exploding Handgun Myths*, (Boulder, CO: Paladin Press, 2009): Trigger Manipulation, DVD.

[255] "I prefer to know exactly when it [pistol] goes off [fires]…After your shooting skills have been developed to a high level, it's difficult to get a surprise break. You know what the hammer and sear relationship feels like." See Matt Burkett, *Practical Shooting Manual* (Scottsdale, AZ: Hotshots Publishing, 1995), VII-23.

"Now what you will notice is that a lot of shooters will tell you or a lot of schools will tell you that the shot should surprise you. Let me tell you what, if you are coming in to rescue my family that shot should not surprise you. You should know right when that shot is about to break," said Chris Costa. See Magpul Dynamics, *The Art of the Dynamic Handgun* (Columbia, SC: Panteao Productions, 2009): Disc 1, Chapter 6, Seven Fundamentals, Trigger Control, DVD.

When using the trapping technique against an adversary "...the firer must know precisely when the weapon is going to fire." See Department of the Army, *Rifle Marksmanship M16-/M4-Series Weapons* (Washington, DC: August 2008), 7-41.

"Many of our experts have advanced the theory that they do not know or do not want to know just when the hammer is released. I cannot agree with this as I want to know, and do know, when the hammer is released." See J. Henry FitzGerald, *Shooting* (Boulder, CO: Paladin Press, 2007), 49. Originally published in 1930 by J. Henry FitzGerald.

"If anyone ever tells you let it be a surprise shot—you can shut down right there. I don't pull this weapon out expecting it to surprise me when I pull the trigger. I know I am pulling the trigger. I know I am trying to stop a threat. So, I am not looking for surprises there. I was already surprised and that is why I had to get it out. So, we need to get that kind of terminology out of our head and we need to stop that myth of—if you let it be a surprise shot you can't anticipate it. It's bull, and it's not the way to train for operating in the real world and trying to save yourself." See Phil Motzer, *Crucible High-risk Environment Training II Volume 4: Combat Handgun*, (Boulder, CO: Paladin Press, 2010): Trigger Manipulation, DVD.

"We do not press-press-press the trigger and there is no such thing as a surprise break. Our subconscious mind knows within a few milliseconds of when the shot will fire because it is perfectly timing the shot." See Bill Rogers, *Be Fast, Be Accurate, Be the Best* (Rogers Shooting School Publications: Jacksonville, FL, 2010), 80.

[256] International Association of Law Enforcement Firearms Instructors, *Standards & Practices Reference Guide for Law Enforcement Firearms Instructors*, (January 1995): 267-268.

[257] Bill Rogers, *Be Fast, Be Accurate, Be the Best* (Rogers Shooting School Publications: Jacksonville, FL, 2010), 80.

[258] Department of Justice, *Violent Encounters*, 2006, (Washington, DC: FBI, 2006), 47.

[259] U.S. Department of Justice, *Violent Encounters*, 2006, (Washington, DC: FBI, 2006), 127.

[260] Bill Rogers, *Be Fast, Be Accurate, Be the Best* (Rogers Shooting School Publications: Jacksonville, FL, 2010), 82.

[261] National Rifle Association, *Law Enforcement Handgun Instructor Manual* (Fairfax, VA: Handgun Handling Techniques, Edition 6.1, 2006), 5.

[262] In the Line of Duty, "(OH) Kehoe Brother's Shoot-Out," *Volume 4 Program 8 Video*.

Lenny Magil Productions, "Move! Shoot! Live!," (San Diego, CA: GunVideo, 1997), *Item #X0172D DVD Video*.

[263] Bill Rogers, *Be Fast, Be Accurate, Be the Best* (Rogers Shooting School Publications: Jacksonville, FL, 2010), 101.

[264] Travis Haley, *Make Ready with Travis Haley: Adaptive Handgun* (Columbia, SC: Panteao Productions, 2010): The Draw, DVD.

[265] Keeping the non-firing hand open and the fingers loosely spread will provide a stronger grip as the hands join. See Matt Burkett, *Practical Shooting Manual* (Scottsdale, AZ: Hotshots Publishing, 1995), VII-33.

[266] Robert K. Taubert, *Rattenkrieg! The Art and Science of Close Quarters Battle Pistol* (North Reading, MA: Saber Press, 2012), 117.

[267] Robert K. Taubert, *Rattenkrieg! The Art and Science of Close Quarters Battle Pistol* (North Reading, MA: Saber Press, 2012), 117.

[268] National Rifle Association, *Law Enforcement Handgun Instructor Manual* (Fairfax, VA: Handgun Handling Techniques, Edition 6.1, 2006), 3.

[269] Matt Burkett, *Practical Shooting Manual* (Scottsdale, AZ: Hotshots Publishing, 1995), VII-33.

[270] Matt Burkett, "Practical Shooting Volume 4," (Scottsdale, AZ: How to Shoot Faster!, 2003), DVD Video.

[271] Glock Inc., *Glock Pistol Transitional Instructor Workshop Course Outline*, (Smyrna, GA: 2012): 5.

[272] Matt Burkett, *Practical Shooting Manual* (Scottsdale, AZ: Hotshots Publishing, 1995), VII-31.

[273] Glock Inc., *Glock Pistol Transitional Instructor Workshop Course Outline*, (Smyrna, GA: 2012): 5.

[274] Shoulder Holster: "A suspension system or harness that goes over the strong-side shoulder and across the officer's [or civilian's] back positioning the holster below the armpit of the support hand side. Shoulder holsters include vertical carry (muzzle pointed downward), horizontal carry (muzzle pointed rearward) and upside-down carry (muzzle pointed upward)." See International Association of Law Enforcement Firearms Instructors, *Standards & Practices Reference Guide for Law Enforcement Firearms Instructors*, (January 1995): 215.

[275] Cross-Draw Holster: "A holster designed to be worn at the waist on the opposite side from the shooting hand. To draw, the shooting hand crosses the body to grip the firearm. Cross-draw holsters are popular for plainclothes wear and for transporting prisoners." See International Association of Law Enforcement Firearms

Instructors, *Standards & Practices Reference Guide for Law Enforcement Firearms Instructors*, (January 1995): 214.

[276] Kathy Jackson, *The Cornered Cat: A Woman's Guide to Concealed Carry* (White Feather Press, 2010), 86.

[277] Glock Inc., *Glock Pistol Transitional Instructor Workshop Course Outline*, (Smyrna, GA: 2012): 5.

[278] Travis Haley, *Make Ready with Travis Haley: Adaptive Handgun* (Columbia, SC: Panteao Productions, 2010): The Draw, DVD.

[279] Timothy D. Blakeley, "Personal Notes from the Firearms Training Session," *U.S. Marshals Fugitive Investigator's Course,* (Federal Law Enforcement Training Center, Brunswick, GA: 2005): 6.

Glock Inc., *Glock Pistol Transitional Instructor Workshop Course Outline*, (Smyrna, GA: 2012): 5.

[280] Out of Battery: "A firearm is said to be out of battery when the breeching mechanism is not in a proper position for firing. The condition of a firearm in which the breech mechanism is not sufficiently closed to safely support the cartridge or seal the action for firing." See International Association of Law Enforcement Firearms Instructors, *Standards & Practices Reference Guide for Law Enforcement Firearms Instructors*, (January 1995): 275.

[281] Glock Inc., *Glock Pistol Transitional Instructor Workshop Course Outline*, (Smyrna, GA: 2012): 5.

National Rifle Association, *Law Enforcement Handgun Instructor Manual* (Fairfax, VA: Handgun Handling Techniques, Edition 6.1, 2006), 6.

[282] In the Line of Duty, "Trooper Coates Shooting," *Volume 1 Program 4*: DVD.

[283] Interview with police adviser while at the Kandahar Regional Training Center in Afghanistan, author first heard the term 5s-by-25s, 2008.

[284] Urey W. Patrick, and John C. Hall, *In Defense of Self and Others* (Durham, NC: Carolina Academic Press, 2010), 165.

[285] Grip: "The portion of a firearm designed to be grasped by the shooting hand in normal operation. In handguns: the handle for holding the weapon in the shooting hand; also, a panel or covering attached to or enveloping the grip frame." See International Association of Law Enforcement Firearms Instructors, *Standards & Practices Reference Guide for Law Enforcement Firearms Instructors*, (January 1995): 50.

[286] Wendy Kierstead, *Law Enforcement Safety Handbook*, (Brunswick, ME: Burnswick Police Department, 2006): 64.

[287] Sergeant Chris Hice of the Rialto Police Department in California by telephone with the author, February 21, 2012, confirmed the pistol as a Smith & Wesson Sigma.

Wendy Kierstead, *Law Enforcement Safety Handbook*, (Brunswick, ME: Burnswick Police Department, 2006): 64.

[288] Photograph courtesy of Wendy Kierstead. See Wendy Kierstead, *Law Enforcement Safety Handbook*, (Brunswick, ME: Burnswick Police Department, 2006): 64.

[289] Kathy Jackson, *The Cornered Cat: A Woman's Guide to Concealed Carry* (White Feather Press, 2010), 87.

[290] The Concealment Shop, Inc., "Holstered Handbags," *Feminine Protection Handbags*, http://www.theconcealmentshop.com/Handbags.php (accessed September 22, 2012).

[291] U.S. Marine Corps, *Pistol Marksmanship* (Albany, GA: November 2003), 2-15 and 2-16.

[292] National Rifle Association, *Law Enforcement Handgun Instructor Manual* (Fairfax, VA: Handgun Handling Techniques, Edition 6.1, 2006), 9.

[293] Department of the Army, *Rifle Marksmanship M16-/M4-Series Weapons* (Washington, DC: August 2008), 7-43.

U.S. Marine Corps, *Rifle Marksmanship* (Albany, GA: March 2001), 3-9 – 3-10.

[294] National Rifle Association, *Law Enforcement Handgun Instructor Manual* (Fairfax, VA: Handgun Handling Techniques, Edition 6.1, 2006), 8.

[295] International Association of Law Enforcement Firearms Instructors, *Standards & Practices Reference Guide for Law Enforcement Firearms Instructors*, (January 1995): 244-145.

[296] International Association of Law Enforcement Firearms Instructors, *Standards & Practices Reference Guide for Law Enforcement Firearms Instructors*, (January 1995): 244.

[297] Robert K. Taubert, *Rattenkrieg! The Art and Science of Close Quarters Battle Pistol* (North Reading, MA: Saber Press, 2012), 103.

[298] International Association of Law Enforcement Firearms Instructors, *Standards & Practices Reference Guide for Law Enforcement Firearms Instructors*, (January 1995): 244-145.

[299] International Association of Law Enforcement Firearms Instructors, *Standards & Practices Reference Guide for Law Enforcement Firearms Instructors*, (January 1995): 244-145.

[300] Phil Singleton, *3 Day Tactical Pistol for Hostage Rescue, High Risk Warrant and Drugs Raids*, (Warrenton, VA: Singleton International): 38.

[301] Phil Singleton, *3 Day Tactical Pistol for Hostage Rescue, High Risk Warrant and Drugs Raids*, (Warrenton, VA: Singleton International): 18.

[302] Robert K. Taubert, *Rattenkrieg! The Art and Science of Close Quarters Battle Pistol* (North Reading, MA: Saber Press, 2012), 99.

[303] Steve Anderson, *Refinement and Repetition: Dry Fire Drills for Dramatic Improvement* (Steve Anderson, 2003), 8.

[304] Paul R. Howe, *The Tactical Trainer* (Bloomington, IN: AuthorHouse, 2009), 94.

[305] Dean T. Olson, "Improving Deadly Force Decision Making," *FBI Law Enforcement Bulletin*, (February 1998): 8.

[306] Department of the Army, *Combat Training with Pistols, M9 and M11* (Washington, DC June 2003), 2-21.

[307] Department of the Army, *Combat Training with Pistols, M9 and M11* (Washington, DC June 2003), 2-21.

Erik Lawrence, *Tactical Pistol Shooting*, (Lola, WI: Gun Digest Books, 2005), 93.

[308] Phil Singleton, *3 Day Tactical Pistol for Hostage Rescue, High Risk Warrant and Drugs Raids,* (Warrenton, VA: Singleton International): 31.

[309] The instructor had participated in Operation Nimrod in 1980 in which he stormed the Iranian Embassy. See Phil Singleton, *3 Day Tactical Pistol for Hostage Rescue, High Risk Warrant and Drugs Raids,* (Warrenton, VA: Singleton International): 30.

[310] Phil Motzer, *Crucible High-risk Environment Training II Volume 4: Combat Handgun*, (Boulder, CO: Paladin Press, 2010): Reload, DVD.

[311] Jeff Gonzales, *Combative Fundamentals, an Unconventional Approach* (Cedar Park, TX: Trident Concepts, LLC, 2002), 63.

[312] Phil Motzer, *Crucible High-risk Environment Training II Volume 4: Combat Handgun*, (Boulder, CO: Paladin Press, 2010): Manipulation / Remove, DVD.

[313] Jeff Gonzales, *Combative Fundamentals, an Unconventional Approach* (Cedar Park, TX: Trident Concepts, LLC, 2002), 63.

[314] "Current magazine tubes have a four-sided metal liner that usually falls free from the receiver when the magazine catch is depressed." See Glock Inc., *Armorer's Manual*, (Smyrna, GA: 2009): 61. Operators cannot depend on *"usually falls free"* when reloading. Operators must depend on *always* when reloading. An operator that strips the magazine from the receiver will always have an empty magazine well to insert the replacement magazine.

[315] Underhand Technique: The pistol in an upright position is rotated 45 degrees toward the ground and the non-firing hand's pad and fingertips grasp the slide pulling rearward until the slide is stripped from the non-firing hand.

[316] Glock Inc., *Glock Buyer's Guide Professional Edition*, (Smyrna, GA: Glock Inc., 2012): 39.

[317] Matt Burkett, *Practical Shooting Manual* (Scottsdale, AZ: Hotshots Publishing, 1995), VII-45.

Brian Enos, *Practical Shooting* (Clifton, CO: Zediker Publishing, 1991), 56.

National Rifle Association, *Law Enforcement Handgun Instructor Manual* (Fairfax, VA: Handgun Handling Techniques, Edition 6.1, 2006), 16.

[318] Travis Haley, *Make Ready with Travis Haley: Adaptive Handgun* (Columbia, SC: Panteao Productions, 2010): Tactical Reload, DVD.

[319] U.S. Marine Corps, *Pistol Marksmanship* (Albany, GA: November 2003), 2-9.

[320] National Rifle Association, *Law Enforcement Handgun Instructor Manual* (Fairfax, VA: Handgun Handling, Edition 6.1, 2006), 18.

[321] Jeff Gonzales, *Combative Fundamentals, an Unconventional Approach* (Cedar Park, TX: Trident Concepts, LLC, 2002), 60.

[322] Ring's Manufacturing, ""Home," *Blueguns,* http://www.blueguns.com/default.asp? (accessed September 22, 2012).

[323] U.S. Department of Justice, *Violent Encounters*, 2006, (Washington, DC: FBI, 2006), 105.

[324] National Rifle Association, *Law Enforcement Handgun Instructor Manual* (Fairfax, VA: Handgun Handling Techniques, Edition 6.1, 2006), 13.

[325] Brian Enos, *Practical Shooting* (Clifton, CO: Zediker Publishing, 1991), 58.

North Carolina Justice Academy, *Private Protective Services Firearms Training Manual Student 5th Edition* (Salemburg, NC: Module 5 Night Firing, 1998), 3.

[326] U.S. Department of Justice, *Violent Encounters*, 2006, (Washington, DC: FBI, 2006), 104-105.

[327] "A stoppage is an unintentional interruption in the cycle of operation; e.g., the slide not moving forward completely. A stoppage is normally discovered when the pistol will not fire. Most stoppages can be prevented by proper care, cleaning, and lubrication of the pistol." See U.S. Marine Corps, *Pistol Marksmanship* (Albany, GA: November 2003), 2-13.

[328] "Malfunction: "Failure of a firearm to function as designed because of a mechanical defect or malfunction, as opposed to a stoppage caused by shooter error." See International Association of Law Enforcement Firearms Instructors, *Standards & Practices Reference Guide for Law Enforcement Firearms Instructors*, (January 1995): 273.

[329] "A malfunction is a failure of the pistol to fire satisfactorily or to perform as designed (e.g., a broken front sight that does not affect the functioning of the pistol). A malfunction does not necessarily cause an interruption in the cycle of operation. When a malfunction occurs, the pistol must be repaired by an armorer." See U.S. Marine Corps, *Pistol Marksmanship* (Albany, GA: November 2003), 2-13.

[330] National Rifle Association, *Law Enforcement Handgun Instructor Manual* (Fairfax, VA: Handgun Handling Techniques, Edition 6.1, 2006), 27.

[331] Alan Ramsey, Director of Training for Glock provided the information during the Advance Armorer's course held at Glock Inc., in Smyrna, Georgia, in a face-to-face conversation with the author, January 26-27, 2010.

[332] Robin Taylor, Bobby Carver, and Mark Passamaneck, *The Glock in Competition*, (Bellingham, WA: Taylor Press, 2010): 106-107.

[333] Glock Inc., *Glock Professional*, (Smyrna, GA: 2012): DVD PowerPoint Slide 114.

[334] Double Feed: "Double feeds (the releasing of two rounds at once from the magazine) are typically caused by damaged or improperly dimensioned magazine lips (weapon malfunction) or, in weapons with tubular magazines, a faulty cartridge interrupter (weapon malfunction). See International Association of Law Enforcement Firearms Instructors, *Standards & Practices Reference Guide for Law Enforcement Firearms Instructors*, (January 1995): 287.

[335] National Rifle Association, *Law Enforcement Handgun Instructor Manual* (Fairfax, VA: Handgun Handling Techniques, Edition 6.1, 2006), 28.

Phil Motzer, *Crucible High-risk Environment Training II Volume 4: Combat Handgun*, (Boulder, CO: Paladin Press, 2010): Remedial Action, DVD.

[336] Glock Inc., *Instructions for Use Glock Safe Action Pistols All Models*, (Smyrna, GA: March 2011), 31.

Battery: "Also in battery. The condition in which the breech of the action is fully closed in proper position for firing. If firing occurs with the breech not fully closed, the firearm is said to have fired out of battery." See International Association of Law Enforcement Firearms Instructors, *Standards & Practices Reference Guide for Law Enforcement Firearms Instructors*, (January 1995): 263.

[337] Glock Inc., *Glock Pistol Transitional Instructor Workshop Course Outline*, (Smyrna, GA: 2012): 7.

Phil Motzer, *Crucible High-risk Environment Training II Volume 4: Combat Handgun*, (Boulder, CO: Paladin Press, 2010): Immediate Action, DVD.

[338] "...the fact that there is no need to look at the weapon to apply the procedure, and consequently the fact that it works as well in the dark as in the daylight." See International Association of Law Enforcement Firearms Instructors, *Standards & Practices Reference Guide for Law Enforcement Firearms Instructors*, (January 1995): 289.

[339] Glock Inc., Glock *Instructor Workshop*, (Smyrna, GA: 2012): 7.

U.S. Department of Justice, *Violent Encounters*, 2006, (Washington, DC: FBI, 2006), 103.

[340] Robert K. Taubert, *Rattenkrieg! The Art and Science of Close Quarters Battle Pistol* (North Reading, MA: Saber Press, 2012), 66.

[341] Jeff Gonzales, *Combative Fundamentals, an Unconventional Approach* (Cedar Park, TX: Trident Concepts, LLC, 2002), 105.

[342] Jeff Gonzales, *Combative Fundamentals, an Unconventional Approach* (Cedar Park, TX: Trident Concepts, LLC, 2002), 105.

[343] International Association of Law Enforcement Firearms Instructors, *Standards & Practices Reference Guide for Law Enforcement Firearms Instructors*, (January 1995): 289.

[344] International Association of Law Enforcement Firearms Instructors, *Standards & Practices Reference Guide for Law Enforcement Firearms Instructors*, (January 1995): 289.

[345] Phil Singleton, *3 Day Tactical Pistol for Hostage Rescue, High Risk Warrant and Drugs Raids,* (Warrenton, VA: Singleton International): 37.

[346] "In the Overhand method, the Support Hand's four finger wrap over the top of the slide with the ejection port facing away from the body." See National Rifle Association, *Law Enforcement Handgun Instructor Manual* (Fairfax, VA: Handgun Handling Techniques, Edition 6.1, 2006), 16.

[347] Precision Gun Specialties, "Product Overview," *Saf-T-Trainers,* http://www.precisiongunspecialties.com/strainer-main.html (accessed September 22, 2012).

[348] Glock Inc., *Glock Pistol Transitional Instructor Workshop Course Outline*, (Smyrna, GA: 2012): 7.

National Rifle Association, *Law Enforcement Handgun Instructor Manual* (Fairfax, VA: Equipment and Ammunition, Edition 2.1, 2006), 4.

[349] Glock Inc., *Armorer's Manual*, (Smyrna, GA: 2009): 82.

[350] Glock Inc., *Glock Pistol Transitional Instructor Workshop Course Outline*, (Smyrna, GA: 2012): 7.

[351] Glock Inc., *Instructions for Use Glock Safe Action Pistols All Models*, (Smyrna, GA: March 2011), 11.

[352] Glock Inc., *Glock Pistol Transitional Instructor Workshop Course Outline*, (Smyrna, GA: 2012): 7.

[353] Administrative Loading: With the pistol holstered, the magazine is inserted in the magazine well. A push, pull, sweep is performed. Remove the pistol and chamber a round by pulling the slide to the rear and releasing. The pistol is returned to the holster. The magazine can be topped off by removing he magazine, inserting one round and perform a push, pull, sweep again. See North Carolina Justice Academy, "Specialized

Firearms Instructor Training," *Service Handgun: Operation and Use* (Salemburg, NC: July 2010): 12-13.

[354] Glock Inc., *Glock Pistol Transitional Instructor Workshop Course Outline*, (Smyrna, GA: 2012): 5.

[355] Glock Inc., *Armorer's Manual*, (Smyrna, GA: 2009): 82.

[356] U.S. Department of Justice, *In the Line of Fire*, 1997, (Washington, DC: FBI, 1997), 8.

[357] Flinch: "A spasmodic physical reaction caused by the shooter's anticipation of the explosive sound or recoil of a weapon just prior to the actual discharge, causing inaccuracy in shooting." See Enforcement Firearms Instructors, *Standards & Practices Reference Guide for Law Enforcement Firearms Instructors*, (January 1995): 267.

[358] Muzzle Blast: "The sudden air turbulence and pressure exerted at the muzzle of a firearm by the rush of hot expanding gases and air on firing, often perceptible to the shooter or another person near the muzzle as concussive pressure or blast of air. The term is also used to refer to the sound or report accompanying muzzle blast." See Enforcement Firearms Instructors, *Standards & Practices Reference Guide for Law Enforcement Firearms Instructors*, (January 1995): 65.

[359] Bill Rogers, *Be Fast, Be Accurate, Be the Best* (Rogers Shooting School Publications: Jacksonville, FL, 2010), 87.

[360] Bill Rogers, *Be Fast, Be Accurate, Be the Best* (Rogers Shooting School Publications: Jacksonville, FL, 2010), 88.

[361] Brian Enos, *Practical Shooting* (Clifton, CO: Zediker Publishing, 1991), 92-94.

[362] Bill Rogers, *Be Fast, Be Accurate, Be the Best* (Rogers Shooting School Publications: Jacksonville, FL, 2010), 86.

[363] Advantage Arms Inc., "Conversion Kits," *Glock Conversion Kits*, (2009), http://www.advantagearms.com/mm5/merchant.mvc?Screen=CTGY&Store_Code=AA SOS&Category_Code=GLK (accessed September 22, 2012).

[364] Advantage Arms Inc., "Recommended Ammo," *Recommended Glock Ammo*, (2009), http://advantagearms.hostasaurus.com/mm5/merchant.mvc?Screen=CTGY&Store_Cod e=AASOS&Category_Code=GLKRecommended (accessed September 22, 2012).

[365] Rimfire: "A cartridge in which the priming mixture is placed in the enclosed cavity formed by the folded protruding rim of the head of the case, as in .22 caliber rimfire cartridges." See International Association of Law Enforcement Firearms Instructors, *Standards & Practices Reference Guide for Law Enforcement Firearms Instructors*, (January 1995): 179.

[366] "Do not "Dry Fire" this kit. The only time this kit should be dry fired is when it is required for removal." See Advantage Arms Inc., *.22 Caliber Rimfire Conversion Kit for the Glock Pistol*, (Valencia, CA).

[367] Bill Rogers, *Be Fast, Be Accurate, Be the Best* (Rogers Shooting School Publications: Jacksonville, FL, 2010), 93.

[368] Bill Rogers, *Be Fast, Be Accurate, Be the Best* (Rogers Shooting School Publications: Jacksonville, FL, 2010), 85.

[369] Brian Enos, *Practical Shooting* (Clifton, CO: Zediker Publishing, 1991), 83.

[370] Brian Enos, *Practical Shooting* (Clifton, CO: Zediker Publishing, 1991), 83.

[371] Bill Rogers, *Be Fast, Be Accurate, Be the Best* (Rogers Shooting School Publications: Jacksonville, FL, 2010), 88.

[372] Brian Enos, *Practical Shooting* (Clifton, CO: Zediker Publishing, 1991), 83.

[373] Matt Burkett, *Practical Shooting Manual* (Scottsdale, AZ: Hotshots Publishing, 1995), VII-14.

Brian Enos, *Practical Shooting* (Clifton, CO: Zediker Publishing, 1991), 94.

Saul Kirsch, *Thinking Practical Shooting* (ISBN 90-808805-3-1: Double-Alpha Academy, 2005), 26.

[374] Brian Enos, *Practical Shooting* (Clifton, CO: Zediker Publishing, 1991), 94.

[375] Brian Enos, *Practical Shooting* (Clifton, CO: Zediker Publishing, 1991), 94.

[376] "These .22 caliber guns are not in any way playthings or toys. They are very effective guns, and when the student learns to handle one of these well, he [or she] can also handle the regular .38 guns about equally well, and easily develop into mastering all of the larger calibers also. These are the guns with which I train my police classes for all of the early speed development exercises." Ed McGivern, *Ed McGivern's Book of Fast and Fancy Revolver Shooting* (New York, NY: Skyhorse Publishing, Inc., 2007): 29.

[377] From the ready gun position at the 3-yard line, the SWAT operator must fire 1 shot in 0.5 second and from the 7-yard line fires 2 shots in 0.75 second. See North Carolina Justice Academy, *In-Service Firearms Qualification Manual* (Salemburg, NC: November 2009), SWAT Pistol Course, Stages 1 and 2.

Bill Rogers, *Be Fast, Be Accurate, Be the Best* (Rogers Shooting School Publications: Jacksonville, FL, 2010), 93.

[378] Jerk: Also trigger jerking. "The sudden yanking or similar movement of a firearm's trigger by the shooter, in an effort to discharge the firearm at the precise time the sights align with the target, usually causing a bad hit on the target." See Enforcement Firearms Instructors, *Standards & Practices Reference Guide for Law Enforcement Firearms Instructors*, (January 1995): 272.

[379] Bill Rogers, *Be Fast, Be Accurate, Be the Best* (Rogers Shooting School Publications: Jacksonville, FL, 2010), 95.

[380] Robert K. Taubert, *Rattenkrieg! The Art and Science of Close Quarters Battle Pistol* (North Reading, MA: Saber Press, 2012), 79.

[381] From the draw at the 7-yard line, the SWAT operator must fire 1 shot in 1.5 second. See North Carolina Justice Academy, *In-Service Firearms Qualification Manual* (Salemburg, NC: November 2009), SWAT Pistol Course, Stages 1 and 2.

Bill Rogers, *Be Fast, Be Accurate, Be the Best* (Rogers Shooting School Publications: Jacksonville, FL, 2010), 101.

[382] Bill Rogers, e-mail message to author, December 5, 2011.

[383] Bill Rogers, *Be Fast, Be Accurate, Be the Best* (Rogers Shooting School Publications: Jacksonville, FL, 2010), 93-94.

[384] Federal Bureau of Investigation, "Law Enforcement Officers Killed and Assaulted," (Clarksburg, WV: *Table 36 – Distance Between Victim Officer and Offender, 2001–2010,* October 2010), http://www.fbi.gov/about-us/cjis/ucr/leoka/leoka-2010/tables/table36leok-feloniously-with-firearms-distance-victim-offender-01-10.xls (accessed September 22, 2012).

[385] Department of the Army, *Combat Training with Pistols, M9 and M11* (Washington, DC June 2003), 2-24.

[386] Call: "The ability or act of the shooter in "calling the shot," i.e., estimating the approximate location of his [/her] hit on the target, without inspecting the target itself, by noting the position of the sights at the instant of firing. In traditional marksmanship training, the ability to call the shot is considered an essential ability for self-coaching and development of marksmanship skill." See International Association of Law Enforcement Firearms Instructors, *Standards & Practices Reference Guide for Law Enforcement Firearms Instructors*, (January 1995): 239.

[387] Saul Kirsch, *Thinking Practical Shooting* (ISBN 90-808805-3-1: Double-Alpha Academy, 2005), 17.

[388] In the Line of Duty, "Trooper Coates Shooting," *Volume 1 Program 4 Duty Sheet and Lesson Plan.*

U.S. Department of Justice, *In the Line of Fire*, 1997, (Washington, DC: FBI, 1997), 64.

[389] National Rifle Association, *Law Enforcement Handgun Instructor Manual* (Fairfax, VA: Section C, The Fundamentals of Handgun Marksmanship , Edition 6.1, 2006), 12.

[390] Glock Inc., *Armorer's Manual*, (Smyrna, GA: 2002): 12.

[391] Glock Inc., *Glock Pistol Transitional Instructor Workshop Course Outline*, (Smyrna, GA: 2012): 5.

[392] Bill Rogers, *Make Ready with Bill Rogers: Reactive Pistol Shooting* (Columbia, SC: Panteao Productions, 2010): Reloading, DVD.

[393] U.S. Department of Justice, *Violent Encounters*, 2006, (Washington, DC: FBI, 2006), 104.

[394] A drop pouch is a bag with an open top attached to the operator's vest or belt used to hold magazines after they are removed from a firearm.

[395] North Carolina Justice Academy, "SWAT Operator," *Firearms Use in Tactical Operations* (Salemburg, NC: January 2008): 20.

[396] S.T. Action Pro Inc., *Safety Warnings for Use of Action Trainer Dummy Rounds*, (Cocoa, FL), 2.

[397] International Association of Law Enforcement Firearms Instructors, *Standards & Practices Reference Guide for Law Enforcement Firearms Instructors*, (January 1995): 290.

[398] Timothy D. Blakeley, "Personal notes from the Antiterrorism Combat Shooting session," *Antiterrorism Combat Course*, (Tel Aviv, Israel: 2008): 5.

"The kneeling position is generally used when correcting a weapon malfunction." See Department of the Army, *Rifle Marksmanship M16-/M4-Series Weapons* (Washington, DC August 2008), 7-43.

Phil Singleton, *3 Day Tactical Pistol for Hostage Rescue, High Risk Warrant and Drugs Raids,* (Warrenton, VA: Singleton International): 44.

[399] Phil Singleton, *3 Day Tactical Pistol for Hostage Rescue, High Risk Warrant and Drugs Raids,* (Warrenton, VA: Singleton International): 42-44.

[400] Phil Singleton, *3 Day Tactical Pistol for Hostage Rescue, High Risk Warrant and Drugs Raids,* (Warrenton, VA: Singleton International): 42.

[401] J. Henry FitzGerald, *Shooting* (Boulder, CO: Paladin Press, 2007), 346. Originally published in 1930 by J. Henry FitzGerald.

[402] Glock Inc., *Glock Pistol Transitional Instructor Workshop Course Outline*, (Smyrna, GA: 2012): 10.

[403] Magazine Safety, also called a Magazine Disconnect: "A type of safety device found on some semiautomatic firearms that prevents the firing of a chambered round unless the magazine if fully inserted into the firearm." See International Association of Law Enforcement Firearms Instructors, *Standards & Practices Reference Guide for Law Enforcement Firearms Instructors*, (January 1995): 62.

[404] Glock Inc., *Instructions for Use Glock Safe Action Pistols All Models*, (Smyrna, GA: March 2011), 1.

[405] The 3 to 4 second exposure technique is based on a combat tactic provided by Coalition Forces (CFs) to the Afghanistan National Police when running from one

position of cover to another as observed by author at the Kandahar Regional Training Center (RTC) in 2008.

[406] Phil Motzer, *Crucible High-risk Environment Training II Volume 4: Combat Handgun*, (Boulder, CO: Paladin Press, 2010): Remedial Action, DVD.

[407] Paul Howe, *Make Ready with Paul Howe: Advanced Tac Pistol/Rifle Operator* (Columbia, SC: Panteao Productions, 2010): Masking Targets, DVD.

[408] "On February 28, 1997, an intense confrontation between two heavily-armed bank robbers and the Los Angeles Police Department was seen on television worldwide. The incident that lasted 44 minutes, resulted in the wounding of twelve police officers, two civilians and the demise of the two suspects." See The Los Angeles Police Department, "10 Year Anniversary of the North Hollywood Shootout," in *LAPDOnline.org*   [paragraph   five],   (2011) http://www.lapdonline.org/february_2007/news_view/34831 (accessed September 22, 2012).

[409] Robert K. Taubert, *Rattenkrieg! The Art and Science of Close Quarters Battle Pistol* (North Reading, MA: Saber Press, 2012), 128.

[410] Robert K. Taubert, *Rattenkrieg! The Art and Science of Close Quarters Battle Pistol* (North Reading, MA: Saber Press, 2012), 126.

[411] North Carolina Justice Academy, *Laws Governing Concealed Handgun and Use of Deadly Force*, (Salemburg, NC: 2011): 21.

COMBAT SHOOTING PHASE 2

7

The Combat Shooting Phase 1 chapter provided a foundation for fighting with a pistol. However, other skills will further enhance operational survival.[1] In this chapter, an operator will read about how to fight from the positions of kneeling, prone, rollover prone, reverse rollover prone, supine, and contact. In addition, an operator will read about how to verbally challenge, use cover, fire with one hand, engage moving and multiple targets, close the distance, low light fire, fire and reload while injured, and clear stoppages with one hand. An operator utilizing the kneeling, prone, rollover prone, reverse rollover prone, supine, and contact positions at various distances must fire at maximum speed, but within *required* accuracy.[2]

Operators frequently ask. "At what distance should the sights be used?" The answer is from 1 yard (0.91 meter) to the maximum capability of the pistol.[3] Use one method of sighting with the exception of being at arm's reach from the adversary.[4] The sights are placed within the line of sight providing the best possible accuracy. The aligned sight image is *superimposed* on the target as the firearm comes into the line of sight and the trigger is pulled. Time and distance normally allows for greater clarity of the sight picture. The only variable in the sighting method is possibly closing one eye long enough to *clarify* the superimposed sight image ensuring an effective hit on the target. Closing one eye will occur *only* when the operator is physically capable and not experiencing an alarm reaction as previously pointed out in the Combat Shooting Phase 1 chapter. The goal therefore is to shoot with *both* eyes open with clarity of the sight picture.

There is not a particular ready position or shooting position that will cover every situation. The operator must be aware of three factors relating to an adversary:

1. *Weapon* the adversary is using.

2. *Distance* to the adversary.

3. *Environment* the adversary is operating.

After accessing the three factors a responsible decision on how best to deploy a pistol can be made. The entire decision process can occur in a split second although the weapon, distance, and environment are being mentally assessed. This is because of the extraordinary ability of the human brain to *subconsciously* process information. An operator may not *consciously* recognize that decisions are being made and carried out. The fact is in life-and-death situations many times the subconscious brain assesses information and acts on such information faster than the conscious brain can interpret. An operator may describe this experience as, "I just reacted without thinking." This can also contribute to lapses in memory.[5]

LIVE FIRE DRILLS

Live Fire: Target Discrimination and Challenge

The ability to shoot *discriminately* is one thing that separates responsible operators from their adversaries. This discretion is dependent on an operator's ability to pay attention to subtle differences and exercise good judgment. The adversary on the other hand will shoot indiscriminately. They will *not* make careful distinctions, but will shoot haphazardly without forethought or remorse.[6] The mark of a professional operator is the ability to use a firearm responsibly and effectively.

The use of a firearm does not mean just having to fire. The use of a firearm also includes the presentation of the weapon system. When a pistol is pointed at someone—normally one or two things occur. Either the trigger is pulled or commands are given. One exception to this is covert operations in which a firearm is pointed at a potential threat without commands given. However, the situation has not escalated to the point of using deadly force. When reasonable in view of the circumstances engage any imminent threat. Not engaging will likely result in serious bodily injury or death to an innocent person. However, operators must also have the necessary discipline to give a verbal challenge when appropriate. That appropriateness is dependent on it *not* endangering the operator or innocent people.[7]

The drills that follow are conducted from the holster at a distance of 7 yards (6.4 meters) with 3 to 5 rounds fired in 2 to 2.5 seconds at a human silhouette target. The scoring lines on the target should be subdued. The response times account for drawing and firing the first shot in 1.5 seconds and 0.25 second split time for subsequent shots. An additional 0.5 second may need to be added to the times depending on the type and complexity of the retention devices on the holster.

1. On the instructor's verbal command of "reaching for a gun" or "attempting to point a gun at you" or "pointing a gun at you" or "coming at you with a knife" or "beating you unconscious" or "active killer located" or some other similar phrase the operator will draw and shoot the target.

2. On the instructor's verbal command of "suspicious person discovered hiding" or "burglary suspect coming out of store" or "car chase—suspect wrecked" or "traffic stop—driver getting out of vehicle, not listening to commands" or some other similar phrase the operator will draw (from a high ready position— trigger finger on receiver) and give a verbal challenge. The challenge may be "I have a gun, do not move!" "Police, do not move!"[8] "U.S. Military, do not move!" or other agency appropriate challenge.

NOTE: The above commands are used *specifically* for discrimination training. Other training is conducted using standardized range commands such as load and holster, fire, ceasefire, and unload and holster.

The operator fires only when a deadly force scenario is described. The drill builds a mental record of what are deadly force encounters. The brain has the ability to compare past training to a real-life situation and decide when to fire or challenge. The trigger finger during challenge commands must be on the receiver. The suggested distance to the target is 7 yards (6.4 meters), but operational requirements will dictate specific training distances. This training also works well with turning or appearing photographic targets in conjunction with the instructor's verbal commands. The mind will have not only have an audible imprint, but also a visual imprint.

A team the author was on in Afghanistan took small arms fire after a suicide bomber detonated. Within a few minutes of the explosion and the small arms fire, the rear security yelled "Stop!" several times to an approaching person dressed in a burqa (head to toe covering with an opening for the eyes worn by females). There were attacks against Collation Forces (CFs) in which males were disguised in a burqa. The author maintained his sector of responsibility and had confidence that a fellow team member would do the same. The next thing the author heard was "Preparing to fire warning shot!" An Afghan police officer ran from an alley and grabbed the woman who came close to experiencing a warning shot. Yelling a verbal challenge not only warns the person being yelled at, but also provides information for other team members as well. A warning shot was an acceptable force response within the rules of engagement (ROE) for military personnel in that area of operation (AO).

Tell people who you are and what you want them to do. Learn survival phrases in the language native to the AO. The author while a police trainee in the Dallas Police Department Academy had to learn survival Spanish. People of different cultures generally understand the word "Police." In Spanish, it is "Policía." In German, it is "Polizei." In Polish, it is "Policja." The English pronunciation emphasizing the first two letters prevents the announcement from mistakenly sounding like "Please." This is especially true when the police officer is under duress and yelling police, police, police! It can sound like please, please, please! No matter the law enforcement agency: city, county, state, federal, or national, each should announce with the word "Po-lice." The same thought process applies to clothing identification. Have clothing clearly marked with the word "Police."

Live Fire: Precision Shooting

The drills are conducted at a distance of 5 yards (4.57 meters) with 5 rounds fired from *high ready* position with the arms extended at the target. The goal of the *one-hole* drill is to fire precision shots as quick as the operator can while maintaining a 1-inch (25.4-millimeter) group. Use the center of the circle as the first aim point and the first bullet hole as the subsequent aim point.

Assume a fighting stance, obtain a two-hand grip, and keep both eyes open. Control the natural respiratory pause and the wobble area while establishing a sight picture. Take up the slack, apply pressure, and pull the trigger. Do not blink as the pistol fires. See the front sight lift out of the rear sight and reset the trigger during recoil. Establish a second sight picture and fire the next shot. Practice the drill until achieving competence.

Another variation of the one-hole drill is to add a coach. The operator while in a fighting stance establishes a point of aim. When the coach gives the command *fire,* the operator will fire the pistol and hold the trigger to the rear. The coach will then give a command of *reset* for the operator to reset the trigger. In between commands, there will be a 2-second pause and would sound as follows: fire…reset…fire…reset…and so on until 5 rounds are fired. Use the same fundamentals of shooting as explained in the previous paragraph.

COVER AND CONCEALMENT

Operators as a matter of habit need to identify and utilize cover whenever practical, especially during a deadly force encounter. The operator needs to use cover because he or she is a living target for an adversary. The best cover not only stops or deflects the adversary's weapon, but also *minimizes* the operator's exposure while *maximizing* the adversary's exposure. Cover can sometimes be used to buy time for making tactical decisions, such as continuing with the fight, or break contact.

It is common knowledge in law enforcement that cover is something that will stop or deflect an adversary's bullets. Equally important is the emphasis on selecting cover that also provides a position from which to mount a *counterattack.* It does little good to hide behind cover with the head down while an adversary closes the distance and kills the operator. Likewise, cover that maximizes distance provides an advantage for the operator to impart superior shooting skills on the adversary.[9] The ultimate goal of using cover is to minimize the operator's exposure while attempting to engage the adversary with effective fire.[10]

Shooting from behind cover uses the same shooting skills as when not using cover. The difference is that behind cover there is an object in front of the operator. Shooting effectively from behind cover is manipulating a pistol around the object. There are a couple of methods for using cover. The first is to expose only a minimum amount of the *body* for a minimum amount of *time* (less than a second).[11] The second method is to expose enough of the body to ensure a stable fighting position, dominate the use of cover, and control the area of responsibility.[12] An operator should be aggressive and give up the area of responsibility only at his or her discretion.

Make fast deliberate movements (out and back in) and do *not* linger from behind cover *unless* controlling the area of responsibility. Lingering from behind cover without having control of the operational area affords an adversary adequate time to get a sight picture and fire. However, getting behind cover after shooting an adversary is giving up control of an area that was just fought over. Refrain from getting behind cover automatically when having control of an area and reloading.[13] Move from one position of cover to another *only* when there is an advantage for doing so. There needs to be a plan to withdraw from cover and utilize available cover and concealment along the egress route. The pistol would likely be kept in a ready or carry position dependent on the circumstances when moving from cover.

Constantly use cover to improve survivability.[14] Using cover is the physical relationship between the operator, cover, and the adversary. The operator's body must remain behind cover and not expose any part except as necessary to counterattack. To counterattack: (1) obtain a line of sight from the eye to the adversary, (2) make sure the muzzle is clear of the cover, and (3) obtain a superimposed sight picture and fire. The only part of the operator's body exposed is the firing hand, eye and a small portion of the head. Cover can be used with the standing, kneeling, or prone positions. The prone position can limit the operator's field of view. The prone position can also be slow to get into and out of while wearing an equipment vest with ballistic plates.

Close cover is reachable in about 2 seconds.[15] Examples of cover are 18-inch (457.2-millimeter) trees, masonry walls, dirt embankments, vehicle engine compartments, utility poles, utility boxes, fire hydrants, drop mailboxes, etc.[16] A powerful firearm or repeated bullet hits can quickly turn cover into concealment. Certain types of cover can stop or deflect pistol rounds, but is ineffective against rifle rounds. As a rule it is best to stay off cover at *least* arm's length and use the leaning out technique.[17] (Figure 7-1) An operator leaning out with his or her pistol extended will likely see the adversary first. The adversary should see the operator's muzzle first. This method also provides a work area to reload and clear any stoppages. Equipment or a pistol protruding past cover can signal to an adversary the operator's location.

Figure 7-1 *Arm's Length from Cover*

The operator might want to switch his or her pistol to the hand that corresponds to the side of cover being used.[18] When firing from the left side of cover the operator to minimize body exposure uses the left hand as the firing hand. When firing from the right side of cover the operator to minimize body exposure uses the right hand as the firing hand. This technique is an option only for an operator that can *competently* fight with a pistol in either hand—a skill that should be possessed.[19] The benefit of switching to the hand that corresponds to that side of cover is negated *if* an operator takes excessive time to make the shot.[20] The skill of fighting with a pistol with either hand can be developed by shooting realistic courses of fire with the hand on the dominant eye side and then with the hand opposite the dominant eye within the same time standards.[21]

Do *not* bend the elbows so much they stick out from the body. Leaning out from cover with an elbow stuck out is presenting a target to an adversary. Keeping the elbows close to the body makes the operator a smaller target and lessens the chance of bumping doorframes and walls when clearing rooms. Any police officer with an arm or leg stuck out from behind cover got shot with a fast moving paint ball during the cover drill in the U.S. Marshals Fugitive Investigator's Course. The police officer's mistakes were apparent from the instructor's vantage point inside the acrylic plastic protected booth. (Figure 7-2) From the adversary's vantage point, an operator's mistake is an opportunity to kill him or her.

Figure 7-2 *U.S. Marshals Cover Training Course*

When firing from cover stay conscious of the pistol's position to prevent causing a stoppage. A common mistake is allowing the slide to rub against cover (wall, building, car, etc.). Doing so can prevent the slide from functioning and possibly rip off the front sight. To expose less of the body it may be better to shoot on the side of cover than over the top. Shooting from the side may also limit the number of adversaries that can see the operator at any given time forcing a one-on-one fight. Shooting over the top of cover would likely expose the operator to multiple adversaries simultaneously. However, each situation will dictate the best firing position or a position forced by the tempo of the fight.

Vary the firing position *if* possible on each engagement of fire. An operator from behind cover can fire in the standing position and then the kneeling position to vary the position of the muzzle flash signature. This may prevent an adversary from predicting the operator's next firing position. The standing and kneeling positions are fast to get into and out of and allows closing the distance on an adversary to be done quickly. The standing and kneeling positions maximizes the operator's field of view of the operational area.

Be quick and deliberate when changing positions and handling the pistol. The goal is to keep an adversary guessing what position gunfire will come from next. Do *not* be a predictable target for the adversary. An operator may be forced to move back behind cover because of overwhelming fire from an adversary or not having control of the operational area and needing to reload. Quickly move behind cover to deny the adversary an opportunity to obtain effective hits. Take care of what needs taking care of behind cover, set-up again, slice the area *if* necessary, shoot as necessary, and collapse the sector or area to take control. Be aggressive and dominant the area of responsibility.

Make sure there is no conflict between the *line of sight* and the *line of bore* when firing from cover.[22] Canting a pistol from behind cover may worsen the line of sight and the line of bore issue. This occurs when there is a clear line of sight to the threat or target, but the muzzle is pointing at the surface of the cover. The sights clear the cover, but the muzzle does not. The bullet will impact the cover's surface. Splatter can occur according to the hardness of the cover material. The splatter may blind the operator or a nearby team member. One of the author's academy classmates on the range at the Dallas Police Department fired a shotgun from cover and blew a hole in the plywood barrier. The trainee stood behind cover, peeked his head out, pulled the trigger, but never moved the shouldered shotgun. The plywood gave way—concrete or steel would not have been so forgiving.

The term *fatal funnel* in law enforcement is commonly used to describe a doorway. The term has the connotation for some that stepping into a doorway is a death sentence. What is the difference between using a doorway versus a wall as cover? The material surrounding the doorway, i.e., wood, thin metal, brick, concrete, etc., dictates whether the doorway is concealment or cover. The Israeli antiterrorism combat doctrine utilizes a doorway as a cover position to fight from when surrounded by appropriate material. Inappropriate material such as thin wood, sheetrock, vinyl siding, etc., will not stop bullets. An adversary partially exposed can still be shot center mass. The operator only has to visualize the hidden shape of the adversary behind the wooden fence and shoot through the boards in the center mass area. (Figure 7-3) Center mass is not only what is visually available to the operator, but also what is ballistically available.

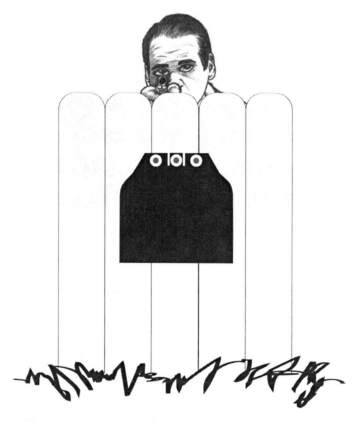

Figure 7-3 *Example of Correct Sight Picture*

The goal is for the operator to see the adversary first. Accomplish this by visually dividing a room into sections to clear it from the doorway. The technique is called *slicing the area*. There are two variations: *incremental slice,* and *quarter slice*. The incremental slice is taking small incremental sidesteps and is popular in law enforcement. The quarter slice is taking larger sidesteps slicing in *45-degree* segments. An example would be to divide the entryway of the room at 45 degrees and then 90 degrees. This method requires less movement by the operator and still affords the capability to duck back behind cover quickly.

Both methods can use the *leaning out* technique in which the operator's upper body leans sideways (20 to 30 degrees)[23] at the waist to maximize the view around the corner. To maintain balance the foot on the side of the cover is placed forward while leaning out. Firing from the left side of cover, an operator's left foot would be forward and behind cover. (Figure 7-4) Firing from the right side of cover, an operator's right foot would be forward and behind cover. (Figure 7-5) The pistol is held under the line of sight to maximize the operator's field of view. The operator may also have to take a quick step out from cover *instead* of leaning out after locating an adversary to have a stable shooting position to engage the adversary effectively. The operator from the adversary's perspective is there one second and not the next.[24]

Figure 7-4 *Left Side Cover*   ***Figure 7-5*** *Right Side Cover*

An operator in the *kneeling* position must be capable of using cover effectively. The knee even with the *outside* edge of cover is up and the knee *inside* of the cover is grounded. This may or may not be the normal kneeling position dependent on which hand is used for firing and the side of cover being used. Keeping the knee up that is nearest the edge of cover provides better stability. As an example, keep the right knee up with the foot flat and the left knee grounded when firing from the right side of a barricade. Keep the left knee up with the foot flat and the right knee grounded when firing from the left side of a barricade. Moving the outside foot over and keeping it flat on the ground allows sliding the grounded knee over. This technique is useful for remaining in the kneeling position while providing the means of moving laterally. Moving laterally allows slicing of an area incrementally while kneeling. An operator may need to move out from a vehicle being used as cover to see and dominate more of the operational area.

NOTE: Concealment is *not* cover. Concealment (foliage, sheetrock walls, darkness, etc.) will hide the operator from view of an adversary, but will *not* stop bullets. Know that whatever object is used as cover that it will in fact stop the adversary's weapon system.

FIRING POSITIONS

The priority for an operator using any firing position is to provide an *immediate* response to a life-threatening situation initiated by an adversary. Use cover the body can conform to and provides an effective firing position when time and circumstances allow. This will provide the best protection against the adversary's weapon system. There are firing positions described in this section that allow shooting underneath vehicles, over street curbs, and behind the wheel of a vehicle. These positions allow the operator to fight, but on a lower visual plane. The sitting position and prone position should be avoided *if* possible because of a loss of maneuverability in the event an operator had to move quickly to a new location.[25]

The body's position when reloading in the prone position may need to change to access the magazines. Move deliberate and quick when changing positions or stripping magazines from a pistol. The body's position when clearing stoppages may need to change, but continue to maximize the use of cover. The operator whether reloading or clearing a stoppage must do whatever is necessary to get the pistol back up and running. A firing position is not always voluntarily assumed by the operator, but can be forced by the adversary (operator tackled to the ground or overwhelming fire).

NOTE: The firing positions can be practiced using dry firing. Three 8-inch circle paper targets can be put on a wall and spaced vertically for standing, kneeling, and prone positions. The center of each target should be in the operator's line of sight when in each of the positions.

DANGER: Depending on the height of the berm/backstop or interior configuration of an indoor range, a target may need to be set at ground level when live firing in the prone positions to prevent rounds from exiting the range![26]

Kneeling

In general, use a kneeling position that will help put effective rounds on the adversary. This also includes two operators assuming mutually supporting high (standing) and low (kneeling) firing positions to bring more firepower on the adversary.[27] There is little if any value for the Special Weapons and Tactics (SWAT) officer or military operator to train on a position unusable while in full tactical gear. Properly layered gear can help negate some of the difficulties caused by equipment when in the kneeling position. It is preferred to train in methods that can be used while wearing any uniform.[28]

The supported kneeling position is more stable than the unsupported kneeling position, but the unsupported kneeling position is more stable than the fighting stance. The supported and unsupported kneeling positions offer the advantage of further lowering the body's center of gravity and profile (smaller target). Tactically the kneeling position can act as a visual indicator for other team members that a reload is occurring. The kneeling position can also assist in adapting the body to a barricade for cover and recover from physical exertion (rest).

The *unsupported kneeling* position allows the body index to remain in the same position as when in the fighting stance. (Figure 7-6) The unsupported kneeling position allows the operator to turn at the waist to traverse a wide area. The unsupported kneeling position works well while dressed in civilian clothing, police duty gear, and in full tactical gear. The bulk of an equipment vest can sometimes make it difficult to fire from a supported kneeling position.

Figure 7-6 *Unsupported Kneeling Position*

The *supported kneeling* position is assumed by placing the non-firing side arm at the bottom of the triceps muscle against the non-firing side knee. The operator will likely have to sit back on the non-firing side foot to get low enough to place the non-firing side triceps muscle on the knee. (Figure 7-7) This requires flexibility and may be uncomfortable for some operators. A common *mistake* is to set the elbow on the knee, which causes wobbling. The supported kneeling position also limits the ability to traverse with a pistol and reduces the operator's field of view.

The *double kneeling* position is probably the quickest kneeling position to assume. However, quickly and forcefully driving both knees to the ground (concrete, pavement, gravel, etc.) runs a risk of injury *if* protective equipment is not worn. Bend both knees simultaneously lowering them to the ground, or place one knee on the ground and then the other to assume the double kneeling position. (Figure 7-8) The same upper body index is maintained as when standing. The upper body leans forward to absorb the recoil by keeping the ears in front of the shoulders and the shoulders in front of the hips. The hips and knees are angle slightly to the rear to maintain better balance.[29]

There are two methods for assuming the kneeling position with one knee up.[30] First, step back with the firing side foot and lower the firing side knee to the ground. The non-firing side foot does not move. The body drops straight down into the kneeling position. This method allows assuming the kneeling position within the personal space the body is taking up. This means the body is not moving left, right, forward, or backward. The body is remaining in the same area as when standing. This method works well on a firing line or in a shoot house. The operator is not stepping in front of the firing line or in front of another operator in a CQC environment.

Figure 7-7 Supported Kneeling Position

Figure 7-8 Double Kneeling Position

Second, step forward with the non-firing side foot and simultaneously lower the firing side knee to the ground. Some operators or instructors may think that it is more natural to ground the firing side knee by stepping forward with the non-firing side foot.[31] Consider the issue of the operator moving forward into an unknown space, as opposed to dropping the weight from underneath the body straight down in the known space currently occupied. An operator behind cover may not be able to move forward. The forward movement near multiple operators could also create a safety issue (moving in front of another's muzzle). The upper body position is maintained (arms straight and sights aligned) when moving from the fighting stance into a kneeling position.

Humans are binocular beings designed to fight in the forward position. Any of the three kneeling positions allow the body to remain in a forward fighting position, but the operator's mobility is reduced. Lowering the hips while kneeling can vary the height of the body's profile. The unsupported kneeling positions allow transitioning to the left and right by rotating at the waist. Maintaining aggressive control of the pistol while tightening the body's core will reduce the tendency to swing the sights past a target. Use the non-firing hand to push against the knee to assist in getting up from a kneeling position. This is especially helpful while wearing heavy equipment.

The drills are conducted at a distance of 7 yards (6.4 meters) with 3 to 5 rounds fired at a human silhouette target with subdued scoring lines.

Transitioning to the Left Side: From the unsupported kneeling position quickly snap the head to focus on the left side target, turn the upper torso 90 degrees to the left with both arms naturally locked, and point the muzzle directly at the target. (Figure 7-9 through 7-11)

Figure 7-9 *Kneeling Firing Position (left)*   **Figure 7-10** *Look to Identify (left)*   **Figure 7-11** *Turn to Face and Fire (left)*

Transitioning to the Right Side: Quickly snap the head to focus on the right side target, turn the upper torso 90 degrees to the right with both arms naturally locked, and point the muzzle directly at the target. (Figure 7-12 through 7-14)

Figure 7-12 Kneeling Firing Position (right) **Figure 7-13** Look to Identify (right) **Figure 7-14** Turn to Face and Fire (right)

Transitioning to the Rear: Quickly snap the head to the *non-firing* side to focus on the rear target. Bring the pistol close to the body (carry position) and turn the upper torso toward the non-firing side. The non-firing side knee will move upward from the ground and become the forward knee. As the torso continues to turn 180 degrees from the original position, the firing side knee is grounded. Extend the pistol into the line of sight with both arms naturally locked. The muzzle points directly at the target and the operator is now in the opposite direction of the front position. (Figure 7-15 through 7-17)

  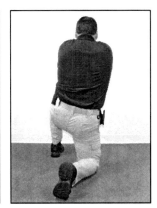

Figure 7-15 Look to Identify (rear) **Figure 7-16** Turn to Face (rear) **Figure 7-17** Extend Arms and Fire (rear)

Transitioning Back to the Front: Quickly snap the head to the *firing side* to focus on the front target. Bring the pistol close to the body (carry position) and turn the upper torso toward the firing side. The firing side knee will move upward from the ground and become the forward knee. As the torso continues to turn 180 degrees from the original position, the non-firing side knee is grounded. Extend the pistol into the line of sight with both arms naturally locked. The muzzle points directly at the target and the operator is now in the opposite direction of the rear position. (Figure 7-18 through 7-20)

Figure 7-18 Look to *Identify (front)*   **Figure 7-19** Turn to *Face (front)*   **Figure 7-20** Extend *Arms and Fire (rear)*

Prone

The *prone* position may be appropriate when there are multiple adversaries at a distance or a lack of available cover. As a rule, assume the prone position *if* in a kneeling position and cover will still not protect the body. The prone position enables the operator to fire from a stable position while being a smaller target. An operator may be roughly one-sixth the size prone as when standing.[32] This results in the operator being a harder target to hit, but with a reduction of maneuverability. The prone position when practiced must allow use of cover from either the right or left side (ambidextrous) while still limiting the body's exposure.

The operator's visibility of the operational area may be reduced when wearing a ballistic helmet and in the prone position. Maintaining the prone position for an extended period can fatigue the neck and arms. The prone position can be an effective fighting position in combat, but it is susceptible to ricochets.[33] This is especially true if the bullet strikes a hard surface within 20 feet (6 meters) of the operator.[34] However, using the prone position behind an elevated obstacle such as a raised curb, particularly one near a storm drain reduces the chance of being hit by a ricochet bullet.

"In a small Midwestern city a uniformed police officer responded to a burglar alarm ringing at a corner liquor store. Two suspects emerged through the front door, and one suspect appeared to have a gun in his right hand. The officer assumed a prone position in the street and shouted, "Police officer, halt!" The suspect immediately fired at the officer. A .38 caliber bullet hit the concrete pavement 6 feet in front of the officer, ricocheted, and entered the officer's skull 2 inches below the bill of his cap."[35]

Complete drawing the pistol from the standing position if possible prior to assuming the prone position. Keep the trigger finger on the receiver and the muzzle pointed toward the target.

There are two techniques for assuming the prone position. To use the *first* technique, quickly bend the knees, extending the non-firing hand down toward the ground and forward. Lower the body forward and down until the non-firing hand touches the ground and the bottom of the firing side forearm is on the ground controlling the descent. Push both legs back keeping the feet in line with the body and extend both arms forward. The feet are positioned so the ankles lay flat on the ground or as much as possible with the toes pointing out to the sides. An alternate position for the toes is to point directly to the rear with the instep on the ground. To use the *second* technique, move to a double kneeling position extending the body and firing arm forward. Continue to lower the body forward and with the non-firing arm break the fall controlling the descent into the position.

With both techniques, the bottoms of both forearms are on the ground and preferably *not* the elbows. Establish a two-hand grip. The head remains down between the arms and behind the pistol. The neck will feel strained from the head being upright, but keep it as low as practical between the arms. (Figure 7-21)

Scan the operational area before getting up from the prone position. Get up by bending the elbows bringing the extended arms back toward the body. Push off with the non-firing hand and if necessary use the bottom of the firing side forearm to help. Push the body up and bring the firing side knee under the body. Raise the pistol to the join position. Swing the non-firing side foot forward grounding it and establishing a kneeling position. Establish a two-hand grip, scan the area, stand, and scan the area again.

Figure 7-21 *Prone Position*

NOTE: It is common in recreational shooting to see shooters place their non-firing hand on the ground and kick both feet back allowing the body to slam to the ground.[36] This technique although quick to assume is unrealistic for an operator carrying 30 to 60 pounds (13.6 to 27.2 kilos) of equipment. There is also the issue of landing hard on debris in an operational area causing a self-inflicted injury.

Keeping the feet in line with the body is to prevent inadvertently exposing the legs from behind cover. Control the recoil by keeping the bottom of the forearms on the ground while pushing forward with the arms and the wrists locked. Only raise the pistol off the ground when necessary. Bending the elbows up or down provides flexibility while shooting targets at various elevations.[37] However, shooting on the elbows *will* result in a loss of stability and reduced recoil control to some degree. The pistol can be held in the right or left hand according to the side of cover being used. This option is dependent on the urgency to shoot and the operator's ability to shoot effectively with either hand.

However, under the stress of combat a pistol will likely be fired with the hand on the same side as the dominant eye.

Lessen the effects of weight on the body by bending either knee bringing it toward the chest removing pressure off the diaphragm. This technique is especially useful after physical exertion such as running from one position of cover to another. This prone position closely resembles the prone position while firing a carbine. The prone position does limit the operator's mobility and visibility and therefore is not a desirable position to remain in for an extended period. Some operators may find the prone position uncomfortable and prefer an alternative prone position *if* conditions allow.

Rollover Prone

The *rollover prone* is a firing position that adapts well to shooting under cover low to the ground such as underneath a vehicle. When using the rollover prone roll the body to the firing side to support the weight of the body. Operators should use caution and *not* point the muzzle at themselves when assuming the position. The rollover prone position is comfortable, but in the open may expose too much of the operator's body to gunfire.[38]

Complete drawing the pistol from the standing position if possible prior to assuming the rollover prone position. Keep the trigger finger on the receiver and the muzzle pointed toward the target.

To assume the rollover prone position stand at a 45-degree angle to the target. Bend the knees and extend the non-firing hand down toward the ground and forward of the body. Lower the body forward and down until the non-firing hand touches the ground and the bottom of the firing side forearm is on the ground controlling the descent. Push both legs back keeping the firing side foot in line with the body and extend the firing arm forward. Roll the body over to the *firing* side and bring the non-firing side knee up toward the chest. The non-firing side foot can lie on the back on the firing side knee or remain on the ground near the knee. Some operators may find it faster to move out of the position by *not* crossing the leg. The bottoms of both forearms may be on the ground dependent on the operator's flexibility. Establish a two-hand grip. The magazine floor plate or the web of the hand should be on the ground if possible. The head naturally rests on the firing side bicep in line with the pistol. There should be little if any strain felt on the neck. Assumed a two-hand grip and acquire a sight picture. (Figure 7-22)

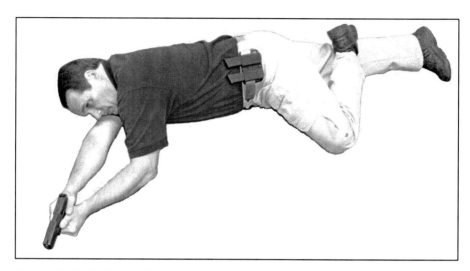

Figure 7-22 *Rollover Prone Position*

Shooting in the rollover prone position with both eyes open and focusing on the target will cause the two images of the pistol to stack one on top of the other. This occurs because the eyes are rotated 90 degrees from the horizontal axis to a vertical axis. The eye next to the firing side bicep creates the image on top and the other eye creates the image on the bottom. (Figures 7-23 and 7-24) The operator will use the top image to establish a sight picture. An operator with a right dominant eye should fire with his or her right hand and lie on the right side of the body. An operator with a left dominant eye should fire with his or her left hand and lie on the left side of the body. This is so the dominant eye is used for aiming with both eyes open.

Scan the operational area before getting up from the rollover prone position. Get up by bending the elbows bringing the extended arms back toward the body. Push off with the non-firing hand and if necessary use the bottom of the firing side forearm to help. Push the body up and bring the firing side knee under the body. Raise the pistol to the join position. Swing the non-firing side foot forward grounding it and establishing a kneeling position. Establish a two-hand grip, scan the area, stand, and scan the area again.

Left-Hand Operator
Left Eye Image *(top)*
Right Eye Image *(bottom)*

Right-Hand Operator
Right Eye Image *(top)*
Left Eye Image *(bottom)*

Figure 7-23 Left hand operator in the rollover prone position focusing on the target while seeing superimposed sights.

Figure 7-24 Right hand operator in the rollover prone position focusing on the target while seeing superimposed sights.

Reverse Rollover Prone

The *reverse rollover prone* position is a variation of the rollover prone that has the feet facing in the same direction as the muzzle. The position of the body is reversed from the rollover prone as the name indicates. Use the reverse rollover prone to remain concealed behind narrow cover while shooting under objects close to the ground. The most common use would be behind the wheel of a vehicle and firing under the vehicle chassis. The operator must be careful not to cause a self-inflicted gunshot because the knees and feet are forward of the muzzle.

Complete drawing the pistol from the standing position if possible prior to assuming the reverse rollover prone position. Keep the trigger finger on the receiver and the muzzle pointed toward the target.

Ground the knee on the side of the body that will be supporting the weight. Assume the reverse rollover prone from the *firing* side by grounding the firing side knee. Bend over extending the non-firing hand down on the ground and the firing side forearm on the ground to help support the upper body weight. The non-firing hand is grounded close to the pistol, but not in front of the muzzle. Kick the grounded knee under the body and roll onto the firing side. Assume the reverse rollover prone from the *non-firing* side by grounding the non-firing side knee. Bend over extending the non-firing hand down on the ground to support the upper body weight. Keep the pistol up and pointed toward the target. Kick the grounded knee under the body and roll onto non-firing side. In both cases keep the knees bent and out of the line of fire to prevent a self-inflicted gunshot. The hands move to the join position and assume a two-hand grip. The head remains off the ground and the pistol in line with the dominant eye. (Figure 7-25)

Figure 7-25 *Reverse Rollover Prone Position*

Scan the operational area before getting up from the reverse rollover prone position. Get up from the *firing* side by bending the elbows bringing the extended arms back toward the body. Push off with the non-firing hand and if necessary use the bottom of the firing side forearm to help. Push the body up and bring the *firing* side knee under the body. Raise the pistol to the join position. Ground the non-firing side foot forward establishing a kneeling position. Establish a two-hand grip, scan the area, stand, and scan the area again. Alternatively, get up from the *non-firing* side by bending the elbows bringing the extended arms back toward the body. Push off with the non-firing hand. Push the body up and bring the *non-firing* side knee under the body. Raise the pistol to the join position. Ground the firing side foot forward establishing a kneeling position. Establish a two-hand grip, scan the area, stand, and scan the area again.

Supine

Having to shoot in the supine position (on the back) could be a result of accidentally falling or from an attack. In either case, tuck the chin against the chest when falling to prevent the back of the head from slamming against the ground. Such an impact could result in being knocked unconscious. Obviously, an unconscious operator would be defenseless. Being knocked to the ground does *not* mean a counterattack is no longer an option. The ground is not the preferred place to be, but a counterattack is possible. An operator on the ground *must* take decisive action to survive.

Deadly force is appropriate when an operator is on the ground and being viciously attacked or threatened with a deadly weapon. Such attacks can put the operator in a position of being knocked unconscious with a single punch at any moment or incapacitated from gunshots by the armed adversary. There are also grabbling techniques used to get an opponent on the ground, beat them unconscious, or use a joint lock capable of breaking bones. In any case, when such techniques are used by an adversary against an operator—disfigurement or death is a real possibility.

Deployment of a pistol to engage the adversary is still an option even with limited mobility. Just be aware the bullet's trajectory may be skyward. There are three key principles when attacked: (1) *defend*, (2) *counterattack,* and (3) *control*. When on the ground defend against the incoming attack *if* possible. Some examples of defending are quickly moving to avoid being struck, using the hands and elbows to deflect blows, and going to the fetal position to fend off kicks. The goal is to avoid damage to the body and move to a position for a counterattack.

The counterattack in this case is the deployment of a pistol. It is preferable to *simultaneously* defend and counterattack.[39] Defending and counterattacking simultaneously puts the operator on the offensive and a step ahead of his or her adversary. It is inconsequential that shots fired are from the supine position *if* the rounds are striking the adversary. When on the ground do *not* try to sit up and fire as it may waste valuable time. Strive to stay low and raise the head only enough to obtain a sight picture. The same principles of shooting while supine apply as when standing.

Bring the pistol into the line of sight, acquire an appropriate degree of sight picture clarity, and pull the trigger. Operators using threat level 4 body armor may find it useful as a field expedient rest for a supported firing position. An important point is to fire from a position that does *not* cause a self-inflicted gunshot. Keeping the knees down and feet spread allows the operator to traverse the pistol without the fear of causing a self-inflicted gunshot.

If a fight occurs at *contact* distance on the ground, hold the pistol close to the body and fire at the adversary. This is the same principle as the Retention Position used to prevent a gun takeaway. Preferably, point the pistol quickly and fire directly at the adversary's head. Hold the pistol in whatever position that provides a tactical advantage to shoot the adversary in the head and does *not* cause a self-inflicted injury.

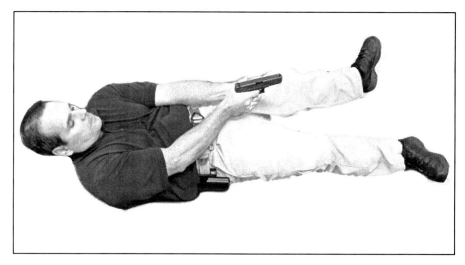

Figure 7-26 Supine Position

Complete drawing the pistol from the standing position if possible prior to assuming the supine position. Keep the trigger finger on the receiver and the muzzle pointed toward the target.

To assume the supine position, quickly bend the knees and extend the non-firing hand down toward the ground and rearward of the body.[40] Lower the buttocks until the non-firing hand touches the ground and the body leans back. Keep the chin tucked and the back curved forward while rolling backwards. This *controlled* rolling movement is to prevent the head and back from slamming against the ground. The legs extend forward with the knees apart to prevent a self-inflicted gunshot. The hands move to the join position establishing a two-hand grip. The head remains off the ground the pistol's sights are in line with the dominant eye. (Figure 7-26)

To get up from the supine position, begin by scanning the operational area. The operator can quickly get up from the supine position by rolling to the *firing* side, planting the bottom of the firing side forearm and the non-firing hand on the ground, bring the firing side knee under the body. Alternatively, roll to the *non-firing* side, place the non-firing hand on the ground, and bring the non-firing knee under the body. Scan the area while keeping the muzzle pointed in the appropriate direction, stand as necessary, and scan the area again.

Squatting

An operator may need to reduce his or her exposure to an adversary, but not be able to assume or want to assume a kneeling position. The ground may be uneven, littered with broken glass, or undistinguishable from a lack of ambient light. The advantages of squatting are simplicity, quickness, and silence.[41] The squatting position is useful when shooting over a passenger vehicle's hood or trunk.

The squatting position allows the operator to utilize the cover while maintaining mobility. There is a deeper bend in the knees than when in the fighting stance, but the upper body maintains the same index as when shooting in the fighting stance. (Figure 7-27) An operator should squat low enough that the body conforms to the object used as cover, but refrain from the buttocks touching the calves. Squatting too low can be uncomfortable, unstable, and reduce mobility.

Sitting

The author, during a U.S. Marshals simulation course, found himself sitting on a floor and drawing his pistol. He was handcuffing a suspect in the prone position. In a split second, another suspect came into the room and fired a blank round at the author's cover officer. The author quickly spun from a kneeling position and fell on his buttocks. He drew from a seated position and protected himself as a spontaneous reaction. He drew his pistol and presented it in the same manner as when standing. The author as a police officer on numerous occasions had to draw his pistol in the line of duty while seated in a police vehicle.

The point is the arms will likely be extended with the sights aligned in the line of sight and the trigger pulled regardless of the operator's position. The *unsupported* seated position from the waist up is the same shooting position as if standing. (Figure 7-28) However, the *supported* seated shooting position calls for the triceps to rest on the knees. In reality this is not a technique an operator armed with a pistol in combat would likely use. The supported seated position may be a shooting position, but that does not mean it is a good fighting position. The unsupported seated position reduces the operator's mobility, but does offer the advantage of remaining in it for an extended period. Realistically an operator could find him or herself sitting in a vehicle or at a dining table and firing from a seated unsupported position.

Figure 7-27 Squatting Position   **Figure 7-28** Sitting Position

NOTE: The seat belt in some instances puts pressure against magazine catch releasing the magazine when wearing a holster on the waist and sitting in a vehicle. Pull on the magazine floor plate periodically to ensure it is seated. This is especially true for police officers because they spend extended periods seated in a vehicle. A magazine found not seated requires an examination to its cause and the problem fixed.

One-Hand

The priority in a life-threatening attack is to put effective hits on the adversary. This is best accomplished by using two hands when firing. Operators should practice dropping items such as a citation book, entry tool, flashlight, grocery bag, etc. and establishing a two-hand grip. However, a response to a close quarters ambush or moving a person out of the line of fire can require firing with one hand. Shooting one-handed reduces support of the pistol by 50 percent. The reduction amplifies hand movement before firing and the felt recoil after firing. An operator should consider these weaknesses and return to a two-hand grip at the earliest opportunity. Using two hands in most situations will provide the best chance of hitting an adversary.

Dominate Hand Firing: When firing at a *contact* distance the non-dominant hand may be used instinctively to protect the face and neck area. When firing in a fighting stance using one hand at distances other than contact a non-dominant hand will probably be held naturally at the side. Holding the non-firing hand against the thigh *prevents* a pendulum effect that can destabilize the body resulting in muzzle movement.

There is a video from a dashboard camera showing a police officer putting his hands in front of his face and neck area when on the ground and being shot.[42] A police officer's actions in another shooting incident were self-described as "I put my left-hand up to protect my head and start firing in the direction where I could see the muzzle flash coming from."[43] This instinctive response needs to be included in training at a contact distance while firing with one hand. There are other incidents captured on video that police officers held one hand down at their side.[44] This response is likely because of the body instinctively maintains a *balance* between the dominant side and non-dominant side. Holding one hand down at the side also needs to be included in training while firing with one hand.

WARNING: Anchoring the non-dominant hand in front of the chest only increases the chance of getting the hand struck by an adversary's bullet. There is no instinctive or tactical reason for the technique.

When protecting the face and neck with the non-dominant hand it is bent about 45 degrees at the elbow. This position for the non-dominant hand is similar to holding a flashlight at shoulder height. It is *not* necessary to cant the pistol when holding it in the dominant hand and using the dominant eye since they are on the *same* side of the body. Canting the pistol in this case may cause the wrist to break to the outside and the muzzle to point off target. When firing with the dominant hand it is best to leave the pistol upright.[45] The dominant arm will be straight and naturally locked out at the wrist and elbow as when firing with two hands. This method will provide sufficient stability to fire accurately.

Complete the one-hand draw in the fighting stance using the grip and extend steps as follows:

Grip: Move quickly into a fighting stance. Simultaneously move the non-dominant hand down to the side against the upper thigh or in front of the face and neck area as the firing side hand goes forward and high on the back strap gripping the pistol. The fingers apply equal pressure gripping from front to rear pulling the back strap against the palm. The elbow is close to the body. (Figure 7-29)

Extend: Pull the pistol straight up from the holster to chest level and rotate it 90 degrees. Push the pistol forward within the line of sight between the dominant eye and the target. (Figure 7-30) Lock the wrist and elbow with the arm naturally extended. See the aligned sights as a single image superimposed on the target.

Figure 7-29 Grip   **Figure 7-30** Extend

The fighting stance as a rule does *not* change when shooting with one hand.[46] The body will normally remain squared to the target. The author has seen police officers on the firing line change from a *static* squared stance to a *static* bull's-eye shooting stance (angled) when firing with one hand. Not only is it unnecessary—tactically it is wrong.[47] Taking a step forward to assume a bull's-eye shooting stance in close quarters may put the pistol in arm's reach of the adversary. Changing to an angle standing position is also wasting time needed to win the fight.

Non-dominant Hand Firing: The previous marksmanship methods in this chapter apply equally to the non-dominant hand. There are advantages for being able to fire a pistol competently with the non-dominant hand. Tactically it can be advantageous not to expose the operator's body from behind cover to an adversary. Furthermore, if a dominant arm injury occurs the operator will have the ability to defend him or herself. The main difference between firing the pistol with the dominant hand versus the non-dominant hand is canting the pistol *slightly* to roll the sights into the line of sight.[48] (Figures 7-31 and 7-32)

Figure 7-31 Non-dominant hand (front)

Figure 7-32 Non-dominant hand (side)

This allows for the aligning of the sights with the *dominant eye*. A slight canting of the pistol should feel comfortable for most operators. The pistol cant is limited to 30 degrees[49] and 20 degrees is probably a good compromise. It is natural for the body to align the pistol with the dominant eye. The goal is to leave both eyes open. However, to improve sight image clarification it may be necessary to close the non-dominant eye. Closing an eye can occur *if* the operator is physically capable and not experiencing an alarm reaction. However, the goal of combat shooting is to shoot with both eyes open.

Figures 7-33 and 7-34 show the pistols canted at 20 degrees. An operator holding the pistol canted in the non-dominant hand and both eyes open while focusing on the target will cause the two images of the pistol to appear angled. These angled images occur because the pistol from the upright position is canted toward the outside. The dominant eye creates the image closest to the centerline of the body and the non-dominant eye creates the image on the outside. The operator will use the image closest to the centerline of the body to establish a sight picture.

Left-Hand Operator
Right Eye Image / Left Eye Image

Right-Hand Operator
Right Eye Image / Left Eye Image

Figure 7-33 A left hand operator using the right hand and focusing on the target while seeing superimposed sights.

Figure 7-34 A right hand operator using the left hand and focusing on the target while seeing superimposed sights.

The author just before a firearms qualification at Dallas Police Department talked to a fellow officer about canting the pistol when firing with the non-dominant hand. The officer confessed he felt the rounds fired with his non-dominant hand were wasted. The officer went on to say he did not have control of the pistol and trying to align the sights by bending the wrist was uncomfortable. The author explained the body's natural tendency to align the pistol with the dominant eye could be enhanced by slightly canting the pistol. The officer after the qualification thanked the author for the advice and admitted to shooting a career high score.

To help develop muscles used to grip the pistol for combat shooting try this exercise.[50] While in a fighting stance hold an *unloaded* or *inert* pistol extended in the line of sight of the dominant eye using one hand. Contract the muscles of the firing hand by pulling the three fingers wrapped around the pistol's grip straight to the rear equally and centerline of the pistol. Let the trigger finger naturally curve in and position itself on the trigger. Squeeze the three fingers hard until the pistol trembles, relax until trembling stops. Maintain the rearward pressure for five breaths and release. Then repeat the exercise five times or until becoming fatigued. Be sure to breath throughout the exercise and rest for five breaths between each set. Perform the exercise with each hand and slightly cant the pistol's sights into the dominant eye's line of sight when practicing with the non-dominant hand.

Retention

Use the retention firing position when an adversary is at arm's reach. It may be the adversary is attacking by viciously punching, kicking, using an edged weapon, blunt object, or trying to gain control of the operator's pistol. In the three Federal Bureau of Investigation studies: Killed in the Line of Duty, In the Line of Fire, and Violent Encounters "...when unarmed offenders removed service weapons from officers, they shot or attempted to shoot the officer in every instance."[51] No operator is expected to take a beating, perhaps hospitalized, and all in the mere hope of not being killed with his or her own handgun.[52] A life-and-death attack at contact distance calls for hand-to-hand combat skills combined with an extremely fast draw followed by rapid multiple shots until the adversary is no longer a threat.

An operator should practice the retention position at 1 yard (0.91 meter) from a target. Hold the pistol canted just under the chest with the butt of the grip pressed against the body. Canting prevents the slide from hitting the body and provides a solid platform so the slide cycles properly. (Figures 7-35 and 7-36) How far the pistol is pulled back will depend on the flexibility in the shoulder and the circumstances of the situation.

Figure 7-35 Retention (front)

Figure 7-36 Retention (side)

The target area is any exposed center of mass on the adversary's body. However, there is a likelihood the operator's non-firing hand will be pushing or striking the adversary's face, neck, and chest. To prevent a self-inflicted gunshot shoot the adversary's pelvic griddle (hips and groin). A gunshot to the pelvic griddle is a devastating injury that normally results in not being able to stand. However, the adversary may still have use of his or her hands even after sustaining the injury. Be committed to shooting the adversary until he or she is no longer mentally or physically capable of continuing a deadly attack.

WARNING: A compensated pistol fired from the retention position can injure an operator. The injury occurs when the longitudinal openings point at the operator's body. The openings release a significant muzzle blast and particulate capable of causing serious bodily injury when the pistol fires.[53] Read the manufacturer's safety instructions before firing a compensated pistol.

CONTACT SHOT

The contact shot is not to be confused with the retention firing position. A *contact shot* is placing the muzzle of the pistol against an adversary's body and pulling the trigger. The bullet not only causes damage, but also the muzzle blast entering the body.[54] What if the muzzle contacts the adversary's body and the pistol will not fire? The slide will likely be *out of battery*.[55] Pull the pistol back slightly and pull the trigger again—the pistol should fire. An advantage of having a handgun mounted light that extends past the muzzle is the *standoff* effect. The pistol will not come out of battery because the flashlight makes contact when held against an adversary's body and not the muzzle.

A contact shot may need to be used when an operator comes to the aid of another operator engaged in a hand-to-hand fight with an adversary. The adversary may be using an edged weapon against the operator or trying to take his or her firearm. Normally it is not an option to use a pistol to shoot from a distance at such an adversary that is fighting with another operator. A better option may be to close the distance putting the muzzle against the adversary's head and firing. The responding operator must be mindful of the bullet's trajectory in the case of over penetration to prevent hitting the victim operator.

Another technique is to approach the adversary from behind. The responding operator will use the fingers on the non-firing hand to grab the adversary's jaw pulling it rearward trapping his head against the operator's body. The operator puts his or her muzzle against the adversary's head and fires. Stabilize the head *only* long enough to place the muzzle in the desired location and fire. There can be no hesitation between the time of pulling the head (stabilizing) and placing the muzzle. Do both simultaneously. The operator must fire the shot at such an angle that if the bullet over penetrates it does not hit his or her hand securing the adversary's jaw or hit the victim operator.

A contact shot used correctly is an effective survival option during a deadly hand-to-hand fight. Firing with the muzzle against the adversary's torso can cause significant damage, but causes more damage when held to the head. An operator in a life-threatening hand-to-hand fight should see the contact shot as a means to end the attack quickly.

The operator with speed, surprise, and aggression should place the pistol against the adversary's body or head and pull the trigger until the attack stops. In a clinch[56] situation, quickly placing the muzzle under the adversary's head and shooting may be the best option. The adversary may not even be aware of what the operator is doing until it is too late. This is especially true in a dark environment. However, the same holds true for the adversary using the contact shot against an operator.

STRIKE AND TRANSITION

The author while investigating drug activity had one person detained and a crowd began to gather. From that crowd one person came quickly toward the author. He reflexively palm struck the person in the chest knocking him back about 6 feet (1.82 meters). The man as he staggered back had a look of rage in his eyes, but the author had transitioned to his pepper spray. The man decided not to make a second run and the one-hand palm strike in this incident worked as intended. The author transitioned to his pepper spray because the man was unarmed. He could have as easily transitioned to his pistol if circumstances warranted.

The *strike and transition* force option can be performed with one or two hands. Perform the technique using violence of action. A palm strike is deliverable to the chest or face. In another incident while serving drug related arrest warrants, three females attacked the author. He immediately shoved *both* palms forward striking one of the females in her face resulting in a bloody nose. That stopped the attack, arrests were made, and the female struck by the author was subsequently convicted in court.

Using both hands will provide twice the striking area than one hand. Use the strike and transition to get the adversary away and hopefully off balance so a weapon can be accessed. A sidestep combined with a forceful two-hand strike violently knocking the adversary away and hopefully to the ground will have the greatest chance of success.[57] It also coincides with solving one problem at a time. Get the adversary away and then transitioning to a weapon. (Figure 7-37 through 7-39) This type of shoving tactic has been captured on video from a dashboard camera.[58]

The strike and transition technique might be the appropriate response to a *deadly* spontaneous attack. The operator should move with speed and agility. The operator sidesteps *if* possible while violently striking the adversary knocking him or her off balance and preferably on the ground.

Simultaneously the operator draws and drives the pistol into his or her line of sight acquiring a sight picture and fires multiple shots into the adversary's high center mass or any other exposed area. Shoot until the adversary is no longer a deadly threat. Scan the surrounding area visually and audibly for additional adversaries.

Figure 7-37 Standing   ***Figure 7-38*** Strike   ***Figure 7-39*** Extend

SHOOTING AT MOVING TARGETS

Especially for police officers and military operators training should include some type of surprise targets that move. Preferably use human silhouette targets capable of charging, retreating, bobbing (quickly appearing and disappearing), and traversing. Traversing targets are especially useful in duplicating an adversary moving at either right angles or oblique angles. Those with an interest in operational survival will find it easy to integrate practical scenarios and moving targets. Using previous incidents within the organization as a guide is an excellent starting point for practical scenarios.

The Federal Bureau of Investigation's annual publication of Law Enforcement Officers Killed and Assaulted contains a narrative of how officers were killed and can be used as a guide for practical scenarios. Make sure scenarios are winnable for the operator.[59] Not that scenarios are designed to be easily won by the operator, but the scenarios should be winnable. Operators do *not* need to be taught how to die, but making bad decisions can result in a simulated death in a scenario. Successes and failures both provide learning lessons.

An adversary is not likely to stand still to be shot by an operator. An adversary in a deadly force encounter at the first opportunity will move in an attempt to gain a position of advantage to kill the victim. The adversary must be stopped before gaining that advantage. It is considerably more difficult to shoot a moving target than a static target. However, there are methods that can be employed to reduce the difficultly. The methods advocated are with the understanding that using deadly force is reasonable.

Follow-through is crucial to get hits on the adversary when using the tracking or trapping method. This is especially true for the tracking method. The follow-through allows the operator to maintain a continuous sight picture on the adversary. There are three steps to shooting a moving adversary: (1) index on the center of mass, (2) track the adversary, and (3) maintain a sight picture. An operator that can see a continuous sight picture while focusing on a moving target will experience a newfound level of marksmanship previously thought impossible. The operator no doubt will wish he or she had been doing it all along.

Tracking

An armed adversary running from one place to another to gain a tactical advantage is a fast moving target.[60] However, a moving adversary is susceptible to being shot at two points: (1) the moment of moving from a position (gaining speed) and (2) the slowing down at a new position (losing speed).[61] As the adversary is running, maintain a sight picture while pulling the trigger.[62] The operator can fire additional follow-up shots at the adversary *if* the first burst misses. This is called *tracking*.

An operator may find it useful to place the sights on the leading edge of an adversary that is moving at right or diagonal angles 15 to 20 yards (13.71 to 18.28 meters) from the operator.[63] Usually there is no tactical advantage to place the sights on the leading edge of an adversary while firing at 7 yards (6.4 meters) or less which is the distance common of police involved shootings.[64] Tracking requires moving the pistol while pulling the trigger and can be challenging even for experienced operators.

Trapping

Being able to anticipate the adversary's next position allows an excellent opportunity to engage him or her. An example would be an adversary that committed murder and coming out of the building and getting into a getaway vehicle.[65] The adversary would likely move from the building to the driver's door or *if* a driver is sitting in the vehicle then the passenger's door. Maintaining a sight picture on the car's door and shooting the adversary after coming in view would be *trapping*.[66]

The tactic will also work on an adversary moving *slowly* in a continuous direction. Place the sight picture in front of the adversary. Once the adversary comes into the line of sight, pull the trigger in a controlled, but sudden manner. Operators who can pull the trigger without reacting to the firearm discharging may fire better using this technique than tracking because the pistol is held steady. Take any slack out of the trigger before firing. Holding the breath is likely to occur just before pulling the trigger.

SHOOTING AT MULTIPLE TARGETS

Shooting at multiple targets is shooting one target at a time compressed into a short time frame.[67] The body's natural response to stress is useful for increasing survivability when engaging multiple adversaries. An automatic impulse from the brain causes the arm and hand to stop when the pistol reaches the line of sight. The key point in training is to allow natural movement: eyes, head, and body. Do not force unnatural movements. Keep the upper body stable and *if* possible transition by pivoting at the knees. There must be a superimposed sight image on *each* target before, during, and after firing.[68] The natural ability of eye-hand coordination combined with a superimposed sight image is extremely fast in engaging multiple targets.

When faced with multiple adversaries the operator's ability to transition from tunnel vision to scanning is critical for survival. There are combat doctrines that advocate assessing the adversaries and then shooting the most dangerous adversary first.[69] In reality, the first adversary *recognized* as a threat will probably be the first one shot.[70] Many times this is the closest adversary, but *not* always. The eyes pick up movement first, and the adversary moving would probably be first to get the operator's attention.[71] The operator will likely experience tunnel vision and be visually focused on the adversary being engaged. Only after that adversary is stopped will the tunnel vision subside and the capability of scanning for additional adversaries return.

The operator will need to shoot, move, and communicate to stay ahead of the adversaries. The operator might be able to maneuver putting one adversary in the other's line of fire. The operator might also be able to put obstacles that can be used as cover in between the adversaries. The operator must be prepared to fire multiple rounds at each adversary to ensure hit probability and to stop any attack quickly. This is done with overwhelming violence of action at maximum speed to *prevent* other adversaries from mounting simultaneous attacks. The operator does not let up until the adversaries are incapable of fighting. The operator scans the area and fires at any remaining adversaries. This sequence continues until there are no more adversaries posing a deadly threat.

After shooting the last known adversary, scan the area and assess, making sure the area of responsibility is clear. This is especially important before leaving cover and moving across the area. The operator must dominate his or her area of responsibility. Target Focused Sighted Shooting with practice can be used out to the maximum effective range of the pistol. Firing at distances beyond personal capabilities should *not* occur. Capabilities are realized through training and mandated qualification courses.

Maintaining situational awareness to assess the situation may provide crucial information allowing the operator to make necessary preparations—ever how slight. One of those preparations is for an operator to use a carbine *if* he or she has knowledge of armed adversaries in an operational area. However, combat has a tendency to begin and end. It is highly *unlikely* that during combat an operator would be capable of using a pistol to fight back to where a carbine is located.[72] A police officer as an example would probably *not* be capable of retrieving a carbine from the trunk of a police vehicle once the gunfight begins. The police officer's handgun will likely have to be used to finish the fight.

NOTE: A common practice in recreational shooting is to transition between targets by letting the recoil carry the pistol over to the next target. An operator in combat must confirm that the adversary when shot is no longer a threat *before* transitioning to the next adversary.

MOVING OFF THE LINE OF ATTACK

Moving off the line of attack is used primarily to defeat the ambush in close quarters. An adversary will *assess*, *prepare*, and *act* when attacking an operator.[73] The adversary assesses where the operator is located, prepares a position of advantage readying the weapon, and then acts completing the attack. The operator does *not* have to wait for the action to occur and can interrupt the attack at the assess stage or prepare stage. The least desirable stage to interrupt is the act stage, because at that point the attack is already underway. The attack could be with a blunt object, knife, or firearm. The operator needs to get off the line of attack and make an explosive movement to his or her pistol.[74]

The operator moves as fast as humanly possible in a direction that is off the line of attack while drawing and suddenly stops as the pistol is on the adversary. (Figures 7-40 through 7-42) The explosive movement changes the *operational flow* in favor of the operator. The movement may be forward, rearward, laterally, diagonally, or anywhere in between in relation to the adversary. The operator faces the direction he or she is moving (no running backwards). The operator from suddenly stopping and then shooting will likely have his or her feet far apart. After the adversary is no longer a threat, scan the area for additional threats, and reset the feet returning to a fighting stance. The operator is prepared for the next movement *if* required. Assess the adversary and scan the area again.

Figure 7-40 Standing   *Figure 7-41* Move   *Figure 7-42* Extend
and Draw

Captured on video from the dashboard camera was this type of counterambush tactic.[75] An attacker reaching for a handgun was shoved by a state trooper who broke contact momentarily with his attacker. The trooper to gain distance from his attacker and avoid being shot ran in a zigzag pattern only long enough to draw his pistol. The trooper with his pistol in hand abruptly turned facing the attacker, stopped, and shot him.[76] This is an excellent example of a police officer making an explosive movement while simultaneously drawing his handgun. A deputy in another incident was captured on a video from the dashboard camera during a traffic stop moving off the line of attack, stopping, and returning fire.[77] The ability to draw while moving as fast as humanly possible is a fundamental skill that every operator should possess.

The explosive movement can also be used to move beside and in front of a person to provide protection or to a position of cover. A range drill for teaching this is to have a person stand on the firing line. The instructor will call "move right!" The operator will run to the right side of the person, draw, and fire a specified number of rounds at specific targets. Repeat the process on the left side with the command "move left!" Finally, the operator will run in front of the person and stop, draw and fire on the command of "move front!" This drill helps to teach how to move and shoot around other people. Perform the same drill with similar objects found in the operational area and routinely used as cover.

The environment will dictate how far *if* any that an operator can move off the line of attack. A police officer conducting a traffic stop and shot at on arrival to the driver's window will instinctively want to move off the line of attack. The police officer gains nothing by moving off the line of attack and into the path of a moving vehicle. The police officer in this instance needs to prepare in advance for moving off the line of attack. The police officer should offset his or her police vehicle from the violator's vehicle to provide a safety lane. The police vehicle should be parked to provide a tactical advantage by having a safety lane wide enough for the police officer to move off the line of attack without fear of being struck by a passing vehicle.

CLOSING THE DISTANCE

There are situations that call for quickly reducing the distance to an adversary. Sometimes reducing the distance is the most effective tactic and should be an option taught in training. To reduce the distance between an operator and an adversary use the technique called *closing the distance.*[78] There are *two variations* of closing the distance. The operator will do one of two things: (1) the operator will run at full speed, come to a complete stop and shoot; or (2) the operator shoots (ballistic cover) while quickly moving to gain a position of advantage. A police officer in one incident thought he was running while shooting at a suspect. The police officer in reality ran, quickly stopped, and then shot the suspect.[79]

In the *first variation* of closing the distance, the operator will at the first opportunity providing a *superior* tactical advantage, run, stop, and engage the adversary. The operator may need to do so because of poor visibility from smoke, dust, etc., masking the adversary, or to move in front of innocent people to get a clear shot. The key components to this Israeli technique are velocity (running at full speed), quickly stopping in a stable firing position (usually the fighting stance), and immediately shooting the adversary. Stop quickly by stamping each foot back and forth.[80]

The *stamping*[81] *technique* maximizes stability (helps prevent the feet from flying out from underneath the body). In a disruptive environment with unstable surfaces such as rocks, sand, mud, and wet grass—operators are susceptible to falls. Stamping is learned by quickly moving forward one step and stamping one step. Stamping one step is striking one foot hard against the ground and then the other. After correctly moving forward one step and stamping, add two steps on each side, then three, until five steps is reached, and then run at full speed for longer distances and quickly stop. The stamping technique has also been described as a sprint forward and shuffle, or stutter step to stop the forward momentum.[82]

WARNING: When running or moving with a pistol in hand, hold the pistol between the waist and chest. Keep the trigger finger on the receiver and the barrel pointed at the ground (carry position). Do *not* point the muzzle in the air, especially in city environments with multistory buildings. Running with a two-hand grip on the pistol creates an unnatural side-to-side motion.

In summary, accomplish the recommended technique in three steps:

1. Break the velocity (running at full speed and stopping).

2. Move into a stable shooting platform (fighting stance).

3. Engage the target (use a sight image superimposed on the target).

Closing the distance is an effective tactical maneuver that has been captured on dashboard videos. A police officer used the technique of closing the distance, quickly stopping, and firing.[83] Regrettably, it can also be used against police officers.[84] A former Vietnam combat veteran murdered a deputy by effectively firing a rifle and closing the distance. The suspect during the initial engagement ran toward the deputy, stopped and fired. In a subsequent engagement, he outflanked the wounded deputy by using his vehicle as cover, and taking several quick steps while firing.

In the *second variation* of closing the distance addresses the issue of what if the first or second operator entering a room is immediately met with gunfire. The appropriate action is to take the necessary number of quick steps to get out of the doorway to allow other operators in the room to get as many guns on the adversary as possible and secure the room.[85] The operator will continue to fire while stepping out of the team's path. This is not the continuous slow walking and shooting taught in some tactical training programs. The objective is not to slowly walk and shoot, but to engage the adversary while quickly moving only far enough to create a gap so other team members can flow into the room.

An operator must be capable of maneuvering at a realistic speed expected under operational conditions and shoot a target also maneuvering. When training on the range use the command "Move!" Operators will get accustom to hearing it and respond immediately.[86] The operator's core needs to be tight to maintain the upper body index while quickly moving and then shooting. The operator after making entry in a room would need to take a side step, stop, and shoot in order to make a *precision* shot on an adversary masked (concealed) by an innocent person.[87] The operator should allow his or her lower body to negotiate terrain naturally and the upper body to maintain an index to engage the adversary effectively.

NOTE: A human has a tendency to flee or stand and fight. A Special Air Service (SAS) soldier and instructor explained room clearing to the author as, "Make entry, plant, and shoot."[88]

It is in the best interest of the law enforcement community to embrace effective tactics. Closing the distance to gain a tactical advantage is one of those tactics and a viable option under certain conditions. Some firearms instructors have no problem teaching shooting on the move. The technique has the feet walking a narrow path forward heel to toe, and backward toe to heel. Walking with the feet so close together reduces the body's ability to balance from side to side. Instability of the body is an undesirable condition when firing a pistol.

The *heel to toe* and *toe to heel* while shooting techniques are too dangerous to use *if* the training area is uneven or littered with curbs, poles, cans, bottles, limbs, or rocks. Why teach techniques that are dangerous to use under realistic conditions? Why teach a technique that requires a flat sterile range for it to be performed safely? Walking slowly toward the muzzle of a firearm is an effective method to test body armor.[89] When is the last time a dashboard video has captured a police officer using the tactic of walking slowly toward an adversary that was shooting back? Operators should be proficient at moving to shoot more so than trying to shoot on the move.

NOTE: Study the environmental conditions and movements of operators in combat. Look at what got them killed and what saved their lives. Then build a practical training program that promotes operator survival in the worst of circumstances.

FOOT PURSUITS AND SHOOTING

Armed civilians and military operators are not normally involved in foot pursuits commonly occurring in law enforcement, but the information is useful to any operator pursing an adversary on foot. The resolve and commitment of an adversary to kill an operator during a foot pursuit should *not* be underestimated. In an interview with a detective, a suspect admitted during a foot pursuit he had set up in *three* different locations to ambush the police officer.[90]

Simulation training and *live fire* training should include how to pursue an adversary on foot and engage him or her with a pistol. Such training tests the operator's firearm proficiency, fitness, and agility. Fitness and agility are attributes often required by an operator during dangerous situations. Without a doubt, there is a certain amount of risk when conducting dynamic training. Nevertheless, risk adverse leadership that prevents realistic training weakens the operator survival program of the organization.

Environmental Conditions

Operators need to practice running in similar environments in which they work. A solution to this issue is to construct an obstacle course on-site at the firearms range. The obstacle course needs to represent the common obstacles that operators negotiate in their area of operation. At the Dallas Police Department during foot pursuits police officers routinely jumped chain link fences. The author during a foot pursuit had climbed a chain link fence, jumped from another fence onto a roof, ran across the roof, and from the roof jumped to the ground. In another incident, he climbed to a second story balcony to gain entry into an apartment.

The point is to make the obstacle course realistic to the operational environment. Another option is to use a state mandated physical agility test for police officers. Begin the training with the operator running the obstacle course. Using North Carolina's Police Officer Physical Abilities Test (POPAT) as an example, the operator would run the POPAT course as described in the next section. The operator immediately after completing the POPAT course would view a picture of a suspect and move to contact.

Police Officer Physical Abilities Test (POPAT)

Begin the test with the operator in a vehicle seated on the driver's side with the seat belt on and a hand at the 2 and 10 o'clock positions on the steering wheel. Give the operator two street names.

1. The operator on the command "Go" removes his or her seat belt, gets out of the vehicle, and runs 100 yards (91.44 meters) in a straight line, and then back to the rear passenger side of the vehicle.

2. The operator opens the rear door, removes the seat belt from the 150-pound (68-kilogram) dummy or bag, and pulls it from the rear passenger area of the vehicle. The operator drags the dummy 50 feet (15.24 meters) placing it gently on the ground at the staircase. The body drag must be done walking backwards while grasping the dummy under both arms.

NOTE: Course personnel will need to close the rear passenger door and reposition the weighted bag or dummy on the ground beside that door.

3. The operator runs up and back down a staircase (five steps on each side) three times, and touches each step.

4. The operator runs 25 feet (7.62 meters) from the staircase to a door that has 50 pounds (22.6 kilograms) of resistance and pushes it open using body force.

5. The operator once through the door performs 20 military style push-ups and 20 sit-ups (feet held).

NOTE: Push-ups and sit-ups are standardized with no exceptions for age or gender.

6. The operator runs back to the staircase and again runs three times up and back down touching each step.

7. The operator runs 25 feet (7.62 meters) from the staircase to a 40-foot (12.19-meter) long enclosed culvert and crawls through on hands and knees. Black plastic is hanging on each end of the culvert—dark inside.

8. The operator once out of the culvert again performs 20 military style push-ups and 20 sit-ups (feet held).

9. The operator runs 100 yards (91.44 meters) and returns 100 yards (91.44 meters) back to the rear passenger door of the vehicle where the weighted bag or dummy is positioned.

10. The operator drags the bag or dummy 50 feet (15.24 meters) placing it on the ground at the staircase, recites the two street names given in precisely the same order stopping the clock. An operator that *cannot* remember the two street names must run another 100 yards (91.44 meters) and return 100 yards (91.44 meters) stopping the clock. (Figure 7-43) Timed Score: Minimum time for completion of the course is 7 minutes and 20 seconds. This concludes the North Carolina's Police Officer Physical Abilities Test (POPAT).

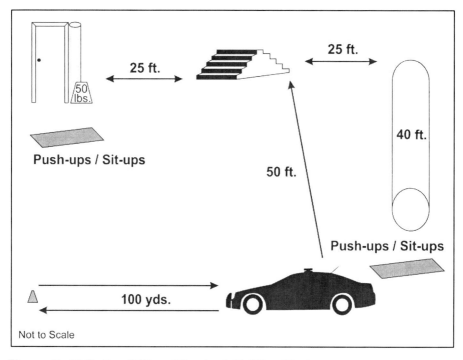

Figure 7-43 Police Officer Physical Abilities Test

The operator for value added training is then shown a color picture for 5 seconds of an armed suspect. The operator moves to contact with the suspect by sprinting to the 10-yard (9.14-meter) line on the firing range where an array of threat and no-threat targets are located. The operator must quickly draw and decide which target is the suspect and justifies deadly force. The operator fires a 5-shot burst at maximum speed. The operator should reload when appropriate and use positions of cover if available while engaging other threat targets if identified. Using cover effectively should provide some protection for the operator from the *simulated* line of fire of the threat targets and reinforce the ability to shoot, move, and communicate. The shot group on any threat target should be within required accuracy. Fatigue combined with the 10-yard (9.14-meter) distance and target discrimination requirement will test the integrity of the operator's shooting fundamentals.

Stamping Technique Applied to Foot Pursuits

The stamping technique is a controlled method for an operator to stop and engage an adversary while in a foot pursuit. The adversary will typically use two techniques to shoot at a pursuing operator. The first is running and simultaneously pointing the pistol over the shoulder and firing. The second is to stop running abruptly, hide, and fire at the operator (hasty ambush). An operator can use the stamping technique to stop quickly and assume a stable position to engage the adversary.

An operator cannot afford the luxury of being irresponsible and firing wildly as does the adversary. Operators must concede that shooting while running is *not* an option.[91] Running in this context is a rapid movement of the legs while shooting at a fleeing adversary. The focus is on the operator's ability to quickly stop and assume a stable firing position to engage the adversary.

To go from running to a fighting stance, lower the body into a crouch by bending the knees (lowers the center of gravity) and quickly shorten the stride by stamping each foot hard against the ground (back and forth). As the non-firing side foot makes the final step and slides to the outside just in front of the firing side foot, (wider than shoulder width) maintain the fighting stance and draw the pistol to engage the adversary. The body will have a natural tendency to stop in this position on flat ground. However, the feet will naturally adapt to an environment and may not be in the described position. The goal is to be in a stable firing position to engage an adversary effectively.

DANGER: Do not pursue directly behind an adversary because there is a greater chance of being struck by gunfire. To counter this risk run *offset* from an adversary anytime terrain allows. Change to a different offset position *if* possible each time an adversary looks back.

LOW LIGHT SHOOTING

Flashlights are used primarily to *navigate, locate adversaries, identify adversaries*, and *engage adversaries*.[92] A strobe light or bright white light can disorient an adversary. One manufacturer recommends an LED flashlight have at least 50 lumens to overwhelm the dark-adapted vision temporarily of an adversary.[93] Shining the light in an adversary's eyes can result in temporarily blindness.[94] A person must be identified as a threat *before* taking action. An operator at night using a flashlight will probably need to be about 15 yards (13.71 meters) or closer to identify what is in an adversary's hands.[95] The farthest distance from the target for night qualification with a pistol is 15 yards (13.71 meters) for law enforcement officers in the State of North Carolina.[96]

The flashlight in law enforcement is frequently used to conduct building searches and perform nighttime traffic stops. It is important to have a flashlight even during the daytime. A darkened basement or abandoned building when searching will require a flashlight. Flashlight techniques for this reason go beyond the description of shooting at night.[97] A more appropriate description is *low light* shooting techniques. It does not have to be dark to practice low light shooting techniques. An operator can practice the techniques in the daylight to correct skill problems and build procedural memory. However, the techniques at some point must be practiced in the dark to verify their effectiveness and the operator's skill.

WARNING: Exposure to strobing lights may cause dizziness, disorientation, and nausea. About 0.00025 percentage of the population suffers from photosensitive epilepsy and may experience seizures or blackouts triggered by strobing lights. Go to www.epilepsyfoundation.org to find more information about photosensitive epilepsy. An operator that had symptoms linked to photosensitive epilepsy should consult a doctor before using a strobing light.[98]

A flashlight is a tool that when properly deployed can increase the operator's survival. An operator in a lit area can use a flashlight to scan into dark areas. The operator in a lit area is already visible and turning on a flashlight does not give away his or her position. An operator on the other hand already in a dark area should *not* use a flashlight unless necessary. The darkness provides concealment, but it is lost once the flashlight is activated. Do *not* move from a lit area to a dark area without using a light *if* possible. This is especially true for a dark area that may conceal an adversary posing a danger. Maintain visual contact when an adversary is located by flooding the area with light to avoid having to relocate him or her.[99]

An operator that practices shooting or qualifies at night may notice a tighter shot group in comparison to daytime shooting. This occurs because the operator is not distracted with the visual noise prevalent in daylight. The light also helps the operator focus on a smaller area of the target. Some flashlights have an adjustable beam from a narrow to wide dispersion. Do not adjust the beam so wide that it is difficult to identify people and objects. Light will bounce off light colors and it can be beneficial. Shining a flashlight at a white ceiling may provide illumination for an entire room.[100]

Police officers routinely place a flashlight under their arm for lighting personal workspace (issuing citations, field note taking, etc.). A flashlight that has a *constant on* capability by turning the head or pressing a switch near the head provides for efficient manipulation when tucked under an arm. The flashlight held under the firing side arm when reloading is not the preferable method, but it does allow the arm and hand handling the magazine to move freely.[101] Other options are to put the flashlight in the waistband, pocket, or on the ground *if* kneeling.

When reloading *if* circumstances allow—turn off the flashlight and return it to the holder (preferable method). Using a momentary switch ensures the light will automatically go off simply by removing pressure off the switch. There is a greater chance of dropping a flashlight tucked under the arm or in the waistband when running. Some operators in Special Operations consider dropped equipment—lost equipment.[102] A dropped flashlight can result in a blown lamp. Keep a spare lamp and batteries nearby for any light source used operationally.

Operators, especially police officers need to use a three light system: (1) firearm mounted light, (2) primary light, and (3) backup light.[103] A convenient backup light is a small flashlight clipped to the inside of a pocket.[104] (Figure 7-44) Dropping, damaging, or losing a primary flashlight confirms the importance of a backup flashlight. The flashlight must also be easily accessible. Present the pistol first and then the flashlight when presenting a flashlight in conjunction with a pistol.[105] An operator during a deadly force encounter may have trouble manipulating a flashlight and pistol together.[106] The pistol obviously has a higher priority.

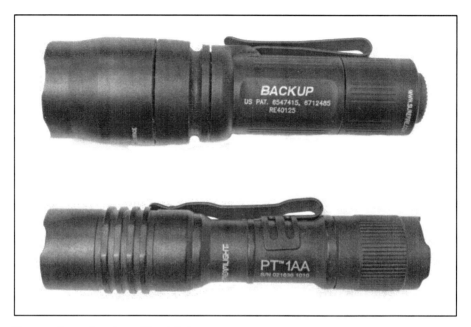

Figure 7-44 *Backup Flashlights*

Flashlight Techniques

Flashlight techniques must work when firing a pistol with hands that are covered in fresh blood, rain, or sweat. This requirement is the foundation of flashlight techniques used for self-protection. How should a flashlight be held? That will depend on how the flashlight is going to be used. Flashlight techniques are used much more often for searching than shooting. Use techniques that work efficiently and feel natural. A flashlight with a switch near the head works well with the side-by-side technique. A flashlight with a tailcap switch works well with the shoulder technique and the offset technique. (Figure 7-45)

Operators should *not* overcomplicate using a flashlight. Turn it on and point it at whatever needs to be illuminated. The more natural the position feels the less fatiguing it will be to use. There are three types of flashlight activations: (1) *proper activation* (PA) of turning on the light for a tactical advantage, (2) *improper activation* (IA) of turning the light on whether intentional or unintentional resulting in a tactical disadvantage, and (3) *accidental activation* (AA) caused by mechanical failure of the light that could not be humanly anticipated. Police officers generally hold a flashlight in their non-firing hand allowing for switch activation and the firing hand to remain free. Some flashlight designs are more user friendly in comparison to others when using a *two-hand* grip with the pistol.

Figure 7-45 *A flashlight with a tailcap switch used with the syringe technique (top), and a flashlight used with the inverted-L technique (bottom).*

Although there are several flashlight techniques listed in this section—an operator would do well to find one that is natural and simple to use. An operator being shot at in close quarters combat will have little *if* any concern for his or her flashlight and may drop it as in the case of a state trooper captured on a dashboard camera.[107] It certainly is not worth hanging on to a flashlight and trying to manipulate it with a pistol and being killed for doing so.

Shoulder Technique: The shoulder technique is a natural method to use a flashlight. (Figure 7-46) The shoulder technique has probably been around since police officers began making traffic stops and illuminating the interior of vehicles. The shoulder technique provides a quick and effective method when rapid firing a pistol and reduces fatigue while conducting searches. The shoulder technique also allows the operator to see the pistol sights and use daytime shooting skills at night.

Offset Technique: Using offset technique[108] with the palm facing up allows the thumb to turn on or off a flashlight equipped with a tailcap switch. The offset technique with the light held forward and away from the body is a variation of the shoulder technique. (Figure 7-47) Some operators and trainers may view the offset technique as obsolete. However, the following suspects' statements give credence the technique is a viable survival option, especially while searching in the dark for an armed adversary.

Figure 7-46 *Shoulder Technique*   **Figure 7-47** *Offset Technique*

A police officer was shot in the chest while scanning a backyard for a suspect. When interviewed about the attack, the suspect said, "I fired at the flashlight."[109] A police officer in another incident had chased a suspect through a courtyard and had lost sight of him. The police officer was shot in the chest and leg while using a flashlight in an attempt to locate the suspect. When interviewed about the police officer having a flashlight, the suspect said, "Yeah, it was lit up; that's how I noticed him. He's easy. For one thing, he's got a flashlight, and he's got on black, the word *police* lit up like a reflector."[110] Holding a flashlight close to the body or leaving it constantly on under certain conditions can be detrimental to an operator's survival.

Side-by-side Technique: The pistol and flashlight are side-by-side and level so the operator can engage a target or adversary. The thumb or a finger is on the side-mounted on/off switch. A flashlight specifically designed for the syringe technique also works. The twist tailcap switch from the on position is turned counterclockwise slightly to the off position. The thumb applies *side* pressure against head of the light resulting in counter *side* pressure against the tailcap activating the light. The thumb of the flashlight hand is straight and the pad below the thumb's first knuckle presses underneath the firing hand thumb and against the grip of the pistol with either flashlight. (Figures 7-48 and 7-49)

Figure 7-48 *Side-by-side Technique (front)*

Figure 7-49 *Side-by-side Technique (close-up)*

A variation of the technique is to leave the hands separated with the light pointing forward and the pistol in a high ready or low ready position. This is probably one of the most *practical* and *efficient* techniques to use. The technique can be used with a flashlight that has a tailcap switch push button, but does *not* twist to an on or off position. However, the flashlight would have to remain constantly on and that is *not* recommended. The tailcap switch that does not twist on and off cannot be operated while holding the flashlight using this technique.

Syringe Technique: A flashlight specifically designed for the syringe technique works with a two-hand grip.[111] (Figure 7-50) An efficient method to present the flashlight is to have the bezel down in its holder and the tailcap pointing up. The non-firing hand will grasp the light with its barrel in between the index finger and middle finger. Assume the thumbs forward grip with the ring and little fingers against the firing hand in the normal location. The light points forward and turns on and off with rearward pressure of the index and middle fingers pressing the tailcap switch against the palm of the hand.

Inverted-L Technique: A small 90-degree angle head flashlight (L flashlight) is another light that works with a two-hand grip.[112] The on/off push button switch is located on top of the head of the flashlight. The index finger wraps around the grip/battery compartment (barrel) and under the head with the back of the barrel resting against the front of the middle finger. (Figure 7-51) The method to present the flashlight is to have the barrel down in a holder and the head pointing forward. The index finger wraps under the flashlight's head and the light is pulled from its holder. The hands join with the lower three fingers wrapping around the firing hand. This is called the *inverted-L* technique.[113] The fingers wrap in the same position as when a light is not used taking advantage of procedural memory. The non-firing hand thumb (thumbs forward grip) pushes down on the switch to turn on and off the light. The *syringe* technique and the *inverted-L* technique are used mainly for searching, apprehending, or engaging dangerous adversaries (known risk).

It is unlikely that a flashlight should remain constantly on in tactical situations. It will likely be better to scan with the eyes combined with momentarily turning the light on (about 1 second) and looking, turning off the light and moving to a new location (preferably laterally), turn the light back on and look, and repeat as necessary.[114] With multiple operators at a location, it may not be necessary for each one to have a light on. The illumination from an operator's light source may provide sufficient lighting for safe movement by other team members. Another technique is to use an *alternating* light technique. One team member will turn on a light and then back off. The next team member will turn on a light and then back off. Both team members will continuously move as the situation allows.

Figure 7-50 *Syringe Technique (close-up)*

Figure 7-51 *Inverted-L Technique (close-up)*

The fingers can be used to cover the lens of the flashlight partially to restrict the light when a small amount of light is required—such as lighting up a walkway.[115] A flashlight can be a double-edged sword. Operators must be aware of illuminating themselves. Light can reflect off cover and laminate the operator. The flashlight needs to be forward of the cover.[116] Likewise, an improper activation of the flashlight could compromise an operator or team's location resulting in disastrous consequences.[117] Utilizing simulation training in conjunction with video recordings for review[118] will help to provide an understanding of when and how to deploy a flashlight. An operator acting in the role of an adversary will probably benefit more from doing so than any other survival training.

A chief of police had attended an instructor marking cartridge course. The chief acting in the police officer role while using a handgun mounted light was shot three times in his hands. The police officer that role-played the suspect said, "I got blinded and shot at the light." The chief said, "My pistol would have been shot out of my hands."[119] A firearm mounted light can also be a disadvantage just the same as a flashlight. It is the operator's responsibility to understand the advantages and disadvantages of the firearm mounted light.

WARNING: The *crossed wrist* technique[120] used with a flashlight and pistol requires crisscrossing the hands. The arm holding the flashlight might sustain a self-inflicted gunshot in a stressful situation. The method also contorts the body and the operator becomes fatigued quickly. When pointing the *flashlight* at the target there is a tendency for the *pistol* to point off the target and vice versa.

Expect the Fight

The last thing an operator needs is to turn on a light and be startled by an adversary. The operator must believe the adversary *will* be located and it is just a matter of when. Such thinking puts the operator in the offensive mind-set to handle the situation and *not* be surprised. The pistol must be ready for immediate use. Muzzle flashes and noise from team members and adversaries alike will affect the personnel present *if* gunfire occurs. To what degree will likely depend on past training, ammunition fired, whether hearing protection is worn, and the severity of an alarm reaction.

NOTE: An operator should not overlook the option of locating a light switch and turning on lights when available instead of using a flashlight. There is also the tactic of flooding an area with vehicle lights (headlights, overheads, and spotlight).

Handgun Mounted Light

Many pistols feature mounting rails cut into the receiver for attaching a light. (Figure 7-52) There are several advantages to a handgun mounted light. The greatest advantage is being able to maintain both hands on the pistol while utilizing the light. A handgun mounted light also provides enough lumens to overwhelm the dark-adapted vision of an adversary temporarily. The light at the operator's discretion can be removed or installed. The light when installed must stay secure even after repeated firing. The light emitter must also be capable of withstanding the repeated jolts from the pistol recoiling.

Figure 7-52 *Handgun Mounted Light*

Law enforcement and the military have tactical pistol lights available with built-in laser and infrared (IR) technology. Infrared allows an operator to see and work in darkness. Using an IR for combat is relatively simple. The helmet mounted goggles or monocular are used to see the target and the firearm mounted laser is used to engage the target. This is an advantage over a white light. A light under the same circumstances would give away the operator's location compromising personal safety and the mission. The night vision goggles to remain secure and provide reliable and consistent use require a headband or helmet.

WARNING: Read the operator's manual for safety instructions and proper laser usage before participating in training or combat.

Some lights are also switchable from the white lamp to a visible laser, infrared illuminator, or laser as an aiming point designator. The light can be switched on or used intermittently. The thumb of the non-firing hand manipulates the light's activation switch.[121] Operators may find a deliberate motion of flipping the switch to up for constant on and flipping it down to off works well instead of trying to shoot while using the momentary function. The thumbs forward grip works well using this technique (non-firing hand thumb).

Some handgun mounted lights are available with a *grip switch*.[122] The switch uses a minimal center-mounted pad allowing the operator to activate the light with finger pressure. The grip pressure on the pistol would have to fluctuate in order to turn on and off the light. Fluctuations in grip pressure, especially in stressful situations could cause a negligent activation inadvertently revealing an operator's location. A former Navy SEAL stated, he found it incongruent that his firing grip had to be adjusted in order to manipulate the light.[123]

One organization that studies human dynamics in high stress, rapidly unfolding encounters using force recommends that officers avoid the switching device as it "…creates risk of an unintended firearm discharge during high-stress confrontations because of its design."[124] The same organization that studies human dynamics suggests "…relying instead on the on-off mechanism that is built into the flashlight itself and can be activated when needed with the non-dominant hand." [125] The manufacturer disagrees with the findings that the grip switch should be avoided and states proper use of the product is dependent on training.[126]

Various companies build quality firearm mounted lights[127] and some with a built in laser.[128] The handgun mounted light uses the same tactical techniques as a long gun with a mounted light. Using the same techniques for the handgun and long gun allows for standardized training and application in the operational area. It is crucial the trigger finger remain on the receiver and the muzzle pointed in the *appropriate* direction. Deployment of the firearm mounted light is usually during known risk situations such as searching or apprehending violent adversaries. Engaging with a firearm mounted light is done by the sequence of eyes, hands, and then exposed center mass.[129]

Do *not* point the handgun mounted light indiscriminately at innocent people. The operator when pointing the light is also pointing the firearm. Doing so in an official capacity that reasonably appeared necessary under the circumstances is lawful. However, *indiscriminately* pointing a pistol at innocent people even in an official capacity might result in a criminal charge.[130] Training an operator on the proper use of the handgun mounted light is necessary to help prevent allegations of misuse or criminal behavior.

The bullet's point of impact between 2 and 10 yards (1.82 and 9.14

meters) *may* be in the center of the light's beam (bore sighted).[131] This is easily confirmable on a firearms range. A handgun mounted light used in conjunction with guide rod laser may also have its dot in the center of the light's beam. This too would need confirming. An operator knowing the bullets impact in the center of the beam may have tactical options that otherwise would not be available. Likewise, it confirms pointing the center of light beam at a person is also pointing the muzzle.

An organization for safety reasons and by policy may recommend *not* removing and replacing the light when the pistol is loaded. There is also an issue of putting a light on a pistol while using a holster designed for one without a light. The pistol cannot be put back in its holster quickly because the light has to be removed first. The removing and replacing of the handgun mounted light during stressful situations would become even more difficult. It is best to use a holster design for the handgun mounted light. (Figure 7-53) There is some loss of ability to conceal the handgun with a mounted light, but it is a nonissue with operators wearing a uniform. Leave a light mounted on a pistol that has a built-in laser to prevent affecting its zero.

Figure 7-53 Left-hand holster for pistol with a light mounted.[132]

The pistol should be vetted using practice ammunition and ammunition carried operationally after installing any handgun mounted light. The added weight of the light may affect functioning and cause stoppages. However, the stoppage issue may not be the light. The cause can be shooting with the wrists and elbows unlocked or using underpowered ammunition. Handgun mounted light techniques should be practiced dry fire and live fire during the day before participating in night live fire. The light beam will not be as visible during the daytime, but the exercise allows operators to remedy equipment problems and technique issues before firing at night.

NOTE: Glock recommends the 11-coil spring for magazines used in G22, G31, G35, and G37 pistols equipped with a light.[133] Do *not* use the older 10-coil magazine spring with these pistol models in conjunction with a pistol mounted light. [134]

Laser Sight Techniques[135]

A *laser* (Light Amplification by Stimulated Emission of Radiation) sight projects a bright colored (red or green) laser beam on a target or adversary marking the aim point, but does *not* serve to illuminate the target or adversary.[136] Technically speaking a laser sight is not a sight in the sense the operator looks through the laser sight. The operator's focus is on the target or adversary and the colored dot is on the intended aim point.[137] The greatest advantage of a laser sight is the ability to keep the operator behind cover while exposing only the pistol to engage an adversary.[138] This tactical advantage alone *is* reason enough to use a laser sight. Even a severely injured operator shooting from an awkward position within the effective range of the pistol only has to hold the laser dot on the adversary and the round will go there.[139]

DANGER: "Laser radiation is emitted from the front aperture of the laser when the switch is activated."[140] Please read the manufacturer's warning labels and do *not* point a laser at someone's eye. Keep the laser pointed in an appropriate direction.

A pulsating (blinking) laser is three times more visible than a steady beam. The pulsating laser works on the same theory as emergency lights on a police vehicle—calling attention to the light. The range of a 5-milliwatt red laser (Class IIIA) before *washed out* in bright sunlight is about 16.4 yards (15 meters). However, in low light conditions the range can exceed 100 yards (91.44 meters) or more. The human eye in bright and low light conditions is more sensitive to the green than red. Green lasers works well indoors, especially where the operator transitions from dark to pools of light and back. The red laser sight can operate in temperatures from minus 15 to 130 degrees Fahrenheit (minus 9.4 to 54.4 degrees Celsius) and use little battery power. The green laser operates in a smaller temperature range of 40 to 100 degrees Fahrenheit (4.4 to 37.7 degrees Celsius) and uses more battery power than a red laser.

NOTE: *Infrared* laser systems for many pistols are available to law enforcement agencies and military units.[141]

The *guide rod laser* which is a laser mounted in a pistol's guide rod is advertised by one manufacturer as having the best possible point of aim to point of impact over various distances. As an example, the point of aim to point of impact at 20 yards (18.28 meters) for Glock compact pistols (19/23/32/38) is 2 inches (50.8 millimeters) and is set at the factory.[142] The guide rod laser sight replaces Glock's recoil spring assembly. No special holster is required because the guide rod laser does *not* change the external dimensions of the pistol or its ability to be concealed.

WARNING: "Safety glasses are recommended during all steps of assembly and disassembly"... of the guide rod laser sighting system.[143]

According to one manufacturer, a first-time installation can take about 20 minutes or less, and a subsequent installation and battery replacement less than a minute.[144] The receiver and slide protect the guide rod laser sight. The laser sighting system for a Glock pistol encompasses the laser diode, lens, solid state electronics, battery cap, recoil spring assembly, batteries, and slide lock. (Figure 7-54) Use of the guide rod laser does *not* affect Glock's warranty. However, remove the laser sight and related components and install factory components *before* returning the pistol to Glock for repair.

CAUTION: The guide rod laser's alignment or function is *not* warranted for ported or compensated firearms or firearms modified from stock factory configuration.[145]

The guide rod laser's activation ambidextrous switch is on the side of the pistol and has three distinct *click* positions.[146] When shooting using the thumbs forward grip with a Glock pistol the switch can be turned on using the trigger finger of the firing hand[147] and off with the thumb of the non-firing hand. Activation of the guide rod laser is a *deliberate* motion of constant on or off. This ensures the operator maintains control of the pistol and laser in the dark. Pulling or locking the slide to the rear automatically turns off the laser sight. This prevents the laser beam from disclosing the operator's location when reloading. The laser sight automatically shuts off after 30 minutes if accidentally activated.

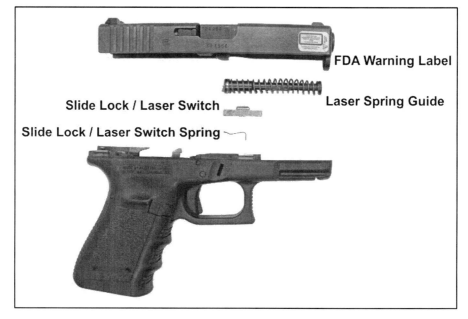

FDA Warning Label

Laser Spring Guide

Slide Lock / Laser Switch

Slide Lock / Laser Switch Spring

Figure 7-54 Guide Rod Laser

There may be opposition to the laser sight because it is an electronic device. However, the guide rod laser sight meets three government tests:[148] (1) Environmental - Department of Homeland Security blowing sand test. United States Navy and Marine corrosion test (salt water fog test) and extreme high-temperature operation; (2) Submersion - United States Navy SEAL submersion to 66 feet (20.11 meters) in salt water for

2 hours test and extreme low-temperature operation; and (3) Durability - United States Military and National Institute of Justice live fire tests and 6-foot (1.82-meter) drop to concrete from various firearm angles.

The laser's window on the muzzle end can get covered with a smoke residue. To clean the window—first *unload* the pistol and turn the laser sight *off.* Remove the smoke film using lens cleaner or alcohol on a cotton swab.[149] The manufacturer recommends after 5,000 rounds to replace the recoil spring on a guide rod laser for a Glock pistol.[150]

NOTE: According to one manufacturer, "Operation of a laser without the required safety labeling may violate federal law. The FDA requires the label supplied with your laser be affixed to the outside of the gun with the arrow pointing to the laser aperture." The FDA is the Food and Drug Administration in the United States.

Both eyes remain open when using the laser sight maximizing peripheral vision. Target Focused Sighted Shooting works well with a laser as focusing is on the target or adversary and *not* the front sight. A visual shift to the front sight can create two laser dots. Operators that understand how to shoot with both eyes open will find it easy to use a laser sight. The most efficient method to use the laser is for the operator to focus on an aim point on the target or adversary and bring the pistol into the line of sight superimposing the dot on the aim point. The operator having to take time to hunt down the dot visually will shoot slower.[151] Shooting with a laser sight at longer ranges can be faster than iron sights for some operators, but it may not produce as tight of a group.[152]

An adversary with a colored dot on his or her chest might see it as a visual prompt and be more prone to surrendering.[153] Most police officers using a blinking laser report a decrease in the aggressiveness of some suspects and they comply with the arrest according to one manufacturer.[154] The de-escalation of a situation without the use of deadly force is a desirable and preferred outcome. However, operators must *not* put themselves and innocent people at risk in an attempt to use a pulsating laser sight as a deterrent when deadly force is reasonable and necessary.

There are also disadvantages to using a laser sight. The device might become misaligned or stop working.[155] While searching with a laser it can give away the operator's location and show the direction of movement. The dot and its beam are visible in smoky, cloudy, misty, or high humidity environments.[156] The washout effect of the dot is also an issue. The dot's visibility can be further diminished in rain, fog, smoke, and when used in conjunction with a white light illuminating certain colors of clothing. Operators should *not* see a laser sight as a replacement of their iron sights.

Operators must become proficient with their iron sights *before* training with a laser sight. Do *not* use the laser sight as an expedient remedy for poor shooting skills with iron sights. Visually hunting for the dot can worsen the effect of tunnel vision. The operator can reduce the effect by *focusing* on the aim point while bringing the pistol into the line of sight and *seeing* the superimposed dot. This is the same method as TFSS, except the operator *sees* the superimposed dot instead of the aligned sights. Confusion can occur when multiple operators are pointing laser sights at the same adversary. As operators move their lasers to try and sort out which is theirs it becomes a *dancing dots* situation.[157] An operator that cannot identify his or her dot should discontinue use of the laser.

NOTE: The laser sight offers tactical advantages that overcome any of the disadvantages. The disadvantages quickly diminish with proper training and deployment.

The laser sight can also be beneficial for dry fire and live fire training. The reaction of a laser dot on a target quickly revels if an operator is flinching. The laser dot provides the operator with immediate feedback. The red dot correlates with align sights revealing where the operator is pointing the pistol. This is important for demonstrating how to keep the muzzle pointed in an appropriate direction. The operator can practice drawing and use the laser to find the most efficient presentation of the pistol from the holster to the target. When shooting and the laser dot moves off the target prior to the shot firing that is an indication of flinching. The laser is also useful for demonstrating how to quickly move off line and shoot while keeping the muzzle level.

Whether a laser sight is chosen or not does not change the fact that operators need to accept "...being "paper" trained with stationary targets, iron sights, and one eye closed will never prepare [them] for the real thing!"[158]

CAUTION: The guide rod laser designed to be used with the Glock pistol requires the firearm to be lubricated as specified in the Instructions for Use Glock Safe Action Pistols All Models manual. Excessive or inadequate lubricant can interfere with the proper function of the pistol and the laser sight.[159]

Night Vision Tactics

The probability that an armed civilian, police officer, or military operator will be involved in a deadly force encounter increases at night since the cover of darkness seems to be the adversary's friend. The painted sights on a pistol are ineffective in a dark environment. This is especially true at greater distances of approaching a residence or business on foot as commonly encountered in law enforcement. The problem gets worse when the adversary has on dark clothing. Self-luminous sights help alleviate these problems. The self-luminous sights will provide a sight image (without using a white light) required for effective accuracy. Not using a white light may also provide a tactical advantage of stealth when making an approach at night.

NOTE: *Cones* in the eyes are concentrated in the center of the retina providing clear, sharp central vision, while detecting colors and fine details in bright light conditions. However, at night the eyes using rods see shades of black and white.[160] *Rods* in the eyes are on outside of the macula and extend to the outer edge of the retina. Rods provide peripheral vision and allow the eyes to detect motion and help to see in low light and at night.

Bushes, structures, and vehicles can cast shadows that can be misleading to the operator. This problem is especially noticeable one-half hour before dark and one-half hour before dawn.[161] Another problem is that at dusk, the different colors become virtually indistinguishable.[162] This could be hindrance when giving an adversary's clothing or a vehicle description. Even with a reduction in vision, an operator can use *dark adaptation, off-center vision,* and *scanning* to improve his or her operational capability in the dark.

Dark Adaptation: The dark adaption method has limited use in a city where there is ambient lighting. Nevertheless, an operator needs to be aware of how long it takes the human eye to become dark adapted. The eyes in a dark area typically need about 30 minutes to become 98 percent adapted.[163] This dark adaptation process conditions the eyes to best function during low light conditions.

Off-center Vision: Objects viewed in the daylight are looked at directly (central vision). However, at night if the object is looked at directly it will be visible only for several seconds. To see an object in darkness it must be concentrated on by looking 6 to 10 degrees from its center (peripheral vision).[164] The 6 to 10 degrees is about the width of a fist at arm's length.[165] This can be easily tested by walking into a darken room and looking directly at an object. The object will appear momentarily and then it fades into the darkness.

NOTE: While in Afghanistan the author's area of operation (AO) came under attack at night and air support was called. He could hear the incoming blacked out attack helicopter, but did not see it. He scanned the night sky using abrupt eye movements and saw the helicopter when he looked 6 to 10 degrees off its center. While working as a police officer he had used the same technique to find suspects hiding in shadows.

Scanning: Ambient lighting such as streetlights or an outside porch light sometimes provides only *momentary* artificial illumination. The occurrence can seemingly cause an adversary to vanish during a foot pursuit at night. What happens is the adversary runs through a lit area and then hides in the shadows. The operator should stop at the dark area where seeing the adversary last. Any potential hiding areas are scanned using a *figure eight* technique.[166] The eyes are moved in a figure eight pattern in short, abrupt, irregular movements over and around the area. The movement of the eyes continues at 4 to 10 second intervals.[167] Using a flashlight might result in the operator becoming an illuminated target or cause an adversary to take off running. The scanning technique may help an operator to spot the adversary without his or her knowledge. The operator could then call for assistance to close-in on the adversary.

NOTE: Night vision is immediately lost at the flash of a white light.

When using a white light and needing to retain night vision close the dominant eye. Open the eye to engage an adversary.

VISION IMPAIRED SHOOTING

Vision impairment is a disruption of the operator's ability to see properly. The vision disruption could be from *foreign matter* or a *physical injury*. Operators using *pepper spray* need to maintain an awareness of overspray and not accidentally spray fellow operators. Another issue for the operator is having his or her pepper spray taken and being sprayed by an adversary.

An operator exposed to pepper spray may still be capable of deploying a pistol. The eye that has the least amount of exposure to the pepper spray can be forced open with the index finger and thumb. (Figure 7-55) This should allow the operator to see enough to locate and engage an adversary if necessary. The eye held open will become the dominant eye, because the other eye is closed from the pepper spray exposure. The operator cants the pistol slightly bringing the sights into the line of sight *if* the eye forced open is the non-dominant eye. Canting the pistol will likely occur subconsciously because of procedural memory acquired during training.

Figure 7-55 *Vision Impaired Shooting*

SHOOTING WITH A PROTECTIVE MASK

The starting point for the operator is to use the most technologically advanced protective mask available. Law enforcement agencies should *not* look for an outdated or surplus military mask for their officers. A protective mask needs to provide the widest possible field of vision in the most compact package. This will allow better utilization of combat shooting skills with a pistol and carbine. Skills that might be necessary even with the presence of smoke or a chemical irritant. Operators with prescription lenses will have to make necessary adjustments to ensure correct vision. This could mean getting optical inserts for the protective mask or wearing contact lenses.

A protective mask restricts the amount of oxygen the body can process during physical exertion. Eyesight is one of the first senses negatively affected by an oxygen deficiency. In addition, muscle fatigue will occur quicker. How much physical exertion an operator can perform needs to be determined in training and not on a mission. Finally, the body's heat can cause condensation to form on the inside of the lens. This was an issue for the author while wearing protective goggles in Afghanistan. He regularly cleaned the lens and afterwards coated them with an antifog solution.[168]

NOTE: Some operators may find they shoot better with a protective mask on. One theory is the mind believes the eyes are protected and the subconscious is not concerned about the concussion from the firearm thus reducing the flinch effect. [169] The protective mask *if* worn operationally should also be worn whether dry firing or live firing.

SHOOTING AND RELOADING WHILE INJURED

Shooting while injured differs from shooting with one hand and uninjured. The non-firing hand can be held in front of the unprotected neck or down at the side while shooting with one hand. Shooting with one hand while *injured* signifies the injured arm or hand is no longer capable of a motor function. The injured arm would likely hang *lifelessly* at the operator's side. Allow the arm to hang lifelessly at the side during training to add realism when performing injured operator shooting drills. Let the simulated injured arm relax and flop around. This is what will likely be the circumstance in an actual incident.

An operator with a holstered pistol and sustaining an incapacitating arm injury will have to gain access to the pistol. Using the dominant side arm is a matter of drawing the pistol. However, using the *non-dominant* arm requires additional measures. To access the pistol, grab the equipment belt and pull it in the direction that will bring the pistol within reach. Pull the pistol out of the holster keeping the pistol grip horizontal and the muzzle pointing down. From the fighting stance or kneeling position brace the top of the slide against the stomach rotating the pistol to get a proper grip. (Figures 7-56 through 7-58)

Figure 7-56 Grip   *Figure 7-57* Brace   *Figure 7-58* Extend

Be careful while bracing the pistol against the stomach *not* to inadvertently stick any fingers inside of the trigger guard causing a negligent discharge.[170] Likewise, be careful *not* to drop the pistol as attempting to catch it could end with similar results as previously stated. The pistol is pushed straight out from the body to the target and *not* swept across in front of the body to the target. The muzzle should *not* at any time point at the operator's body. Another option for drawing may be the operator reaching behind his or her back with the non-dominant hand and securing a grip on the pistol worn on the hip.

NOTE: The operator should have a method of shooting and reloading that is reliable and works efficiently with his or her body type, equipment, and pistol even *if* an injury is sustained.

One-Hand Shooting While Injured

Previously covered were the techniques for shooting with one hand. All the aspects of shooting with one hand apply here with the *exception* of allowing the non-firing arm to hang lifelessly. (Figure 7-59) Do *not* use the unrealistic practice of holding the simulated injured arm against the chest. The operator must train for the worst-case scenario of not having use of the injured arm.

Review the One-Hand Firing Position section in this chapter for specific information on *shooting* with one hand.

Figure 7-59 *Injured Arm Shooting*

One-Hand Reloading While Injured

Placing the pistol between the knees to reload will work in the positions of standing, kneeling, rollover prone, reverse rollover prone and supine. Placing the pistol between the knees is the preferred method because of its versatility and flexibility. Operators may find sitting back on their calves helps to maintain balance while in the kneeling position.

Some operators while holding the pistol between their knees may be capable of releasing the slide. The operator after inserting the magazine, grips the pistol grip, and pushes the top of the slide against the knees releasing the slide. Releasing of the slide is dependent on the vee between the knees to provide enough counterpressure to overcome the pressure of the recoil spring. Using this method may be faster than using the rear sight against an object, but it is *not* as reliable. There may be fresh blood, mud, sweat, snow, or rain on the operator's pants and pistol reducing the ability to exert counterpressure to the slide. Likewise, pushing the slide against the knees can also be painful and cause bruising from practicing.

A more reliable method of releasing the slide is to brace the rear sight against an object. This can be done with the pistol whether it is in the right hand or left hand. Releasing the slide by hooking the rear sight on an object is possible regardless of operator's stature and can be practiced without discomfort. This method is reliable, promotes training uniformity, and develops procedural memory.

To reload using one hand, hold the pistol so the thumb or index finger presses the magazine catch[171] and forcefully move the pistol down and back up, dropping the magazine out of the magazine well. (Figures 7-60 through 7-62)

Figure 7-60 *Press*   ***Figure 7-61*** *Down*   ***Figure 7-62*** *Up*

Secure the pistol in an easily accessible position[172] such as the waistband, holster, or between the knees (*preferred method*). (Figures 7-63 through 7-65) Whatever method is used, it must be reliable and performed efficiently.

Figure 7-63
Waistband

Figure 7-64
Holster

Figure 7-65
Between Knees

Insert the replacement magazine into the magazine well until the magazine catch engages fully (click may be felt). Firmly grasp the pistol and rack the slide by hooking the rear sight against the belt, holster, or heel while pushing downward chambering a round. (Figures 7-66 through 7-68) Regain a sight picture.

Figure 7-66
Belt

Figure 7-67
Holster

Figure 7-68
Heel

WARNING: Body fat hanging over the belt may prevent using it to rack the slide. Skin getting pinched between the rear sight and the belt causes a painful injury. A female operator with a narrow waistline and her belt tilting inward may prevent using the belt to rack the slide.

Shooting with a Flashlight While Injured

It is unlikely that with an arm injury a flashlight would be used. There is a possibility of shoving the flashlight under the armpit of the injured arm. However, an injured arm may not be capable of holding the flashlight. Realistically an operator shot will probably not have any concern for a flashlight. The concern will be to have a pistol in hand to prevent being shot a second time. Attacks on police at night caught on dashboard video reveal *uninjured* officers are more likely to drop their flashlight or hold it down by their side[173]—much less being injured and trying to manipulate a flashlight and pistol together.

CLEARING STOPPAGES WHILE INJURED

Keep in perspective the reason for clearing a stoppage with one hand. It is likely an adversary would have shot the operator who would be in a pain and physically weak. Fresh blood might be on the operator's hands, clothing, equipment, and pistol. The operator's vision may be impaired from dust, dirt, pepper spray, blood, or darkness. The techniques used for clearing stoppages under such conditions must be simple, but effective. The techniques must work with the subcompact, compact, and standard pistols. The drills must also work for operators that are dressed in civilian clothing, police uniform, military combat uniform, and while carrying associated equipment for each manner of dress.

The standing or kneeling positions can be used to perform a tap-rack-ready. The standing tap-rack-ready with one hand is quicker than kneeling. Make sure the muzzle is pointed about 30 degrees away from the body when performing the standing tap-rack-ready with one hand and using the belt or holster to rack the slide. Racking the slide with it straight down can prevent a round or casing from ejecting causing a stoppage. Mentally the operator might find comfort in creating a lower profile by using the kneeling position.

The kneeling position offers the advantage of learning one position to clear any stoppage using one hand. Kneeling also lowers the operator's center of gravity and allows quick retrieval of dropped equipment. The operator in the kneeling position can seamlessly transition from the tap-rack-ready to the lock-clear-reload without changing positions. Swinging the pistol to the rear to rack the slide against the heel forces the ejection port to be upside down and pointing toward the ground. The position allows a round or casing to fall free through the ejection port.

DANGER: The kneeling position during live fire training does require a backstop in front (target location) and behind the operator (contain bullet from a negligent discharge).

When performing a clearance drill it is imperative to keep the trigger finger on the receiver to prevent a negligent discharge. Losing the use of one arm from an injury requires clearing stoppages with one hand. This includes a double feed stoppage. One-hand clearance drills vary greatly from two-hand methods. Safety is paramount while performing these drills with live ammunition. It is strongly recommended the operator be in a position of tactical advantage or behind cover before attempting one-hand clearance drills. The operator must be aware of the distance an adversary can cover during the time it takes for clearing a stoppage. The adversary even at a greater distance can quickly close and attack the operator because of the extra time it takes to clear a stoppage using one hand.

Some operators may not be physically capable of using one hand to move the slide to the rear and push the slide stop lever up to lock the slide. Identify these shortcomings in a training environment and *not* in a deadly force encounter. Operators that physically cannot perform the clearance drill must accept their limitation and realize this technique is not an option. Other options must be used, such as picking up a weapon dropped in the area (normally a battlefield environment), retrieving a long gun from a vehicle, or breaking contact with the adversary by running from the area in a zigzag pattern. "The ability to retreat and fight another day is not an unrealistic thing to do when faced with overwhelming odds."[174]

Hiding behind cover with a nonfunctioning pistol will probably end with the adversary closing the distance and killing the injured operator. The operator must do something. Either make the pistol work or break contact with the adversary. When performing the drills it is *preferred* to use procedural memory and not have to change focus from the operational environment. Nevertheless, a momentary glace at the pistol to speed a procedure is acceptable and immediately afterwards the focus returned to the operational environment.

NOTE: Immediate access to a backup pistol would be tactically preferred over any of the one-hand clearance drills.

Standing: One-Hand Tap-Rack-Ready While Injured

The standing tap-rack-ready takes about 2 to 4 seconds to complete using one hand (right or left).[175] While standing to clear a failure to fire stoppage, complete the steps as follows:

Tap: From the standing position, hit the magazine floor plate against the thigh. (Figure 7-63)

Rack: From the firing side, hook the rear sight on a belt, holster, pocket, or near-by object racking the slide and chambering a round. (Figure 7-70) Keep the muzzle pointed away from the body.

Ready: Regain a sight picture. (Figure 7-71)

Figure 7-69 *Standing (tap)*   ***Figure 7-70*** *Standing (rack)*   ***Figure 7-71*** *Standing (ready)*

Kneeling: One-Hand Tap-Rack-Ready While Injured

The kneeling tap-rack-ready takes about 2 to 4 seconds to complete using one hand (right or left).[176] While kneeling to clear a failure to fire stoppage, complete the steps as follows:

Tap: Go to a kneeling position and hit the magazine floor plate against the thigh. (Figure 7-72) An option is to ground both knees (double kneeling) to eliminate the decision of which knee to ground. Place one knee down and then the other.

Rack: Swing the pistol to the rear and hook the rear sight against the heel and aggressively push the pistol downward racking the slide and chambering a round. (Figure 7-73)

Ready: Stand or remain kneeling and regain a sight picture. (Figure 7-74)

Figure 7-72 *Kneeling (tap)*   **Figure 7-73** *Kneeling (rack)*   **Figure 7-74** *Kneeling (ready)*

One-Hand Lock-Clear-Reload While Injured

If a tap-rack-ready drill did not correct the stoppage then a lock-clear-reload drill is in order. Do *not* waste time attempting another tap-rack-ready drill. If the operator's life is not in immediate jeopardy, a lock-clear-reload drill can be completed using one hand and takes about 10 to 16 seconds.[177] This drill is used to clear a double feed stoppage.

Lock: Go to a kneeling position. (Figure 7-75) An option is to ground both knees (double kneeling) to eliminate the decision of which knee to ground. Place one knee down and then the other. Lock the slide back as follows: Wrap the fingers over the top of the slide and reverse the pistol in the hand. (Figure 7-76) Wedge the back strap of the pistol grip between the calf and thigh behind the knee and with the thumb and fingers grasp the front of the slide tight. (Figure 7-77) When using the *right hand* push the slide rearward and with the *index finger* push up on the slide stop lever. When using the *left hand* push the slide rearward and with the *thumb* push up on the slide stop lever. Allow the slide to move slightly forward to engage the slide stop lever and move the applicable index finger or thumb away. (Figures 7-78)

Figure 7-75 *Kneeling*

Figure 7-76 *Reverse Pistol*

Figure 7-77 *Back Strap Wedged*

Figure 7-78 *Lock Slide*

Clear: Rotate the pistol forward and regain a normal grip. Press the magazine catch and simultaneously violently move the pistol down and back up (shaking motion) dropping the magazine out of the magazine well. (Figure 7-79) Swing the pistol to the rear, hook the rear sight against the heel, and aggressively rack the slide three times to remove any debris or a bad round. (Figure 7-80)

Reload: Reload the empty pistol. Place the pistol between the knees, insert a magazine, and use the palm to seat the magazine ensuring the magazine catch engages. (Figure 7-81) Hook the rear sight against the heel—aggressively push the pistol downward racking the slide and chambering a round. (Figure 7-82) Regain a sight picture. (Figure 7-83)

Figure 7-79 *Down and Up*

Figure 7-80 *Clear*

Figure 7-81 *Reload*

Figure 7-82 *Rack Slide*

Figure 7-83 *Sight Picture*

Pistol Malfunction

A malfunction of the pistol is a mechanical failure such as a broken extractor, ejector, firing pin, etc., requiring a certified armorer to correct.[178] The operator *cannot* clear the malfunction. Although, a Glock pistol with a broke trigger spring can be fired. To do so the operator must not allow the trigger finger to lose contact with the trigger. Losing contact with the trigger will not allow it to reset.

PISTOL MARITIME CAPABILITY

Glock maritime spring cups are *only* approved for 9x19mm pistols and available to military and law enforcement organizations.[179] Maritime spring cups allow for optimum water permeability.[180] Unlike standard spring cups, maritime spring cups ensure water can drain pass the firing pin inside the firing pin channel. This will prevent slowing of the firing pin caused by the creation of hydraulic force inside the firing pin channel. The slowing of the firing pin can cause a light primer strike.

Maritime spring cups and JHP ammunition are *not* for firing with the pistol submerged.[181] The model 17 equipped with maritime cups and loaded with JHP ammunition is for surface use in and around water by operators of special operation teams that required optimum water permeability.[182] There is *dive* ammunition that is waterproof to a depth of about 30 feet (7 meters) for a minimum of 30 minutes.[183] However, the JHP dive ammunition is for use by Special Operations teams that move from water onto land. The design of the JHP dive ammunition does *not* allow for under water firing.

DANGER: Shooting a pistol underwater is dangerous! Do so *only* after receiving professional training in the course of official duties and while wearing proper safety equipment to protect against pressure wave effects of underwater detonation and *never* use hollow point ammunition.[184] The sound waves from a gunshot underwater can easily cause *permanent* hearing loss.

MACHINE PISTOLS[185]

The Glock models 18 and 18C (compensated) are selective fire machine pistols for special operational requirements.[186] The operator must understand the strengths and limitations of a machine pistol to extract its full potential. The machine pistol is available only to law enforcement and military organizations. The model 18 and 18C are Class III firearms in the United States. The initial development of the machine pistol was for the Austrian EKO Cobra *(Einsatzkommando Cobra)* military unit involved in antiterrorism operations,[187] but is also in use for executive protection. The machine pistol is a compact solution in lieu of a submachine gun commonly used in CQC operations. Police special operations use the machine pistol for room entry and building clearing. Plainclothes officers requiring substantial more firepower for special assignments also use the machine pistol.

General Information

The machine pistol has a selector located on the left rear portion of the slide. (Figure 7-84) The selector's *up* position is for *semiautomatic* fire mode and points to "o" marked on the slide. The machine pistol will fire 1 round with each pull of the trigger when the selector is in the up position. The selector's *down* position is for *automatic* fire mode and points to "oo" marked on the slide. The machine pistol will fire continuously until releasing the trigger forward or the magazine is empty when the selector is in the down position. The slide will automatically lock to the rear position on an empty magazine.

Photograph Courtesy of GLOCK Inc.

Figure 7-84 Glock Model 18C Machine Pistol with a 19 round *magazine.*[188]

The automatic rate of fire is 1200 rounds per minute. The *Glock 18 (18C) Select-Fire Familiarization Workshop* course recommends that automatic fire normally be restricted to 7 yards (6.4 meters) or less. The tactical advantage of fighting at the greatest distance (standoff) is reduced when firing in the automatic fire mode. The selector should be in the up position (semiautomatic) position during loading, unloading, stoppage drills, movement, or handling.

Glock makes an extended 33 round magazine for the machine pistol. However, the 33 round magazine with the magazine catch cut on the left side *will* fit in any of the 9x19mm pistols (26, 19, 17 and 34) with the magazine catch positioned on the left side. Magazines designed for a *reversible* magazine catch will fit previous generations. There is also an extended floor plate (plus 2 rounds)[189] and insert that must be used with an 11-coil magazine spring in the magazine for standard frame models 17, 18 and 34.[190] Adding the extended floor plate will increase the standard frame model magazine capacity from 17 rounds to 19 rounds.

Liability Issues

The use of any firearm by an operator, especially a police officer involves a certain amount of liability risk. This is true even when used properly and reasonably. Operators are held not only to a standard of correct target discrimination, but also are responsible for any collateral damage such as destroyed property and injuries. Every operator has an ethical and legal obligation to make sure each round fired will hit its intended target. The operator has the same obligation *not* to fire when there is reason to believe the rounds could miss and endanger others.

It should be noted that because of the automatic fire capability resulting in reduced accuracy and infrequent incidents of use with the machine pistol—especially by American police officers—it will be viewed more critically from a liability vantage point than other commonly used firearms.

WARNING: The manufacturer recommends that only specially trained operators (police and military) operate the model 18 machine pistol because of the additional personal discipline required to shoot safely and effectively in the automatic fire mode.

Machine Pistol Training

Any prospective operator selected for training with the model 18 or 18C machine pistols must already be competent with the semiautomatic Glock pistol. The operator's competency must include the disassembly, assembly, maintenance, drawing, holstering, loading, unloading, stoppage clearance, using cover, combat firing positions and reloading (static and dynamic), movement combined with target discrimination, and any other applicable operationally required skill.

An operator that meets the requirements and will use the machine pistol in an operational capacity should receive additional formal structured training regarding automatic firing techniques and characteristics. Glock recommends the training course include firing a *minimum* of 1000 rounds of ammunition before deploying the operator with the machine pistol in an operational environment. Each operator on completion of the initial training program must regularly train to ensure maintaining a mission appropriate skill level. A *minimum* training standard interval for the machine pistol is every two months.[191]

The model 18 and 18C machine pistols are physically small size automatic firearms. For this reason, initial training begins with magazines loaded with 3, 5, and 8 rounds. This allows an operator to gain experience safely by having to control the machine pistol with increased difficulty.

An operator will have to assume an aggressive forward stance to control the recoil of the machine pistol. Align the toes of the firing side foot with the heel of the non-firing side foot (toe to heel).[192] Bend the knees allowing the body to assume a fighting stance. The shoulders will be in front of the hips with the ears in front of the shoulders. Lock the arms at the elbows and wrists. Grip the pistol using a thumbs forward grip as described in the Combat Shooting Phase 1 chapter. Use a tight grip with both hands when gripping the machine pistol.

DANGER: Shooting with the machine pistol in automatic fire mode from the *retention position* (one hand) can cause a violent recoil rise resulting in a self-inflicted gunshot. There is also the issue when using a compensated machine pistol with particles escaping out the ports (openings in the barrel) injuring the operator.

Carrying Method

Keep the selector in the up position (semiautomatic) when carrying the machine pistol in a holster or storing the machine pistol. Glock also recommends the selector be in the up position when the operator is covering an adversary. This includes situations such as greater distances to an adversary or the close range of innocent bystanders. However, there can be situations that preclude the operator from moving the selector to the semiautomatic position.

It is unlikely the operator reloading during a close quarters engagement with an adversary would take the time to move the selector to the semiautomatic fire position, reload, and then move the selector back to automatic fire position. As Glock noted in its Instructions for Use Glock Safe Action Pistols All Models manual a higher level of preparedness required of operators may at times override safety instructions, but only for those that operate at a higher level of preparedness *and* received proper initial combat oriented training *and* a reasonable amount of periodic training that stresses safe tactical procedures.[193]

Operators need to be aware that some holsters can interfere with the selector when drawing the machine pistol. The selector may move from the semiautomatic position (up) to the automatic position (down) when the pistol is drawn. The release in the holster shown in Figure 7-85 is hitting the selector.

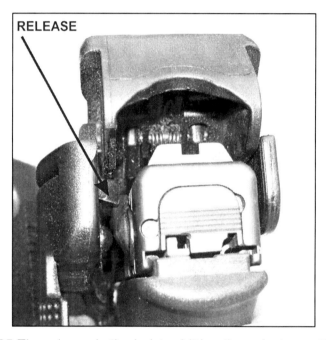

Figure 7-85 The release in the holster hitting the selector on the pistol.

An unknowing operator expecting semiautomatic fire would be surprised with a burst of automatic fire. Worse would be an unintentional injury or loss of an innocent life. Test and evaluate the holster that is going to be used with a machine pistol before using it operationally. Make sure the holster *is* recommended by the manufacturer as the correct model for the machine pistol.

Automatic Fire

Glock recommends that police officers firing in automatic mode be able to keep the entire burst within the target and have no misses. Glock makes this recommendation specifically for police officers, but it is also advisable for other operators. Keeping rounds on the target will depend on the operator's competency and operational conditions, but it is obtainable at a range of 4 to 7 yards (3.65 to 6.4 meters).

To maximize the operator's control of the machine pistol and to *minimize* shot dispersion, use multiple burst fire of 3 to 4 rounds. Using proper trigger control an operator can consistently fire a 2-round burst. Long burst of automatic fire commonplace to military operations are rarely *if* ever used in police operations because missed shots increase substantially.

The pistol when in automatic fire mode is controlled by the operator's timing of the trigger, i.e., trigger control. Trigger control is more abrupt when firing burst in the automatic mode versus the semiautomatic mode. The trigger finger quickly slaps and releases the trigger. The burst duration is dependent on how long the trigger is held to the rear.

Covering Adversaries and Arrest Procedures

Police officers regularly use the universal cover mode (UCM) to hold known risk suspects (dangerous adversaries) at gunpoint. The UCM is holding the muzzle low enough in a ready position allowing a clear view of the adversary's hands. The operator's trigger finger is on the receiver until making a decision to shoot. When tactically possible the operator maintains a position of advantage allowing an unobstructed line of fire.

An operator armed with a machine pistol and covering an adversary keeps the selector in the up position (semiautomatic mode). This allows the operator more control of the machine pistol affording greater precision. The greater precision results in increased safety for an approaching operator that has the job of securing (handcuffing, flex-cuffing, etc.) the adversary.

Hostage Situations and Crowds

As a rule, do *not* employ the machine pistol in automatic fire mode in a hostage situation or with bystanders in close vicinity. These are situations that demand operator restraint and precision shots that minimize danger to the hostage or bystanders. An operator can meet these requirements best with the machine pistol selector in the up position (semiautomatic mode) and the operator utilizing precision shot placement.

Parts Issues

The machine pistol equipped with a polymer recoil spring guide rod and in the automatic fire mode can sustain a rate of fire that can cause the rod to soften and possibly melt. Using the proper burst fire technique in conjunction with effective fire on an adversary will prevent the likelihood that such a rate of fire would ever be reached. It is also unlikely that an operator would carry enough magazines to sustain a rate of fire capable of melting the polymer recoil spring guide rod. However, a demonstration with multiple loaded magazines resulting in a near continuous automatic rate of fire can result in extremely high temperatures for the slide and barrel. The machine pistol requires proper maintenance and inspections as necessary by trained personnel.

CAUTION: After sustained firing (slide and barrel are hot) do not leave the slide back as it can cause a polymer recoil spring guide rod to *set* in a *curved* position after cooling. The fourth generation dual recoil spring is more resilient to heat, but will *not* fit in previous generation pistols.

Additional and Unique Parts

The model 18 machine pistol has 4 more additional parts than the model 17 semiautomatic pistol. The 4 parts are as follows:

1. Selector
2. Selector Pin
3. Selector Spring
4. Selector Spring Bearing

The model 18 machine pistol has 7 unique parts in comparison to the model 17 semiautomatic pistol. The receiver rails and slide rail cuts are at a different height than the model 17. Therefore, a model 17 slide or receiver will *not* interchange with a model 18 slide or receiver. This was done intentionally so the model 17 could *not* be considered a semiautomatic version of the model 18 machine pistol.[194]

The seven unique parts are as follows:

1. Barrel
2. Receiver
3. Slide
4. Slide Cover Plate
5. Trigger Mechanism Housing
6. Trigger with Trigger Bar
7. Spacer Sleeve

Disassembly

To disassemble the model 18 and 18C machine pistols they must be *unloaded* with the selector in the *up* position (semiautomatic mode) *and* the trigger in the *rearward* position. The slide will separate from the receiver in the same manner as a model 17 semiautomatic pistol. Machine pistols use the same cleaning procedures as any of the other Glock pistols.

Selective Fire Familiarization Workshop

The author had the pleasure of completing Glock's training course for the model 18 machine pistols. The course is restricted to police, military, and qualified personnel. Operators must be proficient with a standard pistol before attending the course. Students are monitored closely for pistol handling skills and adherence to safety protocols. The instructor evaluates each student, which receives either a pass or fail. The standards are 100 percent for both the written test and the live fire evaluation and qualification. The student is expected to bring a Glock machine pistol, 3 or more magazines (33 round magazines are optional), a holster that does *not* interfere with the selector, magazine pouch (double recommended), 1000 rounds of factory 9x19mm ammunition, hearing protection, eye protection, appropriate headgear, and seasonal appropriate clothing.

UNARMORED VEHICLES IN COMBAT

Law enforcement probably has more experience at fighting in and around *unarmored* vehicles than any other profession. Many of these encounters occur during traffic stops and sometimes the outcome regrettably is an injured or dead police officer. There are three incidents involving vehicles and gunfire that forever changed survival training for law enforcement officers.

The *first* incident commonly referred to as the *Newhall Incident* occurred on April 6, 1970, in which four California Highway Patrol officers were killed in the Newhall unincorporated area of Los Angeles County, California during a 4½-minute gunfight with two males that reportedly had brandished a weapon in a vehicle.[195] The *second* incident commonly referred to as the *FBI Miami Shootout* occurred on April 11, 1986, in which two Special Agents were killed and five other agents were injured in southwest Miami, Florida, during a gunfight with two robbery suspects.[196] The *third* incident commonly referred to the *North Hollywood Shootout* occurred on February 28, 1997, in which 12 Police Officers and 2 civilians were wounded in Los Angeles, California during a gunfight lasting 44 minutes with two bank robbers.[197] Knowing how to fight from the inside or outside of an unarmored vehicle can be the difference in surviving the encounter or dying.

Inside of an Unarmored Vehicle: Unarmored vehicles are sometimes referred to as *soft-skin* vehicles. There are three options available for an operator *inside* of a functioning unarmored vehicle involved in combat. First, an operator should try to avoid having to shoot from the vehicle. Preferably, drive the vehicle out of the danger area extracting with it the driver and passengers. Second, use the vehicle as a weapon to stop the adversary when reasonable to do so. This will likely mean running over the adversary. This can be problematic if the adversary is shooting at the unarmored vehicle. The closer the vehicle gets the more likely the adversary's accuracy will improve. A suicidal adversary would shoot until being struck by the vehicle. Third, is to shoot from inside of the vehicle. Shooting from inside of a vehicle presents its own set of problems. The best practice is to overcome the problems in training before a life-threatening situation occurs.

Drawing a pistol in a straight line from the holster to the line of sight is not an option from the driver's seat and likely the same for the passenger's seat. The steering wheel and dashboard are obstacles that impede the pistol. Bring the pistol as high as required—usually above the chest to clear the steering wheel and dashboard. Rotate the pistol and join the hands together. Extend the pistol until it stops at the glass surface. Keeping the muzzle close to the glass helps to lessen glass fragment splash back and dissipates the particles to the outside. (Figure 7-86)

Figure 7-86 *Shooting though a windshield.*

Shooting a firearm inside a vehicle increases an already loud noise. The operator and others in the vehicle will likely experience a ringing noise in their ears. The operator before shooting *if* possible should yell for others inside the vehicle to get down and cover their ears. This is especially true for children. Those in the vehicle experiencing an alarm reaction may not hear the shots or hear them at a reduced level. Furthermore, the operator may not have time to give verbal direction. This is where planning and preparation can yield dividends. Teach family members to react without verbal direction to situations involving firearms.

Outside of an Unarmored Vehicle: There is an option for an operator *outside* of an unarmored vehicle to use it as concealment or cover in combat. The operator to use the vehicle effectively as cover has to understand how bullets react when striking the vehicle and the surrounding surface. A ricochet can travel near a hard surface first impacted. This includes vehicle panels (doors, hood, trunk, roof, etc.), vehicle windshield, walls, and concrete floors. When the author attended the Glock Pistol Transitional Instructor Workshop course an instructor demonstrated how a bullet (full metal jacket or hollowpoint) can hit the asphalt or concrete near a vehicle and travel about 6 inches (152.4 millimeters) above the ground, pass under the chassis, and exited the other side.[198]

Skipping bullets under the vehicle parked on a *hard* surface is taught as a method to engage an adversary.[199] The tactic can also be used by an adversary against an operator.[200] The area between the ground and the chassis of a vehicle creates a lit background. Ambient light even in low light situations can still create a lit background. The lit background is disrupted when an adversary walks or lies down behind the vehicle. The eyes easily pick up this disruption of the light as movement. Likewise, an adversary seen going behind a vehicle and disappearing will probably be taking a prone position.

The operator to defeat this tactic fires a round methodically about every 2 feet (0.60 meter) under the chassis of the vehicle. A round that hits the adversary may cause him or her to cry out. The operator will continue to shoot more rounds in that area until the adversary stops making noise[201] (enemy combatant) or is no longer a threat (criminal).[202] The operator adhering to the fourth rule of firearms handling would fire when reasonable in view of the circumstances. This includes having the legal right to shoot and knowing the rounds fired will come to rest in an area deemed acceptable. An example of coming to rest in an acceptable area is one that can safely contain the bullet.

Dirt has a different effect on bullets than does asphalt or concrete. Dirt is softer and absorbs the energy of the bullet. The angles for asphalt or concrete may *not* work the same as for dirt. The Federal Bureau of Investigation in October 1969, published a study titled "Bouncing Bullets." The study found "…the effect of ricocheting off the three surfaces—concrete, asphalt, and turf—seems to indicate that the harder the surface the less the deflection." [203] An operator may consider shooting where the adversary's body meets the ground. Even if a bullet breaks apart, its pieces can hit the throat, eyes, or travel down the length of the adversary's body.

Using underneath a vehicle as cover restricts the operator's view of the operational area. The operator when possible should consider other methods of using a vehicle as cover. Using the frontend or backend of the vehicle may expose the operator only to an adversary that has a line of sight on that *specific* area of the vehicle.[204] An operator crowding the vehicle using the top of the hood or trunk as cover may expose him or herself to a frontal view of roughly 180 degrees.[205]

The hood or trunk may be used as cover *if* precautions are taken. Shooting in the kneeling position and staying back about 3 yards (meters) from the vehicle may prevent being struck by ricochets.[206] The engine block of light passenger vehicles is the only part capable of *stopping* the NATO 5.56x45 millimeter and 7.62x51 millimeter calibers. There may be items in a trunk that are inadvertently capable of stopping rifle rounds, but if possible should not be depended on. The engine compartment of an unarmored vehicle is still the preferred area to use as cover. Where did a deputy feel the safest while being shot at? In the deputy's own words:

> "Bullets were going through the vehicle and out the other side; that's how powerful they were. I felt safest behind the motor and the front wheel well."[207]

What are some things an operator on foot can do to improve his or survivability when pursuing an adversary in a parking lot full of vehicles? An operator can look through windows of vehicles to locate, maneuver, and engage the adversary. Looking through windows will *not* work with vehicles that have dark tinted windows. A quick peek under some of the vehicles may reveal an adversary's location. When maneuvering on an adversary try to parallel him or her by following rows of vehicles using them as cover. This tactic allows the operator to maintain cover and *not* follow directly behind the adversary staying out of his or her kill zone. There may also be an option of shooting through windows to hit the adversary crouching on the opposite side of a vehicle.

Research and Development: Law enforcement and military organizations that stop vehicles (traffic stop, checkpoint, etc.) should research tactics, equipment, weapons, and develop training suited to the task. It is paramount for police officers to carry a firearm loaded with ammunition that will not fragment when shot through a windshield.[208] Police officers constantly encounter vehicles with a driver and passengers. History has established that a police officer might have to shoot through a windshield for self-protection or to protect someone else. That includes an innocent person inside of the vehicle. It is *not* the time to find out after a shooting occurred that issued ammunition fragments when shot through glass.

An organization at minimum should have video documentation on the effectiveness of all issued ammunition against common barriers. That video should have a lesson plan and taught to each operator in the organization. Likewise, the firearms training section should have a vehicle on-site that was shot with issued ammunition showing real-life results. Internal or external *case studies* involving vehicles could also be a part of the lesson plan. This should include operators and adversaries that were injured or killed in and around vehicles. Training should include scenario exercises using airsoft or marking cartridges. Training should be conducted during the day and at night under conditions found in the operational area

PISTOL AS A LETHAL IMPACT WEAPON

Before explaining how to use a pistol as an impact weapon there is one question that requires an explanation. Why would an operator need to use a pistol as an impact weapon? The operator ran out of ammunition or incurred a stoppage or malfunction (mechanical failure) and is in a hand-to-hand fight warranting deadly force. It is a matter of closest weapon—closest target. The operator in the hand-to-hand fight uses the pistol to strike the adversary's facial and cranial areas violently breaking bones in an attempt to cause incapacitation. The reason for striking the adversary as opposed to shooting is the pistol will not fire. It is irrelevant that in a life-threatening situation the pistol becomes an impact weapon. The fact that deadly force is reasonable justifies stopping the adversary by using repeated strikes.

Use the side of the *slide* in a back and forth motion to strike. The slide is a heavy piece of metal similar to striking somebody with a steel bar. Do *not* leave the trigger finger on the trigger when striking. The adversary using a gun takeaway technique can break or tear off the operator's trigger finger *if* left in the trigger guard. However, wrapping the fingers around the pistol grip protects the trigger finger from injury and affords the good control of the pistol to strike effectively. (Figure 7-87) Swinging the pistol with a back and forth motion will provide the greatest striking power and lessen the chance of knocking the pistol out of the operator's hand. The pistol no longer functions as a firearm, but as a club.[209]

Figure 7-87 *Fingers around pistol grip for back and forth striking.*

The author while working patrol in the Southwest Division of the City of Dallas received a call that a male had an AK47 rifle at a motel. The male's room was located and entered using a passkey. The author armed with a 12-gauge pump action shotgun was the first police officer through the door. He closed in on the suspect who was flushing drugs down a toilet. He yelled for the suspect to get on the floor. The second police officer chose to close the distance and went hands-on. The suspect reached for his waist area and the police officer with his service pistol struck the suspect's head (reflexive response according to the police officer). The suspect fell to the floor and subsequently handcuffed by the police officer. From the author's vantage point, he did not see the furtive gesture and therefore did not shoot. However, the strike with the pistol was effective.

For an overhand strike, grip the pistol around the top of the slide and bottom of the trigger guard. From a normal grip rotate the thumb on top of the slide and place the trigger finger in front of the trigger guard with the other three fingers wrapped under it. (Figure 7-88) Use the rear of the slide to strike. Carry out the counterattack with violence of action.

Do *not* strike with the magazine floor plate.[210] The Glock polymer floor plate would likely not cause sufficient damage to stop an adversary. However, the harden steel slide is an effective improvised weapon to use for striking.

NOTE: It is common to see in movies the butt of a pistol (bottom of the magazine for a semiautomatic pistol) used for striking. This is an example that movies are best suited for entertainment and *not* training purposes.

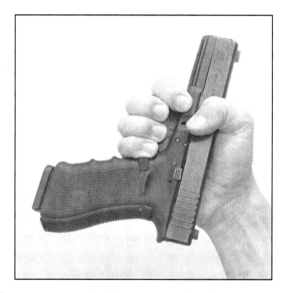

Figure 7-88 *Fingers around slide and receiver for overhand striking*

The muzzle of the pistol can also be used for punching the adversary. This is called a *muzzle punch* and generally used in the standing position. The front of the receiver is what impacts the adversary causing damage as the slide will move rearward. The firing hand fingers wrap around the pistol grip and the non-firing hand wraps around the slide and receiver in front of the trigger guard. (Figure 7-89) Use the muzzle of the pistol to strike the adversary's face and neck area until he or she no longer poses a deadly threat. The face and neck are preferred target areas, but strike any exposed portion of the adversary's body to inflict damage.

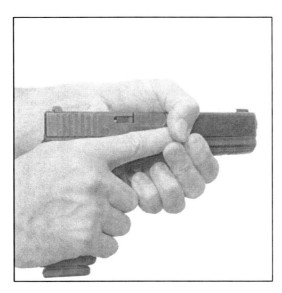

Figure 7-89 *Shooting grip with non-firing hand thumb over the slide and fingers around the trigger guard for muzzle striking.*

NOTE: Some pistols with a manual safety engaged prevent the slide from moving rearward increasing the effect of the technique.

The muzzle punch technique can also be used *if* a stoppage or malfunction occurs at contact distance from a life-threatening adversary. Drive the pistol muzzle violently into the chest, neck, or face area. The operator after striking moves laterally when possible to get out of the adversary's line of attack. Performs a tap-rack-ready and using verbal commands directs the adversary or reengages with deadly force. The thought process for the technique is to strike, move off the line of attack, and clear the stoppage.

As a rule, do *not* use the muzzle punch as a *nondeadly* force option. The obvious reason for not using the muzzle punch as a nondeadly force option is the fear of a negligent discharge resulting in an unreasonable use of force. Even under exigent circumstances in a nondeadly force situation, it is preferable *if* possible to use other nondeadly force options such as a palm strike, front kick, etc.

SUMMARY

The operator's chance for survival improves by utilizing different shooting positions and cover to engage adversaries effectively. The distance to an adversary can be contact to the maximum effective range of the pistol. The strike and transition technique can be used at contact distance. The prone position provides a smaller profile and steady firing position at the maximum effective range of the pistol. There are three types of flashlight activations: (1) *proper*, (2) *improper,* and (3) *accidental.* An operator should be capable of accurately firing with one hand. Use the tracking or trapping methods to engage moving targets effectively. Closing the distance is a method to gain the tactical advantage to control or engage an adversary. The advancing or retreating method of walking slowly while shooting has little if any practical application to operational survival. There may be a need to fire an 8-inch (203.2-millimeter) group or make a precision shot amounting to a 1-inch (25.4-millimeter) group in combat. An operator should be motivated to maintain his or her shooting skills to make the shot that is required. A machine pistol can be an effective weapon for antiterrorism and CQC operations. There is a greater liability issue with a machine pistol and employing it requires bi-monthly training sessions. The most effective area of an unarmored vehicle to use as cover is behind the engine compartment at the wheel well. A pistol can be used as an effective improvised impact weapon in a life-and-death fight.

DISCUSSION QUESTIONS

1. At what specific distance should the sights be used?
2. What are the three factors relating to an adversary on how best to deploy a pistol?
3. Before pulling a trigger what is one thing that separates responsible operators from their adversaries?
4. Discuss why each law enforcement agency: city, county, state, and federal should announce with the word "Po-lice."
5. List the characteristics of best cover.
6. What is the hazard to an operator for lingering outside cover and not having control of the operational area?
7. How should an operator while behind cover change from one firing position to another?

8. Why is it not tactically sound to stick the elbows out to the side when firing a pistol?
9. Describe the conflict between the line of sight and the line of bore when firing from cover.
10. Discuss the term "fatal funnel" and its connotation.
11. What are the two variations of slicing the area that are used to clear a room from a doorway?
12. What are the major drawbacks of the supported kneeling position?
13. What are the advantages of the unsupported kneeling position?
14. When is the prone position appropriate?
15. What firing position adapts well to shooting under cover low to the ground such as underneath a vehicle?
16. Why would an operator most likely be shooting from the supine position?
17. Discuss why an operator should be able to draw from a seated position.
18. Why is it a poor technique to hold the non-firing hand in front of the chest when shooting with one hand?
19. What two steps are used to accomplish the one-hand draw?
20. When is the retention firing position used?
21. Discuss what can happen when firing a pistol with a ported barrel from the retention position.
22. What is a contact shot?
23. Discuss the pros and cons of the strike and transition using one hand versus two hands.
24. Describe the two techniques used for shooting at moving targets.
25. When shooting at multiple adversaries, which one will likely be shot first and why?
26. An operator shooting at one adversary must do what before transitioning to the next adversary?
27. Discuss the technique of closing the distance and its application.
28. Discuss the advantages of integrating foot pursuit training with firearms training.
29. What is the stamping technique and how is it applied to a foot pursuit?
30. Discuss why operators need to use a three light system.
31. List the three types of flashlight activations.
32. List the five flashlight techniques shown in this chapter.
33. Discuss the disadvantages of the crossed wrist flashlight technique.

34. What is the advantage of using the same tactical light mounted techniques for the pistol and carbine?
35. Discuss using night vision tactics, such as dark adaptation, off-center vision, and scanning.
36. Why would indiscriminately pointing a pistol with a mounted light at an innocent person, even in an official capacity likely be a criminal offense?
37. List three examples of how an operator's vision might get impaired.
38. Discuss the importance of testing a protective mask under training conditions before using it operationally.
39. Describe how to shoot, reload, and clear stoppages with a pistol while injured.
40. Is it unlikely that an injured operator engage in a gunfight with a pistol would use a flashlight?
41. Why is it dangerous to fire a pistol under water?
42. Discuss issues related to the machine pistol, such as liability, training, carrying method, covering adversaries and arrest procedures, and hostage situation and crowds.
43. What are the three options available to an operator inside of a functioning unarmored vehicle involved in combat?
44. Where is the most effective area on an unarmored vehicle to use as cover?
45. Describe how a pistol can be used as a lethal impact weapon.

ENDNOTES

[1] Anthony J. Pinizzotto, Ph.D., Harry A. Kern, M.Ed., and Edward F. Davis, M.S., "One-Shot Drops," *FBI Law Enforcement Bulletin*, (October 2004): 20.

[2] Required accuracy is shooting the visually or ballistically exposed areas of the adversary's body that will result in an immediate response quickly leading to total incapacitation.

[3] "As I observe any potential targets, I have already oriented my body to the act; and after I determine that a target is bad, I commit, or *act*, firing the shot. The act itself is pushing the weapon out, taking the slack out of the trigger at the same time, catching the front sight as it comes up on target and dropping it into my rear sight, breaking the shot as this happens." Paul R. Howe, *Leadership and Training for the Fight* (New York, NY: Skyhorse Publishing, 2011), XLII.

"Break it down to sight picture, and there are elements in the sight picture of the rear sight, the front sight, and the target, or dot and the target. That's aiming...Aiming never changes...The basic fundamental that you put the sights where you want the shot, that never changes." Rob Leatham, *Rob Leatham on Pistol Shooting*, interviewed by a representative from GunsForSale.com, YouTube video, uploaded May 20, 2011, http://www.youtube.com/watch?v=CqqhSSiU_j8, (accessed September 22, 2012).

"Reality: When in a "lethal force action" your total focus will be on the weapon in the suspects' hands. The sights will both be a slight blur, *but* enough to align and take the shot." See Phil Singleton, *3 Day Tactical Pistol for Hostage Rescue, High Risk Warrant and Drugs Raids,* (Warrenton, VA: Singleton International): 12.

[4] "The soldier should use his sights when engaging the enemy unless this would place the weapon within arm's reach of the enemy." See Department of the Army, *Combat Training with Pistols, M9 and M11* (Washington, DC June 2003), 2-14.

"You should always use the sights when engaging the threat, the only exception being if this step would place the pistol within arm's reach of the threat." See Erik Lawrence, *Tactical Pistol Shooting*, (Lola, WI: Gun Digest Books, 2005), 119.

[5] Edward C. Godnig, O.D., FCOVD, "The Police Policy Studies Council," *Vision and Shooting,* http://www.theppsc.org/Staff_Views/Godnig/vision_and_shooting.htm (accessed September 22, 2012).

"Other aspects of body-alarm reaction include...a reduced capacity for analytical reasoning and decisionmaking; inability to count one's shots accurately; inability to keep mental track of the sequence of events as they occur; and a reversion to trained behavior." See International Association of Law Enforcement Firearms Instructors, *Standards & Practices Reference Guide for Law Enforcement Firearms Instructors*, (January 1995): 312-313.

[6] George T. Williams, "Reluctance to Use Deadly Force," *FBI Law Enforcement Bulletin* (October 1999): 1.

[7] Urey W. Patrick, and John C. Hall, *In Defense of Self and Others* (Durham, NC: Carolina Academic Press, 2010), 65.

[8] National Rifle Association, *Law Enforcement Handgun Instructor Manual* (Fairfax, VA: Firearm Safety and Range Organization, Edition 6.1, 2006), 8.

[9] Jeff Gonzales, *Combative Fundamentals, an Unconventional Approach* (Cedar Park, TX: Trident Concepts, LLC, 2002), 194-195.

Paul Howe, *Make Ready with Paul Howe: Advanced Tac Pistol/Rifle Operator* (Columbia, SC: Panteao Productions, 2010): Masking Targets, DVD.

Robert K. Taubert, *Rattenkrieg! The Art and Science of Close Quarters Battle Pistol* (North Reading, MA: Saber Press, 2012), 151.

[10] Jeff Gonzales, *Combative Fundamentals, an Unconventional Approach* (Cedar Park, TX: Trident Concepts, LLC, 2002), 120.

[11] National Rifle Association, *NRA Guide to the Basics of Personal Protection Outside the Home* (Fairfax, VA: National Rifle Association of America, 2006), 196.

[12] Paul Howe, *Make Ready with Paul Howe: Advanced Tac Pistol/Rifle Operator* (Columbia, SC: Panteao Productions, 2010): Barricades Pistol, DVD.

[13] Paul Howe, *Make Ready with Paul Howe: Advanced Tac Pistol/Rifle Operator* (Columbia, SC: Panteao Productions, 2010): Barricades Rifle Mods, DVD.

[14] Paul R. Howe, *Leadership and Training for the Fight* (New York, NY: Skyhorse Publishing, 2011), XXXV.

[15] National Rifle Association, *Law Enforcement Handgun Instructor Manual* (Fairfax, VA: Tactical Use of Cover and Concealment, Edition 4.1, 2006), 2.

[16] National Rifle Association, *Law Enforcement Handgun Instructor Manual* (Fairfax, VA: Tactical Use of Cover and Concealment, Edition 4.1, 2006), 3.

[17] The leaning out technique is keeping the body behind cover and leaning out only far enough to get a sight picture on the target. Timothy D. Blakeley, "Personal Notes from the Firearms Training Session," *U.S. Marshals Fugitive Investigator's Course,* (Federal Law Enforcement Training Center, Brunswick, GA: 2005): 7.

[18] Ronald J. Adams, Thomas M. McTernan, and Charles Remsberg, *Street Survival,* (Northbrook, IL: Calibre Press, 1980), 172.

[19] J. Henry FitzGerald, *Shooting* (Boulder, CO: Paladin Press, 2007), 365. Originally published in 1930 by J. Henry FitzGerald.

[20] Paul Howe, *Make Ready with Paul Howe: Advanced Tac Pistol/Rifle Operator* (Columbia, SC: Panteao Productions, 2010): Barricades Rifle, DVD.

[21] J. Henry FitzGerald, *Shooting* (Boulder, CO: Paladin Press, 2007), 88. Originally published in 1930 by J. Henry FitzGerald.

[22] Line of Sight: "The straight line from the sighting eye through the sights to the target or point of aim." See International Association of Law Enforcement Firearms Instructors, *Standards & Practices Reference Guide for Law Enforcement Firearms Instructors*, (January 1995): 193.

"Line of Bore: "The extended bore axis of a gun." See International Association of Law Enforcement Firearms Instructors, *Standards & Practices Reference Guide for Law Enforcement Firearms Instructors*, (January 1995): 55.

[23] National Rifle Association, *Law Enforcement Handgun Instructor Manual* (Fairfax, VA: Tactical Use of Cover and Concealment, Edition 4.1, 2006), 6.

[24] Paul Howe, *Make Ready with Paul Howe: Advanced Tac Pistol/Rifle Operator* (Columbia, SC: Panteao Productions, 2010): Barricades Pistol, DVD.

[25] Ronald J. Adams, Thomas M. McTernan, and Charles Remsberg, *Street Survival*, (Northbrook, IL: Calibre Press, 1980), 163-165.

[26] Robert K. Taubert, *Rattenkrieg! The Art and Science of Close Quarters Battle Pistol* (North Reading, MA: Saber Press, 2012), 217.

[27] Robert K. Taubert, *Rattenkrieg! The Art and Science of Close Quarters Battle Pistol* (North Reading, MA: Saber Press, 2012), 113.

[28] Paul R. Howe, *The Tactical Trainer* (Bloomington, IN: AuthorHouse, 2009), 114.

[29] National Rifle Association, *NRA Guide to the Basics of Personal Protection Outside the Home* (Fairfax, VA: National Rifle Association of America, 2006), 173.

[30] National Rifle Association, *NRA Guide to Basics of Personal Protection Outside the Home* (Fairfax, VA: National Rifle Association of America, 2006), 169-171.

[31] Timothy D. Blakeley, "Personal notes from the Antiterrorism Combat Shooting session," *Antiterrorism Combat Course*, (Tel Aviv, Israel: 2008): 5.

[32] J. Henry FitzGerald, *Shooting* (Boulder, CO: Paladin Press, 2007), 355. Originally published in 1930 by J. Henry FitzGerald.

[33] Ronald J. Adams, Thomas M. McTernan, and Charles Remsberg, *Street Survival*, (Northbrook, IL: Calibre Press, 1980), 163-165.

[34] Urey W. Patrick, and John C. Hall, *In Defense of Self and Others* (Durham, NC: Carolina Academic Press, 2010), 172.

Ronald J. Adams, Thomas M. McTernan, and Charles Remsberg, *Street Survival*, (Northbrook, IL: Calibre Press, 1980), 163-165.

[35] Federal Bureau of Investigation, "Bouncing Bullets," *FBI Law Enforcement Bulletin 38*, (October 1969): 1.

[36] Matt Burkett, *Practical Shooting Manual* (Scottsdale, AZ: Hotshots Publishing, 1995), VII-57.

[37] Department of the Army, *Combat Training with Pistols, M9 and M11* (Washington, DC June 2003), 2-11.

[38] Robert K. Taubert, *Rattenkrieg! The Art and Science of Close Quarters Battle Pistol* (North Reading, MA: Saber Press, 2012), 110.

[39] Boaz Aviram, *Krav Maga*, (Boaz Aviram: 2009), 77.

Imi Sde-Or (Lichtenfeld), and Eyal Yanilov, *Krav Maga*, (Tel Aviv, Israel: Dekel Publishing House), 8.

[40] National Rifle Association, *NRA Guide to Basics of Personal Protection Outside the Home* (Fairfax, VA: National Rifle Association of America, 2006), 211.

[41] National Rifle Association, *NRA Guide to Basics of Personal Protection Outside the Home* (Fairfax, VA: National Rifle Association of America, 2006), 174.

[42] In the Line of Duty, "Trooper Coates Shooting," *Volume 1 Program 4*: Video Recording.

[43] U.S. Department of Justice, *Violent Encounters*, 2006, (Washington, DC: FBI, 2006), 122.

[44] In the Line of Duty, "Perpendicular Shoot," *Volume 3 Program 3*: Video Recording.

In the Line of Duty, "Shreveport Officer Shoots Man with Phone, Not Gun" *Volume 10 Program 1:* Video Recording.

In the Line of Duty, "Brentwood (TN) Bank Robbery and Shootout," *Volume 8 Program 3*: Video Recording.

[45] Matt Burkett, *Practical Shooting Manual* (Scottsdale, AZ: Hotshots Publishing, 1995), VII-5-6.

[46] National Rifle Association, *Law Enforcement Handgun Instructor Manual* (Fairfax, VA: The Fundamentals of Handgun Marksmanship , Edition 6.1, 2006), 9.

[47] Jeff Gonzales, *Combative Fundamentals, an Unconventional Approach* (Cedar Park, TX: Trident Concepts, LLC, 2002), 156.

[48] Matt Burkett, *Practical Shooting Manual* (Scottsdale, AZ: Hotshots Publishing, 1995), VII-5.

[49] Jeff Gonzales, *Combative Fundamentals, an Unconventional Approach* (Cedar Park, TX: Trident Concepts, LLC, 2002), 156.

Matt Burkett, *Practical Shooting Manual* (Scottsdale, AZ: Hotshots Publishing, 1995), VII-5.

[50] The Grant-Taylor Manual, *The Palestine Police Force Close Quarter Battle* (Boulder, CO: Paladin Press, 2008), 25. Originally published in 1943. Reprinted by Paladin Press in 2008.

[51] U.S. Department of Justice, *Violent Encounters*, 2006, (Washington, DC: FBI, 2006), 50.

[52] Urey W. Patrick, and John C. Hall, *In Defense of Self and Others* (Durham, NC: Carolina Academic Press, 2010), 162-163.

[53] Glock Inc., *Glock Pistol Transitional Instructor Workshop Course Outline*, (Smyrna, GA: 2012): 12.

[54] Christian Schyma, "Wounding Capacity of Muzzle-Gas Pressure," *International Journal of Legal Medicine* (2012, 126, No. 3): 371-376.

[55] Out of Battery: "A firearm is said to be out of battery when the breeching mechanism is not in a proper position for firing…The condition of a firearm in which the breech mechanism is not sufficiently closed to safely support the cartridge or seal the action for firing." See International Association of Law Enforcement Firearms Instructors, *Standards & Practices Reference Guide for Law Enforcement Firearms Instructors*, (January 1995): 275.

[56] Clinch: "To hold a boxing opponent's body with one or both arms to prevent or hinder punches." *American Heritage Dictionary of the English Language Online*, 4th ed., s.v. "clinch," http://www.thefreedictionary.com/clinch (accessed September 22, 2012).

[57] Itay Gil, *Protect Krav Maga*, (North Hills, CA: Rising Sun Video Productions): DVD.

[58] The video shows on September 21, 1991, Trooper Andrew Lopez of the Texas Department of Public Safety stopping a vehicle near the Refugio city limits for a traffic violation. After getting out of the vehicle, one of the passengers reached in his waistband for a gun and shot at Trooper Lopez grazing his arm. Trooper Lopez returned fire killing his attacker. See Andrew Lopez Jr., *Shooting During Drug Stop in Refugio, Texas*, YouTube video, uploaded May 28, 2011, http://www.youtube.com/watch?v=InfOgXUJtMA, (accessed September 22, 2012).

[59] International Association of Law Enforcement Firearms Instructors, *IALEFI Guidelines for Simulation Training Safety*, (2004): 26.

[60] Thomas D. Petrowski, J.D., "Use-of-Force," *FBI Law Enforcement Bulletin*, (November 2002): 26.

[61] Department of the Army, *Rifle Marksmanship M16-/M4-Series Weapons* (Washington, DC August 2008), 7-36.

[62] Department of the Army, *Rifle Marksmanship M16-/M4-Series Weapons* (Washington, DC August 2008), 7-41.

[63] The Grant-Taylor Manual, The Palestine Police Force Close Quarter Battle (Boulder, CO: Paladin Press, 2008), 60. Originally published in 1943. Reprinted by Paladin Press in 2008.

[64] National Rifle Association, *Law Enforcement Tactical Handgun Instructor Manual* (Fairfax, VA: The Theory of Shooting Moving Targets, Edition 2.1), 5.

[65] Thomas D. Petrowski, J.D., "Use-of-Force," *FBI Law Enforcement Bulletin*, (November 2002): 26.

[66] Department of the Army, *Rifle Marksmanship M16-/M4-Series Weapons* (Washington, DC August 2008), 7-41.

[67] "All I do is wait until I can see the sights stop on that target. And, it isn't come down on the target, that looks good, reaffirm, now think about pulling the trigger, now look at the sights again. You got to get rid of all that. You put the sights on the target and you pull the trigger. And that's all there is to it." See Rob Leatham, *Rob Leatham - Training with Action Target Plate Rack*, demonstration, YouTube video, uploaded July 7, 2011, http://www.youtube.com/watch?v=_PQ1wpUybHs&feature=related, (accessed September 22, 2012).

[68] Phil Singleton, *3 Day Tactical Pistol for Hostage Rescue, High Risk Warrant and Drugs Raids,* (Warrenton, VA: Singleton International): 12.

[69] Department of the Army, *Soldier's Manual 95B Military Police*, (Washington, DC: Headquarters, Department of the Army, 2002), 3-56.

[70] Phil Motzer, *Crucible High-risk Environment Training II Volume 4: Combat Handgun*, (Boulder, CO: Paladin Press, 2010): Multiple Targets, DVD.

[71] Robert K. Taubert, *Rattenkrieg! The Art and Science of Close Quarters Battle Pistol* (North Reading, MA: Saber Press, 2012), 140.

[72] Travis Haley, *Make Ready with Travis Haley: Adaptive Handgun* (Columbia, SC: Panteao Productions, 2010): Balancing Speed & Accuracy, DVD.

[73] Robert L. Cantrell, *Understanding Sun Tzu on the Art of War* (Arlington, VA: Center for Advantage, 2003), 68.

[74] Travis Haley, *Make Ready with Travis Haley: Adaptive Handgun* (Columbia, SC: Panteao Productions, 2010): Off Line of Attack, DVD.

[75] The video shows on September 21, 1991, Trooper Andrew Lopez of the Texas Department of Public Safety stopping a vehicle near the Refugio city limits for a traffic violation. After getting out of the vehicle, one of the passengers reached in his waistband for a gun and shot at Trooper Lopez grazing his arm. Trooper Lopez returned fire killing his attacker. See Andrew Lopez Jr., *Shooting During Drug Stop in Refugio, Texas*, YouTube video, uploaded May 28, 2011, http://www.youtube.com/watch?v=InfOgXUJtMA, (accessed September 22, 2012).

[76] Trooper Andrew Lopez (retired) of the Department of Public Safety in Texas by telephone with the author, March 20, 2012, confirmed the circumstances of the shooting.

[77] The video shows on Friday, January 6, 2012, Deputy Jeff Nichols and Reserve Deputy Jeremy Conley of the Kalamazoo Sheriff's Office in Michigan stopping a vehicle on East Michigan Avenue after it ran a traffic light. When Deputy Nichols

approached the driver's side window, shots are fired at him. See Jeff Nichols and Jeremy Conley, *Cop Gets Shot at on Traffic Stop*, YouTube video, uploaded January 19, 2012, http://www.youtube.com/watch?v=w9JbdwHvRZo, (accessed September 22, 2012).

[78] National Rifle Association, *Law Enforcement Handgun Instructor Manual* (Fairfax, VA: Tactical Use of Cover and Concealment, Edition 4.1, 2006), 11.

[79] U.S. Department of Justice, *Violent Encounters*, 2006, (Washington, DC: FBI, 2006), 70-71.

[80] An Israeli instructor referred to this as *blocking*, but a more accurate description in the English language is *stamping*. Timothy D. Blakeley, "Personal notes from the Antiterrorism Combat Shooting session," *Antiterrorism Combat Course*, (Tel Aviv, Israel: 2008): 2.

[81] Stamping: "To thrust the foot forcibly downward." See *American Heritage Dictionary of the English Language Online*, 4th ed., s.v. "stamping," http://www.thefreedictionary.com/stamping (accessed September 22, 2012).

[82] Robert K. Taubert, *Rattenkrieg! The Art and Science of Close Quarters Battle Pistol* (North Reading, MA: Saber Press, 2012), 155.

[83] Kansas City Police Department, "Iser Park Shooting," Kansas City Police Department video, September 6, 2009. http://www.kcmo.org/police/Services/ReleasedVideos/index.htm, (accessed September 22, 2012).

[84] In the Line of Duty, "Murder of a Georgia Deputy," *Volume 7 Program 2*: Video Recording.

[85] "I am often asked how to handle immediate threat targets, or a threat that an officer observes that needs to be dealt with immediately up entering the room. In years past, the solution has been to shoot the threat twice and continue to your corner. I now teach officers to commit right or left out of the doorway and put the threat down. I promote servicing the target until it falls, while stepping right or left and creating an air gap that allows three or four to pick up and clear your corner while you are preoccupied." See Paul R. Howe, "CQB: Direct Threat or Points of Domination?" (Nacogdoches, TX : *Combat Shooting and Tactics*) http://www.combatshootingandtactics.com/published/cqb_july_%2006_final.pdf (accessed September 22, 2012).

[86] Phil Singleton, *3 Day Tactical Pistol for Hostage Rescue, High Risk Warrant and Drugs Raids,* (Warrenton, VA: Singleton International): 47.

[87] Paul Howe, *Make Ready with Paul Howe: Advanced Tac Pistol/Rifle Operator* (Columbia, SC: Panteao Productions, 2010): Masking Targets, DVD.

[88] Interview with Special Air Service (SAS) soldier at the Forward Operating Base (FOB) in Lashkar Gah, Afghanistan, 2008.

[89] Paul R. Howe, "CQB: Direct Threat or Points of Domination?" (Nacogdoches, TX   :   *Combat   Shooting   and   Tactics*) http://www.combatshootingandtactics.com/published/cqb_july_%2006_final.pdf (accessed September 22, 2012).

[90] U.S. Department of Justice, *Violent Encounters*, 2006, (Washington, DC: FBI, 2006), 122.

[91] J. Henry FitzGerald, *Shooting* (Boulder, CO: Paladin Press, 2007), 360. Originally published in 1930 by J. Henry FitzGerald.

[92] Ken J. Good, *A Law Enforcement Officer's Guide to: The Strategies of Low-Light Engagements* (Grandview, MO: Strategos International LLC), 12.

North Carolina Justice Academy, *Private Protective Services Firearms Training Manual Student 5ᵗʰ Edition* (Salemburg, NC: Module 5 Night Firing, 1998), 2-3.

[93] SureFire, LLC, "Surefire Products Catalog 2012," (Fountain Valley, CA: Surefire, 2012): 35.

[94] National Rifle Association, *Law Enforcement Handgun Instructor Manual* (Fairfax, VA: Reduced Light Training, Edition 6.1, 2006), 8.

[95] Paul Howe, *Make Ready with Paul Howe: Advanced Tac Pistol/Rifle Operator* (Columbia, SC: Panteao Productions, 2010): Barricades Rifle Mods, DVD.

[96] North Carolina Justice Academy, *In-Service Firearms Qualification Manual* (Salemburg, NC: November 2009), Handgun Qualification Course – 50 Rounds (Night Firing).

[97] North Carolina Justice Academy, *Private Protective Services Firearms Training Manual Student 5ᵗʰ Edition* (Salemburg, NC: Module 5 Night Firing, 1998), 2.

[98] SureFire LLC, Z2-S CombatLight LED Flashlight with Strobe User Manual (Fountain Valley: CA: Revision B 5-7-2010), 1.

[99] National Rifle Association, *Law Enforcement Handgun Instructor Manual* (Fairfax, VA: Reduced Light Training, Edition 6.1, 2006), 13.

[100] North Carolina Justice Academy, "SWAT Operator," *Firearms Use in Tactical Operations* (Salemburg, NC: January 2008): 39.

[101] National Rifle Association, *Law Enforcement Handgun Instructor Manual* (Fairfax, VA: Reduced Light Training, Edition 6.1, 2006), 10.

[102] Jeff Gonzales, *Combative Fundamentals, an Unconventional Approach* (Cedar Park, TX: Trident Concepts, LLC, 2002), 140.

[103] SureFire, LLC, "Law Enforcement Tactical Trinity Catalog," (Fountain Valley, CA: 2011), 1.

[104] SureFire, LLC, "Flashlights," *E1B Back*, http://www.surefire.com/E1B-Backup (accessed September 22, 2012).

Streamlight Inc., "Ultra Compact Tactical Light," *ProTac 1 AA*, http://streamlight.com/product/product.aspx?pid=199 (accessed September 22, 2012).

[105] Phil Singleton, *3 Day Tactical Pistol for Hostage Rescue, High Risk Warrant and Drugs Raids* (Warrenton, VA: Singleton International): 48.

[106] National Rifle Association, *Law Enforcement Handgun Instructor Manual* (Fairfax, VA: Reduced Light Training, Edition 6.1, 2006), 8.

[107] The video shows on September 21, 1991, Trooper Andrew Lopez of the Texas Department of Public Safety stopping a vehicle near the Refugio city limits for a traffic violation. After getting out of the vehicle, one of the passengers reached in his waistband for a gun and shot at Trooper Lopez grazing his arm. Trooper Lopez returned fire killing his attacker. See Andrew Lopez Jr., *Shooting During Drug Stop in Refugio, Texas*, YouTube video, uploaded May 28, 2011, http://www.youtube.com/watch?v=InfOgXUJtMA, (accessed September 22, 2012).

[108] Erik Lawrence, *Tactical Pistol Shooting* (Lola, WI: Gun Digest Books, 2005), 185.

[109] U.S. Department of Justice, *Violent Encounters*, 2006, (Washington, DC: FBI, 2006), 8.

[110] U.S. Department of Justice, *Violent Encounters*, 2006, (Washington, DC: FBI, 2006), 8.

[111] SureFire, LLC, "Flashlights," *Z2-S LED CombatLight*, http://www.surefire.com/Z2-S-LED (accessed February 27, 2011).

[112] Leapers Inc., "Flashlights and Lasers/LT-EL223HL," *Combat 23mm IRB Tactical OPS LED - the "L" Light*, http://www.leapers.com/prod_detail.php?mitem=flash&level1=&level2=&itemno=LT-EL223HL&status=&mtrack=m (accessed September 22, 2012).

[113] The author provided the label "inverted-L" to describe the flashlight technique using a small angle head light. To the author's knowledge, this is the original use of the inverted-L technique when using a small angle head flashlight and a pistol simultaneously. A Boolean search using the Google website did not reveal previous use of the technique or reference to the "inverted-L" label related to a flashlight. See Google, "No results found for "inverted-L" "flashlight technique", http://www.google.com/search?hl=en&q=%22inverted-L%22+%22flashlight+technique%22#hl=en&sclient=psy-ab&q=%22inverted-L%22+%22flashlight+technique%22&oq=%22inverted-L%22+%22flashlight+technique%22&gs_l=serp.12...0.0.0.45612.0.0.0.0.0.0.0.0..0.0.le

s%3B..0.0...1c.wNw0zx88jt0&pbx=1&bav=on.2,or.r_gc.r_pw.r_qf.&fp=5988fe0ce707
769a&biw=784&bih=633 (accessed September 22, 2012).

[114] Phil Singleton, *3 Day Tactical Pistol for Hostage Rescue, High Risk Warrant and Drugs Raids* (Warrenton, VA: Singleton International): 48.

[115] National Rifle Association, *Law Enforcement Handgun Instructor Manual* (Fairfax, VA: Reduced Light Training, Edition 6.1, 2006), 7.

[116] National Rifle Association, *Law Enforcement Handgun Instructor Manual* (Fairfax, VA: Reduced Light Training, Edition 6.1, 2006), 12.

[117] National Rifle Association, *Law Enforcement Handgun Instructor Manual* (Fairfax, VA: Reduced Light Training, Edition 6.1, 2006), 8.

[118] Dean T. Olson, "Improving Deadly Force Decision Making," *FBI Law Enforcement Bulletin*, (February 1998): 8.

[119] Jason Collins, Chief of Police (Retired) of the Mason Police Department in Tennessee conveyed the story while in Afghanistan, in a face-to-face conversation with the author, January 21, 2009.

[120] Erik Lawrence, *Tactical Pistol Shooting*, (Lola, WI: Gun Digest Books, 2005), 183.

[121] "…Lewinski recommends relying instead on the on-off mechanism that is built into the flashlight itself and can be activated when needed with the non-dominant hand." See Force Science Institute, LTD., " Force Science warning: Gun-mounted Flashlight Device Susceptible to Fatal Errors under High Stress," Force Science News #173, (March 11, 2011).

[122] SureFire, LLC, "Switches," *Grip Switch Assembly for X-Series Weapon Lights*, http://www.surefire.com/DG-Remote-Tailcap-Switch-X-Series (accessed September 22, 2012).

[123] Jeff Gonzales, *Combative Fundamentals, an Unconventional Approach* (Cedar Park, TX: Trident Concepts, LLC, 2002), 134.

[124] Force Science Institute, LTD., "Force Science warning: Gun-mounted Flashlight Device Susceptible to Fatal Errors under High Stress," Force Science News #173, (March 11, 2011).

[125] Force Science Institute, LTD., "Force Science warning: Gun-mounted Flashlight Device Susceptible to Fatal Errors under High Stress," Force Science News #173, (March 11, 2011).

[126] Bill Murphy, and SureFire Institute, "The Surefire DG Pressure Switch," (Yorba Linda, CA: *Articles and Studies*), http://www.surefireinstitute.com/images/pdfs/dg_pressure_switch.pdf (accessed September 22, 2012).

[127] Glock Inc., 6000 Highlands Parkway, Smyrna, GA 30082, USA, Phone: 770-432-1202, Fax: 770-433-8719, www.Glock.com.

Insight Operations, 9 Akira Way, Londonderry, NH 03053, USA, Toll-free: 866-509-2040, www.InsightTechnology.com.

Leapers, Inc., 32700 Capitol Street, Livonia, MI 48150, USA, Phone: 734-542-1500, Fax: 734-542-7095, www.Leapers.com

Streamlight Inc., 30 Eagleville Road, Eagleville, Pa. 19403, USA, Toll-free: 800-523-7488, Fax: 800-220-7007, www.streamlight.com.

SureFire, LLC, 18300 Mount Baldy Circle, Fountain Valley, CA 92708, USA, Toll-free: 800-828-8809, Fax: (714) 545-9537, www.SureFire.com.

[128] SureFire, LLC, "Law Enforcement Lights," *X400*, http://www.surefire.com/X400product (accessed September 22, 2012).

[129] Jeff Gonzales, *Combative Fundamentals, an Unconventional Approach* (Cedar Park, TX: Trident Concepts, LLC, 2002), 138.

[130] In North Carolina, the violation is called Assaulting by Pointing Gun. Other states will likely have similar laws. See North Carolina General Statue "§ 14-34. Assaulting by pointing gun. If any person shall point any gun or pistol at any person, either in fun or otherwise, whether such gun or pistol be loaded or not loaded, he shall be guilty of a Class A1 misdemeanor. (1889, c. 527; Rev., s. 3622; C.S., s. 4216; 1969, c. 618, s. 2 1/2; 1993, c. 539, s. 17; 1994, Ex. Sess., c. 24, s. 14(c); 1995, c. 507, s. 19.5(d).)."

[131] Robert K. Taubert, *Rattenkrieg! The Art and Science of Close Quarters Battle Pistol* (North Reading, MA: Saber Press, 2012), 89.

[132] Blade-Tech Industries, "Holsters w/Tactical Light," *Weapon & Tactical Light Holster w/Sting Ray Loop*, http://www.blade-tech.com/Weapon-Tactical-Light-Holster-w-Sting-Ray-Loop-pr-951.html (accessed September 22, 2012).

[133] Glock Inc., *Armorer's Manual U.S. Addendum*, (Smyrna, GA: 2012): 11.

[134] Glock Inc., *Armorer's Manual U.S. Addendum*, (Smyrna, GA: 2012): 11.

[135] LaserMax, "LaserMax First Shot Confidence," *LaserMax Sighting Systems* (2010): 1-22.

[136] International Association of Law Enforcement Firearms Instructors, *Standards & Practices Reference Guide for Law Enforcement Firearms Instructors*, (January 1995): 229.

[137] International Association of Law Enforcement Firearms Instructors, *Standards & Practices Reference Guide for Law Enforcement Firearms Instructors*, (January 1995): 229.

[138] Robert K. Taubert, *Rattenkrieg! The Art and Science of Close Quarters Battle Pistol* (North Reading, MA: Saber Press, 2012), 91.

[139] National Rifle Association, *Law Enforcement Handgun Instructor Manual* (Fairfax, VA: Reduced Light Training, Edition 6.1, 2006), 5.

[140] LaserMax, *LaserMax Installation and Operation Manual*, (Rochester, NY: Police Laser Sight, 1/10 01785-0-1 REV-P): 2.

[141] LaserMax, "LaserMax First Shot Confidence," *LaserMax Sighting Systems* (2010): 22.

[142] LaserMax, *LaserMax Installation and Operation Manual*, (Rochester, NY: Police Laser Sight, 1/10 01785-0-1 REV-P): 6.

[143] LaserMax, *LaserMax Installation and Operation Manual*, (Rochester, NY: Police Laser Sight, 1/10 01785-0-1 REV-P): 1.

[144] LaserMax, *LaserMax Installation and Operation Manual*, (Rochester, NY: Police Laser Sight, 1/10 01785-0-1 REV-P): 11.

[145] LaserMax, *LaserMax Installation and Operation Manual*, (Rochester, NY: Police Laser Sight, 1/10 01785-0-1 REV-P): 2.

[146] LaserMax, *LaserMax Installation and Operation Manual*, (Rochester, NY: Police Laser Sight, 1/10 01785-0-1 REV-P): 4.

[147] LaserMax, *LaserMax Installation and Operation Manual*, (Rochester, NY: Police Laser Sight, 1/10 01785-0-1 REV-P): 6.

[148] LaserMax, "LaserMax First Shot Confidence," *LaserMax Sighting Systems* (2010): 20.

[149] LaserMax, *LaserMax Installation and Operation Manual*, (Rochester, NY: Police Laser Sight, 1/10 01785-0-1 REV-P): 7.

[150] LaserMax, *LaserMax Installation and Operation Manual*, (Rochester, NY: Police Laser Sight, 1/10 01785-0-1 REV-P): 7.

[151] National Rifle Association, *Law Enforcement Handgun Instructor Manual* (Fairfax, VA: Reduced Light Training, Edition 6.1, 2006), 5.

[152] National Rifle Association, *Law Enforcement Handgun Instructor Manual* (Fairfax, VA: Reduced Light Training, Edition 6.1, 2006), 5.

[153] National Rifle Association, *Law Enforcement Handgun Instructor Manual* (Fairfax, VA: Reduced Light Training, Edition 6.1, 2006), 5.

[154] LaserMax, "Home Defense," *For Personal Protection,* http://www.lasermax.com/training/consumer/homeDefense.php (accessed February 17, 2011).

[155] National Rifle Association, *NRA Guide to Basics of Personal Protection Outside the Home* (Fairfax, VA: National Rifle Association of America, 2006), 272.

[156] National Rifle Association, *Law Enforcement Handgun Instructor Manual* (Fairfax, VA: Reduced Light Training, Edition 6.1, 2006), 6.

[157] National Rifle Association, *Law Enforcement Handgun Instructor Manual* (Fairfax, VA: Reduced Light Training, Edition 6.1, 2006), 6.

[158] LaserMax, "LaserMax First Shot Confidence," *LaserMax Sighting Systems* (2010): 2.

[159] LaserMax, *LaserMax Installation and Operation Manual*, (Rochester, NY: Police Laser Sight, 1/10 01785-0-1 REV-P): 3.

[160] American Optometric Association, "Aviation Vision," *The Eye and Night Vision,* http://www.aoa.org/x5352.xml (accessed September 22, 2012).

[161] Department of the Army, *Combat Training with Pistols, M9 and M11* (Washington, DC June 2003), 2-23.

[162] American Optometric Association, "Aviation Vision," *The Eye and Night Vision,* http://www.aoa.org/x5352.xml (accessed September 22, 2012).

[163] Department of the Army, *Combat Training with Pistols, M9 and M11* (Washington, DC June 2003), 2-23.

[164] Department of the Army, *Combat Training with Pistols, M9 and M11* (Washington, DC June 2003), 2-23.

[165] Headquarters United States Marine Corps, *Pistol Marksmanship MCRP 3-01 B* (Department of the Navy, Washington, D.C., 25 November 2003), 10-2.

[166] Headquarters United States Marine Corps, *Pistol Marksmanship MCRP 3-01 B* (Department of the Navy, Washington, D.C., 25 November 2003), 10-2.

[167] Department of the Army, *Combat Training with Pistols, M9 and M11* (Washington, DC June 2003), 2-23.

[168] McNett Corporation, "Product Info," *Op Drops Antifog Lens Cleaning System*, http://www.mcnett.com/Op-Drops-Anti-Fog-Lens-Cleaning-System-P329C94.aspx (accessed September 22, 2012).

[169] Bill Rogers, *Be Fast, Be Accurate, Be the Best* (Rogers Shooting School Publications: Jacksonville, FL, 2010), 88.

[170] National Rifle Association, *Law Enforcement Handgun Instructor Manual* (Fairfax, VA: Handgun Handling Techniques, Edition 6.1, 2006), 31.

[171] Glock Inc., *Glock Buyer's Guide Professional Edition*, (Smyrna, GA: Glock Inc., 2012): 21.

[172] National Rifle Association, *Law Enforcement Handgun Instructor Manual* (Fairfax, VA: Handgun Handling Techniques, Edition 6.1, 2006), 32.

[173] In the Line of Duty, "Trooper Coates Shooting," *Volume 1 Program 4*: Video Recording.
In the Line of Duty, "Perpendicular Shoot," *Volume 3 Program 3*: Video Recording.

[174] Eugene Sockut, *Secrets of Street Survival Israeli Style* (Boulder, CO: Paladin Press, 1995), 33.

U.S. Department of Justice, *Violent Encounters*, 2006, (Washington, DC: FBI, 2006), 100.

[175] The author doubled the time for the one hand drill in comparison to the two-hand stoppage drill. See International Association of Law Enforcement Firearms Instructors, *Standards & Practices Reference Guide for Law Enforcement Firearms Instructors*, (January 1995): 289.

[176] The time was doubled for the one hand drill in comparison to the two-hand stoppage drill. See International Association of Law Enforcement Firearms Instructors, *Standards & Practices Reference Guide for Law Enforcement Firearms Instructors*, (January 1995): 289.

[177] The time was doubled for the one-hand drill in comparison to the two-hand stoppage drill. See International Association of Law Enforcement Firearms Instructors, *Standards & Practices Reference Guide for Law Enforcement Firearms Instructors*, (January 1995): 289.

[178] "Malfunction: "Failure of a firearm to function as designed because of a mechanical defect or malfunction, as opposed to a stoppage caused by shooter error." See International Association of Law Enforcement Firearms Instructors, *Standards & Practices Reference Guide for Law Enforcement Firearms Instructors*, (January 1995): 273.

[179] Glock Inc., *Glock Buyer's Guide Professional Edition*, (Smyrna, GA: Glock Inc., 2012): 42.

[180] Glock Inc., *Glock Buyer's Guide Professional Edition*, (Smyrna, GA: Glock Inc., 2012): 42.

[181] In the 2005 Glock Buyer's Guide Professional Edition on page 46 it states as follows: "Optimum water permeability for secured firing even under water! Only approved for GLOCK pistols in caliber 9x19." In the 2010 Glock Buyer's Guide Professional Edition on page 42 it states as follows: "Optimum water permeability! Only approved for GLOCK pistols in caliber 9x19." The phrase "for secured firing even under water" has been removed. Glock is no longer advertising their 9x19 pistol can fire under water. Just because something can be done, does not mean that it should be done. See Glock Inc., *Glock Buyer's Guide Professional Edition*, (Smyrna, GA: Glock Inc., 2005): 46., and Glock Inc., *Glock Buyer's Guide Professional Edition*, (Smyrna, GA: Glock Inc., 2010): 42.

Speer, "9mm 124gr GDHP Service Ammunition Special Waterproofing Design," *Product Specification Sheet* (Lewiston, ID: 2010): 1.

[182] Speer, "9mm 124gr GDHP Service Ammunition Special Waterproofing Design," *Product Specification Sheet* (Lewiston, ID: 2010): 1.

[183] ATK, *Law Enforcement Ammunition & Accessories 2010 Product Catalog*, (Minneapolis, MN: 9mm Luger SOC, 2010) 6-7.

Speer, "9mm 124gr GDHP Service Ammunition Special Waterproofing Design," *Product Specification Sheet* (Lewiston, ID: 2010): 1.

[184] Speer, "9mm 124gr GDHP Service Ammunition Special Waterproofing Design," *Product Specification Sheet* (Lewiston, ID: 2010): 1.

[185] Glock Inc., *Glock 18 (18C) Select-Fire Familiarization Workshop*, (Smyrna, GA: February 2010): 1-11.

[186] Machine Pistol: "A machine pistol is a fully automatic or selective-fire handgun." See International Association of Law Enforcement Firearms Instructors, *Standards & Practices Reference Guide for Law Enforcement Firearms Instructors*, (January 1995): 59.

Selective Fire: "A feature of some automatic firearms that, by virtue of a selector switch or lever, allow the shooter to choose among two or more of the following firing modes: semi-automatic fire…, continuous automatic fire, or limited automatic (two- or three-shot) burst fire." See International Association of Law Enforcement Firearms Instructors, *Standards & Practices Reference Guide for Law Enforcement Firearms Instructors*, (January 1995): 82.

Glock Inc., "Buyer's Guide," *Glock Autopistols 2012*, (New York, NY: Harris Publications Inc., 2012): 102.

[187] Glock Inc., "Buyer's Guide," *Glock Autopistols 2012*, (New York, NY: Harris Publications Inc., 2012): 102.

[188] Photograph courtesy of Glock Inc. See Glock Inc., *Glock Professional LE*, (Smyrna, GA: 2010): DVD PowerPoint Slide 28.

[189] Glock Inc., *Armorer's Manual*, (Smyrna, GA: 2009): 62.

[190] Glock Inc., *Armorer's Manual U.S. Addendum*, (Smyrna, GA: 2012): 11.

[191] International Association of Law Enforcement Firearms Instructors, *Firearms Training Standards for Law Enforcement Personnel*, (2004): 14.10.

[192] North Carolina Justice Academy, "SWAT Operator," *Firearms Use in Tactical Operations* (Salemburg, NC: January 2008): 21.

[193] Glock Inc., *Instructions for Use Glock Safe Action Pistols All Models*, (Smyrna, GA: March 2011), 1.

[194] Glock Inc., "Buyer's Guide," *Glock Autopistols 2012*, (New York, NY: Harris Publications Inc., 2012): 102.

[195] California Highway Patrol, "Memorial," *The Newhall Incident*, http://www.chp.ca.gov/memorial/newhall.html (accessed September 22, 2012).

[196] Federal Bureau of Investigation, "News," *A Byte Out of History: Fatal Firefight in Miami*, http://www.fbi.gov/news/stories/2011/april/miami_041111 (accessed September 22, 2012).

[197] The Los Angeles Police Department, "Newsroom," *10 Year Anniversary of the North Hollywood Shootout*, http://www.lapdonline.org/february_2007/news_view/34831 (accessed September 22, 2012).

[198] Timothy D. Blakeley, "Personal notes from the 3-Day Firearms Instructor Workshop," *Glock Pistol Transitional Instructor Workshop*, (Smyrna, GA: Instructor Bob McCracken, December 17, 2003): 2.

[199] Paul Howe, *Make Ready with Paul Howe: Advanced Tac Pistol/Rifle Operator* (Columbia, SC: Panteao Productions, 2010): Vehicles as Cover, DVD.

Urey W. Patrick, and John C. Hall, *In Defense of Self and Others* (Durham, NC: Carolina Academic Press, 2010), 172-173.

Devallis Rutledge, *The Officer Survival Manual*, (Flagstaff, AZ: Flag Publishing Company, 1980), 277.

Robert K. Taubert, *Rattenkrieg! The Art and Science of Close Quarters Battle Pistol* (North Reading, MA: Saber Press, 2012), 158.

[200] Ronald J. Adams, Thomas M. McTernan, and Charles Remsberg, *Street Survival*, (Northbrook, IL: Calibre Press, 1980), 179.

[201] Paul Howe, *Make Ready with Paul Howe: Advanced Tac Pistol/Rifle Operator* (Columbia, SC: Panteao Productions, 2010): Full & Partially Exposed Targets, DVD.

[202] Urey W. Patrick, and John C. Hall, *In Defense of Self and Others* (Durham, NC: Carolina Academic Press, 2010), 173.

[203] Federal Bureau of Investigation, "Bouncing Bullets," *FBI Law Enforcement Bulletin*, Vol. 38, (October 1969): 3.

[204] Devallis Rutledge, *The Officer Survival Manual*, (Flagstaff, AZ: Flag Publishing Company, 1980), 276.

[205] Ronald J. Adams, Thomas M. McTernan, and Charles Remsberg, *Street Survival*, (Northbrook, IL: Calibre Press, 1980), 169.

[206] Paul Howe, *Uncovered: The Myth of Cover from Your Squad Car*, (Nacogdoches, TX: Combat Shooting and Tactics), http://www.combatshootingandtactics.com/published/the_myth_of_cover_07.pdf (accessed September 22, 2012).

[207] Deputy Charles Hille recalling one of his actions that occurred on May 9, 1980, during a gunfight involving five men dressed in Army fatigues who robbed the Security Pacific Bank in Norco, California. See Shirlee Pigeon, "The Norco Bank Robbery,"

Riverside   Sheriff's   Association,   (2010)
http://www.rcdsa.org/norcorobbery/robbery.html (accessed September 22, 2012).

[208] Robert K. Taubert, *Rattenkrieg! The Art and Science of Close Quarters Battle Pistol* (North Reading, MA: Saber Press, 2012), 185.

[209] Rex Applegate, *Kill or Get Killed* (Boulder CO: Paladin Press, 1976), 146.

[210] Office of Strategic Services (OSS) Close Combat Instructions: "Demonstrate the correct method of hitting with the pistol (not with the butt)." See Rex Applegate and Chuck Melson, *The Close Combat Files of Colonel Rex Applegate* (Boulder CO: Paladin Press, 1998), 45.

RANGES

8

WARNING: These recommendations are general in nature and *not* intended to be all-inclusive. Consult the necessary *private*, *local*, *state*, and *federal* authorities before opening and operating a range facility.

The *firearms instructor* has overall responsibility of the range and is the ranking official.[1] As a rule, there is one range instructor for every six shooters on the firing line.[2] However, at times it may be necessary to have one range instructor for each shooter.[3] Obey the firearms instructor's commands except when thought to be unsafe. Examples are a command that violates a safety rule or an operator on the firing line that believes the command to be unsafe. The operator needs to immediately call a *cease-fire* and continue after the command has been clarified.

An instructor that repeatedly gives contradictory instructions on the range will likely be regarded as incompetent and unprofessional by the operators. Range commands must be clear and concise. As an example, "We are leaving live fire training and going into dry fire training." There is no doubt about what is occurring. The instructor would then provide additional instructions to the operators.

Ranges should have a first aid bag specifically designed to treat gunshot wounds. The first aid bag must be accessible to operators and firearms instructors. Post emergency response information along with range rules. Any lesson plan provided to operators needs to include the range rules and emergency contact information. A telephone or other method of communication capable of contacting emergency responders is necessary. Restrooms and clean drinking water should be available.

Clean or repair pistols in designated areas. Know the range

boundaries to prevent exceeding its firing limits. Load empty firearms only when told to do so by a firearms instructor. The pistol remains in the holster until told otherwise by a firearms instructor.[4] The muzzle must remain in the appropriate direction for the sake of safety, especially with multiple operators on a firing line. This will prevent pointing the muzzle near or at other operators. Complete the turns and face downrange *before* removing the pistol from its holster. After firing, holster the pistol while facing downrange, and before turning around.

Never *bend over* on the firing line to pick up an object. Bending over reduces the operators field of vision, exposes the head to gunfire, and is tactically unsound. Training protocols may allow for operators on a firing line to pick up dropped items as in a real-life situation. To do so the operator must keep the head up, assume a *kneeling position,* and reach for the item while remaining behind all muzzles.[5] Other range protocols may prohibit any form of picking up equipment dropped when the line is hot. Never move downrange until a firearms instructor calls the line clear, and operators agree the line is clear. It is the operator's responsibility on completion of a training session to verify the condition of his or her pistol as loaded or unloaded.[6] Operators should separate their slides and receivers while on the firing line before going to the cleaning room.

NOTE: An instructor assumes greater liability when vouching for an operator that his or her pistol is unloaded. The assumption of liability takes place when the instructor checks each pistol on the firing line. An instructor may want to consider only giving the command to unload and allow the responsibility of unloading the pistol to remain with the operator.

At the end of the training session, perform a final check of the area to ensure no equipment or firearms are left behind. Check all pockets to make sure they do not contain any live ammunition. This is especially critical when flying commercial airlines as ammunition must be declared *and* in checked luggage. "Violations can result in criminal prosecution and the imposition of civil penalties of up to $10,000 per violation."[7]

WARNING: Before leaving the range, wash hands with soap designed to remove lead and heavy metals to reduce exposure.[8]

INDOOR RANGE

An organization with an indoor range is fortunate to have one. An indoor range provides 24-hour access and allows training regardless of weather. Turning off the range lights provides nighttime shooting during daytime hours. There is also the convenience of converting the range into environments that closely resemble the actual operational conditions, especially urban characteristics that armed civilians and police officers encounter.

Statistics show what many police officers can attest too. Criminals prefer to use the darkness to conceal their unlawful exploits. Over half of police involved shootings occur at nighttime.[9] It is to the operator's advantage to practice with a pistol regularly in low light conditions. With regular practice, an operator can become proficient at hitting moving targets in low light conditions.

An indoor range provides an excellent opportunity for training, but is an expensive endeavor that demands absolute diligence by the owner. The state and local building authorities must approve the range site and construction plans before breaking ground. State and local building code authorities will also have to sign off on the permit before the facility can open.

OUTDOOR RANGE

Building an outdoor range is straightforward to build *if* proper guidance is obtained. The natural lay of the terrain can expedite the range construction process. Property surrounded by a high bank or a hillside is a great starting point. Such property provides on-site soil to build a minimum 15-foot (4.57-meter) tall berm capable of stopping bullets. A side berm is also a good idea and recommended. The height of the berm must be the *actual* soil minus any vegetation. Grass or weeds growing on top of a berm is the *perceived* height, but the *actual* height of the berm is only the height of the soil. The range is preferably enclosed with a fence and perimeter signage warning of firearms training. An abandoned quarry or sandpit could be a viable option. The only property available might be flat ground. In this case, soil for the berm would have to be delivered to the site. There are specific dimensions for building a berm. The methodology of construction is beyond the scope of this book. The National Rifle Association has an excellent manual that provides information on building ranges.[10]

The outdoor range has the benefit of fresh air, fumes quickly disperse, and generally, the noise levels are lower than indoor ranges. Those reasons appeal to many operators that prefer to shoot outdoors. Nevertheless, the outdoor range does have its limitations. Zoning changes can put an outdoor range in danger of closure. Public outdoor ranges normally operate during good weather and daytime hours. Police and military ranges are used at night and in inclement weather except for lightning. The equipment on an outdoor range does have a tendency to deteriorate quicker than an indoor range.

To remove debris and bullets from a dirt berm the soil requires sifting.[11] The bullets do not penetrate the berm far and continuous shooting has a tendency to bring them to the surface. Clean the berm as needed. Sell the bullets recovered as scrap metal to reduce operational cost. What must *not* occur is to allow impacted bullets to collect in one area creating a ricochet hazard. A ricochet is a hazard to any living thing within the range area. Sew the front portion of the berm in grass. This will help reduce erosion. Just as an indoor range would have to be approved by state and local building code authorities, so would an outdoor range.

GENERAL REQUIREMENTS FOR A RANGE

Both an indoor and outdoor range should have a designated control point. The control point is the place where the range caller has a clear and unrestricted view of the firing line, operates targets, and announces the state of the firing line as clear or hot. The control point person turns on a red light *if* available to show the firing status as hot (firing allowed). A green light shows the firing status as clear (no firing allowed). Eye and hearing protection must be worn while on a firearms range.

NOTE: A *closed-circuit television* (CCTV) recording system is recommended for any range activities. Such documentation would be vital if an injury occurred on the range.

There should also be numbered or color-coded 25-yard (22.86-meter) firing positions coinciding with divided longitudinal lanes to the targets. The targets can be spaced 24 inches (609.6 millimeters) apart from scoring edge to scoring edge. An asset to a range is a turning target system with a variable time input capability. A variable time input system allows preset target exposures that are useful for target discrimination training. A public-address system allows the instructor to give range commands that any shooter on the firing line can hear while wearing hearing protection. A lighting system with variable brightness allows for night shooting. Law enforcement training can include police lights, siren noise, and dispatch radio traffic played over a loudspeaker to induce stress.

The firearms range should also have the capability to allow freedom of movement. Flexible firing points allow for dynamic movement advocated for realistic training. A continuum of training should include two-hand shooting at the 25-yard (22.86 meter) line to one-hand shooting at the 1-yard (0.91-meter) line. Training can also include running at full speed across the range stopping suddenly at surprise targets and firing multiple rounds in rapid succession. Only one operator at a time should live fire the drill in order to maintain a safe training environment. A range properly configured and drills ran in an orderly manner will allow a smooth rotation of operators.

DANGER: When shooting *prone* or *supine* take appropriate measures to ensure bullets will not go over the berm. Placing targets close to the ground or laying them horizontally should remedy trajectory issues.

Having flexible firing points allow the operator to practice *moving, communicating,* and *shooting* during training. This is especially important for training in mock operational environments. Before the training begins, carefully check the range for debris that could cause a ricochet or present a tripping hazard. Range transformation is limited only by the instructor's imagination. The range can be transformed into the interior of an urban structure as an example. This transformation can represent a residence or one of the local commercial establishments.

TARGET DISCRIMINATION TRAINING

In the United States, law enforcement firearms training must also include when *not* to shoot. Just teaching how to shoot is not enough.[12] The armed civilian and military operator should also attend training in threat discernment commonly referred to as target discrimination.[13] To receive the maximum benefit from training, operators must understand the concept of ability, opportunity, and jeopardy. In the United States, *ability, opportunity,* and *jeopardy* are the accepted standards to use force.[14] (Figure 8-1) The "shoot or don't shoot" error is the *highest* causation for civil litigation in America regarding the use of police firearms. [15] Legal justification and reasonableness under the circumstances are the standard of the shoot or do not shoot decision.

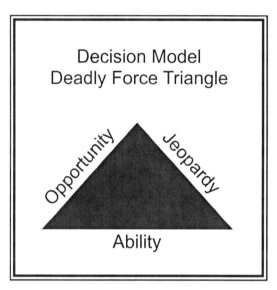

Figure 8-1 Decision Model: Deadly Force Triangle[16]

Look at the entire person first and then his or her hands.[17] In law enforcement, it is common to teach police officers to look at the hands first. Looking at the hands first can cause a mistake in judgment resulting in a friendly fire death (fratricide). Looking at someone's hands first and seeing a weapon will likely produce immediate engagement. What can occur is the person holding the weapon (pistol, rifle, etc.) is *not* a threat, but a friendly. First, observe the whole person, then hands, waistline, immediate surroundings, and finally the person's demeanor.[18]

NOTE: It is not so important to shoot fast as it is to discriminate fast.[19] An operator can shoot only as fast as seeing and articulating the threat.

Target Discrimination Course: In a split second, operators must be able to decide when to use deadly force. Target discrimination training helps to develop an operator's ability to decide quickly. On the range, construct walls out of large sheets of cardboard or lightweight plywood panels that slid snug into stands. The panels need to be at about 6 feet (1.82 meters) high. This method of assembling walls allows for a nearly endless room and building configuration. Three types of targets are used: (1) *threat,* (2) *no-threat,* and (3) *friendly.* The target discrimination classification simplifies the thought process for the operator. The operator will begin at the start point and work through the course. (Figure 8-2) The operator is given the circumstances of a situation and told not to harm innocent civilians.

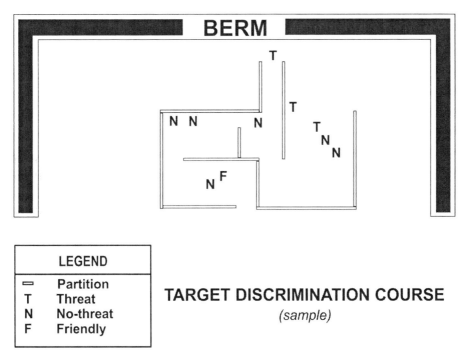

Figure 8-2 Target Discrimination Course

NOTE: Instructors should *not* use no-win scenarios. The operator that keeps being killed (hypothetically speaking) will not learn how to get past the abrupt ending of the scenario. No-win training only reinforces failure.

Awaiting operators will only see a wall and doorway in which they must enter and make life-and-death decisions, i.e. target discrimination. Instructors when using surprise targets must not allow operators to anticipate what is going to happen by standing or moving with the pistol positioned in the line of sight. The operator may have a pistol in the holster or in a ready position according to the circumstances. Obviously, the operator will remain in a firing position to engage the exposed threats when targets appear one directly after the other. When the threat targets in one area have been neutralized the operator should return to a ready position (safety on if equipped) or holster after each engagement. The operator will then continue the course according to instructions provided by the range officer.

A ready position must allow an unobstructed view of the area. Searching with a firearm (handgun or long gun) directly in the line of sight obstructs the vision.[20] The operator would likely have to lower his or her pistol to identify the target and again bring the pistol back into the line of sight to engage. The down and back up motion of the pistol is unnecessary movement that wastes precious time. Keep the pistol below the line of sight for quick target identification. Once a target is identified, quickly raise the pistol, and push it forward into the line of sight to engage. A skilled operator with a pistol held below his or line of sight with the arms extended can engage an 8-inch target at 10 yards in 0.5 second. What happens if an operator turns a corner and presented with a threat at contact distance? The target would be shot from the retention position.

Using a law enforcement scenario as an example, the call is a domestic disturbance. The police officer enters the door accompanied by a range instructor. The police officer's personality will likely decide if the entry is slow and deliberate or more dynamic. The house is crowded with several no-threat targets. At the end of a hallway is a threat target that represents an adversary that thinks it is better to shoot it out with the police rather than go to jail. The police officer must immediately stop the threat target. The house could have other doors that require investigating in addition to the narrow hallway. There can be three-dimensional (3-D) dummies or photograph targets that represent *no-threats* and *threats* occupying the rooms.

NOTE: Realistic looking three-dimensional threat targets can help break the resistance barrier to shooting another human being. Scenario targets with hands separated in two different positions require an operator to see both hands before making a decision to fire.[21] Change hand overlays with and without weapons to force the operator to make a decision during multiple training scenarios.

The police officer has to maintain situational awareness and make a quick assessment. The police officer's appearance is the cue for the scenario to begin. There can be sounds of screams, arguing, and finally gunfire that blare in the background (sounds played over a loudspeaker). The suspect could be waiting in ambush. The innocent family members may partially shield the suspect. The police officer has to negotiate the furniture and the no-threats to get a clear shot on the threat target. The police officer will likely assume a fighting stance and fire at any identifiable threats until the magazine is empty. It is unlikely the police officer will know the exact number of shots fired.[22] Hopefully the police officer will not have any hits on the no-threat targets.

Any no-threat targets shot will require a verbal explanation or written report (course dependent) by the police officer describing how such a tragedy occurred. A real-life police involved shooting that resulted in an innocent civilian being injured or killed would be widely publicized in the media. The discipline of *not* shooting is just as important as when to shoot.[23] The author while at the scene of a suicide bombing and being shot at had a great desire to shoot back, but did not do so. He could not *identify* a terrorist to shoot. The Special Air Service (SAS) team leader (TL) could not identify a terrorist and did not shoot. Sometimes *not* shooting is the best course of action—a vital point to cover during training.[24]

Discrimination training is not just playacting. Discrimination training is to immerse operators in a stressful environment in which life-and-death decisions are made in a split second. Every police and military firearms training program needs to include realistic decision-making.[25] Obviously, discrimination training would also be beneficial to armed civilians. This type of training will challenge and stimulate for the betterment any operator. It is time to move past the "ready on the right, ready on the left, watch your lane!"[26]

Cost: How much does this type of training actually cost? The cost is negligible when combined with imagination and motivated range personnel. The materials are wood, cardboard, old clothes, 3D targets, and photographic targets with the edges trimmed around the figures. This type of training course is *not* going to be detrimental to the department's budget. Nevertheless, administrators must be willing to provide the necessary funds, and allow training time for personnel to maintain their operational survival skills.[27]

NOTE: Cutting the excess target away provides a realistic size to the figures. The author first saw this done during a bus and vehicle assault course taught by a former British Special Air Service (SAS) soldier.[28]

Use human silhouette targets attached to cardboard backing. Target placement should reflect real-life positions that adversaries use. Vertical targets can be placed low to the ground to represent kneeling, horizontal targets to represent lying down and targets flat on the ground (dirt surface) to represent prone. To verify operator skill and to get feedback—use 0.75 inch (19mm) square adhesive *pasters*[29] to cover the holes in targets or frequently replace the entire target. Various faces can be printed using a color printer and given appropriate scenario related names. The excess paper around the face can be trimmed off and the image pasted on a target. This adds adversary identification training within the firearms training program.

Prop Walls and Ventilation: Safety is paramount in any course of instruction and must be balanced with the need for realistic survival training. When in an indoor range, instructors must be conscious of prop walls not interfering with the air ventilation system. Indoor ranges are designed with specific airflow patterns. If there is any doubt concerning the airflow of the range consult an expert in designing ranges. An adversely affected ventilation system allows fumes to linger inside the range. If this occurs, immediately leave the range until the fumes dissipate. Identify what object is interrupting the airflow and make the necessary changes. The eyes will be irritated and over time possibly infected with continued training on an indoor range with poor ventilation.

A well-built indoor range will have excellent ventilation, cement floor, variable lighting, acoustical material, and a backstop that allows shooting within 1 yard (0.91 meter). An indoor range is an excellent firearms training resource for armed civilians, police officers, and military operators. Productive days on the range improve operator competency in operational survival—accept nothing less.

NOTE: At the conclusion of each training session, the instructor should ask if there are any injuries, complaints, or questions.

FIREARMS QUALIFICATION STANDARDS

Some might argue the law enforcement profession is one where mediocrity is accepted. There are police qualification courses that a police officer can miss 15 out of 50 rounds fired and still pass (35 hits x 5 points = 175 and 175 x 0.4 = 70 percent).[30] Others might argue the 70 percentile score is widely accepted by society and the academic community. Nevertheless, the standard translates into a state approved standard that permits a police officer to carry a lethal weapon that misses 30 percent of the time. An argument could also be made the standard needs to reflect the responsibility.

Target Focused Sighted Shooting provides the means to shoot a human silhouette target under low light conditions with extreme speed within effective accuracy. This is what it takes to win a spontaneous up close and personal deadly force encounter. The forebrain (conscious reasoning) is bypassed and the midbrain (primitive reaction) responds.[31] The actions of the operator must be quick. This quickness can only be acquired by pushing past personal comfort zones. A training program must not deter operators from firing at their maximum speed.

Qualification targets can be realistic images of people. Rotate targets of various races and gender to reflect real-life target discrimination. This should negate accusations of inadvertently teaching operators to shoot at a particular race or gender. A threat is *not* a person of a certain race, gender, or age. A threat is what can harm or kill the operator.[32] To allow qualification targets with prominent scoring lines is to undermine the philosophy of combat shooting. This means using targets with subdued scoring lines. Visible scoring lines entice the operator whether consciously or subconsciously to shoot for points instead of stopping effectiveness. Precision shooting the course of fire will take away from how to incapacitate an adversary quickly with a pistol.[33]

A minimum standard for a police officer and military operator is to complete an annual qualification course. The object of in-service training is not to promote an atmosphere of mediocrity, but to test the operator's proficiency. Besides the annual qualification, shooting a combat course should occur quarterly.[34] To perform at maximum capability an operator must practice daily. A daily investment in realistic training for the area of operation will build *subconscious* skills necessary for operational survival.

A police officer or military operator should provide his or her own combat firearms training *if* the agency does not or it is inadequate. Training does not always have to be live fire. Many of the skills used for fighting with a firearm can be maintained without ever firing a shot. Civilian shooters to validate their firearms skills can use their resident state's law enforcement qualification course of fire. The course can be scored pass or fail. Documentation of passing the course can help to negate any accusations of incompetence. An operator that carries a firearm should also carry a card with information for legal counsel (attorney's business card with a 24-hour telephone number).

An acceptable standard for a qualification would be to hit a human silhouette target in the high center mass area 70 percent of the time. The remaining 30 percent would have to be somewhere on the target and not a single miss. The requirement of not missing puts real *stress* on an operator, but the human silhouette target aids in shooting as fast and accurate as possible. This is the type of shooting called for during a deadly force encounter. As already discussed, the preferred target area is from the forehead to the lower sternum. However, multiple hits somewhere on the suspect's body are certainly to the operator's advantage.[35]

SHOOTING RECOGNITION PROGRAM

As a part of the annual qualification, many law enforcement agencies and military organizations offer a shooting recognition program based on individual performance. This is an excellent idea when combined with a challenging and realistic course of fire. The appropriate course of fire with human silhouette targets will discourage attempts to precision shoot the course. The shooting recognition program can be a part of the qualification and regular in-service training program.

A shooting recognition program should also make an allowance for challenging the requirements in one shooting session. An operator that has the initiative to complete the requirements in one session should have the opportunity *if* logistically possible. Evidence of such motivation is a police officer spending personal money on ammunition that will be required to challenge the award program.

From a logistical point, it is acceptable to conduct the qualification and then offer the range to any operator who wishes to attempt the award program's course of fire. An example of a shooting award program would be for a police officer to fire a 50 round qualification course with 90 percent of the rounds in the high center mass on the human silhouette target and remaining 10 percent would have to be somewhere on the target and not a single miss. The police officer would be required to complete the course three consecutive times.

If a 50 round nighttime qualification is mandated, the police officer would have to also shoot it three times just the same as the daytime qualification. This means the police officer would have to supply 300 rounds of ammunition to fire both the daytime and nighttime course three consecutive times.

There is a sense of professional satisfaction for those that earn a shooting award. The U.S. Army acknowledges that soldiers desire to be publically recognized for their *hard work*, *suffering*, and *bravery*.[36] To a police officer that earns a shooting award it is not a trinket, but a symbol of hard work and professionalism. The shooting award standard needs to be high. Standards that are easy to achieve quickly lose their value. "This devaluation creates resentment in those who most deserve the special recognition."[37] Combining a *realistic* qualification course with an awards program gives police officers a sense of satisfaction and confidence.

RANGE TIPS FOR INSTRUCTORS

Egos: The issue of having an ego can apply to an instructor as well as an operator. Instructors should not monopolize training time when *attending* a course presented by another instructor.[38] In addition, operators attending a training course might have more real-life experience than the presenting instructor—something that everybody must be willing to accept without malice. Attending instructors and operators must also accept and respect that it is the presenting instructor's course. A training course is not the place for egos, but should be a place for teaching and learning.

Bias Opinion: The instructor should not ask a question and then *bluntly* say to a student that answered is wrong. It is embarrassing to the student and makes the instructor look like an egomaniac. The author as an example had attended a pistol course taught at a law enforcement regional training conference. The instructor asked, "Who believes in night sights?" Many officers raised their hands. The instructor *adamantly* replied, "I don't!" The instructor then asked, "Who believes in laser sights?" Again, several officers raised their hands. Again, the instructor replied, "I don't!" The body language of some officers revealed their defensiveness toward the instructor and the author had to fight from becoming defensive. The instructor never addressed the advantages or disadvantages of night sights or laser sights.

Operator Motivation: Operators that use their money and vacation time to attend a course want to be there. However, there are operators that have no desire to be at a course and probably see it as a nuance. Instructors need to dedicate their time to the motivated operators who want to be there and not waste time trying to help others that have little or no motivation.

Cell Phones: While training on the range carefully consider whether to allow operators to have cell phones on their person. Not having cell phone will prevent operators from trying to answer a call or return a text. A student who had a phone tried to shoot with one hand and answer his cell phone with the other hand during a course of fire.[39] Not allowing cell phones on the firing line may also prevent operators from being mentally preoccupied about possible incoming calls or texts. There is also the option of allowing cell phones, but they are *not* to be used while on the firing line. The obvious exception is a medical emergency at the range.

Note Taking: Encourage operators to keep a notepad and pen while on the range. It is unlikely that an operator will remember the specifics of training unless documented for future review. More importantly, the information might be applicable to the operator's survival in particular area of operation (AO).

Ammunition Changeover: Provide an opportunity for operators who stay armed professionally to change over from their duty ammunition to practice ammunition and vice versa. This would likely need to be done at the beginning of the course, mealtime, and at the conclusion of the course.

Loading Magazines: Suggest to operators that they can utilize training time more efficiently by using a speed loader to load magazines, and keeping loose rounds in a cargo pocket on the dominant hand side for immediate access while on the firing line.

Range Commands: Do *not* use the word *gun* in the place of *fire* as a range command.[40] Police officers use the word gun to warn other officers, not as an automatic response to shoot. Range commands must be clear and provoke an immediately action as related to the meaning of the word or words. Use standardized commands on the range: load, unload, unload and show clear, fire, cease-fire, etc.

Shooting Relays: Keep lag time between shooting relays to a minimum. This can be accomplished by having a relay on the line firing, one behind the firing line ready to shoot, and another loading magazines. Single operator relays should last about 30 to 60 seconds and resetting the course of fire (targets pasted, bobbers reset, etc.) in about the same amount of time. Break time can be included during the lag time between setting up the courses of fire.

Hanging Targets: Instructors need to remind operators how to hang their targets. The target in an indoor range is normally secured to the bottom edge of the backing board (cardboard). This will prevent the target from being hung too high resulting in rounds impacting into the ceiling's protective baffles—especially while shooting head shots. Hang targets so the point of aim is in the center of the backstop.

Weak Firearm Handling Skills: It is crucial that an instructor stand close enough to an operator that has weak firearms handling skills to *stop* any unsafe movement. An operator that cannot be touched—cannot be controlled.

Record Keeping: Make notes in the training records of operators such as safety violations, inadequate equipment manipulation, poor firearms handling skills, and any corrective or remedial instruction provided. Document the type of firearm and caliber, *especially* if problematic to an operator. The operator's paper target retains the hit information and acts as permanent record.[41]

Rainy Weather: Laminate the written course of fire to protect it from inclement weather. Cardboard targets when wet have a tendency to separate. A piece of tape run along the top of the target will aid in preventing the cardboard from separating. Covering the entire target with a clear plastic bag may be the better option for extended training periods in the rain.

Simulate Low Light Conditions: Operators can wear a pair of welder's goggles to help simulate low light conditions when practicing on an outdoor range during the day.[42]

Leaving the Range: Operators need an opportunity to put their pistols in the desired condition before leaving the range.[43] Obey all laws when making the decision to leave a facility with a loaded pistol. Check for dummy rounds that could be in magazines, pockets, or even in the chamber.[44] After a session of shooting—clean the pistol before carry it for self-protection.

SUMMARY

Firearms instructors have total responsibility for the range and the personnel on the range. Range commands must be immediately obeyed unless doing so would compromise safety. Every person on a range has a *moral* obligation and the right to call a cease-fire for any safety violation. Post on the range information for emergency medical assistance. Indoor ranges offer the advantages of training day or night and in severe weather. Outdoor ranges offer the advantages of training in all types of weather conditions and with vehicles. An outdoor or indoor range can be converted easily for target discrimination training. Administrators should maintain a shooting recognition program in an agency that reinforces realistic firearms skills. Instructors need to keep notes on student deficiencies and improvements.

DISCUSSION QUESTIONS

1. Who is the ranking person on a firearms range?
2. Why is it important to have a telephone or other methods of communication during range training?
3. Where is a pistol cleaned or repaired at a range?
4. Discuss the advantages and disadvantages of an indoor range.
5. Discuss the advantages and disadvantages of an outdoor range.
6. Explain the importance of closed-circuit television (CCTV) recording system on a range.
7. What are the accepted standards to use force in the United States?
8. What error is the highest causation for civil litigation in America regarding the use of police firearms?
9. Discuss why instructors should not use no-win scenarios.
10. What type of training immerses police officers in a stress induced environment in which life-and-death decisions are made in a split

second?
11. Why are various photographic targets used during qualification?
12. Discuss why a shooting recognition program can have a positive influence on an operator.
13. What will make an instructor look like an egomaniac?
14. Discuss why an instructor should dedicate their time to the motivated operators?
15. Explain why instructors need to set ground rules for cell phones on the range?
16. Explain an advantage of note taking while on the range.
17. What device can operators use when loading magazines for a more efficient use of training time?
18. What information should be included in an operator's training record?
19. Explain why an instructor may have to stand close to an operator that is performing a shooting drill?
20. What can be worn to simulate low light conditions?

ENDNOTES

[1] National Rifle Association, *Law Enforcement Handgun Instructor Manual* (Fairfax, VA: Firearm Safety and Range Organization, Edition 6.1, 2006), 2.

[2] International Association of Law Enforcement Firearms Instructors, *Firearms Training Standards for Law Enforcement Personnel*, (2004): 15.0.

[3] National Rifle Association, *NRA Basics of Personal Protection Outside the Home Course: Course Outline and Lesson Plans*, (Fairfax, VA: April 2009), 7.

[4] J. Henry FitzGerald, *Shooting* (Boulder, CO: Paladin Press, 2007), 418. Originally published in 1930 by J. Henry FitzGerald.

[5] National Rifle Association, *Law Enforcement Handgun Instructor Manual* (Fairfax, VA: Firearm Safety and Range Organization, Edition 6.1, 2006), 4.

[6] National Rifle Association, *Law Enforcement Handgun Instructor Manual* (Fairfax, VA: Firearm Safety and Range Organization, Edition 6.1, 2006), 11.

[7] Transportation Security Administration, "For Travelers," *Traveling with Special Items*,   Firearms   and   Ammunition, http://www.tsa.gov/travelers/airtravel/assistant/editorial_1188.shtm   (accessed September 22, 2012).

[8] Esca Tech, Inc., "Products," *D-lead Hand Soap*, (2012), https://www.esca-tech.com/ProductDetail.php?category=1000&productnum=4222ES   (accessed September 22, 2012).

[9] U.S. Department of Justice, *Violent Encounters*, 2006, (Washington, DC: FBI, 2006), 7.

[10] National Rifle Association, *The Range Source Book* (Fairfax, VA: Range Department, January 2004), 1-674.

[11] National Rifle Association, *The Range Source Book* (Fairfax, VA: Range Department, January 2004), I-5-9.

[12] U.S. Supreme Court, *Graham v. Connor*, 490 U.S. 386 (1989).

[13] Dean T. Olson, "Improving Deadly Force Decision Making," *FBI Law Enforcement Bulletin*, (February 1998): 2.

[14] Dean T. Olson, "Improving Deadly Force Decision Making," *FBI Law Enforcement Bulletin*, (February 1998): 2.

[15] North Carolina Justice Academy, "Specialized Firearms Instructor Training," *Civil Liability: Firearms Training* (Salemburg, NC: Summer 2005): 23.

[16] Dean T. Olson, "Improving Deadly Force Decision Making," *FBI Law Enforcement Bulletin*, (February 1998): 4.

[17] "Soldier must visualize the entire target because an armed target could be a fellow Soldier or other friendly." See Department of the Army, *Rifle Marksmanship M16-/M4-Series Weapons* (Washington, DC August 2008), 7-54.

[18] Paul R. Howe, *The Tactical Trainer* (Bloomington, IN: AuthorHouse, 2009), 119.

[19] Paul Howe, *Make Ready with Paul Howe: Advanced Tac Pistol/Rifle Operator* (Columbia, SC: Panteao Productions, 2010): Barricades Rifle, DVD.

[20] Paul R. Howe, *The Tactical Trainer* (Bloomington, IN: AuthorHouse, 2009), 122-123.

[21] Paul Howe, *Make Ready with Paul Howe: Advanced Tac Pistol/Rifle Operator* (Columbia, SC: Panteao Productions, 2010): Masking Targets, DVD.

[22] U.S. Department of Justice, *Violent Encounters*, 2006, (Washington, DC: FBI, 2006), 3.

[23] J. Henry FitzGerald, *Shooting* (Boulder, CO: Paladin Press, 2007), 351. Originally published in 1930 by J. Henry FitzGerald.

[24] J. Henry FitzGerald, *Shooting* (Boulder, CO: Paladin Press, 2007), 306-307. Originally published in 1930 by J. Henry FitzGerald.

[25] George T. Williams, "Reluctance to Use Deadly Force," *FBI Law Enforcement Bulletin*, (October 1999): 2.

[26] Force Science Institute, LTD., "Point Shooting Clarification," *Force Science News* #135 (October 23, 2009), http://www.forcescience.org/fsinews/2009/10/force-science-news-135-%e2%80%9cpoint-shooting%e2%80%9d-clarification%e2%80%a6plus-what-new-gaze-pattern-findings-mean-for-your-training-more/ (accessed September 22, 2012).

[27] Douglas A. Knight, "Perfect Practice Makes Perfect," *FBI Law Enforcement Bulletin*, (June 2007): 7.

[28] The instructor had participated in Operation Nimrod in 1980 in which he stormed the Iranian Embassy. See Phil Singleton, "Singleton International," *About Us,* http://www.philsingleton.com/about_us (accessed September 22, 2012).

[29] Pasters: "Small gummed pieces of paper used to patch bullet holes in the target." See International Association of Law Enforcement Firearms Instructors, *Standards & Practices Reference Guide for Law Enforcement Firearms Instructors*, (January 1995): 248.

[30] North Carolina Justice Academy, *In-Service Firearms Qualification Manual* (Salemburg, NC: November 2009), 12 NCAC 9E .0106 (e).

[31] George T. Williams, "Reluctance to Use Deadly Force," *FBI Law Enforcement Bulletin*, (October 1999): 2.

[32] Itay Gil and Dan Baron, *The Citizen's Guide to Stopping Suicide Attackers* (Boulder, CO: Paladin Press, 2004), 53.

[33] J. Henry FitzGerald, *Shooting* (Boulder, CO: Paladin Press, 2007), 336-337. Originally published in 1930 by J. Henry FitzGerald.

[34] International Association of Law Enforcement Firearms Instructors, *Firearms Training Standards for Law Enforcement Personnel*, (2004): 14.8.

[35] J. Henry FitzGerald, *Shooting* (Boulder, CO: Paladin Press, 2007), 318. Originally published in 1930 by J. Henry FitzGerald.

[36] Department of the Army, *Leader's Manual for Combat Stress Control* (Washington, DC: FM 22-51, September 29, 1994), 3-2.

[37] Department of the Army, *Leader's Manual for Combat Stress Control* (Washington, DC: FM 22-51, September 29, 1994), 3-2.

[38] Jeff Gonzales, *Combative Fundamentals, an Unconventional Approach* (Cedar Park, TX: Trident Concepts, LLC, 2002), 15.

[39] Jim Greene, firearms instructor for Glock Inc., provided the information during the Glock Pistol Transitional Instructor Workshop course held at Glock Inc., in Smyrna, Georgia, in a face-to-face conversation with the author, February 3-5, 2010.

[40] National Rifle Association, *Law Enforcement Handgun Instructor Manual* (Fairfax, VA: Firearm Safety and Range Organization, Edition 6.1, 2006), 8.

[41] Robert K. Taubert, *Rattenkrieg! The Art and Science of Close Quarters Battle Pistol* (North Reading, MA: Saber Press, 2012), 127.

[42] National Rifle Association, *NRA Basics of Personal Protection Outside the Home Course: Course Outline and Lesson Plans*, (Fairfax, VA: April 2009), VII-68-70.

[43] National Rifle Association, *Law Enforcement Handgun Instructor Manual* (Fairfax, VA: Firearm Safety and Range Organization, Edition 6.1, 2006), 11.

[44] National Rifle Association, *Law Enforcement Handgun Instructor Manual* (Fairfax, VA: Firearm Safety and Range Organization, Edition 6.1, 2006), 11.

INDEX

ABOUT THE AUTHOR

The author remains in law enforcement in North Carolina and previously worked at the Dallas Police Department in Texas. While at Dallas Police Department, he patrolled the city's crime laden Southwest and Southeast Divisions and left at the rank of senior corporal. He earned awards that included bravery, lifesaving, professionalism, driving, and marksmanship.

When working in North Carolina as a chief of police in a gang and drug ridden community—the author planned, prepared, and carried out antidrug operations. Those operations led to the arrest and conviction of multiple suspects. One of the suspects specifically targeted was the leader of a violent street gang.

The author to help rebuild Afghanistan's national police force worked as police adviser and trainer for 18 months mostly in the Helmand Province located in the southern area of the country. On March 17, 2008, while moving on foot in the Gereshk district, he survived a suicide attack. The author in September 2008, traveled to Israel and received antiterrorism combat training. He also received high-risk motorcade training in Kabul, Afghanistan.

The author has a Bachelor of Science in Human Services (Specialization in Administration of Justice) degree. He attained an Advanced Law Enforcement Certificate from the North Carolina Criminal Justice Education and Training Standards Commission. He served as a combat engineer and as a military police officer during his 13 cumulative years between the U.S. Army Reserve and the Texas National Guard. He has multiple firearms and self-defense instructor certifications from the North Carolina Justice Education and Training Standards Commission, and the National Rifle Association. He completed Glock's courses for Advance Armorer, Instructors Workshop, and Glock 18 (18C) Select-Fire Familiarization Workshop.

The author completed the North Carolina Justice Academy's *Tactical Training Certificate Program*, and the U.S. Marshals *Fugitive Investigator's Course*. He has received training in physical and electronic surveillance, special weapons and tactics, high-risk apprehensions, active killers, and counterterrorism. His articles have appeared in several publications: Combat Handguns, The Law Enforcement Trainer, The Police Chief, and The Firearms Instructor.

HOW TO ORDER

Retail Orders: To order *retail* copies of this book by Timothy D. Blakeley go to www.Amazon.com, enter the author's name in the search box. On the page that appears, click on the book's title to access details and ordering information. A valid credit card number is required to order.

Wholesale Orders: To order *wholesale* quantities of this book for educational institutions, civilian libraries, military libraries, law enforcement agencies, companies, or other organizations go to www.PoliceTech.com. To speak with a representative, click on the *Contact Us* and call the telephone number provided.

Reporting Errors: Efforts were taken to make this book as complete and as accurate as possible. However, there may be mistakes, both typographic and in content. Please report typographical or content errors by e-mail at info@policetech.com.

Book Reviews: To inform other operators about *Shooting To Survive: How to Fight with a Pistol*, please post a review for it on Amazon.com.

CPSIA information can be obtained at www.ICGtesting.com
Printed in the USA
BVOW010323161112

305592BV00005B/10/P